Confessions OF AN OVERSEAS BRAT

*Adventures
Growing Up in Europe
During the 1960s and early 70s*

Ronald Walker

Confessions of an
Overseas Brat

Copyright © 2018 by Ronald Walker.

All rights reserved.
No part of this book may be reproduced in any form or by any electronic or mechanical means including information storage and retrieval systems, without permission in writing from the author. The only exception is by a reviewer, who may quote short excerpts in a review.

Cover designed by kmh Graphics

ISBN-9781727326178

Printed in the United States of America

First Printing: Dec 2018
Rocket Surgery Productions
Oracle, Arizona

*This book is dedicated to
Master Sergeant John G. Walker
United States Air Force*

Thanks Dad, for everything.

Table of Contents

Forward   pg. 7
Introduction   pg. 9
1. Peñiscola   pg. 15
2. Calle Endrinas   pg. 30
3. Calle Triana   pg. 43
4. It All Began with the Beatles at the Bullring   pg. 56
5. The Beautiful Beasts and Beyond   pg. 79
6. Soul – Both Rubber and Psychedelic   pg. 99
7. Royal Oaks   pg. 118
8. Torrejon Air Base   pg. 130
9. Madrid High School   pg. 144
10. The Glass House   pg. 175
11. Benidorm   pg. 198
12. Canillejas   pg. 215
13. Morocco   pg. 232
14. Breton de los Herreros   pg. 268
15. Off to the New World   pg. 292
16. Myrtle Beach – Round 1   pg. 315
17. Florida Trouble   pg. 339
18. Back to Spain Again   pg. 362
19. Amsterdam   pg. 376
20. Rotterdam   pg. 390
21. Frankfurt   pg. 407
22. Barcelona   pg. 443
23. Madrid Once Again   pg. 459
24. The States for Good   pg. 480
25. Tales of the White Mustang   pg. 495
26. Myrtle Beach – Round 2   pg. 522
27. Finally to Tucson   pg. 539
28. A Final Word   pg. 552
    Acknowledgements   pg. 558
    A Note on Pictures Used   pg. 560
    About the Author   pg. 561

FORWARD

The book that follows: "Confessions of an Overseas Brat," is stylish, accurate, and a lot of fun to read! Ronald Walker grew up as a Military Brat mostly in Madrid, Spain, and in other exotic locations in Europe during the late sixties and early seventies: a time of great political, social, and artistic upheaval of all kinds.

The keywords for Ron's generation were: sex, drugs, and Rock and Roll, and Ron and his cronies explored all of it fully! For me personally, one of the most entertaining stories is about the time that he, his brother and a buddy named Andy made a trip to Morocco with Ron's father during a school vacation. Besides getting a chance to visit this wonderful and ancient country, the boys had one express intention: to buy and smuggle back into Spain a kilo of high-quality Moroccan hashish. Ron's father, of course, knew nothing about this caper. All went well, with no problems developing at customs, but the story was one with edge-of-the-seat anticipation all the way through!

He recounts all kinds of very diverse adventures in this marvelous book—from his first explorations into the hormone-driven world of the teenager, to watching the Beatles perform live at the Bullring in Madrid and how that experience changed his life, to working with some brilliant teachers in high school, to spending a brief time in jail, to camping on an island in the middle of Frankfurt, Germany after spending a summer among the hippies in Amsterdam. He held numerous unusual jobs which included a time spent working as a "carnie" on the Midway in Myrtle Beach and elsewhere, and later working briefly for a circus in Holland, among many others. These are just a few examples of the exciting adventures and experiences that he describes in great detail. And Ron really got around, having opportunities that few American youths had available to them.

Ron has done a splendid job of capturing the essence of life during this most exciting of times. He has also conveyed very clearly what it was like to be a "boy without a country," an experience many military brats share. The feelings of rootlessness, restlessness, and lack of a sense of clear national identity are very common for the children of military personnel who move often. Friendships are hard to form and sustain, when everyone is moving around all the time. Ron actually did a far better job at maintaining friendships than many "brats" do, because he was a very loyal friend who really made an effort to stay in touch with his compadres.

As the book progresses, Ron proves himself to be a kind, sincere, generous, curious, and trustworthy person—with a very appealing and consistent character—someone whom anyone might like to know better.

By Marguerite Wainio
—author of *"The Horses Are Running"*

INTRODUCTION

The following is a collection of stories, anecdotes, and memories of my life as a boy and as a young man. Although they are all true and correct to the best of my knowledge and memory (and only very slightly embellished), the names of most of the characters have been changed to protect the innocent and the not so innocent. And though these events occurred several decades ago now, I have changed the names only to a point where the actual people mentioned will probably recognize themselves, if by nothing else, from the actual story itself.

I use the word "confessions" loosely here, because although only a few of these stories involve actual crimes being committed, there are several that might be construed as being less than honorable or respectable from an adult twenty-first century perspective, but they reflect the innocence and naivety of youth.

There are two reasons why I feel that I must attempt to put to paper these memories and recollections. The first reason is that I, like everyone else alive in the world today, am not getting any younger. Every day that passes brings me one day closer to the inevitable end, and I feel that I must make this attempt now, while I'm in my mid-60s, and before I am unable to do so due to plain old forgetfulness or possible senility. I am not undertaking this endeavor only so I can document my unusual life and upbringing, but also so the other participants in these stories and adventures might have a chance to take a step back in time and relive along with me some of the unusual experiences that we shared.

Secondly, I feel that by my passing along some of these experiences, I may be able to show something to other people that might, in some small way, help them to better understand this strange planet we all occupy. After all, isn't that why we are all here? To try to understand this weird and wonderful world we all inhabit?

At this point, I feel that an introduction is in order. You see, I am an overseas military brat (a United States Air Force brat specifically), and by the time I was twenty-one years old, I had spent almost all my young life living outside of the United States as a "military dependent." My father had put in for overseas assignments since the very beginning of his military career, and due to luck, perseverance, and determination, he had been assigned to various posts all over the world. In fact, I was born overseas, in Lisbon, Portugal, while my father was assigned there with the MAAG program (Military Assistance and Advisory Group).

After Lisbon, my family and I spent a period of eighteen months stateside at an Air Force base near Tampa, Florida. After that my father was assigned to Ankara, Turkey, for another three-year post. After a short stay back in the States, (this time at Walker Air Force Base, New Mexico), he was assigned his final military tour of duty in Madrid, Spain, in January, 1960, when I was just seven years old.

When my dad's tour of Spain was over in 1964, it corresponded with him having completed twenty years in the Air Force, and he became eligible for retirement with full military benefits. By that time, he decided he had enough of the military life, and so he chose to retire in Madrid. His wife and two young sons were delighted with this decision since Madrid in the 1960s was a wonderful and exciting place.

In those days, people around the world still greatly respected Americans and were very interested in their lifestyle and culture. On top of being welcomed wherever we went, life in Spain was very inexpensive and bargains were to be found everywhere. The difference between the two economies (the Spanish and the American) allowed my dad's retirement pay to go a lot further than it ever could have in the States. Prices were low for us everywhere in Spain in those days, and my family was able to live a life of luxury unheard of, except to the very affluent in the States. We had a large house, a maid, and plenty of pesetas to spend.

To supplement his retirement pay as well as to give him something to do, my dad, along with a partner from Puerto Rico, opened a Swiss cuisine luxury restaurant in downtown Madrid called the "Chalet Suizo." It was a four-fork restaurant, meaning that not only were there white tablecloths and a different fork for each course, but there were at least four waiters for each table, one for every possible whim the customer could conjure up. And, as it was the only restaurant specializing in fondues and other Swiss specialties in Madrid at the time, it became quite a lucrative and successful business. The fact that it was owned by Americans lent it even more appeal. The Chalet Suizo became a meeting place for Madrid's elite upper-class society, with many of the rich and famous, both Spanish and foreigners, dining there in four-fork luxury.

Life was good living in a foreign capital during the turbulent 1960s. So good that my family stayed for over ten years, until I, the younger son, had finished high school. Our family then returned to the States in 1970.

In Spain during the 1960s, Generalissimo Francisco Franco was in command of both the Spanish military and the government. He ruled with an iron fist, a true dictator who posted his own private guard, called *"La Guardia Civil"* everywhere. They were always in twos, with their rifles, their dark green uniforms, and their pointed patent leather hats and knee-high boots. They were stationed on almost every block of every city in Spain, as well as along every few kilometers in the Spanish countryside, on bicycles, motorbikes, scooters, or even on burros, if not on foot.

The Spanish Civil War was still fresh in most peoples' memories, and Franco was so determined to prevent any hint of a revolution that he also controlled the media, including the newspapers and the two TV stations available in Madrid. The result was, with these pairs of *Guardias* everywhere, crime of any sort was almost non-existent. One could walk virtually anywhere on the streets of Madrid at any time of day or night without any fear, because crimes were just not committed. Yes, certain infractions of the law such as soft drugs and prostitution occurred, but these were mostly victimless types of laws being broken, and the *Guardias* usually looked the other way for these small infractions.

One of the main differences between life in the States and life in Spain was the sense of honor and respect that Spaniards had that didn't seem to exist in the same way stateside. In Spain for many centuries, (since even before they had finally managed to kick the Moors out of their peninsula), the Spaniards had developed a code of honor among themselves. A man sometimes had nothing but his honor and his family name going for him, but this was usually enough. Even if a man was just a waiter in a cafe, or a street-sweeper, or a garbage collector, he took his job seriously and looked on it as a career and an honorable and important position, as perhaps his father and grandfather before him had held the same job. He had honor and pride, no matter his position in life and society.

To commit a crime against someone, anyone, would bring disrespect on the criminal, his ancestors, and his family name. The only exception to this was the gypsies, but they weren't really considered true Spaniards. And if a crime was committed in Spain, nine times out of ten it was a gypsy who committed it. But these were mostly minor crimes such as pick-pocketing, swindles, and petty thievery. Serious crimes such as murder, rape, or any type of violence were almost unheard of in Spain in those days.

The American community that I and my family were a part of was, in a way, immune to the laws that governed the average Spaniard. Americans in Spain were in their own category as far as the law went. Of course, any major crime would be punished severely by the authorities, but in general, foreigners, and especially Americans, were allowed a certain freedom much different than that in their home country.

Unless the crime involved murder, rape, or severely bad words against the government, the worst an American could suffer would be deportation back to the States. I had several friends while I was in high schools who were arrested for crimes such as selling drugs or stealing motorcycles, and their punishment was just to be sent back to the States to live with relatives before their fathers and the rest of their family were rotated back stateside later.

Near Madrid, there was an American base called Torrejon Air Force Base. Torrejon was established in 1957 and was finally turned over to the Spanish Air Force in 1992. Most of the American community in Madrid was involved in some way or another with the base, which was located about twenty miles from Madrid on the outskirts of the city. This meant that at any given time, there were hundreds of active-duty American military personnel assigned to the base in some capacity or another for about thirty-five years altogether. Most were there for either a three- or four-year tour of duty and, of course, the married personnel brought with them their wives and children (their "dependents," as they say in military-speak.)

On the base itself, there was a small housing area, mostly for officers and essential base personnel, but it was not nearly large enough to accommodate the thousands of military personnel and their dependents. For this reason, there was an American housing area by the name of "Royal Oaks" (known in Spanish as *Encinar de los Reyes*) that was located on the outskirts of Madrid where many of these Americans lived. Many other Americans connected to the base lived "downtown," which is what living in the actual city of Madrid was called.

Not all Americans living in Madrid at the time were active-duty military; many were civilians but still had connections to the base in one way or another, much as my family had after my dad retired. Other Americans were living in Madrid for non-military reasons, and chose to enroll their children in the American school on base, or another American school in Madrid named appropriately, "The American  School of Madrid" or A.S.M. Some were businessmen with families who worked for such American companies as Libby's Foods or General Tire, who were representing their particular businesses in Spain.

Torrejon Air Force Base was much like any American base anywhere in the world. The military wished for their personnel and their families to be happy and content with their overseas living assignments, and they made the base appear to be as "American" as possible. The idea was to keep morale high and keep people from becoming quite as homesick for "The World," as some people called the USA.

For this reason, there were many amenities such as a movie theater, a bowling alley, a library, a snack bar, a golf course, a post office, a bookstore, a church, a barber shop, a teen club, a junior high and high school, and various other businesses and services on base to make the Americans feel more at home.

There was also the "Commissary," which is military-speak for a grocery store, and the "PX" or the Post Exchange, which is military-speak for a department store. Both had American-made goods, and groceries brought in from the States or from American bases in Germany at great expense. In addition, there were the usual "Officers' Club," and the "NCO" (Non-Commissioned) Officers' Club. The military did indeed manage to create a facsimile of a small American town on the outskirts of Madrid. And in this most unusual of locations and circumstances is where I was raised, educated and grew up.

So the following is my story of how I went from boyhood to manhood living in a most unusual time and place, in Madrid, Spain during the 1960s and early 70s. For anyone who was there during that very magical time, my story will be a wonderful and nostalgic trip to the past. For those not lucky enough to have had that experience, my tales will reveal what it was really like living in one of the most exciting cities in Europe, at a time when the entire world was going through such turbulent and profound changes.

Part travelogue, part coming-of-age story, and part personal confessions, these stories not only include my travels and adventures all around Spain, but also across the Straits of Gibraltar into Morocco, and then later my unusual experiences while traveling and working in Holland and Germany. Afterwards, I explain in detail the many difficulties and challenges of trying to adapt to life in the United States after living overseas most of my life.

Being set in that decadent decade of the 1960s and early 70s, sex, drugs, and rock and roll all play a big part in my stories. And I explore all three in detail, from my first time getting to third base, to smoking *kif* in Morocco, to watching the Beatles perform live at the Bullring in Madrid when I was only twelve years old, and how that experience changed my life forever.

I hope that my adventures and experiences leave my readers with not only a deeper knowledge and better understanding of the places and times that I describe in detail, but also what it was like to be a "Stranger in a Strange Land," both in Europe as well as in my own country when I returned to the States to make my life. What follows is truly what it was like growing up as an Overseas Military Brat.

Chapter 1. Peñiscola

"Before the deed comes the thought.
Before the achievement comes the dream.
Every mountain we climb,
we first climb in our mind."
— Royal Robbins

It was summer 1961, and the summer I turned nine years old. The location for this account is Peñiscola, a small village on the coast of Spain. The previous year, in January 1960, my family and I found ourselves living in Madrid, Spain, as my father was stationed there by the United States Air Force. Spain in the early 1960s was a great place to live for Americans like us. The tourist wave that engulfed Spain in the latter part of the decade had not yet begun, and costs were still very inexpensive, since the average Spaniard had not yet been conditioned to equate tourists with *peseta* signs.

Foreigners were still quite rare in Spain in those days, and were viewed by the average Spaniard as being not only interesting, but somewhat of an oddity as well. We as Americans were especially warmly welcomed, because most Spaniards were curious about all things American. This was very likely due to the powerful American film industry that exported their products all over the world so that even the most remote areas had come to know Hollywood and the worlds it created.

My family rented a very comfortable home in a nice area of Madrid for the very modest sum of about 5000 pesetas per month (about $80), and for an additional 1000 pesetas per month (around $16), we hired a maid to do all the housekeeping, cooking, and laundry. That included her services twenty-four hours per day, five and a half days per week. She had Thursday afternoons and Sundays off, in alignment with the local custom. Of course, her pay included free room and board, which was no problem because our house had separate maid quarters with a small bedroom and bathroom, as did most Spanish houses, usually near the kitchen area.

Spain was a true paradise for the traveler in those days. Everything was cheap by American standards, and bargains were to be found just about everywhere, from the price of a glass of *vino tinto* (red wine) or a *caña de cerveza* (a glass of beer) for five pesetas *(un duro)* or about eight cents, to the price of a taxi ride anywhere in the city for less than fifty cents. For these reasons among others, my family enjoyed living in Spain very much. Spain, being one of the most civilized countries in the Western world, had a long and interesting history which included its extensive explorations and conquests of the new world.

All this made Spain an ideal place to get into the local culture, doing everything from exploring the Prado Museum to shopping in the Rastro (the Sunday morning flea market in downtown Madrid). For me and my brother Johnny, who is two years older, life was grand indeed. We were both learning to speak Spanish quite rapidly, due to the facts that most of our local neighborhood friends were Spanish, and also, learning a second language comes quite naturally to the young and impressionable.

During the latter part of the spring of 1961, my father's youngest brother Dale, and his young wife Ruth, came to Spain for a visit. Dale was fourteen years younger than my Dad, so he was around twenty-four years old. Dale and Ruth had both worked for a while in menial jobs in the states, saving their dollars to pay for this trip to Europe. Dale made quite an impression on my young mind, being as they said in those days a "Bohemian," or perhaps better said, a "beatnik." This was long before the term "hippie" came about, but that is indeed what he looked like. He had long shoulder-length hair, a giant mustache, and a demeanor that said, "I'm different, and not the average American tourist." Dale and Ruth had plans to stay in Spain for as long as they could on their limited savings (perhaps an entire year or so) and hopefully he could commence to write the Great American novel.

Dale, as had three out of four of my other uncles, considered himself to be a writer. Or at the least, he was a would-be writer, because by this point, he had not yet published anything for actual money. But he was in beautiful Spain, the land of the conquistadors, and life was fun, cheap, and always an adventure. And he knew that, as had Hemingway and others before him, he wanted and needed to live life fully before he could attempt to write about it.

The previous summer, the Spanish family next door, *Los Belichones*, who had five young children, had become close family friends. Our family and theirs had traveled together to their favorite place for a summer holiday, the small pueblo of Peñiscola on the Mediterranean coast. It is a small town built on a peninsula jutting into the sea about fifty kilometers north of the city of Valencia on the Spanish Costa de Alzahar. The Hollywood movie "El Cid," starring Charleston Heston, had been filmed there a couple of years earlier, and the pueblo had stood in for the ancient city of Valencia in many scenes in the film, including the famous jousting scene on the beach.

The town sits on a rocky outcrop of land connected to the mainland by a long narrow sand spit with beaches on both sides of the spit. A small port with its accompanying breakwater sits on the south side of the sand spit. On the north end of the spit lies a beautiful stretch of white beach that spans from the mainland all the way to the castle-like structure of the original town itself at the end of the peninsula. This beach had swimming and sunbathing facilities, small quaint cafes, and bars with their lively atmosphere of drinkers, guitar players, dancers, and singers. Hand-clappers held court there too. One fellow who was a regular at the cafes had only one arm, but he clapped the loudest, using his one hand against the bare bottom of his foot.

The town itself dates back to the middle Ages, and many centuries ago, as a means of fortification, the residents had used the natural cliff walls at the end of the peninsula, adding gigantic stone walls on the landward side, to make the entire pueblo impenetrable by sea or by land. Gates allowed access to the main town inside the fortified walls and cliffs. The structure was very much of the Moorish design, having been originally designed and built by the Moors, who occupied the Iberian Peninsula for seven centuries.

All over Spain, there are many remnants of the Moorish occupation. Along almost the entire Mediterranean coast of Spain, there still exist a series of stone towers built on most of the promontory points, which in centuries past were used to send messages up and down the coast. They built huge fires in the tops of these towers by the windows, and by covering these windows with blankets; they were able to use a kind of Morse code.

Thus they could communicate messages in a matter of a few hours, instead of it taking days by horse and rider. Of course, this communication system only worked at night for obvious reasons. And Peñiscola was a prime location for one of these communication towers due to its promontory reaching into the sea.

The summer of 1961, after my father took them there for a visit, Peñiscola, Spain, was the place my Uncle Dale and Aunt Ruth chose to stay for a while, realizing this town would be a perfect setting for encouraging Dale's creative writing juices to flow.

They were able to rent a small *piso* (apartment) off a side street inside the pueblo walls for 1200 pesetas or about twenty dollars per month. The owners of the place thought they were getting such a good deal from their renters that they just lived elsewhere while Dale and Ruth occupied their premises for the summer. It was a small three-room dwelling, with old fishnets as curtains and ancient wooden furniture probably dating back to the days of the Moors. They acquired food in the same way the locals did: they went shopping every day to see what was available and they consumed what was fresh each day.

A few small fishing boats were moored at the small breakwater on the south end of the peninsula, and on moonless nights, the fisherman would take their small boats out into the sea with very bright lights attached to car batteries on the bows. Then they would throw their nets overboard and catch sardines by the hundreds if not thousands. These tasty delicacies were for sale in the mornings by the docks, and sold for about five pesetas per kilo, or about eight cents for over two pounds of fresh sardines.

It seemed that a lot of things in Spain at the time cost five pesetas, (also known as *un duro)*. From the price of a beer or a glass of wine, to a kilo of sardines, grapes, olives, or oranges, or a loaf of the local bread called *pan*, and even a decent fishhook.

Since the piso they had rented allowed access to the roof of the building to use as a patio, it became the favorite location for a barbecue. Many an evening was spent cooking sardines on the grill on the rooftop overlooking the town, watching the Spanish sunset in the west, drinking the local vino tinto, or a cold *Mahou* or *El Aguila* beer. Dozens of people would congregate on the rooftop in an atmosphere of fun, friendship, and celebrating being alive. Life was cheap, fun, and interesting, and a real adventure could be had by all.

This is where I found myself that summer of 1961. I'd be turning nine that August and had never before been away from my family. My parents had decided it would be great to have their boys do something interesting and different during the school break that summer, so my older brother Johnny was sent to spend the summer with the Spanish family across the street from our house, who were also good friends of our family's by that time. He was to spend the summer with them in a little town on the Costa Brava, just south of Barcelona.

His experiences that summer vacation differed slightly from mine, for it was decided that I would be spending my vacation with my aunt and uncle in Peñiscola. This was a grand adventure for me, not only because I would be away from my family for the first time in my young life, but because I would be staying with my favorite aunt and uncle, Dale and Ruth. Being not quite nine yet, the world truly looked fabulous, with endless possibilities for adventure and new experiences.

The artist community in the town of Peñiscola was rather small in those days, but there was another person of the artistic persuasion besides Dale living in that small pueblo. Keith Patterson was an aspiring abstract artist from New Zealand, of all places, and he was living there with his young family, trying to create abstract masterpieces on canvas that would make him rich and famous. Keith and his wife, Christine, had two young sons. Jonathan, the older boy, was around my age, and his brother Christopher was about two years younger. The stories I'm about to relate involve just a couple of the many fine adventures that my good friend Jonathan and I enjoyed that wonderful summer so long ago.

The geography and the physical layout of the old pueblo of Peñiscola were quite interesting, and a great challenge to adventurous eight- and nine-year-old boys. The tall rock cliffs at the end of the town acted as a natural barrier against invaders in the days of  the Moors, and by fortifying the landward side of the peninsula with huge walls and an even larger gate, the town was virtually impenetrable by anything less than a full army.

One day Jonathan had a great idea, and he wanted me to partake in this adventure with him. His idea was to start on the beach on the north side of the peninsula near where the rocks began and the sand gave out, and then we'd walk or swim clockwise around the entire seaward side of the natural fortification. He said that we'd have to swim part of the way because the cliffs were so high and steep that it was impossible to walk it. We were accustomed to walking and climbing along the rocks by this point, for we had already spent quite some time down by the breakwater doing exactly this type of activity.

For this endeavor, including all the rock climbing, I required some special shoes like the ones he had. My regular tennis shoes were not going to work. Luckily, my parents had left a small allowance for me, and so off we went to the general store. What we were looking for was a pair of clear plastic sandals. These sandals were worn by many of the locals because not only were they cheap (about twenty pesetas), but they were also very durable, waterproof, and had a great corrugated grip on their soles to help grab the slick rocks better, and keep a body from slipping into the sea while climbing and jumping from rock to rock.

While we were there at the general store (which sold just about anything a person could ever want, it seemed to me), another item caught my eye: a swim mask with a snorkel attached. Jonathan told me that he had a mask and snorkel at one time, but he had left it on a rock and it got swept out to sea, never to be seen again, and his parents just could not afford the fifty-five pesetas for a new one.

So I made my two purchases, the swim mask with the snorkel and a pair of plastic "water" shoes, and we were ready for our grand undertaking of circumnavigating clockwise the entire cliff side of the peninsula, from the main beach all the way around to the breakwater on the opposite side.

After donning my new shoes at Dale and Ruth's piso, leaving my old ones under my bed, I grabbed my new gear, and we ran all the way to the beach, right to the point where the rocks and the sand met. I couldn't wait to try out my mask and see what was under this beautiful sea that was all around me.

I stood in the water up to my waist and asked Jonathan how to work this contraption. He took it from me, rinsed it out with seawater, spit on the inside of the glass and rubbed the saliva all around the glass with his fingers, explaining to me that this helped to keep the mask from fogging up. Then he put the strap around his head and ducked his head underwater, with one end of the snorkel in his mouth and the other end sticking out into the air. After a couple of minutes, I said in a voice loud enough to hear underwater, "Hey, Jonathan, it's my turn already, man!"

He finally emerged his head from the water and handed the contraption to me. After strapping the device around my head, putting the snorkel in my mouth, and biting down on the little wings that stuck out of the mouthpiece, I tried a couple of practice breaths to make sure that it would work and that I could actually breathe through it. Then I stuck my head underwater.

Wow! I had never seen anything like this before in my lifetime! There was a whole other world underwater that I had never seen or even imagined before. There were creatures all over the place, some swimming, some crawling and some just sitting there looking content. Schools of fish of every type and variety were swimming about, doing their thing, seemingly unaware of my presence. Gold ones, striped ones, and even polka-dotted fish were all just going about their business.

On some of the underwater rocks I could see thousands of tiny snail-like creatures slowly crawling along. There were crevasses among the rocks where shadows of strange creatures seemed to lurk. Other animals with strange-shaped shell exteriors were attached to the rocks, and even some weird creatures that didn't look like plant or animal, but instead like something in between. They looked like Hollywood had created them as aliens from another world. A short distance away where the water was deeper, I could see seaweed growing and swaying with the rhythm of the waves.

I found that by breathing slowly and deliberately, I could stay underwater for as long as I wanted to without lifting my head from out of the water. I felt almost like a sea creature myself as I kicked my feet and moved around. I was fascinated by everything I saw. After a few minutes, I could hear Jonathan's muffled voice yelling something, so I stood up in water that came right up to my neck, and looked around. He was saying something about diving down and he wanted to show me how this was done. Reluctantly, I took off the mask and handed it to him.

As he was putting it on his head he said, "Ronnie, if you want to dive down, hold your breath and just do it, but when you come back up, there's going to be some water in the snorkel, so just blow it out when you surface. Like this."

Then he dove down and totally submerged under the water, and about ten seconds later he came up again and as soon as the snorkel came out of the water, he blew into it and a short stream of water shot out of the top of it. In his hand he was holding a nice shiny shell that he had picked up from the sand beneath our feet.

He handed me the mask and snorkel so I could try it. I dove holding my breath, and when I reached the bottom, I grabbed a pretty shell and then, pushing off with my feet, I shot to the surface remembering to blow into the mouthpiece once I surfaced. I managed to get most of the water out of the tube, but there was still some left and I choked a little on it.

He said, "Don't worry, Ronnie, you'll get the hang of it. It just takes a bit of practice."

Immediately I dove down again and saw a large school of small fish swimming by. I swam over towards them and they turned and headed my way and suddenly I was enveloped by swimming swirling life forms all around me. It was an exhilarating experience to be surrounded by hundreds of fish at once, all apparently unconcerned by my presence.

I surfaced and when I took the mask off, I shouted with joy, trying to explain to Jonathan what I had just experienced.

He just looked at me and said, "Yeah, it's a lot of fun, isn't it? Now we'd better get going if we're going to make it all the way around the point before it gets dark on us."

Reluctantly, I started walking back to the rocks and dry land holding the mask and snorkel tight to my chest, having just experienced one of the most fantastic things of my entire young life.

We made our way carefully over the rocks, jumping from one to another, being very careful not to lose our balance, and trying to keep our sandals' grip on the slick rocks. After about fifteen minutes of climbing and jumping from rock to rock, we reached a point where the climbable rocks disappeared for quite a distance. We could see where they picked up again a little further on, but it looked like we would have to swim it for a while, anyway.

I put on my mask and snorkel and jumped in the water, following Jonathan's lead. Once again, I was flabbergasted by the vast number and variety of life forms all around me. I saw all along the bottom and along the submerged rocks hundreds of small round creatures about two or three inches across, with pointed black spines sticking out all over them.

I took the snorkel out of my mouth and shouted to Jonathan, "Look at all those things with the black needles on them. What are they?"

He yelled back, "They're sea urchins. Just make sure you don't step on one!"

Putting the mask back on, I felt lucky to have it with me because the entire bottom seemed to be covered with these things, and it was hard to find a place to step where there wasn't at least one underfoot.

When we finally got to the point where there were more rocks to scramble onto instead of the sheer towering cliff, we decided to take a breather on a large smooth rock, being careful to avoid any black spiny things.

As we were sitting there drying off in the sun, Jonathan asked me with a smile on his face, "Hey, you hungry?"

I just shrugged and said, "Yeah, I guess, a little, why?"

He reached into the pocket of his old cutoff jeans, pulled out a small one-bladed pocketknife, and said, "Watch this!"

He reached over with the knife blade in his hand and put the edge of it next to a roundish, shallow, conical-shaped shell that was stuck to the surface of the rock we were on. Just as a wave gently lapped over that part of the rock, he slipped the blade between the rock and the shell and managed to pull the shell from its hold on the rock. He turned it over and with the tip of the blade he scraped out the insides of the shell and popped it into his mouth.

He smiled and said, "Hmm, very tasty! You want one?"

I said, "Sure, why not?"

He waited a couple of seconds until the next wave lapped at the rock and repeated the process on another shell. He again scraped out the inside of the shell and this time handed it to me. I looked at it, smelled it, and then sucked the juicy creature into my mouth. It was delicious, and I told him so.

I asked him, "What are these things, Jonathan?"

He said, "They're called *lapas* and, as you can see, they're really easy to get. You just have to wait until they loosen their grip on the rock when the water is over them. Here, you want to try it?"

He handed me his knife. I reached over, and at just the right time when the shell was slightly underwater with the next wave and the creature had slightly lifted its shell up from the rock to feed on tiny microscopic things in the seawater, I slipped the blade right under the lip of the shell and pried the helpless creature off the slippery rock.

I scraped the thing out with the tip of the blade and slipped it into my mouth, and after two or three quick bites it was gone. Since the shells were only about an inch across or so, we sat there and each ate about a dozen before we felt we had enough. Later, I was to discover that these things we were eating on that rock that day are called limpets in English, but to me they will forever be called *lapas*.

So off we went again, part of the time jumping and climbing from rock to rock and at other times swimming short stretches where the rocks disappeared under the sea and only sheer cliffs were visible, stretching upwards towards the sky.

After another twenty minutes or so of this, we reached a point where we figured we were at least halfway around the peninsula, and we stopped for another break. Ahead of us were only cliffs as far as we could see, and at this point the waves were growing increasingly higher and stronger, as we had taken the turn around the point, and were exposed more to the force of the open Mediterranean pounding against the cliffs.

I looked at Jonathan and asked him in the boldest voice I could muster, "Hey, do you really want to keep going? It looks like we'll have a lot of swimming to do before we reach the other side."

He looked back at me and said, "You know, maybe you're right. It does look like a long ways to swim, and besides I'm getting hungry; those *lapas* really didn't fill me up. What do you say we turn back?"

Feeling slightly disappointed and a little bit defeated by the elements, we turned back to retrace our route. And looking back at it now, I realize that it was a wise decision for two young boys to make, because there was a real danger of drowning if we had tried to swim the entire length. With nothing between us and the giant waves besides huge rock cliffs for quite a long way, we clearly made the right choice.

To say that Jonathan's family was poor would be quite the understatement. I don't think his father had sold very many paintings at this point in his career, although I do remember my father buying one of his paintings once, not because he really liked it, but out of kindness and to help Keith and his family out financially.

Due to the poor sales of his artwork, the family was trying to live as meagerly as possible. Hunger was a major concern for the family, even more so than for the locals, because almost all the Spaniards had at least enough to eat, but for Jonathan's family, hunger was a major factor in their lives.

Their rent was around twenty dollars per month, and Keith could usually somehow scrounge up that amount around the first of each month, but food for his family was whatever and however it could be acquired.

Getting a real job in Spain was nearly impossible for foreigners in those days since so many Spaniards were out of work, and had been since before the Spanish Civil War in the 1930s, and few employers would hire *un extranjero* (a foreigner) to do a job that a local could do. So one of Jonathan's chores was to help gather food for the family with whatever means was possible, and I was committed to helping him in this endeavor.

Stealing was not an option, since we were not thieves, nor beggars, and besides, all the shopkeepers kept an eye on us. Mostly because we were foreigners but also because we were quite loud and boisterous at times, being as full of spirit as young boys can be, and running all over town by ourselves unsupervised. Occasionally we would allow young Christopher to accompany us on our adventures, but since he was only seven years old, he would slow us down for the most part and we would usually just let him stay at home with his mother, which he seemed to prefer, anyway.

So it came to be that it became my responsibility as well as Jonathan's to help with the food collection activities for his family. Our rounds usually started in the morning by heading down to the docks and hanging around the fishing boats, hoping to catch the attention of a generous fisherman for a handout of a fish or two, directly in competition with several dozen of the town's sizable feline population. If that activity didn't prove productive, sometimes we'd use an old rusty bucket, a piece of discarded fishing line, and a fish head to tie it to, and then we'd be in business.

Around the rocks of the breakwater were many small crabs, dark brown or black in color and ranging from one to three inches across. Our method was quite basic: we just dropped the string with the fish head tied to it among the rocks until a crab would grab the bait with his claw, and then we would gently lift him up and drop him into the bucket.

This usually only worked about twenty percent of the time though since usually they would let go and fall off before we got them into the bucket. At this point, if they were still on land, our job was to grab them with our hands and put them into the bucket, claws and all.

On many occasions we'd be yelling and cussing with a crab claw stuck to one of our fingers, shaking our hand frantically and yelling, "Let go, dang it, let go!" Most of the crabs that were captured this way that made it into the bucket, (along with some that didn't), got slightly squished sometimes, mostly by our accidentally (or not) stepping on them.

But overall, after a few hours of crabbing during the afternoon, and with a minimum of damage to our fingers, we'd have a pretty good catch in our bucket. We'd haul the bucket, half-full of seawater, back up the hill to Jonathan's family apartment, and Christine would be so grateful. She would rinse and then boil the crabs in fresh water until they were soft and at that point, she would crush them and strain them through cheesecloth (to remove most of the shell) and add some seasoning.

The resulting broth with bits of crab meat would be delicious and full of protein. That would be dinner for the Patterson family that evening, along with a loaf of *pan* (bread). And to my delight, they usually invited me.

Another way of scavenging for protein involved a little more preparation and time, but the results would be even tastier! It required fishing poles for this endeavor. Jonathan already had his, but I still had to acquire mine. To get the pole part of the apparatus, we walked down the length of the peninsula to the mainland, which was about two kilometers away, to where a small creek flowed into the sea. This freshwater source is where a grove of *caña* or bamboo cane grew. After selecting an appropriate pole and cutting it down with my pocket knife, and trimming the leaves off, we hiked back to town to the small general supply store. Jonathan knew exactly what to purchase, and for un duro, I bought a large treble hook with an accompanying lead weight. This hook was about an inch long with three nasty looking hooks with barbs pointing upwards.

After purchasing this lethal-looking device, we headed for the port and the breakwater. I already had a fairly long piece of fishing line in my pocket from the crabbing, so I was all set. After attaching the line to one end of the *caña*, and the treble hook with the weight at the other end of the twenty-foot line, I was ready to fish.

This kind of fishing required no bait whatsoever, for the idea was to snag the fishes as they swam by in the water around the port and the breakwater. We could see them swimming in tight schools, only a couple of feet deep, looking for leftovers from the fishermen cleaning their catches or whatever else might be around the port area (perhaps even some squished crabs).

Standing on the rocks of the breakwater, we watched the schools swim by, and then, at just the right moment, we'd cast the line into the water in the direction the school was swimming, wait a second or two until the weight sank the hook into their midst and then, yank as hard as we could at just the right moment to snag one, sometimes in the tail or sometimes the gills. Sometimes we'd even catch two at a

time, but that was rare. Our success rate was around one out of every five casts, but like anything in life, the more I did it, the better I got at it. Ranging in size from two to five inches long, these fish were called *Lisas* by the locals (and smelt in English), and were delicious once gutted, beheaded and fried, and eaten whole, bones and all.

One particular afternoon I remember well, Jonathan and I were at the docks with our *cañas*, and the fishing had not been great so far, for we only had a dozen or so small fish in our bucket. Suddenly, Jonathon, who was standing out on a rock at the end of the breakwater, started yelling with delight. He had caught a monster, and it was squirming on his hook as he jumped from rock to rock to get back to where the bucket was located.

Surely enough, this one must have been the granddaddy of the entire *Lisas* family, for he was at least eight to nine inches long. After removing the hook from the creature's eye socket, we examined it closely. Yes, it was by far the largest *Lisa* that we had caught yet. We were both very excited about our good fortune as well as our excellent fishing skills.

After another hour or so of fishing, we decided to call it a day. The sun was going down over the hills in the west, resulting in another spectacular Spanish sunset, and we were both quite hungry, having had nothing to eat all day but cheese sandwiches for lunch. So once again we trekked up the hill, taking turns lugging the bucket half-full of seawater with our mess of fish, feeling quite proud of ourselves.

When we got back to the Patterson's modest *piso*, we proudly showed Jonathan's mother the mess of fish we had caught. She was very pleased with both of us, especially with Jonathan after she saw the monster fish that he had snagged that day. She told us we would have them for dinner that evening, along with a *tortilla Española* — a delicious pie made in a skillet from eggs, potatoes, onions, and garlic that she had made earlier in the afternoon. And we'd be having dinner as soon as Keith got back from his studio, where he had been working diligently all day on his latest masterpiece.

Since she knew that I had caught my fair share of the fish in the bucket, she invited me to stay for dinner that evening. She sent Jonathan and me into the bathroom to wash up for dinner, and we scrubbed our hands almost red trying to get the stink of fish off of them, but only managing to remove most of the visible fish scales and guts from under our grimy nails.

When we finally finished with our hand washing chore, we headed for the large wooden kitchen table where the family meals were taken. Keith was already seated at the head of the table as well as Christopher in his seat, and Christine was in the process of frying up the last of the tasty fish. After we were all seated with a platter of steaming fish and the two-inch-thick *tortilla Española* in front of us, she began to dish out dinner.

Then Jonathan said in a loud, almost whining voice, which was very unlike him, "Well, I think I should get to eat that large fish since I'm the one that caught him."

Then Christopher piped up, "I think I should get to eat him, since I'm the youngest and I still got all the most growing to do."

Then Keith said in his booming voice, "Now boys, you both know that I've been working hard all day on my painting, and I'm famished, so I should get to eat that big fat fish myself."

We all looked at each other, with Christopher almost ready to start crying and Jonathan with tears of rage in his eyes, and then we all looked at Christine. She had a fork in her hand holding the monster fish on it, ready to dish out our dinners on our plates.

She looked at all four of us hungry males and said in her sweet and kind feminine voice, "Well, gentlemen, you're all being very greedy and are not at all watching your manners. This large fish should go to our esteemed guest, Ronnie."

The three male members of the Patterson family looked at me with envy in their eyes as she placed the monster fish on my plate.

I just grinned and said, "Thank you very much, Mrs. Patterson."

I dug in. And to this day, I don't remember ever eating a more tasty fish. It was absolutely delicious!

Chapter 2. Calle Endrinas

"There may be no fool like an old fool, but our observation has been that the young fool runs him a pretty close second.
—Robert Elliott Gonzales

When we first arrived in Spain from the states in January 1960, the family's first residence was the Hotel Aitana on *Avenida Generalissimo* in downtown Madrid. This was the hotel where most American families stayed until they could secure permanent quarters: either on base, in the Royal Oaks housing area, or as our family did, by renting a house in downtown Madrid.

We had to wait for our "household goods" to arrive via ship from New York to Barcelona, and then into Madrid by truck. Then we moved into our first house in Madrid, on a street named Calle Endrinas.

Our "household goods" consisted entirely of items that the U.S. military had allowed us to bring with us for this overseas assignment. My parents, with the help of professional movers, had loaded these items in large shipping containers before we left Walker Air Force Base outside Roswell, New Mexico, where we had lived for about eighteen months before my father was assigned to the MAAG mission in Madrid. These items included furniture, clothing, appliances, and other miscellaneous household goods. The military spared no expense in trying to make this kind of move as easy as possible for its families, realizing that having one's personal items around would do a lot for morale and make the transition to living in a foreign country much easier.

The military even allowed my father to ship his car to Madrid as well, which he picked up in Barcelona the same time that the rest of our stuff arrived. Unfortunately, the car that my dad had owned in New Mexico was a 1957 Chevrolet station wagon, with a bright red and white paint job. Although it was a really nice car, it was much too large for the tiny streets of Madrid and, of course, it stuck out like a sore thumb.

Almost all Spaniards drove small SEAT automobiles, which were similar to the FIAT brand made in Italy, but instead were made in Spain. In fact, these Spanish-made cars were the only automobiles that were not taxed heavily due to Franco's desire to keep Spanish auto workers employed. It was good for the Spanish economy obviously, but the three models that were available all became rather redundant among drivers.

The models of cars that SEAT produced were the SEAT 1500, the 850, and the 600. These numbers designated the size of their engines in cubic centimeters. Only the 1500 had four doors, and was used for taxi cabs,

government and police vehicles, and by larger families. The 850 was only slightly larger than the 600, but it had slightly more pep than the 600 did.

Due to the small narrow streets in Madrid and the traffic situation, many Spaniards drove motorcycles, motor scooters, and motorbikes. In fact, it was not unusual to see an entire family of five riding down the street on a Vespa scooter with a sidecar. The father would be driving, with one child standing on the floorboards in front of him, another riding behind him on the seat, and the wife riding in the sidecar holding the baby. This was quite cheap and efficient transportation, except that whenever it rained, it could prove to be a challenge.

Our family's huge lumbering Chevy looked like a monster among the tiny SEATS everywhere, and was difficult to drive on certain streets and even more difficult to park, but my Dad made do with what he had. However, it wasn't too long before he sold it and bought a SEAT 1500, a lot more efficient and not nearly as conspicuous. And he was able to sell the Chevy for a very nice profit, since imported cars were not only rare and quite the novelty, but also only the reasonably wealthy could afford them since the import tax was around one hundred percent for cars that were not manufactured in Spain.

This meant that in order for a Spaniard to own an imported car, they required him to pay the cost of the car, plus an equal amount to the government of Spain for allowing him to own it and drive it. Needless to say, most Spaniards drove SEATS. Due to a special trade deal with France however, French vehicles such as Citroen, Renault, and Peugeot somehow got around the severe tax, so there were quite a number of these French-made cars on the Spanish roads and streets as well.

My parents had fallen in love with Spain, and Madrid in particular, while my Dad was stationed in Lisbon, Portugal in the early 1950s (where I happened to be born in 1952). They had taken several trips to Spain during the three years they were in Lisbon, and each time they had found it to be even more enchanting and special. His assignment to Lisbon was unusual because there wasn't an actual American base anywhere in Portugal, so he worked with the MAAG program, which was directly connected to the American Embassy in Lisbon.

As he did in Madrid, he wore civilian clothes and worked with the local military bureaucrats. In Lisbon at the time, there was a family from each branch of the American military: one from the Air Force (our family), one from the Army, and another from the Navy, and there were several Marine units assigned to guard the American Embassy itself. His job consisted of a lot of public relations work with various members of the Portuguese military. His tuxedo got a lot of use at the many official functions with various foreign dignitaries at the embassy in Lisbon. For this reason and because of prior overseas assignments he had while in the Air Force, Madrid did not seem as strange as a place as it would have to someone who had never had these types of military duty assignments before.

Our family quickly settled into our house on Calle Endrinas. We even got a Dachshund we named Rudy, and life became interesting, fun, and quite an adventure for the entire family. Our house was a large single-story duplex with a big yard and maid quarters for our new maid, Victoria. Within a few months we had neighbors on the other side of the duplex. Larry and Josie Tucker were an American couple who were very good friends with my parents and coincidentally had lived right upstairs from us when we lived in Ankara, Turkey while my dad was stationed there in the mid-1950s.

Ankara was a choice assignment at the time due to the exchange rate between the American dollar and the Turkish lira. It seemed Americans couldn't spend all the lira that their dollars could buy, and most Americans there spent money like drunken sailors. There were parties that were legendary, especially among the many Americans who lived on "Alcohol Hill," which included my family.

Larry and Josie had been my parents' best friends for many years and were a very unusual couple, even among all the different kinds of people that my parents had gotten to know throughout their many travels and adventures over the years. He was a large gregarious man from Maine who chain-smoked Lucky Strikes and loved to drink dry martinis. He worked for an American company that sold supplies to the NCO and Officer's Clubs at Torrejon Air Force Base, similar to the job he had in Ankara. Josie was a pretty blond originally from Brussels, Belgium, who spoke five languages fluently and several others quite well. Everyone involved was quite happy that once again they had become our neighbors, and we all looked forward to more great times with the Tuckers.

In 1958, my family, along with Larry and Josie, took a trip through Europe from Ankara to Brussels, Belgium, to attend the World's Fair that was held in that fair city that year. We went through Greece, Yugoslavia, Italy, Germany, Switzerland, Luxembourg, and France on the way, and we stayed with Josie's family once we arrived in Brussels. Even though I was only six at the time, it made quite an impression on me and I remember most of that trip to this day.

 While in Germany, all four males in our traveling party bought matching German-style *lederhosen* pants with suspenders which we all wore proudly while in that country. Then when we reached Switzerland, we guys all got matching Swiss Alps-style hats with red and yellow feathers in the band which we also wore proudly while touring the Swiss Alps. The trip was an adventure for all of us and we all enjoyed the grilled lamb in Greece, the Swiss fondue in Switzerland, and the great local cuisine while traveling through France.

While in Greece, we stopped and visited some friends of my parents as well as Larry's and Josie's who lived on the beach just outside of Athens. They were able to show us around and took us to all the tourist sites including the Acropolis and the other monuments of ancient Greek history. By the time we reached Belgium, countless photographs were taken of us standing in front of castles, fountains and monuments all across Europe. All of this considerably influenced my developing mind as one can imagine.

Expo 58, as that year's World's Fair was known, featured "The Atomium" exhibition, a giant model of a unit cell of an iron crystal. It especially impressed me because we were able to walk through and explore the various corridors and spheres that represented an atom. And there were pavilions from countries all over the world, almost equally impressive, but the one that stuck in my mind the most was the Atomium. It was so futuristic and unusual.

I remember another exhibit made especially for kids that represented a miniature city, and everything was small to adjust to the scale of children. Houses, streets, and even cars were child-sized, and they allowed children to drive these small kid-sized "cars" (actually modified go-carts) around the houses and through the streets. This world was just about perfect for us smaller humans.

Larry and Josie became such good family friends that my brother and I ended up calling them Uncle Larry and Aunt Josie, and they had an enormous influence on our lives for many years to come. Larry seemed to take a special shine to me for some reason, probably because I was the youngest and was always asking him questions about the world around me, being a very curious and inquisitive child. With no children of their own, I imagine they both liked having two young boys around. A few years later Josie found she was pregnant at age forty-one, and gave birth to a beautiful daughter they named Lynn, who would become the apple of Larry's eye.

Life was a marvelous experience for all of us while living on Calle Endrinas in 1960-2. Not only was I absorbing the Spanish language like a sponge, but I was growing very fast and I was full of curiosity and wonder about my new surroundings. All our neighbors (except for the Tuckers) were Spanish, which was the fourth language I had been exposed to by the young age of seven.

While in Portugal we had a young black nanny named Lea who had migrated to Lisbon from the Cape Verde Islands, a Portuguese colony off the west coast of Africa, and she took care of me as a baby, speaking to me in Portuguese of course. When we were in Turkey, we had a "house-boy," (a male version of a maid that foreigners employed in Turkey), named Haime who watched over me most of the day and talked to me in Turkish. I even learned to do the Muslim prayers five times a day right alongside him.

My family spoke to me in English, so by the time Spanish started entering my brain, I was used to translating words in my head automatically. But what came out of my mouth could sound a little strange to the ear sometimes. That all these languages were mixed up in my young brain might be the reason that a couple of years later, while in the third grade, I was sent to "Speech" class once a week along with the stutterers and the lispers.

At first I thought I would be taking a class on how to make speeches in front of the public, and I wondered about this because I was one of the few kids in my grade that was chosen for this special class. But it turned out that it was just special training to try to teach me to speak better English.

My issue was that I couldn't pronounce my "Rs" properly and was diagnosed with something called a "lazy tongue." Whenever someone asked me my name, after I told them, I'm sure that they thought my name was "Wonnie Walkaw." Thankfully, I outgrew this slight speech impediment, but to this day I still have trouble rolling my "Rs," though I still speak fluent Spanish otherwise. I'm sure that all this exposure to languages at such an early age helped enormously when I learned French in just one year's time a few years later when I lived in Alicante, on the coast of Spain.

In the summer of 1962, my family, again along with Larry and Josie, took a camping vacation to southern Spain for two weeks. There was a beautiful campground called "Camp Columbus" set among the pine trees close to the U.S. Naval Base near Rota. This camp was maintained by the American military for use by their personnel as well as the occasional tourist. There were several cabins for rent and many tent sites available. The camping area was a short walking distance from the Atlantic Ocean, with a very nice beach and rolling sand dunes as far as the eye could see.

There was also a swimming pool, a playground for kids and a small store on site. We rented two cabins, one for our family and the other nearby for Larry and Josie. We soon settled in for a very nice vacation  amidst the trees. The adults relaxed under the cool pines with cocktails in hand as Johnny and I ran all over the place, exploring all the possibilities for further adventures.

Quickly, we made friends with the other children who were there. There were many Americans of course, but also many Spanish families, and a sprinkling of vacationers from such northern European countries as Germany, Holland, England, and the Scandinavian countries.

The amazing thing about this particular landscape was that among the tall pines lived a species of native chameleon. I was fascinated by these chameleons since I had never seen such creatures before. The fact that they could change their color depending on the specific shade of green or brown of the background they were sitting on was amazing to me. What was even more amazing was their ability to move their eyes independently, and 360 degrees, to literally be able to see in every direction at once.

Millions of years of evolution had allowed these lizards to develop to be perfectly suited to their environment. The fact that they moved very slowly through the trees also made it very difficult for any predator such as birds or other animals to be able to see them.

Most of the chameleons averaged around six to eight inches long and the trees seemed to be full of them; one just needed to be patient and wait until they moved slightly in order to spot them among the branches. Their camouflage was so effective that they could even blend their skin in with the particular grain of the bark they were perched on. Of course we captured several of them, and had countless hours of fun placing them on various backgrounds and watching in fascination as within a minute or so, they would blend in exactly with whatever surface we placed them on. There were exceptions of course. If I tried placing one onto a red plaid shirt for example, the poor creature had a very hard time trying to match that kind of background.

One particular chameleon I captured was different from the rest. He was only about four inches long, and was obviously a juvenile, so I named him "Junior." I kept him in a shoebox, and when our vacation was over, I talked my parents into letting me take him home. Once back at our house, I fixed up a small cage for him in my room with several branches for hanging on to and a water bowl.

I fed him insects I was able to catch, such as flies, grasshoppers, and crickets. He had an enormous tongue that he would use to capture the bugs by lashing it out and wrapping it around his helpless victims. When I was unable to catch insects to feed him, he seemed to enjoy a few Cheerios or the occasional small piece of raw hamburger meat.

Sometimes, after I made sure that Rudy the Dachshund was safely indoors, I'd take him out to the backyard and watch him walk around in the grass, seeing how he perfectly changed his skin color to match any particular shade of green. A few times I actually saw him stalk an insect. By being very still and almost invisible, he'd wait patiently until they were just close enough and then lash out with his long sticky tongue to capture his prey. To a ten-year-old boy, this was fascinating. I even took him to school one time for "show and tell," and I found out that I wasn't the only one who thought Junior was charming and a lot of fun to watch.

I kept Junior for about four months until one day he decided to just stop eating. It didn't matter what I put in front of him; he showed no interest in it whatsoever. He acted unusually slow and lethargic and then, after about a week, he died. I was devastated.

I asked my mom why he died, and she said, "Well, Ronnie, sometimes wild creatures don't do very well in captivity after a while. They miss their freedom and they miss being with their own kind. Or maybe he just got sick; it's hard to say, honey. But I know it wasn't your fault because I know that you took very good care of him."

She helped me find an old cigar box to put him in along with his favorite branch that he liked to hang on to, and a handwritten note. The note read as follows:

"Junior the Chameleon, You were a very nice pet and a good friend of mine, I'm sorry that you died and I will miss you. Thank you for being my friend, I hope you are in a place where you can be with others of your kind. Your good friend, Ronnie."

I sealed the cigar box with scotch tape and took it to an area near our house that the kids in the neighborhood called "Bear Canyon" (although it wasn't a canyon and there definitely weren't any bears), and I dug a hole in the dirt under an old gnarled tree and I put Junior's box in it. I said a few words much like what I wrote in the note before I covered him with dirt and stuck one of his favorite branches into the dirt pile.

I noticed a couple of Spanish kids a short distance away watching me as I did this, but I thought nothing of it. The next day I went back to Junior's grave and saw that someone had dug up the cigar box, as it was lying there by the hole, empty.

I felt violated at that point. I couldn't understand how anyone could do something like this. I told my mom about what had happened, and she said that perhaps the kids who watched me bury the box were curious and just wanted to know what was in it. Maybe they thought it was something of value. Or, she said, it could have been a dog that smelled it, dug up the box, and ate poor Junior's remains. I realized that I should have either buried the box deeper or somewhere where there was no one around to watch me.

On the other hand, as they say, "boys will be boys." One of the favorite things to do in our neighborhood involved fire crackers and lizards. While living on Calle Endrinas, I had a good buddy by the name of Terry Ybarra. He was a Mexican-American boy, and his parents were from San Antonio, Texas. His dad was in the Air Force like mine was, and his family lived a couple of blocks up the street from our house.

He was a rather dark-skinned kid with very dark eyes and straight jet black hair. Our maid at the time, Encarnacion, (or Encarna, as we called her for short), who lived with us for many years, thought he was black. She called him "el Negrito," even though I told her that he was not a Negro, but a Mexican-American.

Obviously, she had never seen a Mexican-American before, and had never seen anyone as dark as he was except for the occasional African she'd seen around Madrid. He was even a shade darker than the local Spanish gypsies that she had always seen around.

Encarna had replaced our previous maid, Victoria, who unfortunately my dad had caught stealing, and had to dismiss. Encarna became like a member of our family, and we became like members of her family as well. Over the years, on several occasions we went out to the town of Avila where she was born and raised, and while there we got to know her family who lived on a *finca*, a farm just outside of that beautiful ancient town.

Terry and I hung out together almost every day after school, and sometimes we'd get into some slight mischief around the neighborhood. One of our favorite activities was to walk up to the tiny store on the corner where they sold all kinds of wonderful things, such as candy, cigarettes, snacks, magazines and the most amazing things for young boys: firecrackers! Yes, for just one *duro*, (five pesetas, or about eight cents), we could buy a package of two dozen "*petardos*," which were small firecrackers with half-inch-long fuses. I imagine they were called "*petardos*" because the slang word in Spanish for "fart" was "*pedo*", and so a *petardo* would translate as something like "an enormous fart."

These little farts were lots of fun, especially for ten-year-old boys. The fuse would last only three or four seconds, but that was plenty of time to get it away from your fingers before it blew up. They weren't that powerful, but plenty strong enough to make a satisfyingly loud bang when they exploded.

Now what I'm about to relate to the reader I am in no way proud of whatsoever, but for the sake of honesty, I will relate it in detail. There was a large empty field near our street and we'd spend countless hours playing around the old abandoned construction debris that littered the lot. Such things as broken red bricks, chunks of old concrete, and pieces of rusty rebar and other leftovers from construction jobs were cast away there, forgotten and neglected.

This was a perfect habitat for lizards. There were hundreds of small lizards from two to six inches in length roaming the field, and hiding under and around this debris, trying not to get caught and eaten by the many birds, as well as the neighborhood cats and dogs that frequented the area. What Terry and I would do when we caught a lizard, and we had a supply of *petardos* in our pockets is that we'd grab the lizard right behind its head until it opened its mouth, then we'd stick
a *petardo* all the way down as far as it would go, light the fuse, and then throw the entire thing up in the air as far as we could, and watch as the lizard's guts and blood would fly everywhere.

For some reason that only young boys can understand, this was great fun for us. And it wasn't until a few years later that I realized that these poor lizards were very close cousins to my beloved "Junior," whom I had just buried a short time before I was committing these atrocities against the world of reptiles.

To this day, I have a deep affinity for the reptile world, perhaps due to the awful atrocities that I committed against their kind so many years ago. Whenever I see a snake on the road who is trying to cross it without getting run over, I cooperate fully in helping it to reach its goal, even if that means stopping my car and waiting for it to complete its journey. Perhaps this is my way of trying to pay it backwards for the terrible crimes I committed with lizards as a young boy living on Calle Endrinas.

On another occasion, I committed a different kind of atrocity that I later deeply regretted, but this time, it was against glass windows. My brother and I were playing around this same empty field when we decided that all the nice round rocks lying around would come in handy for some other kind of despicable action. Across the street from the field was an old abandoned house, very common in the various neighborhoods of Madrid in those days. This particular house had large windows facing the street, and sported large "Xs" marked on them with soap, to show that they were there and not missing.

I'm not sure if it was my idea or my brother's, but one of us got the notion of using those Xs as target practice. We each gathered up a handful of nice round rocks from the field, walked across the street and stood on the sidewalk, getting ready to try our hands at target practice. After each of us had thrown five or six rocks, it turned out that we both had a pretty good aim, because all three front picture windows were smashed, leaving broken glass all over the place. Neither one of us felt particularly proud for some reason though; as a matter of fact, suddenly we both felt scared, ashamed, and mortified to realize that we had done something that we were sure to regret.

Sure enough, within a few seconds after the sound of the breaking glass, a large, older, heavyset man with a dark mustache came running around from the back of the house and started yelling at us. We both took off as fast as our legs could carry us and, without looking back, ran straight to our house, breathless and scared out of our wits by the time we reached home. We ran to our own backyard to catch our breath before entering the house very nonchalantly, acting as if nothing was wrong.

A couple of minutes later, the doorbell rang and my mom went to answer it. It was the large man who was yelling at us and chasing us earlier. He had followed us all the way home and was visibly quite angry. He began to yell at my mom that two young boys had broken some windows of the house up the street which happened to be one of the properties that he watched over. He had followed these two *gamberros* (hoodlums) to this house and was demanding retribution or, he threatened, the *Policia* would be involved.

She went to get Dad, who had just finished taking a nap in the bedroom, and he came to the front door asking what this entire ruckus that was going on was about. The large man told my dad what he had told my mom and then went on to say that if he was not paid 4000 pesetas for the damages, he would contact the police. My brother and I were cowering in the kitchen, overhearing everything that was going on.

My dad then yelled, "Johnny, Ronnie, get up here right now!"

We did as we were told and came to the door and looked at the large man standing at the entrance.

When he saw us, he pointed at us and screamed out, "*Si, son estos dos muchachos que rompieron las ventanas de la casa!*" (Yes, those are the two boys who broke the windows of the house!)

My dad then asked us, "Boys, is this true? Did you guys break the windows that this man is talking about?"

Johnny looked up at my dad and said in the bravest and the most honest voice he could muster, "No, Dad, it wasn't us. We were hanging in the backyard all afternoon, playing catch."

My dad then said to the large man, (in Spanish of course), "My son has just told me that he and his brother did not do what you accuse them of doing, sir."

Then the man said in a voice that was getting more angry by the second, "But sir, I heard the windows break and I came around from the back of the house and I saw them running away and I followed them here! I know that they did it, without a doubt!"

My dad then said something that has stuck with me in my memory for over half a century now. In a loud and firm voice he said to the man, "Sir, my sons have been raised properly by their mother and me, and we have taught them both integrity and honesty, and if they say they did not commit this crime, then I believe them, and you must be mistaken. And that is all there is to say about it, so good day to you, sir!"

And he closed the door in the man's face. The man then rang the doorbell again, and my dad opened it again and said in an even louder and firmer voice, "Sir, we have nothing else to discuss. Please leave the premises."

And he closed the door again. After that, we assumed that the man just walked away, because we never heard from him again or, thankfully, from the police either.

Johnny and I maintained our deception for many, many years and planned to never reveal to either him or my mom the truth about what happened that afternoon. But finally, about thirty or so years after the event, I was visiting my father at his house one day and, after sharing a few cold beers with him, I asked him if he remembered that day in Calle Endrinas when the windows got broken.

He said, "Well, Ron, actually I remember it very well. Why do you ask?"

I replied, "Well, Dad, I've got something to confess to you. Johnny and I actually did break the windows of that house that day. I don't know why we did it, but we did, and I'm so sorry that we lied about it."

He looked at me with a look that only a father who really loves his son can give and said, "Well, I knew you boys had done it all along; I could tell that you were both lying through your teeth. But frankly I didn't want to pay for those damn windows so that's why I pretended to believe you. And besides I knew that someday your guilt would get to you and you would confess."

I just smiled, reached over and gave him a big hug, and said, "Thanks, Dad. I love you, hombre."

Chapter 3. Calle Triana

"Any man's life, told truly, is a novel."
— Ernest Hemingway, Death in the Afternoon

By the beginning of 1963, my family and I had moved to a different house in Madrid. There were new buyers for our rental house on Calle Endrinas and they wanted to move in themselves, so we were asked to find other accommodations. After a month or so, we moved into a large three-story duplex on Calle Triana, just a few blocks from Plaza Peru. Much to my delight, this was where the American Theater was located, and now I could walk easily to the theater to see movies. American movies then became a major influence on my limited understanding of American culture and ways of life.

Our new place consisted of half of a large building that was divided into two separate houses that shared a common wall between them. Each house had its own separate yard, garage, driveway, and fence, and each had its own separate entrance. About a block away was Calle Alfonso XIII, named after Alfonso XIII, the King of Spain from 1886 until 1931. It was a major thoroughfare, and many businesses were located along this wide and busy street. One of these businesses was, of all things, a movie studio.

Samuel Bronston Studios operated for many years in Spain and was  responsible for such Hollywood epics as "El Cid," "King of Kings," and "The Fall of the Roman Empire." Bronston was a pioneer in the practice of locating epic-scale productions in Spain to reduce the massive costs involved. The success of his films inspired him to build the studio near our house in Madrid as well as a gigantic studio in Las Rozas, just outside of Madrid.

The cost of the construction of the film studios as well as the box office failure of "The Fall of the Roman Empire" combined to leave Bronston in financial difficulties and in 1964, he had to stop all business activities. Soon after that he filed for bankruptcy and ended up abandoning both of his movie studios in the Madrid area.

This left a huge area (which occupied several city blocks) very near our house on Calle Triana that was formerly the movie studio. Kids from our neighborhood, both Americans and Spaniards, would climb the wall that surrounded the place and find all kinds of movie paraphernalia and artifacts, such as old plastic swords and shields buried in the dirt from the many "Gladiator"-type movies filmed there. This was fantastic fun for young boys, as one might imagine.

As it turned out, the house right behind ours on Calle Triana, across the wall that divided the two houses, was a sound studio and audio production facility. While Bronston Studios was open, the facility did audio production work there for some of those movies. After Bronston closed, they then worked for one of the two Spanish television channels and dubbed American, British, and other non-Spanish speaking films into Spanish to air on local television.

On many occasions, both during the day and at night, we could hear sounds of their production work coming from the other side of the wall. We'd hear a line of dialogue in English, then a few seconds later, the same line done in a different voice, translated into Spanish. This never was a real nuisance because it was usually so faint that it did not really bother our household. But they worked at night a lot, and I remember many nights falling to sleep hearing faint English lines of movie dialogue followed by the same line repeated in Spanish. It was almost like getting free Spanish lessons!

Our new house was huge compared to the single-story house we lived in on Calle Endrinas. It had three floors; the top floor had three bedrooms and a bathroom, and the middle floor, which was just above ground level, had the main dining room, the living room, an office for my dad, and a den with a fireplace and bar. Downstairs in the basement floor were the kitchen, the laundry room, the maid quarters (which included both a bedroom and bathroom), and another smaller dining room as well. Connecting the kitchen and the main dining room upstairs was a dumb-waiter operated by a pulley system.

Of course, we brought our maid, Encarna, with us from Calle Endrinas to our new house and she was thrilled with her new accommodations, which were not only larger, but were separated from the rest of the family, who slept two stories above her. And like all live-in maids in Spain at the time, she had every Sunday and every Thursday evening off. Her pay of 1000 pesetas per month (plus free room and board) allowed her to save every month, and eventually she opened a *perfumeria* (perfume and cosmetics store) in her hometown of Avila many years later.

And Encarna had become almost like a member of our family very quickly. Not only did she do all the cooking, cleaning, and laundry, but she also taught us a lot about Spanish language and culture, as well as the Spanish cuisine and the Spanish way of life.

She was an excellent cook whose specialties included *Tortilla Española, Pescado Frito, Calamares en su tinta, Caldo a la Madrileña, Gambas aljillo, Croquetas de jamon y queso, Papas bravas, Albondigas,* as well as a delicious *Paella* on special occasions. Of course, she'd make just about anything we wished for, from a sandwich or a nice fresh salad to a complete breakfast. It was almost like having a restaurant right in our own house. She'd go shopping every other day or so and buy whatever was fresh and looked good for that evening's meal. Dinner time was always an interesting adventure with her introducing us to different Spanish dishes that we had never tried. And if we all liked it, she would make it more often.

Johnny and I loved our new house; not only was it bigger than our previous home, but the yard was larger with huge trees in the backyard, perfect for climbing and building tree forts in. We also liked the fact that many other American families lived in the neighborhood, (probably because the American Theater at Plaza Peru was so close), and we quickly became friends with most of them, especially the ones that had kids around our age.

We boys had both gotten new bicycles for Christmas the previous year, and it wasn't long before there was a group of American juveniles riding around the neighborhood on bikes, doing what kids do the world over. Our house had a large garage which was separate from the main house and half of it was underground, as the driveway sloped down at the end of it into the garage. It wasn't totally subterranean, but about five feet of it was lower than the surrounding area.

On top of the garage was a nice patio where we would enjoy meals *alfresco* on warm summer days. Of course, my parents enjoyed many cocktail hours sitting around the table on our top patio, and my brother and I would occasionally join them for a glass of wine mixed with *gaseosa* (a clear 7-UP type of beverage) purchased in one liter bottles.

My dad always parked the car on the street, so this garage became our hangout and was also where we stored and worked on our bikes. There was quite a competition at the time among the neighborhood boys to see who could "trick out" their bike the most. We all started with the most basic and easy trick which was to use a clothespin to attach a playing card to each wheel so that when the bikes spokes turned, it would make a cool fluttering noise that we all thought sounded like a motorcycle. And, of course, we added all kinds of accessories to our bikes such as different types of horns, some of which were air-powered as in squeezing the bulb made them squawk. Others were the typical ring-a-ding bell type, and still others were battery-powered and made a loud buzzing noise whenever the button attached to the handlebars was pressed.

And every decent bike had to have a light system, with both a headlight in front and a red tail light in the back. These were either battery-powered, requiring two D cells, or ran off a small generator which was attached to the front tire so that when the tires rotated, it powered both the headlight and the tail light. But these were not as popular as the battery-powered ones because they would only work while the bike was in motion, and we liked to shine our headlights all the time, not just when the bike was moving.

Of course, this required using a lot of batteries and when they went dead, so did our lights. One of the most popular styles of bikes in those days was what was called a "Spyder," made by Sears. Schwinn also made a similar bike known as a "Stingray."

These types of bikes had several things in common besides the fact that they looked so cool to us. They all had the long seats known as "banana seats," as well as the high-rise "ape hanger" handlebars. Many had the "sissy bar" which was a frame that fit behind the seat so that the rider could lean back. This style of bicycle was inspired by the "chopper" style of motorcycles that were becoming popular in California at the time. The banana seat itself usually came in outrageous colors, some even with tiger stripes, bright sparkles, or some other such eye-catching finish. This type of bike was very popular among the boys in our neighborhood, and they even made one for girls that were usually pink with a low-rise cross bar. The best ones had a three-speed gear shifter attached to the cross bar which made them even more fun to ride.

Some kids, such as my brother and I, modified our existing bikes to make them look and ride like "Stingrays" by adding the high handlebars and the banana seats to our old style "regular" bikes. We'd order the parts from the Sears catalog, and then install them ourselves, which was a lot cheaper than buying a new bike. Countless hours were spent in our garage modifying and customizing our bikes to get them just right. All this tinkering with bicycles was a great introduction because within just a few short years, I owned and rode actual motorbikes and motorcycles — but more about that in a later chapter.

There was a rather steep hill near our house on Calle Triana that became the center of a lot of our adventures. The street this hill occupied was about two blocks long and we'd ride our bikes down it to see just how fast we could go, often reaching very high speeds. And like most streets in Madrid, it had a sidewalk, which we would ride on because there was some moderate traffic going up and down this residential street, and nobody wanted a collision with an oncoming car. Most times, we felt fairly safe riding on the sidewalk except when there was foot traffic, but we'd usually manage to avoid the occasional pedestrian or two.

This hill was not only where we would race our bicycles but also became the location of our version of "soap box derbies." These small gravity-powered race cars were becoming very popular in the States by the early 1960s, and we had our own neighborhood version of these races.

The first soap box that we saw around the neighborhood was created by a chubby kid named Albert who had "borrowed" the wheels from his kid sister's baby buggy and had built a contraption 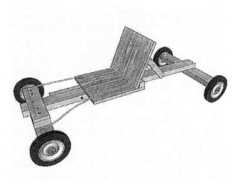 using these wheels along with a few pieces of old discarded lumber. It was a very basic device with each wheel attached to the end of a two by four. The front one attached to the frame with a bolt that would allow it to swivel so it could be steered. The steering was done by setting one's feet onto the front two by four and moving them in the direction one wanted to go.

After watching Albert as he rode his racer down the hill, another kid had the idea of attaching a piece of rope to the front axle and using it to steer instead of his feet. This was a great idea and by the next day, Albert had made the modification. After a short while there were several of these contraptions in the neighborhood, enough to start having races.

Some of us kids didn't have a kid sister with a baby buggy, so we'd try whatever we could find that was round and would roll. These included bicycle wheels and tires, but these proved to be way too big to be very practical. One kid had somehow procured a shopping cart and had taken the wheels off it to build his car. Another kid, Stevie, had decided that since he had nothing else to use, he thought he'd try using his skates, the type that attached to your shoes with a skate key. He had two pairs of skates (having once again "borrowed" the second pair from his little sister), and he screwed one skate each to the bottom of each end of the two by fours, and ended up having a pretty nice ride.

One day after his sister demanded her skates back; he tried something different, since he now only had one pair of skates. He did away with the axles and just attached one skate each to the front and to the rear of the frame. He tried sitting on the frame and it rolled downhill fairly well with him on it. But, of course, without a front axle he was unable to steer it at all, and the first few times he rode it down the hill, he fell off at considerable speed and almost injured himself.

Then Stevie, the great visionary that he was, decided to try standing up on his device and riding it down the hill. And *Voila!* The first skateboard in Madrid was born. He quickly realized that just by leaning one way or another, he was able to steer the thing, and it was great fun to stand up while riding instead of sitting down on it with your butt cheeks mere inches from the cold hard pavement.

Within a few weeks, every kid in the neighborhood had followed suit. Most of us had old skates sitting around in the closet, and we all got them out and attached them to an old piece of wood and soon we were all riding these new gadgets all over the place. A new kid named Joey who was hanging around the neighborhood had just arrived in Madrid from Southern California, and as soon as he saw us riding on these things, he told us that what we were doing was called "sidewalk surfing" in California. We thought that was a pretty cool name for it and we called our new devices "sidewalk surfboards," until we later discovered that they were actually just called skateboards. Within a few years, skateboards would become commercially available, with special wheels on the bottom, and in all kinds of shapes, sizes, and colors.

About this time, during the early 1960s, everything from Southern California became very popular all around the world it seemed. The Beach Boys, Jan and Dean, The Ventures, The Surfaris, and other musical groups from California were creating a new sound along with a youth sub-culture that was very appealing to many teens and pre-teens of the era. Songs about surfing, cars, and girls seemed to symbolize that California "fun in the sun," happy-go-lucky lifestyle. And even though we did not live in southern California, we caught glimpses of it through various sources. Comics and magazines were a great way to catch a little of this new phenomenon, as well as movies at the American theater.

Television to us was practically nonexistent since Spanish TV consisted of only one channel at the time, which was the state-sponsored station with mostly government news coverage and other boring stuff, at least to us American kids. A second Spanish station launched in 1966 and

was a more commercial station that aired old movies (mostly the kind produced in Spain showing the glory and greatness of Spain's history), along with an occasional comedy or variety show.

Every Sunday, depending on the season of the year, the station would air live either the weekly

Futbol (soccer) game from *Estadio Bernabeu*, (the soccer stadium, which was not far from our house), or the weekly bullfight, which was usually from *Las Ventas* Bullring in Madrid.

It was a strange experience being in a bar or a cafe on a Sunday evening around the neighborhood of the stadium when a live Futbol game was in progress, and the place had the game playing on a TV set behind the bar. One could hear the roar of the crowd on the TV, then a second or two later, one could hear it coming from the thousands of people who made up the crowd in the stadium. It took longer for the sound to travel through the air to reach our ears than it took for it to be transmitted and broadcast to the TV set.

Everything on TV was in black and white of course, because color television didn't begin until 1974 in Spain. By the time they launched the second station, there was a demand for other programming, and that is when an occasional American TV program would appear. "Bonanza" and "Mission Impossible" reruns from the U.S. became very popular among the Spanish viewing audience, along with many American-made Hollywood movies, all dubbed into Spanish of course. Some of this work was very likely done by our next-door neighbors.

Another source of American culture, along with DC and Marvel comic books such as "Superman," "Spider-man," and "The Fantastic Four," was MAD magazine. These were all available at the newsstand on base right alongside the latest copy of "Stars and Stripes" (the American Armed Forces newspaper).

At that young age, we American pre-teens thought that MAD was almost the funniest thing in the world. I remember the cover of the January 1961 issue had the numbers of the New Year in large numerals and then in small print it read, "For the actual year, please turn magazine upside down." And, of course, it said the same thing upside down as it did right side up. The image of Alfred E. Neuman, with his gap-toothed smile and motto, "What, me worry?" along with other regulars like "Spy vs. Spy," and the fold-in back page, were all considered by us to be hilarious satire (even though we probably didn't even know the meaning of that word at the time.) We just thought it all to be both incredibly funny and a lot of fun.

The fact that our house on Calle Triana was only two short blocks from Plaza Peru, where the American theater was located, contributed greatly to my understanding and appreciation of American culture. This theater was provided as a benefit to the American Service personnel who lived in "downtown" Madrid. There were also two other American theaters in the Madrid area at the time: one at Torrejon Air Base, mostly for the active duty airmen and officers who lived on base, and another in the Royal Oaks housing area for the Americans who lived there.

The Plaza Peru Theater was a very nice modern theater with a large auditorium downstairs and a balcony upstairs where the teenagers would usually sit to "make out." There was also a nice snack bar that offered not only popcorn but the latest in American snacks and candies as well. I allowed only Americans with Military ID cards inside the theater, the only exception being for someone who was a "guest" of someone else who had an American military ID. These ID cards were issued to everyone connected to the American military presence in Spain, regardless of age. All "dependents" (as families of military personnel were called) had their own cards and were required to show them to enter any American military facility.

The theater showed five or six different movies every week, along with a Saturday matinee. Weeknights there would be two showings of the same feature: first, at six in the evening, and the next one starting at around eight. Mondays and Tuesdays would be the same movie, but Wednesdays through Sundays they would show a different movie each night.

Each show always began with a short film of the "Star-Spangled Banner," with a minute and a half of that music blaring through the loudspeakers with lots of shots of American flags waving in the air and of bombs bursting in the air. Everyone in the theater was required to stand up during this song and remove their hats if they happened to be wearing them. Most people also put their right hands over their chests near their hearts during this prelude to the filmed entertainment. And before the main feature, they would show previews of upcoming movies as well as "newsreels," which were short news stories about what was going on back in the States with a variety of subjects from politics to celebrity gossip.

Saturday's matinees would begin at ten in the morning and sometimes last for three to four hours. After the obligatory standing for the "Star-Spangled Banner," several cartoons would follow, the usual ones that could be seen on any Saturday morning on almost any American TV station in the States at the time. These included such cartoons as "Bugs Bunny," "Tom and Jerry," "The Roadrunner," etc. Following four or five cartoons, there would be a science fiction serial such as "Flash Gordon" or "Buck Rogers in the 25th Century." But sometimes there would be a western serial such as "The Lone Ranger" or "The Cisco Kid."

After this they previewed the coming attractions of the movies that would be shown later that week, and then finally the main feature would begin. And all this cost the pricey sum of 15 cents for kids under age 12 and a whole quarter for adults. My mom would toss me a quarter every Saturday morning (popcorn was a dime) and off I'd go on my bike to this other world, so much different from the one all around me right outside the doors of the theater.

The American Theater at Plaza Peru was very much a social scene as well, and kids were not the only people who would show up to enjoy a good movie. In fact, sometimes they showed movies that had an "R" rating, but that was unusual. Most were the G or PG variety, but adult-themed movies were available occasionally. Such Hollywood movies as "Psycho," "The Day of the Triffids," and "Dr. Sardonicus" as well as many, many others stick in my mind to this day.

Sometimes the theater would have a "special night" when a visiting celebrity who happened to be in town would show up at the theater; usually on the night that they were showing a movie that he/she happened to be in. One night I was at the theater preparing to watch "Ben Hur" (which was filmed in Spain), when I saw a long line in the lobby in front of a man who turned out to be Steven Boyd, who played the role of "Messala" in that film. I stood in line and got the man's autograph, and then a little later I walked into the auditorium and watched him on the big screen acting in the movie. My young mind realized something that evening that I'm still trying to understand to this day concerning fame, celebrity, and personality.

One Friday evening I was at the theater with my brother watching a movie, but we never got the chance to see the end of it. The date was November 22, 1963, and I was eleven years old, and my family had been living at our house on Calle Triana for a little less than a year. About a half hour into the main feature that evening, the movie stopped, the lights came on in the theater, and an announcer said over the P. A. system, "Due to a national emergency that has just occurred in Dallas,

Texas, all active duty American military personnel must immediately report to their duty stations and await further instructions. The remainder of tonight's film will not be shown. Please evacuate the theater in an orderly and safe fashion."

My brother and I rushed home and told my Mom what had happened at the theater but she had already heard the news and had already turned on our large Grundig radio/record player and was listening intently to the Armed Forces radio station broadcasting from Torrejon. My dad had already reported to the Air Ministry where he worked following his orders. Our nation's President, John F. Kennedy, had just been shot in the head during a motorcade in Dallas. The three of us sat around listening until way past midnight, horrified by the news and wondering what would happen to our country and the world.

The next couple of days seemed to get even worse if that was possible. We listened to more of the Armed Forces Radio broadcast and learned that the murder suspect, Lee Harvey Oswald, had been shot himself while being transported from the Dallas City Jail to the Dallas County Jail, by Jack Ruby, a Dallas nightclub owner. Soon after that, we learned that Vice President Lyndon Johnson had been sworn in as our new President. These were very trying times for the United States and indeed for the entire world.

Spain, being 99% Catholic, considered Kennedy to be the greatest of all U.S. presidents, and took the news of his death very hard. There were masses held at every church, and people all over the country prayed for him and his family. The pictures in the newspapers of Kennedy's young son, John Jr., at his father's funeral brought tears to the eyes of many Spaniards and Americans alike. It truly was a very strange transition time for the entire world and seemed to mark the ending of a very innocent time and the beginning of a more turbulent, and world-changing decade: the remaining years of the 1960s and early 1970s.

A few months after President Kennedy's assassination, our household had quite the shakeup as well. My father received word from his brother Dale that two Dale's friends were to pay us a visit in Madrid. My Uncle Dale, along with his wife, my Aunt Ruth, had spent almost a year in Spain the previous year. They had spent about half of that time on the coast in the little town called Peñiscola, and the other half in a small *piso* in a cheap neighborhood of Madrid. My dad had gotten word that Robert and Martha, Dale's friends from the States, were soon to pay us a visit.

Coincidentally, this visit from Robert and Martha coincided with a trip that my folks had been planning for quite some time to Switzerland. My parents, at this point, were still in the planning stages for opening a Swiss restaurant in downtown Madrid that was to become known as *El Chalet Suizo*. They had taken several trips to Zurich and the Swiss Alps to do research for the dishes that were to be offered at the restaurant. So within a day or so of our visitors' arrival, my parents had to leave for a week in Switzerland, and left our house to my brother and me, our maid Encarna, and Robert and Martha.

To my young eyes, and to just about anybody's eyes, I imagine, Robert and Martha were an impressive-looking couple. Robert was over six feet tall with a long flowing beard, very long hair, and fierce, deep piercing eyes. Martha was equally impressive with her waist-length hair, slim figure, and a gentle demeanor about her that radiated calmness, composure, and tranquility, in contrast to Robert's wildness and impulsiveness. These two were "hippies" before there was such a thing. Both in their mid-twenties, they were in Spain for travel, adventure, and to experience life and all it had to offer.

Robert had been in the Merchant Marine, had met my Uncle Dale in San Francisco a few years earlier, and they had become great friends. Robert had worked his way across the Atlantic on a commercial ship on this trip, but Martha had a little money, so she paid for a flight to Barcelona, and she met up with Robert there. They both had their backpacks on, their passports ready, and were eager for a grand tour of Spain, Portugal, and Morocco.

Our house on Calle Triana had a large room that we called the den. It had the fireplace, a couch and chairs, the stereo, and the fully stocked bar that my dad had set up. It also had French-style doors that locked from the inside. This is where Robert and Martha set up their own headquarters. For the next five or six days, they rarely left the den, except to tell Encarna to bring them more food. They almost emptied the bar of all libations including most of the wine that my dad kept there, as well a lot of the hard booze such as rum, gin, vodka, and whiskey. They kept the doors locked at most times and had the stereo cranked up loudly to help cover up the sounds of their wild lovemaking all night and most of the day.

There was also a peculiar odor coming from the room that I had never smelled before. It had a unique smell that did not exactly stink, but did not smell very pleasant either; it was a sort of stinky-sweet odor that I later realized was pot. They did not light up in our presence, however, but only smoked it behind the closed doors.

When Encarna asked them what the strange smell was, Robert told her that it was just "Turkish" cigarettes they were smoking. Encarna had never been exposed to such a thing before and didn't know what to do besides believe him. But she was not happy with these two *Jovenes Americanos,* (young Americans) in her house, disrupting the household she was in charge of maintaining, and was quite visibly upset the entire time they stayed with us.

The following week when my parents returned from Switzerland, she told my dad what had been going on, and my dad, being the gentle and diplomatic type of person that he was, just told them that it might be better if they got on their way. The next day, they loaded their packs onto their backs and got my dad to drive them to the southern outskirts of Madrid, where they hitchhiked south to southern Spain, and later to Morocco. Years later we found out through my Uncle Dale that Robert and Martha had ended up settling in a hippy commune in northern New Mexico, near Taos, and had continued to live their "alternative" lifestyle.

Much to my delight, I was able to visit them there on several occasions later in my life and saw that they had not only maintained their chosen lifestyle for the rest of their lives, but had also built their own house on a plot of land. And later when their children got older, they built houses for each one of them on the same property. They raised a beautiful family, and they continue to this day to live life by their own rules and as they choose.

This visit that we had from Robert and Martha and from my Uncle Dale and Aunt Ruth the previous year was the beginning of my realization at that very early age that there did exist alternatives to the typical American lifestyle. The American life that was depicted in the glimpses I had perceived from movies, school, and the occasional trip back to the States to visit relatives, was obviously not the only American lifestyle or way of life.

Later in the decade as a teenager, and then later in my life as a young man, I explored these "alternatives" myself to a much greater degree. And as a matter of fact, this alternative lifestyle became a large part of whom and what I was to become as an adult.

Chapter 4. It All Began with The Beatles at the Bullring

"After silence, that which comes nearest to expressing the inexpressible is music."
— Aldous Huxley

It all began with the Beatles at the bullring. On the second of July 1965, the Beatles performed at La Plaza de Toros de Las Ventas Bullring in Madrid, Spain. I was fortunate enough to see that concert, and it affected me profoundly for the rest of my life.

In the early 1960s, the Beatles arose from Liverpool, England and within a few short years became the biggest and most famous band in the world. Their 1965 European tour began on 20 June 1965 in Paris and included fifteen concerts over nine dates because in several cities, they played two shows. They chose the bullring in Madrid because it was the largest venue in all of Spain, holding almost 25,000 people. The Madrid show was their second to last show of their tour; with their very last show to be held in Barcelona the following day.

To say that this Beatles show overwhelmed me would be quite an understatement. I was only twelve years old at the time, soon to turn thirteen, and my young mind was able to recognize not only the power and influence that these four young lads from Liverpool exuded, but I also was able to see the joy and excitement that their music brought to so many people. I've been asked over the years what I remember most from that concert, and I still remember almost every detail about the show.

Their set list included songs that I had heard on the radio countless times, (as well as half the world, it seemed), including such hits as,

"Twist and Shout," "She's a Woman," "A Hard Day's Night," "Baby's in Black," "Can't Buy Me Love," "She Loves You," "I Feel Fine," and "Ticket to Ride." The Beatles had played on the Ed Sullivan show in February 1964, but since we were living in Spain during that time, (where TV was so limited), I had missed that famous performance when so many other people first saw the Beatles perform.

My father had been able to get tickets for the show through a poker-playing friend of his who had two daughters who were both around our ages, so my brother and I had "dates" to the first concert of our young lives. One of them had brought a pair of binoculars along so we passed them around throughout the show to use to zoom in on the action. I remember when it was my turn to use them, I focused on Ringo playing his drums and I watched as he shook his head to the beat, his hair flying all around, especially the hair on the back of his head. It was the longest hair I'd seen on any man up to that point in my short life.

I looked at his drum set and saw these words on the bass drum, "Ludwig - The Beatles." I was unfamiliar with the Ludwig drum company that put their name on all their bass drum heads, so in my mind I thought that they were comparing themselves to the famous classical musician, Ludwig Van Beethoven, which made perfect sense to me at the time. It wasn't until later that I learned it was just the brand of drums Ringo used.

I also zoomed in with the binoculars on the guitars the lads were playing, trying to figure out what kind they were, because I somehow thought that the equipment they used was very significant to the power and ability that they demonstrated. I tried to figure out what kind of guitar John Lennon was playing. Since he was wearing the black "Beatles" suit that they all wore during their live performances, and since the Rickenbacker 325 that he had strapped on was all black, except for the white pick guard, I thought that his guitar was shaped like the pick guard, the shape of a teardrop, since the rest of the guitar blended in with his black suit.

George's guitar was an Epiphone Casino hollow body and Paul was playing his famous Hofner violin-shaped bass guitar. They all had their guitars plugged into their Vox AC-100 Super Deluxe amplifiers, also known as Vox "Super Beatles." Vox designed these amplifiers especially for groups like the Beatles who were playing for audiences of 10,000 or more. And they seemed to work quite well, because I could hear the music just fine, even over the screaming and yelling of thousands of fans.

I remember that a lot of the people attending the show could not sit down once they started to play. Many stood up and danced in the aisles, twisting and gyrating to the music. Others stood on their seats to be able to see better, and then the people behind them had to do the same to be able to see as well. I would estimate that over half of the audience did not stay in their seats during the entire show.

The tickets cost about what a bullfight would cost: 250 pesetas or around four dollars. Those four dollars that my father spent on my ticket would change my life almost more than any other experience I would ever have, because from that day on, I realized that what those four guys were doing that day is what I wanted to do. I wanted to have that ability to make people feel that way. I wanted to make people feel the excitement and exhilaration that I experienced on that day. And I have pretty much been trying to do so ever since, in one way or another.

The very next day after this incredible experience, my brother and I decided that we would form a band. So along with two of our neighborhood friends, another pair of brothers named Randy and Wally Padilla, we wasted no time getting started. The Padilla brothers were the same age as my brother and I, Randy being my brother's age, and Wally my age. They lived a few blocks from us and their family also included an older sister named Linda, who was already in high school, and a younger brother named Charlie. Their father was a pilot, originally from Panama, but was in the U.S. Air Force and flew military aircraft from Torrejon Air Base to various other bases around Europe, mostly to Air Force and Army bases in Germany.

They had a large house, as most Americans in Madrid had, with a nice big garage, perfect for our fledgling band to practice in. Randy had taken a couple of guitar classes by this point and so he was to become our "lead" guitarist. My family had a Spanish acoustic guitar around the house that Johnny was learning a little on, so he would be the "rhythm" guitarist. And a year or so earlier when Johnny expressed interest in learning the guitar, my parents hired a Spanish guitar teacher to come to our house and give him an hour lesson once a week for a few months. Immediately after his lesson, he would show me what he had learned, and this way we got two lessons for the price of one.

But Wally and I couldn't decide who would be the drummer, so we decided to both be drummers. We went down to the local music store in downtown Madrid and used our allowance money to each buy a couple of tambourines, a pair of drumsticks, and a little brass cymbal. We took the small metal jingles off the tambourines to make them sound more like actual drums and put them on a chair and hit them with our new drumsticks. As far as where the cymbal went, we somehow mounted it to a pencil tied to the back of the chair and were able to strike it with our drumsticks as well. So we had two very primitive drummers and drum sets in our original band.

Later I would switch to bass guitar, and Wally would get a real drum set, but that wasn't until the next year. Randy was a very smart and capable guy, so he got the idea to take the acoustic nylon strings off his Spanish guitar and put steel, electric guitar strings on it. He next purchased a pickup for the guitar that he mounted and wired over the hole in the front. He now had an "electric" guitar.

For an amplifier, he took an old radio/record player that his dad let him have, and somehow put an input on the back of it where he was able to plug in his new electric guitar. For a microphone, he used one of his dad's military walkie-talkie-type two-way radios with the push-to-talk microphone, and he used tape to hold down the talk-button so it would stay on all the time. He taped the mike to the end of a broomstick which he tied to a straight-back chair, and that was his mike stand and microphone. It actually worked when he plugged it into his homemade amplifier. We would spend countless hours in the Padilla's garage, with these primitive instruments and equipment, trying to make music and, if nothing else, we had a lot of fun trying.

Around this time there was a worldwide phenomenon of kids trying to make music. In the States, in England, in Spain, and really all over the world, there were countless kids forming bands and playing music. Obviously, we weren't the only ones who were trying to be the Beatles. Before the Beatles, I had always enjoyed music and listened to such singers as Elvis Presley and Fabian, and other "teen" idols, but with the Beatles, we realized that we might actually be able to do it ourselves. Elvis had a band behind him, as did the others, and their bands were sometimes really orchestras, with countless horns, keyboards, and other mysterious (at least to us) instruments. But with the Beatles, we saw that just four guys could do it all; write, perform, and play all the instruments themselves to create what we came to call, "rock-and-roll."

Soon after the Beatles created their worldwide phenomenon, along came countless other bands in their wake, including many great bands that were maybe as good as or even better than those four lads from Liverpool. Not only were there the "British Invasion" bands such as The

Animals, The Kinks, The Rolling Stones, The Hollies, The Who, Herman's Hermits, The Yardbirds, The Zombies, The Spencer Davis Group, The Dave Clark Five, and many others, but there were countless American bands as well.

Bands such as The Loving Spoonful, Paul Revere and the Raiders, The Ventures, The Byrds, MC5, The Mamas and Papas, The Beach Boys, Simon and Garfunkel, Creedence Clearwater Revival, Bob Dylan and so many others were emerging in the States, creating all kinds of sub-genres of music including surf, folk, psychedelic, pop, soul, and various combinations of them all. The early to mid-1960s was a very prolific time in the development of modern music, and the influences of those early bands are still felt today in popular music over fifty years later.

Of course, these bands were the ones who were successful. There were thousands of others that never made it out of the garage. And most of the successful ones, at least the ones who were making records and were on the radio, were slightly older than us by a few years. By this time, we were barely in our teens and the bands on the radio were in their early twenties for the most part. There were exceptions, though, such as one band whose members were almost our exact age. They were called Dino, Desi, and Billy, and were the sons of the famous Hollywood celebrities named Dean Martin and Desi Arnaz. They had a couple of songs on the radio (mostly Bob Dylan covers) and were only twelve or thirteen at the time. But I'm sure their famous parents had a lot to do with their success, of course.

At about this time, 1964-65, is when my parents were starting to have some marital issues. The reality of the situation was that my dad was starting to feel a little restless and unfulfilled with his marriage. Being the *dueño* (owner) of a very fancy restaurant that was becoming very popular among the elite and the upper crust of *Madrileño* society enabled him to have a roving eye, as they say, and being the man of integrity that he was, he didn't want to "cheat" on his wife, so they decided to separate before he actually did so.

I remember the way he described it to my brother and me one evening. He sat us down and explained to us that a marriage can be like an archer that releases two arrows at the same time, they might go along side-by-side for a while, but eventually they split up and each goes their own way. He said that he and my mother were like that; that they had been together for over twenty years, and that now they found themselves going in different directions.

They decided to try a separation and see what happened. What this meant to our family was that my dad was to stay in Madrid to keep running the restaurant and keep up the house we were renting, and my mom, my brother, and I were to go to live in the Spanish coastal town of Alicante for one year. Since there wasn't an American or even a British school in Alicante at the time, my brother and I would be enrolled in a French school.

Although we didn't speak French at all at this point, we would have a special tutor so we'd learn it very quickly, and we'd finish the year adding another language to our skills. They ensured us that it was to be a grand adventure since we would be living in an apartment right on the beach in a little town just outside of the city of Alicante called Albufereta.

So in the middle of that summer of 1965, we packed up our stuff and headed off to spend a year on the beach in Alicante. Johnny and I were reluctant to go since we would miss our friends in Madrid and besides we were just getting our band together. But the decision was made, so off we went.

Sure enough, the *piso* (apartment) that we rented was right on the beach and on the fourth floor which was the top floor of the apartment building. We moved into our spacious *piso*, with its wraparound terrace and views towards both the north and the east of the deep blue Mediterranean Sea. I even got my own room since I elected to occupy the maid's quarters of the apartment. Since I had always loved the beach and

all the adventures and opportunities it presented, I was actually content with my parents' decision and ready for another exciting chapter in my young life. Having the beach only steps from my house opened many possibilities, and I was ready to explore them all!

We started our tutoring sessions every day with a private French tutor, and these sessions continued twice a week even after school started. The original school had occupied a building in downtown Alicante, but the year we arrived, the school had been moved to a larger campus on the outskirts of the city just a short distance from Albufereta, so we could walk to school. Although we were young, (I had just turned thirteen and Johnny was fifteen), it was still hard to learn a new language in such a short time. I had learned Spanish quickly, but I was only seven when we arrived in Spain, and at that age, I was probably more able to absorb new things quickly. Nevertheless, by the end of that school year we both spoke fairly decent French.

The reason that there existed a French language school in Alicante in the first place is rather interesting. In 1962, there was a revolution in the country of Algeria, which is only 220 miles from Alicante across the Mediterranean Sea. After this war, many of the French Algerians could not return to France, since many were criminals in France, and that's why they left the country to live in North Africa in the first place. They called these kinds of Frenchmen, *Pieds-Noirs*, or literally "Black Feet" in English.

The reason for this nickname is that these people had one foot in Africa and the other in Mother France, and they existed all over Africa, from Algeria to French Morocco to Mali to Mauritania to Senegal to Madagascar. Because these French Algerians had spent many decades in Africa, they developed their own distinct accent, called appropriately enough, *L'accent pieds noirs.* This particular French accent was quite different from a Parisian accent or one from Marseilles and quite distinctive. This became the French accent that we learned.

The *Nouvelle Ecole Francaise D'Alicante* (New French School of Alicante) was mostly filled with children of these French ex-patriots that had left Algeria during the war and had settled in the city of Alicante in Spain. I'm not sure exactly why so many of these French Algerians couldn't return to France, because this sort of thing was just not discussed among the kids at the school. I got the feeling that many were possibly criminals who had fled France to Algeria to avoid prosecution perhaps, and after the

war had found that they could not return to their homeland.

They considered my brother and me rather strange at our new school, not only because we were Americans but also because we spoke pretty poor French for the most part, especially for the first few months we were there. So we had to communicate using Spanish with the other kids which, luckily for us, most of them spoke fairly well. The main issue for my brother and me was that most of the teachers wouldn't allow Spanish spoken in the classroom, so at times we were treated rather like the "short bus kids" as they are called these days, by some of the teachers.

I remember one teacher, Monsieur Calvert, whom I had for French History class. He was an older French gentleman, slightly bald with a drooping mustache who always wore the same old tattered gray suit, vest, and tie. And luckily it was gray because he chain-smoked *Gauloises* cigarettes, and for some reason, he never would use an ashtray. He held the cigarette in his mouth the entire time and when the ash got long enough, pure gravity would cause the ash to fall onto his chest, or wherever it landed. Traditional *Gauloises* were short, wide, unfiltered, and made with dark tobacco from Turkey which emitted a very strong and distinctive aroma that permeated the small classroom.

As Monsieur Calvert lectured to the class, we all sat there watching the ash on his cigarette get longer and longer and wondering when it would drop off, and where it would land, but most of the time, it was a pretty sure bet it would land on his suit jacket, his vest, or his tie. Sometimes he would walk between the rows of old wooden desks, explaining in a loud voice the virtues and superiority of the French civilization, while his students cowered every time he walked by, hoping the ash wouldn't land on them. When the cigarette reached a point where it was so short that it threatened to burn his mouth or ignite his mustache, he would simply drop it to the floor and stomp it out with his foot. Then he would light another one. I guess he had about as much respect for the school janitor as he did for his students.

Monsieur Calvert could never quite comprehend the fact that I didn't speak or understand French very well. I'm sure that he just thought I was slightly retarded and/or just lazy whenever I just replied, "*Je ne sais pas*" (I don't know), whenever he asked me something. And for some reason, he would constantly call on me to answer his questions, more than any other student in his class. He became quite visibly upset with me when all I could say was that I didn't know. Although I didn't understand what he was saying most of the time during his lectures, I did understand plenty of what he was saying about me in his frustration, such as "*Stupide Americain!*" and probably using even much stronger language than that, I'm sure.

But Monsieur Calvert was the exception because almost all the other people at the school, both teachers and students alike, were very kind, as well as being curious and interested in us, mostly because we were Americans. Americans were few and far between in those days in Spain and we were sort of a novelty, I suppose. We were constantly asked where in the States we were from, and for lack of a better answer, we'd usually reply that our dad's family was from Texas, because that question can often be difficult to answer for a military brat. Their immediate reaction to that was to reach for an imaginary gun at their hip and say something like, "Cowboy!" or maybe say something about John Wayne. This was yet another example of the power and influence that Hollywood was having around the world.

Our classes included some complicated subjects (at least for those of us accustomed to an American kind of education), such as Latin, Advanced Algebra, and French History. I have to admit that our education may have suffered somewhat during that one year at the French school. In fact, when we returned to Madrid the following year and enrolled in Madrid High School (the American High School at Torrejon Air Base), they did accept my credits for the previous school year since I was only in the eighth grade, but my brother had to repeat the tenth grade because they did not accept his credits from the French school. In order to graduate from high school, they required one to have a certain number of approved credits in certain courses.

The fact that we both learned another language during that year far outweighed the "American-style education" we might have missed at an American accredited school. Not only did we learn to speak and understand fairly good French during that year, but we also learned a lot about French culture, history and people, as well as gaining a different perspective on life and the world by seeing things through a totally different cultural lens for an entire year.

We managed to make friends easily by being young, receptive, and open to everything new. Of course, our interest in all things musical played a big part in the friends we chose. We met two French Algerian kids at our school who, like a lot of the other kids, were very interested in us when they found out that we were American. Serge and Yves were both about our age and, like us, were very interested in playing rock-and-roll music. So naturally we decided to create a band with them.

Spain is a much different country than the U.S. in so many ways. For one thing, in Spain there is no minimum drinking age as there is in the States. Anyone, of any age, can simply go into a bar, a café, or a restaurant and order whatever they care to drink. The consumption of alcoholic beverages is looked at much differently in the Spanish culture. They figure that if someone is old enough to be able to walk into a place and reach the bar, then they should be able to order whatever they want. Alcoholism was rarely a problem among Spaniards, perhaps because they did not make such a big deal of drinking as people do in the States.

Johnny and I had both consumed all kinds of beverages by this time in our lives and had learned to respect them and what they can do. Many times after being at the Chalet Suizo, for example, we had made it home slightly intoxicated from indulging in a little too much wine or champagne, depending on the function going on there that particular night. So we learned from a very early age to respect alcoholic beverages and what they can and cannot do.

Another big difference between alcohol consumption in Spain and the States was that, unlike some areas in the States, alcohol was available absolutely everywhere in Spain. Almost every place of business sold alcohol, whether it was a cafe, restaurant, ice cream parlor, snack bar, or nightclub. And, as I said, there was no "drinking age" whatsoever. There were exceptions; if a nightclub had entertainment that was considered "adult" in any way, then one had to be eighteen years of age to enter. But the Spanish entertainment was not "adult" in the American sense of the word, which suggested topless dancers or nudity.

This kind of thing was just not allowed during Franco's reign; even Playboy magazines were forbidden and not sold anywhere in Spain. What was meant by adult type of entertainment is what would be called a burlesque show in the States where slightly off-color or dirty jokes were told and women might dance in sexy (but not topless or nude) costumes. So apart from these specialized nightclubs, from a very early age, my brother and I were allowed to go almost anywhere we wanted to, and we did. And we learned what overindulgence in alcohol can lead to, so we learned about those consequences at a very early age.

One place we began to frequent regularly while living in Alicante that year was a nightclub very near our *piso* called *Club Blanco y Negro*, or the Black and White Club. It was less than a block from the beach and it featured live music on the weekends. It was an outdoor place with tables all around the stage and with a large dance floor in front of it, which got quite lively on weekend evenings. The house band that played there almost every weekend was called *Los Duques* or "The Dukes" in English.

They were a Spanish four-piece rock-and-roll band with the usual Beatles setup of a lead guitarist, a rhythm guitarist, a bass guitarist, and a drummer. The main singer and rhythm guitarist was named Paco, and he had flaming red hair, which was actually not that uncommon among Spaniards, especially those that came from the Northwest coast of Spain. The Celts settled and populated that area many centuries before, and their descendants are still in abundance. Paco had a great band together, and all the members were quite talented. The guys in the band were probably in their late teens or early twenties and had that same urge to play rock-and-roll as my brother and I did, but they were actually doing it and getting paid for it.

Their set lists included songs by the latest British and American bands such as The Rolling Stones, The Beatles, The Kinks, The Ventures, and many others. Paco would do his best with singing in English, and although he spoke very little English at all, he was able to phonetically pronounce the sounds he heard on the record, and then reproduce them adequately enough while singing on stage. They also played songs by Spanish rock-and-roll bands which, by this time, were getting a lot of airplay on the radio as well as performing all over the country. Spanish bands such as *Los Brincos* and *Los Bravos* were their inspiration because those guys were Spaniards like themselves who had made it playing their own kind of rock-and-roll music.

Every weekend we would find ourselves either on Friday or Saturday night (sometimes both) down at the *Blanco y Negro* watching and listening as *Los Duques* did their thing, all the while trying to learn the art of playing music in front of a crowd of people, and how to get them dancing and enjoying themselves. We'd usually get there right after finishing our dinner, and they would have just finished their first set, so we'd stick around until their last set which was over usually around midnight. After the first couple of weeks of this, we were approached by different members of the band between their sets, and we would chat with the guys and let them know that we were interested in what they were doing and we really wanted to do it as well.

When they found out that we were Americans, they became very friendly towards us, since everything American was of great interest to most Spaniards. We started discussing new music and the fact that we had lots of records we had bought from the record bins at the PX at Torrejon Air Base, and they became even more interested. It usually took several months for records from the States to reach the record stores in Spain, so we had records from some of their favorite bands that had not been released in Spain and they had not even heard yet.

After a while, we became quite good friends with members of *Los Duques,* and they would come over to our place and go through our record collection and listen to songs that they would then figure out how to play, and end up performing them at the club, even before they were on the radio in Spain. Paco was the most interested and would listen intently to the records and take notes in a notebook he always carried with him. He would write down phonetically how he would pronounce the words while the lead guitarist Jose, would be strumming on an acoustic guitar, figuring out the chords to the song. Often by the following weekend, the band would have the songs down and be performing them at the club!

Since they knew that we went to Madrid quite often to visit our dad and friends, they gave us money and asked us to purchase some new records at the PX for them. We'd return from a trip to Madrid with a dozen or so of the newest 45 RPM records by various artists, and they would end up being the first band in Alicante to cover these new songs. Johnny and I both felt proud that we could help these guys with their fledgling music careers, even in this small way.

One day Paco, Jose, and Tony, the band's bass player, were over at our place listening intently to "Set Me Free" by the Kinks, and figuring out how to play it, when Tony mentioned that he was thinking about buying a new bass guitar. He had eyes on a Hofner bass much like the violin shaped one that Paul McCartney played. It was a little cheaper version with the same hardware but shaped like a regular cutaway hollow body guitar. He knew that I was interested in playing bass and so he offered his old bass to me if I wanted to buy it from him. My eyes lit up, and I told him that I would ask my mom for the money that evening. The price he wanted was 2000 *pesetas* or about thirty-two dollars.

It wasn't the greatest bass guitar, but it worked for a beginner like me. It was solid red with a black pick-guard and had one pickup, one volume knob, and one tone control, very basic but functional and efficient. I knew it had a sweet mellow tone by the countless hours I had heard it played in their band at the club. The brand name was *Invicta,* a Spanish-made brand of lower to mid-range quality instruments. That evening I was excited but a little apprehensive to broach the subject to my mom, knowing that money was tight and it was a lot of money after all. But I had a plan, I would tell her that by my owning this instrument I would be able to play in a band and very possibly even make some money playing music one day, much like *Los Duques* were doing at the *Blanco y Negro* club, and that then I would be able to pay her back. It didn't take too much persuasion since my mom could see the excitement I felt, and she knew that any kind of musical ability on my part could only benefit me and be a positive influence in my life.

Within a week, I was a proud owner of an electric bass guitar. Of course, I could barely play it and, since I didn't have an amplifier yet, I could hardly hear it while picking the strings. But, I was on my way. Shortly after this, my dad showed up for one of his monthly visits and surprised Johnny by bringing him an electric guitar. My dad knew that he had wanted one badly since all he had at this point was the old acoustic Spanish guitar with nylon strings that we had around the house for years, so he thought he'd surprise him with this electric.

He had found it through a friend of his in Madrid who had dabbled in jazz guitar playing and had recently bought a new one, so my dad had gotten a good deal on it. It was a large, full-size, hollow-body, two-pickup electric made by Gretsch. It was the kind of guitar that jazz musicians preferred, and it had a rich full mellow sound, much like an acoustic guitar only much louder of course.

But Johnny was devastated. He didn't want a hollow body jazz guitar; he wanted a solid body rock-and-roll electric guitar, made to make sounds like the Ventures with their surf rock sound or the lead guitar sounds that would come out of Dave Davies of the Kinks. He wanted a Fender or a Mosrite or at the very least a Hofner electric like our friend in Madrid, Randy Padilla, had recently gotten. Randy's dad had picked up a nice Hofner two-pickup electric while on one of his regular runs to Germany flying for the Air Force. Hofner was a German brand of musical instruments, and they also made a line of them in Spain. But the German-made ones were far superior, and comparable to the famous Fender brand of guitar from Fullerton, California.

So, rather reluctantly, my dad took the Gretsch hollow body back to Madrid, hoping that he could get the money back from the friend who had sold it to him. Of course, today that Gretsch hollow body electric would probably be worth thousands of dollars, because not only was it a true classic, but Gretsch made and still makes some of the finest guitars in the world. And so, a few weeks later, my dad showed up again, this time bringing with him a Hofner three-pickup electric guitar with a sunburst finish just like the one Randy had but with one pickup more. He had talked to Randy's dad and had gotten him to pick one up for him the next time he had flown to Germany. Johnny was elated; not only was it a beautiful guitar and just the one he wanted, but it had one more pickup than Randy's.

At this point, my brother and I both had our instruments; him with his nice Hofner electric and me with my beginner's bass, only we had no amplifier and we could not really play them without one, at least loud enough to be heard. My family always had the latest copy of the Sears and Roebuck's catalog around the house since my mom was always ordering something or another out of it. She would order clothes for herself and for us boys around Christmas time and other things such as drapes and household items throughout the year.

We were always looking in the Sears catalog for things we could use and maybe get her to buy for us. By this time, the powers behind Sears and Roebuck had caught on and realized that all these young people were making bands, so Sears had recently started selling a large assortment of musical instruments, along with bell-bottom pants and ponchos. The most recent issue of the catalog had several pages devoted to this relatively new phenomenon, and they had added a line of electric guitars and amplifiers to their existing line of band instrument such as trumpets, trombones, and violins. In fact, their house brand of guitars and amplifiers called "Silvertone" were once considered cheap and poorly made, but these days they are considered classics and are collector's items, and some are worth a considerable amount of money.

After looking at the latest Sears "wish-book," we decided on an amplifier that would work for us as well as being one that we thought my mom could afford. It was a Silvertone three-channel, twenty-five-watt amp with one twelve-inch speaker and three inputs: one for guitar, one for a microphone, and another for keyboards. Since we didn't have a keyboard, we thought we'd use that input for my bass. It cost sixty-five dollars, and we somehow got my Mom to agree to buy it for us, once again telling her that we might actually be able to make some money off this gear once we had a band going and had gotten some paying gigs. Within a month, dad showed up again, this time bringing with him this beauty of an amplifier, and we were finally ready to get our band going.

Our French Algerian friends from school, Serge and Yves, were ready as well. Serge was actually a very talented and naturally gifted musician and could play guitar better than almost anybody we knew at the time. And Yves was a pretty good drummer although he didn't have an actual drum set yet. Serge had a cheap *Invicta* electric guitar along with a small practice amp that his parents had bought for him the previous Christmas.

His father owned a small French-style cafe/restaurant on the outskirts of Alicante, not far from Albufereta, and worked very hard at his business. Sometimes Serge would help him out by washing dishes and cleaning up around the place to earn some spending money for himself.

Yves lived with his mother and didn't seem to have a father around. They really didn't have much money either and so could not afford a drum set, but like Wally and I had done in Madrid, he had a couple of tambourines and a pair of drumsticks. But he had recently heard about a guy from our school that was selling his set and only wished he had the money to buy it. He told us about it and we thought we might be able to again ask my mom if she'd help us out. It was only 1000 pesetas, (around sixteen dollars), so once again we were able to talk her into "lending" us the money so we would be able to have the basic equipment to complete our band.

To call these drums a "drum set" was actually stretching it, because it consisted of just three pieces of gear. It had an old skinny, noisy snare drum on a rickety rusty stand, and a bass drum that looked like it originally served as a marching band instrument that someone banged on with a mallet. It was over three feet tall and only about eight inches wide, with a bass drum pedal held together with wire that squeaked loudly every time it was stepped on. It had one rusty bent up cymbal about ten inches across that sounded only slightly better than a trash can lid. There weren't any tom-toms with the set, but Yves had two tambourines that he somehow hooked to the bass drum so he could bang on them occasionally. There was also no high-hat and so the one rusty cymbal got quite a workout whenever we played. And for a microphone we had managed to find a recording mike from someone's old tape recorder, and by using Randy's old trick, we tied it to a broom handle then attached the broom to a straight-back chair.

We set up all our gear in our spare bedroom and we were ready to rock! Serge knew quite a few songs for a fifteen-year-old kid, and he patiently tried to show Johnny how to play the right chords while he played the leads. He had even written an instrumental song which he called "Melody." It was in the style of The Ventures or The Shadows (an English band that also specialized in instrumentals). The chord progression was the same as a hundred other songs with C, Am, F and G, but Serge and I invented a very nice three-octave lead melody that went perfectly along with the chords. We practiced that one over and over again until we had it down. For my bass part, I just tried to find the root note on the bass, and plucked it every now and then to the beat, as I did with all the songs we played.

Serge had also figured out the opening lead part, and most of the chords to "Day Tripper" by The Beatles, and we tried that song repeatedly until it almost sounded like the original. Another Beatles song that he had figured out was "Michelle," and he could sing the French part great, but the part in English sounded just like a French kid who didn't speak English trying to sing it — which he was. Another song we managed to get down very quickly was "La Bamba," by Richie Valens, since it was all in Spanish and he could sing it all the way through without sounding too strange. It was only three chords, so it was pretty simple to play, except for the lead, but Serge negotiated it pretty well.

Johnny tried singing a few songs by the Rolling Stones. "As Tears Go By" was one that we were able to play more or less correctly, and "Paint it Black" also found its way into our repertoire. The Stones' great song, "Satisfaction" had come out that summer of '65, so naturally we attempted it. Even though Serge could play the opening riff, the rest of it we never quite got figured out completely.

We all agreed that The Kinks were the best band of all, and we tried their classics, "All Day and All the Night" and "You Really Got Me," but Johnny had trouble sliding the F barre chord all over the fret board and constantly complained about his wrist hurting. Serge seemed to be able to handle it all right though, so we did put those on our set list. Serge sang most of the songs, not only because he knew how to play and sing them at the same time but he had also figured out how to sing phonetically in English, much like Paco, the lead singer from *Los Duques*.

As I mentioned before, this phenomenon of young teenaged boys getting together and trying to form bands and play music was worldwide. Not only were there countless bands in the States and in England, but there were plenty in Spain as well. Every weekend, there were new bands popping up and playing anywhere they could, in nightclubs, little cafes, restaurants, and, of course, at dances. On Sunday afternoons, dances were held at a large outdoor cafe in downtown Alicante near the port area. The four of us went diligently almost every week to watch these bands play for their audiences (who were mostly young teenagers of the city), to try to get some tips and to check out the competition. This music scene was very exciting for both the audience and the bands that participated, giving both a chance to experience this thing called "rock-and-roll."

Many of these bands played songs in Spanish as there were many Spanish bands that were beginning to make a name for themselves and getting airplay on the radio. The Spanish band Los Bravos had a huge worldwide hit with their song "Black is Black" in 1965, even though their lead singer, Mike Kogel, was from Germany. And Los Brincos were a huge success in Spain and were sometimes called the "Spanish Beatles." Los Shakers was another very popular band from that era that would translate many of the Beatles' songs into Spanish and have enormous hits with them.

Spanish radio was experiencing a new revival, as were stations all over the world, with this new phenomenon known as rock-and-roll. It truly was an exciting time for music and popular culture in general, and it would continue for the rest of the decade and on into the next ones.

There were even "fanzines" available at the local news stands. I remember wandering the streets of downtown Alicante and coming across a small stand that sold newspapers, gum, candy, and cigarettes, and seeing a cover for one magazine that merely said, "Los Rolling" in large letters and had a picture of those five guys, looking mean and sexy, with Mick's lips being most prominent. I guessed that the publisher of the zine hadn't gotten the memo that they were called "The Stones" for short, instead of "Los Rolling." And of course The Beatles' name was pronounced by most Spaniards as "Los BE-AT-LES," as the word would be pronounced in

Spanish. The musical and cultural wave that followed shortly after the original "British Invasion" continued for many years in Spain before other types of music became popular in later decades, such as New Wave, Punk, and Heavy Metal.

We four guys, two Americans and two French Algerians, all living in Alicante, Spain in 1965, needed a name for our band. We all thought long and hard about this because we realized that our name would be a big part of our success if we ever had any. Every time we got together to practice we would kick around names, but could never seem to find one that all four of us liked. Finally, we came up with "The Jaxx," thinking that it sounded a little like our favorite band, "The Kinks." And we kept that name until one day we realized that in Spanish the "J" is always pronounced like an "H" and that would make our band sound in Spanish like "The Hacks" — probably not too good!

But after thinking a while longer, we finally came up with the name that stuck and the one we would use for our one and only gig. We decided on *Los Espiritus,* or The Spirits, in English. We all thought that name sounded very special because everything had a spirit to it, especially our music. I guess we never realized that we might be considered real drunks naming ourselves after booze, especially with one member named Johnny Walker!

One Sunday afternoon the four of us were down by the port in Alicante to watch yet another young Spanish band entertaining the crowd at the weekly dance when one of us noticed a flier on the wall near the entrance to the cafe. It said that a "Battle of the Bands" was coming up soon, and the organizers were looking for local bands to take part. The concert would include several judges and the first, second, and third place winners would win cash prizes, and the first-place winner could even win a possible recording contract.

This *Batalla de las Bandas* was to take place in the courtyard of *El Castillo de Santa Barbara,* or the Santa Barbara Castle. One could not fail to notice this impressive castle situated on an outcropping overlooking the city of Alicante. It is one of the largest medieval fortresses in Europe and covers the complete summit of *Benacantil* Mountain. Originally built by the Moors in the tenth century, Santa Barbara Castle had everything one would expect from a castle: cannons, a palace, dungeons, a moat, the ruins of a small church, and a famous lookout tower. The views from the castle were magnificent, and on a clear day one could see all the way up and down *La Costa Blanca* of Spain. This amazing place was to be the setting for the first and only gig that *Los Espiritus* ever played, and the first time any of us had ever performed music in public.

Serge wrote down the phone number from the flier, and the next day he called it. After talking a few minutes on the phone with the organizer, he had managed to secure our first gig. He told us that all we would have to bring with us would be our guitars, because they would provide all the other gear, including amps, a drum set, and a P. A. system. He took down the name of our band and asked how many members were in it and where we were from.

Serge told us that he seemed to be impressed when he told him that two Americans and two French Algerians made up the band. He told Serge that each band would get to play three songs and the judges would announce the winners at the end of the evening. The concert would be held on a Saturday afternoon starting at four p.m., and last until all the bands had played, depending on how many bands signed up.

All four of us were very excited, and we got together to practice almost every other day after school until the day of the show. We discussed which three songs we would play, and it was finally decided that due to our unique backgrounds, we would play one song in English, one in French, and one in Spanish. These three songs were "Day Tripper," "Michelle," and "La Bamba."

Since we only had one microphone during our practices, we hadn't even thought about background vocals up until then, but we decided that Serge would just sing lead on all three songs, and if there was an extra mike on stage at the show, Johnny and I would sing background vocals on "La Bamba," anyway.

The day of the "Battle of the Bands" arrived, and we loaded up our guitars into my mom's little yellow SEAT 600, and off we went. Serge's parents were taking him up to the castle and planned to pick up Yves along the way. We all got there early, around 3 p.m., so we found each other easily in the small crowd that had gathered before the main crowd showed up.

We carried our guitars in their cases, along with Yves' drumsticks, over to the area behind the stage, and talked to a young guy there and told him the name of our band. We were told that we would be performing in eleventh place out a total of twenty bands that were registered to perform that evening. To make it fair, the judges had lined up the bands in the order that they had registered, so as not to have a "headliner," or show any other favoritism.

The stage was set up towards one end of the castle's huge courtyard, and there was an area behind the stage where we could safely leave our guitars. So we left them there and went off to watch the other bands play before it was time for us to go on.

The place was gradually filling up, and by the time the first band started right at 4 p.m., the courtyard was filled to near capacity with close to a thousand people. All the seats were taken, so the four of us just stood on the sidelines near the stage with some other young guys. Before the first band went up to play, the emcee of the event, some older man wearing a suit and tie, walked up on stage, took the mike off the stand, and made a long announcement welcoming everyone and mentioning the various sponsors of the event which included an ice cream company, a couple of local restaurants, and a music store.

He then read off the names of the judges, who they were, and what they did, and who, coincidentally, seemed to be the owners of the fore-mentioned businesses. After that he wished everybody a good time and thanked them again for coming down to this fabulous *Batalla de las Bandas.* He then thanked all the hard-working young people in the bands for taking part, and reminding them that first prize would be 5000 pesetas, second prize would be 3000 pesetas, and third would be 2000.

He then announced the first band this way: "*Damas y Caballeros... Los Gatos Negros!*" And four young Spanish guys just a little older than we were came on stage to the sound of loud clapping and cheers from the crowd. Their set was pretty good, but I didn't recognize any of the songs. All of them were in Spanish and they played them with enthusiasm and style. After their three songs, they exited the stage to the sounds of more applause. Then the emcee came up on stage again and made a few more quick announcements, while the next band came up with their guitars and plugged into the amps, and their drummer sat behind the drum set and got it adjusted to his particular liking. Then the emcee presented the next band, *"Los Diablos."*

It went on this way for over two hours while we stood there getting more and more nervous as time passed. They had told us the name of the band we would be following, and for us to come around back stage right after they began, to get ready for our set. When the emcee finally announced, *"Los 5 del Barrio,"* we made our way through the crowd to the backstage area and found our guitar cases, feeling nervous and apprehensive as we got our guitars out. Meanwhile, *Los 5 Del Barrio* were making a fine racket indeed, for they even had a sax player who was honking away for all he was worth. By the time they finished their third song and exited the stage, we climbed up the three steps to the lip of the stage and stood there waiting to be announced.

Then, while the four of us walked onto the stage and plugged in our guitars, and Yves sat down behind the drums, the emcee strolled up to the mike and said the following, (in Spanish, of course), "Ladies and Gentlemen, we now have a very special group for your musical enjoyment. These four young men are unique among this evening's performers because none of them are Spanish! Yes, indeed, two of them are originally from French Algeria, just across the sea from our beautiful city of Alicante, and the other two are brothers all the way from the United States of America! May I present to you... *"Los Espiritus!"*

Serge walked up to the mike and said in Spanish, "Thank you very much; we are thrilled and honored to be here to perform for you this evening. We will be performing our three songs in three different languages; Spanish, French, and English, and we hope you enjoy them all."

He started playing the opening guitar riff to "Day Tripper." Yves came in with a little drum roll on the snare and soon we were all playing the song to the best of our ability. I remember that all I really contributed was the bass root note and tried to keep it in time with the others. Johnny strummed the chords to the song for all he was worth and then Serge started singing, "Got a good reason, for taking the easy way out."

I looked over the crowd of people and saw the recognition of the song in their eyes and the smiles on all their faces, and I felt something that I had never felt before in my young life: a feeling of pure joy. For the first time in my life, I was experiencing the ability to put smiles on all those peoples' faces, and I watched in fascination as they all started moving to the beat, and some brave couples even began to dance in the small area right in front of the stage. I had found my element, and this feeling was even better than I had ever imagined it could be. My memories of seeing The Beatles perform live at the Bullring in Madrid just a few months earlier came back to me, and I thought to myself, "This is it — the best feeling in the world!" My nervousness and my feelings of self-doubt disappeared immediately as I continued rocking out with our band.

By the time we finished "Day Tripper," we could tell we had the crowd on our side. They were clapping and cheering with all their might. When Serge played the opening chords to "Michelle," I looked around at the crowd and once again I saw the recognition in their eyes and soon many were singing along with the song. Serge sang both the English and the French parts of the song, and of course the French part sounded much more authentic than the English part, but the people lapped it up, anyway.

By the time he started playing the opening guitar part to *"La Bamba,"* people started cheering. And as we had planned, during the chorus part, Johnny and I shared the extra mike on stage and sang the background vocals of *"Bail-a Bamba, Bail-a Bamba."*

We ended the song with a *Beatlesque* flourish by letting the last chord ring out and carry throughout the courtyard. Serge then said into the mike to the sounds of cheering and applause, *"Muchas gracias, muchas gracias por todo,"* and we walked offstage, all four of us having had our lives changed forever.

Feeling quite proud of ourselves, we put our guitars back in their cases and walked back to where our parents were sitting towards the back of the crowd, and they greeted us with many congratulatory remarks, and I remember my mom saying, "Oh, I'm so proud of you boys, all of you did so well!"

Johnny just shrugged and said, "Well, we'll see how well the judges think we did."

Then my mom asked me, "So, Ronnie, did you have fun?"

I looked her in the eye, smiled, and said, "It was the most fun I've ever had in my life. It was a real blast!"

We waited around another couple of hours watching the other bands perform until all of them had played and they were ready to announce the winners. Not surprisingly, we did not win first place, or second, or even third. But there were twenty bands playing that day, almost all of them far older and more experienced than we were. And many had already played lots of actual gigs at bars, cafes, and dances around town. We may not have been the only band that was playing its very first gig that day, but probably one of only a few.

After announcing the first, second and third place winners, the emcee announced that the judges had decided to give honorable mentions to the next seven bands, for a total of ten being recognized that day. He then went through the list of the next seven performers by name and mentioned a little about them and why the judges had selected them. Of the fourth one he announced (the band that would come in seventh out of twenty), he said, "Because of their fine performance, their excellent choice of songs, and for being all *extranjeros* (foreigners) in our fine city of Alicante, *Los Espiritus!*"

So for our first and only live public performance in front of a real audience, we came in seventh place out of twenty. Not bad for four kids who had more desire than actual ability at this point. We were elated and started patting each other on the back, excited and feeling quite proud of ourselves, and determined that we did have a future in playing "rock-and-roll."

After we picked up our guitars from the backstage area and headed to the parking lot, my mother said again enthusiastically, "I'm so proud of you boys; you all did really great!"

I replied, "Well, Mom, maybe one day we can pay you back for helping us buy the equipment after all!"

She just smiled and said, "Well, we'll see, Ronnie, we'll see."

Within a few months after this one and only performance by *Los Espiritus*, my family and I moved back to Madrid, and coming along with

us was none other than Serge, who would go on to form a band in Madrid with my brother called The Beautiful Beasts, who would have considerably more success, and a lot more gigs than *Los Espiritus*.

Chapter 5. The Beautiful Beasts and Beyond

*"For the great things are not done by impulse,
but by a series of small things brought together."*
—Vincent van Gogh

When returned from Alicante after spending over a year there living on the beach and attending a French school, Johnny and I were eager to resume our regular "American"-style lives with our friends, at our old American school. Unfortunately, Johnny was told at MHS (Madrid High School) that he would be required to repeat the tenth grade for the simple fact that he did not earn any "credits" at the French school. And a certain number of credits were necessary in order for him to graduate from this American accredited high school. He was disappointed to have to spend another in school but took it in stride and soon became as eager as I was to start school.

I, luckily, did not have to repeat a grade because in the eighth grade, I was not really earning high school credits yet, so much to my delight; I was enrolled in the ninth grade at MHS. And I was more than ready to start this next chapter of my life — high school!

Within a week of our arrival back in Madrid, and getting settled in and enrolled in school, Serge, our friend and lead guitar player from Alicante, arrived to stay with us and to help keep intact the band that would be sure to lead us all to vast riches and worldwide fame. Serge didn't really seem interested in school anymore since he really thought that this band that we were forming would lead him to a life where further schooling was unnecessary. We would soon all be living in the lap of luxury, being big rock-and-roll stars!

He moved into the spare bedroom upstairs, and I moved into the downstairs maid quarters, because by then we only had our maid Encarna working part-time for us, mainly to do the laundry and house-cleaning. I was happy to move into her old quarters because it gave me privacy, being two stories below the other bedrooms, and having my own private bathroom.

Within the first couple of weeks of school starting, Johnny met a guy from one of his classes by the name of Steve Rodgers. He was a drummer with a nice Slingerland drum kit and lived in Canillejas, which was a small pueblo on the outskirts north of Madrid. Many Americans lived in Canillejas at the time due to its location on the way to the base. There were some very nice houses there as well as several apartment buildings that housed a good number of American families, including some teachers who taught at the schools on base.

Steve and Johnny seemed to hit if off immediately, especially once Johnny told him about Serge, the amazing French Algerian guitar player from Alicante who was staying with us, ready to make a band that was bound to go somewhere big. Steve in turn told Johnny about a friend and neighbor of his by the name of Manolo Angeles. Manolo was a Spaniard from a fairly well-off family in Canillejas, who played excellent bass guitar, and they had been jamming a little together in Steve's bedroom over the summer and were both looking to start a great band. Before long Steve and Manolo brought their gear over and set it up in the garage of our house on Calle Triana, and it became the central practice room for this new developing band.

Johnny, Serge, and I had a long conversation shortly after arriving back in Madrid about playing music together. It was decided by consensus that since I was quite a bit younger than they were, and probably the most unskilled musician among us, Johnny and Serge would go ahead and make a band without me and that I would pursue my own musical endeavors with guys around my own age. This didn't bother me because my old buddy Wally Padilla who played drums was still around the neighborhood, and he was eager for us to start playing music together again.

Johnny and Serge were both playing through their old small amps from *Los Espiritus* days in Alicante, and Manolo had a Hofner bass guitar and small bass practice amp. But it was soon decided that if they were to make a professional band and play in public and actually get paid for it, they would require some decent professional gear. The question was how they were to acquire it with no money and no gigs as of yet.

Manolo had a good friend from Canillejas by the name of Martin (Tin Tin) Martinez, who was a couple of years older than the guys in the band, and he had told Manolo that he wanted to become their manager. Tin Tin was a smooth-talking kind of guy, already out of school, and even wore a suit and a tie everywhere he went. He also claimed to know just about every night club owner in Madrid and because of that, he said he was the perfect guy to manage this up-and-coming rock-and-roll band. And he showed proof of this by showing the guys in the band several business cards of night club promoters that he carried in his wallet.

This was good enough for the guys and so he became the manager of the band, and it was agreed that he would take twenty percent of any earnings that the band would make. This seemed like a good idea for everyone involved because frankly not too many other options were available at this time, and the guys just wanted to play music. Besides, any gig was better than no gig.

The question of professional equipment came up again soon after everyone agreed that Tin Tin would be their manager. Tin Tin understood as well that in order to play out in front of large audiences, it would be required to have professional gear, including better guitar and bass amps, and a decent P. A. system with a decent mixer, microphones, stands, speakers, etc. Tin Tin didn't have any money to invest, since one reason he wanted to become a manager of a band was to earn some money to help him out with his finances. His only real job at the time was working part-time with his father's accounting and book keeping business.

It was decided that Johnny would talk to our dad and Manolo would talk to his dad and see if perhaps the band could get a loan from them to buy some gear, which they could then pay off when the earnings from playing gigs started coming in. Serge didn't have any money since his parents barely had enough to send the sixty dollars per month to my parents for his room and board. And Steve didn't seem to have a father around and was being raised by a single mother, so money was not available from his folks either.

I remember well the conversation Johnny had with my dad because I was involved as well. It was decided that he would lend Johnny the money for a good professional guitar amplifier and half the money towards the P.A. gear, and Manolo's dad would help him buy a good bass amp and the other half of the money for the P.A. system. The deal also stipulated that if I got a band together and got a gig that I could use the gear for my band's performance as long as it wasn't on a night when Johnny's band was playing a gig.

So the four guys in the band, along with Tin Tin and both fathers, decided to all meet at a musical instrument store just off the *Gran Via* in downtown Madrid, to shop for the gear necessary for a fledgling band to play in public. They ended up (after shopping and negotiating for several hours) with a VOX AC 50 guitar amplifier and a VOX Foundation bass amp. They also purchased a SUNN 8-channel 200 watt P.A. head, two column speakers with monitors, three Shure microphones with stands, and an echo/reverb unit for the P.A. system. Altogether it came to just under $2000. The VOX guitar amplifier that Johnny got alone was over $600. With this gear, the four guys in the band, along with Tin Tin, felt they had the right equipment to be able to play just about any size venue in Madrid besides the *Las Ventas* Bullring, perhaps.

Besides the necessary gear, the guys had to come up with a good name before they could be called a real band. Downtown Madrid has a flea market that has probably been open since the middle ages called *El Rastro*. It is open every Sunday morning and has countless stalls and thousands of shoppers looking for bargains. Anything and everything can be found there, and it's a popular place for tourists and locals alike to spend several hours every week. Said to be the largest flea market in Europe with up to 3500 different stalls, it extends through several blocks in one of the city's oldest working-class neighborhoods. There are bargains with everything from furniture to clothing to antiques, along with souvenirs and a wide range of other goods, both new and used. Antique shops line the  surrounding streets to take advantage of the bustling crowds and the wonderful lively atmosphere every Sunday morning.

This market is ultimately what inspired the name for the band. One Sunday Manolo and Steve were at *El Rastro* looking around and they came across a vendor who was selling genuine sheepskin vests with the fur on the outside. He told them that he raised sheep on the outskirts of Madrid, and whenever he butchered one to eat, he cured the hide. One average-sized sheep had just about enough fur to make one large vest. After the guys tried a couple of these vests on and saw how really different and unique they were, they bought one for each member of the band, as a way to identify themselves and to look more interesting.

When Manolo brought the four vests to the band's next rehearsal, the other guys immediately liked them, and after the four of them tried them on and looked at each other, they knew they had something. Steve then said, "Man, we look like some real beautiful beasts with these things on." Johnny looked at him and said, "That's it, we are the Beautiful Beasts. That's the name of our band!" He went on to explain to Manolo and Serge who spoke very little English what it meant in Spanish, "Las Bestias Bellas." Of course, it didn't sound quite the same in Spanish, but they all thought it was a great name in English, and so they had finally found a name for their band. And at every gig they would perform, they wore their sheepskin vests and soon this type of vest became quite popular among the fashionable Madridleños, both Spanish and American alike.

When Tin Tin came over for their next rehearsal, he saw the vests and thought it was an amazing idea and a fantastic name for the band. He scheduled a professional photo shoot for the following week at a studio he knew of, and the band got some promotional photos to help get them some gigs. With a little more practice, the band was ready to go!

Coincidentally, both guitarists in the band, along with the bass player, all played *Hofner* guitars. Johnny played the German-made one his friend's father had brought down from Germany the previous year while we were still in Alicante, and Serge had finally convinced his folks to buy him a Spanish-made Hofner that had more knobs and buttons on it than any of the guys had ever seen. Manolo's bass was a Spanish-made Hofner similar to the famous violin-shaped one that Paul McCartney played with the Beatles, but it was the

single cutaway model instead. These three instruments, along with their new gear, made them a force to be reckoned with among the other bands in Madrid at the time.

Since Johnny wasn't much of a singer, except for occasional background vocals, and Steve was always behind his drums and so was limited to background vocals as well, it was decided that Manolo and Serge would do most of the vocals in the band. Serge was rather shy and spoke very little English, but Manolo had a different kind of personality. He was quite flamboyant, very good-looking and charming, with a deep solid voice, and he did speak a little English and so could handle the lead vocals better than Serge.

His personality and stage presence are what made him the perfect front-man, along with the effect that his good looks and charm had on the many females in the audience. Being a natural showman, he quickly learned how to work the crowd into a frenzy, at times setting down his bass and grabbing the mike off the stand, getting on his knees and moving and gyrating like a young Elvis Presley on a good night. This never failed to impress the guys and girls alike in the audience and they all felt that they were in the presence of someone extraordinary and extremely talented — and they probably were. And, being the only Spaniard in the band, he quickly became the favorite of the four Beasts with most of their audiences.

Virtually all the songs on the band's repertoire were in English, with the exception of "*La Bamba*." Their set list included such mid-sixties classic rock songs such as "Wild Thing," "Steppin' Stone," "Wipe Out," "Gloria," "Midnight Hour," "Long Tall Sally," "Kansas City," and of course, lots of covers by The Beatles, The Rolling Stones and The Kinks. Manolo had such charisma and showmanship that on certain songs, the girls in the audience acted like they were watching The Beatles perform, by screaming and crying out shamelessly.

Tin Tin made good on his promise and before too long, the guys were gigging out almost every weekend. Not only did he get the band shows on Friday and Saturday nights, but a lot of the nightclubs where they played were what were called "maids'" bars, and had live shows on Thursdays and Sundays, the typical nights off for the city's maids. These bars were especially set up as places where the maids of Madrid could attend safely without shame and go on their nights off to enjoy themselves and possibly meet a potential husband. So a lot of the gigs were on Thursday and Sunday evenings as well as Fridays and Saturdays. The nightclubs and venues where they played were located all over Madrid because Tin Tin seemed to know them all. Some were downtown near *La Gran Via*, others were in poor working-class neighborhoods such as *Vallecas*, and others were in places like *Canillejas* on the outskirts of Madrid.

The Beasts were popular and a big success right from their very first show. Spanish people had a thirst for American and English music, what with the huge popularity of British bands like The Beatles and The Stones. Also wildly popular were many American bands like the Beach Boys and the Byrds, who were selling millions of records around the world and becoming popular just about everywhere as well. Manolo's stage presence along with the lead guitar skills of Serge made the band a solid and very entertaining group, and the fact that the Beasts had two Americans and a Frenchman in the band made them even more interesting and intriguing to the average Spanish audience.

The four boys in the band became quite good friends by spending so much time rehearsing and performing together, and they really enjoyed each other's' company, so they spent a lot of time together that was not related to the band. Being typical teenage boys and living in such a vibrant and exciting city as Madrid definitely had its advantages.

I remember one rare Saturday evening when the band didn't have a gig, when Manolo, Serge, Johnny, I, and a friend who hung out with the band sometimes by the name of Scott Wilson were in our garage listening to some new records that Scott had brought over with him after a trip to London. Manolo suddenly had an idea. He suggested that we all go to "*Un Bar Americano.*" An "American" style bar in Spain at the time meant that the bar was much different that a regular bar in Madrid, where food as well as beverages were served to all types of customers, both male and female. "*Un Bar Americano*" was something totally different indeed.

Instead, this was the kind of bar frequented by an exclusively male clientele, and was where the "working" girls of Madrid liked to hang out. In fact, they worked behind the bar serving drinks, and it was known that these women were the kind who could be rented by the minute or by the hour, depending upon your supply of *pesetas* and your sexual stamina.

There were usually three or four girls behind the bar and when one of them made a deal with a customer, there would usually be an upstairs or a downstairs area of the bar, or sometimes just a private room somewhere nearby, where the customer and the girl could find some privacy for as long as it took. These bars were everywhere in Madrid and they weren't just for the purpose of acquiring a female for one's sexual pleasure, but were also just places where lonely men could go to have a drink and chat with a woman, very often older men whose main topic of discussion seemed to be how their wives just didn't understand them.

There was one of these establishments not far from our house, just down the street from Plaza Peru (where the American theater was located), by the name of *"Bar Americano Carmencita."* So this was the place where five teenaged boys (one Spanish, one French Algerian, and three Americans) headed that evening. Manolo took the lead for he was quite familiar with these types of places and knew what to expect. Since there is no minimum drinking age is Spain, anybody could go just about anywhere at any time, so getting into the place would pose no problem. I had never been to such an establishment before so I was getting excited and anxious as the five of us walked the several blocks to the place.

Now the "working girls" of Spain were not always "girls" in the strictest sense, because many of them were mature older women often way past their prime in their chosen profession. Many had been widowed without a pension, left without any skills to speak of, and they needed to make a living somehow or another. Others had been into this kind of life and work most of their lives and now didn't have any other idea of how to make a living, so they continued to work the world's oldest profession. Almost all of them were very good-natured and always had a good sense of humor about their line of work. After all, a lot of their job merely consisted of cheering up the older men that were hanging around the bar looking for a sympathetic ear. They all received a regular wage for tending bar and only performed any other type of favors for generous "tips" from the clientele.

So with Manolo leading the way, we walked into the place like we owned it. Manolo's confidence and swagger gave us all a sense that this was perfectly natural, like we did this kind of thing all the time. The five of us walked up to the bar where there were three female bartenders behind the bar. All three were the older, chubbier type of women who had long ago passed their prime of beauty and sexuality, but still retained the knowledge and expertise on how to excite and tantalize the male of the species. All three were wearing the skimpiest of outfits; their ample breasts were threatening to fall out of their blouses and each had enough makeup on to probably last younger women a month.

As we crowded around the bar, the oldest and the chubbiest of the three leaned over with her ample rack almost totally exposed and asked, "*Buenas tardes caballeros, que quieren tomar?*" (Good evening, gentlemen, what would you like to drink?)

Manolo looked at her and said with a devilish grin, "*Para mi, yo quiero una teta!*" (For me, I'll have a tit!) And he leaned over the bar, grabbed one of her breasts, pulled it out from her blouse, and started sucking on it!

Everyone in the bar (including the wench) burst out laughing. The lady allowed about ten seconds of Manolo's suckling until she finally said, "*Basta con eso, por ese tipo de bebida, cobro mucho mas!*" (Enough of that, for that type of beverage, I charge much more!)

While everyone was still laughing out loud, Manolo said, "*Pues, en ese caso, cinco cervezas entonces.*" (Well, in that case, just five beers then.)

We all found bar stools and sat down to continue admiring the view of the ample cleavages presented to us by the three bartenders.

But Manolo was just getting started. Before long, he was in deep negotiations with the lady whose flesh he had just sampled. After a few minutes, they finally came to a mutually agreeable price of 500 pesetas for her to take him downstairs for a quickie. With his typical male Spanish bravado and machismo, he continued to discuss the intimate details of their upcoming sexual encounter.

He told her, "*Mira, la problema es que tengo una polla muy, muy grande y no se si puedo meterlo todo en tu chocha!*" (Look, the problem is that I have a huge, huge prick and I don't know if I can put it all in your pussy!)

The lady just smiled her most seductive of smiles and said, "*No hay problema, yo creo que si se puedes meterlo todo, y un huevo tambien!*" (No problem, I think that you will be able to put it all in, and a testicle as well!)

By this time, the five of us were laughing uncontrollably along with the rest of the patrons in the bar. And the phrase that she told Manolo that evening became the catchphrase for the band whenever they encountered anything remotely difficult whether it was learning a new song or trying to make it to a gig or putting up with any of the countless other problems that a band might have.

And so, *"Y un huevo tambien!"* became the battle cry for the Beautiful Beasts whenever any problem arose. If Manolo had been writing his own songs by this time, I'm sure that would have been the name of one of his first songs.

Neither Manolo nor any of the rest of us ever went downstairs with any of the ladies that evening, but we all had a great time, including the ladies who worked there. And I learned that after so many generations of putting up with the Spanish male's machismo and arrogance, the Spanish female has learned how to balance the fragile male ego with plenty of humor, kindness, and compassion.

One would think that being in a popular rock-and-roll band would include many benefits; including lots of adoring female fans who would be more than willing to exchange certain favors for the privilege of hanging out with rock and rollers. But, then, one must understand the cultural and social interactions of Spain during the 1960s.

There were two kinds of females in Spanish society, and with very little fluctuation between them. The first was the kind that the boys met at the *Bar Americano*, and these were women with very loose morals, who were considered "floozies" and were looked down upon by the general population.

It was rare for such a woman to get married because the typical Spanish man wanted a virgin as his wife. Once deflowered, if she wasn't married, a woman was considered to be *"una puta"* (a prostitute), or at the very least, a loose and immoral person, not worthy of anything but working in *"un Bar Americano"* perhaps, or even worse, walking the streets looking for customers.

The other type of females in Spain at the time (by far the majority) was the kind who, because of the above-mentioned unwritten rules, were determined to remain virgins until marriage. Perhaps the main reason that there existed so many of the *"Bar Americanos"* in almost every neighborhood in Spain is because of this great distinction. If a man wanted to explore some of his natural sexual desires, it was only possible with the "loose" type of females easily found almost everywhere. Of course, there were exceptions, and any rule, written or unwritten, is made to be broken. But the types of females that were willing to break these rules usually were foreigners or tourists and definitely not the typical Spanish girl, especially not the maids and other Spanish girls that made up the band's typical audience at their shows.

This was the social system that existed at the time, and lasted until Spanish society finally opened up considerably after the death of Francisco Franco in 1975. Then, things really began to change, not only the sexual mores of the society but also art, music, literature, and every other type of self-expression exploded after Franco's death when more freedom was finally allowed.

Although it seemed to the members of the band that their group lasted for years, in reality, The Beautiful Beasts only lasted about seven months before breaking up. As in many cases like this, before too long all the members of the band regretted it. Afterwards, they realized that they had something very special, and a certain chemistry existed between them that was not only magical but also very difficult to recreate with other musicians.

The reason the band broke up was because certain outside influences crept in and affected their decisions. The mother of Steve, the drummer, decided that it would be better for her if the band was to replace Johnny with her other son Tommy (Steve's younger brother) who also played the guitar. She was enjoying the few dollars that Steve was earning and contributing to their household and figured that if her other son was in the band, it would double that income. So she convinced Steve to demand from the other guys that Johnny had to go to make room for Tommy. He convinced Manolo that it would be a good move since three of the four members would all live in Canillejas and it would make it easier to rehearse, get to gigs on time together, and make it much easier for everyone overall.

What Steve or his mother failed to consider was that without Johnny in the band, their rehearsal place (our garage) would be gone, along with half the equipment that the band used to perform. Tommy didn't have a professional amplifier or the means to acquire one, and Manolo had only part-share in the P. A. system that the band used, so their gear would be limited and this would make it impossible to perform truly professional shows. Steve claimed that soon they could buy more gear, and besides, he was sure that Johnny would sell his half of the P.A. system by allowing them to pay him off in monthly installments. And he was sure that they could easily find another rehearsal space.

When Johnny found out that the band wanted him out, he was heartbroken, to put it mildly. Not only was the band a lot of fun and allowed him to have some very magical and wonderful experiences, but he really thought that they were all friends and would continue to be regardless of anything. Even though he and Manolo had promised to pay their respective fathers back for the loan they had given them to buy the equipment, in actuality very little was being paid back and they still owed most of it at this point. Other things came up to spend their band earnings on such as taxi rides to and from shows, replacing guitar strings, picks, and cables, buying rounds of drinks after the shows, or just enjoying the fruits of playing for money instead of working for it.

So when it got down to the nitty-gritty, and the band met in our garage one afternoon to discuss the details of the band's breakup, a rather ugly scene ensued. Johnny refused to give up any of the gear he owned, even with a promise from the others that they would make payments to him or my dad for the balance owed on it. He decided that he would continue to play music and possibly form another band at some point, and that he needed his gear for that purpose.

All of this rather confused Serge. He rightly knew that if Johnny was not a member of the Beasts, then the chances of him being able to stay with our family were rather thin. But when you're young and dumb, sometimes you make mistakes that you regret soon afterwards. He figured that he could find another place to stay in Madrid, and besides, he still had the dream of becoming a rich and successful rock-and-roll performer and it was just a matter of time before his dreams would come true. So he rather reluctantly agreed to the band change up and went along with Manolo and Steve. The next day after the band's breakup, he was asked to leave our house and shortly after that, having very little money, and no one willing to take him in, he took a train back to Alicante to help his father with his restaurant there, never to be seen again by anyone in Madrid.

It wasn't long before Johnny started having other musicians come over and jam in our garage. Some of the best guitar players from our high school would come over and play and hang out. Some guys were already in bands or forming bands and Johnny played with many of them, but never did he reach the level of success around town that the Beautiful Beasts had enjoyed.

For one thing, Tin Tin was Manolo's best friend and of course he offered his management services to Manolo and the new band that he was trying to put together with some other Spanish guys from Canillejas. As far as The Beautiful Beasts were concerned, once Johnny was out, the band never performed again. Steve and his brother Tommy, having no professional gear to play on, stayed in their bedroom playing to each other while Steve tried to join other bands.

After a couple of months went by, out of the blue one evening, Johnny got a phone call from Manolo asking him if he wanted to get together and jam with a hot new guitar player from Canillejas. He told Johnny that this guy, Javier, was as good as Serge was and possibly even better, and was into a lot of new sounds that were just becoming popular, called "Psychedelic" music. Jimi Hendrix had just released his first album and his style of rock music was just beginning to be played on the radio. "Hey Joe," "Fire," "Stone Free," and some of Hendrix's other songs were really starting to blow peoples' minds, both musicians and audiences alike.

Johnny told him that he might be interested and suggested his friend Scott Wilson to play drums since Scott had acquired a drum kit and had shown up to jam with Johnny in our garage a few times. Manolo knew Scott very well from the days when he used to hang out with the Beasts, so he agreed. The next day, Manolo showed up with his gear along with this young Spaniard by the name of Javier. Scott came over as well and brought along with him an American guy from ASM (American School of Madrid, where they both went to school), by the name of Ted, who played trumpet of all things!

Ted was also a pretty good singer, both lead and backgrounds, and he was a tall, lanky guy with Buddy Holly-style glasses and a very open and friendly personality. From the first song they played together, they knew that the old musical magic was back between Johnny and Manolo. Scott turned out to be an excellent drummer and Javier played lead guitar as well as any of the guys had ever heard, and he knew all the licks to almost every song they tried. With the addition of a horn into the band, they could play songs that were a lot different from just the two guitars, bass, and drums setup.

"Soul music" was also very popular during this time in the 1960s, with such artists as Wilson Pickett, The Temptations, The Four Tops, Otis Redding, and other similar acts being played all over the radio and jukeboxes. Now with the trumpet in the band, they could cover certain songs a lot better than they ever could without a horn. Songs with great horn parts like "Midnight Hour," "My Girl," and "Knock on Wood" all made it on their set list, along with other styles like Hendrix and Eric Clapton. After a few practices, the band had a pretty solid set list with quite the variety of music.

Tin Tin was still around as their manager and was eager to get the band gigging. This time around, the band members decided to only give him ten percent of their earnings, because, after all, there were now five guys in this band. Besides, Tin-Tin had a few other bands he was managing by then, and the guys had discovered that ten percent was the regular going rate for a band manager.

This was the summer of 1967, known in the States as "The Summer of Love." The whole "Hippy" phenomenon was just beginning, and society was changing almost on a daily basis, it seemed. The "Love-ins" and other happenings in San Francisco were gaining world-wide attention, "Carnaby Street" fashions were all the rage in London, and the world was transforming itself into something no one had ever seen or could even imagine yet. The Beatles released "Sergeant Pepper's Lonely Hearts Club Band" later that year, which changed the way music was recorded and produced, and music was at the forefront of this huge and fantastic Cultural Revolution.

It was Scott who came up with the idea for the name of the new band. Scott's mother was an American lady from a well-to-do family in Connecticut who had married a retired British Naval Admiral after her husband had passed away a few years earlier. They lived in a very nice *piso* near *Plaza Castilla* in one of the nicest areas of Madrid, and Scott was not only a very smart and well-educated young man, but very charming and good looking as well.

His idea was to make their rock-and-roll shows truly spectacular events; similar to what was going on with bands like the Grateful Dead and Jefferson Airplane in San Francisco at the time. He suggested that they keep the sheepskin vests since similar types of garments were becoming very fashionable in London and elsewhere. He knew this to be a fact first-hand because he regularly traveled to London to visit his father's family and always made a point of visiting Carnaby Street while he was there.

His idea for the band's name was "Freak Out." And the idea was not only to dress in the wildest clothes possible but also to paint their faces with all kinds of messages and sayings, such as "Peace," "Love," and other assorted designs and markings. His idea was for the band to be totally different, such that if someone saw their band perform, they would never forget the experience.

Tin Tin was a little doubtful about the band's name as well as their look, but really had not much of a say in any of it. Besides, the guys thought, what did a guy who wore a suit and a tie every day know about fashion or about anything cool for that matter? But before too long, he had scheduled a photo shoot for the band on the outskirts of Madrid with wide-open spaces and mountains in the background. Soon he was also busy getting them gigs at the usual clubs as well as making some great fliers to put all over town advertising their shows.

The first gig for the new band was at a club downtown right off *La Gran Via* called "Tin Pan Alley." It was an old nightclub that had been there for several decades and had originally specialized in jazz music, but within the last few years, the owners had changed the format to include rock-and-roll music as well.

This place was not one of their typical Beautiful Beasts gigs at a maid's bar, but instead was more of a regular nightclub where businessmen would go to have a drink after work, or a place where a guy could take a date to impress her with his impeccable taste. It was a rather small dark place with a horseshoe-shaped bar on one side and lots of red velvet couches and tables with white tablecloths on the other side. Sharply dressed waiters in stiff white coats served drinks. A small elevated stage with the usual stage lights had a backdrop of a mural scene that looked like it could have been

Bourbon Street in New Orleans. In fact, their business card and their advertisements always featured the following saying: *"Un Rincon de Nueva Orleans en Madrid"* — a corner of New Orleans in Madrid.

The band arrived right on time to set up for their nine to one gig which consisted of three sets of about an hour long each, with a twenty-minute break between each set. Three hours of music was a lot for a beginning band, and the guys knew that they'd probably have to repeat their first set to be able to complete the night. They began their first set with the usual standard songs that they had played with the Beautiful Beasts, including "Midnight Hour," "Kansas City," "Wild Thing," and "Gloria."

They seemed to be received rather coolly by the audience, but they just figured that this crowd was not really a rock-and-roll crowd. By the time they started their second set, with some of their newer material — songs like "Hey Joe," "Sunshine of Your Love," and "Stone Free" — they realized that they were just clearly not reaching any of the audience with their music. Several gentlemen got up and walked out with their dates while frowning at the doorman.

By the third and final set of the evening, when they started repeating some of their earlier songs, they knew that they would not be invited back for another gig at this place. The average Spanish businessman was just not quite ready to be entertained by five young guys with the wildest possible clothes on and their faces painted up with flowers and words in English that they didn't even understand. By the end of the night, the only people left in the place besides the band members were the waiters, bartenders, and the manager.

The manager being the civilized and decent man that he was, did pay them the 5000 pesetas for the show, but gave them a few words of advice while they were packing up their gear, *"Muchachos, la proxima vez que vienes a tocar en un lugar como esto, quite esa mierda de maquilaje de sus caras y no tocas tan fuerte y baja el volumen un poco. Y buena suerte!"*

"Guys, the next time you come to a place like this to perform, take that shitty makeup off your faces, and don't play so damn loud and turn the volume down a little! And good luck!"

Of course, none of this fazed the members of "Freak Out" whatsoever. Their only reaction was something to the effect of, "Man what a square, what does that old man know about music, anyway?"

Tin Tin didn't have much to say at the end of the night either, but just collected his ten percent and said only this: "Well, we'll see how the show goes next week. I got you a gig at *Las Palmas* next Sunday." This was a maid's bar in the *Vallecas* neighborhood where the Beasts had played often and were always a huge success.

Unfortunately, the following Sunday things didn't improve that much from their previous gig. Instead of the crowd dancing and carrying on as they used to do, they just stood there with their arms crossed and stared at the five guys on stage. It seemed that the spectacle of their appearance far outweighed any sounds that they emitted. Performing music in public in front of an audience is a two-way experience, similar to dancing or sex. In all three of these activities, there are two participants, and a give and take situation, but if one of the participants is not taking part, then it can become boring and dull for the one who is into it.

This was the situation that "Freak Out" found themselves in at almost every one of their gigs around town. The one exception was the one gig that Scott got for the band at ASM.

School had already started up again by then, and The American School of Madrid had regular dances every other Saturday night during the school year, weather permitting, because the dances were held outdoors in the parking lot of the school.

The ASM campus was located on the outskirts of Madrid not far from the small pueblo of Aravaca. Unlike MHS (Madrid High School), ASM was not affiliated with the American military, but instead was a private school that offered an "American" style of education to the kids of American businessmen or American Embassy staff who lived in Spain.

Children of other nationalities attended as well, many connected to foreign embassies. Of course, English proficiency was required in order to attend classes, but the student body was quite diverse, with many different languages and cultures represented. There were even a few African and Arab kids studying along with the kids of parents who worked at such American companies as Libby's Foods and General Tire that had offices in Madrid.

The students from ASM and MHS did not tend to mix socially very much as there was no football game rivalry or other sports competition between them. MHS teams played their rivals at the other American base schools in Spain, such as the Air Force Base located in Zaragoza and the Naval Base in Rota. ASM didn't have much of a sports program to speak of, but it was an excellent school academically, since only the best of American accredited teachers and school personnel worked there.

The students at MHS who were not kids of active duty military personnel were more likely to associate with the ASM crowd. These kids almost always lived in downtown Madrid. My brother and I were lucky in that we had friends at both schools, though we both attended MHS.

Scott attended ASM, and he somehow got the band a gig at one of the Saturday night dances there. A stage was set up in the parking lot in front of the school and all vehicles were temporarily sequestered to a vacant lot next door. The ASM campus was located in a rather rural area, with open country all around and the nearest town of Aravaca several kilometers away. The dance was to start at seven o'clock, which was right around sunset, and the school had set up bright lights on tall poles to shine down and illuminate the entire parking lot. There were booths set up selling snacks and beverages, and a general ambiance of fun and festivity with streamers, balloons, and colorful signs everywhere.

Shortly after seven, the Master of Ceremonies came up to the stage, stood in front of the microphone and, after a little squeal of mike feedback, said, "Ladies and gentlemen, boys and girls, welcome to the second parking lot festival and dance of the year at the American School of Madrid. I'd like to welcome everybody here. I can see we have a great turnout tonight with lots of people ready to dance and have a great time.

"Please remember to use the trash receptacles provided for just that purpose. This will make clean-up much easier for Señor Garcia and his crew tomorrow. And please, everybody, I know you will all be on your best behavior, but just as a reminder, there is no alcohol allowed on campus as you well know. So please, everyone have a great time, and without further ado, I present to you for your entertainment and dancing pleasure: Freak Out!"

The five guys in the band quickly walked onto the stage and plugged in their guitars as the crowd quickly gathered around the front of the stage. Most of the people stood there with their mouths agape as they saw what was before them. Not only did the band all have their faces painted up with bright colors and designs, but all five of the guys were wearing their sheepskin vests, and Manolo even had a pair of sheepskin chaps on as well. He looked like something that no one had ever seen before. Two of the guys had hats on; Scott was wearing a white cowboy hat with bright feathers sticking from its band, and Javier was wearing a Spanish wide brim, black, gypsy-style hat. The band's look was somewhere between sixteenth century pirate and nineteenth century American wild west cowboy.

The opening three chords of "Wild Thing" carried across the parking lot, powered by the powerful VOX amps and the 200-watt SUNN PA head set at level 9, just at the bare threshold of starting to feed back. Manolo stepped up to the mike and sang with all his might, "Wild thing, you make my heart sing. You make everything, groovy."

And the crowd went nuts! They started screaming with delight and they all started dancing, not caring if they had a partner or not. Just the pure power, energy, and volume of the band made people not only want to dance and move but also made the audience realize that they were facing a force to be reckoned with. When the time came for the solo of the song, which on the original recording by the Troggs was performed on a flute, Ted played it on his trumpet note by note, and adding a special quality to the song.

By the time the last chord echoed across the parking lot, the band knew that they had the audience eating out of their hands. They kept the volume and the power up throughout the evening because they realized that performing outdoors was totally different from playing indoors where there were walls that would bounce the sound back around the room. But outdoors, the sound just carried on to infinity across the Spanish countryside.

By the time the band took its first break and stepped off the stage, there was a small crowd of people, (mostly girls), waiting for them, hoping to get a chance to chat with one of the guys in the band. Manolo seemed to get most of the attention, being the lead singer and the best looking of the five members, but since he spoke very little English, he didn't have much to say except to the few girls who spoke Spanish, which disappointed a number of the other girls!

So this musical act that was so unsuccessful at performing in a nightclub full of Spanish businessmen, had finally found an appreciative audience in a mostly American teenaged crowd. They had finally found their target audience. The band played once more at an ASM dance later that semester, but before too long, the weather would not permit more outdoor dances until the following spring, and by then the band had broken up.

The gigs that were possible for them were so limited that Manolo and Javier realized that they would be better off playing in a more traditional band performing at the maid's bars and the other regular nightclubs around Madrid. They formed another band of all Spanish guys and with Tin Tin's help got back into gigging fairly regularly around Madrid again.

A couple of years later, we heard that Manolo had quit the music business and had moved to Israel and joined a kibbutz. While working on a farm there, he had fallen off a tractor and had landed in front of the heavy tires while it was rolling, and both of his legs were damaged to such a severe degree that they had to be removed, and he spent the rest of his days in a wheelchair. What a terrible tragedy for such a talented, exciting and charismatic performer. My brother and I both wept when we heard this news, and to this day, I still feel a pang of sorrow when I think about his tragic fate.

Johnny, Scott, and Ted continued without Manolo and Javier, but it was just not the same without their front man in the band. They continued to put a band together whenever a gig arose, but these were so few and far between that a regular permanent band was just never formed again.

But the memories of both bands, The Beautiful Beasts and Freak Out!, will live forever in the memories of the band members, as well as the various audiences that were lucky enough to see them perform live. Such was the power of rock-and-roll!

Chapter 6. Soul – Both Rubber & Psychedelic

"We dance for laughter, we dance for tears, we dance for madness, we dance for fears, we dance for hopes, we dance for screams, we are the dancers, and we create the dreams."
— Albert Einstein

I had my own adventures playing music during these most interesting of times. Having the use of my brother's professional music gear whenever his band was not using it opened up many possibilities for my own fledgling musical endeavors.

Within a few days of my return to Madrid from Alicante and starting school again, my old friend from the days before we had moved, Wally Padilla, and I started jamming again. He had since acquired a second-hand set of cheap drums, and I had my *Invicta* red bass, along with the Silvertone amplifier we had ordered from the Sears catalog the year before, so we had the basic gear with which to start making some loud noise together.

A new kid had recently moved into our neighborhood by the name of Bryce Lester. He was our age and in our grade at school and he played a little bit of guitar. Bryce was physically the opposite of Wally. Wally, being of Panamanian descent, was rather dark-complexioned, as well as being less than five feet tall, and his voice hadn't even completely changed yet. Bryce, by contrast, was over six feet, two inches tall at age fourteen, and every day his five o'clock shadow appeared around two in the afternoon. Bryce also had a very deep but awkward-sounding voice.

He lived very close to my house, and his house had a large basement which was originally the maid's quarters, where his bedroom and bathroom were located. This was the place that we claimed as our rehearsal and practice space since The Beautiful Beasts were using our garage for their purposes and kept all their own gear there.

Bryce had a nice Hofner electric guitar, along with a small amp that his parents had given him for Christmas the previous year, and he had been learning quite a bit on it since then. So the three of us set up our gear in his basement room and started to make some noise. We had somehow acquired two microphones, one with a boom stand, which we plugged into our guitar amps so we were ready to go. It was decided that Wally would be the lead singer because he had a very sweet, almost angelic voice. Since he hadn't quite completed puberty yet, his voice was still high, clear, and pure. We set up the boom stand by his drums and the other mike in the center of the room for Bryce and me to share, and we started playing music.

The first song we tried was "(I'm Not Your) Steppin' Stone" by the Monkees with its easy four-chord progression. Wally really had the lead vocal down perfectly, until it came to the bridge of the song, when Bryce didn't have a clue how to play the lead part on the guitar. So Wally just sang the lead guitar part in his high, clear voice, which seemed to work okay. The next song we tried was "Gloria" by Them, and its three chords were easy for Bryce and me to play together. He had even mastered the easy lead lick in the middle of the song. "Wipe Out" by the Ventures was another song we were able to play together fairly well, since it was an instrumental. Wally even had the drum solo down to perfection, having practiced that classic drum part countless times ever since he had gotten his drum kit.

We also worked up quite a number of other songs, including "Day Tripper" by the Beatles, "Get Off My Cloud," and "As Tears Go By," by the Rolling Stones, "House of the Rising Sun," by the Animals, and "Well Respected Man," "You Really Got Me," and "All Day and All the Night" by the Kinks, as well as "My Girl" by the Temptations, "Louie, Louie" by the Kingsmen, and "Wild Thing" by the Troggs. Before too long we had almost twenty songs together that we could play well enough to at least make them recognizable to the average listener.

Within a month or so of twice weekly practices, we thought we were ready to perform in public. At Torrejon Air Force Base where we all went to school, there was a "Teen" club located not far from the high school where, during the school year, they held dances for teenagers on the weekends. It was also a place for teenagers to hang out after school.

The building featured a snack bar, a large dance floor with many tables and chairs around, and even a couple of sofas. There were also two

pool tables, and a few pinball machines, and a chess set and other board games were also available. It was a very popular place for the teenagers to spend time, and it was considered a safe and secure place by the parents as well.

They set aside Saturday nights for the high school dances, but on Friday nights, they staged dances for the junior high school kids. This is where and when we thought that we might be able to perform our first shows in public.

So one Tuesday afternoon right after school, the three of us walked over to the Teen Club and asked if we could talk to the manager. We sat down at one of the tables and before too long an older well-dressed gentleman came out and, introduced himself as Mr. Anderson, and asked if he could be of assistance. We had decided previously that I was to do the talking since my brother was in a working band and we thought that might carry some weight somehow.

I said, in the manliest voice I could muster, "Hello, Mr. Anderson, my name is Ronnie Walker, and these are my friends Wally Padilla and Bryce Lester. The three of us are freshmen at MHS and we have gotten a rock-and-roll band together and would like to be considered for playing at the junior high dances on Friday nights."

He looked at the three of us with a gentle smile and asked, "Well, Ronnie, it's nice to meet you boys. Tell me, how long have you guys been playing together now?"

I said to him with all the sincerity I could muster, "Well, sir, it's been over a month now that we've been practicing together and we can play over twenty songs already. We're really pretty good. My brother plays in a band called the Beautiful Beasts, and they play all over Madrid. They even have a manager and everything."

Mr. Anderson smiled and asked, "Well, that sounds very impressive Ronnie, so what's the name of your band?"

I said without hesitation, "Rubber Soul, sir. And my brother Johnny has told me that we can use his equipment when we play in front of people. He has a VOX amp and a real nice microphone and speaker system."

He replied, "Well Ronnie, we have our own P. A. system here with speakers and microphones, so all you guys would have to bring would be your guitars, amps, and drums. And we don't pay very much either, only fifty dollars for the entire band per night; would that be all right?"

I look at him straight in the eye, and say, "Yes, sir, that would be okay, I guess. When would you like us to play?"

He thought for a moment and said, "Well, let's see, we have the Stompers playing this Friday, and the following Friday the Four Clovers are supposed to play, so how about the following Friday night the twenty-third; will that work out for you guys?"

I replied eagerly, "Yes, sir, that will be fine. What time should we be here?"

He says, "Well, the band is supposed to play from seven till nine, but get here a little early to set up your gear and do a sound check if you like, okay?"

With a grin that reached from ear to ear, I replied, "All right, that sounds great, Mr. Anderson, we'll be here."

He just smiled his gentle smile again and said, "Okay then, guys, we'll see you on the twenty-third, and if things work out and the kids like you, we'll see about letting you guys play some more dates in the future maybe. We can always use a variety of talent around here, you know. And we like to let everybody get a chance."

The three of us stood up, and I reached my hand out and shook his hand. The other guys did the same, and I said, "Thank you so much, sir, we'll see you then. Goodbye now. And thanks again, I know you won't be disappointed."

The three of us walked out of the Teen Club with big smiles on our faces, and Wally said, "All right! We got a gig! A real chance to play in front of people, plus we're going to get paid for it! And fifty dollars, that's a lot of money. Let's see, that's over sixteen dollars each! Hell, the allowance my Mom gives me is only eight dollars a week! This is double that! This is great!"

Bryce looked at me seriously and said, "Ronnie, why did you tell the guy that the name of our band was Rubber Soul? I thought we were still thinking about our name, man. I like the name that Wally came up with a while back which was 'Phil & the Blanks.' Remember that one?"

Wally replied, "Yeah, but the trouble is, we don't have anyone named Philip in the band, remember? I liked the one you came up with, Bryce, but again we don't have someone named Richard in the band."

And Bryce said with his usual smirk, "Oh, you mean 'Dick and the Pants'? Yeah, I liked that name a lot too, heh, heh."

I look at them and replied, "Well, I had to tell him something, and that was the last name we had been thinking about, wasn't it?"

Bryce frowned and said, "Well, I thought we hadn't totally agreed on a name yet. But I guess that one will have to do for now."

Wally grinned and said in his high voice, "Well, I like it, man. I think it sounds cool!"

I say, "Yeah, me too. I like it because it has two different meanings, you know. One meaning is like having a shoe that has a rubber sole instead of a leather one. Plus the idea of having a rubber soul, kind of like an elastic spirit, you know? It sounds cool."

Then Bryce said with a weird smirk on his face, "It has another meaning as well, you know, you guys."

"What's that, man?" asked Wally.

"Well, just think about it," replied Bryce with a very serious look on his face. "If you bang a girl with a rubber on, then all your spermies get caught in the rubber, right? And the souls of the babies that those sperms could have made would be called Rubber Souls, get it?"

Wally and I just looked at him with the same bewildered look on our faces, and Wally said, "Jeez, man. Only you would think of something like that! That's the only thing you ever think about, isn't it, is banging girls!"

Bryce just shrugged his shoulders and agreed. "You'd better believe it, little man, you'd better believe it."

I interrupted, "Cripes, I just thought of something, guys. What if everybody thinks that all we play is Beatles songs, because of the Beatles album, Rubber Soul?"

Wally mulled this over for a second and said, "Ah, don't worry about it, Ronnie. We do play a few Beatle songs but I don't think people will think that all we can play is Beatle songs because of our name. Besides let them think it, who cares? The Beatles are the coolest band ever, man!"

"I guess you're right," I replied as we continued walking towards the bus stop to catch our ride back to Madrid, each of us deep into his own thoughts about what we had gotten ourselves into.

We practiced several more times before the date of our first the gig came around. And we wrote down on paper two set lists, figuring that we'd play for about forty-five minutes, then take a half hour break, then come back and play for another forty-five minutes, and that would make the two hours.

We figured each song was around three or four minutes long, so we'd have to have at least twelve or so songs for each set. But then we realized that we only had eighteen songs really worked out well enough to play in front of people, and a few more that just didn't sound quite right to play in public yet. So, we figured we'd just have to repeat a few towards the end of our show.

Wally had a great idea for the end of the first set. He suggested that we do "Wipe Out" for the last song, and he could extend the drum solo in the middle of the song for as long as we liked, and that could add another four or five minutes to that set. We tried it in rehearsal and when it was time for his drum solo, he just kept it going for over four minutes. Finally, he nodded at Bryce and me and we came in and finished up the song. We did it again and this time, Bryce timed it on his watch and it came out as just over seven minutes long.

"That should work," Bryce says, "And people really like drum solos, man."

Friday the twenty-third finally came around, and we were as excited as kids on Christmas morning. We got to the Teen Club way early; in fact, instead of going home after school that day, we just walked over there after school and hung around until we were scheduled to play. My mom had helped us get Johnny's VOX guitar amp and Wally's drums out to the base a couple of days before when she had gone out there to do some shopping. She had dropped the gear off in the Teen Club's back storage room so we'd have it there the night of our gig. Bryce and I had brought our guitars with us on the bus to school that morning and put them in our lockers until after school.

We had told all our friends at school about our show, and we asked all of them to come check it out, but most of them showed very little interest in going to a *junior high school* dance, saying something about having no desire to hang out with a bunch of little kids, after all they were in *high school* now. Besides, most of them were planning on going to the Teen Club the next night for the high school dance, when one of the coolest bands in school, "The Stompers," which was made up of all juniors and seniors, were going to play.

We had the gear set up way before our start time of seven o'clock. We even did a short (one song) sound check to test everything and make sure all the gear was working well, including the really nice P.A. system that the club provided. There wasn't an actual stage in the club, but instead there was an area near the left side, in front of the dance floor and near the big floor-length windows, where the bands performed. With the dance floor right in front of the band, we were at the same level as the audience would be, hopefully dancing to our music.

Right at seven o'clock, Mr. Anderson, the manager of the Teen Club, stepped up to the microphone and with a slight squeal of feedback, said in his best announcer voice, "Ladies and gentlemen, boys and girls, for tonight's entertainment and for your dancing pleasure, I present to you a band whose members are all ninth graders from MHS... the Rubber Soul!"

Wally adjusted his drum throne slightly and said into his microphone, "Thanks very much for having us, Mr. Anderson; we really appreciate the chance to play here at the Torrejon Teen Club. Our first song is one by the Monkees, called "Steppin' Stone," and we hope you like it."

We start playing the intro of the song, and all four chords of the song sounded in tune and together. Bryce was strumming the barre chords for all he was worth, and I was matching my bass notes right along with him. And since there were three microphones with the P.A. system, each of us had our own microphone, so we all began singing at the same time, "I, I, I, I, I'm not your steppin' stone."

The kids had by this time formed a half-circle around us, and as soon as we started singing the song, I saw the recognition in their eyes and smiles appeared on almost all of their faces. The girls started moving a little and swinging their arms, and soon a group of four or five were dancing away right in front of us, not even caring if they had a partner or not. By the time the bridge of the song came around, there were about twenty or so kids dancing to the song, and very few of them appeared to have a partner. It didn't matter; it was the sheer simple joy of the music that made them want to move and dance. Again, this was the power of Rock & Roll!

After a couple more songs, including "House of the Rising Sun," which seemed to be a lot of kids' favorite, it was time for a real slow song, so we started playing "As Tears Go By," by the Rolling Stones.

Since it was a slow song, they really couldn't dance by themselves, so the girls went back to their seats and waited until someone asked them to dance. Before too long, about a dozen couples were slow-dancing to the song.

By the time we took our break between sets, and after Wally's five-minute drum solo on "Wipe Out," all three of us were feeling pretty good about ourselves and how things were going. While Wally was chatting with his younger brother Charlie and some of his junior high friends, Bryce and I went over to the snack bar to grab a couple of soft drinks, and while standing in line, we were approached by two eighth-grade girls. They introduced themselves as Kathy and "Birdie."

Kathy was a tall blond girl with glasses and Birdie was a rather short, chubby girl with dark hair who told us her real name was Dolores. She explained that she went by the nickname Birdie, because, as she said, "Why would anyone ever go by that goofy name?" I thought to myself, "Well, 'Birdie' is certainly not much better." But, of course, I didn't say it out loud.

She seemed to take a particular shine to Bryce for some reason, even though she was less than five feet tall and rather chubby, and Bryce was over six feet two inches, thin, and gawky. But it turned out that they really hit it off and started to date shortly after that meeting, and became a couple and were together almost throughout high school, until her family rotated back to the States in her junior year, when Bryce was a senior.

Kathy and I didn't seem to hit it off whatsoever, but that was okay, because I was dating girls that went to ASM and besides, I wasn't ready to spend all my time with one girl for the most part. And, as I kept telling Bryce and Wally, I was into playing music for the "art" of it, not just to be able to pick up chicks.

Our next and last set went over pretty well, considering that Bryce kept making goo-goo eyes at Birdie the whole time and getting very distracted by her. We had to repeat several songs from our first set, and Wally did his long drum solo again to "Wipe Out," but the kids didn't seem to care; all they wanted to do was dance, flirt, and giggle, or so it seemed.

A few minutes after nine p.m. we ended the last song, and we got a nice round of applause. Then the kids started to leave, and we began to pack up our gear to put it into the storage room, when Mr. Anderson came up to us and said, "Well, you guys did real well tonight, and the kids really seemed to like you. Here's your pay." He handed me an envelope with fifty dollars cash in it.

Then he said, "How would you guys like to come back and do another show? It looks like I've got next month on the twenty-eighth open."

I smiled at him and said, "Sure, absolutely, Mr. Anderson, we'd be happy to."

He replied, smiling too, "Okay, boys, we'll see you again on Friday the twenty-eighth then. I'll go ahead and put you down on the calendar."

"All right, and thank you very much, Mr. Anderson; we really appreciate it," I replied.

"You're welcome, guys. Glad to help out."

After he walked away, Wally said, "Wow, Ronnie, we seem to have been quite the hit tonight. And he even asked us back for another show. This is way cool, don't you think?"

"Yeah, man. You're right, it went even better than I expected! What do you think, Bryce, old buddy?"

Bryce just shrugged his massive shoulders and said, "It was cool, man. And I met this really nice chick too. I think she might be the type to put out, too."

Wally looked up at him and retorted, "That really is all you think about, isn't it, man?"

Bryce smiled his most wicked of smiles and said, "You'd better believe it, little man."

Rubber Soul played three more junior high school dances at the Teen Club that year, but those gigs were nothing like that first time when the three of us felt we were on top of the world, playing music to a live audience, and actually getting paid to play it!

The following summer, between our freshman and sophomore year, Wally got some bad news. His family was going to be moving back to the States. His father had gotten a transfer to an Air Force Base somewhere in Florida, and they would be leaving by the end of the summer.

This kind of thing happens all the time with Military Brats. It seems as soon as a kid starts making good friends or starts to do something worthwhile, it's time to pack up and go somewhere else and start it all over again. Every three or four years seems to be the pattern with most military families, but that's the job, and most people just take it in stride. Besides, there's not much you can do about it, anyway.

We played a few private parties that summer before Wally had to leave. We played for free at Birdie's birthday party one Saturday evening at her house in Royal Oaks. And even though she was not quite a freshman in high school, she did know how to throw a decent party.

There was some booze, but it was kept very low key because her parents were around. A lot of the kids spilled out from the living room, where we were set up, onto the outside patio where cigarettes were being smoked and some serious petting was going on.

It was great having Birdie hang around the band because she even managed to help get us a gig that summer at the Royal Oaks pool. There was a very nice pool in center of the Royal Oaks housing area, where all the kids would hang out during the summer, and they had "pool parties" every other weekend or so. Usually older high school bands would play at these parties, but she managed to talk the manager into allowing us to play one time.

It was a Saturday afternoon from four until six, and it only paid  twenty-five dollars, but we were never too choosy about what a gig paid because we just wanted to play. We would have played for free as we did on many occasions, but a little money never hurt. So, we set up our gear under the shade of the Ramada in front of the snack bar, and the place was as crowded as I'd ever seen it.

There seemed to be close to a hundred kids there, of all ages and grades. Young kids were running around the pool, constantly being yelled at by the lifeguards on duty, "Slow down, no running allowed on the pool deck!" Other people were just sitting on towels in the sun working on their sunburns. And, of course, a lot of the boys just sat around ogling the girls, trying not to be too obvious about it. A great time was being had by all.

We had worked out a short set of songs that we called our "surf set," which consisted of three instrumental songs in the "surf" genre. We started out with "Pipeline," with its gnarly, fuzzy, bottom-string lead guitar part. And after a lot of practice, we had finally worked out the classic Ventures song, "Walk, Don't Run," and even though we always messed up the middle part of it, we could fake it well enough to make the song recognizable at least. And of course, we ended the set with "Wipe Out," with Wally's great four-minute-long drum solo.

We played this "surf set" twice during our two-hour gig, but the second time, people seemed to like it even more than the first time we played it. We had a good-sized crowd of kids dancing the "Watusi," "the Boogaloo," and the "Swim" within a couple of feet of where we were playing in the shade. At times I had to hold my bass close to my chest and watch where I pointed it in fear that I might bang some kid in the face with the headstock. But once again, like every time we played in front of people, a great time was had by all, audience and band members alike.

By the end of that summer, Wally had left Madrid and the band that I had formed with him and Bryce had disappeared as well. School started, and Bryce and I gradually began to drift apart. He spent most of his time hanging out at Royal Oaks with his girlfriend, and I moved on to other things in my young life.

One day I met this guy in my Shop class at school and we started talking about music and forming a band. His name was Ramon Douglas, and he said he played guitar. He lived out in Royal Oaks and had a friend and neighbor who played drums, Nick Rynowski. Ray was a typical American teenager of the times, with slightly greasy hair smeared down onto his forehead to help cover up the zits that kept popping up there, and the same military-issue glasses that we all seemed to wear at the time.

Nick was a good-looking guy, with blond hair, a great smile, and a good complexion. He had a decent "Slingerland" gold sparkle drum kit that his dad had recently bought for him, and he and Ray had been looking for a bass player to complete their band.

They had Nick's drums set up in his bedroom, and that is where I showed up one day with my bass guitar and my little Silvertone amp. Ray played an "Airline" electric guitar (from Montgomery Wards) which had three pickups, and he had a small practice amp. He was really into a new band that had recently come out of California called the Doors, and he was trying to figure out some of their songs from their debut album.

I set up my gear and Ray showed me how to play "Light My Fire," but, of course, we couldn't play the opening organ part without a keyboardist. So, we just omitted that part of the song and went right to the verses and chorus. Next we tried, "Break On Through," and after he showed me the opening bass riff on his guitar, I was able to play it well enough on my bass, and the song came together sounding pretty good.

"Twentieth Century Fox" was another Doors song we were able to work out as well.

We went through some more songs, most of which I already knew, such as "Wild Thing," "Stepping Stone," and "House of the Rising Sun." My experience playing with Rubber Soul was helping me a lot in this new band. We also worked out a song by the Jimi Hendrix Experience called "Hey Joe." Ray showed me the bass pattern and it went along perfectly with the chords he was playing. He even played a little lead guitar part that sounded great to all three of us, but didn't sound close to the lead that Jimi did on the song.

I told the guys about my brother's band, The Beautiful Beasts, and the fact that they had a manager and were gigging pretty regularly all over Madrid. Ray then asked me why I didn't ask Tin Tin to manage us as well. I thought about it for a minute and told him I would talk to Tin Tin about it soon, because it sounded like our new band was coming along pretty well, and before too long we'd be ready to play out.

A few weeks later, after several more rehearsals with this new band, Nick said that he wanted to have a party at his house the following Saturday night, and he wanted us to play. Ray and I agreed, and we got two set lists together for our debut performance. A lot of the songs were the same ones that I was playing with Rubber Soul, but there were many new ones as well, since Ray had a different style and ability than Bryce had. He was also the lead singer, and it looked better for a band when the front man wasn't hidden behind the drum kit, as it was when Wally was the main singer.

Nick could be a rather loud and rowdy guy sometimes, especially when there were girls around whom he was trying to impress. The night of his party, his parents had gone to a bowling tournament on base and left the house for several hours that evening. Of course, the booze was broken out almost as soon as his folks stepped out the door, and before too long, the party started getting a little wild. There were around twenty-five kids there that night and everyone seemed to be having a great time drinking and dancing.

We had set up in the living room, and there were even kids standing outside in the yard listening who hadn't been invited to the party, but could hear our music, and had come around just to listen. The first set went okay, and while we were taking a break between sets, Nick started chugging Bacardi rum straight out of a bottle, and by the time our next set was to begin he could barely stand up, much less play the drums adequately.

By the third or fourth song, he was playing in such a sloppy way that Ray just put his guitar down and fumed, "Nick! You're drunk as a skunk, man! It sounds like shit and I'm not playing anymore! That's it! Fuck it!"

Nick stood up behind his kit and said to Ray, "Hell, I'm not *that* drunk, man!" And he proceeded to fall all over his drums, sending stands and cymbals crashing and drums rolling all over the living room floor. The dozen or so kids standing around the living room all start laughing hysterically as Nick crawled over towards the couch where he heaved himself onto it and proceeded to pass out.

I leaned my bass against my amp and said to Ray, "Well, man, it looks like tonight's show is over, huh?"

He just gave me a look like I was stating the completely obvious, and replied, "Yep, well, it was fun while it lasted, I guess."

He put his guitar into its case and I did the same. We both left Nick's house with him sleeping away on the couch, and the crowd was leaving too, mumbling some obscene things about our band and about Nick especially.

Monday morning at school, Nick was ashamed of himself and as apologetic as a person could be. He promised us that such a thing would never happen again, and he told us both that he would never drink again at a gig, at least not until after it was over. Of course, Ray and I forgave him and asked him what happened after we had left on Saturday night. He just smiled and told us that his little sister had helped him get to bed and had cleaned up the house by the time his folks got home so, luckily, he didn't get in any trouble. He also told us that he would never touch a bottle of rum again in his life; he could promise us that.

Around this time, I was able to get a new and different bass guitar. The one that I had wanted to own since the day when I saw The Beatles perform at the Bullring in Madrid was the famous Paul McCartney, violin-shaped Hofner bass guitar. To me and millions of other bass players, it seemed to be the coolest bass around, and it was played by Paul, the most famous bass player in the world.

I managed to save a little money from the gigs that I had played and along with my allowance, had saved almost half of the $180 cost of the guitar. The rest was chipped in by my dad, who knew that this was something that mattered so much to me that I was not going to stop mentioning it to him until I owned it. He also figured that he had spent a lot on my brother's equipment and it was the least he could do to help me to get my dream bass. When I brought it home from the store, I really thought that I had reached the big time, with this beauty in my hands to play!

Our little band had a stroke of luck soon after the disastrous gig at Nick's party. It turned out that Ray's dad knew the guy who managed the Royal Oaks Theater. This theater was in the part of Royal Oaks where there were also the elementary school, a snack bar, a gym, a library, several baseball fields, and other educational and recreational facilities set up for the American military and their dependents who lived in the Royal Oaks housing area.

The theater itself was a large building that showed American films and was a very popular spot for people to hang out because, like the American theater near Plaza Peru in Madrid, American movies were shown every night of the week. The snack bar next door was another popular gathering place for people of all ages. Somehow, Ray's dad had talked his friend, who was the manager of the theater, into allowing our band to rehearse occasionally on the stage of the theater.

So, one Sunday afternoon we brought our gear down the hill from Nick's house and set it up on the big stage of the Royal Oaks Theater. Jimmy the manager was there, and he told us that we only had a two-hour window before he had to prepare for that evening's film presentation. We managed to go through the entire set list that we had together at that point. Unfortunately, we didn't have a P.A. system, but we made the best use of our guitar amps by plugging a mike into each one. Trying to fill that huge auditorium with only one twelve-inch speaker and one ten-inch speaker from our guitar amps was a challenge to say the least, but we made the best of it by turning everything up to ten on the volume knobs.

It sounded rather distorted until we adjusted the two amps to just fill the few first rows of seats. When we began playing, the entire place was empty, because Jimmy had left the auditorium mumbling something about the fact that he didn't like this loud rock-and-roll music much anyway. He went up to the projection room to hang out, saying he would be back in a while to let us know when to knock it off.

But by our third song, a small crowd had begun to gather near the front of the stage. Ten or twelve kids had heard the musical sounds from outside by the snack bar area, had let themselves in through the side exit, and were enjoying this free rock-and-roll show. Most of them were young girls, and they were having the time of their lives moving and dancing to the music we were playing.

Ray was doing his best Jim Morrison imitation, growling and shouting into the microphone, and the girls seemed to be eating it up. When he sang the chorus of, "Twentieth Century Fox," a few of the girls started screaming and acting like they were at a real rock-and-roll concert. Having a live audience, especially of young teenaged girls, certainly gave us the incentive to play the best we could. But, of course, this was a just practice session, and we had to stop occasionally during the middle of the song for Ray to show me the chord changes and the bass notes to fit them. Then we'd start the song over from the beginning until we thought we had it down well enough. This seemed to annoy our small audience slightly, but they still stuck around and continued to enjoy our sounds.

When we took a short break about halfway through our set list, we climbed down from the stage and three girls were standing there, waiting to chat with us. One older girl who was around our age told us her name was Kathy and her little sister's name was Sharon, and her sister's friend's name was Debbie. Kathy was a real "Chatty Kathy" type, and kept up a nonstop barrage of words, allowing us only an occasional "huh huh."

When she finally came up for air, we told her we were really thirsty and we wandered off to go down to the snack bar for a soft drink. When we got back, she and the other girls were still there. She started up again with the non-stop talking and giggling, and only stopped when we climbed the stairs, got back on stage, and turned our amplifiers on again. Right before we started the next song, I heard her say to her sister, "Gee, these guys are really quiet. They must be really shy or something, don't you think?"

We were able to have one more practice session at the Royal Oaks Theater before Jimmy told us that his boss didn't like the idea of a band practicing there because of insurance regulations, so we would have to find somewhere else to rehearse. We practiced in Nick's bedroom again, but only when his dad wasn't around, because he thought we were too loud and the noise bothered him considerably.

One afternoon, right after one of the Beautiful Beasts practice sessions in our garage, I was finally able to get a chance to talk to Tin Tin about becoming our manager. I told him about our band and the fact that we were getting pretty good, and that we were playing some songs by the Doors and the Jimi Hendrix Experience.

He told me that he'd like to hear us before booking us for any jobs, so I told him where and when we practiced.

He showed up right on time the following Saturday and I introduced him to Ray and Nick. Neither of them spoke that much Spanish, and Tin Tin's English skills were limited, so I had to do a lot of translating. He listened to a couple of songs and told us that he would indeed like to become our manager. He would get twenty percent of any job that he booked for us and he would also help us get our gear to the shows by using his van. He said that he would take charge of all promotions and advertising for the band as well.

He knew about the agreement I had with my brother about using his gear for shows when his band wasn't playing, and he knew that with this gear, we could play just about any venue in town. He asked what the name of our band was, and I told him that we were still working on the name but I'd let him know before the first gig that he got for us. We all shook hands and he left telling us that he would let me know when he got something booked.

After he left, Nick and Ray seemed very excited about having a manager for our band and we started to discuss our band's name again. We had to continue to brainstorm a name, because Tin Tin was talking about getting us gigs very soon, like within a couple of weeks or so.

Ray said he really liked his idea which was "The Windows," but Nick and I told him that we thought it sounded too much like "The Doors." Nick came up with "The Whatever," but Ray and I thought it sounded too much like "The Who." We also discussed the idea of just keeping the name of my old band, "Rubber Soul," but we decided that since I was the only original member, people who had seen the original band might think that something was wrong, what with only one guy left from the original band.

Finally, I said to the guys, "You know, guys, what kinds of music do we all really like the most?"

Ray instantly replied, "Psychedelic, man. Hendrix, Jefferson Airplane, The Doors, that kind of thing."

And then Nick chimed in, "My favorite kind of music is Soul Music, James Brown, Wilson Pickett, Otis Redding, all those guys, man."

"Then that's it, guys! Psychedelic Soul! What do you think? Instead of Rubber Soul, we just change one word and get a totally new meaning! Psychedelic Soul, I like it! It sounds cool as hell, man!" I must have sounded very excited.

Ray said, "You're right, Ron, that is a cool name, and it does really describe our music well too. I like it."

"Hey, I'm cool with it if you guys are," Nick added.

"Okay, then, it's decided: We are Psychedelic Soul!" I said the name with a flourish.

Then Nick said, "Shouldn't it be *The* Psychedelic Soul?"

I said, "No man, without the *The*, just plain Psychedelic Soul."

Ray agreed. "Psychedelic Soul doesn't sound very plain to me, man! It sounds really cool and far out and wild, man! We are Psychedelic Soul!"

Within a week or so, I got a call from Tin Tin telling me that he had booked a gig for us at a place called the "Yola Club." He told me that it was a "Maids" club and that the gig was for the following Sunday from five to nine p.m., and it paid 5000 pesetas (about eighty dollars), minus his twenty percent, which would leave us with 4000 pesetas for the three of us. Not bad for three fifteen-year-old kids for just playing music, I thought.

He told me that he wanted to print a hundred fliers to put up around the area of the club and other parts of town. He said he would be using his regular printer, and that the fliers would only cost around 100 pesetas, and that he would cover them. But he needed to know the name of the band before he could have them printed.

I told him we had come up with a great name, and that it was "Psychedelic Soul."

He asked me to repeat it and so I did. He then asked me if I would spell it for him. So I slowly spelled it out for him, "P–S–Y–C–H–E–D–E–L–I–C S–O–U–L."

He then said, *"Muy bien, Ronnie, ya tengo escrito. Los papelitos van a salir cojunudo, macho!"* "Very good, Ronnie, I have it written down. The little fliers are going to come out really cool, man!"

The day of the show, we arrived at the club fairly early to set up and to do a sound check, and plastered all over the wall outside of the place was the following:

ORGANIZACIONES GADY
Presenta en
YOLA CLUB
2514 Calle Los Molinos
Domingo 17 de Julio, a las 5 de la tarde,
Presenta el gran cojunto musical Americano
"PFYCHETELIC FOUL"
Magnifico Baile para la Juventud
Precios Popularisimos

Now one of several things could have happened. First, the lousy telephone connections in Madrid at the time left a lot to be desired. Or two, my Spanish skills, especially when it came to pronouncing letters in Spanish, was less than perfect; or three, Tin Tin just plain wrote it down wrong.

When Nick and Ray saw the fliers all over the outside of the building, they had a good laugh, and soon the three of us were tearing down several of them for souvenirs of our first big gig at a Spanish club.

The show went over fairly well, even with the confusion over our name. Our mostly Spanish audience didn't speak a word of English, much less could they read a word of it, so to them the name of our band didn't matter, anyway.

The Yola Club was a large cavernous building with one main room with a very high ceiling. The stage was lifted and set against one wall about halfway up to the tall ceiling and was accessible by a set of stairs. Our heads were about a foot or so from the ceiling due to the height of the stage and the closeness of the ceiling. But this arrangement did make it possible for the band to be seen from anywhere in the large dance hall.

Several hundred people were there that night, mostly maids from the area, along with working-class young men hoping to meet a young lady, or at least have a dance or two with one. As in places like this all over the world, the sexual tension and flirting going on was thick, with the young *macho* Spaniard males competing for the attentions of the demure, virginal young ladies.

There was a bar on the premises, and some of the young men would drink quite a lot of beer or wine to bolster their courage to be able to go up to a complete stranger and ask her to dance. The bar did a great business, and the club patrons did a good business as well charging about fifty pesetas (about eighty cents or so) entrance fee for the males, and about half of that for the *señoritas*.

What with the huge popularity of The Beatles and other English bands in Spain and indeed all over the world, we Americans at least sang in the same language as these much more famous and accomplished bands. But what we mostly provided was loud and exciting music that people could dance to, and do what young people have been doing for countless centuries: strut, flirt, and try to find a mate.

We played four forty-five-minute sets. After our first set we took a break, and the three of us walked down the steep stairs to the dance floor, and before we could reach the bottom, there were several young ladies there, not much older than we were, holding pens and papers. They wanted our autographs! We were amazed and delighted, and were willing to sign our names with a flourish on their sheets of papers, followed by the name of our band spelled correctly this time.

At the end of the night, after we got paid by Tin Tin, the three members of Psychedelic Soul were feeling pretty good about themselves, to say the least. The three of us had just experienced something that was to stick with us for the rest of our lives, regardless of what we did or how accomplished we were to become as musicians.

As Paul McCartney said so famously in an interview many years later: "Musicians and athletes are the only people that get paid to play, everyone else gets paid to work!"

It was a great feeling indeed, to get paid to play instead of to work. And many years later when I was searching for what I wanted to do for a living, I definitely kept this in mind.

Chapter 7. Royal Oaks

"Youth cannot know how age thinks and feels.
But old men are guilty if they forget what it was to be young."
— J. K. Rowling

Royal Oaks, also known as "Roaks" for short, was a housing area near Madrid where many Americans lived, almost all of them connected in one way or another with the nearby Torrejon Air Force Base. In Spanish, this area was known as "El Encinar de los Reyes." "Encinar" in Spanish is an Oak grove, and "de los Reyes" translates as "of the Kings." Many people who lived in Royal Oaks during those years truly felt like "Kings" at times.

Being an American living in Spain during the 1960s and 70s certainly had its advantages, not only because of the great exchange rate between dollars and pesetas in those years, but also due to the fact that Americans were considered to be extraordinary people to the average Spaniard and were generally treated accordingly. American movies and TV shows were seen worldwide in almost every civilized country in the world, and Spain was no exception. The Hollywood machine was cranking them out and American culture, celebrities, and lifestyle were shown as positive and exciting influences on the rest of the world. They strongly felt the American sphere of influence in Western Europe where the United States had so many military bases. This feeling of being special and different from the local people, combined with the enormous amount of respect from the Spanish population, made it fun and exciting for Americans to live in Spain in those days.

At any given time, there were close to a thousand Americans living in Royal Oaks, most if not all for only the three- or four-year duration of the average tour of duty for the servicemen who were stationed at Torrejon. Royal Oaks was the housing area where the servicemen who had families, also known as "dependents," lived. If they were young single "airmen," then they were usually confined to living in quarters on base, or an apartment in downtown Madrid.

So Royal Oaks was, in a way, a small pocket of the American life on the outskirts of Madrid. And though I never lived there, I did spend a lot of time there over the years because I had many friends who lived there, as well as many activities and events that I attended there on a regular basis.

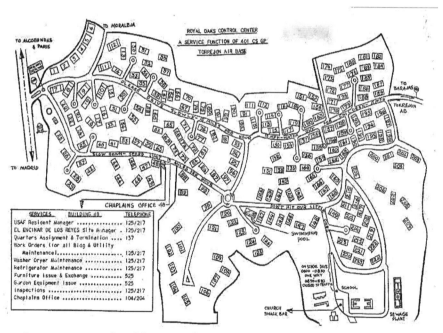

As one can see by this map, there were over 200 different buildings in Royal Oaks and most of them were four-plexes. There were four separate apartments to each building, with two downstairs and two upstairs, and each one with either an outside patio for the downstairs apartments, or a *terraza*, or balcony for the upstairs ones. All had carports and yards with very nice landscaping and green lawns during the warmer months.

Some buildings had only one or two units per building and these were located towards the entrance of the housing area, located near the main highway towards Madrid, and were reserved for officers and their families, which is another distinction that the U.S. military puts between officers and enlisted men. These units were either single-story buildings with one residence each, or two story duplexes with each residence occupying an entire floor.

Regardless where one lived in Royal Oaks, it was a pleasant and healthy place for families to live and the U.S. Military did their best to try to provide a small slice of Americana for their active duty personnel and their families. There were many facilities that contributed to the effort to replicate a small town in the States, such as an elementary school, a movie theater (which doubled as a church on certain days), a snack bar, a swimming pool, a small park with swing sets, a gymnasium, and several baseball fields, including the dugouts.

And since technically this was still Spanish territory, there were also several businesses owned and operated by Spaniards that did a fairly good business catering to their mostly American clientele. These included a small store located right on one of the two main roads that ran through the housing complex, which were known as the high road and the low road.

This little store sold various grocery items, including fruit; hence its name was "La Fruteria", or the fruit store. This was the place where many of the residents of Royal Oaks would go to buy all kinds of things, including snacks and sodas, and even beer, wine, or hard liquor. It also became a location for a lot of people looking for a place to just hang around, and to see and be seen at.

There was also a place just on the outskirts of Royal Oaks called the "Stables." Like any Spanish business that gathered a regular crowd of people, they had a small bar there, serving beverages of all types as well as a few *tapas* sometimes. And the owner didn't seem to mind serving underage kids because technically there is no minimum drinking age in Spain. They figure that if you're old enough and tall enough to reach the bar, then they will serve you. The Stables was not only a place where one could rent horses by the hour to ride around the nearby countryside, but also where one could get a drink or two, accompanied by the ripe smell of horses and horseshit which were stabled right next door to the bar.

Another thing that Spaniards would do around the Royal Oaks area was graze sheep. Sheep, along with their shepherds and accompanying sheep dogs, are a common sight all over Spain, including the outskirts of most major cities. They provide a service in keeping the weeds and grass at an acceptable level, at the same time providing fodder for these flocks of mutton on the hoof. It was not unusual to see flocks roaming the empty fields around peoples' houses and around the various buildings in Royal Oaks.

The shepherds were usually good-natured gentlemen who were willing to discuss the ways of the world with anyone willing to give them the time of day. At times while driving, one would have to wait a few minutes until a flock of sheep could safely cross the road in front of cars. But this was life in Spain, and people would normally just take it in stride, unless they were in a great hurry. Then the honking would begin, usually in a useless effort to hurry the flock along.

Spanish entrepreneurs had some other ways of making a few pesetas from the American population living in Royal Oaks. All it took was a cart and a horse, and on a sunny Saturday afternoon, it was possible to give some kids rides around the block for a few pesetas each, much to the delight and fun of the many kids hanging about.

There were other types of activities the military provided for their personnel and their dependents, all in an attempt to recreate the wholesome American values they believed were necessary to maintain morale for the hundreds of Americans living in this foreign land.

Baseball during the summer was always a great activity that both the kids and parents could enjoy. The kids by playing on teams and leagues, and the parents by attending the games, or coaching a team, or being umpires, or just by helping with the snack bar near the baseball diamonds.

My brother Johnny was on a Little League team called "The Spartans," and was a pretty good second baseman and shortstop. There were other teams in the Royal Oaks league with such names such as "The Trojans," "The Warriors," "The Aguilas," and "The Matadors." During the summer months, games were held once a week and practices were twice a week. Some people (mostly the parents) seemed to take the games quite seriously, and there was always plenty of excitement at the weekend games, with big crowds rooting for their favorite team.

There was another league for the younger kids who weren't quite old enough to play in Little League called the "Pee Wee League," and that's how I came to participate in baseball during those years. We were kind of like the minor league players waiting to get old enough to play in the real Little League. We didn't generate the same excitement as the older players, but we still did have a lot of fun taking part in America's favorite pastime.

With the baseball teams, the gymnasium, the movie theater, the swimming pool, the snack bar, and other activities in Royal Oaks, there was always something to keep the young people occupied and out of trouble. Nevertheless, there were  some kids who were able to find trouble without having to look too hard for it. And as young people are around the world, in any situation and environment, they will find ways to test their limits, their families, and their world.

There was an activity in Royal Oaks among the teenagers who lived there at the time that was unique to their particular environment and situation that was called a "woodsie." A "woodsie" was basically a party held in the woods. The woods that were used for this activity were not far from the community area where the theater, snack bar and gym were located. There was a small creek that had water in it at times during the rainy season, and the area of woods used for "woodies" was just past this mostly dry creek bed.

These woods were thick, but not so thick that one couldn't walk through them fairly easily, yet they were thick enough to conceal who or what was going on back inside them behind the trees. This was the area where sometimes young people would gather to drink, to party and to make out.

I remember one particular evening when I was able to partake in a "woodsie" that left a lasting impression on me. The experiences that leave a lifelong impression on people generally are the kind where something quite extraordinary happens to them, or they do something for the very first time. In this case, it was the first time that I had gotten to third base, so to speak, and I'm not talking baseball here.

I had a good friend the summer before I was a freshman in high school whose name was Jonathan Cross, and he lived with his family in Royal Oaks near the entrance since his father was an officer. They lived in one of the duplexes and had the entire top floor to themselves. I used to spend the night with him and his family at their house occasionally on weekends and during the summer.

His father was a commander in the U.S. Navy, as there were several members of other branches of the Armed Forces besides the Air Force that were connected with Torrejon Air Force Base. Probably because he was assigned to a ship, Jonathan's father seemed to be rarely around. He had an older sister named Kathy and a younger brother named Paul and his mother was very nice and seemed to like having me around, so I spent a lot of time with this family, and Jon and I became great friends.

One lazy Saturday afternoon, Jon and I were hanging out at the snack bar area and we started talking to two young girls about our ages. They said their names were Marcy and Linda and they were both in the eighth grade. We didn't know them from school because they were in junior high school and Jon and I were already freshmen in high school.

Marcy was skinny and flat-chested, with blond hair and a few pimples on her face, but she was very cute and quite talkative. Linda had darker hair, a fuller figure, and was not quite as talkative. Both girls seemed very friendly towards Jon and me so we spent a couple of hours chatting with them while drinking cherry Cokes at the snack bar that afternoon.

When they said something about having to get home to have dinner with their families, Jon asked them if they would like to have a woodsie that night. Neither of them knew what he was talking about, and Marcy asked him what a woodsie was.

Jon said in a very sincere voice, "Well, a woodsie is when a group of kids gets together in the woods right over there," as he pointed in the general direction of the woods behind the snack bar, "and have a real fun party, hanging out in the woods where no one can see. You girls interested?"

Marcy giggled and looked at Linda and asked her, "I don't know, what do you think, Linda?"

Linda asked, "Well, what time would this woodsie begin, anyway? I'm spending the night at Marcy's house tonight, and I don't think her parents would let us out again after we have dinner, would they Marcy?"

Marcy said with a little giggle, "No, of course not, but we could always sneak out if you really want to go. I've done it before, I just open the window of my room and crawl out, and the folks never even know I'm gone!"

With a little smile, Linda replied, "Okay, guys, we'll do it, but you'll have to wait for us outside the window and walk with us down to the woods, all right?"

Jon says, "Sure, no problem, so what house number do you live at, Marcy?"

"I live in 96-C, downstairs, just up from the circle, on the left. And my room is the one right next to the patio, not the one behind because that's my parent's room. So what time are you guys going to meet us?"

Jon smiles and says, "Well, anytime you want. What time do your folks go to sleep?"

"Usually around eleven or so but it might be later since it's a Saturday. They usually stay up a little later on weekend nights. How about at midnight just to make sure, okay?"

He gave her a big grin and said, "Okay, midnight it is then, and we'll make sure to bring some refreshments, as in the alcoholic kind! What do you girls like, rum, gin, vodka?"

Linda replied with a giggle, "Well, I always like screwdrivers, they're my favorite, plus I like the name, hee hee."

"Okay, screwdrivers it is then. We'll be waiting right outside your window at midnight, and don't be late," Jon said teasingly.

Marcy retorted with, "Oh, don't worry, we'll be there, and don't forget the refreshments! See you guys later tonight."

Marcy then stood up and said to Linda, "Okay, we've got to go, I don't want to be late for dinner tonight. And we'll see you guys tonight then, right at the stroke of midnight!"

Jon smiled again. "Okay, we'll see you two lovely ladies tonight then."

As they walked out the door of the snack bar, we both gave them a little wave and I turned to Jon after they left and exclaimed, "Wow, man! It looks like we're going to have a woodsie tonight! All right! This is gonna be great, man!"

Jon looked at me with his devilish grin and said, "Hell, Ronnie, since I did all the talking, I get dibs on Linda, okay? You cool with that?'

"Sure, Jon, no problem, man. I think Marcy's kinda cute anyways."

He grinned again at me and said, "Shoot, she's flat as a board, man. Linda's the one with the nice big titties! Anyway, we gotta get ready. We'll stop at the *fruteria* and get a bottle of Bacardi and I know my Mom has a carton of orange juice in the fridge at home. You got a couple of bucks to chip in for the rum, don't you?"

"Yeah, sure man, I'll chip in, don't worry. Man, this is gonna be a blast tonight, don't you think?"

He replied again with his devilish grin, "Absolutely man. It's going to be great, I can feel it. And we'll see how much these girls put out tonight."

Later that night, a few minutes before midnight, Jon and I were standing in front of house number 96-C. He was wearing his olive green Boy Scout backpack (official B.S.A.) and inside it he had a flashlight, an old yellow blanket, and a liter-sized bottle of Bacardi that we had bought at the *fruteria* on our way back to his house for dinner. I was carrying a paper sack with a quart of Minute Maid orange juice, and a plastic container full of ice cubes along with four small plastic cups from his kitchen cupboard.

Right before midnight, we watched as the window of the room next to the patio slowly slid up, and the two girls carefully stepped over the window sill, whispering very quietly to each other.

Jon whispered, "Marcy, Linda, we're over here, girls."

They started walking towards us, and Marcy said in a whisper, "Oh, I see you guys made it; we were wondering if you'd show up or not. We thought maybe you two were just playing with us."

Jon said with a smile, "Don't worry, plenty of time for that later, girls. Let's get going, okay?"

So, the four of us start walking down the sidewalk towards the snack bar area and the woods behind it, and we naturally fell two abreast, with Jon and Linda in front and Marcy and me just behind them.

Marcy looked at me with a smile and asked, "So, Ronnie, have you ever been on a woodsie before?"

I looked at her shyly and say, "Oh, yeah, sure, lots of times, it's always a cool time. Hey, look at what I got in here, I sure hope you like screwdrivers!"

And I opened the paper shopping bag and showed her what was inside.

She gave me a shy look and whispered, "Actually, I've never had one before. Are they good?"

"Oh, yeah, sure," I said, "They taste just like orange juice. You like orange juice, right?"

She replied, "Yeah, I have a glass every morning with my breakfast, don't you?"

"Yeah, most mornings anyway," I said.

We were still chatting away by the time we get to the snack bar area, which was totally dark at this time of night, with nobody around. There was a half-moon shining in the sky, just enough to be able to barely see where we were going. Jon stopped and reached into his pack to get the flashlight out and said, "Okay, follow me, I know where to go."

We followed him as he stepped over the half wall which divided the snack bar area from the creek bed and the woods beyond. By the time we reached the creek, we could see that there was hardly any water in it at all, but the four of us take turns jumping over it, anyway. A few steps later, there was a slight incline upwards, and that is where we headed.

Within a couple more minutes of walking, Jon said, "Okay, this is it, right over under this tree is the best spot. Nobody can see us at all here."

He set the pack on the ground, reached in, took out the blanket, and spread it out on the ground, saying to me, "Get those drinks going already Ron, you're the bartender tonight, you know."

I set the paper bag on the ground and started making drinks, putting a few ice cubes in each cup, along with about half rum and half orange juice, and start passing them around saying, "Here ya go girls, try these on for size."

Marcy took a sip of hers and said, "Oh, that tastes pretty good, I like it."

Then Linda tasted hers and laughed. "You put rum in this drink. That's not a screwdriver, a screwdriver is made from vodka not rum! Man, guys!"

"Well, sorry, they ran out of vodka at the *fruteria*, so we got rum instead, but it's all right, it tastes great to me," Jon said while taking a long swig from his drink.

Linda took another little sip and said, "You're right Jon, it doesn't taste too bad at all, really. Actually, I kind of like it."

We sat down with Jon and Linda leaning by the tree and Marcy and I sitting next to each other at the other end of the blanket, and I looked up and saw that Jon had his arm around Linda's shoulders and was starting to nuzzle her neck with his nose.

I slowly put my arm around Marcy's shoulder and pulled her towards me tightly, all the while sipping on my drink with my other hand. We started kissing passionately until I finally set my drink on the ground, being careful not to spill it. I then put both of my arms around her and held her tightly against my chest.

After a few minutes of this, I checked my drink and realized that all I had left was ice cubes in my cup and I said, "Well, I'm ready for another, that one went down so well. Anybody else want a refill?"

Jon says, "Sure, I'm ready and Linda's almost done with hers too. Here you go, bartender." He handed me their cups.

As I was making fresh drinks for everyone, I realized that I was starting to get a little drunk. And as I looked around, I realized that I was probably not the only one. Jon and Linda were laughing hysterically about something or other that he had said, and Marcy was just staring into the sky with a dreamy look on her face.

As I handed around the cups with the fresh drinks, I said, "Wow! Maybe I'm making these a little too strong, because I'm starting to get a little woozy here. Anybody else?"

Jon replied with a big grin, "Hey, man, that's the idea, isn't it?"

Within a few more minutes, we were all starting to get into it. I had gotten Marcy's blouse totally off and I was feeling her little titties, while Jon had Linda's blouse off and her shorts down to her knees at that point.

I heard Linda moaning slightly as he rubbed his hand over her bush. Following suit, I tried to unbutton Marcy's pants, but she kept telling me, "No, no, I can't do that. Stop it, please."

I looked at her with a passionate plea in my eye and asked, "Well, cripes, Marcy, why not? Come on, honey."

She just gave me this look and said, "Listen, I just can't let you do that, I'm sorry. You can't do that, but you can feel my titties all you want."

So I continued to feel her little breasts, bending over and kissing them a little, and getting more frustrated and hornier by the moment.

A few more minutes passed by, and I tried again to unbutton her pants, and again she said, "Listen Ron, I told you before, I just can't do that. Now knock it off, please!"

By this time, Linda had overheard our conversation and said to me, "Hey Ron, if you want to feel a pussy, I'll let you feel mine if you want."

I looked over at her and said, "Okay, sure, if it's all right with you, Jon."

He said, "Sure, man, I don't mind. Go for it, man!"

So I got up and sat right next to Linda, while Jon got up and walked away, saying something about going to take a leak.

I slowly reached my hand over and put it right onto Linda's bush and felt something that I had never felt before up to that point in my young life. And I understood then and there why this most wondrous of all things was called a "pussy."

It felt warm, soft, slightly furry, and absolutely wonderful. I felt around and gradually inserted one finger right inside her and felt the warm wet smoothness of her female organ and it felt absolutely incredible to me.

She looked up at me and asked, "Well, what do you think?"

I just said, "Wow, that's really something, that's for sure."

"Is this the first time you've ever felt one, Ronnie?" she asked me.

"No, of course not, I've felt lots of them before," I lied between my teeth. "But yours feels really nice, Linda."

By this time, Jon came stumbling back up from the creek bed where he had gone to relieve himself and said, "All right, I just made room for another drink!"

He went over to the paper sack with the booze in it, lifted the bottle of Bacardi out, looked at it, and exclaimed, "It looks like we got just about enough for one more drink each left here. Who's ready for another?"

"Yeah, I'm about ready, how about you girls?" I asked as I got up and stepped over towards Marcy again.

Linda said cheerily, "Sure, I'll have another. All I got is cubes left in my cup."

Marcy, however, said, "I think I've had enough guys; I'm feeling real woozy here, sorry."

Jon said, "Okay then, I'll just empty the bottle," and he mixed the last three drinks, finishing up both the rum and the orange juice.

I sat down again next to Marcy, thinking about the experience I had just had, relishing the feeling of having done something that I had only dreamed about for quite a while, and remembering the creamy silkiness of what I had felt. I reached up to scratch my nose, and I smelled something on my finger that I had never smelled before. It didn't smell bad, but not quite good either, just really strange and different from anything I had ever encountered before.

And I thought to myself, "So this is what a pussy feels like and smells like, wow! Absolutely amazing! Who would have thought it?"

To this very day, I remember that ground-breaking evening in the Royal Oaks woods, and the experience I had that night. I admit I have continued ever since trying to figure these things out, one of life's greatest mysteries, incredible as they are, and absolutely wonderful and amazing indeed! And as the French are known to say, *Vive la Difference!*

Chapter 8. Torrejon Air Base

"Life is all memory except for the one present moment that goes by so quickly you can hardly catch it going." — Tennessee Williams

Torrejon Air Base, also known as T.A.B. by the people who worked there, lived there, or went to school there, was not a typical American overseas military base. It opened officially on June 1, 1957 and was finally was turned over to the Spanish Air Force on May 21, 1992. During those thirty-five years of existence, many thousands of American military personnel and their dependents had spent time there.

Over the years, improvements were made to the facilities available on the base, including the shopping center which featured the PX and the commissary, and an excellent full-service hospital where most of the doctors were military officers. The doctor who delivered a woman's baby might also have been a captain or a colonel in the U.S. Air Force. This hospital offered great care for active duty personnel and their dependents. The U.S. Military did indeed want to take good care of their people.

Some other facilities on the base included the Officer's Club and the NCO Club. These were places where either military officers or non-commissioned officers could hang out, have a drink or dinner, and socialize with each other. The military has always been very keen on separating the officers from the "troops" or, better said, the members of the military who had a college education and the servicemen who did not. Whether that is a positive or a negative stance is debatable; however, that's the way it worked.

Other facilities that weren't so class conscious were: a bowling alley, a golf course, a movie theater, a thrift store, the service club (which had a cafeteria and a lounge for anyone to enjoy), and various other places around the base for the purpose of maintaining happy and productive military personnel. I had the opportunity to enjoy most of these facilities at one time or another during the years when I attended school on-base, or was there for various other reasons.

Almost all the buildings on base were made of red brick, and many, such as the high school I attended, were converted three-story barracks that had initially provided housing for the many airmen assigned to the base. All over the base, there were exposed pipes running to and from almost every building. They were insulated and painted silver to reflect the intense Spanish sun and provided a steam-based heating system for the buildings. They were set up on supports and seemed to run everywhere on base, with extreme right angles and sometimes small foot bridges to allow pedestrians to able to walk over them.

One of my earliest memories of Torrejon Air Base was the Fourth of July 1961. As I mentioned before, the powers that be had decided that all the military servicemen and their families needed to have plenty of American culture and traditions available to them, for fear that otherwise, they might "turn native," or yearn for life in the United States. So the Fourth of July was celebrated with much pride, tradition and patriotism, and featured an outstanding fireworks show.

The morning of the Fourth, I went with my family — me, my older brother Johnny, and my parents — out to the base for a day of celebration, American-style. We loaded up in the '59 red and white Chevy station wagon that my Dad had brought overseas as part of his military transfer and headed out to the base, expecting a great day spent celebrating America's birthday.

They held the day's festivities in an open field approximately three hundred yards square that was near the golf course. This field provided plenty of room for the fireworks show that was to begin at dark, and for parking for the many hundreds of spectators. The area was near a small snack bar where the usual food and beverages such as hot dogs, hamburgers, and sodas were being offered for sale. There was also a machine that dispensed cold Budweiser by the can for twenty-five cents each for the adults in the crowd who wished for something a little stronger than soft drinks and had neglected to bring their own coolers.

Some people brought their own barbecue grills so they could cook their own assorted meats including steaks, hamburgers and chicken. Other families, including my own, brought their own folding card table we filled with all sorts of wonderful things, including cold fried chicken, potato salad, and a great assortment of desserts and goodies. No one ever went hungry on the Fourth of July at T.A.B.!

I, eight years old at the time I am describing, just wanted to play, run around, and explore. After a full lunch of my mom's great cooking and plenty of Fanta orange soda, I headed off with another kid about my age by the name of Tommy to the edge of the lot where the festivities were being held. A small irrigation ditch ran alongside the road and held a few inches of running water most of the year. What a delight it was for kids my age to explore and splash around in the puddles that formed along the small waterway.

To our delight, Tommy and I first found lots of tadpoles swimming in the puddles and later, after more exploring and getting our feet wet, we found actual frogs! We spent hours catching these small green frogs, then carrying them to another nearby puddle to release them there, thinking that we were having a heroic effect on their survival somehow. We were having such fun pretending to be amphibian scientists that we didn't notice that the sun was dropping low on the horizon.

My mom did notice though, and she started worrying, so she sent my older brother Johnny to look for me. This was the last thing he wanted to do though, since he had been spending the afternoon talking and flirting with several girls about his age, who he was just beginning to get interested in at this time in his life. After much protesting, he agreed to go look for me. It didn't take long for him to walk the perimeter of the grounds and after a while he found me and Tommy by the ditch with our shoes and socks soaking wet, but with looks of delight and excitement on our faces.

"Look, Johnny, we got frogs!" I said in a very excited voice, holding one out for him to see. Though for some reason, he couldn't understand our great excitement, and he just said in a loud, authoritative voice,

"Come on, you little squirts, Mom sent me to find you, let's get going!"

He wanted to get back to talking with the nice dark-haired girl that he was becoming infatuated with and didn't want to waste any more time dealing with his goofy little brother.

So I said, "Okay, come on, Tommy. We better get going, I guess."

Johnny looked at our wet feet and said in his most annoying, bossy voice, "Mom's going to be mad at you for getting your socks and shoes all wet, you know."

I didn't say anything as we slowly walked back to the main crowd.

Johnny, using his bossy voice again, said, "Hurry up, you little pipsqueaks, the fireworks are gonna start soon and I don't want to miss them!"

By the time we got back, the crowd was growing anxious with anticipation for the show that was soon to begin. I said goodbye to Tommy as he headed off to be with his own family and I sat down on the blanket my mom had spread out on the grass for us.

Before too long, music swelled through the large speakers that were set up near the snack bar area, and the show began. The music was almost all patriotic songs, such as "America the Beautiful," "My Country 'Tis of Thee," and "The Star-Spangled Banner." The "rockets' red glare" were indeed bursting in the air, accompanied by the loud "oohs" and "ahs" that the crowd emitted after each new round of bursting colors and exploding lights.

My dad sat on the blanket close to my mom and sipped his cold Budweiser while she sipped on a glass of wine. My brother and I both sat cross-legged, Indian style, and stared in awe at the spectacle. All eyes in the crowd were fixed on the sky, mesmerized by the explosions of color and sound going on above them, when suddenly, my Mom began to shriek at the top of her lungs. She jumped up from the blanket, screaming and patting her skirt with both hands, trying to get something off her. I quickly realized with dismay that the frog I had put in my pocket earlier had escaped and had jumped onto her lap!

The people all around us heard her screams, and they turned to look in our direction. My dad finally saw the frog jumping away and reached out to grab it.

I shouted, "Dad, don't hurt him, he's mine!"

My dad then said in a loud voice for all the people nearby to hear, "Don't worry, folks; it's just a little frog, nothing to worry about."

While many of the people around were giggling hysterically, Dad asked, "So, Ronnie, this beast is yours, you say?"

And I told him, "Yeah, Dad, I caught him by the ditch over there. I thought I would take him home for a pet, maybe."

He smiled at me and said in a more gentle voice than he had used before, "Well, son, frogs don't make very good pets actually, so why don't we return him to where you got him? And let him live out his life in peace with his fellow frog friends."

So, holding the poor frightened frog in my own two hands, being careful not to hurt him, I ran back to the stream and gently placed him back in the same puddle where I had found him. By the time I returned, the fireworks show was starting to wind down and the "Grand Finale" was just beginning.

When I settled on the blanket again and looked upwards, the sky was full of red, white, and blue, all exploding at once in a grand spectacle of light and sound. And down at the far end of the field where the pyrotechnical crew had set up their headquarters earlier in the evening, there was another fiery spectacle to behold. It was a giant American flag, thirty feet across, done in blazing sparkles of red, white and blue, a replica of our flag, including the fifty sparkling stars. It seemed to burn and burn forever, and it was still smoldering when the crowd dispersed and headed towards their cars.

As we finished folding up our blanket and packed up to leave, I approached my mom and said, "Wow, Mom, I'm really sorry that little Froggy frightened you so bad. He didn't mean to."

She smiled the smile that only mothers know how to give and said in her soft, gentle voice, "That's okay, Ronnie, I guess I was probably more surprised and embarrassed than scared, anyway. Did you enjoy the fireworks show?"

With a sigh of relief that she wasn't mad at me, I replied, "You betcha, Mom, it was great, one of the best days of my life!"

Torrejon Air Base would impart many other memories to me, including my couple of years of junior high school, and another four of high school. All this schooling required daily bus rides to and from the base from wherever my family was living at the time in Madrid. Each trip averaged about one hour each way, due to the many stops the buses would make to pick up other students, combined with the usual heavy traffic and the twenty miles or so of distance from the outskirts of Madrid to the base. This two-hour daily commute left a lot of time for other things besides just looking out the window. A lot of kids would use the time to work on their homework or chat with the other kids on the bus.

Myself, I liked to talk with the drivers. Often I would choose the seat up front right across from the driver and talk to him about his life, his job, and whatever else he had on his mind. This special seat right across from the driver became prime real estate for the bus rides to and from school because I wasn't the only rider who was curious and interested in what the driver had to say. But not all the riders had such a good command of the Spanish language as I did, or that much interest in what the driver might have to say, so I occupied the "shotgun" seat on a fairly regular basis.

Often on a chilly morning, one particular driver would offer me a shot of cognac from the small bottle that he kept under his seat. I usually declined his offer, but I watched as he helped himself to a short shot to ward off the cold. Even though the buses had heat, he would still feel the need for a warm-up. It did make him a little more talkative, though, and he would go on about his life, politics, his wife, his family, and whatever else was on his mind at the time.

It was interesting chatting with the bus drivers because they could give their own perspective on life in Madrid, and what it was like to work for the American military as a civilian employee. It was a good job that paid reasonably well, and it left a lot of free time while they waited for school to let out, followed by the drive back to Madrid from the base.

Since all the buses had certain routes and schedules, each one had an assigned area in or around Madrid where they picked up and delivered students. Usually the same drivers drove the same routes, so it became possible to get to know the drivers well after an entire school year. We even gave small presents at Christmas time to show our appreciation of the bus drivers' dedication to delivering us to and from school safely and on time.

Getting a ride to and from the base was not hard, even if I was unlucky and missed the bus in the morning, or if I stayed after school for an event or activity. There was a commercial bus that ran from various locations in Madrid to the base, and a return bus that I could pick up at the base that would take me right into Madrid. Of course, this bus wouldn't drop me off near my house, like the school  bus did, but another local bus or a *tranvia* (streetcar) ride would get me home fairly quickly.

Or, for a ride back to town from the base, as a last resort if I didn't have the few coins for public transportation, there was always hitch-hiking. There was even a series of benches with signs over them designating where one wanted a ride to that were located just on the outside of the base entrance. This is where one could just sit and wait until someone stopped and would give me a ride to wherever one was headed.

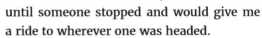

The signs read Roaks, Torrejon Apartments, Canillejas, or Madrid. But I would usually use the hitch-hiking method as a last resort, not only because I almost always had the bus fare but also because being a shy young fellow, I didn't relish sitting for almost an hour with a stranger trying to think of something to talk about.

One of my favorite places on base to hang around was the shopping center area. Not only was this where the PX was located, as well as the commissary, but there were other places of business there too, including a bookstore, a movie theater, a barber shop, a cafeteria-style restaurant, and other assorted services and facilities.

All these places required showing a military ID card to enter, but since mostly Americans were the only people on base anyway, this rarely proved to be a problem. It was possible to bring a guest on base that didn't have an ID card, but that required stopping at the main gate and signing the guest in. Most people that had ID cards were American active duty military personnel or their dependents, but there were a few that were neither, but still had special ID cards that allowed them limited access on base. These were usually kids who went to school on the base but were not directly affiliated with the military. Some were kids of American or foreign diplomats, or kids of American businessmen with some connection or another with the base. These people wanted their kids to have an "American" education and were willing and able to pay a hefty tuition in order for their kids to go to the American school on base.

This was the situation that my parents found themselves in as soon as my dad retired from the Air Force in 1964. Not being active duty military anymore, the free schooling that my brother and I had received while he was active duty went away. I remember very well the discussion that my family had shortly before his last day as an active duty member of the U.S. Air Force. It would have been much cheaper to just enroll my brother and me into a Spanish school right around the corner from where we were living, but after much discussion, it was decided that my parents would pay the five hundred dollars tuition per semester that would allow us to continue receiving a one hundred percent American education.

The concern was also about our college education, and whether an American university would give us credit for a Spanish education from a Spanish school. The tuition that my parents had to pay per year to keep my brother and me in the American school on base was quite a financial hardship for them. But they realized it was necessary if we were to continue our education in a college in the States after we finished high school.

A couple of other places on base where I spent considerable time were the service club and the bowling alley. The service club was a large one-story building where there was a very nice cafeteria-style restaurant, and also a large area with facilities for airmen to enjoy their time off from work.

This club featured a lounge area with several pool tables, tables with chess sets and other board games, pinball machines, and other types of recreation for the many young airmen stationed at Torrejon Air Base. Technically, high school kids were not allowed in the lounge area, but they rarely enforced the rule.

On many occasions during high school, I would skip a class or two, or maybe the entire day and just walk over to the service club cafeteria and hang out. There was always someone else like me who was skipping class as well, and we'd sit around drinking coffee and discussing the world's problems together.

There were two brothers whom I remember very well who also spent a lot of time at the service club for some reason. Their names were Phillip and Michael, and these brothers were not only quite eccentric, but were both geniuses in their own particular way. Phil was a classic guitar virtuoso and had studied under Andres Segovia, the famous Spanish classical guitarist. Phil went on to have a very successful career as a classical concert guitarist and ended up performing all over the world for many thousands of people during his career.

Mike was a pool and chess aficionado and was an expert at both games. He seemed to be constantly in the lounge area of the service club playing one of these games, usually for money, with the many servicemen who hung around there, and he'd almost always win. He carried around his own pool cue in its dark leather case and was always ready for a game with anyone at any time. I wasn't much of a player, but I enjoyed watching him play against the countless airmen, most of whom were only a few years older than he was as a high school student, watching as he beat them most of the time. He became known as quite the pool shark, and after a while, it became harder and harder for him to find a game because his reputation always preceded him.

He chain-smoked Kent cigarettes, had long, dark, greasy hair, and always wore a black vest over a white shirt, with a black beret on his head. He looked as eccentric as he truly was, and because I was the kind of person naturally drawn to the unusual and the strange, I spent many hours sitting in the cafeteria with him drinking coffee, smoking cigarettes, and talking about every subject in the world.

Around lunchtime, the cafeteria was quite busy with almost every table occupied with people eating their lunches, or just hanging around. There were a lot of loud conversations, dishes being moved, and various other noises that a crowded place can make. But Mike still always spoke with a soft gentle voice, almost a whisper I had to strain to hear at times.

One day, we began to discuss the powers of the human brain and how these powers allowed him to win both at pool and at chess. He was telling me that, in his opinion, science had only barely touched on the incredible abilities of the human brain.

Taking a long drag from his Kent, he said to me, "You know, Ron, there are things that just cannot be explained in this world, and I'll show you what I'm talking about right now if you'd like."

I looked at him closely, took a sip of my coffee, and said, "Okay, Mike, I'd like to know what you're talking about, man."

He replied with a glint in his eye, "All right, let's do an experiment right now, okay?"

"Sure, why not?"

"Okay, both of us just stare as hard as we can at the back of the head of that lady over there with the white blouse on, do you see her?"

I looked where he was looking, and I saw an older lady eating a bowl of soup about three tables away from our table, facing away from us.

"Yeah, I see her," I whispered.

"Okay, now just keep looking at the back of her head, and concentrate on nothing else besides her head, all right?" He said this with a mischievous look in his eye.

"Okay, Mike, I'm doing it, man," I said quietly while staring intently at the back of the lady's head.

"Hang on and watch what happens," he whispered.

Within about twenty seconds or so, the lady turned her head and glanced all around with a strange look on her face.

"See what I mean, man. We created that, don't you see? We made her turn her head around, she felt our vibration," he said in his soft voice.

"I don't know, Mike, maybe it was just a coincidence, man. It's really hard to tell," I told him with a doubtful look on my face.

He looked at me as if I really couldn't see the obvious and said, "Okay, my man, let's try it again. See that airman over by the window with his uniform on?"

"Yeah, I see him. The one eating the hamburger, right?"

"Yes, that's our target this time. Just keep staring at his head and think of nothing else, okay?"

I did as I was instructed and sure enough, within about twenty or thirty seconds, the guy turned his head and looked all around the cafeteria as if somebody had just called his name.

"See what I mean, man," he whispered.

"Wow, that's uncanny, Mike," I replied.

"I know it is. This just demonstrates the power of the human brain, right?"

"I guess so. It's weird, but it still could just be a coincidence, you know," I said tentatively.

"Well, it only seems to work when people are by themselves for some reason. If they're with other people, they're distracted by conversation or other people's vibes, and it just doesn't work. They have to be alone."

"All right, let's try it one more time," I proposed. "How about that kid over there reading his comic book, let's try it on him, okay?"

"No, it also doesn't seem to work too well on people who are reading or otherwise distracted, it's gotta be someone who is just sitting there, letting their thoughts wander," he whispered. "But go ahead and pick someone else, man."

I took a good look around the crowded restaurant and I noticed a pretty girl about our age sitting by herself four tables away and I said, "Okay, how about that girl over there by herself with the dark hair and the yellow blouse?"

Mike looks at me and whispers, "No, she won't work either. Pretty girls are used to having people looking at them intently all the time, so it doesn't seem to affect them much. Pick someone else. And it has to be someone who is looking the opposite direction, so they can't notice that we're staring at them, okay?"

This time I noticed a rather heavyset older man sitting by himself almost halfway across the room from us and I asked Mike, "Is that chubby guy way over there with the blue shirt too far away you think?"

"No, distance doesn't seem to matter much, he'll work. Now just stare at the bald spot on the back of his head for a while and we'll see what happens."

After about thirty seconds of both of us staring intently at the man's head in complete silence, the man put his sandwich down, turned his head, and gazed around with a perplexed look on his face.

"There you go, man," Mike said to me with a grin. "You see what I mean now?"

"Wow, man! I'm really amazed. How do you account for this phenomenon? What is it that creates this?" I asked him.

"I really don't know," he replied. "It's just gotta be some sort of mental energy or something that most people don't even know exists. And with both of us doing it, it seems to increase the vibration or whatever it is and the results are even better than if I just do it by myself. Pretty weird, huh?"

I looked at him and whispered, "Really weird. Wow, Mike, thanks for this demonstration. I really think I learned something today, you've really blown my mind, man!"

He just grinned and said, "Hey, that's what I'm here for, man."

I realized that I had just received a very valuable lesson from him that afternoon. To this day I'm still trying to figure out how and why such strange phenomena can exist, as well as other similarly strange and inexplicable things that I've seen in my life.

The service club wasn't the only place where I spent a lot of time, either while skipping classes or just hanging around after school. The base bowling alley was another one of my favorite places, not because I was that much into bowling, but because it was one of the few places on base where there were slot machines!

Technically, of course, it was illegal for minors to play the slots, but the manager and the other employees at the bowling alley usually looked the other way when high school kids put a few coins in the machines. Besides, I was quite sneaky about it, by only playing when an employee wasn't around, and if I saw one approaching, I'd stop playing and just wander away until he passed.

There were several nickel slots around a corner from where the main desk was located, hidden from the view of the employees, who spent most of their time behind the counter, renting bowling shoes, charging bowlers for their games, and conducting other such bowling alley business. These were the machines I played the most often, and I really got into it for a while. I even saved my lunch money to go and put it into the slots after school sometimes. I erroneously believed that there was some skill involved in playing slot machines. I believed that by pulling the handle just right, I could affect the outcome of the spinning wheels behind the glass somehow.

Of course, slot machines, like almost all forms of commercial gambling, are a pure game of chance with really no skill involved, and are set so that the "house" will usually always come out ahead.

It was the thrill of possibly hitting the jackpot that kept me putting my nickels into the machines. The jackpot only paid a hundred and fifty nickels, which is $7.50, but it seemed like a lot of money at the time, especially since it was possible to win it with only one little nickel. I'd drop my nickel in and slowly pull the handle with just the right finesse that I thought would roll the fruits or bars around and put them all on the same line, or at the very least get one or two cherries, which would either pay me two or three nickels back on my investment of one nickel.

I learned to not be too greedy either; if I hit three oranges (which paid ten nickels), or two bars (which paid twenty coins), I'd stop, collect my winnings, and walk away. Most of the other players around would stand there and put all their winnings right back into the machine and end up losing it all. To me that was the most frustrating: to come out ahead and then throw it all away again. So I learned gradually to quit while I was ahead, and this turned out to be a great lesson in other aspects of my life as well.

The problem with hitting the jackpot (three bars) was that in order to collect the winnings, one had to see the attendant. The machine would only spit out a maximum of fifty coins, so the remainder of the jackpot, another five dollars, had to be collected at the desk, and since I was not old enough to be legally playing the machine, this created a problem if I did actually hit the jackpot.

Lo-and-behold, one afternoon after school, I dropped in just four nickels and I finally hit the big one. The jackpot! I walked quickly over to a garbage can in the corner and found a discarded paper coffee cup, and after turning the cup upside down to drain out the last few drops of old coffee, I scooped up the fifty nickels that the machine spit out and looked around. Luckily, nobody seemed to have noticed, especially not the employees working that day. I looked around and noticed a young airman not more than five years older than me, standing by himself, drinking a beer and looking quite relaxed. I carefully approached him, all the time keeping one eye on my machine with the jackpot on it.

I looked him directly in the eye and said in a low voice, "Excuse me, sir, I was wondering if you might help me out here. I just hit a jackpot on that nickel machine over there and I'm not quite old enough to collect it. I'll split it with you if you go to the attendant and say you hit it, what do you say?"

He looked at me, smiled, and said, "Okay, kid, that sounds good to me. You just stand over there out of the way and let me handle this for you."

So after walking by my machine to verify that what I had told him was true, he walked over to the counter where the attendant was handing an airman a pair of bowling shoes, and waited politely until the attendant looked at him and asked him, "What can I do for you, sir?"

He smiled and said to the guy, "Hey, I just hit a jackpot on that nickel machine over there and I'd like to collect it, okay?"

"Sure, no problem, sir," the guy said, and he grabbed a nickel and a five-dollar bill from the register and followed him over to my machine.

He looked at the three bars displayed behind the glass and said to the airman, "All right, and congratulations on hitting the jackpot. Here's your five dollars," and he handed the guy the five-dollar bill.

He then dropped the nickel he'd brought from the register into the machine, pulled the handle, and said, "Gotta clear it, you know."

The airman said, "All right, thanks very much, I appreciate it. That was pretty damned easy."

"Sure, no problem, glad to be of service," the attendant said as he walked away.

As soon as the attendant rounded the corner out of view, I walked up to the airman and said to him, "Thanks, man, you're a real lifesaver. I don't know what I would have done if you weren't standing there."

He just looked at me and said, "Okay now, kid, so how are we going to split this?"

I pointed to the coffee cup almost full of nickels and replied, "Well, listen, I got over fifty nickels right here in this coffee cup. How about if I give you all of it, and you give me the five-dollar bill?"

"Well shit, kid," he said, "I don't feel like hassling with getting change and all that, so that should work I guess. Besides, I can use the change to play that machine you hit on. It looks like it might be getting hot."

I handed him the paper cup full of nickels and he handed me the five-dollar bill and we shook hands and I walked away, five dollars richer for my efforts, feeling lucky and a bit wiser to the ways of the world.

Chapter 9. Madrid High School

"Musical training is a more potent instrument than any other, because rhythm and harmony find their way into the inward places of the soul."
— PLATO, The Republic

"Madrid High School" or "Torrejon High School" was located at Torrejon Air Base and was established and operated by the U.S. Department of Defense. Most of the students were U.S. Military dependents (primarily Air Force). However, the school was also open to U.S. Embassy dependents, and U.S. government contractor dependents. In later years, the school became more widely open to other Americans and, in some cases, Spanish and other foreign students. The school should not to be confused with the American School of Madrid, located near the small town of Aravaca on the opposite outskirts of Madrid from Torrejon. This high school was (and still is) a privately run school.

In early 1954, American military personnel with school-age children began arriving in Madrid. At first, parents enrolled their children in the available schools (the American Institute, the British Institute, and Spanish schools). These soon reached their saturation point, and temporary arrangements were made for school space while a more permanent location was being prepared.

This more permanent location was an apartment complex that occupied an entire city block in Madrid. This same complex also housed the in-town branches of the PX and Commissary, and many apartments in the block were occupied by personnel who lived in town. One of the four streets that bounded the complex was called Avenida del Generalissimo Franco (it has since been renamed as an extension of *Paseo de la Castellana*). Thus, the entire complex was often referred to (informally, and primarily by Americans) as the "Generalissimo" building.

In November 1954, the high school, which had been located at 18 Calle Juan Bravo, was moved to 7 Avenida Felix Boix, and the first official graduating high school class was the Class of 1955. When the next school year started in September 1955, the junior and senior high school (grades 7-12) moved around the corner to 37 Calle Doctor Fleming. To the best of my knowledge, the high school's formal name was then "Madrid Dependents' Junior-Senior High School," but it was usually referred to as "Madrid High School" or "MHS."

In September 1959, the high school moved to a converted barracks on Torrejon Air Base. For several years after the move to Torrejon, the high school continued to be known as "Madrid High School" until 1971 when the name was officially changed to "Torrejon High School."

In the late 1960s, a dormitory was opened for high school students whose parents were stationed in locations where there were not enough people to justify opening (or continuing) an American high school. A converted barracks very near the campus of the high school on Torrejon Air Base served as the dormitory. Many of these students, known informally as "dormies," had left their families in such areas in Africa or the Middle East to attend high school at Torrejon in order to experience an American-style education.

In the early 1990s, the U.S. acceded to Spain's desire for greater sovereignty over what had always officially been a joint air base at Torrejon, and the U.S. presence there began to be phased out. As a result,

Torrejon High School graduated its last class in June 1992, and the school then closed its doors forever.

I am a proud graduate of MHS, class of 1970. I spent all four years of my high school career at MHS. Every year of my formal education (except for two) before I began college, was at DOD schools in and around Madrid and Torrejon. The two years that are the exceptions are the year I spent in first grade at Walker Air Force Base in New Mexico, and my eighth-grade year which I spent at a French school in Alicante, Spain.

As with everything else located on Torrejon Air Base, the military tried as hard as possible to create an environment similar to that of a small American town, and the high school was no exception. Such all-American activities as Friday night football games were a big part of life at Torrejon. The team was called the Madrid Knights and the school colors were red and silver. The team played their rivals at other American bases in Spain, including Rota Naval Station and Zaragoza Air Base, as well as Kenitra Air Base in Morocco.

Of course, there were other sports as well, including basketball, baseball, track, and soccer. But it was the football team (as is usually the case at American high schools everywhere) that got the most attention and support from the students and the community as a whole.

I never played many sports in high school since I was interested in other activities such as music instruction and language classes. However, for the many guys who did, there was a lot of competition to excel in sports. They played sports not only to become popular, but because the prettiest girls in school were always on the cheerleader squad and none of them would have even dreamed of dating some guy who wasn't a member of the football team (preferably the quarterback), or at least someone from the backfield.

As in any high school anywhere in the world, there were cliques, and the universal need for teenagers to belong to a certain group became a motivating factor in much of what the kids would do both in and out of school. Everyone had the need to belong to something; some group they could identify with and where they felt they were accepted for who they were or at least who they were trying to be. Basically, it came down to two main groups, and one might fit into either one or the other, it seemed. The two groups at MHS at the time were known as the "jocks" and the "freaks." Many (if not most) kids tried to belong to both groups, but ended up really belonging to neither.

As the word signifies, the jocks were the All-American football-playing guys with their letter jackets and their pretty cheerleader girlfriends, or at least the people who wanted to belong to this group. To be a successful member of this group required either talent or looks, or even better yet, both. One could take part in sports without being the star quarterback, of course, and many guys did. And it was possible to go out for the cheerleading team and make it even if you weren't the best-looking girl in the school, but it certainly helped if you were very attractive.

But not everyone who went to school was able to play sports well or was pretty enough to be on the cheerleading squad, and this left a lot of students unable to participate in the All-American experience. So a lot of these kids ended up belonging to the other group that I'm referring to as the "freaks."

During the latter part of the 1960s, the world was going through many changes, in almost every aspect of society. These included fashion, music, language, and the culture itself, which was transforming from something that it was before into something that it was to become. Life on an American Air Force base overseas was no exception. Of course, some students at MHS, like kids anywhere and everywhere, were pushing the limits of what society in general allowed or considered appropriate. One of the main symbols of this changing society was the length of hair on guys.

Long hair during this time was not only fashionable, but it also became a badge of identity and gave a sense of belonging to something more — to this group known as "freaks." The hairstyle of guys having bangs hanging onto the forehead began with the Beatles earlier in the decade, and almost every guy had this hairstyle at one time or other. But to have really long hair was absolutely forbidden. Anything that went over the ears or hung past the collar was considered to be a violation of the dress code and was reason to be expelled until an appropriate haircut was had, and approved by the assistant principal.

During my time at MHS, our assistant principal was Mr. Gerald Bloom, and he became the most hated man on campus because his job was to enforce the dress code rules, and he seemed to do so with obvious glee and pleasure.

He was a short, balding man, and he was unwilling to allow any slack when it came to the length of a guy's hair. One Monday morning in 1968, he went around the school and handed out pink dress code violation slips to about one half of the entire male student population on campus. These students were to *immediately* go to the base barbershop and get haircuts before they would be allowed to attend any more classes that day. The barbershop on base had a long line of dozens of high school boys standing outside for the entire day, since Mr. Bloom didn't notify the barbershop of his intentions ahead of time, and only the one regular barber was on duty that day.

I was one of Mr. Bloom's many victims that day, along with most of my friends and many of my other fellow students. The rumor going around at the time was that Mr. Bloom had received orders from the Base Commander himself to issue these ultimatums for haircuts. It seemed that the Base Commander (who was in charge of literally everything on base) had seen some high school guys around the base with hair that did not meet military issue regulations.

He had spoken to the Principal of the high school, Dr. Gogo (yes, that was his actual name), and Dr. Gogo had delegated the responsibility of haircut duty to his assistant, Mr. Bloom. My guess is that he didn't want to be the most hated man on campus so he passed the buck to Mr. Bloom to secure that honor. Dr. Gogo also had a son and daughter in the same school, and I'm sure he was concerned about this fact as well, since he didn't want the student body to dislike his kids because of what he did.

In a way, I suppose this was all a good thing because the next semester in 1969, the student body elected an outgoing and open-minded student council president by the name of Dan, and the platform that Dan ran on that year was that he would finally make some changes in the archaic and anachronistic dress code rules. He won by an overwhelming majority and before too long; he was able to somehow make substantial changes to the dress code at the high school.

For the first time in the school's history, longer hair was allowed on the male students. Before this, the rules were exactly the same for dependents as for servicemen, in regards to having a military-style haircut. A military-style haircut is short on the sides, not touching the eyebrows in the front, and not touching the collar in the back. So finally, after the changes were made, the guys at school could start looking like they were living in the 1960s and were not confined to looking like they themselves were in the military.

Another accomplishment that Dan achieved that year was to get the dress code changed for girls as well. For the first time in the school's history, girls were allowed to wear slacks to school. Before this, dresses and skirts were mandatory. The female portion of the student body rejoiced and finally had a choice regarding the clothing covering the bottom halves of their bodies. Needless to say, Dan was the most popular guy on campus for the rest of that year, and I'm sure he would have been elected Student Council President the next year as well, if he had not graduated in 1969.

Things changed rapidly after this major transition in the dress code at MHS. By the time my class graduated in June 1970, there were male members of my class who stepped up onto the stage to receive their high school diplomas with their hair down to their shoulders, a far cry from just a year and a half before.

Fashion is always a big deal for high school students and young people in general because of their instinctual need to feel like they belong to a certain group. The length of hair on guys was only part of the fashion revolution going on during the 1960s. Clothes were also a big part of it as well. Young people felt a need to be different from their parents' generation and part of that difference was in the clothes they wore. I was never much of a "clothes horse," but there were many who were. I didn't even think too much about the clothes I wore, as long as they were efficient and did their job of protecting me from the elements, until one day when I was sitting in my homeroom class next to a guy named Wayne. Now Wayne was a real clothes horse kind of guy and everyday he wore a very nice "outfit."

He looked at me that morning and said, "Hey, Ron, I see you're wearing the same exact clothes you had on yesterday, what's the deal with that, man?"

I looked back at him and replied, "I don't know Wayne, these clothes were not really that dirty yet so I wore them again, why?"

"Because you gotta look sharp man, that's why. Look at me for an example. I always look good because I know how to dress. I mean, look at you, man, you're wearing a red plaid shirt with dark green corduroy pants. They just don't match, man!"

I looked down at my pants and said to him, "I guess I never really thought about it too much, Wayne."

"Look at what I got on now, man. I got my white 'high water' Levi's jeans on with a light blue shirt and now look at my socks; they're the same exact shade of blue as my shirt. You see how everything is coordinated? And unless I get my white jeans really dirty today, I won't put them in the dirty clothes yet, but probably wear them again later in the week with a different color of shirt and socks. And tomorrow I'll wear my black jeans with a yellow shirt with my yellow socks and that way I can look cool every day. Where do you get your clothes anyway, man?"

I looked down at my worn corduroys and said, "Well, my mom usually buys them for me at the PX or from the Sears catalog. Why do you ask?"

"Well, I used to have a pair of corduroys just like that until my mom donated them to the thrift store a while back because they're so out of fashion these days, man."

My cheeks started to burn with embarrassment because I knew that my mom, in order to save quite a few dollars, shopped regularly at the base thrift shop, where just about everything cost pennies to the dollar. I was pretty sure that the pants I had on were a pair that she had gotten for me there and probably did belong to Wayne once.

I just looked at Wayne, trying to hide my embarrassment, and said, "Well, Wayne, thanks for the fashion tip, buddy, I'll try to keep it in mind."

He just smirked and replied, "Well, I'm glad to help out, my friend, glad to help out."

That evening when I got home, I told my mom what had happened in homeroom period that morning and how embarrassed I was, and that I didn't want her to shop for me at the thrift store anymore. And that from now on, I was going to shop for my own clothes!

I got the Sears and Roebucks catalog from out of the hall cabinet and I asked her if I could order some new clothes. She looked at me with a look that only a mother could give and said, "Okay, Ronnie, I was going to order a couple of items anyway, and I guess you could use some new clothes, so how about if you choose two pairs of pants and two shirts and we'll put in the order, all right?"

I opened up the Sears catalog to the clothes section which I never paid much attention to up till now. Sears had quite the selection of clothes for all members of the family and all in the latest fashions. I chose two pairs of bell-bottom pants, one a pale blue and the other a light green color, along with a dark blue long sleeve shirt and a light yellow one that had pin stripes as well.

My mom looked at my selections and went ahead and placed the order. Within a couple of weeks, the box arrived. She handed me the new clothes from the box and I excitedly tried the new shirts on. They fit just right and had the long tails to tuck into the pants that I liked.

But when I tried on a pair of the bell-bottom pants, they just didn't feel right, and I said to her, "Mom, these pants don't feel right on me, they're way too baggy."

She came over and slipped her finger in the waistband and looked at the length and said, "Well, they look just right and they're your exact size. They look great on you."

"Well, I don't like them, they feel way too baggy on me. Can't you fix them?"

She looked at the pants again and then at my face and said, "No honey, they fit perfectly. I'm not going to try to fix them, there's nothing I can do. You're just going to have to wear them as they are. And besides they look great on you."

"Well, I can't wear them like this, they're just way too baggy on me. Look how much room is down here at the bottom of them."

She just smiled and said, "Honey, they're supposed to be that way, they're bell-bottoms."

"But they don't have to be belling all over, do they? And look how low they sit around my waist and look at the size of these belt loops!"

"Well, honey, that's the fashion now, and you're supposed to wear a wide belt with them, see, that's why the loops are so wide. We should have ordered you a wide belt to go with them, I guess."

"Well, I don't know about this whole fashion thing, anyway. I think they look stupid!"

She looked at me and used her stern voice, "Well, we paid good money for those pants, and you're going to wear them, kiddo!"

The next day I put both pairs of pants in a grocery bag and I went over to my friend Bryce's house nearby, and I asked him if his sister was around. He looked at me and asked, "Yeah, she's upstairs, but what do you want with her?"

"I just want to talk to her about something; can you go get her, please?"

"Okay, whatever man," and he walked upstairs and came back with his sister Cindy, who was about two years younger than we were and rather pretty, except for strangely resembling her brother a bit too much.

I looked at her and said, "Listen Cindy, here's the deal. I understand that you have your own sewing machine and you know how to sew pretty good, is that right?"

She gave me a quizzical look and said, "Yeah, I have a sewing machine, and I like to sew outfits for myself sometimes. Why do you ask?"

"Well," I said, as I took the two pairs of pants out of the bag and showed them to her, "Can you fix these for me? They're just way too baggy around the thighs. I'll pay you a dollar each, if that's okay?"

She looked at the pants and said, "Sure, I guess so, if that's what you want. But you don't have to pay me, I'll fix them for nothing if you'd like."

"That would be real nice of you, Cindy, I really appreciate it a lot. All they need is the thigh areas tightened up a couple of inches or so, okay?"

She just gave me a funny look and said, "Okay, I can have them ready tomorrow if you like. But once I do this, I'm going to have to remove the material from the inside so it doesn't show through, so there will be no going back after they're done, all right?"

"Yeah sure, Cindy, no problem, I'm sure I'll like them fine once they're fixed, and thanks again."

The next day, I walked over to pick up my new "fixed" pants and again I offered to pay her the two dollars for her efforts. Again, she declined payment which was all right by me because I only got 500 pesetas (about eight dollars) per week allowance, so I felt pretty good about not having to pay for these pants alterations.

When I got home, I went upstairs to my bedroom and tried on the blue pair and then the green pair and they felt pretty tight around the thigh area which made the bell bottoms look even more pronounced. But they felt right to me and as I stood in front of the mirror, I thought that I must look pretty cool now.

So I left the green pair on and went downstairs and found my mom sitting in the living room, having a cocktail and smoking a cigarette with her friend and neighbor Josie. I walked into the room and did a little parade over to the coffee table and back, swishing my butt as I walked by. And I asked, "Well, what do you think, ladies? Pretty nice pants, don't you think?"

Josie started giggling and my mom asked, "Are those the same pants that we got you from Sears, honey?"

I looked at her and said, "Yeah, Mom, I got Bryce's sister Cindy to fix them for me, what do you think? They look pretty cool now, don't they?"

Josie couldn't stop giggling, and said, "Well, at least you can tell that you've been circumcised, Ronnie! Ha ha!"

My mom looked closely at the crotch area and said, "Yeah, you're right Josie, they are pretty tight, aren't they? Is that the way you really want them, honey?"

"Yeah, Mom," I said, "They fit just about right now, nice and snug and not so darn baggy!"

"Okay," she said with a smile, "you're the one who has to wear them, and I hope you enjoy them like that."

Josie smiled and giggled some more and said, "Well, I guess the girls will know what you're packing, anyway!"

I walked out of the room and went back upstairs, wondering exactly what she had meant by that last comment, but I thought I had a pretty good idea.

The next day I wore my new green bells along with my yellow striped shirt to school, and in homeroom class I sat down next to Wayne with a little smile on my face. He looked at me and said, "Wow Ronnie! Cool outfit! But where did you get those pants, man?"

I stood up and did a little spin and told him, "I ordered them from Sears but I got some alterations done professionally. What do you think, pretty cool, huh?"

He did a little swish with his left hand and said, "Absolutely! Very cool Ron, I like them a lot! They look really nice on you!"

And he stared at my crotch area with a funny look in his eyes that I couldn't quite figure out.

Years later, I realized that Wayne was most likely gay, and had enjoyed my new pants probably more than I had even realized.

Two weeks later, I was wearing the blue pair and had pulled them up as far as they would go, because they kept feeling like they were resting too low on my waist, and then I bent over to pick up a pencil I had dropped during Math class, and the butt of the pants split right between the cheeks! Luckily, I had a pair of sweatpants in my gym locker, and after asking Mr. O'Neil if I could be excused for a few minutes, I wrapped my sweater around my waist and tied the sleeves together in the front and then walked over to the gym to change into my sweatpants. For the rest of the day, I had to explain to my teachers what had happened and why I was wearing sweatpants in class. I never got the blue pair fixed, and I never wore the green pair again either, fearing the same thing might happen, and knowing it would be a real disaster if I happened to be somewhere without a backup pair of pants to wear.

This lesson in clothing has stuck with me ever since, but I still don't place a lot of importance on the clothes I wear. I actually think the "fashion" industry is just another way for corporations to take one's hard-earned money for something that is unnecessary and requires spending for clothes that, a few seasons later, will be regulated to the trash barrel or the thrift store.

So now I purchase most of my clothes at thrift stores, regardless of what the Wayne's in the world might think, except for underwear and socks, of course. Not only are thrift store prices for clothes a fraction compared to the price of new clothing, but also there seems to be a lot more variety and selection at a good thrift store than at any regular retail store. I also feel that I'm helping the environment by not purchasing things new, but instead recycling items that otherwise would end up in landfills.

But high school was much more than just about fashion lessons and haircuts. Like any school, the main purpose of its existence was education. Madrid High School attracted a high caliber of teachers, and many of the teachers that I had while attending MHS were exceptional. Many spent most of their teaching careers at Torrejon working for the Department of Defense, not only because it was a good job and quite rewarding but also because they got to live the good life in a European capital with three months off from work every summer to explore and travel all over Europe.

Many kept their jobs at MHS for many years and some even for decades. They raised their families in Madrid and enjoyed a much different life than if they had been teaching at a school stateside. Some teachers really immersed themselves in the local culture and made living in Spain their life.

I was lucky enough to get to know several teachers on a personal level over the years, and I am a much better-educated person because of it. The teachers and classes that I enjoyed the most and got the most out of taught subjects I was interested in and was good at. Since my personal preferences leaned towards the arts, social studies, and languages, these were the subjects and teachers that I learned the most from.

Although there were many teachers at MHS that I learned a great deal from and enjoyed their classes, there were three that were my favorites and that stick in my mind the most. These were Gordon Glaysher, the music teacher; Raymond Mortimer, the social studies teacher; and Elizabeth Vallet, the writing and languages teacher. There were several others that I remember fondly as well, but these three were the most memorable and left a lasting impression on me and my developing mind.

Music had been a big part of my young life ever since I was fortunate enough to see the Beatles perform live at Las Ventas Bullring in July 1965 and I witnessed the power and influence of music on audiences. The day after seeing the Beatles perform, I decided that I wanted to be involved with music, and so I have been for my entire life, one way or another, for better or worse.

With this deep interest in music, when I started ninth grade I took beginning band class, and my teacher was Mr. Gordon Glaysher. We were fortunate enough that the school provided band instruments to the students who desired to learn music, and this kept expenses down for the parents. But the choice of instruments was limited to the number of students that desired to learn that particular instrument.

GORDON C. GLAYSHER, MUSIC

When I saw the list of instruments that I could learn, I immediately chose the saxophone because I had seen rock-and-roll bands with Saxes in them and I thought that of all the band instruments available to students, the sax was the most relevant to rock-and-roll. But I was very disappointed to find out that all the Saxes the school had were already checked out to other students, and the next closest thing was the clarinet. True, a clarinet did have a reed much like a sax, and one squawked into it to make it sound, but to me it was very square and just wasn't what I wanted to learn to play. But Mr. Glaysher assured me that if I stayed in band class, eventually a sax would become available for me, either the following semester or the next school year by the latest.

Mr. Glaysher at this point had been teaching music for several years and had acquired the skills and the patience to teach students basic rudimentary music lessons, as well as to teach advanced students who played in the school's marching band and the high school jazz band. Mr. Glaysher was an accomplished musician in his own right, and he played the trumpet professionally in jazz bands all over Europe during his free time.

He must have had the patience and the temperament of a monk to be able to stand in front of a class and listen to young students trying to master the most basic musical skills. My ears started to hurt after only a few minutes of sitting in a class with twenty or so other kids, all of us trying to see who could make the most noise with their particular instrument. But Mr. Glaysher's perseverance and dedication to teaching music motivated him year after year, and class after class, to instill into hundreds (if not thousands) of students the joys and appreciation of music.

We began with the most fundamental music lessons, such as learning half notes and quarter notes, the various time signatures, and learning what the notes on the lines were. Gradually, after an hour a day, five days per week, the students in his classes began to learn the magical language of music.

After many years of teaching music, Mr. Glaysher had a system down that was not only quick and efficient but also fun for the students. He had an enormous amount of patience to be able to advance a student with no knowledge of reading music to the point where he or she was proficient on an instrument in a relatively short time. I'm not sure how he was able to teach six hour-long classes every day and endure the squawking and the bleating of the instruments of his young students. I realize now that his love of music and his belief that learning music could and should be a fundamental part of a young person's education were a big part of his patience, endurance, and motivation.

It wasn't until the following year that I finally got a saxophone to play. By then I'd had two semesters of clarinet and was ready to graduate to the sax. I started on the alto sax my sophomore year instead of the tenor I wanted because that was the only one available. I was fine with that though. The following semester I got to play the baritone sax which is the big one that rests on the ground while being played and takes considerably more breath, and it became my instrument of choice for band class.

I realize now the wonderful gift that he gave me, along with countless other students over the years, of the love and appreciation for music. I had been learning to play bass guitar and had been playing in rock-and-roll bands for a short time by then, but I had no idea what real music was all about until Mr. Glaysher showed me, and for this I owe him an enormous debt of gratitude.

Mr. Glaysher was not only a great music teacher, but he was also a very nice and decent man as well. Once he invited my brother and me over to his house on a Saturday afternoon to visit him and to meet his family. They lived not too far from our house, right off Calle Arturo Soria (known by Americans as "Suicide Lane," due to the amount of traffic and the narrow lanes of this major thoroughfare). So one Saturday, Johnny and I took the *tranvia* (the streetcar) up to Arturo Soria and we got off and walked the couple of blocks to the address that he had given us. It was a rather large two-story house with a nice front yard with tall trees, and very well-landscaped with rose bushes and other nice vegetation.

Johnny rang the doorbell and Mr. Glaysher answered the door wearing an old sweatshirt and blue jeans and invited us in. I was rather taken aback since I had never seen him outside of school and he always wore a white shirt and tie while in class. He introduced us to his lovely wife, and she offered us some iced tea which we accepted gratefully.

He then showed us around the house; a large grand piano was the centerpiece in the living room, and after a while we sat down on the sofa and began to chat. He asked us about our musical efforts playing in bands and Johnny told him about his band The Beautiful Beasts, and how they were playing fairly regularly around town. Then Mr. Glaysher mentioned the jazz band that he played with during summer vacation and the fact they sometime got gigs in Italy and France as well as in jazz clubs all over Spain.

Two young girls then came into the living room from outside and he introduced us to them. They were his daughters, and both were barely in elementary school but were very well-behaved and courteous to his house guests. After a few more minutes of chatting, we told him we had to leave to get home in time for dinner, and so he politely showed us out and we thanked him for a very nice visit and for showing us his home and family.

While walking back to catch the *tranvia* home, Johnny and I felt amazed and delighted that we had been invited to visit our favorite teacher outside of the classroom and we both felt very privileged. We had learned that teachers are just ordinary people outside of the classroom, with lives and families much like our own.

The following year, I again took band class, and this time I was playing the baritone sax in the intermediate band and was learning more about music and improving my skills on the sax. Band became my favorite class, and I began to meet other like-minded students who not only loved music but also considered Mr. Glaysher their favorite teacher.

In 1968, during my junior year in high school, there were a lot of changes going on in the world as well as in our school. "Sergeant Pepper's Lonely Hearts Club Band," the famous Beatles album, was released the previous year, and it changed popular music forever, and the album cover changed fashion forever. Mustaches, sideburns and beards became very popular for men and our teachers at MHS were no exception. Over the Christmas break that year Mr. Glaysher decided to grow a mustache and not just an ordinary one either, but a real whopper! It was the giant handlebar kind that hung over his lip, one that George Harrison might have worn at the time and been proud of.

 A couple of weeks after the break, a student named Steve, who was known to be a big joker around campus and was in Mr. Glaysher's first class of the day, decided he would have a little fun with his favorite teacher. He cut out twenty-five giant black mustaches from thick black construction paper. He then handed them out to every student in the class and passed along a roll of scotch tape to stick these paper mustaches over the upper lip of every mouth in the class, including the girls.

Mr. Glaysher was often known to be a few minutes late to his first class, so Steve had plenty of time to hand them all out and get everybody wearing them by the time Mr. Glaysher walked into the classroom. The stunned look on his face as he gazed upon his first period's students all wearing these giant black mustaches was worth the considerable effort Steve had put into the joke. Someone in the class had a camera and took a picture at the exact right moment to capture the look of surprise on Mr. Glaysher's face and a copy of that photo was tacked to his bulletin board for the rest of the semester.

I wasn't the only person who considered Mr. Glaysher to be a great teacher. I don't think any student that he had over the many years that he taught music at MHS will ever forget him or ever have any regrets at having taken music, band, or chorus classes with him. He was not only a great teacher who excelled at teaching young people the basics of the language of music, but he was also an extraordinary human being with a spirit and a personality that made everyone remember him fondly. Many of his ex-students went on to become professional musicians and were lucky enough to be able to play for a living instead of working for one, thanks to the devotion, patience, and the love for his subject that Mr. Glaysher had, and was able to transmit so well to his students.

...

Another teacher whom I remember quite fondly was Raymond Mortimer, who taught social studies and U.S. history at MHS. It was rumored that Mr. Mortimer was secretly a member of the American Communist Party; secret because if his employers, the Department of Defense, were to become aware of this information about him, his job would certainly have been in jeopardy. Communism and communists were generally not looked upon very favorably by many Americans during the turbulent years of the 1960s, and especially by the American military. If it had been known that a card-carrying member of the Communist Party was actually teaching the developing minds of young students on an American Air Force Base, heads would certainly have rolled.

So he kept his political affiliations under wraps, but this did not prevent him from discussing his views in the classroom with his students. He used the official U.S. History textbook that was required for him to teach from, but only used it as a general guideline for his courses. Actually, he used it to point out to his students the fallacies in it, and how the history of the United States and the entire world was actually much different from what the history books would have you believe.

His teaching style and his rather revolutionary personality was perfect for influencing the minds of his young students, especially with all that was going on in this most turbulent of decades. He was able to cover all the major issues of the day with his own particular insights and points of view, including civil rights, the Vietnam War, racism, the corruption in government, and many more issues, with sincerity and with a totally different view from that of the mainstream. He tried to teach his students to think for themselves and not believe the bullshit that was broadcast or published about what was happening in the world, but instead to find out for themselves what was really going on, and not to take anyone's word for it, including his own.

Mr. Mortimer's ability to show his students how to look outside the box and not take anything for granted was a far more valuable lesson than the various dates and events of U.S. history that the course work tended to dwell on. He was a man of courage, convictions, and integrity, and these attributes were remembered by his students far more than anything from the textbook.

He showed his students that it was okay not to believe in everything that society and the older generation was trying to make young people believe, and that it was imperative for people to think for themselves, especially during these most culture-changing of times. Mr. Mortimer too, by this point, had changed his grooming to reflect the times in which we were living, along

Raymond Mortimer, Social Studies

with a few other teachers at MHS. He grew a beard that made him look even more like the 60s radical that he actually (and secretly) was.

He was also a big rock-and-roll fan, which I found out in a very strange and unusual way. My locker during my junior year was right down the hall from the entrance to his classroom. One day, as I was standing in front of my locker looking for my History textbook, he was walking to his classroom. He stopped to chat with me briefly and was carrying something under his arm. He asked me if I had the latest album by the Rolling Stones, "Beggar's Banquet," and I looked at him closely and replied that I hadn't yet gotten it. He handed me the record that was under his arm and told me that I could have this copy because he already had the record at home, and he didn't need two copies. I was quite surprised, to put it mildly, thanked him very much for his generosity, and told him that I couldn't wait to play it.

Listening to the album later at home all the way through, I realized that it made perfect sense that a man of his political persuasion would like the album so much, especially considering that the two standout tracks on the record, "Sympathy For The Devil" and "Street Fighting Man," were both songs about revolution and political turmoil.

I felt quite honored and grateful that Mr. Mortimer had singled me out of the hundreds of students that he taught to give me this incredible gift. I tried to figure out why he chose me to give this album to, and could never figure it out. Could it be because I happened to be standing there in front of my locker as he was walking by? Or was there another reason that I couldn't quite understand? It's not like I was his favorite student or especially talkative in class or in any other way had made myself stand out from all the other students he taught. I generally kept a very low profile in high school. I rarely raised my hand unless there was something I totally disagreed with or had a serious question about. My shyness and lack of confidence made me

try to blend in and not stand out in any way whatsoever.

This was further confusing to me because at the end of the school year, I realized that I had failed my U.S. History class; I had gotten a big fat F! It was the only class that I had ever failed in my entire four years of high school and it quite surprised me. I usually got fair to good grades all the way through school. I would coast through all my classes and rarely do any more than was required (or sometimes even less if I felt I could get away with it).

I only did homework during my homeroom class or sometimes on the bus to or from school, and even though I never tried to excel in any way, I had always managed to get passing grades up to this point. I was warned by Mr. Mortimer before the class ended that if I didn't pick up the pace and turn in the reports and homework required that I would be facing getting an F in his class, but I just shrugged it off and didn't do the work, thinking that at worst I would skate by with a D.

The problem was that U.S. History was a required course to pass to graduate from MHS. Without getting a passing grade in this class, one just didn't graduate. So the following year, I was required to take the same class over again and ironically enough I got Mr. Mortimer again, and I was even assigned the same seat that I had sat in the year before. By this time I was a senior, and sitting in class with all these juniors made me feel a little strange, but I had no other choice about it.

On top of this, it was an even more serious matter because after my graduation from high school, my family had made plans to return to the States and make our lives there. My brother and I would be enrolled in college and my parents would go on with their separate lives. Unless I passed this class, I would not graduate, and this would disrupt my parents' plans as well as my brother's life and indeed our entire futures. My family was not prepared to spend another year in Spain just so I could finally finish graduating from high school.

So in my senior year of high school, I became determined that I would pass this class, since not only my future relied on it, but the rest of my family's as well. But as the year progressed, and I came closer to the end of my high school career, I began to slack off again on my homework and other assignments I was given.

I was doing okay in all my classes except for U.S. History with Mr. Mortimer, and he was very much aware of my situation. Towards the end of the semester and my final few weeks of high school, he sat down with me and told me that unless I would do a special assignment for his class, the work I had done so far was just not good enough to earn a passing grade in his class. In desperation, I asked him what I could do to ensure that I passed his class. He told me that the final project was an oral report that all students were to give in front of the class about any subject of their choosing. If I did the report and got a passing grade on it by showing that I had actually put some time and effort into it, he would give me a passing grade.

For several days I thought about what subject I could do a report on that was of interest to me and that I'd be able to give an oral report on in front of the entire class. I had two weeks until the day when I'd have to do my report, so I decided on a subject that, for some reason, I'd been interested in for quite a while, although it had absolutely nothing to do with U.S. History.

My good friend Andy, with whom I had spent a lot of time during the last couple of years, both in and out of school, had given me the idea. Andy lived with his mother, who was Italian and was an elementary school teacher on base, and his four siblings, but their father never seemed to be around. When I asked about the whereabouts of their father, I was told that he spent most of his time living and working in Madagascar and was able to visit his family in Madrid only on vacations and special holidays.

He always brought gifts from Madagascar for his children whenever he returned for a visit. These items (mostly native works of art) were lying about his house and I always found them to be of great interest. I'm not sure what Andy's father did for work, but I knew he was a French citizen and Madagascar used to be a French colony, so I figured that probably had something to do with his work on that island nation, which had recently changed its name to the Malagasy Republic after gaining independence from France in 1960.

So now that I had my subject in mind, I went to Mr. Mortimer and asked him if he thought the subject of Madagascar would be okay to do my report on. At this point, he just wanted me to pass his class and to be able to get along with my life, and he seemed to be pleased that I had found a subject I was interested in, so he gave his approval on my choice of subjects, as long as I showed that I had put considerable effort into my presentation.

I spent quite a lot of time during the next couple of weeks in the library doing research and compiling as much information as I could about Madagascar. I even came to like the sound of the word since it just made such perfect sense from my weird ecological perspective as in: "Mad! A **gas** car!" Cars shouldn't run on gas, this is sheer madness!

I spent more time and effort on this report than anything I had ever done in my entire school career. I ended up knowing more about Madagascar than the Malagasy people themselves, probably. It is the fourth largest island in the world and had (at the time) only six million inhabitants. The fact that the island had split from the African mainland some 88 million years ago, which had allowed native plants and animals to evolve in relative isolation, so that over 90% of its wildlife is found nowhere else on Earth, was all fascinating to me. The more research I did, the more interested I became about this most unusual of places. I found the lemurs especially interesting; with over one hundred separate species living on the island, each finding its own separate niche in the island's complex ecosystem.

Everything about the place seemed to be unique; from the people themselves who came from a blend of Austronesian (Southeast Asian) and Bantu (East African) roots, to their language (Malagasy) which was only spoken by the inhabitants of the island. It was also one of the main suppliers of vanilla and cloves in the world. The more I researched, the more fascinated I became with its history, geography, flora, fauna, and people.

All my trips to the library and all the research I did on the subject made me realize a very important life lesson. If one is truly interested in and enjoys something, then it rarely seems like work, but is almost always fun, enjoyable, and a positive experience. This became an invaluable lesson to learn for later in life when I began to think about what I wanted to do for a living and how I was to make my way in the world.

By the time of my oral presentation in front of the class, I knew I was prepared, because I had made several homemade maps and charts about such subjects such as the geography, the history, the distribution of population, the types of crops grown, the four distinct climate zones of the island and just about anything else one could possibly want to know about the place. I stood in front of the class with my stack of poster size drawings and charts and felt confident that I was going to nail it. How could I not? I had taught myself more about this subject than probably anyone else in the school ever had; of this I was absolutely certain.

I knew my subject so well by this point that my enthusiasm, my interest, and my excitement were contagious. I could tell that I had the other students' attention during my entire report. After going on for about fifteen minutes, explaining all that I had taught myself about this island, I concluded with the following very profound statement: "In conclusion, ladies and gentlemen, I believe that the island of Madagascar is not only one of the most fascinating places on earth, with its unique flora and fauna, comparable to such places as the Galapagos islands (where Charles Darwin first came up with his idea of natural selection and the theory of evolution), but also due to its low population numbers, its vast untouched wilderness, and its varied climate, it has the possibly of becoming an alternative place to immigrate to, where there still exist vast open spaces and opportunities for establishing a new life and a new society, much like many people are already doing on the great island continent of Australia."

I think I threw the last part in about Australia because my brother had recently been discussing immigrating to Australia with his good friend Scott Wilson, who had a family member there that owned a sheep ranch and had invited Scott and Johnny to come and work on his "station."

I heard a smattering of applause when I was done and a grateful look from Mr. Mortimer that indicated to me that I had done it, that I could be sure that I would graduate in a few months and my family's and my future would not be held up by my lack of studying. I felt quite proud of myself as I made my way back to my desk carrying my stack of charts and maps, knowing that if I really put my mind to it, I could accomplish almost anything.

I ended up getting a mere "B plus" on my report, since it seemed that Mr. Mortimer really didn't give out "A's" very often, but I felt that I had accomplished something very important. Not only was I the school's resident expert on Madagascar, but I had also shown myself that I was capable of a lot more than I had previously thought, and that I was able to do anything at all once I put my mind to it and just did it. Again, this was a most valuable lesson for later in life when not just a grade was on the line, but my job and very livelihood.

I thank Mr. Raymond Mortimer to this day for failing me in his class the first time I took it and making me have to take it again my senior year. Not only was I able to sit through another year of his political ramblings and discussions that helped to open my eyes to a lot of what was going on in the world at the time, but he also made me realize that there actually can be pleasure in learning. My self-confidence was boosted, as I realized that I could do anything in the world, if I just put in enough energy and my mind to it. Thanks, Brother Ray!

Another teacher who made a really great impression on me during high school was Elizabeth Vallet. She was an African-American woman married to a French jazz musician from Paris, and they were living in Madrid while she was teaching various classes at MHS, including English, creative writing, and French, while Mr. Vallet continued to try to make a living playing jazz. She taught French because the school wanted to offer French language classes as well as Spanish, and she was the only member of the faculty that spoke any French at all. She had lived several years in Paris with her husband before beginning work with the Department of Defense and had learned a considerable amount of Parisian French. Although she was not an expert and by far was not totally fluent in the language, she was the best that MHS could come up with to teach their French classes.

When I returned to Madrid after spending one year living in Alicante on the coast of Spain, and attending a French school there, I thought that I would take French at MHS. It would be a very easy course to pass, I thought, since I spoke French fairly well from my time in Alicante, and I should be able to breeze through the class.

Elizabeth Vallet
English, Creative Writing

MHS only offered two French classes, French I and French II, and not any advanced French classes at all due to Ms. Vallet's limited French writing and reading skills. So, I figured that I would take French I and earn a good grade very easily.

As I've mentioned before, during my school years I was never really an outspoken student or a guy who wanted much attention due to my basic shyness and lack of confidence, but for some reason I made an exception in Ms. Vallet's class. Having spent the previous year going to a French school as well as getting extensive tutoring in the language the entire time, I had the French language on my brain, and when I heard her speak French to the class in her Parisian accent which was slightly Americanized by her slight southern drawl, I was appalled. Her pronunciation at times was just plain awful to my ears, and I let her know on a regular basis. I couldn't just sit there and hear her butcher the French language the way she was doing, so I'd constantly raise my hand to correct her.

It was not only her bad pronunciation of certain words and phrases, but she also seemed to lack basic verb conjugation skills, and a quite limited vocabulary. I just couldn't sit still when I heard her try to wrap her tongue around certain phrases and words.

A few weeks into the semester, she asked me to stay after class and have a "rap session" (her words). So I stayed behind after the rest of the students left the classroom and sat down at one of the desks in the front row while she sat on top of her desk facing me. She asked me why I was constantly interrupting her class, and couldn't I understand that she needed to maintain a certain air of authority and professionalism in her class.

I had explained to her at the beginning of the semester that I had just returned from living a year in Alicante where I had attended *"Le Nouvelle Ecole Francaise D'Alicante."* There, I was force-fed the French language in order to attend the school, including almost daily tutoring by a French professor, and I explained that the French language was something I took very seriously.

She told me that it was obvious that I had a certain command of French and was quite proficient in it, but she could not tolerate me constantly interrupting her class anymore. I apologized and told her I understood her point very well, that sometimes I just couldn't help myself, but I would try to keep my comments to a minimum in the future. She thanked me and let me go.

But I just couldn't help myself, it seemed. Whenever I heard something come out of her mouth that was just plain wrong, I raised my hand and let her know the proper way of saying it. The other kids in the class probably thought I was a show-off and was just giving her a hard time, but I really didn't want these other students to learn things that were just plain wrong. Her pronunciation I could tolerate for the most part, but when she made grammatical and conjugation errors, I almost always raised my hand to correct her.

It finally reached a point where she called my mother to set up a parent-teacher conference about my disrupting her class so often. I heard all about it when I got home from school because my mom wasn't used to being called down to a teacher's classroom to discuss my shortcomings. I tried to explain to my mom that Ms. Vallet was just plain awful with the French language and I spoke it much better than she did, and that it was really hard for me to sit in class and hear her butcher such a beautiful language the way she did on a daily basis.

My mom explained to me that if I didn't want to get kicked out of her class, I was to immediately stop correcting her the way I was doing, and that Ms. Vallet had told her that even though she was limited in her French language skills, she was doing the best she could, and she was getting paid to teach the class, not I. And this was my final warning. The next time I corrected her in class, I would be seeing the principal about it, and would not be allowed to return to her class.

I reluctantly promised her that I would not disrupt Ms. Vallet's class anymore, and I would just have to learn to bite my tongue whenever I heard her say some atrocious thing in the French language. My mom again tried to explain to me that sometimes in life, things just aren't fair, but there is often not very much we can do about it.

Luckily the semester was close to being over with only a few weeks left, and I was able to stay silent in her class for the remainder of that time. But the next semester, I decided not to take French II as I was planning to because I realized that not only would I not get very much out of it, but I would risk getting in serious trouble with Principal Gogo.

I really did like Ms. Vallet as a teacher and a person, so the following year, I took a beginning creative writing class with her and I enjoyed it very much and got a great deal out of it. It was my first attempt at writing anything from my imagination instead of just book reports and papers for other classes. I realized during her class that writing could be fun as well as very creative, as long as I was writing about something I was interested in, instead of just what I was forced to write about. And even though I had disrupted her French class to a point where I was close to getting kicked out of it, she treated me with kindness and respect in her writing class and I got straight A's all the way through it.

During this time, in the late sixties, fashion was going through remarkable changes, and Ms. Vallet made the most of it. Every day in class it was always a treat to see what she would be wearing. She preferred very bright colors and wore a lot of African-style clothing with full flowing skirts and long colorful scarves, sometimes with huge dangling earrings and jingly necklaces. She was a remarkably intelligent woman, and I  learned to have a great deal of respect and admiration for her, despite her lack of proficiency in the French language.

Coincidences are something I've always been very interested in and quite fascinated by. I often try to understand the deep meaning, if there is one, behind these strange phenomena. A good example of this is an incredible coincidence that involves Liz Vallet and me. In the spring of 2013, almost forty-three years after I graduated from high school, I saw Ms. Vallet again. I had friended her on Facebook a year or so before then, and I knew that she had retired in Spain. I told her that I was planning a trip back to Spain and that I'd like to look her up.

It had been almost forty years since I had last been to Spain, so it was a very exciting trip for me. My oldest and dearest friend, J.P., who I have known and remained friends with since the ninth grade, had an apartment in Madrid and that is where I stayed. I was there about a week with him at his *piso* near Las Ventas, and we went around Madrid every day looking up old places that I remembered, including the various places where I used to live in Madrid. It was a marvelous experience and brought back many memories, and I was able to see the amazing changes that Spain had gone through during the previous four decades

The second week I spent in Spain, J.P. and I traveled around to different places in Spain that I remembered so well from having lived there so long ago. We went by train and bus to Valencia, Peñiscola, Benidorm, Malaga, Marbella, Torremolinos, Gibraltar, Cadiz, and Alicante. And it was in Alicante, where she was living, that I was able to look up Liz Vallet. I contacted her when we reached Alicante and we agreed to meet at a small cafe just downstairs from her apartment building. The strange thing is not only did she retire in Alicante, but she was living in the little town of Albufereta, just a few kilometers north of downtown Alicante.

Albufereta was the same small town where I had lived for over a year when I was in the eighth grade and attending French school. The apartment building that she was living in was right next door to one of the *pisos* that my family and I had lived in way back in 1965! What a remarkable coincidence that she had ended up living in the almost exactly the same spot where I had lived. And, ironically, because of the French language skills I had acquired there, I had given her such a hard time in her classroom the following year at MHS.

In 2013, she was getting on in years and was using a walker to get around, but her mind was as sharp as ever. Her husband had passed away a few years earlier, and she lived alone, but she had regular visits from both of her daughters. She was very well known and liked around the neighborhood, and the owner of the café where we met and with whom we chatted with for a while as we waited for her to come downstairs, only had great things to say about her.

We ended up spending several hours that afternoon getting reacquainted and reminiscing about the old days at MHS. I asked her if she remembered me from her French class and the fact that she had to call my mother into her class to discuss my disruptions, but she didn't seem to remember what I was talking about. She did vaguely remember me though; especially when I told her that I had attended a French school just a couple of kilometers from where we were sitting. And when I told her that I used to live on the ninth floor of the building right next door to the one she was living in, she agreed that it was an incredible coincidence.

She had brought with her from her apartment an MHS yearbook from 1969, and we paged through it to help bring back memories. We discussed her long and eventful teaching career with the Department of Defense and some of the other places she had lived and taught school besides Madrid. It turned out that she had spent over a decade living in Japan after Madrid, and she spent some time telling us about her life there. She also talked a lot about her two daughters and their families and how much they

meant to her. We had very nice visit, and it became one of the highlights of my trip to Spain that year.

I stayed in touch with Mrs. Vallet on Facebook until a couple of years later, when I saw a posting by her daughter saying that Elizabeth Vallet had passed away. I felt sad but realized that she had lived a wonderful life, had traveled and lived in some fantastic places, and had lived her life on her terms and as she wanted. She had found true love and had raised two beautiful and brilliant children, and she had a career where she not only taught young developing minds, but she also had a profound impact and a positive influence on so many peoples' lives. What more can anyone say about anyone's life? R.I.P. Elizabeth Vallet.

I had some other very interesting teachers at MHS, all of them different and unique in their own ways. One who comes to mind was Mr. Louis Moreno, my typing teacher. I not only got to spend an hour per day learning to peck at a keyboard, but I also liked his class because I was one of the few males in the class, since typing skills at the time were almost exclusively for female students who might go on to become secretaries or other kinds of office workers. The interesting thing about Mr. Moreno was that he was obviously a gay man, but no one made a big deal of it or even seemed to really care, which was unusual for those days.

John O'Neil was another teacher at MHS who left a lasting memory. I had him for math class and I owe my complete lack of understanding and appreciation for anything beyond basic mathematics to him. He would literally sleep in class on a regular basis. He would give us an assignment that would last the entire hour, then proceed to prop the newspaper in front of his face and fall sleep until the bell rang at the end of the class.

John J. O'Neil, Mathematics

It might have been because his class was the first one in the morning, and perhaps he was just plain sleepy or maybe hung over from the night before. But I never really missed much on advanced mathematics courses such as algebra and trigonometry since I never found much use for such subjects the rest of my life, anyway. Besides, when he was sleeping I didn't have to listen to the boring lectures that he'd give us every occasionally, and try so hard to understand those complex theories of mathematics.

Mr. O'Neil had a son named Mike who was a really nice guy and would at times hang out at the Glass House and places like that where my friends and I would congregate. He never really seemed to fit in, though, maybe because his father was a teacher and not a particularly well-liked one at that, and maybe he felt that the kids treated him differently because of it. He used to love motors of every sort, and he had a very nice *Bultaco* motorcycle that he'd race around with, always showing off how fast it was compared to the little mopeds that my friends and I had. Many years later I heard that Mike had died in an automobile accident in Madrid not too long after he graduated from high school. He was racing down Arturo Soria in a very fast sports car that he had recently bought and had a bad accident that killed him. This was a tragic ending to a very nice guy.

Another teacher who left a lasting impression on me was Carlos Aparicio, the Spanish teacher. I took advanced Spanish classes with him for a couple of semesters because it helped my Spanish language skills and because it was an easy course to pass for someone who spoke fluent Spanish already. (I had reasoned the same thing with French and Mrs. Vallet, but it didn't quite work out!)

Mr. Aparicio was rare among the Department of Defense teachers in that he was a local, a Spaniard. He was very well-educated and spoke perfect English. He had a degree in law but I think he found his calling teaching American high school kids the Spanish language. He was very well-liked because of his outgoing and very positive personality and with his extremely good looks; he was especially admired and liked by many of the high school girls who took his classes. He thought of himself as a sort of cross between a Spanish playboy and James Bond (or at least the actor who played James Bond at the time, Sean Connery).

CARLOS APARICIO, SPANISH

His classes were always an adventure because he would always have a quick smile and a joke (usually off-color) for everyone around him. The classes were mostly just sitting around and having conversations in Spanish, and he would correct students whenever he heard a bad conjugation or another grammatical error. He taught vocabulary, and I was able to learn to say things in Spanish that I probably never would have otherwise. I learned quite a lot from Mr. Aparicio and not just about improving my Spanish language skills, but about life, humor, and how to carry oneself in this world. Muchas gracias, Señor Aparicio!

There were many other teachers that come to mind and that I also have fond memories of including Mr. Gerald Walth, the shop teacher. I think the most important lesson I learned from him was that I figured out that I didn't think I wanted to become a carpenter, a metal worker, a mechanic, or any other kind of similar occupation when the time came for me to choose my life work one day. He was a nice man and knew his subjects well, but I came close one day to slicing off my finger on a table

Gerald Walth
Industrial Arts

saw and I realized that it was probably only a matter of time before something like that actually happened, even though Mr. Walth stressed enforcing the utmost safety practices around all the various machines in his classroom.

Another teacher who comes to mind is Mr. Harvey Paulin who taught science and biology, and who was very well-liked by all of his students. He went on to teach at a Department of Defense school at an Air Force Base in the Azores islands for many years after leaving MHS.

Mr. John Malik, who taught Russian and Science classes, I became personal friends with a couple of years later, after I got out of high school but was still living in Spain.

Mr. John Morris taught English and was another deep thinker and a very intelligent man who had the ability to make his students think for themselves and was also very well-liked by almost every one of his students.

Mr. Charles Guthrie was a kindly older gentleman who also taught English and reminded many students of their grandfathers. He was also the coach of the high school golf team; yes, they actually had a golf team at MHS!

Overall, I consider myself to be very lucky to have had so many intelligent, dedicated, and professional teachers while I was in high school. Not only did I learn a lot about the subjects that they taught, but they also taught me many important life lessons as well. These lessons included patience, honor, integrity, perseverance, how to think for myself, and how to be a better human being, which very well might be the true meaning of being a great teacher. I offer a deep and heartfelt thanks to all of them, for I would not be the man I am today without their help, their dedication, their knowledge, and their kindness.

Muchas gracias to all of them! And Viva MHS!

Chapter 10. The Glass House

> *"Only two things can reveal life's great secrets:
> Suffering and love."* — Paulo Coelho

The Glass House, officially known as "Cafe Jeylo," and as "Cafeteria Oliverri" at one time as well, was a bar and a cafe not far from Plaza Castilla in the *"Generalissimo"* area of Madrid. It was in a neighborhood where many Americans and foreigners lived, and this little cafe was called the Glass House because there was a large room outside, between the sidewalk and the street which was entirely enclosed in glass. The purpose of this structure was for patrons to indulge in one favorite European pastime: sitting at a sidewalk cafe and watching people walk by. The Glass House enabled them to do so in virtually any kind of weather. Many people, including me, learned to spend a great deal of time participating in this activity, simply by mastering the skill of nursing a beer or a soft drink for hours.

In the summer when the weather was great, there was no reason to sit inside a glass-enclosed building, so the owners of the cafe removed the glass enclosure and it became just another sidewalk cafe in Madrid. This particular cafe happened to be one of the more popular hangouts for American high school kids, both from MHS (Madrid High School) and from ASM (American School of Madrid).

Many of the teenagers lived in the area and in the late 50s and early 60s, the American military complex occupied the same city block as the Glass House. So this little café had been popular with Americans for quite a long time. When I used to spend so much time there in the mid to late sixties, one could usually find a crowd of American kids hanging out almost any afternoon or evening. On the weekends, it became the place in Madrid for high school kids from Royal Oaks to come and party, as well as the kids who lived in "downtown" Madrid.

The manager and head waiter of the place was Marcelino, and he welcomed the crowds of American students who made the place a regular hangout, as long as they comported themselves in a respectable manner, which was usually the case. On very rare occasions, some guy would have too many *cuba libres* and would start to act obnoxious and Marcelino would have to ask the fellow to leave, but most people who hung around there had respect for him and his place and rarely created any problems.

The prices at the Glass House were comparable to almost every other place around town and were cheap by American standards. *Un chato de vino tinto* (a small glass of red wine) or *una caña de cerveza* (a glass of draft beer) both cost *un duro* (five pesetas or about eight cents.) A bottle of Coke, Fanta, or Pepsi was about 10 pesetas, so it was cheaper to drink beer and wine than soft drinks, and that is what many people did.

They also served great hamburgers, french fries, and other American-style food for very reasonable prices. One of the cheapest things on their extensive menu, which included all kinds of Spanish cooking as well, was *huevos fritos con papas*, or fried eggs with potatoes. This plate came with a big slice of *pan tostada*, (toasted bread), and cost 25 pesetas or around thirty-five cents. I ordered this plate regularly, not only because of its nutritional value but for its monetary value as well. My 500 pesetas (eight dollars) weekly allowance went a long way at places like the Glass House.

It was at the Glass House that I experienced something for the first time that was to become a big part of my life for many years to come. Even though I knew it was illegal, I had wanted to try pot for a long time. I was just fifteen and a sophomore in high school, but I felt I was quite wise for my age. After spending most of my short life living overseas, I had seen and experienced things that most kids my age had never even heard about.

There was quite a lot of cannabis around Madrid in the 1960s, almost all of it imported from Morocco, which was only nine miles across the Straits of Gibraltar from southern Spain. It usually came in the form of hashish, since that form was more compact and hence easier to smuggle, but occasionally one could find a substance called *kif*, which was what many Moroccans themselves smoked on a daily basis. Because it's a Muslim country, it is technically forbidden to consume alcohol in Morocco, although it is accepted and allowed in the "modern quarter" of many cities, so there are some bars and nightclubs that do have alcoholic beverages for sale. But because it is so close to Europe, Morocco does not have the extreme puritan Muslim ethics that are found in such countries such as Saudi Arabia, where it is illegal and totally prohibited.

Having been colonized by both Spain and France in the past couple of centuries has added to the relative sophistication and modernization of the typical Moroccan. Yet because alcohol has been traditionally forbidden, Moroccans over the centuries have developed their own particular method of relaxing, especially in the old quarter of most cities. They smoke this substance called *kif* which is basically the finely chopped flowers of the female cannabis plant mixed with a small amount of black tobacco. They smoke it in long-stemmed pipes with small clay bowls called *sebsis* which most Moroccan men carry around with them tucked into the long robes called *djellabas* that most of them wear.

It seemed to me during my two trips to the fair country of Morocco that many of the locals seemed to spend a lot of their time hanging around cafes, smoking *kif* and sipping mint tea (to coat the throat with mint and make it easier to keep smoking).

Traditionally in Morocco, the smoking of *kif* took the place of cigarettes, since it did contain a small amount of strong sun-dried black tobacco, as found in certain Spanish and French cigarettes like *Gauloises*, *Gitanes*, *Celtas*, and *Ducatos*. In Morocco the art of smoking *kif* over the centuries has reached a very high level of sophistication, tradition, and skill.

However, I, at age fifteen, was not experienced whatsoever. But one Tuesday evening I found myself hanging out at the Glass House, having a cold beer and trying to find something to do. Tuesday evenings were rather slow at the Glass House, with a lot of the local kids at home early on a weeknight doing homework or some other useless waste of time — as it seemed to me, anyway.

So I found myself having my second caña of *El Aguila* beer while sitting in one of the booths when a fellow by the name of Dick walked in with a smirk and an attitude. Dick was a year older than I was and was known for having a reputation of being sort of a J. D. (a juvenile delinquent). He was the kind of guy who seemed to always be in trouble of some sort and didn't seem to care about very much at all besides having a good time in life.

He sat down in my booth across from me and said, "Hey, what's up, Walker?"

"Not too much, Dick, what are you up to tonight?"

"Well, I've been getting a little buzzed tonight, want to join me?"

He could tell by the look on my face I had no idea what he was talking about, so I ask, "Um, what do you mean, Dick?"

"Yeah, man, I got some killer *kif* with me. Wanna try some?"

Then he pulled out his pack of Marlboros, pulled one out that looked different from the others and showed it to me. It was slightly wrinkled, and the tip was twisted into a point.

"Sure, I guess so."

"Okay, come with me outside then, and leave your beer on the table, we won't be long." He got up and I followed him out the door, telling Marcelino, the barkeep who was busy reading his newspaper, that we'd be right back.

We walked to the alley behind the bar and after a quick look around, Dick used his Zippo to light up the Marlboro that was emptied of its tobacco and filled with *kif*, took a long drag, and then passed it to me, saying, "Here ya go, kid, take a long drag and hold it in."

I had recently begun experimenting with smoking cigarettes, so I knew how to inhale and I knew well the slight dizziness I had experienced after smoking cigarettes, but I had no idea what effects this type of smoke would have on me. I took a long drag and immediately noticed the strong flavor and the peculiar smell the smoke had, much different from the Kents and Parliaments that I used to sneak from my Mom's cigarette box on the coffee table at home. I held it in as he had instructed and then let out a long exhale, trying not to cough, which I just barely managed to do.

I passed the cigarette back to him as he asked me, "Hey, is this is the first time you've done this?"

"No, man," I lied, "I've gotten high lots of times before."

We continued to pass the Marlboro back and forth until it burned down to the cotton filter. At which point he tossed it to the ground, stepped on it with his shiny, black Beatle boot, and said, "Okay, let's get back inside, all right?"

As we walked back into the Glass House, I started experiencing some things that I had never felt before. The entire world seemed to have changed considerably; colors seemed more colorful, and sounds were brighter. In fact, everything suddenly felt more intense and more alive, almost vibrating and shimmering.

As we sat back down in our booth and I took a sip of my beer, I started feeling very strange indeed. And Dick must have noticed it because he asked me, giggling, "Hey man, you all right, you look a little pale there."

I replied with a voice that suddenly didn't sound like mine, "Wow, that stuff was really powerful, man."

"Yeah, man, but it's just regular Moroccan kif, are you sure you've done this before?"

"Yeah, but I don't remember feeling like this before, man! This is intense!"

He looked at me with his wicked grin. "Don't worry, you'll be all right, just relax, man."

I wasn't feeling very alright though, or relaxed either, for that matter; something had changed in my mind, my thoughts seemed different, as if they were coming from someone else's brain, and I was just a spectator to my own mind.

I got up and said to Dick with a voice that continued to seem like someone else's, "Here, man, take the rest of my beer, I'm not feeling too good. I think I'll be going home now."

He looked at me with the same smirk on his face and told me, "Okay man, you take it easy now, all right?"

I looked at him with eyes that suddenly seemed to be seeing way too much for some reason and replied, "Okay, Dick, I'll be seeing you around."

He gave me a strange look and said, "Okay, I'll see you later kid, and don't freak out too much, heh heh!"

I walked out of the place, heading for the *tranvia* (the streetcar) stop, which I always took the few kilometers home to my family's *piso*. It was not too far past the *Estadio Bernabeu*, the main soccer stadium in Madrid, just down the *Castellana* from the Plaza Castilla area, where the Glass

House was located. As usual, the *tranvia* was crowded, with no place to sit, so I was relegated to standing, holding on to the overhead metal bar that ran the entire length of the streetcar.

It was only about a ten-minute ride to my stop, but it seemed to me to take several hours. Not only that, but while standing there holding onto the overhead bar, swaying with the movement of the electric tram, I looked around, and I was sure that the entire crowd of people was staring at me. Not only that, but I believed they somehow knew that I was high as a kite. I tried to act normal, but it took a lot of self-control to not freak out totally. I breathed a sigh of relief when we finally reached my stop and I was able to exit without losing my cool.

As I walked the block or so up to my house, I felt the chill of the evening and pulled my pea coat up closer around me, trying to get myself together to face my family in the condition I was in. After riding up the elevator the six floors to our apartment, as I got out and the door closed behind me, I could not remember riding the elevator at all. I opened the door with my key hoping that my mom was already in bed. But, no, not much luck for the wicked there.

She greeted me from the living room couch, looked up from her book, smiled, and said, "Hi, dear, where have you been?"

I replied in a voice that still didn't seem to be my own, "Oh, just up at the Glass House for a while, but I don't feel very well. I'm going to bed."

Just then my older brother Johnny walked into the room, took a good look at me, and said with a smile, "What's wrong, Ron, you look a little green. Are you lovesick? Maybe you got a new girlfriend or something?"

I turned away and walked off towards my room, thinking to myself, "Yeah, I'm lovesick all right, with a girl named Mary Jane!"

As I closed the door behind me, I suddenly realized that I was famished, as if I hadn't eaten for days. So I went into the kitchen and made myself two baloney and cheese sandwiches with mustard and grabbed the largest dill pickle out of the jar and headed back to my room, thinking, "Maybe I'll just make it through this after all."

Another bar that was popular among the Americans and foreigners around Madrid was a little place just around the corner from the Glass House, heading up towards the Plaza Castilla, just a thirty second walk from the Glass House. It had a different "official" name, but everybody just called it the "Horseshoe Bar," because it had a large horseshoe-shaped bar in the main room. Here you could sit at the bar and look directly into the faces of the patrons' sitting across from you.

What was most unusual about the place was that because of the narrow sidewalk in front of it, there wasn't room for outside tables, so they had an upstairs sitting area instead. Up a short flight of stairs, there were several tables with chairs and open windows, which you could sit by and look down on the pedestrians below. This was a slightly different experience than watching the walkers go by at ground level since they really couldn't see you watching them unless they looked up.

Sometimes on weekend evenings, the Glass House would fill to capacity, since it only had four booths and just a few tables. On many occasions, people could find nowhere to sit, so they would just go around the corner and hang out at the Horseshoe Bar instead. The Horseshoe Bar had an excellent jukebox with all the latest records by both British and American artists. They even had an extension speaker for the upstairs area where things could get very lively on weekend evenings when the place would fill up with American teenagers drinking and dancing to the loud tunes.

There was another place near the Glass House that was also very popular with American kids. It was just down the street a short way, right around the corner, and just past the taxi stand. It was officially called something else, but it seemed like everybody just called it *Jefe's*, which means "the Boss's." It was a bar only, in that food was not prepared or served. One could get a bag of potato chips or a few peanuts, but it was mostly just a place to have drinks. The name *Jefe's* came from the place right next door, which was a billiard parlor with pool tables and several pinball machines. It was run by a really old guy who just went by *Jefe*. My friend Bill was playing pinball in the place one day and asked the old guy what his name was and his response was, *"Yo soy el jefe de aqui!"* I am the boss of here! So

Jefe It was from then on, and the bar next door ended up with the same nickname.

I had quite a range of experiences and adventures hanging around that place, which for some reason was more of a hangout for the kids from ASM than from MHS, and I ended up making a lot of friends who went to ASM. And unlike the kids at MHS, who were mostly children of American servicemen stationed at Torrejon Air Base, the ASM kids were a slightly different crowd. Most of their parents were American businessmen working for American companies doing business in Spain. Some were connected with the American Embassy in Madrid and yet others were kids of American parents who were just living in Spain for one reason or another.

I think I got along so well with the ASM kids because many of them, like me, were in Madrid for the long haul, and had been living there for many years, not just the regular three- or four-year tour of duty that the American servicemen and their families usually had. Not only that, but many of the MHS kids lived in Royal Oaks, and rarely went into Madrid. They usually spent most of their time out at their American enclave or on base at Torrejon. Unlike me, most of these kids had hometowns back in the States somewhere and that is where they'd return to live and make their lives once they had finished their adventure of living overseas for a few years.

There is something about living in a foreign country as a young person that is unlike any other type of upbringing. For one thing, we were foreigners in a land that was not our own, and not the one where our parents and grandparents and the rest of our families lived while growing up. We felt different, and we were different from the masses of people all around us every day, the "locals." And we knew that we were not the same kind of people as our cousins and other people our age back "home," wherever that might be. Many of us didn't have a real home in the States, for we had rarely spent any time there during our entire lives. It was a strange type of existence and many of us felt displaced and without any of the roots that most people take for granted. But most of us felt that this was a small price to pay for being able to live an extraordinary life overseas

Of course, the number one priority for most teenagers of a certain age is to fit it, to find other people that one could relate to and who could relate to us. In the case of Overseas Brats, these other people that we were looking to fit in with were others like us, that were in the same boat as us, and experiencing this same unusual upbringing.

But unlike living in the States, where everyone around was pretty much like me, and I could make friends with just about anyone, the people that I could relate to in this environment I'm describing, were very limited. Sure, it was possible to become friends with the "locals," in this case the Spanish population, and indeed I did have many friends that were Spaniards, but it was a different kind of friendship both for me and for the Spanish person involved. I was different than they were and they were different than me. If a Spanish person had a friend who was an American, then they had an American friend and felt that their relationship with me was special and not the same as with their regular Spanish friends. A lot of times it was difficult to know if a Spanish person wanted to be my friend because they really liked me or because I was an American.

For this reason, many of the American kids living in "downtown" Madrid at the time found that we could make friends with others like ourselves, others who felt like misfits as well. I became friends with all sorts of people during my time in Madrid. At times it almost felt like some sort of United Nations of different people among my friends. One was a French guy, whose mother had left France for Spain during World War II and had never gone back. Another guy was of German descent, whose parents had left Germany for South America after the big war and now found themselves in Madrid.

A girl I was good friends with was Cuban and had left Cuba for Spain along with her family when Castro took over. Another buddy was half-Japanese, from the time his dad had spent there during the war, and another close friend was Turkish, whose father worked at the Turkish Embassy in Madrid. Others were Puerto Rican, Greek, Swiss, British, Norwegian, and a host of other backgrounds and nationalities. These were the people who felt similar to me. We were all in our own way, "Strangers in a Strange Land." (Robert Heinlein)

So Jefe's bar became a gathering place for many of these displaced youth in Madrid at the time and I found it becoming my favorite place to hang out. It was not a very large place, with just one main bar in the front, but it had a rather large room in the back that was reached by climbing a couple of stairs from the main area. This is where the jukebox was along with about a half dozen tables with chairs, and a few booths done in faux red leather with black trim that looked so old it could have been from the previous century.

This place was full of kids much like me almost every afternoon and evening. The jukebox was stocked with the latest rock-and-roll records by the latest groups that we were all into, including The Doors, Jimi Hendrix, The Beatles, The Stones, The Yardbirds, The Who, The Kinks, The Animals and many, many others that kept the place rocking.

There was a regular crowd that gathered at the place most afternoons after school as well as on Friday and Saturday nights, so it became the main gathering place for that group of kids, which consisted of mostly ASM students, but there were a few of us that went to MHS as well.

Jefe's, along with the Glass House and a couple of other places nearby, was located in an area where a lot of Americans lived, near Plaza Castilla and Avenida Generalissimo. In fact, ASM had their campus in this same area until 1967 when they moved to their new location out near Aravaca, on the northwest outskirts of Madrid. So prior to that year, the students only had to walk a couple of blocks after school to find a place to hang out. Since many still lived in the same area after the school moved, and rode buses to and from school, they still kept hanging out in the same places after school as they did before the campus was moved.

There were several other places besides Jefe's and the Glass House where American kids would gather in this same area, including the Woolworth's department store's cafeteria, which was located just a block or two down from the Glass House. Since Woolworth's was an American-style store, the cafeteria was American-style as well, with counters where one could sit, along with booths and tables. The food was also American-style and consisted of hot dogs, hamburgers, french fries, pies, ice cream, and other such delights, similar to what would one find at a lunch counter at a Woolworth's in the States.

I never spent a lot time there because of the crowds of shoppers that were usually there and besides, I knew better places in the neighborhood which I preferred. But for a small slice of "Americana," there weren't a lot of other places like it in Madrid. Usually one could find a few Americans having a coffee or a snack and feeling like they were back at home. The store itself sold the usual things one would find in a Woolworth's anywhere, but with more of a Spanish flair, including souvenirs and postcards from Madrid and all over the rest of Spain.

There were several other hangouts where Americans spent time in the neighborhood as well, including a bar by the name of the Red Lion. It was a very popular place for British tourists because it was decorated as an old English pub and of course, the main activity there besides drinking pints of English stout and ale was playing darts, and they had teams and tournaments regularly. A lot of American servicemen as well as Spanish businessmen seemed to frequent the place but, again, it wasn't my favorite place since I knew of other establishments that had patrons more like me.

With so many places around the neighborhood to choose from, I still preferred Jefe's, and it became my favorite hangout. When the back room filled up with a couple of dozen slightly inebriated American teenagers on a Friday night, I truly felt in my element there with so many other kids my own age and in my same situation. There was a camaraderie that existed between us and we all felt a sense of belonging to this place, this time, and these people.

One Friday evening, something happened to me at Jefe's that changed my life forever, both for good and for bad. It was a typical Friday night at Jefe's and the place was happening, with lots of people hanging out and enjoying themselves, but this was an evening when I enjoyed myself perhaps a little too much!

A week or so earlier, a friend named Doug had told me about these pills that one could buy at almost any *farmacia* in Madrid. A *farmacia* in Spain is a drugstore that sold a variety of products any drugstore would sell, in addition to having over-the-counter drugs available. In Spain at the time, there were very few drug problems, besides a few tourists who might be caught bringing hashish back from Morocco. For this reason, one could go into any *farmacia* and purchase just about any drug over the counter, as long as one had a good story to tell the pharmacist about what it would be used for.

A good explanation if one was asked was that the pills were for your grandmother, who was bedridden and unable to come to the store and purchase the drugs herself. And because there just didn't exist much of a drug problem in Spain, nine times out of ten the pharmacist would sell whatever you wanted because he had no suspicions that they could possibly be used for anything else besides their stated intended purpose.

The pills that my buddy Doug had recommended to me and that he had tried and liked so much were called *Dormadinas* and were sleeping pills — probably barbiturates. They were available in a pack of twelve and cost about 100 pesetas (about $1.60) for the dozen. What my friend had told me to do was to take a couple and drink a couple of beers and that I'd get very high very quickly.

So that Friday afternoon, I went to a *farmacia* not far from my house and asked the clerk wearing his white smock for a package of *Dormadinas*. He looked at me, noticed that I was probably not a Spaniard, and asked me what I wanted them for. I told him that my mother had asked me to get some for her because she was having a hard time falling asleep and was not feeling well and that's why she sent me.

He went behind the counter and brought out two packages and asked me if I'd like the small pack with a dozen pills or the larger one which contained fifty. I told him the small one would do for now and he told me that it would be 95 pesetas altogether. I paid the man and walked out of the place with my supply of drugs in hand, ready to try them that night.

At *Jefe's* that night, I ran into Doug and I showed him the pack of *Dormadinas* I had scored that afternoon and I told him how easy it was to do.

He just looked at me and said, "See man, I told you it would be easy as hell! Now just go easy on them and don't take too many, especially if you're going to be drinking with them, okay?"

"Sure, man," I said, "Thanks for turning me on to them, and I'll let you know how I like them."

After buying a *caña de cerveza* from Antonio, the barkeep, I headed downstairs to the basement where the bathrooms were located. I went into the men's room with my glass of beer and opened the package of pills and took two out and went ahead and swallowed them with the beer I was holding and headed back upstairs to see what was going on.

There was a good crowd that night at *Jefe's* and people were enjoying themselves as usual, drinking and smoking cigarettes and busy flirting with the opposite sex. My good friend Mike from ASM seemed to really like the song "Break on Through," by the Doors, because he kept playing the song over and over again on the jukebox, while dancing wildly to it and singing along. I sat down and started to chat with a couple of people and before I knew it, my beer was gone.

I didn't remember drinking it, but somehow there was no more liquid in my glass. So I got up and headed to the bar to order another one and suddenly, I felt a rush of euphoria like I had never experienced before. It felt great, a sort of dreamy feeling, and I felt like I was floating around the room instead of walking. I felt more confidence than I had in a long time and the world was a warm and beautiful place where everyone was my best friend. I loved it!

After a while my beer ran out again and this time, after buying another one, I headed back downstairs not only to pee but also to take a couple more of these happy pills. After coming back upstairs, I sat around for a while longer until my beer finished and I repeated what I had done earlier. An hour or so later, I was feeling no pain whatsoever and my friends all thought I must have been drinking a lot more than I regularly did because I was having a real ball, slapping people on the back, telling them how much I loved them, and basically making a real asshole of myself. But I didn't care; I was feeling great, and that was all that mattered.

The fourth time I went downstairs, I barely made it without falling down the stairs, but I somehow managed to make my way to the toilet. I looked at my pill pack and realized that I still had six left in it, and that I had only taken half of the package so far. I swallowed two more and went ahead and unbuttoned my pants to pee. The pants I wore that night were the kind with buttons instead of a zipper, and for some reason, when I was done relieving myself, I couldn't seem to get coordinated enough to button the buttons, no matter how hard I tried.

I staggered out of the bathroom with my pants hanging right above my knees and somehow I made it upstairs. Antonio saw me staggering around with my pants still hanging almost to my knees and said to two guys sitting at the bar, *"Mira ese jilipollas, se ha tomado demasiado, saquele de aqui ahora mismo!"* "Look at that asshole, he's had way too much to drink, get him out of here right now!"

So the two guys came over and each of them grabbed me under the arm and escorted me out to the parking lot in front of the place.

One of them said to the other, "Man, this guy is really sloshed, let's just leave him over there between those cars, he'll be all right once he sleeps it off."

"Yeah, you're right, he's really fucked up, let's get him over there," the other guy answered.

All of this seemed to be happening to me in a dream.

They took me over to a space between two parked cars and dumped me on the ground. I rolled over and managed to get myself halfway under one of the cars, with my pants still around my knees, and then I totally passed out.

As was related to me later, the two guys who had hauled me out of the place went back in to the bar and started to chat about the poor kid who had had way too much to drink.

The first guy said, "He couldn't even get his pants up, man! Sure is lucky he had his tidy whities on! Ha ha!"

The other guy laughed, "Yeah, otherwise that kid would be displaying his family jewels to the world!"

"Yeah, well, that's what you get when you can't hold your booze, man! Poor kid, he's going to be hurting tomorrow for sure! You know maybe we should go out and check on him, just to make sure he's okay, what do you think?"

"You know maybe you're right, man, let's go see how he's doing."

So the two guys set their drinks down, told Antonio they'd be right back, and headed out to the parking lot again.

Right at this time, Scott Wilson, a good friend of my brother's, was walking into the bar with another friend of his and he asked the two guys walking out, "Hey, guys, what's up, where you guys going so quick?"

The first guy said to Scott, "We're going to check on this kid that's passed out over there, just to make sure he's okay. We had to carry him out of the bar a while ago 'cause he was so fucked up, man!"

Scott followed them over to the car that I was lying halfway under, and seeing me lying there passed out with my pants still around my knees, said to them, "Hey, I know him, that's Johnny Walker's little brother, Ronnie, what the hell happened to him?"

One of the guys said to Scott, "I don't know man, he came up from the bathroom that way, and could barely stand up so Antonio asked us to get him out of the place, so we got him over there between the cars. I'm sure he'll be all right once he sleeps it off."

Scott looked at me and then at the two guys standing there and said, "I know this kid, and he doesn't get that fucking drunk, man, something else is going on here. Here, let's see if we can rouse him."

He bent over me and rolled me out from under the car and reached down to try to pull my pants up and felt the pill package in my right front pants pocket. He reached in and pulled it out and said, "This guy's been taking *Dormadinas,* man! Shit, I don't know how many he's taken, but there are only four left in this pack! We'd better call an ambulance, he might have fucking OD'd!"

The first guy who had helped drag me out of the bar said to Scott, "Nah, man, he'll be all right, just let him sleep it off. I don't want an ambulance and the cops and shit showing up here, man! I don't want to get in any trouble, you know."

Scott looked the guy in the eye and said, "Listen asshole, he might have taken a fucking overdose. He could die right here, is that what you want, you shit for brains?"

Seeing the serious look in Scott's eye, the guy said, "Hey, man, do what you like, I don't care, but I'm getting out of here before the cops show up. I don't want any part of this shit!"

He and his buddy started walking towards the Glass House very quickly, totally forgetting about the drinks they had still waiting for them inside *Jefe's.*

Scott looked at them leaving and shouted, "All right you fucking chickenshits, get the fuck out of here then, I'll take care of this now."

He walked into *Jefe's* and said to Antonio, *"Mira Jefe, dejame usar su telefono, tenemos un problema bastante serio alli fuera."* "Listen boss, let me use your telephone, we got a pretty serious problem right outside."

He called the emergency number and within fifteen minutes, an ambulance showed up to the parking lot. Scott and some other people were standing there waiting for them. Scott handed one of the paramedics the more than half-empty package of *Dormadinas* and told him that these were what he thought I had been taking. They put me on a gurney and rushed me to the nearest hospital with the lights flashing and the siren wailing, still unable to wake me up.

Once in the hospital, they rolled me into the emergency room and they immediately stuck a long tube into my stomach and began pumping the contents out of it. Needless to say, I survived this ordeal and the next thing I knew, I was waking up in a hospital bed with my parents hanging over me both with very worried looks on their faces.

After they made sure that I was okay, my mom asked me, "Ronnie, why did you take so many of those sleeping pills, honey? Were you trying to kill yourself or what?"

I looked at her and said, "No, Mom, I wasn't trying to kill myself. I was just trying to get high, that's all."

"But why so damn many?" my dad asked in a very stern voice.

"Well, I took a couple, and I felt good, so I kept taking them to keep feeling even better. Dad, I'm sorry."

He gave me a very concerned look and said, "Well, son, you took a total of eight barbiturates, that's enough to kill a person. You're lucky that Scott called the ambulance, and they were able to pump your stomach when they did; otherwise you'd be dead. Do you understand that, son?"

"I'm sorry, Dad," I replied tearfully, "I wasn't trying to kill myself. I just was trying to get higher is all."

"Well, there are much better ways to get high than taking an overdose of pills, that's for sure! Now you have to promise me that you'll never do this again, do you understand?"

"Yeah, Dad, I promise," I said sincerely.

And to this day, I have a hard time taking any kind of pill and only do so when absolutely necessary. I owe my life to Scott Wilson, who with his courage and intelligence was a hero that night, and did indeed save my life. Thanks, Scott! I owe you my life, man.

A few years after all this had happened, and after my brother and Scott had missed their opportunity to move to Australia and make their lives there, I heard that somehow Scott ended up in the U.S. Army. I'm not sure if he enlisted or got drafted, but knowing him, I suspect that he was drafted. Sometime after that, I heard that again he was a hero, this

time in Vietnam. I'm not sure of the circumstances, but I understand that he came back from Vietnam in a body bag. He just didn't make in out of that damn place alive.

When I heard this news, it devastated me. Not only had Scott saved my life, but by being such a close friend of my brother's for so many years, he had a profound effect on me as well. His personality, his humor, and his love for life had a big influence on me and my development as a human being. He will forever be missed by all who knew him.   R.I.P. Scott Wilson.

At the age of fourteen or so, I was not exactly a really good-looking kid, with my scrawny frame, big glasses, and occasional acne, but for some strange reason, there were a few girls my age or a little younger who seemed to like me. I was developing my personality, and I was unconsciously borrowing from people around me whom I respected and admired, such as Scott Wilson, for example. When I say borrowing, I was actually just watching them and observing what people liked about them, and I'd try to copy what they did in my own personal way.

I realized that most people seemed to like those who had a sense of humor, so I tried to develop one for myself. I learned jokes that I could remember and tell and I always tried to laugh when other people tried to be funny even if sometimes they weren't so much. I also realized that people naturally gravitated towards someone who had a positive and uplifting outlook on life and were not negative and complaining about something or other all the time.

So I tried to develop these traits in myself in order to be well-liked and have more friends. I realized that self-confidence is the key to just about everything in life, and this was one trait above all that I tried to cultivate the most, which was difficult for a basically very shy kid like me. But I smiled a lot at people and always tried to have something good to say about everything and everybody and I think this is why I managed to have some kind of limited luck with the opposite sex.

The first real girlfriend I had was a girl a year younger than me by the name of Sevi. She went to ASM and was in the eighth grade while I was in the ninth. She lived in the *Generalissimo* area in a very nice *piso* with her mother and younger sister, and she had long dark hair and was very pretty, with big dark eyes. I thought I was in love, which I guess I was. Their *piso* had a nice view of El Estadio Bernabeu (the Real Madrid soccer stadium) from their balcony.

We spent a lot of time together at her house when her mother wasn't home, as well as hanging out together at the various places around the neighborhood, including the Glass House, *Jefe's*, and Woolworth's. She truly was my first true love, and I was very happy whenever we were together. She seemed to like me very much as well, since she told me that I was her very first real boyfriend and that she was still in the process of figuring out this whole boyfriend/girlfriend thing as well.

We experimented quite a lot and discovered the differences between the sexes but never went "all the way," as she would say, as we were young, and neither one of us was in a major hurry. Well, actually I was probably in a little more of a hurry than she was, but that was okay because I was in love and that's all that really mattered.

Around this time, I learned a lesson in life that has stuck with me ever since. It seems quite unfair, but I learned the hard way that if a guy has a girlfriend, then for some reason, other girls immediately find him to be much more attractive. If a guy (for all practical purposes) is unavailable, then other girls sometimes want him to be their boyfriend. Perhaps it's the challenge involved or just the ability to claim victory over another person (in this case the original girlfriend of the guy) that makes it more desirable to go after a guy that is already "taken" over a guy who is still available. And this is what happened with me and Sevi. Since I didn't go to school with Sevi and could only see her after school and on the weekends, there were many other girls that I saw around on a regular basis. One girl by the name of Katie rode the school bus with me, and we used to chat sometimes during the long bus rides to and from the base every day. Katie was a rather pretty girl with long light brown hair and a very nice smile. She had an older sister named Laura and a younger one, Shirley and all three girls rode the same bus that I did.

During one of our chats one morning, I casually mentioned that I was going with this girl named Sevi who went to ASM. Katie said that she knew her or at least had met her several times around town, and she too thought she was very nice. But I noticed a change in Katie as soon as she found out that I had a girlfriend. Suddenly she was friendlier towards me and wanted to chat with me almost every day. I was flattered by her attention and so I kept talking to her every day on the bus for several weeks.

So gradually and subtly, she somehow made it seem like it my idea to break up with Sevi and go out with her. I'm not sure how she did that — by using her considerable female charms, I imagine — but before I knew it; I was convinced that I would have a far better life, be more popular, be better looking, become a better person, get better grades, and be much happier overall if I broke up with Sevi and started going out with Katie.

Of course, it broke poor Sevi's heart when I gave her the bad news that I'd be breaking up with her. We were sitting in the Glass House one afternoon after school and I just told her that I had met another girl and since I didn't want to cheat on her; I was doing the honorable thing and letting her know I couldn't go out with her anymore. She asked me who the other girl was and, being honest, I told her who it was, and she took it not at all as I'd thought she would. She was furious, upset, disappointed, and so mad at me I really thought she was going to physically hurt me.

She ended up calling me every name in the book, and stormed out of the place, crying and carrying on like I'd never seen her act before. Immediately I felt shame, anger, and a great disappointment with myself for letting go of this beautiful sweet girl whom I really loved and had never had any problems with whatsoever, and who was obviously in love with me as well. How could I have done this to her, and indeed, to myself? What possible motivation could I have to do this awful thing to this innocent girl? What had possessed me to break this poor girl's heart when she had done nothing to me besides love me and care for me with all her heart? I'm still asking those same questions today and, as of yet, I still have found no answer.

Katie and I lasted less than two weeks before she moved on to another victim and the next conquest for her. Before our first date, which was to a dance on base, we were discussing our plans on the bus ride home from school and she asked me, "So, Ronnie, what clothes do you think I should wear to the dance on Friday?"

I just looked at her and replied, "Heck, Katie, I don't know, how am I supposed to know?"

She looked at me and said, "Oh, yeah, that's right, you don't know all my outfits yet, do you?"

"Um, no, I guess not."

"Well, I'll just wear my nice plaid skirt with my red sweater, how does that sound to you?"

"Whatever, Katie, whatever you'd like."

A couple of weeks later, it turned out that the next guy she set eyes on was my brother, who of course rode the same bus. I think Johnny lasted less time than I did as Katie's boyfriend before she just went on to the next victim after him. I think she had some serious self-worth issues going on, and needed to feel pretty and desirable, and her way of doing this was to constantly have new boyfriends all the time. But there are only so many guys out there and eventually they all caught on to her true nature and most left her well enough alone.

I tried to talk to Sevi again after Katie and I split up, but she wanted nothing to do with me at that point. In fact, she had even told all her friends what I had done to her, and that I was very bad news and to keep away from me. I was only fourteen, had my heart broken twice and had learned a valuable lesson the hard way. Thankfully, I wasn't discouraged for long since I was young and resilient and there were indeed more fish in the sea, just waiting to be caught.

The next girl whom I started seeing on a regular basis was named Megan, and she also went to ASM. She was a very pretty girl with blond hair and blue eyes and she lived in Aravaca near the campus of ASM. I had met her at one the big parties that her brother would throw regularly at their house. It was a huge place with a big swimming pool and several thousand square feet of living space. Obviously, her father had a great job or was very wealthy (or both probably), because the family even had a chauffeur to drive the kids around wherever they wanted to go. It was a small Spanish car, not a limousine or anything like that, but it certainly saved them on taxi fares and besides it was a way of her folks knowing where the kids were, or at least where they were dropped off.

The second party that I attended at their house was after Megan and I had been seeing each other for a while and we spent the entire time lying down, wedged behind the couch in the living room, between the wall and the back of the couch, pressed tightly together and making out. It was a strange experience lying so close to her while other people were sitting on the couch, literally inches from where we were, but not knowing we were there.

She was an unusual girl because she had no eyelashes at all for some reason. I asked her about what had happened to her eyelashes and she said something about accidentally burning them off one time, but that they would grow back eventually, but it would take some time.

Since she lived all the way out in Aravaca and going to school there at ASM, she would have the chauffeur drive her to our rendezvous after school, which was usually at the Glass House or *Jefe's*. We preferred *Jefe's* because there was more privacy there and we could do what we liked to do together which was to make out a lot. She liked having a boyfriend and I think I was her very first one. She liked a lot of physical contact, cuddling and holding each other tightly, kissing and fondling each other.

Again, we never did go "all the way," but we definitely enjoyed each other's company.

One afternoon, the chauffeur dropped Megan off by the taxi stand near the Glass House where I was waiting for her, and as usual he said he'd be back to pick her up in two hours. So we walked hand in hand over to *Jefe's* to spend a couple of hours together. As we walked up the couple of stairs to the back room of the place where the jukebox was and the tables and booths, we noticed that we were the only people in the place besides Antonio, the bartender.

We ordered a couple of cokes as we sat down in a booth and started making out as we usually did, nothing too serious, just kissing and holding each other, and whispering sweet nothings in each other's ears. After a few minutes, Antonio came up to us and asked us if we'd like to have some more privacy. I asked him what he had in mind, and he told us that there was a special table set up downstairs where we could be sure we were not disturbed by anybody. I looked at Megan and asked her what she thought and she said something like, "Sure, why not, it might be fun to be more private."

So we picked up our drinks and followed Antonio down the stairs where the bathrooms were and where old tables and chairs, cases of empty beer bottles and sodas, and some other unused bar equipment were all stored. And indeed, there was a nice booth set up in one corner all cleaned up and ready for our use.

So we sat down and continued to do what we had been doing upstairs and about five minutes later, we looked up and saw Antonio coming down the stairs with a very strange look on his face. He had his zipper open on his pants and he was pleasuring himself as he said something about what a nice place he had set up for us and maybe we should show some appreciation for his efforts.

I stood up immediately, shocked at what I was seeing, and started shouting at him for all I was worth, *"Cochino! Que piensas que estás haciendo, jilipollas! Vete de aqui! Sin verguenza! Cabron! Hijo puta!"* "You pig! What do you think you are doing, asshole! Get out of here! You're shameless! Bastard! Son of a whore!"

I was as angry as I'd ever been at anyone in my life, and he could see that I wasn't going along with the little plan that he had cooked up (whatever it might have been), and he turned around and ran back up the stairs muttering something about how sorry he was.

I looked at Megan and said to her, "Let's get the hell out of here! This guy's a fucking pervert!"

She stood up while buttoning her blouse, "You're right Ronnie, let's get out of here right now! That guy scared the hell out of me!"

Megan and I never went back to *Jefe's*, and the few times I ever did again, Antonio would never look me in the eye, and always had an embarrassed and shameful look on his face. One evening I was in the place with a couple of friends and I told the story about what had happened that one afternoon to my friend Mike, and Mike got very upset and told me I should go up to Antonio and demand an apology from him. I had already had a couple of beers by this time in the evening, and so with his encouragement, I went up to the bar and had the following conversation with him, (translated from Spanish...)

"Hey, Antonio, I think I deserve a deep apology from you for what happened that afternoon when I went downstairs with my girlfriend. You scared her terribly and I don't ever remember being so mad and upset. Don't you have anything you'd like to say to me?"

He looked at me and suddenly the shameful and embarrassed look he had around me before disappeared and he said the following in response: "Listen, sonny, what happened that afternoon was entirely your fault. After all, you were the one that had agreed to go downstairs with your little girlfriend and do shameful things together there in private. All I did was help you out and give you the privacy that you wanted so badly. So I actually did you a favor."

I gave him a look of astonishment and said, "And it's my fault that you were there fondling yourself on the stairs like that, scaring the hell out of my poor girlfriend?"

"Well, I figured that is what you two wanted when you agreed to go downstairs like that. I wasn't doing anything, anyway. Nothing would have happened if you hadn't gone downstairs like that!"

I looked at him again with a mixture of disgust and astonishment and shook my head and said to him, "Listen, you fucking asshole, don't try to turn things around here. You did something awful and disgusting, and I should report you to the fucking police! Except I know they'd probably never believe me, but if I ever hear about you doing something like this again, I will report it to the American military police, and they'll believe me! And your ass will be in jail like you deserve to be! Asshole!"

He looked at me and said, "I will not be talked to this way in my place. You get out of here right now and never come back. I don't ever want to see you in my place again, so leave right now!"

My friend Mike, who was standing right next to me this whole time, could tell that I was getting angrier and angrier by the second. He put his hand gently on my shoulder. "Come on, Ron, it's just not worth it, man. Let's just get the hell out of here, okay?"

We walked out of the place and my hands were shaking, I was so upset and angry. Mike said to me while trying to calm me down, "Fuck that place, man! And fuck that guy! Come on, let's go over to the Glass House and see what's going on over there."

I did return a few times again to *Jefe's*, but only when there was something special like a party or something going on and there were a lot of people there. Antonio never made eye contact with me and the subject never came up again.

A month or so later, the school year ended and Megan's father was transferred back to the States. Megan and I promised to write often and keep in touch. I received a couple of letters from her in Connecticut, and I responded to every one of them; then the letters stopped coming and I'm sure that she moved on with her life, and I did as well.

I learned another very valuable life lesson from this whole experience with Antonio and *Jefe's*. The fact that the "truth" is only what someone believes it to be, and anybody can make themselves believe just about anything if they have reason enough to do so.

I also learned that this world we live in can sometimes be a cruel, nasty, and wicked place full of people who have no honor and no respect for anyone else besides themselves, and sometimes not even that. I promised myself that I would never become one of those kinds of people, no matter what I did or what kind of person I was to become. And that I would always try to be a person with honor, integrity, and dignity because that is the kind of person I wanted to be, and the kind of people that I wanted to surround myself with as well. And I have strived to do so ever since, with varying degrees of success.

Chapter 11. Benidorm

"Everybody needs his memories.
They keep the wolf of insignificance from the door."
— *Saul Bellow*

Benidorm is a seaside resort on the eastern coast of Spain about fifty kilometers north of the city of Alicante, along the Valencia region's famed Costa Blanca. Until the early 1960s, Benidorm was a small fishing village. Today the town is one of Europe's and Spain's biggest holiday resorts and is responsible for a significant chunk of Spain's large tourist industry, with five million tourist arrivals per year.

The mid to late 1960s, when I spent some time there, was before masses of tourists had discovered it and made it one of the most popular vacation destinations in Europe. The advent of "package" tours in the late sixties is what really put Benidorm on the map as a travel and vacation destination. Suddenly, cold and weary people from places such as Britain, Belgium, Holland, Germany, and the Scandinavian countries could finally afford a week or two's stay in sunny Spain. With the hotel and air fare included for one low price, it made fun in the sun accessible for just about anyone. Tourists could not only get away from the dreary cold weather up north, but could enjoy the wonderful white sand beaches, partake in great traditional Spanish cuisine, and frolic amidst the fabulous nightlife that the coast of Spain offered.

Benidorm's two main sandy beaches, *Playa Levante* and *Playa Poniente*, are backed with palm-lined promenades and rows of skyscrapers, with their ground floors full of things for tourists to partake of, including shops, restaurants, bars, and nightclubs. The very mild winters and hot dry summers of the region also make it a perfect place to hang on the beach and get sunburned, which many tourists seemed to like to do.

The first time I went to Benidorm was during spring break of my sophomore year of high school, and I was amazed by the amount of tourism and the infrastructure set up for these masses of tourists. I had been to the coast of Spain before: in Peñiscola when I was much younger, as well as Alicante, where I had lived for over a year just a couple of years earlier, but these places had not prepared me for Benidorm. There seemed to be more foreigners than Spaniards in the town and almost everywhere, one could hear many languages spoken at once.

During the 1960s, Benidorm became a vacation destination for many high school kids from both MHS and ASM. It was the place to go for both spring break and summer vacation. Most kids just got on the train at the *Atocha* station in Madrid, and seven or eight hours later, got off in Benidorm. Many pooled their finances and rented a room or a small *piso* for the duration of their stay. They always had a great time hanging at the beach, visiting the many nightclubs all over town, and partying like there was no tomorrow. It became almost a rite of passage for many MHS kids to go to Benidorm and return with fabulous tales of drunkenness and debauchery. The party began as soon as the train left the station, and some arrived at their destination already nursing their first of many hangovers.

My first trip there involved a group of friends who were staying at a campground near the outskirts of town. It was the cheapest way to go, because a campsite cost a fraction of what a room would cost, and lots of people could fit in a campsite with various tents and vehicles. It was a short walk to the beach and to the main town, and we were young, strong, weren't in a hurry, and didn't have a lot else to do.

There were about five or six of us friends sharing one campsite and we had one vehicle between us. It was an almost brand-new 1967 Volkswagen "Campmobile." One of the guys' fathers had recently bought it in Germany (where these vehicles were made and were much cheaper than anywhere else), and he was planning on taking it with him when he rotated back to the states the following year. In the meantime, he had driven it to Benidorm for his son and his friends to enjoy.

The van had a very nice set-up for camping, with a small fridge, a sink, a stove, a foldout bed, and a top that popped up so one could stand up in it. Of course, Alan, the guy whose father owned the van, got to sleep in the nice bed, and the rest of us guys were relegated to our sleeping bags and tents, but we made the best of it and no one complained, since we all got the use of the stove and the fridge, and the rent was definitely right.

The second day we were there, we all went down to the beach and spent all day swimming in the warm Mediterranean Sea, sunbathing and watching the pretty girls in their skimpy swimsuits. We returned to the campground just before dark to prepare dinner, and I knew that I had gotten way too much sun. I was as red as a beet and I didn't feel very well at all. I was running a fever; I had chills and felt sicker than I had in a long time.

My friends were very worried about me, so my good friend Erik went to the owner/manager who lived in a small house at the entrance of the campground and told him about my situation. He was an older and wiser man and was convinced by Erik's tone of voice to come take a look. He got one look at me lying on my sleeping bag in the tent and knew that I was in bad shape, with a severe case of sunstroke. He told us that there wasn't much that could be done besides trying to keep me cool and hydrated and off the ground, and that I'd be all right in two days or so.

So Alan, being the kind and generous guy that he was, told me I could use the bed in the camp-mobile since it was off the ground and considerably cooler than either one of the tents. One of the guys had an electric fan that was plugged into an outlet in the van and I was able to have it blow on me while I lay there with a wet rag on my forehead.

The guys took good care of me and sure enough, in a couple of days I was feeling better, but I learned to respect the power of sunshine and the strong possibility of radiation poisoning with too much exposure to the sun, which is what a case of sunstroke actually is. I had a bad sunburn and my arms and legs and face were peeling, but I recovered in enough time to enjoy a few days of enjoying Benidorm before we had to return to Madrid. Coincidentally, that same VW van and I were to have other adventures together later in my life — but more on that in a later chapter.

My next trip to Benidorm was the following summer, and this time I went with my brother and one of his friends, Scott Wilson. We stayed at a small *piso* with several guys, including two English guys who were friends of Scott's who had been in Benidorm for several months by this time. They were named Ian and Matthew and were a few years older than we were, in their early twenties. They were both from London and they both liked to smoke hash a lot. In fact, it's what they seemed to do pretty much all day long.

Being slightly older (and British), they had a much different world view than we American high school kids. I had a long conversation with Ian one afternoon and I was picking his brain about what it was like in England. He told me that hash was plentiful there in London but was not as cheap as it was in Spain. The average price for good Moroccan hash was about one dollar per gram in Spain but was over twice that or even more in England. A five-gram chunk of hash was about the same size as a matchbox and was often sold in a matchbox to avoid having to weigh it every time.

He told me that he had been indulging in this activity for several years now and that his parents knew about his smoking, but they didn't seem to mind all that much. They just figured that if that is what he wanted to spend his hard-earned money on, then so be it. Of course, they had to be very discreet and were very careful about who they got it from and who they shared it with, both in England and in Spain. And they both seemed to really like Spain, not only for the cheaper prices on hash but also because of the warm climate, the great cheap seafood, and the pretty girls everywhere.

Ian and Matthew had a strange and different way of talking with their British accents, at least to our ears. They had one expression that they used between them that for some reason they thought was incredibly funny. It was, "Long-haired fellow, definitely yes, long-haired fellow, definitely yes, yes, yes!" This was used to indicate that someone was "cool" and that the person indicated with the long locks would be okay to discuss such things as the price and quality of hash. They used it so often that it caught on with us American high school guys and we started using it as well whenever we saw anyone with even slightly long hair.

One afternoon, I had just returned from the beach and walked into the small living room of the *piso* that we shared, and as usual, Ian, Matthew, and Scott were hanging around smoking hash and listening to music, when Scott walked up to me holding a matchbox in his hand and said, "Hey, Ronnie, look at the good shit we got today, check it out, man."

He handed me the matchbox. I took it from him; slid open the lid, looked inside, and saw a live cockroach, the same size as the box, with its little antennae waving at me. I jumped back about four feet in one step and drop the box to the floor while the guys roared on the floor laughing. After that it became a joke to hand me a matchbox whenever I was around and watch my reaction. It was all in good fun and I laughed just as hard as everybody else did.

Since I was the youngest of all the guys in the *piso*, they also looked after me after considerably to make sure that I kept out of trouble, which I managed to do for the most part. Ian and Matthew ended up visiting Madrid later that year, and I saw them again. During that visit, they helped my friends and I partake in another adventure that I will cover in a later chapter.

There is a small uninhabited island off the coast of Benidorm, called, appropriately enough, *La Isla de Benidorm*. It's located about three kilometers from the seafront and tourists can take boat rides from the mainland to the island to visit its wildlife, notably its population of wild peacocks. Due to these birds, it is sometimes also known as Peacock Island.

In 1966, a water-skiing facility called "Cable-Ski Benidorm" was created, becoming at that time the first cable water-ski system in the world. It consisted of four towers interconnected by a cable that enabled water-skiing without the use of a boat, and it was just a short distance from the Benidorm beachfront skyline. The entire circuit traversed over one kilometer and did a loop to take the skier back to the starting point: a platform anchored in the bay. Since I never was much of a

skier, either water or snow, I never attempted the cable-ski device, but plenty of other people did and it became one of the main attractions in Benidorm during the summer.

One sport that I did enjoy and that I really liked to partake in was snorkeling. I had started snorkeling as a young boy spending some time in Peñiscola, and I had continued during the time when I lived in Alicante. I was always fascinated by the incredible variety of life forms that could be seen as soon as I put my flippers and mask on and put my head under the water. In Benidorm, there was an area perfect for snorkeling just on the north side of the bay. There were lots of rocks there and it was away from the throngs of people hanging around the main beach.

One sunny afternoon during the following summer, when I returned again and spent a lot of time in Benidorm, I went to this area with a good friend of mine that everybody called Moose. He had some gear with him that I could use, including flippers and a mask, and he even had a small spear gun with which he was hoping to be able to catch some dinner. The area was great for this type of activity because not only were there a lot of large half-submerged rocks around, but there was also a considerable amount of seaweed, perfect for various types of fish and other aquatic creatures to congregate.

Moose had the spear gun, and I was following him while he slowly swam around looking for prey. There were several schools of smaller fishes around, but nothing large enough for him to try his spear gun on. The water was only about waist deep, so occasionally we would stand up and empty the accumulation of water that sometimes got under our masks and adjust our straps to try to prevent this small leakage.

After about a half an hour of snorkeling, I was standing up with my mask in my hands, spitting saliva into the inside of it to try to keep it from fogging up so much, when I felt something on my right leg. It felt a

little like seaweed brushing up against my leg, but it had a somewhat different feel, like something was actually sticking to my leg, not just brushing up against it. I put my mask on again and leaned over and looked down, and I saw *un pulpo* (a small octopus), with all eight of its arms suddenly wrapped around my leg!

Moose told me later that he had heard my yell and when he stood up and looked in my direction, it was the first time he had ever seen anybody walk (or actually run) on water. As soon as I saw what was on my leg, I immediately headed for shore as fast as I could with the *pulpo* still stuck to my leg, yelling and cussing the whole time. Somehow, with the help of my flippers, I don't even think I touched the bottom, but instead I just flew across the surface of the water.

When I got to shore and out of the water I tried desperately to try to pull the thing off my leg, but it had wrapped itself around me tightly and was not letting go. Finally, Moose showed up and between the two of us, we were able to yank the creature off my leg. I looked down and saw small round marks where the creature had used the suction cups on his arms to attach himself to my leg.

Moose was laughing hysterically the whole time; for some reason, he thought my reaction to being attacked by a *pulpo* was very amusing, especially the miracle I had performed of being able to walk on water. But once he calmed down somewhat and stopped laughing, he put the creature into a bucket he had brought along and we took a good look at it.

It wasn't that large a *pulpo* actually, only about three feet long or so from its round slimy head down to the last tentacle on its eight legs (or arms, depending how one looks at it). I had eaten *pulpo* in bars and restaurants before and knew that they were delicious when prepared properly, but otherwise could be very tough and chewy, much like trying to eat rubber bands. But since it was the only thing we had "caught" (or rather, had actually caught *me*) that day, Moose was determined to take it home and eat it.

When we got the octopus back to his place, Moose cleaned it very well, then he put it in a mixture of lemon juice and fresh water and let it soak for several hours, then he cooked it in a special sauce with more lemon, onions, garlic, and peppers and it came out to be quite tasty, even though it was a still little chewy, but that's the nature of *pulpo al aljillo*.

Moose was one of the guys that summer that was able to get a job in Benidorm. There was a chain of hamburger places in Spain called "Wimpy's," with several locations along the coast of Spain, especially where a lot of British people lived. It was a British fast food franchise and was named after the chubby sidekick of "Popeye's" in the comic books, who wore a bowler hat and was always eating a hamburger. Moose, along with my brother, and several other friends, had been able to get jobs at the location in Benidorm and by supplementing their money with part–

time work, they were able to extend their vacation for almost the entire summer. So I hung around the "Wimpy's" a lot that summer, because it was possible for those working there to discretely slip their friends some free meals when the boss wasn't around.

Benidorm was a very modern place by most standards. And because of the huge amount of tourism that was beginning to appear there and the vast amount of money that was pouring into the town, a lot of innovative companies started very modern and almost futuristic types of businesses, at least for the 1960s. Not only was Benidorm the location of the world's first cable-ski system, but there were other very modern innovations and businesses as well.

There was one cafeteria right across from the beachfront that had instituted a new and unique way of selling products to the public. Instead of having waiters coming around and asking people what they wanted, then returning a little later with those items, the customer would sit down at a table and then walk up to a glass-enclosed conveyor belt with different things to eat and drink behind small windows, and with the name and price for each item right below the window.

The customer would then just open the window with the item he desired, reach in and remove it and take it back to his table. There was a man in a white jacket making notes of everything the customer removed from the windows and would present the customer with his bill before he left. The kitchen staff would keep busy checking what items were being removed and constantly replenishing them. Beverages such as coffee or soda with ice would be hand-delivered by the waiters in white, but all food items were on the conveyor belt, which was constantly slowly moving by, enabling the customer to see all the choices available.

The name of the establishment was *La Cafeteria Del Futuro,* or something like that, but it never really caught on all that well. No one knew for sure how long the food items had been sitting there behind the window, and even though there were hot lights that kept the food warm, it was still a mystery sometimes about how fresh it was or wasn't. And the prices were actually a little higher than a comparable place with the same items due to the novelty of the place, but in all actuality, the prices should have been lower since the customer did half the work of bringing his own food to his table.

Another very modern element found in Benidorm were the discotheques. Again, because of the enormous amount of foreign capital coming into the town recently from the drastic increase in tourism, there was intense competition between businesses, and the discos were no exception. There were three very modern discotheques located in one triangular-shaped plaza downtown, and they all competed for the disco-goers' *pesetas*. Because of this, each one tried to outdo the other with the latest in sound and light systems.

Two in particular come to mind that seemed to have the most innovative and modern sound systems and light shows. The *007 Club* had a James Bond kind of atmosphere with several bars and a huge dance floor with pulsating colored lights and even strobe lights and "black" lights, both of which were becoming very popular. The *Piper's Club* was in direct competition and it also had the latest in modern technology to appeal to their patrons. We were never sure whether the "pipe" in their name was about the "Pied Piper" or about a different kind of pipe used for smoking, even though their logo indicated the former.

The music played at these discotheques was not what we now know as "disco" music, but instead was the latest in Rock-and-roll, soul, psychedelic, blues, and any other modern music that was easy to dance to. And all by the latest popular groups and singers, played at a volume and through a sound system that made it impossible not to want to dance like crazy. And these places were where single people went to meet other singles of the opposite sex, so there was a lot of dancing with strangers and heavy drinking going on.

There was usually a small cover charge and the prices for drinks were slightly more than at other places, but it was a small price to pay for experiencing the latest in entertainment technology. The discotheques of Benidorm became legendary all over Europe for the amazing nightlife they offered the party-goers of the time. The excitement of dancing wildly to the latest music while being bombarded by strobe lights and under black lights created an otherworldly atmosphere unlike anything else, especially after downing a few *cuba libres* and perhaps a toke or two of hash.

One Saturday afternoon, my friend J.P. and I were hanging around the beachfront after having just finished eating a free Wimpy's burger that our buddy Dave had managed to slip us, when we saw these two very beautiful girls slowly walking by. They looked like they were rather lost and didn't seem like they were really going anywhere in particular, so J.P. and I started up a conversation with them. It turned out they were sisters and were from Oslo, Norway, and they both spoke perfect English and were in Benidorm for a family holiday. The oldest was seventeen and her sister was fifteen, and both had long blond hair, blue eyes, and seemed to be quite friendly towards us, especially when we told them we were Americans.

They told us that their parents were in a bar having a few drinks and they were just taking a walk around trying to find something to do. They also told us they had been in town just a few days by then for a one-week holiday. They'd soon have to return to cold and gray Norway, but in the meantime, they were enjoying themselves in sunny Spain.

We chatted for quite a while before they asked us what a fun thing was to do around town after dark. J.P. asked the older girl, whose name was Helga, if they had been to the 007 Club yet, and she replied that they had been nowhere besides the beach and out to eat with their parents so far, but she and her sister Franny would really love to go clubbing if they had someone to take them because their parents wouldn't allow them to go alone to a place like that.

So J.P., in all his wisdom, told her that he and his friend Ron would be more than delighted to accompany them to the disco if they'd like. Helga said that would be very nice but that we'd be required to meet their parents before we could take them out. J.P. said that would be no problem whatsoever, so off the four of us went off to find their parents who were drinking in a nearby bar.

It didn't take long to find the bar where Helga and Franny's parents were. It was a small bar just a couple of blocks from the beachfront and was a place frequented by lots of other Scandinavians, including a good number of Swedes and Danes, as well as Norwegians. The girls' parents were in a happy mood when we approached them, since they were in a lively conversation in Norwegian with another couple about something that we couldn't understand. They were quite friendly to us after Helga introduced us and she told them that we'd like to take them to the 007 disco that night. Helga's father took a good look at us and said that would be fine as long as we got them back at the reasonable hour of midnight. We assured him that we would and that we'd make sure that they did not get in any trouble whatsoever and that they would have a great time.

We left the bar with the two sisters and accompanied them back to their hotel and told them that we'd pick them up at eight o'clock right inside the lobby of their hotel. They thanked us and said they had to get ready but they were looking forward to going with us that night, and they'd see us then.

J.P. and I walked away feeling that we had really lucked out that afternoon, getting dates with these two incredibly beautiful Norwegian sisters, who were not only very attractive but seemed to be very nice and friendly as well. We were very excited when we went back to the *piso* where we were staying to get a shower and change clothes for our big date that night.

J.P. was the kind of guy who couldn't live without his tunes, so back at the room we were sharing; he had his portable Panasonic record player going all the time we were there, playing the stack of albums he brought with him from Madrid. One of the albums that he had with him was one that had just recently been released called "Electric Ladyland" by the Jimi Hendrix Experience. One of the songs on the album was Jimi's version of a Bob Dylan song entitled, "All Along the Watchtower." The third verse goes like this:

> *"No reason to get excited,*
> *The thief he kindly spoke,*
> *There are many here among us,*
> *Who feel that life is but a joke."*

While listening to Jimi's version of this song, he said, "Hey, Ronnie, you know this song is about us, don't you, man?"

I gave him a blank look, "Um, what do you mean, J. P.? How is this song about us?"

"Well, listen to the verse here, man, can't you hear Jimi singing, 'Norwegians to get excited'?"

I start laughing hysterically and said, "You're right, man, 'Norwegians to get excited', that is what it sounds like and it pretty much matches our situation right now, doesn't it?"

He looked at me and laughed too and said, "You're right, I'm starting to get pretty excited about some Norwegians, aren't you?"

"You'd better believe it man, you'd better believe it!"

So a little before eight that night, we headed off to the hotel where Helga and Franny were staying, both of us feeling a bit apprehensive but getting pretty excited about these Norwegian ladies, regardless of what Jimi said about no reason to be. Scandinavians, including Norwegians, had a reputation in Spain at the time as being very promiscuous and very sexually liberated, so we both felt that we very well might have an extraordinary evening waiting for us indeed.

They were right on time waiting for us in the lobby of their hotel and they looked even more attractive than they did that afternoon at the beachfront. Helga had on a light blue mini-skirt and her hair was hanging down past her shoulders. Franny was wearing a bright yellow pair of hot pants and she had her hair up in a nice pile on her head. They both looked incredibly beautiful, and we told them so, to which they said "Thank you," in a very polite, shy, and unassuming way.

J.P. and I had decided earlier that since he was almost two years older than I was, he would go for the older sister, Helga, and I would take her younger sister, Franny, which was fine by me because I thought she was the cuter of them, anyway. So when we walked over to the 007 Club along the sidewalk, he walked next to Helga and I walked next to her sister, chatting and getting to know each other a little better. It turned out that Franny was to be in the tenth grade when school resumed after the summer break and she loved animals very much, especially horses. She thought one day she might become a veterinarian. I told her about my school in Madrid and the fact it was located on an American Military base and then she asked me if I was interested in one day being in the military. When I told her absolutely not, especially with the war in Vietnam going on, she understood my feelings immediately.

When we got to the entrance of the discotheque, the large burly man at the door wearing a white shirt and black tie took our cover charge fee, which was 100 pesetas each. Once inside the place, we were bombarded with extremely loud music, flashing pulsating lights, and throngs of people dancing on the huge dance floor.

We made our way to one of the bars and ordered beers for us and *Cuba libres* for the girls. We made our way slowly over to one of the few remaining unoccupied tables and the four of us sat down. We had to get very close to each other to make ourselves heard over the deafening music and I got a whiff of Franny's sweet perfume while talking right into her ear.

After a couple of songs went by, the DJ played a song by the Stones titled "Paint It Black," and I asked Franny to dance. So we went up to the dance floor, and we did not leave until almost a half an hour later when we were both so exhausted and thirsty that we were forced to retreat to our table to wet our throats, both of us sweating profusely, even though the place had decent air conditioning. I excused myself and got up to use the restroom and while walking to it, I stared intently at the posters hanging on the walls, and with black lights shining on them, they looked surreal, especially a couple I noticed that were prints by the artist Peter Max. The black light effect made the posters seem even more psychedelic than they actually were, and I stood there a long time just staring at them.

When I finally made my way back to the table, Franny asked me what had taken so long and I told her about the posters with the black lights. She insisted on seeing them, so I took her by the hand and led her through the crowd over to where the art prints were located.

She took one look and said, "Oh, wow!" We stood under the black lights for a few minutes as she marveled at how the colors of her clothes had changed under the effect of the lights and she noticed how my lips seemed almost black, and everything that was white seemed to glow.

Meantime J.P. had bought another round of drinks for all of us, so we went back to the table and sat down again while chatting over the loud music and getting to know each other better. The girls seemed to be enjoying themselves immensely, but after a couple more hours and several drinks later, it was time to go.

As we stepped out of the club, J.P. glanced at his watch and noticed that it was only a little after 11, so he suggested we all take a stroll down to the waterfront and look at the sea for a while before taking the girls back to their hotel. The four of us sat down on the wall along the beachfront and chatted some more while we watched the moon set over the Mediterranean Sea. I put my arm around Fanny and she leaned her head against my shoulder and suddenly everything seemed just about perfect for that one moment. Here I was with this beautiful and wonderful girl who I was starting to fall in love with, along with my best friend and his girl and we were watching half of this yellow moon slowly setting into the sea. It was a magical moment and forever will be ingrained in my mind.

But as all wonderful and magical moments do, it ended way too early, as J.P. looked again at his watch and told us that if we were to make it back to their hotel before their curfew, we had better get going. So the four of us reluctantly got up and slowly walked back to the hotel, arriving just a few minutes before midnight. Before saying good night, J.P. asked the girls if they'd like to try the Piper's Club the next night. They nodded their heads enthusiastically and so it was agreed we'd meet the next night at the same time and same place.

The next night was a repeat of the night before but instead of hanging out at the 007 Club, we were at Piper's Club all night. Their sound system and lights were comparable to the 007 Club, but they also had go-go dancers dancing in large cages which were hung from the ceiling. Girls in tight mini-skirts and go-go boots would climb small ladders to get inside them and spend half the night gyrating and dancing away inside these cages. I wasn't sure if they were actual customers, or were employees of the club hired to dance, or maybe they were a combination of the two. Either way, it did add something to the atmosphere to see these beautiful girls high overhead dancing away inside cages.

Again we danced until we were drenched in sweat even though the air conditioning was working fine. Now and then the DJ would play a slow song, and that's when I always made sure that we got up to dance. Franny seemed to like the slow dancing as much as I did because she always put her head on my shoulder as we made slow circles around the dance floor, holding each other tight with the lights flashing and the music ringing in our ears.

There was one area of the dance floor that had lights actually set into the floor. It had a series of two-foot square clear glass tiles, each with a different colored light flashing inside the floor that were synchronized with the music somehow, so the flashing lights would be perfectly in beat with whatever song was playing. The clear glass acted almost as a mirror at times when the lights briefly went out for a moment between flashing, so it was possible to look down and see the reflection of whoever was standing over them. The girls in their mini-skirts didn't seem to care that much that one could look down and see all the way up to their panties since they were too busy dancing and enjoying themselves, but it was quite a treat for a sixteen-year-old boy like myself.

The night came to an end too quickly and again we walked the girls down to the beach for a little while before taking them home. This time before the night ended, I gave Franny a long and very wet kiss after we had walked along the beach for a while with the waves gently lapping the sand. She seemed to enjoy it as much as I did and I felt that we were really getting somewhere in our relationship even though we had only known each other for two days.

The next day we met them again, but this time during the day for a beach date. We found an unoccupied umbrella on the beach during the late afternoon and the four of us sat under it trying to squeeze together to all fit under the sparse shade that it provided. J.P. and I were delighted to spend the afternoon with these two beautiful girls, especially since they were both wearing the skimpiest of bikinis. Of course, we spent a lot of time in the sea, swimming and splashing in the waves, which I was grateful for because the cold water helped to keep down the semi-erection that I seemed to have had all day long. I kept hoping the girls wouldn't notice the little pup tent I had pitched in my bathing suit.

Right before sunset, we went over to a cafe overlooking the sea for a drink and a snack, and watched the sunset changing the blue Mediterranean Sea to a hundred different colors.

I asked Franny, "So Franny, how do you like Spain and Benidorm in particular? Has it met your expectations so far?"

She looked at me and gave me her wonderful smile which made her entire face light up and replied, "Well, Ron, it has been absolutely wonderful, and I think I've had the best time of my life here. It has been even nicer and more wonderful than I thought it would be. When we return to Oslo tomorrow, I will bring with me not only a very nice tan, but many great memories as well, thanks to you and J.P."

I looked at her with a devastated look on my face that I couldn't control and said, "Tomorrow? You're leaving tomorrow already? I can't believe it!"

"Yes, we have to go to the airport in Alicante early in the morning to catch our flight back home. I'm sorry we have to leave also, but you knew we are only here for a week-long holiday, right?"

I tried to compose myself and looked at her with all the sincerity I could muster and said, "Well, I just wish we could have had some more time together, we were just starting to get to know each other."

"I know Ron, I feel the same way. But maybe we can talk our folks into coming here again next year for a holiday and we can see each other again, perhaps?"

"Okay, I guess that will have to do then," I sighed disappointedly.

I looked at her and she looked at me and we both knew that the probability of that happening was so slim as to be next to none, but we smiled at each other anyway and I rubbed my eyes trying to keep the tears from forming, realizing another very important life lesson at that moment.

Life is fleeting and we're only here for the moment, nothing more. Life and love can both be very cruel and callous to our feelings, our ambitions, and our desires. Our wants and needs are almost always controlled by outside forces, and all we can do is to try to make the best of the circumstances and situations that we find ourselves in. And try to remember what a very wise man said once, 'Just keep on keeping on.'

As we walked the girls back to their hotel for the last time, all four of us were feeling rather down and sad, each in our own thoughts and wondering why life could be so unfair at times. But when it came time to say goodbye in front of the lobby, I put my arms around Franny and gave her the longest and deepest kiss I'm sure that she had ever gotten in her short life. I told her, "Franny, I just want to let you know that I really think you are the most wonderful and beautiful girl that I have ever met in my life and I am so sad that we have to part like this, but you and the time we spent together will always be a special memory in my heart, forever."

She looked at me with her eyes sparkling and whispered, "Ron, I feel the same way, you will also always hold a special place in my heart as well. But who knows, maybe we will see each other next summer."

I looked at her, trying to hold back my tears, and said, "Yeah, maybe, you never know."

J.P. and I watched as the girls walked into the lobby and then they both turned around and gave a little wave and Franny blew a little kiss in my direction and gave me her wonderful smile for the last time.

We walked away each feeling a lump in our throats and thinking how things could have been different if only we had a little more time with them. And I then realized that this might be the last time I would see Benidorm. Later that summer I would turn seventeen, and then in September, I'd begin my senior year in high school. The following summer, I would graduate, and the plan was for my family and me to return to the States and for me and my brother to start college there and begin our lives in our home country.

J.P. looked at me, smiled, and said, "Well, I guess there are no more Norwegians to get excited about, huh, Ronnie?"

"Yeah, I guess you're right, John, I guess you're right, man. Too bad though, huh?"

Chapter 12. Canillejas

"The whims of youth break all the rules."
—Homer, the Iliad

Canillejas is an ancient village near Madrid, Spain, lying to the northeast of the city on the way to Barajas International Airport and Torrejon Air Force Base. In the days when I knew the area well, it was the last suburb before reaching the *campo*, or countryside. Heading towards the center of the city, its main street becomes the Calle de Alcalá, which has many of Madrid's landmarks including Las Ventas Bullring, Retiro Park, and eventually ending at La Puerta de Sol. Today there is a Metro (subway) station in Canillejas and it's one of the last on the number five line of the Madrid Metro system. But in the 1960s and 70s, there was only a *tranvia* (streetcar) that connected the town to the center of Madrid.

The main *autopista* (highway) that runs to Barajas, Torrejon, Alcalá de Henares (the birthplace of Miguel de Cervantes), and points beyond, is just to the north of the old main town of Canillejas. This highway divides the older original section of the town from the newer and more modern area on the north side of the highway which is where many Americans and other foreigners lived. This was also where a housing area known as *Las Palomas* (the Doves) was located.

The reason so many Americans lived in Canillejas was because of its proximity and easy access to Torrejon Air Base. Las Palomas was an area with several apartment complexes, but there were spacious homes in the area as well, which many Americans rented, with large yards, garages, and plenty of room for their families.

Since the town is located on the outskirts of Madrid, and near open country, there was a campground on the north side of the highway called *Camping Osuna*, as well as a hotel by the same name. The campground today is full of modern RV's and motor homes, but in the late 1960s and early 70s it was mostly people camping in tents. There was the occasional VW camp-mobile (like the one we used to camp in Benidorm), and other types of homemade campers and vans.

This place did attract the budget tourist, sometimes even the backpacker kind, and at times there were rather strange young people staying there, from just about everywhere in the world. It could be an adventure to walk down among the shady trees of the campground to see what was going on. One just never knew what kind of people would be staying there. Most of the time, they were very friendly and open to interesting conversations. I envied the freedom that some of these people enjoyed, and it made me want to do the same perhaps someday.

The Hotel Osuna, on the other hand, had a different clientele, because the hotel was a rather fancy place with a swimming pool, a very nice restaurant, and a meeting center where business conventions were held regularly.

The old part of Canillejas was much different from the newer part on the other side of the highway, for in many ways it was a typical Spanish village with most of its population consisting of working-class families living in apartment buildings, along with the usual number of bars, restaurants, and other businesses. But since it was outside of the city of Madrid proper, it did have a very typical Spanish small-town feel. Walking around the streets of old Canillejas was almost like walking back in time, to a simpler Spain, much less complicated and busy than the modern city only a few kilometers away.

But on the other side of the highway and across the bridge where the Americans and other foreigners lived, it was quite a different place. Being very modern with newer apartment buildings and houses, these places with their swimming pools, tennis courts, beautiful grounds, and all the modern conveniences of the twentieth century were luxurious compared to the village across the highway.

There were two reasons why I spent a lot of time in Canillejas in the late 1960s. The first reason was that my mother had become very good friends with a very nice Spanish lady by the name of Maruja who lived in Canillejas, in the Las Palomas area. Maruja's husband, Jose, worked for

MovieRecord, which was a Spanish company that provided foreign films for the Spanish television market.

Maruja and my mom had met at the Chalet Suizo restaurant, the restaurant that my parents owned in downtown Madrid. Maruja was an entertainer and played guitar and occasionally sang at various venues around town. Her focus was mostly Spanish folk songs, but she sang some contemporary songs as well. She was well liked by all who knew her, and she seemed to know just about everybody in Madrid at the time.

She had a son about my age by the name of Juan, and I quickly became good friends with him and his group of friends in Canillejas. They would often throw elaborate parties and would invite a mixture of Spanish and American people. Occasionally, they would have a barbecue and would roast an entire lamb outside on an open fire. It would take all day long to cook the beast, and it would always be accompanied with lots of beer and sangria.

The sangria would be made up in a large washtub and would consist of dozens of bottles of *vino tinto*, several bottles of brandy, various fresh fruit slices such as lemons, oranges and limes, and then a couple of cups of sugar. They would then add lots of ice to keep the mixture cold all day long until the lamb was finished cooking and the feast could begin.

These parties always included lots of singing, dancing, and guitar playing. Juan was a very accomplished guitar player like his mother, but the guitar usually was passed around for anybody to try a song or two. These parties would always last until the early morning hours and everyone would have a great time.

Juan's friends consisted of a group of Spanish guys that lived in Las Palomas and were a great bunch of people to know. Paco was their ringleader but the other guys, Miguel and Luis, were just as interesting. I learned a lot from these guys, not only about what it was like to be a young, fairly wealthy, and good-looking Spaniard living in Madrid, but also a lot about modern Spanish culture as well. Paco was quite political and he would carry on heated discussions for hours about Franco and the evils of tyranny and Fascism.

As in most parts of the world during the 1960s, Spain was also in a state of cultural change and was becoming something new and different. Indeed, the youth revolution was alive and well in Spain in the turbulent 1960s. Long hair, rock-and-roll music, and drugs were all a part of Spaniards' lives at the time, but with a unique and distinctly Spanish flavor. And I embraced it all as just another example of the incredible changes that were going on in the world at the time.

The other reason I spent a lot of time in Canillejas was that I became great friends with a schoolmate by the name of Bill Johnson who lived in a very nice house in Canillejas with his large family. He and I seemed to hit it off from the first time we met in a classroom at MHS, and we ended up spending a lot of time together. His family was from South Carolina, and he and his family would end up being a very strong and influential part of my life for many years to come.

One thing that Bill and I had in common was our love for motorbikes and motorcycles. I had always liked bikes of all kinds since I was very young; my friend Wally Padilla had a *Solex* motorbike for a while. These types of mopeds were usually used by postmen and for other delivery services and the *VeloSoleX* Company had been around for a long time, originally based in Paris, France. The Solex was a bicycle with a small motor resting on the front wheel of the bike. One would pedal it like a bike but could engage the motor to help get up hills or when one's legs got tired.

There wasn't a drive chain as on most motorbikes, but instead the motor turned a rubber wheel that, when lowered onto the front tire would turn the tire and move the bike forward. Of course, Wally and I tried to soup up the one he had, but with its small engine, it never really went much faster than one could pedal a bicycle. Nevertheless, it was a lot of fun and the first type of motorbike I ever rode.

Among my friends in Madrid, there was a group of us that all had motorbikes or mopeds, of all types and styles. The laws in Spain at the time allowed anyone, regardless of age, to ride a motorbike if the cubic displacement of the engine was less than 50 cubic centimeters. Many manufacturers made motorbikes with 49 cc engines to appeal to this group of people. Another law was that if a bike was over 50 cc's, but less than 75 cc's, one had to be sixteen years of age to ride it, so there were quite a few 74 cc bikes as well. And neither of these two sizes of bikes required a driver's license or permit to operate, nor a license plate of any kind, just a bill of sale or a title if one was stopped, to be able to prove ownership if necessary.

Anything larger than a 75 cc bike was considered a motorcycle and not just a moped and required at least a motorcycle license and registration of the bike to operate it. The Spanish motorcycle industry was (and is to this day) one of the greatest in the world, especially when it comes to smaller two-stroke engines, both for the street and for the dirt (off-road riding). Spanish manufacturers such as Bultaco, Montesa, and Ossa had claimed almost the entire market at the time, especially in Europe. Other brands such as Ducati (made in Italy) had a line of similar bikes but the ones from Spain were the most popular among the people I knew.

The reason Spain had such a large selection of motorcycles, motorbikes, mopeds, and scooters was that these machines proved to be not only economical to buy and operate but also because they were great in traffic, especially in large cities where the number of vehicles on the small narrow streets could be overwhelming at times. The difference between a moped and a motorbike can be confusing, but the basic rule is

that mopeds always had pedals and almost always had an open area between the knees where the gas tank usually goes on a motorbike. Also, most mopeds only had one gear, so there wasn't a clutch or a gear changing device; one just turned the throttle on the right handlebar to accelerate and used the front and rear brakes to stop. These bikes were almost always 49 cc's and were used by just about anyone, including women and older children. They were an alternative to riding a bicycle and were fun and economical to ride.

A motorbike, on the other hand, had a gas tank in the area between the knees and a long seat suitable for two passengers. Some had pedals like a moped but not always. They also almost always had a transmission (usually with only three gears) with a clutch on the left handlebar, and the throttle on the right handlebar. The gearshift was usually controlled by a lever near the left foot, while the back brake was controlled by a lever by the right foot, just like a regular motorcycle. Some models (like Ducati) had the gear shifter mounted on the left handlebar that was operated by twisting the controller while pulling in the clutch next to the gear shifter.

A very popular brand of this type of motorbike in Spain was a brand called *Derbi*, which was a favorite among most of the people whom I knew and rode with. One reason they were so popular was that the cylinder

heads between the 49 cc and the 74 cc were interchangeable; that is to say that one could take the cylinder and the head off a 49 cc motor and put on a 74 cc cylinder and head and have a more powerful and faster motorbike that looked like just a 49 cc model. Derbis were the only bike that we knew at the time that we could "soup up" like this with very little effort, since a new head and cylinder only cost a few hundred pesetas but would make the bike 50% more powerful and faster. Of course, it still only had three gears, so when we got the bike up to faster speeds, the third gear would wind out and make a high-pitched whine waiting to be shifted into the next gear (the fourth) that it just didn't have.

There was nothing like the thrill of taking a 49 cc Derbi that had been upgraded to 74 cc's out on a straightaway, or better yet on a long downhill grade, and winding that third gear out to a point where one would wonder if the cylinder would explode right out of the head, which these types of modified motorbikes would sometimes do. That was all part of the thrill and the excitement of riding these types of bikes. There were no helmet laws in those days, so any wipe-out could be devastating to say the least, especially when speeds could reach over 100 kilometers per hour or more.

The sport of racing motorbikes and motorcycles was and still is very popular in Spain, both street racing and off-road racing. The races were divided into different categories depending on the size of the motors and

the engine displacement. The smallest size was the 50 cc category, and these special racing bikes looked much different from the factory-made ones. The street racers had a fairing on the front to help with wind resistance and very thin wheels and tires, along with a stripped-down frame to help cut down on the weight. The less weight, the faster the bike could go. And just as with horse racing, the smaller the rider, the faster the bike could go as well. Derbi was one of the main manufacturers of these small bikes and usually won most of the races in the 50 cc category.

My favorite kinds of motorbikes were the off-road types rather than the street-racing kind. There was nothing like the freedom of having a machine that allowed you to go virtually anywhere, over any terrain and without even the need of a road. This kind of bike was made specifically for this type of application and they usually had up-swept fenders to keep mud and other debris from getting stuck between tire and fender, higher handlebars to keep the rider in more of an upright position (necessary to be able to rise off the seat to avoid some of the major bouncing), and an up-swept muffler to avoid the possibility of the muffler being submerged if the rider was crossing water of any kind, which these machines were capable of doing to a certain extent. Of course, knobby tires were essential on an off-road bike to help get better traction on a dirt surface.

Bultaco made a small 100 cc off-road bike called the *Lobito* (the little wolf) that was a favorite among fledgling motorcyclists like myself and others. Of course, they made off-road bikes with larger engines as well, such as the Bultaco Scrambler 250 cc. Other manufacturers such as Ossa and Montesa had their own lines of both street and off-road bikes as well, and there was great competition between the various manufacturers to outdo the competition and to create a better machine that was capable of winning the races that were held regularly all over Spain.

One reason Canillejas was so popular among the friends I knew who loved motorbikes (especially the off-road type), was that since the town was on the outskirts of Madrid, there was plenty of open *campo* (country) to ride in. To the north and west of *Las Palomas*, there was open land for many square kilometers with nothing but open fields with small dirt trails and paths that the sheepherders would use to move their sheep from one area to the next, or the occasional horse or burro would use, possibly pulling a wagon.

This area on the outskirts of the city was also notorious for the bands of gypsies who would occupy these areas for certain lengths of time. Gypsies in Spain were like gypsies anywhere, in that they would roam the countryside and set up their camps wherever there was open land, yet close enough to a population center where they could ply their trades to make some money. Spanish gypsies usually rode in caravans of several families along with their wagons, horses, burros, dogs, chickens, etc.

They would find a place that suited them and just set up their camp, apparently unconcerned about whose land it was or what it was being used for. If and when they were asked to move, they would simply pack up and find another location that worked for them.

Throughout history, gypsies had their own separate society and rarely if ever would they intermingle with anyone who was not a fellow gypsy. In Spain and in many other countries of the world, the gypsies were looked on as slightly less than full citizens, and if there existed any type of discrimination that Spaniards exhibited to any other people, it was most likely towards the gypsies. This was because if there was a crime committed anywhere in Spain, it was usually something that a gypsy did. They were notorious pickpockets, swindlers, and petty thieves, and were generally looked down on by most of Spanish society. Perhaps for this reason, they lived on the outskirts of society, both realistically and figuratively.

The few encounters I myself had with gypsies were usually of very little consequence. I left them alone and they in turn left me alone. But it was interesting and a slight thrill when riding motorbikes around the outskirts of Madrid to the north of Canillejas and coming across a gypsy camp and seeing just how different and ancient their culture and society was. They were opportunists; if an old abandoned building was around, they would set up their camp near it and use it for a windbreak and

perhaps to house their animals. And if any chance came up to make a few pesetas, they would jump on it and do whatever they had to in order to survive.

But I personally felt that they seemed to have a sense of honor among themselves, and a dignity and mystery about them that was hard to pinpoint exactly. Their culture almost predates modern history, being that their origin is lost in antiquity and the fact that today they exist in almost every corner of the world.

Ironically enough, a great deal of the culture of Spain is closely tied to the mystery and traditions of the gypsy and these have influenced many things that people consider truly "Spanish," such as *El Flamenco*. Both the dance and the music had their origins in gypsy culture and history. I found them to be quite a fascinating people and culture.

Indeed, I did ride quite a few mopeds, motorbikes, and motorcycles during my time in Spain, not only around the outskirts of Canillejas, but around other areas of Madrid as well, thanks mostly to my good friend Bill Johnson. Bill was a fanatic when it came to bikes; it seemed that he could never have enough of them, so he would steal them, and sometimes I would help him.

The garage next to his family's home was often filled with up to a dozen different bikes at a time. He told his parents that they belonged to friends of his, and that he was working on them in his spare time, doing tune-ups and other minor repairs. They bought his story because there were always a lot of guys hanging around the garage along with the many bikes.

It started innocently enough. One day Bill and I were hanging out near the Glass House and he spotted a nice Montesa 49 cc motorbike leaning up against a telephone pole near an alley. We were looking at it and just admiring its nice lines when Bill noticed that it didn't have a lock on it. Most motorbikes in Spain at the time used a type of lock that is usually used on bicycles, the long thick cable kind that wraps around one tire or the frame and attaches the bike to a pole, a fence or to a bike stand. Few motorbikes had any other kind of locking device, such as a key to start it or a handlebar lock.

So, he looked at me with a mischievous look and said, "Hey, Ron, let's take it for a ride, you want to?"

I looked back at him with what I imagine was a rather bewildered expression and asked, "You mean, just like, take it?"

"Yeah, man, let's just ride it around for a while. If anyone says anything, we'll just say that we thought it was our buddy's bike, and he said we could ride it, okay?"

I thought about it for a moment and finally said, "All right, what the hell, let's do it, man!"

He took the bike and started to push it down the alley and said, "Let's get it out of here a little bit before we start it up, just in case the guy's around and hears it."

I walked along beside him while he pushed the bike down the alley for a while, then he stopped, climbed on the saddle, opened the gas valve to allow the gas to enter the carburetor, held the clutch in to make sure it was in neutral, kicked the pedal, and it started right up. He looked at me and said, "Hop on, man, let's go for a ride!"

I climbed on the back and we slowly rode away. After a few blocks, he stopped and turned around and asked me, "Hey, you want to come out to my house for a while?"

I said, "Okay, sure, I guess."

We rode the bike all the way out to Canillejas. When we got to his house, and he opened the garage door and started to put the bike inside, I asked him, "Um, hey Bill, so you're not going to return the bike until later tonight then, I guess, huh?"

He looked at me with a sheepish grin and said, "Hell, Ron, I'm not going to ever return it, I'm going to keep it, man."

"But, isn't that like stealing then?"

"Yeah, I guess so, you got it, man. I'm just going to keep it here and ride it around here, and I'll never get caught, the owner's many miles away from here. It's cool, don't worry, man."

I gave him another funny look and said, "Okay, Bill, I guess you know what you're doing, man."

This was the first of the many bikes that Bill would steal over the next year and a half. I helped him with a couple more during that time, but usually he did it on his own. It seemed like whenever I went over to his house, he had at least one more bike in his collection.

After a while he got tired of being able to take only the bikes that were left unlocked, so he came up with a system that worked out pretty well for him. He was able to figure out that almost all bike locks used in Spain were made by only two manufacturers, *Batu* and *Atlas*, and each company only had a total of four different keys each for their locks. So with a set of eight keys, he could unlock almost any bike lock in the city. Of course, to own every key, he had to buy eight locks with keys (while comparing each new one with the collection of keys he already had), but by doing so he could unlock almost any motorbike. The locks were cheap enough, costing about 200 pesetas, or a little over three dollars. Gradually he built his collection up to a point where he had a set of eight different keys that could open virtually any lock on any bike. This opened up the possibilities enormously, and he could be a lot more selective in the bikes he swiped.

One Sunday morning, Bill and I went down to the *Rastro* just to look around and see what kind of bargains we could find. We took the Metro down to *La Latina*, the area around this most famous of flea markets, which has been in continual operation for over four hundred years. We weren't looking for anything in particular, but just walking around the stalls and seeing what was for sale. We stopped at a sidewalk cafe and sat down for a coke, and before too long Bill looked at me and said, "Hey Ron, you see that nice Bultaco over there?"

I looked in the direction he was and I saw a Bultaco *Mercurio* sitting by itself between two cars. I said, "Yeah, man, I see it, looks like a nice one. What is it, a 125?"

"Yeah, I think so, it's a beauty; I want it, man! It looks like all it has on it is a *Batu*, and I got my keys with me."

He smiled and reached into his pocket and pulled out his key ring jangling with his eight magic keys.

We finished up our Cokes, paid the waiter, and we slowly and nonchalantly approached the bike. While I stood there between the cars casually looking around, Bill knelt down with his key chain in his hand and within about thirty seconds, he found the right key for the lock. He climbed on it, reached down, turned the gas lever on, adjusted the choke on the carburetor, and kick-started it. It started on the second kick, and then he turned around and said, "Hop on, man. Let's get out of here."

I got on the back of the seat, making sure the foot pegs were down, and off we drove.

We rode all the way out to Canillejas, driving very carefully and making sure we didn't go over the speed limit. When we got to his house, instead of taking the bike into his garage, we took it out into the *campo* for a while and see what it could do. We started off by heading down our favorite trail. He opened the bike up on a straightaway and we started moving faster than I had ever gone on a bike up to that point. He was winding out the fourth gear to the degree where the motor was making a high-pitched squeal and the countryside was flashing by.

When a sharp curve appeared ahead, he pulled in the clutch and down-shifted to third, and the squealing became even more intense. Finally, we got to an old whitewashed abandoned ruin of a building and we stopped for a short rest. We both dismounted the *Mercurio* and Bill said, "Shit, man, this thing is fast as hell, isn't it?"

"No kidding, this bike hauls ass, doesn't it? How fast do you think we were going there?"

"I don't know but we were pegging it at a hundred clicks, which is all the speedometer goes up to."

"Wow, man, that's like sixty-five miles an hour! Shit!"

He looked at me with his wild grin. "Yeah, man, this one's a keeper for sure."

We got back on and took off again, but after just a couple of seconds he stopped and said, "Uh oh! Shit!"

"What's the matter?" I asked.

"It looks like the clutch is fried. It's just not working anymore. Watch, when I let it out, it doesn't do anything."

He put the bike in first gear, and then slowly let out the clutch and the bike lurched and stopped.

"Crap!" I exclaimed, "What are we going to do?"

"Well, we can try to baby it back home and hope that it makes it, I guess. Give me a push so we can at least get it into first, and I'll just shift without the fucking clutch."

I got behind and pushed the bike while he had it in neutral, and once it got rolling a little he jammed the gearshift into first and the bike started going.

He yelled, "Hop on, Ron. I'm holding the brake to hold her still!"

I climbed back on and away we went, with Bill shifting the gears without using the clutch, and each time there was a crunching noise when he shifted. We headed back towards his house but after just a couple of kilometers, the bike just died. The engine ran but it just wouldn't go into gear anymore. We got off and looked at it and Bill said "Well, shit man, it looks like we're walking now, crap! Maybe we should stash it somewhere and I can come back later and try to strip some parts off it. Everything is good on it except the fucking clutch."

He looked around and saw an area not too far from the trail with some tall grass and he pointed. "That might work, we just want to get her out of sight in case one of those gypsies comes by and strips it first, come on, let's get it over there."

So we pushed the bike over to the high grass and laid it down flat right in the middle of the grass, then we gathered some loose grass and brush and did our best to cover it up. We walked back to the trail to see if we could still see it, and we could see one of the handlebars sticking up out of the grass, so he went back and turned it so it wasn't as visible, until finally he was satisfied.

"Well, that's about the best we can do, I guess," he said. "I'll ride the *Lobito* out here again tomorrow or the next day and see what I can get off of it. Of course, I can't carry a lot with just my backpack, but I'll see what I can get, anyway."

We started walking back to his house when he suddenly laughed and said, "Hell, Ron, let the gypsies have it, I don't care. I can always get another one!"

"Yeah, I guess you're right, man, why deal with a broken bike, anyway? There are too many good ones out there, right?"

"Right on, man, right on!"

Bill never sold any of the bikes he stole, with one exception. There was a guy who lived in Canillejas named Jeff who was a year older than we were, and his family was scheduled to be rotated back to the states soon. He knew that Bill had a lot of bikes and that he could acquire them easily as well. So he put in an order for a specific bike that he wanted to box up with his family's household goods.

What Jeff wanted was a Bultaco 250 cc *Metralla*. This was one of the most beautiful street bikes that Bultaco made, and he wanted one to take back to the states with him and have the U.S. Military pay for the shipment. He told Bill that he was willing to pay him two hundred dollars for a *Metralla* in good condition. So Bill went on a search, and before too long he had an almost brand-new one sitting in his garage. Jeff came over and looked at it, rode it around the block a couple of times and paid Bill two hundred bucks in cash right then and there.

He told Bill his plan was to drain all the fluids out of the bike, break it down as much as possible by removing the handlebars and the tires, and then he thought it would fit into a heavy wooden box small enough to be shipped along with his family's household goods. And when he got it back to the States, he would have to register it anyway and all he needed was a bill of sale that Bill was happy to provide. Bill later told me that he felt a little guilty about doing the deal, but it was the easiest two hundred bucks he had ever made.

But all things must come to an end, and Bill eventually got busted. He let his passion for motorcycles get in the way of his number one rule — "Don't shit in your own front yard" — also known as don't steal bikes from your own neighborhood, because it very well might come back to bite you. And that's exactly what happened.

After about a year and a half of swiping bikes from areas of Madrid far from Canillejas, and then carefully riding them out to his house and storing them there in his family's garage, and only riding them around his home turf, one day he broke his own rule and paid the price, big time.

The summer between our junior and senior years in high school, we were hanging around Canillejas one sunny afternoon in a small bar that was just below the bridge that went over the *autopista* that connected the old part of Canillejas to the newer part. This bar was so small that it only had three bar stools and one pinball machine, and one small table with two chairs that overlooked the highway through the open door. We spent a lot of time in this little bar not only because it a nice friendly place, but it was only a couple of blocks from Bill's house and was one of the only places to get a drink in the newer part of Canillejas, besides the Hotel Osuna. The place was frequented by a few local kids as well as *obreros* (workmen) who would sometimes stop in for a quick one after work, along with a few Americans and other foreigners who lived in the area.

On that fateful afternoon that changed Bill's life forever, we were standing at the pinball machine taking turns and trying not to tilt it while we gently shook it to get the ball to do what we wanted, when Bill glanced outside the door after hearing the sound of a motorcycle riding by. He immediately stopped playing and quickly stepped outside to see what kind of bike it was that was riding by. He caught a good glimpse of it before it took the corner to the right to head towards *Las Palomas*. He realized that what he saw was a bright yellow and black Ossa Stiletto 250 off-road bike, and it was almost brand new. I could see him almost starting to drool as he became more and more excited.

He looked at me with his eyes wide open and exclaimed, "Man, did you see that bike? It was an Ossa 250! Just like the one I've been looking for! I gotta have it; it's my dream bike, man!"

I replied with a slightly questioning tone of voice, "Yeah, Bill, I've seen that bike around before a couple of times, I think the guy that owns it is some rich Spanish guy that lives up there in *Las Palomas* in one of the buildings near Juan."

"Oh, really?" he asked in a tone of disbelief, "and you didn't tell me about it?"

"Well, I really didn't think you'd be interested in it since it is in your own neighborhood and everything, man."

"I don't care, I gotta have it! I've only seen one ever before and it was impossible to get since it was parked right in front of two *Guardia Civil* at the time. You say the guy lives up there in *Las Palomas*?"

"Yeah, I think so. I saw the guy riding around on it when I was up visiting Juan last week."

"Well, I'm going to get it, damn it. I love that bike!" He said this with a glint in his eye.

"Okay, man, but if I was you I'd definitely get one from a different side of town. Remember your rule of not shitting where you eat. I'm not going to help you with it, that's for sure. You're on your own with this one, man."

He looked at me with a look I'd never seen before, as if he was obsessed (or maybe possessed); I wasn't sure.

"Okay, Ron, you can sit this one out if you like, but I'm gonna get it for sure. I just gotta have it, man. It's only the second one I've ever seen."

And sure enough, a few days later, I went over to his house and as soon as I got there he said, "I gotta show you what I got in the garage, man."

We walked over to the garage and he swung open the door and there it was, the Ossa 250 sitting there in all its yellow and black glory.

"Isn't she a beauty, man? Look at her lines and look how sweet she is," he said as he ran his hands all over the gas tank and seat. "This is the nicest bike I've ever had, man!"

I asked, "So is this the same one that belongs to the guy from *Las Palomas*?"

"Yeah, I just walked up there the night before last with my keys and it was just sitting there with two *Batus* on it, one on the front wheel and the other on the back, but no problem for the magic key ring," he explained, giving me his big grin.

"But Bill, man, what if he sees you riding it around?"

"Oh, don't worry, I'm only going to ride it out in the *campo*, man; I won't get caught, no way if I just stay out there with it."

"Okay, man, but you'd better be careful is all I gotta say."

"Ah, don't be a pussy Ron, wanna go for a ride?"

"Nope, not on that thing, no way, man."

"Okay, the hell with it, we'll leave it here then. You take the *Derbi*, and I'll take the *Lobito*, and we'll go out riding for a while. I think there's a new gypsy camp up by the old house we can check out, all right?"

"All right, sure, let's go." I said as I walked over and got on the nice red *Derbi* sitting there. "Is there enough gas in this one?"

"Yeah," he said with a grin, "I got my old man to get me a gas can on base at the auto parts place, so I keep them all full now, and ready to go. *Vamanos hombre!*"

So we took off for a nice long ride and it turned out to be the last motorcycle ride in Spain that I ever shared with Bill.

A couple of days later I went out to Canillejas to see him, and as I walked up to the door of his house, he came out to greet me and he had a really miserable look on his face.

I asked him, "Bill, what the fuck is wrong, man?"

He gave me a long sad look and said, "You were right, Ronnie, I should have never taken that fucking Ossa. The police showed up here yesterday and wanted to look in the garage and they found it. Fuck!"

"Oh my god, man! Shit, what happened?"

"Well, they came back with a big van and took every last bike out of the garage. It turns out that someone who knew the guy who owned the Ossa saw me riding by on the way to the campo yesterday and called the police. They came to the neighborhood and set up a stake-out, and just waited until I rode by on my way home. I'm busted! God damn it, man!"

"Oh shit, Bill, what are they going to do to you?"

He gave me another deep look and said, "Well, I told them that it was me and me alone that took all those bikes. I didn't say a thing about you helping me with a few, so don't worry, Ron."

"Thank God," I thought to myself with a sigh of relief, realizing how close I had come to being in some serious trouble.

"So, what do you think will happen to you, man?" I asked him.

"I don't know yet, the cops said I have to go down to the police station tomorrow and put in a plea. We'll just have to see what happens, I guess."

"Shit Bill, goddamn it, man!"

"Well, all good things must come to an end eventually, I guess," he said with a look of resignation, "and I guess my bike stealing streak is over, man."

I tried to put on my bravest face and said to him, "Well, you're an American citizen, so I doubt if they're going to throw the book at you, and besides you're still a minor, right?"

"That's all true, my friend. I sure hope they go easy on me, because I can't see myself sitting in a Spanish prison for years, that's for sure."

"Well, good luck, amigo, and anything I can do, don't hesitate to ask, okay?"

"Okay, Ron, I appreciate it brother, that means a lot to me. Hey, but you'd better go now, since my folks don't really want my friends around right now, all right?"

"I understand. I'll see you later, all right?"

"Yeah, I just hope it's not from a fucking jail cell, man!"

Thanks to the fact that Bill's dad was a Chief Petty Officer and in charge of a lot of things at Torrejon Air Base, Bill ended up not going to jail. The fact that he was a minor had something to do with it, but his dad had to go in front of the Base Commander. The Commander was able to pull a few strings, and the result was that Bill was just deported out of Spain, much to his relief. Within a week, he had left Madrid and gone to live with his grandmother in South Carolina. He would have to finish high school there and wait until his dad and the rest of his family rotated stateside the following year.

A couple years later, I hooked up with Bill again in South Carolina, but those adventures will be covered in a later chapter.

Chapter 13. Morocco

*"Do not bite at the bait of pleasure,
till you know there is no hook beneath it."*
— THOMAS JEFFERSON

Ah, Morocco... what a wonderful, beautiful, and strange country! A place of mystery, which conjures up images of belly dancers, shish-kebabs, Kasbahs, and scenes from the Arabian Nights. Although I've only taken two trips there during my entire life, I feel that I know it fairly well, due to the profound effect those trips had on me. Growing up in Madrid, I had heard of Morocco since I was quite young, and I couldn't wait to visit this fascinating and mysterious place.

When I was around ten years old, I knew a kid named Sammy from school who had just come from Kenitra Air Base in Morocco, where his father had been stationed prior to Torrejon Air Base. Kenitra was originally known as Port Lyautey during World War II; it served as a staging area for many Allied operations in North Africa and the Mediterranean theater of operations. The United States Navy and the United States Air Force were based there with their specialized aircraft.

Following World War II, the airfield was expanded to become a major U.S. Naval air station in 1951. Starting in the 1960s, the base became a United States Naval Training Command, and would be called that until it closed and was turned over to the Royal Moroccan Air Force in 1977. During this entire time, many Americans worked and lived in this otherworldly country.

The American base in Morocco was not nearly the size of Torrejon or other bases in Europe, but they did have an American school there for some years and would play football games and other sporting events against bases in Spain, including teams from Torrejon, Rota, and Zaragoza. This inter-base contact between students of these two vastly different countries made for quite interesting conversations and interactions between the players, coaches, and everyone else involved.

Sammy had lived in Kenitra for a while and told me a few stories about the place, and he always made it sound like a place that was totally different from anything I'd ever known. I told him about my having lived in Ankara, Turkey, as a young child, so we felt we had something in common. Both of us being about ten years old at the time and being kids, of course the first thing he told me was how to say a few cuss words in Arabic. "*Didamuk*" meant an asshole or a very despicable person. And "*Walet*" meant a young boy which was what he was probably called quite often when he was out among the locals. He had other stories to tell me about how different the Moroccans were from Europeans, Americans, and just about everyone else he had known in his young life. And as so often happens with military brats, before too long, his father was reassigned elsewhere, and he and his family moved on, never to be heard from again, at least not by me.

A few years later, what really made me want to go to Morocco was the smoke. After first trying pot when I was fourteen, I was very interested in going to the source of this magical substance.

There is a *cerveceria* (a brewery) in Madrid located at the Plaza de Santa Ana which is a very historic cafe, bar, and hangout. Its name is *La Cerveceria Alemana*, (the German Brewery), and it first opened its doors in 1904 when a group of German manufacturers decided to open a bar exclusively devoted to tasting beer. Its decor has remained virtually unchanged up to this day, although the Prussian fireplace and the large Bavarian mirror that adorned the walls in the early years are gone.

Since those early years, it has always been a place where writers, artists, intellectuals, bullfighters, and celebrities have gathered to drink beer or coffee and have great conversations. It has seen the likes of such people as Ava Gardner, who lived in Madrid from 1952 until 1967, drawn there by her romance with the famous bullfighter Luis Miguel Dominguin.

Another famous American to partake of the brew at *La Alemana* was none other than Ernest Hemingway, who was also attracted to the place due to his love for bullfighting. Hemingway's favorite table was near the window and to this day remains one of the choicest seats in the cavernous room of this most famous of bars.

In the late sixties and early seventies, the *Alemana* and the Plaza de Santa Ana area became a gathering place for "suspicious-looking foreigners, with long hair and tattered jeans," as the press of the time described them. They were the hippies, who for quite some time disturbed the classic atmosphere of the place—which in part revolved around bullfighting—to the horror of its regular visitors who were not too keen on changes of any sort in the patronage.

This was the place in Madrid where I found out that it was possible to purchase illegal substances such as *hashish* and *kif* if one knew the right person and appeared to be *cool*. The *Alemana* was not the best or my most usual place to procure these substances, but on several occasions I did try, and once I actually did succeed in scoring.

There were many long-haired fellows who frequented the establishment and sometimes I could find just the right one to help me out with what I was looking for. But just being in the place was an experience; to go in and just sit and soak in the history, the atmosphere and some of the strange characters that hung around the place was always worth the trip of going down to that area of Madrid, regardless of the outcome.

But the usual way that myself and my small group of my friends that smoked were able to obtain these substances was basically through each other. There were around a dozen people or so in this little group and we would all look out for each other. What we would do was rotate taking trips to Morocco and we'd bring hash back with us. We would all chip in and give our combined money to the person who was about to take the trip, and when that person returned, we would split up the hash, each according to how much he had contributed.

Prime Moroccan hashish (known as double zero, indicating its purity) sold for about two hundred dollars per kilo in Morocco. This came to about twenty cents per gram when purchased by the kilo, a little more if purchased in smaller quantities. Since hash sold for an average of one dollar per gram in Spain and even more in the rest of Europe, this was a substantial savings. Not only was the price so much lower, but we could have a steady supply and avoid the risk of being busted by someone pretending to be a dealer who hung around such places as the Plaza de Santa Ana.

Of course, the person who actually made the trip to Morocco and brought the stuff back risked a lot as well, but for some reason nobody in our group ever got caught bringing anything back. The Spanish government made it quite clear that the minimum jail time was eight years in prison for trafficking or possession of drugs, so we just figured that you might as well take the big risk, if the punishment was the same for either offense.

One guy in our group had a red passport. His father worked at an embassy in Madrid and his passport was red, indicating that he was a diplomat's kid, and therefore was not subject to any search when crossing international borders. Naturally, he took more trips than any of us because he had no fear of being searched. He almost always had a friend accompany him, and once my brother made the trip with him and was rewarded with a very good supply of the product they brought back, much more than the equivalent of his contribution to the money pool.

It was a good system that worked out very well for the guys in our little group. If we each chipped in ten or twenty dollars or whatever we could afford, when the person returned from a short trip to Tangiers, Rabat, or Marrakesh, we would have enough to last us several months or even longer. If the trip was only to bring hash back, then the trip was quite short, perhaps only a couple of days, and would usually involve a short airplane trip from Barajas airport in Madrid to a city in Morocco, and then just a matter of stuffing a kilo or so down the pants or the multitude of other more ingenious methods that smugglers use, and taking the return flight to Madrid to share the bounty with everyone that contributed.

When the two-week Christmas break came along in my junior year of high school during the winter of 1968, I, my brother, and a friend from school decided we wanted to make this trip ourselves. My brother and I managed to talk our father into taking us on a ten-day trip to Morocco in his SEAT 1500 and we also talked him into bringing along Andy, our friend from school. My dad knew that Johnny and I had been experimenting with pot, and he was curious about the substance himself. He didn't want to try it in Spain where it was illegal, but rather he preferred to try it where it was semi-legal as it is in Morocco. Of course, we did not tell him about our plans to smuggle a kilo of hashish back with us.

So, we brought out the map and planned our trip. We decided that due to time restrictions, we would stay in the northern area of Morocco only but still try to see as many of the cities in that area as possible. Our plan was to go to Algeciras first, a large port in southern Spain near Gibraltar where the car ferry can be taken to either Tangiers in Morocco, or to the small Spanish enclave town of Ceuta. Although Ceuta is in Africa, it is actually a part of Spain, just like the other small enclave Spanish town of Melilla further down the Mediterranean coast. These two small towns were similar to what Gibraltar was to Great Britain, a part of their Mother country, yet were actually in a different country.

Our plan was to take the ferry to Ceuta, and then about ten days later, come back from Morocco through Tangiers, and in between, we would drive through the ancient cities of Fez, Meknes, Rabat, and Casablanca. The distance from Algeciras to Ceuta is only about twenty-two kilometers and from Tangiers back to Algeciras is about twenty-eight kilometers, so the ferry ride would be quite short on both ends of our trip.

Johnny, Andy, and I told our group of friends of our plans for Christmas break, and we collected about two hundred dollars from the usual contributors and we assured them that we would do our best to bring back the best quality possible. Andy got permission from his mom to take the trip with us, and he was as excited to go as Johnny and I were. He had never been to Morocco before either, but had heard so much about the place, including the culture and the smoke.

We had a full two weeks off from school for Christmas vacation plus the weekend on either side of the break, so we were rather open on our return date, but we figured around ten to twelve days total for our journey. The morning of our departure, we loaded one small suitcase each into the trunk of the car and took our places. Since Johnny was the oldest and since Andy was a little more my friend than Johnny's, he and I sat in the back seat, and all of us were ready for a grand adventure.

My dad didn't like to drive a long eight- or ten-hour drive every day, so our trip was a leisurely one and we took our time to see the sights along the way. The first night we spent in the wonderful ancient city of Córdoba, which was on the way to Algeciras where we would board the ferry across the straits of Gibraltar to another continent... Africa!

Córdoba was famous in the 1960s as being the birthplace of the most famous bullfighter in modern times, Manuel Benitez, also known as *"El Cordobés."* His fame as a matador was due to his daring and courage, along with his unorthodox acrobatic and theatrical style in the bullring. By the time of his first retirement in 1971, he was the most famous and highest-paid bullfighter in history. He was known as the "Beatle" of the bullring due to his youth, his dashing good looks, and his Beatles-style haircut.

A significant moment came near the beginning of his career in 1964 when he made his first appearance at Las Ventas Bullring in Madrid. It was one of the first bullfights to be televised and so was watched by millions of people instead of the usual thirty thousand or so that this largest of Spanish bullrings could hold, and he made quite an impression. The bullfight ended with him being nearly fatally gored on the horns of the bull named *Impulsivo*. Yet, only twenty-two days later, El Cordobés returned to the ring to fight again, insuring his place in the annals of history in the art of bullfighting.

We reached Cordoba early enough in the afternoon to find two rooms in an inexpensive hotel near the center of town and had plenty of time to explore the town before having dinner at a nearby restaurant. We went down to the Guadalquivir River that flows through the city and admired an old bridge that was built by the Romans over 2000 years ago and was still in use. Originally Córdoba was a Roman settlement and then was colonized by the Moorish armies in the eighth century. Its architecture reflected its Moorish origins, a taste of what we would see much more of once we crossed the Straits of Gibraltar into Morocco.

The next morning, after a restful night with Johnny and my dad sharing one room and Andy and I sharing the other, we again headed south towards Algeciras. Approaching the *Bahia de Algeciras,* as the Spaniards call this huge bay near the southern tip of Spain, also known as the Bay of Gibraltar by the British, we could see the famous rock rising above the surrounding land and sea. It was an impressive sight and we could see how this piece of real estate has invoked so much controversy and complex history over the ages.

We wanted to stop and visit the Rock, but at the time it was not permitted to go to Gibraltar from Spain. It has been a British Overseas Territory since 1713 when the Treaty of Utrecht ceded the area to Britain "in perpetuity." This 6.7 square kilometer area has a population of around 30,000 Gibraltarians who, despite Spain's claim to sovereignty, want to remain British citizens and under British control.

Its unique location as the northern pillar of the "Pillars of Hercules" has been throughout history, and still is, an extremely important and strategic location for trade and commerce. Today almost half of all seaborne trade in the world passes through this strait, and the economy is largely based on tourism, gambling, financial services, and cargo ship refueling and repair services. During the 1950s, Franco had tried unsuccessfully to annex Gibraltar back to Spain, and when he was unable to do so, he closed *La Linea,* the border that connects it to mainland Spain, making it impossible to cross into Gibraltar from Spain (or to Spain from Gibraltar). This border with Spain was finally reopened in 1985 and today commerce, trade, and travelers can cross easily and openly.

We knew beforehand that it would be impossible to visit Gibraltar due to the political turmoil, so we were not too disappointed that we could not visit the 'Rock' on this trip. At the time the only way to enter Gibraltar was either by ship or airplane from another country besides Spain, such as Morocco or Great Britain. Nevertheless, we did enjoy the view of this most impressive of landmarks from across the bay in Algeciras.

Arriving quite late to Algeciras, we learned that it was too late to take the ferry to Ceuta, but we found the ferry office and bought our tickets for the next morning's crossing of the Straits of Gibraltar. After going out for dinner and spending a quiet night at a small hotel near the ferry terminal, we got in line early the next day, ready for our sea voyage to Africa!

We could easily see the coastline of the African continent from Algeciras and it looked like another world across the Straits, both mysterious and inviting. A large and impressive mountain range loomed in the distance across the blue waters. We drove the car onto the ferry, left it in the bowels of the ship, and made our way up onto the deck. Once we got underway, the mountain range in the distance got closer and closer as we made the voyage over to Ceuta.

The trip took just under two hours altogether and from the deck we saw schools of dolphins following in the ship's wake, and we wondered if they used the ship to help propel them through the water more easily, or if they merely enjoyed riding the wake that the ship's propellers made while cutting through the water. They were a delight to watch, these wonderful mammals of the sea, and they made our voyage even more exciting.

We reached Ceuta, disembarked from the ferry, and slowly drove off the ship and onto dry land. The busy port terminal looked pretty much like any other Spanish port town, although there were even more Arab-looking people around than we had seen in Algeciras, and we were surprised that there was apparently no one to check our passports or papers, so we just drove off the ship without stopping and kept on going.

After driving south for a couple of kilometers, we did reach the border between Spain and Morocco. At this point, there was a regular guardhouse with custom agents and a checkpoint. We showed the guard our passports, and he asked where we were going and how long we were planning on staying in Morocco. My dad spoke to him in Spanish and told him we were tourists from America living in Madrid and we were planning to travel around for a week or so and then return to Spain from the port of Tangiers once our trip was done. The guard smiled at us, stamped our passports, welcomed us to Morocco, and told us to have a nice trip.

Once we headed south away from the border crossing, it started to look and feel very much different from Ceuta. Suddenly we felt like we had stepped back in time. Everywhere we saw people who looked like they could have been living thousands of years ago. Most of the men were wearing long robes, called *djellabas*, and the women wore similar attire but most had veils covering their faces as well. Some people were dressed "European" style, but most were dressed in the traditional Moroccan clothing. Most of the men had head coverings of some sort, either round colorful skullcaps, or turbans of some sort. The ones who didn't have a head covering wore djellabas that had hoods that served to cover and protect their heads.

There were donkeys everywhere, some with a single rider, others pulling small two-wheel carts, and others loaded down with cargo and produce of all kinds. The closer we got to Tetouan, the first real town heading south from Ceuta, we felt more and more like we were in a time warp, or at the very least, in a totally different kind of a place than any we had ever seen before. We were fascinated by everything we saw and to our Western eyes, it was just like we had stepped into a scene from an old Biblical movie such as "The Ten Commandments."

Of course, there were modern twentieth century things such as cars, trucks and many motorbikes, but the overall atmosphere felt like an ancient and unchanged world, as if the modern world had never quite reached this place as it had elsewhere. Like almost everywhere else in the world, there were red and white Coca-Cola signs in front of the cafes, but they were in Arabic, a strange and undecipherable writing that to our eyes looked like scribbling that we knew was read from right to left.

When we finally reached the town of Tetouan, we drove around trying to get our bearings. We had decided earlier that we would spend our first night in this town and we boys were all eager to purchase some *sebsis* as well some *kif* to put in them. We drove around a little while longer until we found a small hotel near the "old quarter" of town. There was also the new quarter of town, which had modern buildings, streets, restaurants, bars, shops, and businesses that can be found just about anywhere, in any city in almost any country in the world. Many people there were dressed in the latest European fashions and the place pretty much looked like any other city or town.

Alcoholic beverages were served in the cafes and bars and there were even a few nightclubs available for those wanting to experience some nightlife. The restaurants have waiters with crisp white uniforms, and offer varied items on their rather extensive menus, including French and Spanish cuisine along with typical Moroccan food. The sidewalk cafes appeared to be identical to the ones that were seen all over Europe. There was traffic on the busy and wide streets along with street lights and stop signs and taxis and a general busyness of people going about their lives that existed in just about any modern city.

The old quarter, by contrast, had basically remained unchanged for thousands of years, and had very narrow streets or alleys actually, with tall white-washed walls casting shade below against the fierce North African sun. Unlike any modern towns where the streets are laid out in some kind of organized fashion, in the old quarter of Moroccan towns, the streets appeared to us to be totally haphazard with no pattern; a maze of apparently never-ending corridors and pathways going every which way. Vendors either had small shops along these narrow pathways where they displayed their wares, or they just set their items out for sale along the sidewalks of these paths.

In the old quarter, there was very little that appeared to be from this century. There were no bars, only cafes, but none sold alcoholic beverages of any sort, only tea and coffee. The restaurants usually sold only one or two items and no menus were to be found. They sold what they had that day and if you were hungry, then that is what you ate.

There were very few motor vehicles of any sort due the fact that the extremely narrow streets prevented anything larger than a donkey, a bicycle or a small motorbike. Yet there were all kinds of goods for sale, such as carpets, hats, baskets, metal and ceramic pots and cookware, clothing of all sorts, groceries, including all kinds of fresh produce, spices and other dried goods, and an assortment of every imaginable type of leather goods; hassocks, handbags, wallets, pouches, shoes, and purses. Anything and everything was available for purchase, and the prices were always negotiable since there were rarely price tags on any item.

We realized that very few Moroccans spoke English, but most spoke French and Arabic, of course, and many spoke fairly good Spanish as well. At the hotel we found that my dad was able to use his Spanish with the clerk in the lobby to rent us two modest and inexpensive rooms at the *Hotel Maroquin*. As soon we set our bags down in our rooms and looked around, we boys were ready to go out and explore the town. My dad told us that he'd like to settle in and maybe take a little nap after such a long day, but for us boys to go out and explore. And we knew that it would be much easier and safer to "score" if he wasn't around.

It was only the middle of the afternoon, and we were not ready yet for dinner, having eaten sandwiches from our cooler for lunch earlier, so we had several hours to kill before having to worry about our stomachs. So we told him we'd be back in a couple of hours and left him in the room and went out to explore.

While walking down the two flights of stairs from our room to the street level, all three of us felt an increasing level of excitement and apprehension. Here we were for the first time in Morocco! In North Africa! This was the place we had heard so many stories about and where we were about to sample some of the fabled Moroccan *kif*, right from the source.

We started walking towards the center of the old quarter, which was only a block or so from our hotel, and before too long we were immersed in the narrow streets, stopping and inspecting all the different items that were for sale. Several times we were accosted by young Moroccan boys asking if we needed a guide, but we declined, saying that we were not going far and besides we were staying quite close so we could find our way back to our hotel.

After walking around for a while and looking at innumerable stalls, we finally found one that sold what we were looking for. We came across a small shop that had a display of *sebsis* and *skuffs*, which were the small clay bowls that were inserted at the end of the pipe stem where the kif was packed.

The man attending the stall saw our excitement at seeing his display and asked us in Spanish, "Hello gentlemen, how many do you want to purchase today? Here we have the finest sebsis found in all of Morocco."

Johnny, being the oldest of us, replied, "Well, we would like to buy one for each of us, so that would make three altogether, can you give us a good price for three?"

The man smiled and said, "Of course, sir, I can give you the best price in all of Morocco for these fine sebsis. The smaller two-piece ones are twenty dirham and the longer three piece ones are thirty dirham, and the *skuffs* are one dirham each. Take your pick, and I'll make you a good price." The exchange rate was around 10 dirhams to the dollar, so we knew the prices were quite fair.

We proceeded to go through the dozens of *sebsis* he had for sale and we each selected one that we liked. I chose a two-piece dark green one with a very intricate design carved into the wood and Johnny and Andy each chose one too. We each counted out five *skuffs* each and then Johnny looked at the gentleman and asked, "Very well, sir, we have made our selections, we have two of the two-piece kind and one three-piece one, along with a total of fifteen skuffs. That should come to eighty-five dirham, am I right?"

"Yes, that is correct, sir; I see that you have a good mind indeed. That comes to eighty-five dirham. And now, are you gentlemen interested in purchasing something to go into the *skuffs* you bought?"

We all looked at him and then at each other and then Johnny replied politely, "Perhaps sir, do you happen to know where something like that could be purchased?"

He looked around, up and down the narrow street and told us, "Yes, but it requires you to enter my shop to be out of the public view. Would that be acceptable?"

"Very well, let's see what you have, sir," Johnny told him as we also looked up and down the street.

"Follow me, gentlemen," he said as he turned and walked into the shop.

We followed him into the shop and stepped behind a curtain that he had hung from the ceiling and into a private area out of view of the street. He went to a corner and brought out a large paper sack and showed us what was inside. We looked and saw about a kilo or so of *kif*. He told us that it was all ready to smoke and was premixed with around ten percent black tobacco, which is the way that Moroccans prefer to smoke it. All three of us reached our heads over the bag and took a good sniff and we all nodded our heads in agreement.

Johnny once again took the lead in our negotiations. "But, sir, we don't want to buy so much; we would just like a small amount to sample while we are here in Morocco. Maybe this much." And he put his hands together to form a circle about six inches across.

"Very well," the man said, "I suppose I can do that if you'd like." He then took a piece of newspaper and folded it into a funnel-shaped container, then reached into the paper sack containing the *kif* and grabbed several large handfuls which he put into the newspaper and expertly folded up into a portable package.

"Very well, gentlemen," he said as he handed Johnny the package. "That is fifty dirham worth; is that sufficient for your needs?"

"Yes, sir, that is just about right," Johnny told him, "So we now owe you one hundred thirty-five dirhams, correct?"

"Yes, I see that you are still good at your mathematics skills. One hundred and thirty-five dirhams exactly, sir."

Johnny reached into his pocket, counted out the bills, and handed them to the man, and we all said thank you very much and then Johnny put the newspaper pouch into his jacket pocket and we stepped out into the street again with big smiles on our faces.

"Thanks again, sirs," the man said as we waved and headed on back to our hotel, eager to sample our purchases.

When we reached our hotel, we climbed the two flights of stairs to our floor and we went into the room that Andy and I were sharing. We sat down on the two beds and Johnny opened up the folded newspaper and we each grabbed our sebsis, inserted a *skuff* into each one, and we lit up. Almost instantly the world began to glow and the colors in the room became warmer and more brilliant and then slowly everything became a little stranger and more interesting than it was before.

We had brought with us from Madrid a brand new item that I had acquired at the PX on base. It was a Panasonic portable cassette tape player, and it was one of our favorite items. We had several tapes with us including Led Zeppelin, Jimi Hendrix, and the Beatles. We put in Led Zeppelin's latest, and "Communication Breakdown" came on. Suddenly all three of us were mesmerized by the sounds emerging from the little speaker. Jimmy Page's guitar and Robert Plant's screech got to us on a primordial level and within seconds we were rocking out as never before.

Before the first side of the tape was over, we heard a knock on the door and suddenly we got paranoid. I reached over and turned down the tunes to a level where the machine was barely audible, and Johnny went to the door and opened it slowly just a crack. My dad was standing there, and he said, "Hey, what's going on in here, troops?"

Johnny opened the door the rest of the way to let him in and said, "Well, Dad, we scored already."

He took a sniff of the air and says, "Yes, I can tell by the odor in here. It certainly didn't take too long, did it?"

Johnny looked at him while indicating the bed where Andy was sitting and said, "Yeah, Dad, we just went out to buy some *sebsis* and the same guy sold us some *kif*. You ready to try some?"

He sat down on the bed next to Andy, "Okay, I guess now is as good as time as any. Let's see what you got, guys."

Johnny opened the folded newspaper and showed Dad the pile of *kif* inside and said to him, "Take a whiff of this, Dad."

He leaned over and put his head near the paper and sniffed and asked, "So is that what it's supposed to smell like, kind of stinky, are you sure it's not rotten?"

All three of us started to giggle, and I said, "No, Dad, it's supposed to smell like that. I think it smells sweet in a way."

"Okay, well, let's see now. So what am I supposed to do here?"

Andy filled his *sebsi* and handed it over to Dad with a shy smile and said to him, "Here you go, Mr. Walker, I'll light it for you, just take a toke and hold it in for a little before letting it out."

My dad held the *sebsi* with both hands while Andy leaned over and put his Bic lighter flame to the *skuff* and my dad took a long drag. He was used to smoking tobacco since he did smoke cigars regularly as well as a pipe occasionally. He started to cough a little but caught himself and held it in for a few seconds before exhaling a big puff of smoke.

He looked at us and said, "Um, a rather nice flavor actually, isn't it?"

"Here, have another one, sir," Andy said as he reached over again with his Bic.

Dad took another toke and again let out another cloud of pungent smoke. "Thanks, Andy. It really does have a nice taste, doesn't it?"

Andy reached over and knocked the ash into a small brass ashtray on the table and filled himself a bowl and lit up.

I reached over and turned the volume up slightly on the cassette player and filled my *sebsi* as well from the pile inside the folded newspaper, "Well, what do you think, Dad?"

"How long is this supposed to take, I don't feel anything yet, guys."

Johnny then filled his *sebsi* and handed it to Dad, gave him a smile, and told him, "Well, sometimes it takes a little while for first timers; here, have another one." And he lit the bowl with his Bic.

Dad took a couple more tokes and then said, "You know, I don't know about you guys, but I'm suddenly starving. What do you say we go out and have some dinner?"

"Okay, sounds good to me, let's go," I exclaimed, as I stood up and turned off the cassette player.

Andy said, "Yeah, I'm pretty hungry myself, actually."

"Me too!" Johnny chimed in.

"All right, *Vamanos entonces, muchachos*," Dad said as he stood up and headed for the door.

The four of us walked out into the hallway and headed down the stairs to the street level. As soon as we emerged onto the sidewalk, Dad looked around and said to us with a very confused expression on his face, "You know, I don't remember going down the stairs, but here we are on the street, so I must have, but I don't remember it. That's strange."

The three of us young ones began to laugh, and I said, "Well, Dad, it appears that you very well might be a little stoned."

"Yeah, maybe so, guys, maybe so," he said with a little smile, as we started walking towards the nearest restaurant.

After a nice meal of chicken and couscous, we headed back to the room and again we broke out the *sebsis* for an after-dinner smoke, and I got the cassette player going again, this time with "Are You Experienced?" by the Jimi Hendrix Experience.

When the song, "The Wind Cries Mary," came on, Dad said, "So Ron, that's Jimi Hendrix, huh?"

"Yeah, Dad, I've told you a little about him, what do you think of it?"

"Well, I like that song, but the others seem a little wild and crazy to me, like a lot of noise and not a lot of music. But I think I know what he's saying with that song."

"Yeah, what do you think he means, Dad?" I asked.

"Well, he sings, 'the wind cries Mary', and then he sings later, 'the wind whispers Mary,' then at the end he says, 'the wind screams Mary,' obviously he's thinking that the wind is speaking his girl Mary's name, right? So it's a type of love song, right?"

"Yeah, Dad, but Mary means marijuana, Mary Jane, don't you see?"

He gave me a very thoughtful expression and said, "Okay, yeah, I think I get it now."

"So, Dad, speaking of an experience, what do you think of the experience of getting stoned for the first time?"

He shrugged his shoulders and said, "Well frankly, I'm a little disappointed. I guess maybe I expected too much. All it really did was make me feel confused and a bit disoriented, and very weird. Is that what it makes you guys feel?"

I looked at him and replied slowly, "Well, that's what getting stoned is all about, Dad. But the more you do it, the more used to it you get, and the better it goes because you learn to use it to help you concentrate on certain things, like music for example. It makes music sound much better for some reason. It allows you to get into things more and makes everything deeper and more profound, I guess."

He gave me a thoughtful look. "Well, Ron, frankly, I think I'd rather just have a nice glass of brandy. But I would like to see what sex is like while on pot, that might be interesting, I think."

"Well, maybe sometime you can try that, Dad," I laughed, as I took another toke from my *sebsi*.

"Yeah, maybe so Ron, maybe so, someday."

The next day, we were up early and on the road by mid-morning on our way to the city of Fez, the next stop on our itinerary. Fez is an ancient city, founded in the year 789, and was the capital city of modern Morocco until 1912, when Rabat became the capital, and remained the capital after Morocco achieved independence in from France in 1956. Due to the number of universities located in the city, Fez has been called the "Athens of Africa" and the "Mecca of the West."

Today it is a bustling commercial center and the second largest city in  the country. It is known as the birthplace of the headgear known as the "Fez." Initially, this red hat with the black tassel was a symbol of Ottoman modernity, but over time came to be recognized as an "Oriental" cultural identity sign. Seen as exotic and romantic in the West, it became a part of luxury smoking outfits in the United States and the United Kingdom around the turn of the twentieth century. Today this type of formal headgear is worn in many parts of the world and has become traditional for many of the world's Muslims.

The city of Fez seemed to be a huge city compared to the small towns we had seen in Morocco so far. The city's Medina (old quarter) was so large that it is the world's largest car-free urban area, with over 70,000 people living in this "old quarter" where the only transportation was by donkey or by foot. The huge and complex networks of alleyways and back streets lead in some cases to dead ends. Or they may lead to small squares with cool fountains and a variety of food stands, or sometimes doorways with an assortment of artisans creating their works of art. This fantastic place that has changed little for several thousand years and walking around the old quarter was like walking back into time.

We found a small hotel on a main road but only a block or so from the old quarter, and when the four of us walked in with our bags and approached the desk, my dad discovered that the clerk didn't speak much Spanish, only French and Arabic. Johnny and I stepped up to the desk and with the French language skills we had learned in Alicante a couple of years earlier, we were able to secure two rooms on the third floor with two beds each.

Dad looked at both of us as we were walking up the stairs to our rooms and said, "Boys, with your language skills, you will never have a problem communicating with anyone, anywhere in the entire world. I hope you realize what an advantage you have with these skills."

I looked at Johnny and then at my dad as I changed my suitcase from one hand to the other and said, "Yeah, I guess you're right Dad, unless we go to Timbuktu or somewhere like that!"

Andy laughed, "Actually Ron, they speak French in Timbuktu, my dad has been there and he said it was a pretty cool place."

My dad smiled and said, "See, there you go, Ron, like I said, you'll be fine just about anywhere in the world!"

"Maybe so Dad, maybe so," I answered with a smile.

We settled into our rooms and soon the sebsis were broken out in the room Andy and I shared, and after a while we started developing an appetite. So we all headed down the three flights of stairs and towards the Medina hoping to get a typical Moroccan dinner. We walked around for quite a while and several times we were approached by young boys wanting to be our "guide." We turned them all down saying that we thought we could find our way around well enough to not need their services.

We kept walking, and it seemed like around every corner was another strange sight and another stall selling exotic and beautiful goods. Occasionally we heard shouting up ahead, and we saw a donkey coming towards us piled high with raw leather, produce, or assortments of other products, and we were forced to lean tightly against the walls or find another alley to quickly duck into in order to get out of the donkey's progress down the middle of the small narrow street, while its owner walked behind it slapping the ass's ass with a small stick, yelling in Arabic.

We stopped at one shop that sold all kinds of leather goods and I stared at the wallets for sale. The proprietor approached me and started a conversation with me in French. I told him I was just looking, but he wanted to be very helpful and told me that Moroccan leather goods are the best in the world and can be made out of just about any animal on earth, including cow, sheep, goat, camel, ostrich, gazelle, rhino, snake, and many other types of skins. He proceeded to tell me that Fez has one of the world's oldest tanneries still in operation and dates back to the twelfth century and remains virtually unchanged in their manufacturing of quality leather. The products that are made from their leather range from shoes, slippers, handbags, suitcases, hassocks, wallets, jackets, *kif* pouches, and many other quality products.

I picked up a typical Moroccan wallet which had a golden hue to it and was very soft to the touch, and I asked him what kind of leather it was made from. He looked at me with a smile and said in French, "Ah, young sir, I can see that you have a very good eye for the quality leather. This particular wallet is made from the skin of a camel. And it will easily last you for the remainder of your young life."

I picked up another wallet which had a reddish color and asked him what type of leather it was made from. He looked at me closely and said, "Ah, young sir, this fine wallet is made from the skin of a desert gazelle from the northern slopes of the Atlas Mountains in Southern Morocco. It also should last you the remainder of your days on this Earth. I highly recommend it."

As I held the two wallets in my hand and examined them a little more closely, the shopkeeper looked closely at me and said, "I shall give you a very special price for both of these fine wallets, both of which are made of the finest craftsmanship, only eighteen dirham for each, when you purchase both. A very good price, young sir."

I set the wallets down, looked him in the eye, and said, "Sir, I only require one wallet since I have only one place to put my money and other things, but I could perhaps buy another for one for my mother for a Christmas present."

"Ah yes, young sir, Christmas, I have heard of such a thing that Christians celebrate during this time of the year. Yes, either one would make a fine present for anybody, including your mother, young sir."

Again I stared him in the eye and said, "I will give you twenty dirham for both of these wallets."

"No young sir, you misunderstand me, they are only eighteen dirham each, not twenty."

"No, I will give you twenty dirham for both together, not each."

"Oh no, sir, that is not possible."

I turned to walk away and said, "Very well, sir, I shall look elsewhere for a better price, thank you."

The shopkeeper held up both wallets and said as I was walking away, "Very well sir, for you I give a very special price, these fine wallets for only thirty dirham for both. Very special price for you, young sir."

I turned around and again I took the wallets from him and touched the smooth, silky softness of the fine leather, and told him, "Twenty-five dirham is what I will pay and not one dirham more."

"Very well, young sir, I can see that you are a determined and resourceful young man, I will let them both go to you for only twenty-eight dirham, but I will be not making any money at that price. But I like you, so they are yours for twenty-eight. Very well?"

I reached into my old wallet in my back pocket and took out twenty-eight dirham and counted them out to him and said, "Thank you, kind sir; it is my pleasure to do business with you."

"No, the pleasure is mine, young sir," he said as he wrapped the two wallets in a piece of newspaper and handed them to me. And I realized that I had indeed gotten a pretty good bargain since I remembered seeing the same wallets being sold by Moroccans at the Rastro in Madrid for about three hundred pesetas, over three times the price I paid for them here at the source. And as I 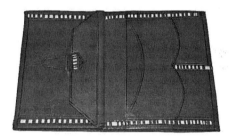 walked away with my purchases, I realize that the bargaining skills I had learned at the Rastro had again paid off quite handsomely indeed.

I caught up with my brother, Andy, and my dad who were looking inside a shop that had countless rugs and tapestries for sale. My dad was trying to speak Spanish to the shopkeeper who had a limited degree of proficiency in the language, so Johnny was helping him converse in a mixture of Spanish and French. My dad thought he knew quite a lot about oriental carpets due to the time our family had spent in Turkey and where he had purchased several expensive high-quality rugs.

After some more discussion, he ended buying a medium-sized rug measuring around one by two meters for just three hundred thirty dirham, or about thirty-three dollars. He also had managed to bargain the shopkeeper down from considerably more, and he felt he had gotten a good deal on the rug. He told us that he had a place for it near his desk in his home office.

A little later, Johnny and Andy were looking at an extensive collection of sebsi pipes at a shop next door to the carpet seller. Some of the stems were unique works of art, intricately carved and painted with an assortment of different colors and designs. They were discussing the fact that it would probably not be a good idea to bring back the sebsis that we had bought earlier and had already used since they would smell of *kif* and perhaps could cause problems at the border upon entering Spain.

So it was decided that we would all purchase new sebsis to bring back with us that were unused and had no smell or residue of *kif* to worry about. If we were asked about them at the border, we would say that they were souvenirs. Once again, we each selected a new sebsi and were able to get a great deal on three of the nicest ones the shopkeeper had for sale.

By this time the four of us were getting quite hungry, so we started looking for a place to get a meal. We walked around the Medina for a while longer until we came across a small hole-in-the-wall kind of establishment that appeared quite intriguing, as it looked like the kind of place where locals ate. The place consisted of a large room with one five-meter-long wooden table with wooden benches along each side of it to sit upon. The wooden table and benches were so worn that they looked like they could have been around since the days when Christ walked the earth. As we walked into the establishment, we noticed a large pot simmering with something bright orange in it, and we greeted the man standing by the entrance with the standard greeting, "*As-salamu alaykum,*" (Peace be upon you.) And he responded with the standard response, "*wa 'alaykumu as-salaam,*" (And upon you, peace.)

We took our seats along the long bench and in French, Johnny asked him, "Good day, sir, what do you have for four hungry and weary travelers?"

The man replied, "*Aujourd'hui, nous avons la soupe de carrottes,*" (Today we have carrot soup.)

Johnny then asked him, "*Autre chose?*" (Anything else?)

"*Pain,*" (bread) was the reply.

Johnny said politely, "*Tres bien, quatre servant s'il vous plais.*" (Very well, four servings please.)

The man came back with a huge wooden bowl in each hand, which looked like they were about the same vintage as the table and bench we were sitting on, and placed them in front of Johnny and my dad, and then returned with a bowl in each hand for Andy and me. He then came back again with four huge slices of dark unleavened bread on a wooden platter and sat it down in front of us.

We looked in our bowls and saw a rich steamy stew consisting of carrots and more carrots inside a meaty broth of undetermined origin. We each grabbed a metal spoon that was provided on the platter with the bread and dug in. It was wonderful, and a matter of fact, we all agreed that it was the best carrot soup that any of us had ever tasted. We dipped big chunks of the bread into the soup and bit into them with relish. We looked around us and saw that indeed the other two customers in the place were also eating the carrot soup as well. There was nothing else served in the place, no Coca Cola, or even mint tea, just carrot soup.

When we finished our bowls of soup, as we were getting ready to leave, Johnny asked the gentleman how much we owed him and he replied, "*Huit dirham, s'il vous plais.*" (Eight dirham, please.)

My dad handed the man a ten-dirham bill and said, "*Merci beaucoup, monsieur,*" and we walked out of the place with all of us stuffed on carrot soup and happy that we had spent under one dollar total for the four servings of soup with bread.   "*Merci beaucoup,*" indeed!

After this nice meal, Dad was feeling a little drowsy, so we walked back to the hotel with him so he could take a nap. We told him that the three of us were going to walk around a little more and possibly get some mint tea somewhere, and that we'd see him back at the room in a couple of hours. We left him snoozing on the bed and off we went, unencumbered by an "adult," at least for a little while.

Earlier we had seen an appealing-looking cafe near the soup place and so we headed there. As soon as we walked into the cafe, we could tell by the odor in the place that *kif* was being smoked inside. We found an area near the back where everyone sat on the floor, using cushions to sit on and to lean against the wall, and short tables on which to place the hot glasses of mint tea. The only ashtray in the entire room was a glass jar, half-full of water placed in the center of the room, and this is where the smokers would aim when they finished a *sebsi* full of *kif*. They would blow into the stem and the ashes of the pipe would fly across the room and land right in the jar.

I never once saw anyone miss, and there was always a fizzing sound as the embers of the ash landed in the jar of gray water. I could tell that these were some very experienced and talented *kif* smokers indeed. We sat down at a small brass table only a few inches above the carpeted floor and ordered three mint teas from the gentleman serving and after they arrived, we sat back and broke out our own *sebsis*. We each had our own along with a small supply of *kif* in our pouches and we sat back against the cushions along the wall and proceeded to do as the locals were doing.

We did get a few strange glances from the dozen or so locals in the place, but after a couple of minutes they seemed to just ignore us. Almost all the gentlemen in the place seemed to us to be wise and grizzled old men, but probably were only middle-aged. The smoking was a personal thing, and the *sebsis* were not passed around or shared in any way. I

guess the thought of sharing a *sebsi* was as strange to them as the idea of sharing a glass of mint tea.

The tea was served on a brass tray in medium-sized glasses, each with boiling hot water and stuffed with fresh mint leaves, along with a large bowl of dark sugar with spoons to add sugar to one's particular taste. Most seemed to like the tea very sweet and added several spoonfuls to each glass of tea. The mint had a kind of menthol affect and coated the throat with a fresh mint taste and helped the *kif* smokers to indulge in their favorite activity with a minimum of coughing and discomfort.

Looking around a little more, we realized that the cafe appeared to have two sections. There was an area in the far back that we hadn't noticed before where the younger smokers seemed to be congregated. This area is where we heard quite a lot of laughter and conversation going on, much different from the stony silence we heard around us where the older smokers were located, puffing away silently on their *sebsi*s.

The half of dozen or so younger men in the back of the cafe were getting quite animated and excited over something one of them had said. They were all laughing and carrying on like they had just heard the funniest thing in the world. Strange Arab music could be heard in the background, which gave the place a very exotic atmosphere, at least to our senses.

We noticed that some of the younger guys in the back were not only laughing and carrying on, but we also noticed that two of them were acting like they were in a relationship of some sort, since they were holding hands and sitting very close to each other. We noticed later on several other occasions, this display of obvious homosexuality between younger males of the Moroccan population, and we were surprised to see it so publicly displayed. But no one seemed to care or gave it much notice and they just carried on acting like a young couple in love, giggling and behaving like they were having the best of times.

Later that evening, after returning to the hotel room, we discussed this strange phenomenon with my dad and after some lengthy discussion, we surmised that what we had witnessed in the back room of the cafe was probably a very common activity among Moroccans and in the Arab world in general. We realized that because of the very strict and severe Muslim religion, with its total separation of the sexes starting right before puberty, and the fact that women are sometimes treated almost as merchandise or at best as second-class citizens, the average young male in Morocco and other Arab countries is in a situation similar to what men are faced with while in prison in the Western world.

Women are not only totally separated from the males and dress in a way in public such that one literally cannot even see their faces, much less any other part of their bodies. Also, the fact exists that in order for a man to have a wife (or several, depending on the man's wealth and social status), he purchases his wives much as one would purchase any other commodity, such as a house, an automobile, a donkey, or a business. He might trade two camels and a donkey and several thousand dirhams for a young virgin. And if he is wealthy and can afford it, he is entitled by law to have up to four wives at a time.

So this situation can be quite a detriment to the average young and lower-income man. Having few resources, the average man's possibilities of acquiring a wife can seem to be almost impossible. As in a Western country's prison system, some men just decide that any sex is better than no sex, so they start going with their own kind, which is other lonely and horny young men.

The fact that wealthy and affluent men can have up to four wives at a time also contributes to this situation by making that many fewer women available to the average man. Of course, I'm sure that the approximately ten percent of the general population who are naturally homosexual has something to do with it too, but at least the "real" homosexuals (the ones that are just born that way and their sexuality is not necessarily a product of their environment), are not discriminated against so much as they are in other countries and cultures. This tolerance of homosexuals seemed to run contrary to other aspects of the culture which seemed to us on the most part to be rather primitive and anachronistic.

The next day we continued on our way across the Moroccan countryside. Our next stop was the city of Meknes, which was only about an hour's drive from Fez, so we were able to get there fairly early in the day, giving us the time to explore the city in depth. We were impressed by the architecture of the city and the different mosques that seemed to be everywhere.

The Koran prohibits any art form that shows people or even animals, so Moroccan art consists mostly of geometrical patterns and designs and they tend to use buildings and other surfaces such as rugs, carpets, jewelry, leather goods, tapestries or just about any other item as canvasses for their art. Some of the mosques around the town of Meknes had amazing detail on the walls and doors.

After having a wonderful dinner of

lamb and couscous at a local restaurant that evening, we again returned to our hotel and indulged in more *kif* smoking until late at night, while listening to great rock music on our portable cassette player.

The next morning, we headed out to Rabat, the capitol of Morocco, which was quite modern compared to the other cities we had seen so far on our trip. The city seemed to be full of government buildings everywhere and there wasn't a lot else to see. That night, after some discussion, we decided not to head on to Casablanca the next day, as our original plans called for, since we all decided that we'd like to spend more time in Tangiers before heading back to Spain. Besides, Casablanca was a several-hour drive south of Rabat and we would end up doubling back through Rabat again to head north to Tangiers, so it was decided by all of us to forgo visiting the famed city of Casablanca on this trip. We had all seen the famous movie with Humphrey Bogart and we were certain that we'd probably have trouble finding Rick's Cafe, anyway.

So, the next day we were on our way to Tangiers! Guarding the Straits of Gibraltar and located at the northernmost tip of the continent of Africa, the city has for centuries been Europe's gateway to Africa and its blend of cultures and influences is unique in the entire country of Morocco. For much of its history it wasn't governed by Morocco, or really any country.

In fact, from 1923 to 1956 Tangiers was only loosely governed, and for years, literally almost anything was permitted. People could do whatever they wanted so long as they were well-mannered about it. Being just a short ferry ride from Spain, all kinds of strange people from all around the world found drugs, sex, and an affordable lifestyle set against an exotic background. The area has always carried a rather sleazy and underground reputation, due to its time as a semi-independent international "free" zone and as an open port that attracted foreigners, artists, thieves, smugglers, and spies, who contributed to its somewhat dismal reputation for centuries.

By the 1950s, Tangiers had the reputation as a place where anything could be bought for a price, and this element attracted the likes of people such as William Burroughs, Allen Ginsberg, Jack Kerouac, and other members of the 'Beat' generation. Later in the 1960s, members of the Rolling Stones and other famous celebrities and musicians went there to find inspiration and to smoke *kif* and hashish. William Burroughs once said, "Tangiers is one of the few places left in the world where, so long as you don't resort to robbery, violence, or some form of crude antisocial behavior, you can do exactly what you want."

This was the place where we planned to make our big score of hash to bring back to Spain with us. We had the two hundred dollars that our friends had contributed back in Madrid, and we planned to purchase one kilo of the best hash we could find and between the three of us, we'd somehow sneak it all across the Straits of Gibraltar and back to Spain.

Driving up from the south, we entered the outskirts of the city with the usual assortment of donkeys, camels, mangy dogs, and strange people who looked like they had just climbed off a time-machine from the eleventh century. Since we were planning on spending two nights in Tangiers, we did take a while to find the right hotel. We wanted to be near the old quarter, yet with easy access to the modern part of the city as well, so we found a modest hotel called *"L'Hotel Centrale"* that fit our purposes. As usual, we got two rooms with two beds each and after settling in, we went out to explore this most mysterious and exotic of cities.

As soon as the four of us started walking around, we were accosted by young boys wanting to be our guide. After the third or fourth boy approached us, we decided to accept the offer of a young fellow about ten years old by the name of Ahmed. He assured us that for only five dirham (fifty cents), he would not only show us all around the city all afternoon but also by already having a guide, we could avoid being approached by anyone else.

Soon we were immersed in the maze of small streets and alleys of the Souk of Tangiers, led by Ahmed who spoke great Spanish so we could all communicate with him. He seemed to be not only proud of his city, but he also had a vast knowledge of the history of the city and where to go for whatever we wanted. Soon we were lost and could never have found our way out of the area without the help of our young guide Ahmed.

After wandering around and looking in shops at different goods for sale, my dad decided to purchase another carpet. He seemed to have a thing for oriental rugs since the days when we lived in Turkey and he was always on the lookout for a quality rug at a good price. After being directed by Ahmed to a carpet shop that he claimed to be the best in all of Tangiers, he successfully negotiated with the shopkeeper and bought a very nice rug about one meter by three meters. He had it rolled up and wrapped in brown paper and Ahmed carried it over his shoulder for him until we returned to our hotel.

When it began to get dark, we headed back to the hotel to get ready to go out for dinner, but before we went upstairs to our rooms, Johnny and I were able to talk to Ahmed out of earshot of my dad and asked him if he knew a place to purchase hashish. He told us that he did and so we agreed to meet him the next day for that purpose.

The next day, we told my dad that we wanted to do some exploring on our own for a while, so the three of us headed out from the hotel and met up with Ahmed near the hotel at noon as we had planned. Again, we followed him through a maze of alleyways, and finally we reached an area which was more residential than commercial. There was a minimum of storefronts and shops around—instead just doorways along the small narrow streets.

Finally, we reached a particular doorway, and Ahmed knocked on the door with three short knocks. After a minute or two of waiting, a man opened the door and looked at the three American teenagers and one much younger Moroccan standing there.

He spoke quickly with Ahmed in Arabic and after a short conversation, he said to us in Spanish, "Good day, young sirs, my name is Mohamed, I understand that you would like to purchase one kilo of Moroccan hashish, is this correct?"

Johnny looked him in the eye and replied, "Yes, sir, we would like one kilo of the best available. I understand that one kilo will be two hundred American dollars; is this correct?"

"Yes, one kilo of the best Moroccan hashish, the double zero, is two hundred American dollars. Do you have the money with you now?"

"Yes, we do," Johnny said. "Can we take a look at it now, perhaps?"

"Oh, no, I do not have that amount with me here. We must go to retrieve it."

"Very well," Johnny said. "And where do we go to retrieve it?"

"We must go to a cafe on the outskirts of the city and that is where we can get this amount of one kilo of the best hashish in Tangiers. So follow me, we shall take a taxi to the location."

Mohamed told Ahmed something in Arabic and the younger Moroccan said to us, "It has been very nice to be your guide today sirs, I must go now, and it will be ten dirham for my services please."

Johnny reached into his wallet and handed him a ten dirham bill and thanked him. Mohamed seemed to be getting a little agitated and said, "Hurry, we must go now, follow me quickly."

He started walking off at a brisk pace through the maze of small streets and alleys with the three of us trying to keep up until we reached an area nearer the new quarter of the city where there were taxis parked along the street. He climbed into the front seat of one while the three of us piled into the back of the little car, and he told the driver something in Arabic and off we went, dodging traffic, pedestrians, and an occasional camel or donkey.

After driving for about fifteen minutes, we reached the outskirts of the city where the traffic and pedestrians became noticeably thinner, until finally we stopped in front of a small cafe with a Coca-Cola sign in front, with the logo in both English and Arabic.

Mohamed again said something to the driver in Arabic and then said to us in Spanish, "This taxi will wait here to give us a ride back to the center of town. Now we must enter this cafe and I will retrieve the kilo. Come now."

The four of us walked into the tiny cafe and sat down at one of the four small tables. Mohamed ordered four mint teas from the proprietor and soon we were sipping boiling hot sweet mint tea. He seemed to get more and more agitated and excited with every minute that passed by. He exchanged a few words in Arabic with a gentleman sitting at the table near us and then he turned to us and said, "Now this man here will go and retrieve the kilo and I shall wait here with you until he returns. Is that satisfactory?"

We looked around the place and Johnny said to him, "Yes, I suppose that will be fine. Do want the money now then?"

"Yes, please hand it to me under the table so no one can see the transaction, please."

Johnny slowly took the ten twenty dollar bills out of his wallet and passed them to the man under the table, out of sight of the other four or five patrons sitting in the cafe. And then Mohamed stood up and said something to the man he spoke with upon entering the place and they stepped outside.

The three of us were getting a little worried at this point because we realized that if he was just to walk away suddenly, there was not too much we could have done about it. So we were very relieved when after a minute or two he stepped back into the cafe and joined us again at our table.

He looked at us and said, "Now we shall wait a short while until my friend returns with your hashish."

He then took a dagger from his belt that we had not seen up to this point because it was hidden under his *djellaba*, and removed it from its sheath and slammed it into the wooden table in front of us, making the table wobble slightly with the impact of the knife point sticking into the tabletop. He did this several more times and was getting more and more agitated and excited and his voice got louder as he talked in Arabic and, of course, we had no clue as to what he was saying.

The few other patrons in the cafe looked our way and smiled and returned to their mint tea and *kif* smoking as the three of us began to tremble in our desert boots, getting extremely nervous and wondering if we were going to get out of this place with our lives intact. If the man's intention was to intimidate us, he had succeeded very well because I don't think any of us had ever felt as scared or as nervous as we felt sitting there around that table.

About fifteen minutes later, the fellow that Mohamed had sent for the hash walked back in and came over to our table and sat down and said something to Mohamed as he reached under his *djellaba* and pulled out a package wrapped in newspaper. He held it under the table and Mohamed said, "Very well gentlemen, which one of you wants to inspect the package? You must not look at it here but instead go the lavatory over there to look at it."

The three of us glanced at each other, and then Andy, who was sitting next to the man with the package said, "I will, I guess."

The man handed the package to Andy under the table and Andy put it under his jacket and zipped it up and then stood up and said, "Okay, guys, I'll be right back."

He walked over to the door at the back of the cafe labeled "W. C." while Johnny and I waited at the table getting more and more nervous by the minute. After a couple of minutes, Andy returned to the table and said to us, "Yeah, it looks okay. It looks like powder instead of chunk, but I guess it's all right, man."

Mohamed looked at the three of us and said with a big smile on his face, "Very well, young gentlemen, our business here is complete. The same taxi is waiting outside to take you back where we left. And don't worry, it is paid for completely. Good day to you and happy smoking!"

The three of us stood up and walked out of the cafe feeling very relieved to be away from the place and away from the dagger still stuck in the tabletop. We found the taxi waiting for us and climbed in. The taxi driver took off without a word and we settled in for the ride back to the central part of Tangiers. We were dropped off in an area near the new quarter that we recognized, and then we walked the couple of blocks to our hotel.

As soon as we entered the room Andy and I shared, Andy opened his coat and sat the package on the bed and opened it up. Wrapped in newspaper was about one kilo's worth of a powdered spice similar to curry but with a different smell and texture. We were not exactly sure what it was, but it was definitely not hash! We looked closer and smelled it and we finally recognized it as being one of the various cooking spices that we had seen for sale in the small shops in the old quarter. They are sold by the kilo and included cumin, saffron, cinnamon, paprika, turmeric, nutmeg, cardamom, and ginger, among several others. It very well could have been "*Ras El Hanout*," which is a mixture of ground spices used in many Moroccan kitchens.

The three of us looked at each other and Johnny was the first to speak, "Oh, shit! We got ripped off man! Fuck!"

Andy looked like he's about ready to cry and said, "God damn it, man! I'm so sorry, I only took a quick look at it and it looked okay I thought. Shit guys, I'm so sorry, it's all my fault, man!"

Johnny and I looked at each other and I shrugged my shoulders and I told Andy, "Shit man, it just as easily could have been one of us. It's not really your fault, the guy was so damn intimidating, I was scared shitless the whole time myself, and I know you guys were too."

Johnny looked at us and with a sad look on his face. "Well, the guys back home are going to be pretty damn pissed off that we got ripped off, but what can we do about it? We can't really go to the police now, can we?"

"Yeah, those two hundred dollars are gone, man," I said, "never to be seen again. All we can do is pool our spending money that we have left and get what we can with it. And make sure we don't get ripped off this time."

I reached into my wallet and counted out about twenty dollars in dirhams, and put it on the bed next to the fake hash and said, "I got this much, what do you guys have left?"

Andy reached into his pocket and pulled out a few bills and counted them out and said, "It looks like I got about the same, maybe a little more. How about you, John?"

Johnny did the same and put his stack of dirhams on the bed. He counted it all together and said, "I count exactly five hundred and seventy dirhams, plus I got the twenty-dollar bill I keep for emergencies in the hidden pocket of my wallet, so all together we got about seventy-seven dollars or so. It should be enough to buy something anyway to bring back with us."

"Okay," I said "No more shopping for anything for the rest of the trip, all of this money has got to go towards our next purchase, to try to get as much as we can for all the guys back home that chipped in."

Andy said with a sad look on his face, "Listen, when we get home, I'll try to explain to the rest of the guys what happened, and I hope I can get them to understand."

I thought for a moment and said, "Listen, we can't be totally broke for the rest of the trip. Dad's going to be suspicious if we have absolutely no money left at all and he's got to give us money for cigarettes, tea, and stuff. We got to keep a little in our pockets for the rest of the trip, man."

"Okay, you're right Ron." Johnny said. "We should each keep about five dollars or so for our spending money until we get home; that should be enough, right?"

"Yeah, that seems about right," I said, "since we do have a couple of days left before we even get home."

Johnny counted out fifty dirhams for each of us and again counted the remainder of the stack of bills. "Six hundred and twenty dirhams, but that's with the twenty-dollar bill. Let's make it an even six hundred dirhams for the deal. It's not a lot, but it's all we got, so it's going to have to do."

Andy looked at us and said, "I'm so glad you guys are not pissed off at me, man. I'm really so sorry."

"Don't worry, Andy," I said, "we just have to make sure that this next score is good and we don't get burnt again. Listen, why don't we go down to that place where we saw the freaks hanging out yesterday, the Café Central, I think it was called. We could just ask someone there where to score. The hell with going with another guide, man."

"You know, that's a great idea," Johnny agreed, "Let's just go down there and hang out and ask around and see what happens."

So the three of us put our jackets on and Andy grabbed the package and said, "I'm going to find a place get rid of this shit, man!"

We headed downstairs and as soon as we got onto the street, Andy put the package down on the sidewalk right next to an old man who was just sitting there and we quickly walked away.

Within a few minutes we reached the Café Central, a rather large café in the old quarter, and we found an empty table and sat down and ordered three mint teas. As we were sipping our teas, we looked around the place and we saw several tables with foreigners sitting around sipping tea and smoking *sebsis*. Most of the foreigners were hippy-looking people with long hair and dressed in blue jeans. We nodded at them and they nodded back but seemed to be unconcerned and uninterested in our presence.

After a few minutes, a young Moroccan dressed in Western clothes walked up to our table and said in English, "Good day, gentlemen, how are you today?"

The three of us looked at him and smiled and Johnny said, "Very well, how are you?"

The young man asked if he could take a seat and we indicated with a gesture that it would be fine. "Are you gentlemen looking for something in particular here or are you just enjoying the atmosphere?" he asked.

Johnny looked him in the eye and said, "Actually we were wondering if we could purchase some hashish, perhaps. Would you know where we could?"

"Yes indeed, sir," he replied, "I have some here in my pocket; how much would you like?"

"Well, we have six hundred dirhams; do you have that much worth?" Johnny asked.

"Yes, I do." He reached into his pocket and took out a brick of greenish-brown hash and sat it on the table in front of us. "Let's see, six hundred dirhams would be about this much, I think."

And he broke off two chunks each about the size and shape of an average-sized wallet and said, "Does this look about right, I sell this for three dirham per gram, so six hundred dirhams can buy about two hundred grams and these are about one hundred grams each. Would you like to taste it perhaps before purchasing?"

The three of us smiled and nodded our heads and soon we were puffing away on a *sebsi* full of hash. After a few more tokes just to make sure, we realized that this hash was the real thing and was indeed very nice. So Johnny handed him the money, and he handed Johnny the two slabs and we thanked him very much, and he thanked us very much back and then he got up and walked away, leaving us with big smiles on our faces.

As we were walking back to the hotel to continue sampling what we had just bought, I said, "Man, that was easy, why the hell didn't we just go to the Café Central in the first place?"

Andy agreed, "Yeah, instead of all that bullshit with the other guy and the taxi ride and all that, we should have just gone there from the beginning. Shit!"

Johnny looked at the two of us and said, "Well, we got a pretty good score now, I figure, so even though we lost the two hundred dollars, we got a great deal just now, so in a way it kind of makes up for it. Not totally, but a little."

I calculated, "Well, I figure we spent two hundred and sixty dollars for two hundred grams altogether; that's still over a dollar a gram. That's a little more than you can buy hash for at the *Alemana* in Madrid."

"Yeah, but how often does it work out when you go down there to score and you never do," Andy chimed in.

"Not very often," I agreed, "and it's certainly not for the lack of trying. We've been down there at least a half dozen times and I only remember scoring once."

"Well, at least we got something to take back to the guys," Johnny said.

"Yeah, now we only have to get it back through Spanish customs is all," I said with a worried tone.

"Don't worry Ron, we'll make it," Andy said with confidence.

"I hope so man, I really hope so!"

We spent one more day in Tangiers mostly sitting around the hotel room continuing to sample the hash when my dad wasn't around and the kif when he was. My dad reminded us that he would not tolerate any pot being brought across the border and asked us on the last night if we had any left. We told him we had just a little *kif* left, and we were planning on leaving it along with our used *sebsis* with some hippies we met at the Café Central before heading for the ferry, so there would be nothing to worry about while crossing the border.

Once again, he reminded us of the folly of trying to bring drugs into Spain and the harsh penalties (eight years in prison) for smuggling. We all agreed that it would indeed be foolish to try to bring anything back to Spain, and we assured him that we would definitely not even try.

The morning we were to leave for the ferry and return to Spain, we first took our remaining *kif* (just a couple of dollars worth by this point) and our used *sebsis* to the Café Central and made a young American hippy very happy when we gave it all to him, explaining that we were getting ready to cross the border and just did not want to risk it.

We divided up the two hundred grams of hash into three roughly equal pieces and each of us took our share and slipped it into our underwear, riding right over our crotch area. We had brought loose-fitting pants specifically for this purpose and with our jackets hanging down over our belts, we were confident that what we were carrying was quite well concealed. We wrapped it thoroughly in plastic that we also had brought along with us and then put a small amount of cologne on the plastic to cover up any smell that might leak through the plastic wrap.

The ferry for Algeciras left at noon and we made sure to get there early to purchase tickets for the four of us and for our car. Dad drove us aboard the ship and we spent the short ride on the aft deck looking at the receding African coastline and the ship's wake as we said goodbye to Morocco.

Arriving at Algeciras, my dad drove the car off the ship and onto dry land and into a line of vehicles waiting to go through customs. When it was our turn, my dad handed our four American passports to the customs official who asked us if we were bringing anything back from Morocco. My dad told him that we had some souvenirs including a rug and a few leather goods. The official waved us through and we drove right into Spain, with a great (if inaudible) sigh of relief from the three younger occupants of the car.

When we got back to Madrid and explained to our friends what had happened, not one of them seemed to be overly disappointed. We split up the hash that we had according to the amount that each had contributed, and everyone did get a nice amount of prime Moroccan hash for their small investment. Besides, after a few tokes, everyone involved was indeed very happy and content.

Chapter 14. Breton de Los Herreros

"Throughout human history, as our species has faced the frightening, terrorizing fact that we do not know who we are, or where we are going in this ocean of chaos, it has been the authorities - the political, the religious, the educational authorities - who attempted to comfort us by giving us order, rules, regulations, informing - forming in our minds - their view of reality. To think for yourself, you must question authority and learn how to put yourself in a state of vulnerable open-mindedness, chaotic, confused vulnerability to inform yourself." — Timothy Leary

Calle de Breton de los Herreros is a street in Madrid where I lived the last few years that I was still in Spain with my family. My mom, my brother, and I moved to the apartment in 1967 after we moved from the big house where we had been living on Calle Triana for many years. It was a large penthouse *piso* on the top floor of a six-floor building with a very large *terraza* (patio) wrapping around two sides of the apartment. It had three bedrooms as well as separate maid quarters as most residences have in Madrid.

Since my mom decided to keep our maid only part-time after moving from Calle Triana, I chose the maid quarters for my room. I liked it because it was separated from the rest of the house by the kitchen and dining area, and also because it had its own bathroom and a lot more privacy than the other bedrooms on the other side of the *piso*.

My mom and dad had been separated for a while by then. My dad was still living in his *piso* near the Plaza Peru, and they were able to find the place on *Breton* through a mutual friend of theirs. It was a sub-lease, so the person my parents paid the rent to wasn't the actual owner but instead was just the person whose name was on the lease. He had been living there for so long and had such a good deal on the rent that he was able to move out, sub-lease it to us, and make a substantial profit, at least enough for him to justify moving out. It was understood that we would only be there until the summer of 1970, when according to our family's plans, we were to move to the U.S. after I finished high school.

Part of the deal of the sub-lease was that it would require us to purchase the existing furniture that was in the apartment. The man knew that he'd probably move back in after the summer of 1970, (or possibly sub-lease it again after we left), but he wanted the furniture to stay. And he figured if we actually owned the furniture, we'd be more likely to take better care of it. The furniture was mostly antiques, and he was quite possessive of all of it. I personally thought most of it was pretty darned ugly and not very functional, but we made the best of it and tried not to harm or stain any of it in any way.

Living in a *piso* in Madrid was a little different from living in a house. For the first time, we had a lobby downstairs on the ground floor where the *portero* and his family lived. His job was to keep the building clean and everything in good operational order. His wife regularly swept and mopped not only the downstairs lobby area, but the stairways as well, all six of them! Of course, the building had an elevator, so the stairs were not used very often, but she would still clean them on a regular basis.

The *portero's* job was also to check and make sure that everyone coming and going in the building either lived there or had some business or other reason to be there. The mailboxes were in the lobby area as well and part of his job was to distribute the mail to the different occupants' mailboxes. The word *portero* literally means doorman, but his job was much more than just opening the door. In fact, I rarely saw him open the door at all, since most of the time whenever I saw him, he was lounging behind his cage in the lobby, reading the newspaper and watching his wife sweep and mop the floors. But he was a very nice fellow and always greeted us as we came and went. His name was Sebastian, and we always made sure he got a nice tip around Christmas-time.

The building also had a *sereno*. It was the *sereno's* job to open the locks on the main doors of the buildings after hours. He worked the entire block of the street and seemed to always wear a heavy long overcoat, especially in winter when the temperature would drop overnight. He was a very friendly older man by the name of Tomás, and he would

come running whenever we got home late at night after we called *"Sereno!"* quite loudly. His large ring of keys would jangle and his nightstick would smack against the walls and that is how we knew he was on his way.

This might take several minutes because he would be occupied with another tenant at another building but he would always show up, eventually. At times, he would smell like he had a few sips from his flask of cognac he carried with him to hold off the chill on a wintry night. But often when we came home late at night, we had been drinking as well, so it was great to see someone in the same state of mind as we were before we headed upstairs. Regardless of the time of the year, he was always friendly and eager to get the few pesetas tip we always gave him. And again, around Christmas, my family always gave him a nice tip and a present, usually a bottle of his favorite cognac.

He usually opened the door to the taxi if we came home by cab late at night, which was usually the case, but only if he was in close enough vicinity, and if he made it to the door before we paid the driver and just opened the door ourselves.

Conveniently enough, our piso on Breton de los Herreros was right around the corner from my parents' restaurant, *The Chalet Suizo*. The Chalet was located on *Calle Fernando de la Hoz* and because it was so close; it was easy to walk to whenever there was an event that required my mom to attend, which was quite often it seemed. The manager that my parents had hired was great at his job and they pretty much left the main operation of the restaurant in his most capable hands, but there was always some meeting or banquet or another event that required my parents' participation, so it was nice that it was so close to our new *piso*.

The manager, Paco Manzano, came highly recommended even before my parents first opened the restaurant, since he had worked at various four-fork restaurants all over Madrid before being hired by my folks. He received a small portion of the restaurant's profits, so he was very motivated to make the business a success.

My parents weren't the only owners since they initially began the business

with a friend of theirs by the name of Margarita. She was the divorced wife of a wealthy Puerto Rican businessman who was spending some time in Madrid away from her ex-husband back in San Juan. But before too long she reconciled with her husband and moved back to Puerto Rico, and at that point became an absentee owner. This left all the owner duties up to my folks to perform. So my folks became the *dueños* and were known as *Don John* and *Doña Patricia*.

The Chalet Suizo was the only Swiss restaurant in the entire city of Madrid at the time. Swiss cuisine has many influences, including French, German, and Italian but there are certain dishes that are traditionally Swiss. These include Swiss Fondue, which is probably the most famous Swiss dish, especially the way it was served in the Chalet, where two different kinds of fondue were served.

The first kind was the traditional cheese fondue which consisted of a blend of melted cheeses, wine, and seasonings and served in a *caquelon*, or fondue pot. The pot was heated with a small burner and was set in the middle of the table, and diners would spear chunks of hard bread with long forks and dip these chunks into the gooey cheese in the pot on the table in front them.

The second kind of fondue served was a fondue *bourguignon*, in which pieces of raw meat were cooked in hot oil that was heated in the fondue pot on the table. People seemed to like this fondue since it enabled them to cook their meat to the consistency they desired. And various dipping sauces were provided on the side.

Of course, these meals were served with sides of pasta, salads, and other dishes, and there was a certain etiquette about fondue. If a man lost his bread in the pot, he was to buy drinks all around, and if a woman did, she had to kiss her neighbors. And double-dipping was discouraged; each morsel was to be put in the pot only once, and the long fork was only to be used to transport the food from the pot to one's plate, not to eat with.

Spaniards really seemed to like Swiss cooking, and it became quite the novelty for a while, and the Chalet Suizo was a very popular restaurant in Madrid in the 1960s. With the help and expertise of Paco Manzano and his stuff, it became a place where Madrid's elite would congregate for drinks, conversation, and dinner. It consistently kept its coveted four-fork designation and therefore could continue to charge four-fork prices.

Paco had a team of at least four employees assigned to each table, all wearing matching dark burgundy uniforms with the Chalet Suizo logo  emblazoned in gold on the front. There were the two main waiters, one for the main dish and the other for the side dishes, and another man whose only job was to handle the drinks at each table, standing ready to top off the bottle of wine sitting on the table or bring another drink from the bar. And there was yet another man whose job was to handle the preparation and maintenance of the fondue pot itself and the clean-up after the dinner was over. It could be rather disconcerting to have four gentlemen watching you eat every morsel of your dinner and filling up your water glass as soon as it became less than half-full, but Spaniards love to eat and dining out has always been a national pastime. The clientele of the Chalet ate it up, both literally and figuratively.

After a couple of years of operation, Paco advised my parents and Margarita (who was still in Puerto Rico, but remained a partner in the business) that the small shop right next door was becoming available and he suggested that the Chalet Suizo acquire it, tear down the wall between the existing restaurant and this small store, (which at the time was a small tailor shop) and open an adjacent bar, appropriately to be named "Bar Chalet Suizo."

So after closing for about a month for construction, the business re-opened with a very nice bar attached to the restaurant. It was typical of  Spanish bars, in that it was long and narrow with one long wooden bar running the length of it. And as was the restaurant, it was decorated in typical Swiss decor, with items that my parents had brought back from their travels to Switzerland, which included stag's horns, paintings of the Swiss Alps, and other native Swiss items.

The bar soon became a very popular place for local businessmen to stop by after work to have a *copa* and a *tapa*. Like most businesses of this  nature, it was the atmosphere that brought the people in and kept them coming back. With the popular restaurant right next door, the bar shared the friendly and open environment of the restaurant. And even if a gentleman couldn't afford to eat very often at a four-fork restaurant, at least he could share the ambiance of the place by just having a drink or two at the bar.

From the first grand opening of the restaurant in 1964, the Chalet Suizo had the reputation of being a very popular place for local celebrities and other well-off people to come and dine and be seen among other wealthy and famous people. There was always an event of some sort or another going on at the place, whether it was a wedding reception, a meeting of a local organization, or just a large group out on the town. There was always room for large parties in a festive and fun atmosphere.

Because my parents knew many people in Madrid, including a lot of Americans from their various different social contacts, the restaurant became a kind of meeting place whenever a place was needed in downtown Madrid to have a large gathering. In Madrid in the 1960s, there was a local English language newspaper for the English-speaking community called the "Guidepost," and they often mentioned the Chalet Suizo as one of the nicest places to have a social gathering or just a good time. And both of my parents, being the *dueños* of the restaurant, in turn met more people, and became friends and socialized with many of Madrid's finest citizens, both Spanish and foreigners.

Even though they were separated, they remained a couple in the eyes of the employees of the Chalet, and for the many social functions that were held there. The business became a success as

the result of lots of hard work, Paco Manzano's professional management skills, a little luck, and the excellent social and business skills on the part of both of my parents.

Back at our piso on Calle Breton de los Herreros, Johnny and I were involved in developing our own social skills and everything else, including classes and credits that were required to finish high school. Johnny was only one year ahead of me because they required him to repeat the tenth grade at MHS since the American school system could not accept any school credits for him attending the French school in Alicante in 1965-66. So he was due to graduate in the summer of 1969, and me the following year in 1970.

But that left him with one full year when he would not be in school, and was basically just waiting until the next summer when I graduated, after which we'd all return to the States with Johnny and me planning to enroll in a college in Texas. My parents didn't like the idea of him being idle for an entire year, so he enrolled at the University of Madrid and took some classes there for a semester, but due to several factors he dropped out after the first semester. These included the fact that the Spanish educational system is far advanced over the American one, with students beginning college in Madrid with an education level equal to graduate students in the States.

Another factor was the language. Johnny and I both spoke fluent Spanish, but it was still a second language to us and our writing and reading skills were not at all near college level. And another factor was that Johnny was just not into it very much at all. He had just finished thirteen years of school and really needed a break from the books and studying altogether for a while. But he managed to have a lot of fun that year after high school because he still knew a lot of friends from school, and after almost ten years in Spain, he definitely knew what to do and where to go for adventures and good times.

He tried various endeavors during that year to do something with his life though. His friend Scott Wilson and he were planning on moving to Australia together and working on a sheep ranch that a relative of Scott's owned, but for one reason or another, that plan fell through, and Scott ended up in the American military not too long after that. By the influence and recommendation of a friend of my parents', he also had an opportunity to get into the U.S. Naval Academy in Annapolis, Maryland, but his grades weren't quite good enough and that fell through as well.

Another opportunity arose for him when my mom met an Egyptian man through the Chalet Suizo who was a successful shipping magnate. He owned a shipping line based out of Cairo, with several ships that made deliveries to and from various ports around the Mediterranean Sea. While chatting with him one time, my mom had briefly mentioned to him Johnny's idleness and his love of the sea, and this gentleman suggested that perhaps Johnny would like to work on one of his ships and get his start as an able-bodied seaman. Johnny loved the idea when it was brought up to him because he had always loved the ocean, and he thought it would be a great adventure to work on a ship for a while traveling the seven seas.

Now, there is a sort of "Catch 22" to getting a job aboard a ship in any capacity whatsoever. To work on any ship, a man must have his "seaman's papers," which are basically a log of the various ships he's worked on, what ports of call he's been to, the different jobs he has done aboard ocean-going vessels, etc. And they require any man to have these "papers" in order to get any job on any ship. But how is he someone supposed to get his *first* job without such papers is the catch.

This Egyptian friend of my mom's was Johnny's avenue of landing this first job on board a ship without having any seaman's papers. Being the owner of the ship, all he had to do was tell the ship's captain that this young man would begin as a cabin-boy and for the captain to hire him and put him to work. And as a matter of fact, the Egyptian told him, he had a ship docked in Barcelona that was at that moment taking on a ship-load of eggs to deliver from Barcelona to Beirut, Lebanon. And the return voyage would be a load of textiles from Beirut to Malaga, Spain. The entire voyage would take around five weeks to complete altogether.

Johnny was excited and ready to do it. The Egyptian put in a call to the captain of the ship and made the arrangements for Johnny to begin as a cabin-boy and he was to report to the captain the following week at the ship in port in Barcelona. He packed his small suitcase and spent considerable time preparing for this adventure. He had his passport in hand and a little money that Mom had given him to take the train to Barcelona and to begin his new life working onboard a ship.

He returned about a week later from Barcelona with bad news. It turned out that he had made it to Barcelona in plenty of time and had reported to the captain of the vessel, on the day and time as planned, but the captain (who was an Arab of questionable background and origin), took one look at him and refused to have him on board his ship, with no reason given or offered. And since he was the captain of the vessel, his word was law on board that ship, regardless of what the owner said or desired.

To say that this was a great disappointment to Johnny would be an understatement. He could never understand why the captain refused to hire him, or even to have him onboard his ship. He was dressed nicely and had a decent short haircut, so it was not his looks that were the issue. After thinking about it, he came to realize that it most likely had to do with the fact that he was an American, since some people in the world just did not like Americans at all, due to the politics and actions of the United States government and the implications those policies had been having on the rest of the world.

But life went on and Johnny found other things to occupy his time for the remainder of that year, as did I. My mom would take frequent trips out of town, either with my dad to Switzerland for business purposes or to other places with various friends. And whenever she was ready to leave on a short trip, she would always say to the both of us, "Okay, boys, remember, no parties when I'm gone. All right, you promise, guys?"

And our response was always the same, "Oh, don't worry, Mom, we won't have any parties."

But we almost always did. Some of the parties we had at our place became legendary among our small group of friends. A party at the Walker brothers' house was always a guarantee of a great time to be had by all, and I'm sure some of the people who attended those get-togethers still remember them to this day. Acquiring booze was not an issue for us as it would have been for under-aged kids in the States, because all we had to do was walk downstairs to the *liquoria*, and buy whatever we wanted. And since the group of friends who attended our parties was the same bunch of guys that we shared our hash supplies with so that was never a problem either. At times, there were perhaps two or three dozen people crammed into our living room at one time, with some spilling over out onto the terrace and into the bedrooms.

I know for a fact that at least a few people lost their virginity on my mom's queen-sized bed during one of our parties. The stereo was blasting the latest by Led Zeppelin, The Beatles, The Stones, The Doors, Jimi Hendrix, and many others and formed the soundtrack to all this debauchery, lust, and madness. Drunk as skunks, stoned to the max, and with hormones running wild can be quite a combination for a bunch of teenagers learning the ways of the world and the ways of the opposite sex.

One particular party, the details of which I barely remember, but still sticks in my mind for obvious reasons, was the time when I finally first got laid. Her name was Connie, and she had a big crush, as many girls I knew at the time, on my good friend Mike. Mike was a really good-looking guy and quite charming and that's why so many girls were so crazy about him. Because of this, he had his choice of just about any girl around and so that is exactly what he did.

At one party at our place, Mike and Connie were both there, and she was making it obvious that she wanted to sleep with Mike. But he had several other girlfriends going at the time and he indicated that he just wasn't interested. So she set her eyes on me, thinking  erroneously that perhaps she could get to Mike through me somehow. I never could figure out why she would have thought this, but with me being just fifteen with all my hormones raging, I went along with her and ended up taking her to my room to be alone.

She had far more experience than I had at this kind of thing, but of course I couldn't let her know that, so I pretended that I had done this type of activity lots of times in the past. For some strange reason, my room had bunk beds in it, probably because we rented the furniture and that's just what was there. So we took off our clothes and climbed onto the bottom bunk and proceeded to do what members of the opposite sex do in this type of situation. I was on top trying to do my thing, but I kept banging my head on the top bunk which was only inches above my head as I was propping myself up on my hands while perched over her.

The worst part was that due to this awkward position I was in while trying not to bump my head too hard on the bed springs right above me, my thing kept falling out of her on a regular basis. She helped me to get it back in, but within a very short time, again it would just plop out of her, much to her dismay and mine.

After a while, both of us were getting quite frustrated with this turn of events and so she decided to take charge. She decided that things might work out slightly better if she got on top and so was in more control. This change of position worked out a little better as she was able to lean over me more easily without banging her head on the top bunk as badly as I had been doing earlier, and things eventually proceeded to their natural conclusion.

After waiting so long to do the deed, I felt a little disappointed, I think. It was a lot of fun but I guess I was hoping it would be more than it actually was. I found out later that it's who you do it with, not just the deed itself that makes the most difference.

Connie eventually made the rounds and before too long ended up sleeping with my brother and several of my friends as well, but never with Mike, as far as I know. And I think she eventually finally found a steady boyfriend and I'm sure she made him quite happy, knowing the sort of appetites she had and the considerable skills she had acquired from experience.

These wild parties that my brother and I had at our place when my mom was away kept going on for quite a long time, and we always made sure to clean everything up and show no trace of any partying before she got back from her trips, so she didn't catch on to our shenanigans for a long time. But eventually, all good things must come to an end and that was the case with the legendary parties we held.

One weekend, Mom went away again, and so we called almost everyone we knew over for a get-together that Saturday night. The usual crowd showed up along with some other people that just came along with somebody else but were technically not invited. One particular girl came with a guy named Charlie that we hadn't known very long, but we had invited him over, anyway. She seemed a little sleazy—not in the good way like Connie was, but instead with a kind of criminal element and vibe about her.

She ended up going into my mom's bedroom with Charlie, to do what we all knew people did in there on my mom's big queen-sized bed, and we didn't think much of it at the time. Everyone was partying: drinking, smoking and having the usual great time and things were going wonderfully all night. Finally, in the morning the only people left in the house were just my brother and me along with one buddy sleeping on the couch and another crashed on the top bunk in my bedroom. We all got up and cleaned up the place as we always did, and we were even smart enough to change the sheets on my mom's bed since they appeared to have gotten slightly stained somehow. Luckily, we only used plain white sheets in the house, so she wouldn't notice that someone had changed them once she got home later that evening.

So, Johnny and I were sitting pretty when she arrived home and nothing looked out of place since we had done an excellent job of cleaning up all evidence of our party. Everything appeared to be fine until later that evening after dinner when she came into the living room where Johnny and I were sitting and looked about as furious as we'd ever seen her.

She looked at the two us and said, "Boys, did you have a party here while I was gone?"

Johnny and I both looked at her innocently and he replied as sincerely as possible, "Um, no, Mom, why do you ask?"

"Well, I just took a look at my dresser and I realized that something looked wrong. My jewelry box was not where I usually leave it. And when I looked inside, I saw that my gold necklace and matching earrings are missing! What the hell went on here when I was gone?"

Uh oh! Busted!

Johnny looked at her and said, "Well, Mom we did have a couple of friends over to listen to music last night, but it was just a couple of people, not really a party or anything."

"I don't care how many people came over, I told you not to have anyone here when I'm gone! Now look what has happened! Someone stole my nicest things!"

She looked like she was about to cry tears of rage and frustration, and Johnny and I both felt worse than we had in many years. Feelings of guilt, remorse, and shame overtook the both of us and soon we were on the verge of tears ourselves.

Holding back my tears, I said to her, "Mom, we're so sorry. A couple of people we didn't know very well came over last night and some girl with Charlie went into your room for a while. She must have swiped your things. I know it couldn't have been Charlie because he's a decent guy."

"Well, I expect you to find out who did this and get my things back! And never will you guys ever have any of your friends over to this place ever again, do you understand?"

"We're so sorry, Mom," Johnny said to her in the most sincere voice he could muster and added, "We're going to get to the bottom of this and find out who did it and get your things back for sure."

"I really hope you do, and boys, I can't begin to tell you how disappointed I am in the both of you. I trusted you and now that trust is gone. And it's going to be a long time before I can ever trust either one of you again!"

We never did recover my Mom's gold jewelry; after talking to Charlie, he claimed that he barely knew the girl he had brought along and all he knew was that her name was Susie and that she didn't even go to our school, but he thought that she went to ASM.

After that we rarely had parties at our place again. We did have a few friends over occasionally, but the wild all-nighters while our Mom was out of town were a thing of the past for us. It just went to prove that the actions of one poor, selfish, desperate person can ruin things for a whole group of people, unfortunately.

But our house wasn't the only place where great parties were held in Madrid in those days. Since we hosted parties on a regular basis for a while there, Johnny and I were invited to quite a few parties in return as well. One party remains one of the all-time strangest and memorable experiences of my lifetime.

A good friend of ours by the name of Dave lived in the *Chamartin* area of Madrid, very near my good friend Andy who was the guy who had gone to Morocco with us the previous Christmas vacation. Dave lived on the sixth floor of his particular apartment building, and the previous summer had spent a lot of time in Benidorm, where he had met and gotten to know pretty well the same two British fellows that I had met through Scott Wilson.

Ian and Matthew had come down to Madrid from London and had called Dave's house after checking into a local *pension*. Their plan was to stay around Madrid for a while before heading down to Benidorm to spend the summer. So Dave let some of the people who knew them from Benidorm know that they were in town, and that they had brought something special with them.

Before boarding the flight from Heathrow to Barajas, Ian had emptied out a toothpaste tube and had inserted a small bag with fifty hits of "purple haze" acid. He stuffed some toothpaste back into the tube, put the cap back on and brought it with him to Spain, and he was willing to share this with his American friends who lived in Madrid whom he had met in Benidorm the previous summer. And it just turned out that Dave's parents were going out of town that coming weekend and we were all invited over to his place to indulge in this new and exciting drug.

Altogether there were about ten people there that night, including my brother, Dave, Andy, my friend Bill from Canillejas, J.P., Moose, William, and most of the other guys who were in our little hash-sharing group. There were no females present if I recall, but that might have been a good thing considering how things turned out to go that night.

When Johnny and I arrived by *tranvia*, we were two of the last to arrive. Ian had already distributed one tab of the purple acid to everybody who was there, and he asked Johnny and me if we wanted to partake. Neither one of us had ever tried this stuff before, very much like everybody else in the house, except for Ian and Matthew of course, who were doing it on a pretty regular basis by then. Being cautious of new and unknown things, Johnny and I decided we would split one tab between us, so after Ian gave it to us, we got a kitchen knife from Dave's kitchen and sliced the tiny thing in half. It was only about as big around as a pencil eraser, maybe even smaller, and a bright purple in color.

After putting the tiny things on our tongues, we washed them down with glasses of water and waited. The other guys had dropped theirs about an hour or so before our arrival, but none of them had really started feeling anything yet. In fact, a couple of guys were even wondering if the shit was any good at all. But pretty soon, we could tell that it was pretty good after all.

I soon noticed that our friends were acting very strangely indeed. William, my half-Japanese friend, had wrapped himself in a blanket from Dave's bed and was running around like a crazy man until he ended up hiding in a dark closet for the rest of the night. Bill from Canillejas was outside on the patio looking down from the sixth floor and freaking out over the view. And almost everybody was freaking out, including Johnny and me eventually. I was glad that Johnny and I had only taken a half tab each because we were able to maintain a sort of calmness and equilibrium about us that the other eight guys there seemed to have lost.

What LSD basically does is remove one's ego temporarily, and the person ends up ego-less, which can be very strange to most people the first time. To just exist as a human being, a bag of bones, flesh, blood, and brains without the sense of self can be alarming and disconcerting to say the least. At times I felt that I was merely a casual observer of my own life and my own thoughts, as if I was outside looking in and just seeing myself for the first time, and just watching my life go by in front of me.

Ian and Matthew were the only two who had done this LSD several times before and knew what to expect, so they were fine, but the rest of us who had never done this sort of thing before were tripping heavily. I noticed that for the first time in my life, I could see music floating around in the room as waves of color and vibration. Dave had a stack of albums playing on the stereo that included the usual rock-and-roll records, but he also had an obscure album called "The Moray Eels Eat

The Holy Modal Rounders," by a band by the name of The Holy Modal Rounders, and it had a song on it called the "Bird Song" that was featured in the cult movie "Easy Rider."

That song seemed to really get to me and I went over to the stereo and lifted up the needle several times to replay it and to listen to it again and again. It indeed made me feel like a bird myself and soon I had my arms out like wings and was feeling like I was floating around the room. Their music sounded to me like old-time music but with a strange combination of folk music and this new emerging genre of modern music known as psychedelic.

Most of the guys were doing all right and trying not to freak out too much. Andy sat in a corner most of the evening and didn't say a word to anyone for hours. Dave was trying to keep cool since it was his place and he had to maintain it, but after a while he was tripping heavily as well. The only people who seemed halfway okay were Ian and Matthew, and they went around telling everyone that this was only temporary and within a few hours we'd all return to normal.

And they were right. It took all night, but sometime before dawn, "our rainbows started to turn brown," to use the words of The Holy Modal Rounders. And by the time everybody started leaving to make their way back to their homes and their beds, everyone who was there that night had been changed to a certain degree. None of us would ever be exactly the same again, and all of us were a little more experienced and slightly wiser in the ways of the world and of ourselves after that most memorable of evenings.

Not all the partying in Madrid in those days involved illegal psychedelic drugs. There is a great tradition in Spain to celebrate "*la noche vieja,*" or "the old night." This was the last day of the year, New Year's Eve among English speakers. Spaniards loved to have any excuse to party and to get rip-roaring drunk, and the last day of the year was always a good one. To ensure having good luck during the following year, the Spanish tradition was to eat one grape for each time the clock rang counting in the New Year. And the best place to do this in all of Spain was at *La Puerta de Sol*, which was not only the main center of Madrid but also the place where all of Spain's highways originated, and the measuring of the highways began from. So if you found yourself on a lonely stretch of highway on the outskirts of Albacete, for example, and you saw a highway sign that read "KM 321," that meant that you were exactly 321 kilometers from *La Puerta del Sol* in downtown Madrid.

Every New Year's Eve, this was the best place to be in all of Spain. The street vendors sold small paper cups, each containing twelve grapes, so people were able to ensure their luck and prosperity in the coming year. The crowds started arriving right after dark and the place filled up quickly. The numerous bars and cafes around the plaza were also filled to capacity and people started celebrating early. By the time the big clock on the wall began to ring out its twelve chimes, most people were sufficiently inebriated to welcome the New Year in the proper frame of mind.

It was just one huge outdoor party, and it seemed like over half of Madrid's population was crowded into *La Puerta del Sol*. Everything was crazy, and everybody was as drunk as possible it appeared. Most people had their own bottle with them and by the time the clock started gonging, a lot of sharing of beverages went on, as well as everyone trying to gobble down their twelve grapes before the official New Year began. Every female there got hundreds of kisses and a hug from complete strangers and the happiness and exhilaration was absolutely contagious. Even if you were the rare teetotaler who hadn't had a drink all night, the atmosphere of the place made you feel almost as drunk as the person next to you who had been drinking all night.

It truly was one of the great celebrations of the world. *La Puerta del Sol* is located only a few short blocks from another famous Spanish plaza, *La Plaza Major.* Literally it means "the Old Plaza" and it is indeed old. The origin of the plaza went back to 1577, when King Felipe II hired Juan de Herrera, a renowned classical architect, to remodel the existing *Plaza del Arrabal,* which was becoming quite busy and chaotic.

De Herrera designed it but construction didn't begin until 1617 under the reign of King Felipe III, and for this reason the famous equestrian statue in the middle of the plaza is none other than Felipe III himself. It was completed in 1619 but due to an enormous fire; it was reconstructed again in 1790 and this is the version of the plaza that we can see today. The new statue of Felipe III was not placed in the center of the plaza until 1848.

It was this statue of this king on horseback that almost landed me in jail one evening. One night I went with my friend J.P. down to a place near *La Plaza Major* called *La Casa del Abuelo,* (the house of the grandfather). This bar was famous for their sweet red wine which they carried by the barrel in the bar. It was right near *La Plaza Major* and was also near a place that sold the best *bocadillos de calamares* (fried squid sandwiches) in all of Madrid. These sandwiches were a favorite of mine and J.P.'s, not only because they were extremely tasty but since we were always on a slim budget, they were very reasonably priced as well. They took a bun, sliced it open and toasted it lightly on the grill, then stuffed it full of fried *calamares* (calamari) which were lightly breaded and deep-fried. They were just delicious and two of them would make a meal, and just as with about everything is Spain, they cost *un duro,* or 5 pesetas, the same price as *un chato de vino de Abuelo's.*

This particular night, J.P. and I were at Abuelo's drinking vino tinto by the bucketful it seemed, after indulging in a couple of our favorite *bocadillos* at the place next door, and after a while neither one of us were feeling any pain whatsoever, as they say. We stumbled out to the *Plaza Major* and were standing looking up at the statue of King Felipe when suddenly I had a great idea. I thought it might be the perfect time to get up on the horse and try to ride it sitting right behind old Felipe since there seemed to be just enough room behind him for one more rider.

So after getting a boost up by J.P., I got mounted right behind the King and put one arm around him and the other waving in the air and started shouting for him to get going, and that we weren't going fast enough. "Giddy-up, Felipe!" I kept shouting over and over again, urging him to get our steed moving along. J.P. was laughing harder than I had ever seen him laugh and I was afraid he might wet himself, but I kept at it for quite a while.

However, within about five minutes of my mounting the statue, two *Guardia Civil* with their dark green uniforms and their strange leather hats showed up and neither one of them were laughing at all nor did they look very happy. They shouted at me to get off the statue and started cussing at me as well.

"Cabron, bajate de alli! No tienes verguenza! Ni respecto! Bajate de alli ahora mismo, jilipollas!"

A rough translation would be as follows, "You bastard, get down from there! You have no shame! Nor respect! Get down from there right now, you little asshole!"

I jumped down from my perch immediately and started apologizing instantly. J.P. jumped in and started apologizing as well. He tried to explain that I had way too much to drink of the great vino tinto from *Abuelo's* and did not know what I was doing, and he asked them to please forgive my rudeness and thoughtlessness. Also, that I was a young and stupid American but I meant no disrespect to the King or to Spain.

The older of the two *Guardias* looked at us and said, *"Vamanos, los dos al carcel ahora mismo. Los que no tienen respecto tienen que pagar. Andale, vamanos ya!"*

Which translates to, "Let's go, both of you to jail right now. Those that have no respect must pay. Come on, let's go now!"

Again, I tried my hardest to look sorry as well as respectful as I could, and J.P. again said to them, "We are so sorry, sirs. My friend had a little too much to drink tonight that is all. We were just going home now at this instant. Let us go and you shall never see us again around here in the most beautiful of all of Madrid's plazas."

Then the younger of the two *Guardias* said something to the older one about stupid foreigners who can't hold their *vino*, and finally after a very stern and severe warning to never do anything like this ever again, they finally let us go.

As we staggered gratefully away from them back to the Metro stop to head home, I looked at J.P. and whispered under my breath, "Shit man, I thought we had it there! Thanks for sticking up for me back there."

"Don't worry, Ronnie, they wouldn't have taken us to jail, too much paperwork for them and too much of a hassle. Besides, those guys would rather just go back to standing around and sipping on their cognac anyways!"

Eventually, due to similar horseback riding attempts by other drunken tourists, within a few years of this experience, the powers that be in Madrid decided it would be better if there was a tall and spiked wrought-iron fence around the statue to prevent such shenanigans from happening again. And that is the way the statue sits today.

There was another place not far from the Plaza Major that was frequented by lots of tourists as well as young, hungry, and thirsty local residents. *Las Cuevas de Luis Candela* (the Caves of Luis Candela) was a restaurant that had an unusual history and took its name from the legendary bandit Luis Candela. Candela was the Spanish equivalent of Robin Hood, who according to legend would rob banks and stagecoaches and store his loot in the ancient caves where the restaurant sits today. In the 1940s, the famous bullfighter Felix Colomo Diaz converted the caves into a restaurant and restored much of the original ambiance. Everything about the place reeked of Spanish history and culture, and it had become a major tourist attraction. The waiters and staff wore traditional outfits from the 1800s, and the place had flamenco shows regularly and other attractions for the tourists and others looking for a true Spanish experience.

On very special occasions and when we could afford it, a group of us would go down to the "Caves" and indulge in a little Spanish history and atmosphere. It was rather strange to eat dinner in a place that was basically a cave, with cold, dank and wet rock walls and with the roof being only a few inches above the tallest guy's head. But, it was great fun and a good place to take people from out of town to experience a bit of the true old Spain.

Living in Madrid was quite an exceptional opportunity, and I realize now that being as young and dumb as I was at the time, I probably didn't experience it as much as I could or should have. I went to *El Prado* museum regularly on field trips while in school, but I never really realized or appreciated what I was seeing there. I did get great lessons on the classic Spanish painters such as Goya, Velasquez, and El Greco, and I learned how to distinguish between their styles and some the history of the artists, but to me it was just another boring day at school and at the time I was really into other things as young kids are apt to be doing.

One thing that caught my eye one day while looking at all the paintings in the Prado was the incredible amount of nudity that seemed to be prominent in a lot of the paintings. I asked my art teacher who was leading our tour of the museum why there were so many naked ladies in the pictures, but her reply left me feeling that I hadn't gotten the complete answer. She told our class that the reason there was so much nudity in the art we were seeing was because it was a big challenge for the artists to get the human flesh-tone color absolutely correct, so that is why they painted so many nudes, to be able to demonstrate their command and ability to get this most difficult of colors just right.

I then asked her why they seemed to paint more ladies than men without their clothes on, and she mumbled something about the fact that most (if not all) of these artists were men, so they chose their models to be female. I realized later that the reason why so many artists chose to paint the female figure nude is because (as most men know) the female figure, especially nude, is a work of art in itself, and to try to capture the beauty and loveliness of the nude female form is a noble, honorable, and necessary endeavor for most artists.

My favorite paintings in the Prado were two by Goya that hung on opposite sides of a large entryway between two rooms. On the left side of the doorway was *La Maja Vestida,* or the clothed Maja. And on the other side was the same model but nude, and it was named *La Maja Desnuda,* or the nude Maja. After studying both for quite a while and carefully noticing what she looked like with and without her clothes on, I decided that I really preferred the nude one. To me she looked prettier and more natural, and she had just a slightly different look on her face than in the one where she was dressed.

I did see the most famous of all paintings one time. The *Mona Lisa* by Leonardo da Vinci was on loan for a while from the Louvre in Paris to the Prado and my class went down to see it. The security around the painting was monstrous, with several heavily armed guards around it at all times, and a velvet rope keeping anyone from approaching it too closely.

This is not surprising considering that it is known to be the most valuable work of art in the world, valued at 100 million dollars in 1962 and at nearly 800 million dollars today. The smile on Mona Lisa's face was what our teacher instructed us to look at carefully, but at such a young age, I didn't see what the big deal was about it, or why her expression was so special. I did notice that her eyes tended to follow me wherever I went in the room, but a lot of paintings have eyes that are able to do the same thing, including the one of a Spanish *señorita* hanging in the living room at our house.

There were a few people whom I knew quite well at the time who were really into skiing as in strapping long boards onto your feet and sliding down a snowy mountain on them. My friend Dave was really into it, and one time he invited me along with some other friends to a mountainous area near Madrid called *Navacerrada.* I had been there several times in the past, mostly on day trips with my parents to get out of the city for a while and play in the snow, of which there was always an abundance of in the winter season. But I had never been there for the purpose of skiing until this trip.

Navacerrada is a small town a little over fifty kilometers from Madrid, so it was a short trip by bus or car and it was possible to go there for the day and return to the city by nightfall. It lies at an elevation of almost 1900 meters (about 6300 feet) above sea level so in the winter there was almost always snow on the mountain. There was a ski lift as well as several places to rent the necessary equipment for the sport. There were also several lodges that offered warm fireplaces, stiff drinks, and a friendly atmosphere to combat the often bitter cold that one encountered at the top of the mountain.

Since I had never been skiing before, I was a little apprehensive, yet eager to get my feet wet, so to speak. We got there early in the day and looked forward to a great day of skiing. We bought the ski lift tickets that enabled one to ride as often as one liked up to the top of the mountain and then to ski back down. I went ahead and rented the gear which included the skis and poles, as well as the boots, gloves and the other items to protect one from the elements.

I was eager to get up to the top and ski down, and as I watched people doing it, it appeared to be quite simple. The fellow that rented the gear showed me how to attach the skis to the boots and how to push oneself along with the help of the poles held in the hands, so I thought I had pretty much gotten the basics of it before I even got onto the ski lift. I slowly got myself over to where the ski lift was, and after watching people for a minute, I figured I could probably get myself up to the top of the mountain with a minimum of effort. The lift attendant got me into position along with another person, and when the lift came around, it picked both of us up and took us up and up to the top of the mountain.

The ride was fantastic as well as was the view from way up there on the lift, and I was really enjoying the ride. But before I knew it, we had reached the top, and I watched the other people in front of me as they timed it just right and pushed off at the exact moment to clear the ever-moving lift. So I did what they did and found myself at the top of the mountain where there was a rather flat area, clear of trees, but with lots of thick snow everywhere. The guy who rode up with me and I had chatted on the way up, and after he heard that this was my first time

skiing, he suggested that I begin at an area known as "the bunny slope," which was located right near where the lift turned around and headed back down, without any passengers, of course.

I made my way over to the bunny slope, which I thought was a pretty sissy name, but I kept that to myself. A nice lady was there along with several young kids and she was showing them the basics of how to push yourself along using the poles and to use them to keep your balance as well. I figured that I had that part down already, so I slowly made my way over to the beginning of the big slope, the one that went all the way down to the bottom where I had just come up from on the lift.

I stood there for a few minutes watching as the other skiers took off and headed down the slippery slope. I noticed that they were doing a rather unusual maneuver; instead of just skiing right down the hill, they seemed to be taking their time with it, and going in a slightly zigzag pattern. I figured that since they had made such an effort to reach the top of the mountain by riding the lift and everything that they probably just weren't in much of a hurry to get back down, so they were taking their time with it and enjoying the ride more by taking a little longer with it.

I pushed off and headed downhill. I soon realized that I had forgotten to learn one very important thing: where were the brakes? I kept going faster and faster and I had no idea how to stop! Before too long I was speeding down the hill and passing everyone else who was zigzagging down the hill, and I kept gaining speed. I started yelling at the top of my lungs, "Watch out! I can't stop! Get out of my way! Help!"

People saw me coming and also heard me yelling and were able to move out of my way and I felt lucky that I didn't run anyone over. But I still couldn't stop, but just kept going faster and faster. There are quite a few trees on the ski run in *Navacerrada* and I still don't see how I managed to avoid them all on my long downhill run. I had no idea that skiing involved certain skills such as the "traverse," which is the zigzag maneuver that the other skiers were doing going down the hill which allowed one to control the speed and direction. Another technique that I hadn't yet learned was called the "snow- plough," where the skis are held in a "V" formation with the tips almost touching which allows for slowing down and turning.

But I knew nothing of these skills as I kept speeding down the slope, gaining momentum by the force of pure gravity. I was whizzing by every other skier on the slope and I was still yelling at the top of my lungs, "Get out of my way! I can't stop! Watch it!"

After what seemed like a very long time, but I'm sure was really only a few minutes, I reached the bottom of the slope and it finally leveled out somewhat. I saw a tall snow bank right in front of me where a snowplow had pushed the snow to clear the area in front of the ski rental shack and that was where I was headed. When I reached the snowbank, I deliberately ran into it and fell over to stop my momentum and to cushion my fall.

Luckily, I was all right, with nothing hurt but my pride. Several guys ran up to me asking if I was okay and they looked relieved when I told them I was. One guy asked me what had happened, and I told him that perhaps I needed some lessons before I tried it again and he seemed to agree with me one hundred percent. They eventually walked away and left me to my own devices, and to my shame.

I managed to get the skis off of my feet and carried them along with the poles over my shoulder back to the rental shack and turned them in to the guy working there and told him, "I really don't think this sport is for me; you can have these back. I don't need them anymore."

He gave me a peculiar look and said, "Very well, sir. I'm sorry that this sport isn't to your satisfaction."

I looked him in the eye and said, "It's not your fault, sir, I just don't think I am the snow skier type, but thanks anyway."

I walked away, never to try this silly sport again. I headed over to the lodge and spent the rest of the day sipping brandy in front of the roaring fireplace and nursing my bruised ego. And I realized that I was very lucky and that I could have seriously injured myself or even worse, injured someone else, an innocent but more experienced skier who just happened to be in my way.

I realized something else that day: that I am more of a beach kind of guy instead of the mountain man type, and that I really prefer lying in the sun on a warm beach somewhere watching pretty girls in bikinis instead of freezing my ass off with cold wet snow getting everywhere, including my nether regions, and nothing to look at but girls dressed like they might be going on an arctic expedition somewhere.

And that is pretty much the way I have been the rest of my life, and as I got older, it has also influenced where it is I chose to live later in my life, and that has been preferably somewhere warm and dry. Sometimes one learns life lessons at the most unexpected times and places, that's for sure!

Chapter 15. Off to the New World

"It takes a very long time to become young."
— *Pablo Picasso*

By 1970, which marked the end of that strange, wonderful and decadent decade of the 1960s, my family and I had been living in Spain for ten years. We did return to the States three times during those ten years for visits, always during the summers when Johnny and I were off from school. These summer visits always consisted of visiting relatives and friends in both Texas and Oklahoma, along with a few other places.

The first of those stateside trips was in 1964, right after my dad had retired from the Air Force, and one reason we took the trip then was because the Air Force technically owed him one return trip for his whole family from Spain back to the States. They had paid for him to go to Spain four years earlier when he was on active duty and therefore they were obligated to pay the return fare, which he took advantage of, naturally.

To fly a family of four-round trips across the Atlantic was not cheap, even in those days, so my dad took advantage of every possibility to save some money on traveling, including flying by *Space Available*. "Space A" was part of his retirement benefits package from the military and it meant that as retired ex-military, he could fly on military flights anywhere in the world for free if there was available space on the airplane. They also allowed him to have eligible dependents (his family) accompany him as well. This was a great retirement benefit and saved him many thousands of dollars in traveling expenses over the years. Of course, he used this free travel for just himself too and ended up traveling all over the world for both for business and pleasure for the rest of his life.

My mom could no longer fly with him for free after they got divorced, and Johnny and I no longer could after we turned the pivotal age of twenty-one, but until that point, we indeed did travel on a lot of military flights back and forth across the Atlantic. All were on military airplanes, including some huge lumbering cargo planes, and were strictly to and from U.S. Military bases, both stateside and overseas, but the price was certainly right.

Our first trip stateside in 1964 was on a commercial flight since the Air Force owed my dad a return trip to the States and we went all the way to San Antonio to visit my dad's family for a week or so. But after that we had to pay for the rest of our stateside flights, including to Oklahoma to visit my mom's family and then after that visit, on to McGuire Air Force Base in New Jersey to wait for a Space A back to Torrejon.

My parents believed, and rightly so, that it would be a good thing for John and me to get to know our relatives as much as possible, but of course we had very limited contact with them except for a few days every few years, so it was difficult to even get to know our own close relatives slightly, but this was the price we paid for living overseas. We felt quite different from our relatives in the States, especially our cousins who were around our age, and living overseas made us see the world quite differently than our American cousins ever could. I'm sure that they saw us as being very different from them as well. We did try to relate to our relatives and find things in common besides our family ties, including the modern American "Pop" culture that was going on. We were considered by them to be these long-lost cousins from overseas who needed help in understanding the ways of their modern world.

The next trip back to the states was in the summer of 1969, and things had changed considerably for us and for our stateside cousins by then. We took a C-141 cargo plane flight from Torrejon to McGuire A.F.B. in New Jersey. This was a huge cargo plane and passengers were really an afterthought when it came to the purposes and construction of the aircraft. All seats were along the sides of the large cavernous interior and they strapped us in much like the other cargo was, and we sat facing the other passengers across the vast interior of the plane.

Once at McGuire we took commercial flights to our stateside destinations which began, as was usual, in San Antonio for a week to visit my dad's family and then on to Oklahoma to visit my mom's family. But on this trip John and I brought something along with us to share with our cousins. We managed to put just a little bit of Moroccan hashish into our wallets, but it was enough to give a taste to our American cousins, who were also beginning to sample these types of substances. We suddenly found ourselves quite popular among a certain few of our relatives, particularly the ones who lived in San Antonio and were around our age.

On the return portion of our trip that year, my dad for some reason thought we would have a good chance of catching a Space Available flight out of Charleston A.F.B. in South Carolina that would take us directly back to Torrejon. So we flew commercially to Charleston and ended up waiting for almost a week in a small motel right on the outskirts of the base to catch a flight. He went out to the base every day to see if there might be space available for four people on their daily flight to Europe, and finally there was, but not until the sixth day.

But that week or so that we spent in the motel room happened to be the same weekend that the Woodstock Festival was happening in upstate New York, which was August 15th through the 18th of 1969. We had a little black and white television in our motel rooms and TV was pretty much all we had to do during that week, and when the national news started reporting on the festival, Johnny and I both became glued to the set.

It seemed at the time that things were really changing in the United States and that the hippies would really bring about some profound and necessary changes to American culture. We were fascinated by what we saw, and not only did we enjoy the music coverage, but we were also amazed that half a million like-minded people got together for this festival that ended up becoming a huge and important event that helped to change American culture forever.

The following year, I saw "Woodstock, the Movie" at a drive-in theater in San Antonio, and I got to see what it what that we missed not being there in person. But by looking at the conditions those half-million people endured during that weekend, I'm pretty sure that it was a lot more comfortable watching it on the big screen than sitting around in the mud during the actual festival would have been!

Nevertheless, it was the event that made many people realize that there weren't just a few of these hippy-type people around, but instead there were millions of them and they were everywhere, all around the world, and were becoming more and more visible and outspoken.

In July 1970, my family finally came to the States to embark on the newest chapters of our lives. I had graduated from MHS in June of that year and it didn't take too long for my folks to get everything together to make the move. The first item that they wanted to get accomplished was their divorce, so it was finalized on August 11, 1970, in Grove, Oklahoma.

Coincidentally, this was also their twenty-fifth wedding anniversary, as well as my eighteenth birthday. Yes, I was born on their seventh wedding anniversary, and that date seemed to have a lot of significance throughout their lives, as well as mine, of course.

One reason they wanted to get the divorce finally done was because my mom already had a new fiancée. During our last year in Madrid, my dad had taken a job in Saudi Arabia in order to earn some additional funds to finance our move back to the States. While there, he got to know a co-worker by the name of Jim. Jim was a retired Air Force colonel, and he and my dad became fast friends working together in the desert of Arabia for the Royal Saudi Arabia Air Force, trying to teach them how to run a modern Air Force.

When the Christmas break came around, they were allowed two weeks of vacation, and when my dad asked Jim what he had planned for the break, Jim told him that he had no plans at all since he was a divorced man with really no family. So my dad asked Jim if he'd like to come to Spain with him and meet his family. Jim readily agreed, and that is when he met my mom. They really hit it off and before long they were engaged. But they had to wait until my parents' divorce was finalized to be able to get married.

Within a month of returning to the States, my folks were finally divorced, and each was free to do what they wanted with the rest of their lives. Jim and my mom ended up going to live in Denver, Colorado, where they eventually got married. And my dad soon started seeing an old friend of his from Texas by the name of Juana, and before too long, they became engaged themselves, which made my brother and me both very happy, to see both of our parents with new partners and apparently happy and ready to begin the next stages of their lives.

My brother and I were ready to begin the next chapters of our young lives as well. We had plans for quite a while that Johnny and I would enroll at San Antonio College for the fall semester of 1970, so after getting the divorce completed, and after my mom went on to Denver with Jim, my dad took us to San Antonio to get us all set up for college.

The first thing we did was to search for an apartment close to the S.A.C. campus on San Pedro Boulevard. This was not hard to do because this area of San Antonio had many such places for rent for the many thousands of students that came and went through S.A.C. Before too long we had a quiet place about four blocks from the campus. It wasn't large, but it was very nice, and since it was the first place we had where we would not be living with our parents, it seemed to us to be a palace. It had a small kitchen and a bathroom and a bedroom and everything else we needed to live comfortably. It was furnished, so we didn't even need to try to find furniture, so we were all set.

The next thing to do was to get registered for school, so we went down to the campus and we each signed up for a full load each of eighteen credit hours, which was about six classes. They asked me what my major was going to be, but since I really didn't know, I just put down "Undecided." This seemed to work for the time being, and I took the regular courses that were obligatory, such as English and yet more U.S. History, but they also allowed me to take several electives of my own choosing. Of these I took classes that I thought I'd be interested in which included Psychology, Geography, and an Anthropology class. I really had no idea whatsoever what I wanted to be when I grew up, but I knew that I must decide soon, because that time was rapidly approaching.

After getting us enrolled in college, paying the rent for a month and paying our tuition for a semester, my dad opened a bank account for each of us, deposited $500 in each of our accounts, and then basically said in so many words, "Well, boys, you're on your own now, good luck!" And he left.

We took this rather well considering that neither one of us knew what we wanted to study in college, or even if we really wanted to continue with our education at all for that matter. Also, neither of us had any idea what life in the United States was all about, or how people acted, lived, or what they did with themselves. We did have a couple of relatives living in the city so we did have some people to show us around a little and, of course, we had each other to share this strange and different world with, and we tried to help each other to understand it better.

Also, when we took our final Space A flight from Torrejon to the Air Base in Bangor, Maine, and then on to San Antonio, we were able to bring a souvenir back with us from Spain. Our luggage included an acoustic Spanish guitar, and before leaving Spain, we had taken the strings off it temporarily, and taped a slab of Moroccan hashish to the inside of the guitar facing upwards so as not be seen. We wrapped it several times with plastic wrap and put the strings back on and put it in its case and carried it right through customs.

Military flights are quite relaxed as far as customs goes, so there was really no problem getting this half kilo into the States with us. We discovered that with this substance in our possession we became quite popular among the few people that we let know about it, including the couple of relatives about our age. When several of us all got together to watch the Woodstock movie at the drive-in later that year, we were all in a pretty good frame of mind to enjoy it thoroughly and properly.

But we also wanted to enjoy some of the local herb as well which usually consisted of regular Mexican grass, which was plentiful and cheap in southern Texas, as it was almost everywhere. Our little apartment didn't come furnished with a TV set, unfortunately, and Johnny and I both thought that watching TV was a good way of absorbing more of this strange American culture that we found ourselves in. It also could become something to do with our time besides studying, so we found out that it was possible to rent a small black-and-white TV set for five dollars a month and the company would deliver it, and then come by once a month to collect the rent. So we called the company from a pay phone (since we didn't have a home phone) and ordered one.

The next day, the TV man showed up in his van and when he walked into our place, he instantly knew that we were pot smokers by the lingering smell of hash in the small place. After setting up the TV set in the main room, he asked us if we'd like a toke. Of course, we said sure, why not, so he lit up a joint and passed it around to us. We started talking, and he told us that he also delivered "lids" as well as TV sets. So along with acquiring a TV, we bought a lid from him for ten more dollars, so we could get a taste of what the locals smoked in San Antonio. The next month, he came by to collect the rent for the TV and also delivered another lid for our smoking purposes.

The guy's name was Roger, and we all became pretty good friends. His dad owned the TV rental business, and he just sold grass as a way to make a little extra money on the side. He knew that pot makes most TV shows the funnier and more enjoyable to watch so I'm sure that he had a good number of clients for his delivery services. We also turned him onto a little of the hash we had with us, but we didn't sell any to him because we wanted to keep it for ourselves and only turn people on that we knew were really cool and whom we were pretty sure would enjoy it.

We gradually realized that in Texas, there seemed to be two different kinds of people, at least the ones that we came across in school and elsewhere. The first type was the typical Texans that one sees in the movies, but living in a more modern era. They usually wore cowboy hats and boots, liked "Country" music and talked with a southern drawl, and acted like because they were Texans, where everything is bigger, that they were probably a little better than anybody from anywhere else. They were for the most part rather unfriendly towards the long-haired kind of people that Johnny and I were slowly becoming at this point, since neither one of us had cut our hair for quite some time by then.

The second type of people we came across were more similar to us; that is to say, they also had long hair and enjoyed what we enjoyed, which included smoking pot and listening to rock-and-roll music. We came to realize that this second type of Texan were more to our liking and a lot easier to get along with, at least for us. Of course, the first kid of people was far more plentiful than the second kind, but we were able to distinguish between the two, mostly by the length of the hair on the males. Although as in most things, there were plenty of exceptions. Sometimes we'd meet someone who had fairly short hair yet it turned out they'd be pretty cool. Then at other times, there would be someone who had long hair down to his shoulders, but was a real redneck. We just figured that these kinds of guys just grew their hair long to cover up their red necks!

There were many other lessons that we learned very quickly the first couple of months of living in the U.S. I was amazed the first time we drove through a Jack-In-The-Box restaurant. I just couldn't believe that you talked to the machine on the outside and then drove up to the window to pick up your order. This just seemed totally strange and futuristic to me, and I couldn't believe it was happening the first time we did it. I kept calling the clown-shaped machine that we ordered through "Jack," as in, "Hey, Jack, could I have a burger and fries?" The people I was with thought it was so funny and told me that there were actually people inside the building who took the orders, not a machine outside named Jack.

John started spending a lot of time with a girl named Janie who had a car, so often we had fun riding around with her and her sister. They showed us around quite a lot which was great because we didn't have a car yet, and we realized that transportation was an essential thing to have and a big part of life in these United States.

We explained our predicament to our dad on the telephone one time, and after a while, he told us that there was a car available to us, but we'd have to pick it up from a small town north of Dallas. The car was a 1960 Chevrolet Biscayne and belonged to the lady who he was seeing and she was willing to give it to us since she was not using it anymore. But one of us would have to have a driver's license in order to drive it legally.

Neither John nor I had a license of any sort so it was decided that since he was older, he would get his license first, then he'd show me how to drive, and then I'd get mine. But the problem was, unlike most people in the States, neither one of had ever taken "Driver's Ed" in high school. And the only way he could get a license was to prove that he had so many hours of certified instruction by a qualified instructor. So he ended up going to a local driving school in order to get the necessary credits to obtain the license. This cost almost one hundred dollars but my dad agreed to cover the cost, and then once John was a licensed driver, he could then teach me and give me the necessary hours of lessons for me to get my license.

After the driving school was paid for by my dad, John had to take an hour-long driving lesson from a certified instructor about every other day for two weeks until he could finally obtain his Texas driver's license. Then we had to get up to northern Texas to pick up the car from the house of my dad's friend, Juana, so we ended taking the Greyhound bus all the way there. It stopped at Dallas on the way where we changed buses and then went the rest of the way to the small town where the car was waiting for us.

The car was in great shape being only ten years old and with not that many miles on it yet. And it was huge compared to any car that we had anything to do with in Spain. It was sky blue, had four doors with lots of room, and a very large trunk. It had an automatic transmission which made it easier to drive and we both instantly loved it. At last we felt like true Americans with our very own automobile.

The next day, we got an early start and headed out. We went less than fifty miles before we saw flashing lights behind us and we were pulled over by the Texas Highway Patrol. We were being very careful not to speed, and the car was in good working order with all the lights working, a current license plate, and everything else that we thought was necessary to drive the vehicle, but we got stopped anyway.

The patrol officer was wearing a large white cowboy hat and a pistol on his belt which barely contained his huge gut hanging over it, and he ambled up to the window and asked to see John's driver's license and the car's registration, which he showed him. But when he saw that the name on the registration did not match the name on his very recent driver's license, he grew suspicious and asked in a very unfriendly tone, "Okay, boy, I see that this here automobile is not registered to you, so tell me, where did you guys steal it from?"

John looked at the guy with a look of disbelief and replied in a very shaky voice, "Um, sir, we did not steal it. It was a gift from a friend of my father's and we just picked it up and we're driving it back to San Antonio where we live. And I plan to register it in my name once we get there."

The officer looked at John and then at me and said, "And who is this guy you're riding with, what does he got to do with all of this?"

"Well, sir, this is my younger brother Ron, and he's traveling with me back to San Antonio."

He looked at me suspiciously and asked me, "So, Ron, you got a driver's license?"

I looked back at him very intently and replied in the firmest but politest voice I could muster, "No sir, I don't have one yet."

"And you're not driving then are you, son?"

"No sir, I don't have a license yet. My brother's driving." I repeated.

"Well, do you have any other I.D. with you then, boy?"

I remembered that luckily we had brought our passports with us just in case such a situation arose, so I reached into the glove compartment where we had all the other paperwork and showed him my passport.

He looked at it for a while with a look of suspicion and then said, "It says here boy that you were born in some place called Lisbon, Portugal. Where the hell is that? It ain't in 'Murica is it?"

I mustered my firmest voice and replied, "No sir, it's in Europe, sir."

"So, you one of those illegal foreigners, then are you, boy?"

"No, sir, I'm an American, and that's why I have an American passport, sir."

"You getting smart with me, boy?"

"No sir, I wouldn't do that, sir,"

"Well, you boys just wait here in the car until I come back and don't get out of the car and keep your hands where I can see them at all times, you understand?"

"Yes sir," John said.

After about five minutes, he came back still holding Johnny's license and my passport and said to Johnny, "Okay boys, now tell me where you got the drugs hidden. It'll make things a lot easier on you if you just come clean."

John and I were both just flabbergasted to put it mildly, and John said to him in the most sincere voice possible, "We don't have any drugs, sir."

The Highway patrolman looked at him as if he had just heard the biggest lie in his life and then said, "Well, in that case, I guess you wouldn't mind if I took a little look in that big old trunk, now would ya, huh?"

"No, sir, take a look if you want to," John told him and handed the man the keys from the ignition.

The man took them and walked around to the back of the car and opened the trunk and rummaged around for a couple of minutes and then he came back and said, "How about in the back seat, got any drugs there?"

Again Johnny looked at him with a look of disbelief and told him, "No, sir, nothing there either, sir."

"Then you don't mind if I take a little look then do you, huh?"

He opened the back door and started sifting through the two small bags we had there and opened the small cooler we had there as well.

After slamming the door closed, he handed the keys back to Johnny, he said, "Well, boys, I guess you got those drugs too well hidden for me to find today, so I guess you're good to go. Now get the hell out of here, and don't come down around here no more, you got that?"

"Yes, sir, you don't have to worry about that officer, we definitely won't," Johnny said as he started the car up and slowly drove away, looking in the rear-view mirror to make sure we weren't being followed.

I looked at Johnny and he looked at me and I said, "Man, I'm sure glad he didn't look in my wallet because he probably would have found the joint I got there! Should I light it up?"

I reached into my wallet and pulled out the joint that I had rolled up and had put in there before we had left San Antonio to smoke on the ride back.

He looked at me and said, "Shit Ron, put that away man! Wait until we get on the freeway at least, all right?"

"Yeah, okay man, don't worry, but what a fucking asshole that guy was, huh?"

"Yeah, I was about to shit my pants. How about you?" he asked.

"No way man, I was cool, but the guy really was a fucking dick about it all, wasn't he?"

"About scared the shit out of me, man. And we were lucky he didn't want to look in our wallets, right?"

"I don't think they can do that, can they?"

"They can do any fucking thing they want to, man! Don't you know that?"

"Fuck that stupid pig, man!" I said with conviction. "Just fuck him! That ignorant asshole motherfucker!"

"Yeah, we'd just better be careful from now on because they obviously can pull you over for no reason like they did to us just now. Now that we're driving, we'd better keep on our toes from now on."

And we did for the most part; at least we never got busted in the "blue beast," as we began to call our car. And even though we did get pulled over on a few more occasions, they never found the little stash that we almost always had hidden in our wallets.

The "beast" became indispensable in our lives after a very short time. To be able to drive anywhere at any time was more than just a luxury; instead, it became a necessity. Having a car opened up worlds that were just not possible by walking or taking the bus or even worse, having to rely on someone else for a ride all the time. We soon discovered that unlike in Madrid, where there was a very efficient public transportation system, in this country it was absolutely necessary to have a car. And with our newfound freedom, we discovered that we could go anywhere and do just about anything, at any time.

And that is eventually what we ended up doing. By December 1970, we both had completed one semester of college at San Antonio College, and after discussing our future plans together in detail, we both decided that perhaps college was not the thing for us after all at this time in our lives. We figured that we had both just finished twelve and a half years of school, (actually thirteen and a half for John), and we both felt we wanted to do something besides continue attending yet more school.

Besides, our bank accounts were dwindling quite rapidly, down to just a couple of hundred dollars between us, and our dad had pretty much told us that for now on, we were on our own. But neither one of us had ever had a job before, nor did we have a clue about how to go about getting one. Texas seemed to be a fine place if you were a Texan, but we were not. We didn't know what we were, just that we didn't seem to fit in very well here in San Antonio. We wanted to go somewhere where we could make a new start, and just about anywhere that wasn't Texas. Some place where there were perhaps more like-minded people around and where this damn "Cowboy" culture wasn't so prominent.

So we went home. Home (to the young) is where your mom lives, and so that's what we did. We went back to Mom. We moved to Denver.

My mom and Jim had moved to Denver because even though he was originally from Ohio, he had spent some time in Colorado and he really liked the mountains and the high-country lifestyle. Mom had gotten a job as a telephone receptionist, and they had rented a small apartment near downtown Denver on Washington Street. We talked to her on the pay phone and she told us that she understood why we wanted to leave Texas and that there was an apartment right below theirs for rent and she could try to help us land jobs if that was what we wanted.

So we made the arrangements to leave Texas, and we packed up the beast with all our possessions and headed out very early in the morning. It was just a week or so before Christmas and we didn't bother to check any weather reports, but if we had, I'm sure we might have delayed our trip for a few days. One of the worst winter storms in years was heading south out of Canada and was expected to bring extreme blizzard conditions to all of Colorado and to most of the neighboring area.

We headed northwest and made it all the way to Amarillo where we spent the night in a Motel 6, which did actually cost six dollars in those days, and the next day we thought we could make it all the way to Denver. But shortly after getting on Interstate 25 in Colorado, the blizzard hit, and what a blizzard it was.

We tried to keep on driving in the blinding snowstorm by following the many trucks ahead of us, but after a while we saw them getting off the freeway and parking to wait out the storm which by this time was a complete white out. We couldn't see five feet in front of our vehicle. So we pulled over in a rest area that we soon found just in time, which was already very crowded with lots of trucks and cars, but we were lucky and found a parking place. By this time, it was late afternoon and darkness was approaching rapidly, so we resigned ourselves to the fact that we'd be sleeping in the car that night, but at least we had a bathroom and soda and snack machines nearby.

We made room for the both of us by rearranging our things to put as much of it into the trunk as we could and since the car had two bench-style seats; I got in the back to lie down and John stayed in the front and did the same. But even though we covered ourselves up with almost every piece of clothing and blankets that we had, it was so cold that every hour or so, we had to start the car and run the heater for a while to keep us from freezing.

Needless to say, we didn't sleep too much that night but by the early dawn; the snow had slowed down to a point where we could at least see a considerable distance in front of us, so we moved on. The Highway Department had done their job and had cleared the snow from the freeway to a point where driving was possible again, and we just drove very slowly and carefully all the way into Denver, arriving right before dark.

Our Mom was thrilled to see us and that first night she made room for us on the couch and on the floor of their tiny apartment and the next day, we arranged to move into the apartment right below theirs, which thankfully was furnished and rented by the week. I'm sure that Jim was having doubts about what he had gotten himself into by this point, but he seemed to take it all in stride and genuinely seemed to like us and our presence there. He was divorced himself but had never any children, so he seemed to treat us as the sons he never had. He was a big drinker so I'm sure that helped him to cope with us being in the middle of his newly found domestic situation.

Now we had to find jobs, and this proved to be much harder than we had expected. Since neither one of us had ever really worked anywhere before, we had absolutely nothing to put on a job application for previous employment, so our choices were quite limited to say the least.

But in downtown Denver, which was only a few blocks away, there was something called "The Colorado State Job Service," so that is where we headed. After filling out forms and talking to a very nice lady, she sent us out to apply for a job at an Army Surplus store on the east side of

Denver. The man running the store hired both of us immediately and told us to come in the next day to start work. We went back to our little place and told our mom the good news and she was elated for us. It seemed to be so easy to get a job after all, so maybe we were wrong about the difficulty of finding work. Our job titles were "stock clerks," which sounded very professional to us and we both felt we were on our way to a great job and possibly even a career.

We ended up working at the Army Surplus store for a total of two weeks for the grand sum of $1.10 per hour, which was the minimum wage at the time. After the two weeks were over and we were expecting our paychecks, the owner fired us. He told us that our work was below his standards, so not only did we lose our jobs, but he also refused to pay us. My mom went down to the store and complained and threatened to call the police and the Job Service agency, and then he finally cut us our checks for around seventy dollars each for two weeks of full-time work. Then the checks bounced, and again we had to go down to the store several more times to finally get him to write us checks that didn't bounce. This experience put quite a damper on our enthusiasm for the working world.

After a couple of weeks, John was able to get a job at a Mexican restaurant washing dishes and I kept looking for work. I ended up going down to the Job Service almost every morning to try to get day-work. I wasn't too lucky because most of these jobs involved heavy lifting or heavy labor and the employers would look at me with my small frame and choose other guys who looked stronger and more capable of doing heavy work. But I managed to get hired occasionally and was able to make a little pocket money.

We moved out of the apartment under my mom's place and found a place that was a little cheaper and wasn't right in downtown Denver. Our new place was out on East Colfax Avenue and was right across the street from a "Gentleman's" club by the name of "Tricky Dick's." It was basically a titty bar and not a very fancy one at that. It had a large and colorful neon sign hanging in front of it with a big-breasted lady shaking her ta-tas with the movement of the pink and yellow neon. A lot of sleazy-looking people came and went all the time but we just took it as part of life in the U.S.A.

The apartment was in the basement of a three-story building, and on the ceiling of our place were the pipes for the plumbing for the entire building. These pipes were only a few inches over our heads and water could constantly be heard running through them. The only windows of the place were at eye-level, and all we could see outside was people's feet and legs walking by. But the place was cheap, and that was what counted most to us.

Since I didn't have a full-time job, and barely even a part-time one, I spent a lot of time with Jim helping him get some of his things together. Before leaving for Saudi Arabia a couple of years earlier, he had put a lot of his possessions in a storage locker in Denver and now he wanted to go through it all and get rid of some stuff that he didn't need or want anymore. So I helped him with that and he paid me a few bucks for my help. At least this was better for me than accepting charity from him and my mom, which of course I did as well. I got to like him a lot, and we formed a deep bond and friendship that lasted right up until his death in 1978.

Jim had a friend in Denver by the name of Chris. Chris and Jim were polar opposites of each other, so it was unbelievable that they were such close friends. Chris was an all-out total hippy, with shoulder-length blond hair, a big beard, and he loved to smoke pot. Jim, by contrast, was a straight-laced ex-military man, with the standard G.I. crew cut, and liked to drink gin, and a lot of it. He was about twice the age of Chris, yet these two guys had formed a close relationship and friendship.

They liked to take drives together up into the mountains since Chris kind of fancied himself as a mountain-man type. In fact, one of his sources of income was making very elaborate hiking staffs out of aspen wood which he'd sell at flea markets around Denver, and to the head shops in the nearby college town of Boulder. His other source of income was selling pot and any other kind of drugs he could get a hold of. He was obviously successful at his enterprises because he always seemed to carry his weight financially when it came to his relationship with Jim.

One sunny day, Jim and Chris asked me if I'd like to go with them on a drive up to Aspen for the day. I said I would because I was eager to get out of town and see something besides the slushy streets of Denver. So the three of us climbed into Jim's 1968 Dodge Coronet 440 and we took off for the high country. I was sitting in the back seat and Jim was driving, with Chris riding shotgun. Jim and Chris had had a couple of drinks before leaving (just to clear the cobwebs, as Jim put it), and they also carried a cooler in the front seat between them with ice, tonic, and a half gallon of gin.

Jim was an experienced drinker considering the fact that he had been drinking heavily most of his military career as well as the years since he had retired, and could really hold his booze, but still I got a little worried when we started to reach Independence Pass which is at an elevation of over 12,000 feet. He was starting to slur his words a little and his driving seemed to deteriorate the more he drank, along with the road conditions the higher and the closer to the pass we approached.

There had been ice and snow on the road ever since we had left Denver, but the snow-moving crews had kept the road clear enough for traffic to reach Aspen and other points beyond. Right after we reached the sign that read, "Continental Divide, 12,095 feet above sea level," we hit a patch of ice, and the big Dodge spun around a hundred and eighty degrees, and suddenly we were facing the opposite direction from which we had been heading. Jim finally got the car turned around and slowly pulled over to the side of the road.

All three of us got out of the car and were struck by the bitter freezing cold. Chris wandered off the road a little ways to "see a man about a horse," as he put it, and I looked carefully at Jim and asked him, "Hey, man, are you sure you're all right to keep driving? That was damn close right back there."

He gave me his big grin and said, "Don't worry, Ron, just a bit of black ice I wasn't expecting; it happens all the time, don't worry, I'm fine as can be."

I took a few steps and looked down at the drop-off of several thousand feet on our left and then I look up at the huge mountain towering over us on my right and I said to him, "Well, Jim, you have my life in your hands too, you know, and Chris's as well, so just try to keep that in consideration if you don't mind, okay?"

He got a really serious look on his face, lit up one of his small cigars, and said, "Don't worry, Ron, I'll be fine, now let's get back in the car, it's freezing out here."

"You're right, you're absolutely right, Jim," I said as we climbed back into the car.

We continued on all the way to Aspen and once we got there and walked around a while, the first place we went into was a local bar called "The Red Onion," and since I was only eighteen, I could only have a 3.2 beer (Coors, of course), but Jim and Chris each had another double gin and tonic. Colorado allowed people between eighteen and twenty-one to drink until 1987, but only the weaker beer that contained just 3.2 percent alcohol. It was also the only beer that you could buy on Sundays until 2008 when they changed that law as well. But until they changed the law in '87, Colorado was full of 3.2 bars. I spent a lot of time in these places when I was in Colorado, but the thing I couldn't understand was that all you had to do was just drink more beer to get the same effect, so all it really accomplished was to force younger drinkers to spend a little more for the same buzz which didn't seem quite right to me because this age group generally didn't have as much spending money as the older people tended to have.

After another round of drinks at the bar, Jim decided that it was time to head back home, so we climbed back in the car and headed towards Denver. Thankfully, the bottle of gin was almost gone, and Chris was passed out on the front seat, so I kept a conversation going with Jim so he didn't do the same thing as Chris had done and eventually we reached the outskirts of Denver right before dark. When we finally made it back to the apartment, I had never felt so relieved to have my feet on solid ground in my entire life. And the next time he asked me to go on a drive with him and Chris, I politely declined, telling him I had something else to do.

Although Jim never actually flew fighter jets in the Air Force, he still considered himself a sort of jet pilot. He had started training to be a pilot at the beginning of his Air Force career, but he quickly discovered that due to his poor eyesight, he could never fly himself. But he managed to stretch the truth on occasions when the subject came up and by talking to him, you would have thought that he flew hundreds of missions and single-handedly won several wars by himself. But he still loved to fly, even just as a passenger, and did so whenever he had a chance.

Because of this love of aircraft and flying, he was able to talk my mom into having a very unusual wedding. For some reason the number thirteen was significant to them both, and they considered it to be their "lucky" number. So on June 13th, 1971, at 13:13 pm, they took the "plunge." They got married on board an Aspen Airways flight from Aspen to Denver at an altitude of 14,500 feet, high over the Colorado Rockies. This wedding was so unusual that it made the local newspaper!

Taking the plunge from 14,500 feet

Col. (ret.) James Caton of Denver married Alice Walker of Grove, Okla., and Madrid, Spain, at 13:13 p.m. on Sunday, June 13, 16 minutes out of Aspen board an Aspen Airways flight from Denver. Altitude of wedding vows: 14,500 and a bit rough. Why? The groom, an ex-pilot, told Aspen Today, "The closer you can get to the home office up there, the better." Rev. Ed Beck, a 6'7" Denver Methodist minister, performed the airborne ceremony. Attendants were Lt. Col. Harvard Murphy and Mrs. Betty Perry, both of Los Angeles. The 18 passengers on the regularly scheduled flight seemed to have enjoyed the occasion, especially the champagne which flowed freely, compliments of Aspen Airways and the groom. After a brief honeymoon in Aspen, the couple returned to Denver, prior to moving to Madrid.

Jim and my mom seemed to be very happy together and deeply in love, and my brother and I were very happy to know that our mom was so happy with her new life. Jim would remain a big part of my life until he died just seven years after their most unusual marriage.

Shortly after their strange wedding, they returned to Spain and lived there for a few years before finally returning to the States to make their lives again. But I had a most unusual adventure myself just a few short days before my mom's wedding high over the mountains.

On June tenth, 1971, the popular Rock band Jethro Tull played a show at Red Rocks Amphitheater just outside of Denver, and that show would live in infamy for many years to come. Red Rocks Park outside of Denver, Colorado, is a natural rock amphitheater which had been converted into a permanent concert facility seating over 9,500 people. It is a beautiful place to have a rock concert, but the night I was there it was far from beautiful.

Jethro Tull was one of my favorite bands and I wasn't alone because several thousands of people showed up for the show that did not have tickets, including me. The tickets were sold out many weeks before the concert, but many people thought they would go to the event anyway and at least be able to hear the show from the surrounding hills.

Tull's music was an odd blend of folk, classical, and hard rock that made this British band one of the most popular groups on both sides of the Atlantic. Led by a charismatic flute-playing singer named Ian Anderson, they were quite unique in both their sound and their looks. Their album covers had pictures of the band dressed and made up to look like they were ancient wise men, which went right along with their unusual music and performances. They dyed their long beards and hair gray and with their bizarre clothing; it made them look like they could have come from the Middle Ages perhaps and gave them an anachronistic appearance.

Ian's lyrics, along with his flute playing, which was an unusual instrument for a rock band to feature, spoke of a deep wisdom and a real philosophy. He would stand on one leg in front of the microphone and blow into his flute like he was telling the world some profound and absolute truth, which maybe he was in his own way.

What went down that Thursday night were rocks, bottles, curses, and several varieties of tear gas. "Riot" is a very ugly word, yet there is no other term to adequately describe what went on before and during that concert, and I was right in the middle of it.

My brother and I had driven out to the park right after dark and we soon discovered that we had to park several miles from the actual amphitheater itself, which is a natural canyon-like formation in the mountain allowing an almost perfect acoustic experience.

We had to leave the car among hundreds of others on the side of the road and walk towards the concert area, along with hundreds, if not thousands, of other young people. To avoid the masses of people and police cars along the road, we decided to walk cross-country across open fields in the direction of the concert. While walking along, Johnny lit up a joint and passed it to me and then I passed it to another long-haired guy who was walking along near us. He took a hit and then said, "Hey, you guys want some peyote, man? I got these buttons here that I brought up from the Navajo land, you want one?"

I looked at the guy and what he was holding in his hand and I said, "Sure, man, why not?"

So he handed me a funny-looking little thing, greenish in color and about as big around as an Oreo cookie, with a brownish interior and light green on the outside. I looked at it and asked him, "Hey, man, I've never done this before. What do I do with this thing?"

"Just chew it up and swallow it, man, you might get sick from it but after that the high kicks in and it's intense, man, better than acid and a lot more mellow."

"Okay, thanks, man," I said to the guy as he wandered off with a very spacey look on his face.

I looked at John and said, "What do you say, we split this little thing, huh?"

"Okay, sure why not?"

I took a big bite out of it and handed the rest to him. He took a bite and said, "Man, this stuff tastes like shit! Here, you can have the rest of it if you want."

So I ate the last little bit of the button and swallowed it with a great amount of difficulty because it really did taste terrible. But I did manage to get it all down even though it had a similar texture and flavor as dirt clods, but not quite as tasty.

It took about an hour or so for the peyote to kick in, and thankfully it took a while, because the next thirty minutes were hell on Earth all around me. We were near the back of this huge crowd of several thousand people who, like us, did not have tickets to the sold-out show, but were determined that they were going to get close enough to at least be able to hear the band play. This crowd started rushing forward and the police who were on hand to keep order, seemed to be doing just the opposite, and were trying to push the crowd back.

In the late 1960s and early 1970s, plenty of young people felt as though music was something that shouldn't be commercialized. They were also not above using sheer brute force to rush into concerts as was evidenced at the legendary Woodstock Festival just two summers earlier.

The police, on the other hand, in their desperate and unnecessary need to "maintain order" tried to push the crowd back, and that is when the chaos and violence began. Some people started to pick up rocks and throw them at the line of police who were standing right in their way of having a good time. The police then overreacted, as they tend to do so many times in these kinds of situations, and they sent in helicopters which began dropping canisters of tear gas on the unruly crowd. Some young people on the "front lines," (those who happened to be at the very front of the crowd), picked up the canisters and threw them back at the police standing in front of them, along with more rocks, bottles, and anything else they could grab.

Of course, the tear gas fumes drifted over towards the stage and the almost ten thousand paying fans began to feel the effects of the gas as well. The helicopters flew dangerously low over the crowds of young people who were still just trying to get inside, perhaps to further

Intimidate them and force them to back off and retreat. But we had the numbers and the determination to keep going and, if anything, the police tactics enraged the crowd even more and we just kept pushing relentlessly forward.

Eventually, the police, realizing that they were fighting a losing battle, ended up opening the gates and everyone who was trying to get in just went in, and everyone found a place to be for the concert. People were sitting on the stairs, in the aisles, standing up along the back, and even some climbed the overhanging cliffs to watch the concert. But they all were able to find a place to fit in the amphitheater and settled back to enjoy the show.

Ian Anderson and the rest of the band finally made it onto the stage to loud cheers from the unruly crowd, and the band, along with most of the audience by this time, were all suffering from the tear gas wafting around and many were still choking and coughing, with some people holding their shirts over their faces to minimize the effects of the noxious gas.

The first thing Ian said to the crowd was, "Welcome to World War Three!" And that's what it actually felt like to everybody who was there. In this case, the war was basically between "The Cops" and the "Freaks." But Jethro Tull went ahead and played their full set and it was fantastic and everyone enjoyed the music immensely, despite the tear gas still floating around and the violence and mayhem that had just occurred.

The peyote I had swallowed earlier kicked in shortly after the band started playing and it made the music I was hearing from my position sitting on the ground in the very back of the place probably much more intense than it actually was, and it was very intense to begin with. I felt that my limbs were suddenly made of lead, and it seemed I could barely lift my arms, and when I was able to move my hand in front of my face, I could see "trails" as if it was a film that I was watching and I was seeing every separate frame of the movement.

Things started slowing down, and it seemed that whenever I spoke, my voice was not my own, as if it came from an unknown place outside of my throat. And similar to the acid I had done in Madrid a year or so earlier, I felt like I was just watching my life go by in front of me and that I was participating in it remotely, and somehow I was feeling almost outside of myself. I had puked most of the button up not too long after swallowing it, but enough of it was in my stomach long enough to have its intended effect.

Looking down on this crowd of thousands of people, all grooving to the sounds that these four guys were making onstage, I felt a feeling of belonging to one large entity, as if everyone there had joined together to form one huge single creature, all feeling the same emotions and experiencing this same wonderful and incredible thing.

When the flute melody and the heavy bass line of the instrumental song "Bourée" filled the amphitheater, it felt like it had transported the entire crowd back in time to an ancient, medieval land of wizards, fairies, goblins, and perhaps even hobbits. The song was originally written by J.S. Bach three hundred years earlier and perhaps that added to the magical and mystical feeling the song created among the thousands of people in the crowd.

People all around me were dancing and floating about along with the scent of marijuana smoke mixing with the toxic fumes of the lingering tear gas. I felt a profound calmness and tranquility and a feeling of universal brotherhood that I had never felt before. I sat back and enjoyed the music and the sights as I had never had before, and my mind was truly blown.

One of Tull's songs has a line that goes like this, "It was a new day yesterday, but it's an old day now." The next day the Denver Post had a version of what happened on their front page. And due to the events of that show, unfortunately all concerts were banned from Red Rocks for the next five years.

That Jethro Tull concert at Red Rocks had a profound and influential effect on me in many ways. I was only eighteen years old, but I felt that I had seen something and experienced something that would leave a lasting memory on my young and developing mind. I never saw a concert again without remembering the feeling I had that night while sharing the incredible gift and pleasure of music with so many other like-minded people.

When I had seen The Beatles perform live a few years earlier at Las Ventas Bull Ring in Madrid, it was a very different kind of experience. The Beatles were all about fun, young love, and innocence, but that show at Red Rocks that night was about much deeper and more meaningful things, such as communion, rebellion, anarchy, the human condition, and the endless possibilities of the human spirit. The feelings I felt that night reminded me that anything was possible if enough people got together and put their collective minds towards something, and that music does indeed have the power to change the world.

Not too long after that show at Red Rocks, I left Denver with no regrets and without looking back.

And then I was on to my next adventure.

Chapter 16. Myrtle Beach – Round 1

"The trail is the thing, not the end of the trail.
Travel too fast and you miss all you are traveling for."
— Louis L'Amour

After living in Denver for a while, my mom and Jim decided to return to Spain and make another new life there. I suppose that my mom missed Madrid and wanted a chance to introduce Jim to some of the people and places that she knew and loved so well. Their plan was to fly commercially as far as Charleston, South Carolina, and from there catch a Space A flight right to Torrejon, using Jim's retirement benefits.

I had been exchanging letters with my good friend Bill Johnson whom I knew so well from my days hanging around in Canillejas near Madrid, and he had invited me to come to Myrtle Beach, South Carolina, and stay with him and his family. His parents had just finished building a big house right on the Intracoastal Waterway and there was plenty of room for me if I wanted to come visit for a while. I talked my mom into paying for a flight with Jim and her from Denver as far as Charleston, and then I would go up to Myrtle Beach from there, while they caught their Space A flight to Spain.

Bill, along with his mom, met us at the Charleston airport and after the two moms chatted a while, and I said my goodbyes, I went back with Bill and his mother to Myrtle Beach. As we drove along the South Carolina coast from Charleston up to Myrtle Beach, I was fascinated with what I saw out the window of the car; I had never seen such a landscape before. Some areas seemed almost like swamps with very low-lying land covered with thick vegetation, and other places had standing water of an undisclosed depth among the trees and underbrush. Everything was flat, without a mountain or even a hill to be seen anywhere. Even the air had a different taste to it, for it was thicker, denser, and very humid. The temperature was very hot compared to mile-high Denver, and I was thankful for the air conditioning in Bill's mom's car.

As we approached the outskirts of Georgetown where the "Grand Strand" begins, I could see why so many people liked the area so much. This long stretch of beach goes on for sixty uninterrupted miles with nothing but white sand and blue ocean as far as one can see. The fresh Atlantic breeze tended to keep the thick humidity to a minimum and the warm sunshine felt good on my face as we sped along Highway 17 heading north.

When we finally reached Bill's parents' new house, I was amazed, even though he had told me what to expect. It was a huge three-story A-frame building sitting right on the shore of the Intracoastal Waterway, which is a three-thousand-mile-long inland waterway system that runs along the Atlantic and the Gulf of Mexico. It runs from Boston southward along the Atlantic Seaboard and around the southern tip of Florida, then follows the Gulf Coast all the way to Brownsville, Texas. Parts of the waterway use natural inlets, freshwater rivers, bays, and sounds while other areas are artificial canals. This waterway allows a navigable route for smaller boats along its entire length without many of the hazards and dangers of navigating out in the open sea.

The house was an amazing piece of architecture and Bill's parents had just recently finished the construction of it. The bottom floor (which was considered the basement, even though it was not underground) was huge, and had several bedrooms along with a bathroom, the laundry room, and a huge den area. The second floor was slightly smaller in square feet since the building was an A-frame. It contained the kitchen, the living room, two more bedrooms, another bathroom, another den, and a huge open deck facing the waterway. The top story which was the smallest due to the shape of the building, had Bill's parents' master bedroom and yet another bathroom.

For the several weeks I spent there that summer, the only family members living there were Bill, his parents, and his two younger sisters, one who was still in grade school and the other was in junior high. I had my own bedroom on the basement floor and instantly felt very welcome and also very fortunate to have such a great friendship with Bill, who had become almost like a second brother to me after all the time we had spent together.

The first week or so, Bill showed me around his home and around the bustling town of Myrtle Beach, which was just a few miles from his place. He had just graduated the summer before from the local high school, but he had spent the first three years of high school going to MHS in Madrid along with me and that is where we got to be such good friends. Due to some trouble he had gotten into in Madrid, he came back to the States one year before the rest of his family and had stayed with relatives until his family rotated back to the States. He was taking some classes at the local community college and, like me, was wondering what to do with his life.

A favorite activity of ours during those warm and muggy afternoons at his parents' place on the Intracoastal Waterway was to sit at the picnic table they had set up on the banks of the waterway and watch the boats come and go. We'd usually have a cold Pabst Blue Ribbon in one hand and were sharing a fat joint with the other, of either some good Jamaican or Colombian pot. These seemed to be the only two types available in the area, unlike Texas where usually only lower-quality Mexican weed was available.

We'd talk about the times we had in Spain, some of the mutual friends we had, and some of the wonderful and exciting adventures we had shared there. It was interesting to watch the different types of boats and yachts that would slowly chug by right in front of us, and we'd wave at the captains and they'd wave back, noting the names of the boats and the port they were based out of when not traveling. Most were from northeastern states and were heading to Florida for the winter or on their way back from points south.

Bill was able to borrow his mom's car quite often, so we had wheels to get around. It was a bright yellow 1966 Plymouth Duster, and he liked to drive it fast as hell, of course without his mom knowing the speeds he would get it up to. He also always had at least two motorcycles around that he was tinkering with, so we usually had no trouble finding transportation to get us to and from town.

The town was a vibrant and happening place, especially in the summer months when the population was almost ten times what it was in the winter. Tourists from all over the eastern seaboard, the entire south and even as far away as the Midwest came to spend their summer vacations on the beautiful white beaches of Myrtle Beach. There was also a large Air Force base right outside of town with thousands of Air Force personnel who came and went on a regular basis.

This huge influx of people during the summer caused two things to happen to the local economy. First of all, housing was scarce and quite expensive in the summer, since all these people from out of town were there, and they all had to stay somewhere.

Motels were plentiful and apartments were everywhere as well, but these accommodations catered to the tourist crowd and were not cheap. The second thing these masses of people did for the economy was it created a lot of jobs in the service industry, which was lucky for someone like me who was looking for employment. They needed all kinds of restaurant help, as well as motel workers, cleaning crews, bartenders, and other types of workers catering to the tourism industry.

Another attraction that Myrtle Beach had was a very large amusement park called the Grand Strand. It not only had one of the largest and scariest roller coasters in the country, but also an assortment of other rides and attractions, as well as a midway with a carnival that catered to the tourists who wanted to dispose of some of their hard-earned money. This amusement park also had quite a variety of eating establishments selling the usual assortment of snack foods and drinks to the many thousands of hungry and thirsty vacationers walking about.

A friend of Bill's parents owned a snack bar and arcade right in the center of the midway, so when Bill's dad told me they might need help at the hamburger stand, I went there and instantly got hired as a cook. It didn't take too long to figure out how to cook hamburgers, chili dogs, french fries and other assorted food items, and I was soon working full-time behind the snack bar of the arcade, accompanied by the sounds of the blaring jukebox, pinball machines, and lots of people having fun. It was a great place to work, and I got good at what I was doing and proud of myself for holding a job, earning a decent paycheck, and being able to take care of myself.

I was still staying at Bill's house and getting a ride into town every day for my shift, but I was looking for some place I could stay in town, to not only make it easier to get to work and back but also because I didn't want to overstay my welcome at Bill's parents' place. After a couple of weeks of working there, and having already received two paychecks, I thought I was ready to start looking for my own place.

One afternoon after I finished work, I started talking to a long-haired guy about my age who was hanging around the snack bar and I told him about my predicament of trying to find a place to stay in such a crowded town. He told me he and his girlfriend were staying in a small travel trailer in a trailer park just on the north side of town. I could come and stay that night with them and if I liked it, then we could discuss how much my rent would be to share the place with them.

I told him that I thought that might be a good idea, so off we went walking towards their place. On the way, we stopped at a Pizza Inn restaurant and I bought us a large pizza which the three of us really enjoyed, along with a pitcher of beer. By the time we got to the trailer, it was after dark and I really couldn't see much of the trailer park and when we got to the couple's trailer; I was pretty disappointed because it was very small indeed. It was only around eight by twenty feet or so, and it only had one small bedroom, a tiny bathroom, a small kitchen and a table with two chairs, obviously designed for one or maybe two people at the most.

The guy asked me what I thought, and I told him that I thought it was a little too small for three people to live in and besides where was I supposed to sleep. He pointed to the floor and told me he had some blankets and an extra pillow and I could just crash right there. I was a little reluctant, but by this time it was way after dark and I really didn't have a way to get back out to Bill's place, so I told him I'd stay for the night anyway and see how it went.

After a while, I lay down on the floor of the place and the couple went into the bedroom to sleep. It didn't take long until I fell asleep and the next thing I knew it was morning, and three big ugly guys whom I didn't know and had never seen before were in the tiny trailer yelling at me.

The largest and meanest of the three asked me, "What the hell you doing here, sonny?"

I tried to stand up, and he knocked me back down to the floor with his fist, and I said, "Hey, Curtis and Cindy invited me to stay here last night and I just slept on the floor like they asked me to."

"Well, that little asshole doesn't have permission to stay here, and this here trailer is my place, do you hear? I don't know who you are but you don't belong here, you little fucker!"

He started punching me as hard as he could in the head and shoulders, and I covered my head with my arms as the two other guys joined in, punching me and kicking me as hard as they could while I was lying on the floor with my hands over my head.

I started yelling and screaming, "Hey, stop it! I wasn't doing anything, where's Curtis, he can vouch for me!"

"Well, that little asshole is not here and besides he knows he's not supposed to come around here no more! You must have broken into my place! You little motherfucker!"

By this time I was crying and yelling for them to stop hitting me but the rage they had towards me was fierce and unstoppable and it was like nothing I'd never seen before, and I could do nothing but cover my head and curl into a tight ball trying to protect my vital organs, including my testicles.

After what seemed to be a very long time they finally stopped hitting and kicking me and the largest of the three guys picked me up and threw me out, right onto the pavement outside the trailer while yelling, "Get the fuck out of here you little asshole, and don't come back! You hear?"

I stood there with blood flowing out of my nose and I suddenly realized that there was something terribly wrong with my left arm. I couldn't move it and it hurt like hell. I felt the bone in the area between my wrist and my elbow and I realized that it must be broken. I was standing there with blood running out of both of my nostrils and I could barely see due to the condition of my swollen eyes and I started to stagger as far away from the trailer and from these three guys as I could and tried to make sure that they didn't follow me and continue with the beating.

Holding my left arm with the other one, I slowly walked out of the park and I found myself on the main highway heading north out of town. I stood on the side of the highway and stuck out my good arm with the thumb sticking up. The third car that drove by stopped and the older man inside rolled down the passenger side window and asked me, "What happened to you? It looks like you need a ride, huh?"

I looked at the man and said, "I think my arm is broken. Can you give me a ride to the hospital please, sir?"

"Sure, hop in, son. I'll give you a ride."

So I got in the guy's car while trying not get blood on his seat from my bloody nose and said, "Thank you so much, sir."

"What the hell happened to you, son?"

"Well, three guys just beat me up for no reason, and it hurts like hell!"

"That sounds pretty lousy of them, isn't it, three on one, that's pretty damn chicken shit if you ask me."

He took another look at me and handed me a paper towel he had in his glove compartment and told me, "Don't worry, son, the county hospital is just right down the road here a few miles. I'll get you there in no time."

When we got to the hospital, I climbed out of the car and thanked him for the ride and I went in through the emergency entrance. I walked up to the lady behind the counter and told her, "Ma'am, I think I broke my arm, can you help me, please?"

She took a good look at me and told me, "Oh, my, yes, it certainly looks that way, son. What happened to you?"

"Well, I got in a fight with three guys and I lost," I said with a grimace.

"What did you get in a fight with three guys for? That doesn't sound very smart to me, sonny."

"Believe me, it wasn't my idea, ma'am. They jumped me."

"Well, let's see if we can fix you up. Come this way and we'll have the doctor take a look at you."

And they did fix me up. Luckily it wasn't a compound fracture and only one of the two bones in my lower arm was broken and only in one place, but they put a cast on my arm and told me to come back in eight weeks to have it taken off.

After I told the doctor what happened, I asked him about pressing charges and he told me that I'd have to go to the police station and talk to them about it. He wasn't going to have the police come to the hospital just to talk to me about a fight I had gotten into.

So I left the hospital with a new bright white cast on my left arm and a feeling that life was not very fair whatsoever.

I did make my way to the local police station and asked the officer there if I could charge the three guys with assault or some other type of crime. He told me that he thought it would be a big waste of time, since it sounded like just a fight that I had gotten myself into and I had lost, unfortunately. Again, I felt how unfair the world seemed to be and how things were not particularly going my way, but I eventually got myself out of the dumps and kept on keeping on, which is pretty much all one can do in a situation like this.

When I reported to work the next day, my boss took one look at my arm in its cast and told me I couldn't work there anymore. The State

Department of Health does not allow a cast to be around any food preparation area due to possible unsanitary conditions. He said he was sorry but I that I couldn't work there until I got the cast off of my arm, which would be two months away.

So it looked like I would have to find a job that did not involve any kind of food service. There was an older guy who hung around the arcade fairly often playing pinball and drinking beer with whom I had talked on several occasions. I knew he worked as a "carnie" at a booth along the midway somewhere, so I went walking out along the midway looking for him, thinking that maybe I could work running one of the booths. I found him easily enough, running a beanbag toss game.  He was easily recognizable because the guy had no teeth—none at all—which I had always thought was quite strange. I had asked him one time how he could eat without any teeth in his mouth and he just grinned and said, "Hey, man, I just gum it!"

So I approached this toothless guy and when he got a break from handing beanbags to young suckers, I asked him how I could get a job with the carnival.

He looked at me and said, "Kid, you don't want to work for the carnival. It's really shitty work, doesn't pay for shit, very long hours and there's not even a minimum wage. I'm sure you won't like it at all."

"But, man, I just lost my job at the snack bar due to this damn cast on my arm and I can't work in food service at all for two months, and I really need a job of some kind."

He looked at me and acted as if he had just noticed the cast on my arm and said, "Okay, listen kid, if you really want to work as a carnie, go talk to Richard; he owns several booths around here. He's a skinny blond-haired guy with a beard about my age or so and you can always find him hanging around somewhere. He's usually at the hot dog booth by the Ferris wheel drinking coffee. Tell him you talked to Sonny and he might give you a job if he needs anyone."

"Okay, thanks Sonny, I appreciate it, man."

"Yeah, no problem, and good luck, kid."

I wandered over towards the Ferris wheel, which was the largest thing around besides the giant roller coaster that dominated the skyline of the amusement park, and I found the hot dog stand not far from the ticket booth for the Ferris wheel. And sure enough, there was a skinny guy with blond hair and a short beard sitting at one of the small tables drinking coffee and looking at a magazine. So I walked up to him and asked, "Excuse me sir, are you Richard, by any chance?"

He looked up from his magazine article and gave me a suspicious look and said, "Who's asking?"

"Well, my name is Ron Walker, and I was just talking to Sonny and he told me that you might need some help to work one of the booths. I just lost my job over at Big Joe's snack bar due to having this darn cast on my arm and they won't let me work around food anymore and so I really need to find a job."

He put down his magazine and gave me a good looking over and asked, "How old are you, kid?"

"Well, I'm eighteen, sir, but I'm turning nineteen next month in August."

"You ever worked in a carnival before?"

"Um, no sir, but I'm a quick learner."

"Well, the guy I had running the weight and age booth up and quit on me the other day so I ain't got nobody to run it. Think you can handle something like that?"

"Sure!" I said with all the enthusiasm I could muster.

"Okay, we'll try you out this evening then. Come back at four and we'll get you started."

"Yes sir, where should I meet you?"

"Right here, kid, this is my office. Be here at four, okay?"

"Yes, sir, I'll be here. And um, one more question, sir, how much do I get paid?"

"Well, you get a percentage of what you bring in every day. I'll start you off at twenty percent and if you do all right, I can eventually boost it up to twenty-five. Is that okay with you?"

"Yes, sir, I guess so. And thank you."

I walked away thinking maybe my luck was about to change. And that I'd be doing something besides standing over a hot grill all day frying burgers at Big Joe's.

So right at four, I was standing in front of Richard's "office" and ready to start work. He led me over to the midway and showed me a booth that was set up but not in operation. Then I walked with him over to an area behind the midway where the vendors and the park employees parked their vehicles. We walked up to an old truck that had a large box-like structure on the back of it and he took out a ring of keys and opened up the back. He climbed in and started grabbing boxes of something and handed them down to me saying, "Here, kid, take these boxes, as many as you can. These are your prizes."

I took three of them and stacked them up in my arms barely able to see over them and he grabbed a couple after locking the door and I followed him back to the booth. When we got there, he set his boxes down on the ground in front of the booth and I did the same and then he took his key ring and opened the front panels of the booth and then started opening one of the boxes.

"Okay, kid," he told me, "this is the 'guess your weight or age' joint and it's real simple to operate. What we do is get the customer to bet one dollar that you can't guess his weight within three pounds or his age within two years, get it?"

"Yeah, I guess," I said.

"And if you guess right, he loses his money, got it?"

I started handing him the prizes out of the boxes and I said, "Yeah, I guess so. But what happens if I get it wrong?"

He gave me a look that conveyed that he thought I was a complete idiot and said to me in a low whisper, "It doesn't really matter, kid. Even if you get it wrong, that's okay because these little prizes here cost us less than a quarter each when we buy them in bulk like this, so we're still making money anyways. You get it now?"

"Yeah, I guess so, Richard."

"Well, you still want to get as many possible right if you can, because that saves on our inventory costs, right? And if someone wants to bet five bucks, then he wins one of the big prizes that we have for show, okay? But only if he wants to bet the five, try to keep the bets at one buck, we make more off the small prizes than the big ones, got it?"

"Okay, I understand."

"You use this scale here to prove the weight of the mark, and for his age you just write your guess down on this tablet, then you ask him for his age first, then you show him what you guessed, okay? It's real easy, you'll get the hang of it real quick I'm sure."

"All right, I think I got it," I told him.

Within half an hour or so, I was in operation. Richard gave me a red polo shirt to wear to show that I was an employee of the carnival and gave me a few more tips on how to get the customers.

"Okay kid, you gotta be aggressive, you can't just wait for them to come up to you because nine times out of ten, they'll just walk on by and ignore you. You gotta get in their faces and tell them what you got, make it a game for them, and make it fun. Act like you're a good guesser and challenge them to it, okay?"

"Okay, I think I got it, Richard," I said.

"All right then, get started now, and I'll be watching from over there to see how you're doing for a while, to make sure you're doing it right. And remember, the more money you bring in, the more you make, okay?"

So I became a carnie, just like that.

I kind of liked the job after I got the hang of it. I got to hang out on the midway all evening along with lots of people who were there just to have fun, and most of them were in a good frame of mine, being on vacation and enjoying themselves. I had to keep a positive frame of mind at all times and be willing to get in peoples' faces and challenge them to my game. Most people thought that it was too easy and that I could guess their age within two years, but many people didn't think I could guess their weight within three pounds very easily, so I used the scale a lot. I gradually started getting better at my guesses as well. At first, I only got about half of them right, but after doing it for a while, I got better and got my percentage up to around two-thirds right.

After a short while, I started discovering how sleazy and underhanded the carnival business could be. Within a couple of days, I noticed these little kids walking around carrying these huge stuffed animals, bigger than they themselves were. Their job was to walk around and if someone asked them where they got the prize from, they'd tell them that they won it at the bottle-toss booth or at the balloon dart game, or whatever booth needed to drum up more business. Of course, it was the same kids hanging around all the time, but there were so many new marks every day, it didn't seem to matter too much. I asked one kid how much he got paid per day for walking around carrying the prize and he told me he got a two dollars a day, plus he got to keep the stuffed animal at the end of the season, so he made sure to keep it in good shape.

Of course, every game had its catch. It might have looked very easy, but they were all designed to remove dollars from the mark's wallet. A good example was the basket-toss. They set bushel baskets up on low tables and the idea was to toss softballs into the baskets and if you got three in; you won a big prize, and it was only a dollar for ten tosses. I saw people spending lots of money trying to get the balls into the baskets, but few ever did. The trick was that they set the baskets at an angle so the balls would just bounce right out instead of staying inside.

Another one that got lots of peoples' money out of their pockets was the bottle ring toss. It had empty soda bottles sitting in their crates on tables and the idea was to toss small rings so that they'd fall over the tops of the bottles, but the bottles were so close together and the rings so small around that it was nearly impossible to get one to fall around the bottle. This game was similar to the dart into the balloon game. The darts were sharp enough, but the balloons were only inflated enough to hold air and to look inflated, and it was next to impossible to get a dart to stick into them and pop them.

I think most people knew that nothing was as easy as it looked and were good-natured enough to not complain too much when they never won. At best, they won something that was pretty much worthless, but at least it gave them a small souvenir to take home. But some people did get pretty upset, and occasionally some guy would cause a stink about one game or another. When this happened, several of the guys running the booths would get together and walk over to the guy complaining and intimidate him until he backed down and decided that it just wasn't worth it.

And most of my fellow carnies were some mean and malicious-looking guys. Many were pretty sleazy, with lots of tattoos, scars and dirty clothes that hadn't been washed in a month, much like their hair. But there was a camaraderie that existed between the different carnies and they tended to stick up for each other a lot.

I got paid on a daily basis. Richard would come around every evening right before I shut down the booth and take all my earnings from me. If I had a good day, I would bring in fifty dollars, which would mean ten for me, though usually I averaged a lot less than that. But it was better than nothing and all I had to spend my money on was food, cigarettes, beer, and maybe some pot occasionally.

Since I was still staying out at Bill's house and I didn't have rent to pay, and I still somehow managed to get rides to and from work every day, I guess that I was doing okay. And I really liked the atmosphere of the Midway where I worked. There were always hundreds of people walking around looking for fun, and I was part of the apparatus that provided it for them.

I had always liked the sport of people-watching, so I had a chance to partake a lot in this activity while hanging around my booth all afternoon and evening. There was always a feeling of excitement and people mostly were having a lot of fun, or at least trying to.

Not far from my booth was the "Tilt-A-Whirl" ride, and music would always be blasting from their extremely loud speaker system, so I always had some good tunes to listen to while doing my thing. A big hit that summer was the song by Alice Cooper called, "I'm Eighteen," and I really liked it. The lyrics went something like this:

"I got a baby's brain and an old man's heart,
Took eighteen years to get this far,
Don't always know what I'm talking about,
Feels like I'm living in the middle of doubt,
Because I'm eighteen, I get confused every day,
Eighteen, I just don't know what to say,
Eighteen, I gotta get away,
Eighteen, Eighteen, Eighteen,
I'm eighteen and I like it!"

I was eighteen myself at the time so I related to that song very well, and I'd sing along at the top of my voice whenever I heard it.

I learned very quickly that sometimes it was not a good idea to try to guess a fat lady's weight. There was a fine line between trying to guess it correctly and insulting her, especially if she had a big and mean-looking husband with her. I'd just usually guess way low, and she'd be happy to get her little prize. But these situations were rare, because most overweight people seemed to be reluctant to step on a scale in public for any reason, regardless of the prize involved. Of course, it was harder to try to guess an older person's age than a younger person's because of the higher numbers and possibilities involved. And again, I had to be careful in guessing too high with certain older ladies, but generally it was all in good fun and most of my customers took it with a sense of humor and had fun with the game.

When the end of the summer finally rolled around, it meant the end of the season and the park would be closing down. Richard had told me in advance that it was only a temporary job and when Labor Day came around, it would be over, so I was expecting this. But a couple of days before the park was to close, he approached me and asked me if I'd like to go on "the road" with him. I asked him what this involved, and he told me that during the off-season he traveled around the eastern states, going from one county fair to another, and occasionally to a state fair. He made it sound like a lot of fun and like I'd be able to make a lot of money, so I told him I'd do it. Besides, with my cast still on my arm for another month, my employment possibilities were still very limited.

So I packed my backpack with a few extra clothes, said my goodbyes and thank yous to Bill and his family, and headed out. Richard had his large four-door pickup with the huge box on the back, and an enclosed trailer that he pulled behind his truck. It contained all the lumber and hardware to set up the booths, and everything else he needed to keep his small outfit going. Counting me, he had three employees going along with him.

Stevie was a young guy from North Carolina, a little older than I was, but had been doing carnie work for a couple of years by then. Brian was the other guy. He was probably in his mid-thirties and was from Brooklyn, New York. He had a New York accent and attitude. He was a short chubby guy with long hair and a big bushy beard, and to me he was very intimidating, always pushy and bossy towards everyone. He was Richard's right-hand man and was the guy in charge when Richard wasn't around, and he rode up front with Richard while Stevie and I sat in the back seat of the truck.

The next few weeks became a routine of driving, unloading and setting up the joints, running them for two or three days while the particular fair was going on; then breaking it all down and doing it all over again. Our first stop was Fayetteville, North Carolina, for their county fair and I soon realized that this job on the "road" was not nearly as much fun as just working the Midway had been. Tearing down and setting up the booths became hard work, and they gave me no slack for my broken arm; I was expected to do as much as the other two guys. But I kept at it and did my best to carry my weight and do my share of the heavy work involved.

Our route across the eastern states did not take a linear pattern since we had to go where the fairs were open, and so at times we'd drive hundreds of miles to a location, then double back southwards to a different fair in another state. I got the chance to see a lot of the country that I'd never seen before and I did enjoy the traveling quite a lot.

Richard always got himself a motel room wherever we landed, but the rest of us were confined to sleeping in the trailer. The three of us would crawl into the trailer and crash out. At least the gear was always out and set up, so there was plenty of room, and Richard kept a few old sleeping bags back there for that purpose.

We ate carnival food for almost every meal because that's all there was around. I got used to corn dogs, chili dogs, burgers, and fries for almost every meal. And it wasn't cheap to eat along the midways of these various fairs. These joints were set up to make as much money as possible in the shortest amount of time and then move on, so they could and did charge as much as possible for their shitty food, since they really didn't expect or need many repeat customers.

Occasionally while we were driving on the road, Richard would stop at a diner or a fast food place, and we'd be able to get something different from carnival food for a change, and that was a welcome relief. Sometimes the owners of the food joints along the midway would give us a little discount, seeing that we were fellow carnies, and that did help a lot, but food became one of the most expensive things I spent my meager earnings on. It seemed that almost everything I earned every day went to buy food, with maybe just a little to buy a pack of cigarettes and a couple of beers occasionally. After a while it seemed like I was a slave, only surviving day by day and not seeing much of a future whatsoever, but I was kind of stuck. I only earned enough money every day to exist, and couldn't seem to save even a few dollars.

Brian liked to drink a lot, and he did so whenever possible. We got to talking one night while waiting to fall asleep in the back of the trailer and he told me that he used to be a junkie, but he was able to quit using heroin by just drinking vast quantities of booze. So he spent most of his money on hard liquor and drank himself into oblivion every night to fall asleep. He was a strange guy, and I always felt uneasy around him and tried to avoid him, but it was hard to not be around someone with whom I spent almost every waking hour, and slept only a few feet away from every night.

From Fayetteville we headed to Roanoke, Virginia, and then up through a small corner of West Virginia and into Pennsylvania. It seemed like every place we hit in Pennsylvania had a "burg" at the end of its name such as Harrisburg, Chambersburg, Shippensburg, and McDonaldsburg. The rolling hills of Pennsylvania differed from some of the other country we passed through. It was also grayer and more industrial-looking, with towns that appeared to be almost abandoned, but when we set up for their county fairs, people came out in droves, ready to spend their money and have a good time.

A lot of these county fairs included animal auctions and 4-H type activities. Every kind of barnyard animal was around and at times the stench of animal shit became almost unbearable, especially when we couldn't get away from it, since our trailer was almost always parked in the same parking lot among the vehicles that the farmers and ranchers used to bring their animals to the fair. Yes, indeed; the "glamorous life" as a carnie started to seem not so great after all.

After a week or two of going to different fairs in Pennsylvania, we headed south again and back into Virginia. We were headed to the town of Mechanicsville, right outside of the city of Richmond, for their county fair. Stevie had decided that he had enough of this kind of life and before we got to the outskirts of Richmond, he asked Richard to stop the truck. So Richard pulled over along the side of the road, thinking that he probably had to take a leak or something. But Stevie grabbed his little backpack and started walking down the road away from us. Richard yelled at him, "Hey, Stevie, where you going, man?"

Stevie turned around and yelled back at him, "I've had enough of this shit, man! I'm hitchhiking back home. Later, guys!"

Richard smiled and yelled back, "Well, good luck, Steve my man. It's been great to know you, you little asshole!"

As we drove off, Richard stuck his middle finger out the window and yelled, "Fuck you, you little quitter!" And honked his horn and kept right on driving.

Once we got to Mechanicsville, we set up our booths and got to work, only there was one guy less to do the work, so it took a lot longer than usual. And the next day, once they were set up, and we started working, even Richard had to run one of the booths since we were one man short. As usual, Richard took off to find a motel that night while Brian and I climbed into the back of the trailer to sleep.

The next morning, all hell broke loose. I was awakened abruptly by Richard yelling at me and cussing me out. "Wake up, asshole! Where's Brian at? And what happened to my shit?"

I started rubbing the sleep out of my eyes and looked at him and asked, "I don't know; what the hell's happened?"

"Well, Brian's gone, and he's taken my money and my gun, now what do you know about it, motherfucker?"

"I don't know what you're talking about, Richard. I've been sleeping right here all night, man."

"Well, asshole, when I got here a few minutes ago, I looked in the trailer and saw that he and his shit was gone, so I looked where I keep my petty cash at and the bag is gone. Then I looked where I stash my pistol and it's gone too, motherfucker!"

"Well, I'm sorry Richard, but I had nothing to do with it, I swear, man."

"Oh yeah, well, you were his buddy and I'm sure you knew all about it, now where the fuck did he go?"

"I have no idea, I really don't, man."

"Well, you're out of here! Get your shit and get the hell out of here, right now, you god damn motherfucker!"

"Now hold on Richard, I didn't do nothing. I swear to god, man!"

"Fuck you, you little asshole, get the fuck out of here right now, I don't wanna see you around here no more and don't try to get another job with any of these other joints around here because I'll tell them that you're a fucking thief! You got that? Now get the fuck out, now!"

"Okay, man, take it easy. I didn't do nothing. I don't know what you're pissed at me for; it was Brian that ripped you off. What the hell!"

"You must have known about it, asshole. How could you not? And I had over a hundred bucks in that bag and my thirty-two caliber is worth even more than that. So get the fuck out of here before I lose my temper and beat the shit out of you, you little fucker!"

I grabbed my backpack and started putting my stuff into it, and then I put my shoes on and grabbed my jacket and stepped out of the trailer while Richard was watching me intently the entire time.

I tried one more time to try to reason with him, "Listen, Richard man, I didn't have anything to do with this shit, I swear to god, man. What the hell am I supposed to do now? I got less than five bucks to my name and I can't even work for anyone around here. I'm fucked man, can't you see that?"

"I don't give a fuck, asshole! That's your problem for palling around with that fucking thief. It's your fault, now get the hell off of this lot now!"

So I put my backpack on my back and started walking away towards the park's exit. I turned around one more time, and I saw him watching me from the trailer. I lifted my middle finger at him and yelled, "Fuck you, motherfucker, you're a crazy fucking asshole!"

He pretended to take a few steps towards me and I turned around and started walking as fast as I could away from him, heading for the exit. As I was leaving, I saw two guys who worked the pig iron (setting up and tearing down the rides) and I stopped and told them what had just happened to me, and asked them for advice.

The tallest guy, who had long greasy hair and a huge red birthmark running down his cheek and his neck, looked at me with pity and said, "Well, kid, it looks like you're pretty well screwed now. If he's going to put the black mark on you like that, then no one around here's gonna hire you; that's for sure. Hey, but Richmond's only about ten miles away. Maybe you should just hitch into town and see what you can find there."

I thanked the guys and walked towards the highway. When I finally reached it, I got my bearings and realized in which direction the city of Richmond was, and stuck out my thumb. Within about five minutes, an old man in a pickup truck stopped and asked me through the window, "Where you heading, kid?"

I told him, "To Richmond, sir, you heading that way?"

"Yeah, get in, I'm going right downtown," he said, and so I got in the cab and put my backpack on my lap.

While riding into town I told the guy who looked like a farmer of some sort, about what had just happened to me and he seemed to be mildly interested but not all that sympathetic.

He spit tobacco juice into a paper cup that was sitting on his dash and said "If I was you kid, I'd go to the Salvation Army, maybe they can help you out. Their office is right downtown, I can drop you off right in front if you like." So he let me off in front of the Salvation Army office and after thanking him for the ride, I walked through the front door and approached the man working the desk who was wearing a uniform with a white shirt, a black tie, and red epaulets on his shoulders.

I told him what had happened to me with losing my job with the carnival and being broke and then he asked me, "Well, son, where's your people at?"

I thought about it for a second and then I said, "Well, sir, my dad is in Texas and my mom is in Spain, but I have some friends I was staying with down in Myrtle Beach. I could try to get a job around here somewhere I guess, but I got this cast on my arm and it kind of limits my job opportunities."

"Well, we can put you up for the night in our barracks but it's not too fancy, just a cot, and we can give you a dinner voucher for some chow tonight but that's about it as far as what we can do to help you out. We can also let you use our phone for free if you want to call someone to help you, okay?"

"Thank you very much sir, I really appreciate it."

So I followed him around to the back of the building and he took me to a large room with a couple dozen small cots, all set up in neat rows, and told me to take my pick of the vacant ones. I chose one that looked unoccupied (at least it didn't have anyone's gear lying around near it) and I put my bag down on top of it.

I followed him back to the office, and he went behind the desk and handed me a slip of paper. I looked at it and it had the Golden Arches logo on it and it said something about a Big Mac with fries and a drink for free, so I put it in my pocket and thanked him.

Then he looked at me and asked, "You ready to make that phone call now, son?"

"Yeah, I guess so," I told him as I reached into my wallet and found the number I had written down for my dad's friend in Texas. I handed it to him and he dialed the long-distance number and then handed me the receiver.

"Hello." I heard Juana's voice on the phone.

"Hi Juana, this is Ron, is my dad around?"

"Yeah, hold on honey, I'll get him for you."

About a minute goes by and then I heard, "Hey, Ron, is that you?"

"Yeah, Dad, it's me. I'm calling from Richmond, Virginia. I kind of got myself into a little trouble and I need your help."

"Oh shit, are you in jail?"

"No, Dad, it's nothing like that."

So I went ahead and told him all about my adventures traveling with the carnival and how I got fired for no fault of my own and now I only had a couple of bucks in my pocket and that I'd like to get back to Myrtle Beach where my friend Bill was.

"Well, son," he said in a very serious voice, "It sounds like you got yourself into a pickle, didn't you? Now what do you want me to do about it?"

"Well, I was hoping you'd be able to lend me the money to get a bus ticket back to Myrtle Beach is all, Dad."

"Well, why don't you get a job and pay for your own ticket?" he asked me.

"Well, Dad, I didn't tell you, but I broke my arm while I was in Myrtle Beach last month and I got a cast on my left arm and I can't work hardly anywhere with this damn cast on."

I'm not sure if he just didn't believe me about the cast or he didn't hear me right, but he seemed to ignore what I had just told him, and instead he just said in a very stern and firm voice, "Well, Ron, it looks like you made your own bed, and now you're just going to have to lie in it. I told you in San Antonio that you boys were on your own now, and you're going to have to learn to take care of yourselves and act like real men and make your way in the world. So I can't help you. You're on your own."

I couldn't believe what I was hearing because this was the first time I'd ever heard my father react like this. So again, I tried to plead with him, "But Dad, I can't work with this damn cast on my arm. What am I supposed to do?"

"That's your problem, Ron, not mine. Good luck."

And he hung up.

I was flabbergasted to say the least and a feeling came over me that I had never felt before. It was a combination of anger, sadness, and fear that almost brought me to tears. I also felt abandoned like I had never felt before. I handed the phone back to the man behind the desk and he gave me a look of pity and then asked me, "So, not very good news, huh, son?"

"Yeah, you're right, not very good news at all, I'm afraid. You think I can make another call, please?"

"Yeah, no problem, son. What number you want me to call now for you?"

So I looked in my wallet again, and found Bill's parents' number and I gave it to him, and then he called South Carolina.

Bill's mom answered, and I told her what had happened and what my dad had told me, and I asked her if she could lend me the money to get a Greyhound bus ticket back to Myrtle Beach. She was very nice and told me she would go down to the Western Union office in downtown Myrtle Beach that afternoon and send forty dollars in my name to the Western Union office in Richmond and that I should get it later that afternoon. I thanked her from the bottom of my heart and told her I'd see her the next day after I got back to Myrtle Beach. She told me to call when I got to town and she or Bill would come and pick me up at the bus station. I thanked her again and said goodbye.

I handed the phone back to the Salvation Army officer and thanked him again and asked him where the nearest McDonald's was, and he told me about three blocks away, just right down the street. I started walking in the direction he pointed and soon I was feeling scared and creeped-out. As I was walking along the sidewalk, I saw all these young black guys who were standing around these mean streets of downtown Richmond looking at me as if I was a rabbit and they were all wolves.

I kept my eyes averted from all of them until one particular guy stood right in front of me blocking my way and asked, "Hey, white boy, what are doing down here? This isn't your side of town, now is it?"

I looked at him and said, "I'm not sure what side of town I'm at, sir. I'm not from around here. I just checked into the Salvation Army down the street and they're putting me up tonight because I don't have any money or a place to stay."

He looked at my grubby clothes and dirty hair and said, "Yeah homie, you look like you don't have shit man. But you'd better watch yourself around here, okay?"

"Yes, sir, I will," I told him as he went back to the wall that he was helping to hold up and I kept on walking towards the McDonald's.

I got my free meal and sat down at a booth to eat it and I realized how hungry I really was, so when I was done, I went back up to the register and ordered an apple turnover for dessert with one of my last remaining dollars. Finally feeling almost full, I quickly walked back to the Salvation Army building, being careful to not look at anyone and keeping my eyes to the ground.

I spent a restless night trying to sleep on the cot and the next morning I walked over to the Western Union office and I picked up the money that Mrs. Johnson had wired me the previous afternoon, and then I walked a few more blocks over to the Greyhound station and asked how much a one-way ticket was to Myrtle Beach. The man told me it was $24.50, so I bought the ticket for the next bus that was leaving in a couple of hours and walked over to the coffee shop and ordered a coffee and two donuts for breakfast.

Later that afternoon, I arrived back at Myrtle Beach, feeling pretty down and defeated, but at least I had some friends around. I used the pay phone to call the Johnson's house and Bill answered and told me he was on his way to pick me up. When he arrived, he seemed happy to see me and he seemed amazed after I told him the entire story about what had happened. He told me that if he ever saw Richard at the Grand Strand Amusement Park or anywhere else for that matter, he was going to kick his ass for what he did to me.

The next day, I went back to the doctor's office and had the cast removed from my arm, since it had been just over two months that I had it on. It was a great relief to finally get the damn thing off since it had been itchy and stinky ever since I first had it put on. I looked at my arm and it appeared to have shrunken considerably. The skin was very pale white and wrinkled, but at least the bone had healed, apparently.

The doctor ordered an x-ray just to take a look at the bone and after looking at it; he told me that for some reason, there was a bump where the two pieces of bone had healed together, and that the lower piece of the bone must have shifted somewhat and healed itself to the other piece at a bad angle and had created a small lump in the bone. He told me that he could break it again if I would like, and try to get it to heal without the bump, but I declined, thinking that I definitely didn't want to go through that all over again. I thanked him for his help and he told me that the doctor's bill would be sent to the address they had on file for me, which was the address I gave them earlier of Juana's house in Texas, which I felt really happy about for some reason.

Bill told me that he knew the manager of the "Bell's Burgers" that was right on Ocean Boulevard, across from the beach just down a ways from the amusement park, and that he thought they might be hiring a cook, and that he would put in a good word for me. He also told me that his buddy sold lids of grass right out of the drive-through window to certain customers to supplement his lousy wages managing the burger joint. The next day I went down to the place and got hired immediately. Finally, I got a full-time job doing something that was not going to hurt me in any way, and on top of that I got a free meal every shift. I ended up working for "Bell's" for about four weeks and I got paid once a week, so after that first month had passed, I had saved over a hundred dollars.

I had another good friend whom I knew from Spain with whom I'd been exchanging letters, by the name of Mike. Mike and his little brother Tommy had moved back to the States from Spain with their parents the previous summer as well, and the family had settled in a little town called Siesta Key, just outside of Sarasota, Florida. So I looked at a map and saw that it wasn't really that far from South Carolina, with only one state (Georgia) in between.

By this time, I felt that I was probably wearing out my welcome at Bill's house and even though they had said nothing to me about it; I knew that I couldn't stay with them forever. And besides, I felt restless, as if I needed to see something else besides Myrtle Beach.

So I quit my job at Bell's and planned to head out the next day. The manager reminded me that I would still have one check owed to me and asked me where I would like to have it sent, but I told him to just hold on to it until I came back and picked it up one day soon.

So the next day, very early in the morning, Bill gave me a ride out of town along Highway 17 and he pulled over on a wide spot of the road to drop me off, and we both got out to say our goodbyes. I had got my backpack on and I was all ready to start hitchhiking south.

I gave him a big hug and a handshake and I thanked him again for everything he and his family had done for me and he said "Well Ron, good luck to you, and if you ever make it back around here, you know that you'll always be welcome. I just want you to know that, man."

"Thanks again, Bill. I might be heading back this way soon, it all depends on what Mike is up to down there in Florida. Besides, I still got a check coming to me from Bell's, you know. If I don't get back here to pick it up, I suppose I can always write to them and get them to send it to me, huh?"

"Yes, I guess so, I'm sure they'll do that. But listen, I also knew Mike from Spain you know, and he was always known to be a pretty wild guy, so take good care of yourself and try not to get in too much trouble there, you hear?"

"Yeah, I remember he could be a little crazy sometimes, but I'll be all right; don't worry."

"Okay, man, I'm going to miss you. Hey, you still␣go that little stash of Jamaican I gave you?"

"Yeah, I still got most of it left. It's some good stuff, and I want to turn Mike and Tommy on to it. I'll tell them that it's from you. I'm sure they're going to like it, man."

"All right, Ron, my brother. Again, good luck to you and take good care of yourself because nobody else will, right?"

"You'd better believe it, man. Adios, hermano."

"Okay, now you keep out of trouble, you hear?"

"I'll do my best Bill, don't worry."

And I did try, I really did.

Chapter 17. Florida Trouble

*"Today is the oldest you've ever been,
and the youngest you'll ever be again."*
— Eleanor Roosevelt

Bill climbed back into his car again, waved, and drove north, leaving me standing alone on the side of Highway 17. I stuck out my thumb and the third car that came along was a brand-new bright red Corvette convertible, and the driver who appeared to be a few years older than I, pulled over and stopped. I jogged a little with my pack bouncing on my back until I reached him, and he looked at me closely and asked, "Hey, you heading south?"

"Yes, sir, I'm going all the way to Florida!"

"Hey, so am I, hop in."

I couldn't believe my good luck. And what a ride! I slid in and squeezed my pack in the tiny area behind the seat, and off we went. The guy reached out his hand and said, "Stanley Greenberg, nice to meet you."

I shook his hand and said, "Ron Walker, nice to meet you as well, Mr. Greenberg."

He laughed and said, "Mr. Greenberg is my father, Ron, just call me Stan, okay?"

I laughed as well and said, "Sure Stan, that sounds good to me."

"So where you headed in Florida?"

"Well, I'm heading for a little place outside of Sarasota called Siesta Key. You ever heard of it?"

"Um, no, I can't say that I have, but I know where Sarasota is. It's just south of Tampa, right?"

"Yeah, just past Tampa Bay."

"Well, I'm heading all the way to West Palm Beach, which is on the Atlantic, but I can take you as far as there and you can get a ride the rest of the way easily enough, huh?"

I said with a smile, "I hope so! So far this trip has been really easy, you were only the third car to come along while I was waiting. And thanks, I really do appreciate it a lot."

"Well, Ron, it looks like you're having some good luck here today. Hey, do you drive?"

"Yeah, I do."

"You got a license?"

"Yes, I do; it's from Texas, but it's still good and hasn't expired yet."

"Good, maybe I can have you drive for a while pretty soon while I take a little nap. I'd like to make it all the way to West Palm today."

"Okay, Stan, sure, I don't mind driving at all." And I really wouldn't mind at all. A brand-new Corvette? No problem at all!

We chatted some more and Stan told me that he lived in New York City, but his parents had a second home in West Palm Beach and he was heading down to visit them for a while. I got the impression that his parents were fairly wealthy, especially when he told me that his car was a college graduation present. I also got the impression that he fancied himself to be a kind of "playboy" type of guy, once he started talking about all the beautiful "babes" that he knew in West Palm Beach.

After a while, after driving through Charleston and going inland quite a distance, we reached Interstate 95. He pulled over in a rest area and when we got back, he said, "Okay, Ron, it's your turn now. You think you can handle this ride?"

I looked at him, smiled, and said with all the confidence that I could muster, "You bet I can, Stan."

So he got in the passenger seat and I got behind the wheel and he told me, "All right now, it's just like any other car; just a lot faster is all. It's got an automatic transmission, so there's no shifting gears or anything. Just point it and go, okay?"

"Okay," and off we went.

And what a ride it was! The feel of the car was almost indescribable, and I had trouble keeping it under the speed limit because it just wanted to move and move fast. I actually found that I had to keep reining it in!

Stan folded his seat back and said, "Okay, Ron, just keep it under the speed limit, and wake me up when we cross the Florida line, all right?"

"Sure, Stan. We just stay on the 95 all the way, right?"

"Yep, it's easy driving on the freeway, but just keep it under the speed limit, okay?"

For the next few hours, I enjoyed the feel of driving this wonderful car down the freeway, with the wind in my hair and feeling like a million dollars, or at least like I was riding with someone who might be worth a million, anyway.

Not too long after crossing into Florida, I saw a sign that read, "Jacksonville, 43 Miles," so I pulled the car over at the next rest area, found a space to park, and Stan woke up.

"Where we at, Ron?" he asked.

"Not far from Jacksonville; we just passed the state line a short ways back. I gotta take a leak, I'll be right back, okay?"

"Sure," he said, "And I'll go take one once you get back."

"Okay, and hey, what kind of soda you want, they got a Coke machine up there I see. I'll get you one."

"Hey, that's nice of you, just a Coke or a Pepsi would be fine, thanks."

When I got back, I handed him his Pepsi, and he put it in the plastic drink holder he had attached to his windowsill and said, "Okay, my turn, I'll be right back."

While he was gone, I took out the map that I had in my bag and I studied it. I discovered that West Palm Beach is a little further south than I wanted to go if I was going to take the most direct route to Sarasota. It looked like if I caught State Highway 70 near Fort Pierce, it would take me almost all the way to Sarasota, going right by the north shore of Lake Okeechobee.

When Stan got back, I showed him the map, and he agreed with me that it would be quicker if I just took Highway 70 west across the entire peninsula from Fort Pierce, right over to the Gulf Coast. He took over the driving again and soon we were passing through Jacksonville, and soon after that we were driving along the Atlantic coast of Florida. Even though the freeway runs slightly inland, I still got glimpses of the deep blue Atlantic off to my left. I saw the turnoff to St. Augustine and then a little later, Cape Canaveral to the left and Orlando to the right.

When we finally reached the town of Ft. Pierce, Stan exited the freeway and pulled into a gas station. While the attendant was filling up the tank he told me, "Well, Ron, I guess this is where we part company, my friend. Highway 70 is just over there a ways. Good luck to you and it was great getting to know you. You take good care of yourself, okay?"

I shook his hand and said, "Likewise, Stan, it was a great ride and I really appreciate your kindness. I hope the rest of our trips both go this smoothly."

He drove away with a quick wave of his hand, leaving me once again alone and in a strange place. I looked at my watch and saw that it was only 4:30 or so and I figured I had at least a couple of hours of daylight left, so I thought I would see how far I could get before dark. I went into the little market next to the gas station and bought a few items, including a can of Hormel chili with beans, a box of crackers, some cookies, and a couple of other things to eat. I put the things in my pack and walked over to Highway 70 which was just a short hike away.

As before, I stood on the side of the road with my thumb out and before an hour passed, a pickup stopped, and I hopped in after tossing my pack in the bed of the truck. The old guy gave me a ride as far as the turnoff to Lake Okeechobee, which I saw on my left, stretching south as far as I could see. I got out, thanked him for the ride, and took a good look around. I realized that hitchhiking after dark was not a safe idea, so I looked for a place to crash.

All around me were fields with some crop covering them, but I'm not sure what it was. It was getting dark very quickly; maybe thirty minutes or so before it would be totally pitch black. I saw a small grove of trees growing between two fields not too far off the road, so I headed for them, and I found a small clearing among the trees and I settled down.

I gathered a little wood and dead brush that was lying around and started a very small fire just to keep the chill of the night off me and to cook my dinner. I had my Swiss army knife with me, so I opened the can of chili, sat it on the fire for a while to warm it up and I ate it with a plastic spoon straight out of the can along with some crackers. Still feeling a little hungry, I ate a few of the cookies too. I had a couple of hits from my sebsi and kicked back and relaxed for a bit. I cleared an area of rocks and twigs just big enough to lie down on, took my extra clothes out of my pack and laid them down on the cleared area, put on my jacket, grabbed my little blanket from my pack, used my pack as a pillow, lay down, and fell asleep almost instantly. I was up shortly after dawn and I got back out on the highway.

It took me six or seven rides and all day to get to Sarasota. All the rides were okay, except for one ride with a guy who seemed to be a traveling salesman of some sort in a station wagon. Shortly after I got in, the guy grabbed my leg and asked if I'd like to "have some fun." I got pissed off at him and told him to stop the car, and he finally did after a couple more minutes of me yelling and telling him to stop the damn car.

I got out, slammed the door, and yelled at him to fuck off as he sped away.

The rest of the rides were all right, mostly with old farmer-type guys in pickups. I provided polite conversation with them and got them to drive me as far west as they were headed. When I finally got to the town of Sarasota, I was both relieved and tired.

The term "key" in Florida and elsewhere refers to small barrier islands offshore usually connected to the mainland with bridges. Siesta Key is one of these small offshore islands just south of the town of Sarasota. It's known for its sandy beaches, shallow waters, quaint shops, and cafes, and there are many rich retired folks in their villas along the beach. There are also several private beach clubs and a lot of vacation rentals.

After getting my bearings, I finally got a ride across the bridge and onto the key itself with two long-haired guys in a van who tried to sell me some pot, which I declined. I asked them if they knew two brothers named Mike and Tommy and it turned out that they knew them. It was lucky too because the only address I had for Mike was for his parents' house and it turned out that he and Tommy were both living in a beach house a couple of miles down the road from their parents' villa. They dropped me off right in front of the beach house and I got out and thanked them for the ride. I walked up to the door of the old funky-looking place and knocked on the door, feeling rather apprehensive.

A pretty young lady with dark hair and wearing a bikini answered the door, looked at me oddly, and asked, "Yeah, what do you want, man?"

I smiled and said, "Hello, my name is Ron Walker and I'm an old friend of Mike's. Is he here by any chance?"

She replied carefully, "Nope, he's not here right now, sorry." And she started to close the door.

So I told her, "Um, hold on, please. I traveled all the way from South Carolina to see Mike; do you expect him home soon?"

"Yeah, he should be home pretty soon. Do you want to wait for him, maybe?"

"Sure, that would be great if I could. I've come a long ways to see him."

"Well, how I do know that you're cool, man?"

"Well, I've known Mike for a long time now, I knew him and Tommy when they used to live in Spain."

"Oh, yeah, Mike has told me about those days. That's cool, come on in. I'm Molly by the way; nice to meet you."

She opened the door all the way, and I walked in. The place was a typical hippy den with very little furniture except for an old couch and a couple of mattresses on the floor, and old blankets over the windows for curtains. It was very dark inside with one black light in the corner near a life-sized print of Jimi Hendrix and a few other posters.

Molly invited me to sit down on the old ragged couch in the living room, so I took my pack off and set it down next to me. I took out my pack of cigarettes and offer one to Molly, lit it for her and then one for me, and we start chatting.

She told me that she was Mike's girlfriend, but that they were not really all that serious. She also told me that Tommy lived in the same place and she thought that their parents rented it for them, just so they wouldn't have to put up with their hippy kids' weird ways.

She then lit up a skinny joint and passed it to me, which I accepted and pretty soon we were both pretty high. She had the radio tuned to a rock station from Tampa and they were playing some decent tunes.

She asked me, "So is Mike is expecting you, Ron?"

I laughed and said, "Well, actually he isn't. I left South Carolina before I had a chance to write him and tell him I was coming. I thought I'd surprise him, you know."

"Well, I don't know if he really likes surprises too much, we'll see when he gets here, okay?"

About twenty minutes later, I heard someone approaching the door, so I got up quickly and stood to the side of the front door, hidden from view. As Mike walked in, I came up behind him and gave him a big bear hug with him facing the opposite direction. He struggled free and turned around with his fist ready to clobber me.

I yelled out, "Hey, Mike, it's me! Take it easy, man!"

He looked at me closely and said, "Who the hell are you?"

"Mike, it's me, Ron Walker, from Madrid, man. Don't you recognize me?"

He looked at me a little closer and said, "Ronnie Walker! Is that you, man?"

"Yeah, Mike, it's me, I thought I'd surprise you, man!"

So he finally gave me a big hug and a long handshake and we sat down and started talking. I noticed that his hair had gotten really long, way past his shoulders, which was strange because I had seen him only a little over a year before and his hair wasn't close to being that long then.

So I mentioned it, and he said, "Wow, you gotta see Tommy's hair; it's down to his fucking waist now, man!"

"How the hell did it grow so quickly?" I asked.

He smiled and told me, "Hey, the trick is to never wash it man, it grows fast that way."

We chatted some more, and he reminded me about some of the great parties that my brother and I used to have at our *piso* on Calle Breton de los Herreros in Madrid, and I reminded him about the girl Connie who liked him so much but how she ended up being with a lot of guys including me.

I told him about my trip down from Bill Johnson's place in South Carolina and how easy it had been to hitchhike all the way, and what I had been doing since I had seen him last. He told me that once his family came to Sarasota from Madrid last year, things got worse between his folks and it looked like they might soon be heading for a divorce. He told me they paid for the little beach shack for him and Tommy and they also gave them some money to live on because neither one of them could get a job, and besides Tommy was only sixteen and would still have been in school if he hadn't recently just dropped out.

Right about then, Tommy came walking in. I stood up when he walked in and said, "Hey, Thomas, how are you doing, kiddo?"

He looked at me closely and said, "Ronnie Walker? Is that you, man?"

"Yep, right here in the flesh, man. How are you doing, muchacho?"

"Hell, not bad Ron, and you?"

"Hey, it could be worse, I suppose," I said with a smile.

I took a good look at him and I saw that his hair had grown long; in fact, it was so long it was down to his belt buckle! I'd never seen any guy with hair that long in my life. And he was almost totally blond whereas Mike had darker hair. And since Tom was so young, he couldn't grow any facial hair yet, so he really looked kinda like a girl. But I didn't tell him that.

After a few hours of sitting around and talking, I noticed that something was wrong with these two guys. These brothers that I used to know so well had changed. They both had a different vibe about them, something that I couldn't quite put my finger on, but they had both changed a lot.

Before too long, I realized what it was. Mike got up off the couch and gave me a long look and asked me, "Hey, you want to shoot some smack, man? I got some if you want a shot."

I looked at him with disbelief and told him, while trying not to be too judgmental, "Nah, that's okay, man. I'm good, thanks anyway though."

"C'mon, you gotta try this stuff, man. It'll knock your lights out, I swear to god."

"No thanks, Mike. I'm just not into that shit, that's all, man."

"Okay, suit yourself, more for us then, man."

He broke out his "works" and proceeded to cook up a spoonful of the shit and I watched as he tied his arm up and injected the stuff right into his left arm. I noticed that he was having trouble because there were already lots of holes in his vein, but he finally got it in and released the belt around his arm and then fell back onto the couch with a contented and exhausted look on his face.

Tommy then said, "Okay, my turn."

And I watched as he did the same thing. Then Mike fixed a shot for Molly and she ended up lying back on the couch as well.

Later that night, I found one of the mattresses to crash on and I woke up the next morning and Tommy was gone but Mike and Molly were still there. Again I declined as I watch them fix themselves again, and then Mike asked me if I wanted to go down to the beach for a while.

I said okay, so the three of us got into his old beaten up blue VW Beetle and headed for the beach. While driving there, Mike seemed very mellow—almost too mellow to drive—but Molly was in the front seat with him and she was helping him somewhat by pointing out stop signs, red lights, and other things that he seemed to be unaware of or just plain not caring much about.

It wasn't too long before we got to the beach. We parked in a very crowded parking lot and climbed out of the car. As we walked towards the beach, we were accosted several times by guys asking what we wanted, but we shook our heads to all of them. One guy standing by a VW van said, "Speed, man. I got white crosses and black beauties, take your pick."

Another guy looked at us and said, "I got some great Jamaican weed. Just ten bucks a lid, man."

Yet another guy who looked really wired was saying very softly to everyone walking by, "I got lots of coke, you wanna buy some?"

And some older guy with a long ponytail and a tie-dyed shirt whispered to us as we walked by, "Acid, I got yellow sunshine, only five bucks a tab, man."

By the time we finally got down to the sand, it seemed like we had been offered just about every drug known by mankind within just a few minutes.

We declined everyone's offers, and when we got to the beach, I took a good look around. The place was overrun by people. I hadn't seen such a crowded beach since the last time I was in Benidorm. There were people everywhere, with beach blankets and umbrellas occupying almost every square foot of sand. There was trash everywhere; the sand was dirty from old cigarette butts, paper plates, plastic cups, and all kinds of other ugly stuff.

I looked to my left and about fifty feet away I saw a tall fence going all the way down and right into the water for quite a distance. When I looked to the right, I saw the same thing. But on the other sides of those fences, the beach was empty and immaculate, with no people and no trash at all.

So I asked Mike, "Hey, how come this beach is so crowded and trashy and the ones on the other side of those fences are so clean and empty, man?"

He looked at me as if I was crazy and not quite all there and told me, "This is the public beach man. Those over there are private beaches; don't you see the signs?"

I looked where he was pointing and I saw the signs that he was referring to. There were several of them and they all said the same thing in big red letters.

"Who actually owns those beaches?" I asked Mike.

He looked at me again as if I was an imbecile and said, "They're private, Ron. They're owned by rich fucks that don't want anyone on their private beach."

"You mean they own the beach all the way down into the water? That's unbelievable man! So what happens if you get in the water and just swim around the fence and get onto their beach?"

"You get arrested for trespassing, man. They got security guards that patrol the beach and they will bust you before you even get a chance to enjoy the beach."

"Shit! I've never heard of such a fucking thing! How do they get away with it? The beach should belong to everyone, man!"

He gave me a look of resignation and said with a deep sigh, "Hey, that's what money can do, man. It can actually buy you the fucking beach!"

"Well, they sure can't do that shit in Spain, man."

"Yeah, I know, Ron, we used to live in Torremolinos for a while, remember?"

"Yeah, I remember seeing the pictures of you and Tommy sitting on Timothy Leary's lap when you were real young kids, right on the beach in Torremolinos."

"Yeah, it's unbelievable that both of my parents were good friends with him back then. But look at them now; nothing but a couple of fucking drunks!"

"I'm sorry to hear that, Mike. You think that's part of the problems they're having?"

"Yeah, they both drink like fishes and can't even get out of bed most of the time and when they do, all they do is argue; it's really fucked! I can't stand it, but I can't do nothing about it!"

"I don't know what to tell you, Mike. My folks got divorced as soon as we came back to the States, but they're both doing pretty good now. Each of them got a new partner is why, I think."

He gave me his look of resignation and said, "Well, maybe that's what they ought to fucking do then! Maybe they'd both be happy then, who knows!"

I saw the deep unhappiness and the sadness in his eyes, but I felt helpless to do anything for him. But I said to him, "You know, you gotta quit this heroin shit, it's fucked up, man. Don't you know that? And getting Tommy into it, that's pretty bad."

"Yeah, I know that. Do you think I'm stupid? But he's a big boy, and he does whatever he fucking wants. And I'll quit one of these days when I get my shit together, okay?"

"I sure hope you do, my friend, I really hope so."

But as far as I know, I don't think he ever did, because once I left Florida I never heard from him or his brother ever again.

That evening, I told him that I was going back to Myrtle Beach the next day since I had a check from work waiting for me there. So the next morning we said our goodbyes, and I gave him and Tommy big hugs and handshakes all around and I told them that maybe I would come back down once I got my check, maybe with Bill even, but I could tell that they knew I didn't really mean it.

I started out early hitchhiking back north. The first ride got me just to the north side of the town of Sarasota right on Interstate 75. The next ride got me to the Bradenton exit off the 75, and that is where all the trouble began.

I knew that technically it was illegal to hitchhike on the interstate highway system. And indeed there were signs to that effect posted on the freeway on-ramps to every interstate in the country. The signs don't specifically mention "hitchhikers" but they do prohibit "pedestrians" which is basically what a hitchhiker is when he's standing there trying to get a ride.

The situation that I found myself in near Bradenton was that the ride that I just had, had exited on the Bradenton exit off the freeway and since I wasn't interested in seeing Bradenton, I had the driver let me off while I was still on the freeway, and he kept going after making his exit. So there I was standing on the freeway itself, but not on the on-ramp, where I should have been because it's not illegal to hitchhike on the on-ramp. I realized that I should probably get myself off the freeway itself and stand on the on-ramp, but my logic told me that there were far more cars going along the freeway itself than the few cars that were heading onto the freeway from the on-ramp. So I decided to stay where I was for a little while which turned out to be my downfall.

As I stood there with lots of cars zooming by (which couldn't really safely stop for me anyway, I realized); I looked north, and I saw another hitchhiker not more than a hundred yards from me. He was an older man and I could see that he had two rather large suitcases with him, one of which he was sitting on. By this time, I realized that in order for me to maximize my chances of getting a ride; I had better get as far away from this guy as I could and off the freeway. So I started walking south back towards the exit that my previous driver had taken.

But before I could reach the exit and off the damn freeway, I saw a highway patrolman stop with his lights flashing about halfway between me and the other hitchhiker in front of me. I kept walking trying to get off the freeway, but the cop started to slowly back up along the shoulder of the highway heading right in my direction. I figure that if I began to run, he'd probably get me for fleeing a crime scene or something, so I just patiently waited for him.

Within thirty seconds, he'd pulled up right next to me. He got out and said, "You know that it is illegal to hitchhike on the freeway, don't you, boy?"

I looked at him and tried to give him my most innocent face and I replied, "Yes sir, I know, but I'm trying to get off the freeway. My last ride left me right about here, and I'm trying to get over to the on-ramp over there."

And I pointed to the exit.

He looked at me with very little pity or compassion and just said, "Well, I gotta take you in, because it looks like to me that you're hitchhiking on the freeway."

"But officer, I was just trying to get off the freeway; can't you see that?"

"Come on, get in the car now, boy. And don't give me no lip."

He came over to me and grabbed my arm and started pulling me towards his car. He opened the back door and pushed my head down until I got in. I sat down with my pack on my lap, and I started to sweat bullets. I knew that I still had my pot in my pack, in my little green pouch, along with some rolling papers and my *sebsi* pipe that I had brought all the way from Morocco. I thought about pulling out the pouch and trying to ditch it, but the window and the door had no way of being opened from the inside, so I just sat there and hoped for the best.

He drove north very slowly and stopped right behind the man I had seen with the suitcases. He got out and had a few words with him, grabbed him by the arm and opened the door on the other side and put him in the back seat right beside me. It looked like he got two arrests for the price of one!

He tossed the other guy's suitcases in the trunk of his cruiser and started driving. The other guy seemed totally nonplussed like he could give a shit what was happening to him, but I was just about shitting bricks by this time.

I asked the officer, "Um, sir, what do you think will happen to us? Is hitchhiking on the freeway a serious offense?"

He turned his head slightly and said, "No, you'll probably just get a fine and if you can pay it, you can go on your way today with no problem. But you gotta learn that it's not good to break the law. And hitchhiking on the freeway is a damn crime!"

The other criminal who was sitting next to me finally began to show some interest and asked, "So how much is that fine around here anyways?"

The officer shrugged and said, "I think it's about twenty-five dollars if it's your first offense. And both you guys look like you probably got that much on you."

Soon we were approaching the Hillsborough County Sheriff's Department headquarters. It was a large red brick building with a security entrance that we pulled up to. After a minute or so it opened, and we drove through. The gates slid shut behind us and we pulled up to a large door and we all got out of the car. The officer opened the trunk and grabbed the suitcases and told the older guy to take them. And then the three of us walked into the building.

As the other guy and I stood off to one side, him with a suitcase in each hand and me with my backpack on my back, the officer walked up to the desk and told the man behind it, "Hey, Sam, I caught both of these guys hitchhiking on the 75 not a hundred yards from each other. Got two for the price of one!" And he laughed his little laugh.

The man behind the desk smiled and replied, "Well, Bob, it looks like you made out this time, didn't you? Now you two gentlemen want to come up here one at a time. You there, sir, with the suitcases, leave them there and approach the desk, please."

So the other guy exchanged a few words with the officer and then it was my turn. I walked up to him with my pack still on my back and he yelled at me, "Hey! Leave your gear over there with the suitcases."

So I shed my pack and walked back up to the man. He gave me a bored look and said, "You know, son, that it's a crime for a pedestrian to be on the interstate highway system."

I tried to tell him my story about trying to get off the freeway just when Bob over there decided to arrest me, but he didn't want to hear it. Instead, he interrupted me and said, "Boy, I don't wanna hear it. Do you plead guilty or not?"

"Um, I guess so, but..."

"That's good enough," as he interrupted me again. "Stand over there for the time being."

And he pointed to where the other guy was standing by the wall. I made my way over there and stood next to the other guy.

I could see the guy behind the desk was doing some kind of paperwork, and he then called the other criminal over and had another conversation with him and this time I could see the guy pulling out his wallet and showing the man his identification and they exchanged some more words. I watched as he then handed the officer some bills from his wallet as well.

Then it was my turn, and I approached the desk again and the man said "Son, you got some ID on you?"

I opened my wallet and pulled out my Texas driver's license and he took it from me and started writing some more on his forms and then he said, "Well, Mr. Walker, it's a twenty-five dollar fine for violating the interstate highway safety regulations. Do you have the funds to pay this fine at this time?"

"Yes, sir," I said with a deep sigh of relief, "I have it right here in my wallet." And I again reached into my wallet and handed him the cash, which he took from me and then handed me back a form to sign and a receipt for the money I paid him.

He then looked at me and said, "Okay, that's it, you're good to go. Just stand back over there for a minute while we look through your stuff, just to make sure you don't have any guns or drugs or other contraband in there."

I turned around, and I saw that a different officer had already gotten both of the other guy's suitcases open and he was rummaging through them, pulling out dirty underwear and socks and making little piles of everything that was in there.

After he was done, he told the other guy he was good to go and told him to put the stuff back in his suitcases, which the guy did. Then he started on my backpack.

He unzipped the main zipper and pulled everything out, including my change of clothes, my jacket, my little blanket, my Swiss Army knife, my plastic spoon, my bottle of water, my little kit including my toothbrush, toothpaste, a bar of soap and half a roll of toilet paper and everything else and he put it all on the floor. He then zipped open the small pocket at the front of the pack and pulled out its contents. He began with my extra pack of cigarettes, my map, and my passport and then he pulled out my little green pouch, and opened it up.

He got a big shit-eating grin on his face and looked at me and said, "Hey, now, what do we have here?"

He pulled out my sebsi, the orange pack of Zig Zag rolling papers, and my little plastic baggie of pot.

"It looks like we got ourselves a pot smoker here, don't we?" He said this with obvious  delight. He walked over to me and started reading me my rights after he told me that I was being arrested for possession of marijuana and possession of drug paraphernalia.

Before I knew it, I was booked, fingerprinted and photographed, and sitting in a jail cell in the Hillsborough County Jail, charged with a felony marijuana possession charge. They had weighed the amount of pot and it came in at a little over seven grams (about three joints' worth), and the state of Florida had just recently relaxed their marijuana laws so that less than five grams was a misdemeanor, but anything over that amount was considered trafficking and was a felony charge. Seven grams is about a quarter of an ounce of pot, and an ounce (commonly referred to as a lid), usually sold for about ten dollars on the street just about anywhere. So I was facing a felony drug charge for having in my possession about $2.50 worth of pot.

They told me my trial would not come up for at least a month or more, due to the court system being backlogged because of the large number of these types of "crimes" being committed. And in the meantime, I was to sit in jail, awaiting trial at some unknown date in the future.

So I found myself in a large cell holding almost forty inmates. There were twenty bunk beds to hold the inmates and one large bathroom for all of us to use. It had three toilet cubicles (without doors) and one long urinal. It also had a large communal shower where several inmates could shower at the same time, again without doors or any other sort of privacy.

They gave me a blanket, a pillow, and an orange jumpsuit to wear with "Hillsborough County Jail" on the back of it. They also assigned me two white T-shirts, two pairs of tidy whities, two pairs of black socks, and a pair of black slip-on canvas shoes to wear. They assigned me a bed on the top bunk right over a very large and mean-looking black man. And when I took a good look around after entering the cell, and after putting my blanket and pillow on my bunk, I noticed that about seventy-five percent of the men looked just like my bunkmate.

To say I was totally terrified would be an understatement. I had never felt so afraid, intimidated, lonely, depressed, worried, and angry in my entire young life. The first five of these feelings were due to the specific place and situation I suddenly found myself in, but the anger that I was feeling was due to the archaic laws that had put me in this situation in the first place.

Just a couple of years earlier, I had visited a land where possession and consumption of this prohibited substance was not only tolerated but was practiced by most of the male members of that society on a regular basis. And I saw with my own eyes and learned from my own experience that indulging in smoking pot did not seem to hurt the individual or society in general.

But I had little time to feel sorry for myself because my major concern at the moment was my very survival. My bunk-mate finally spoke to me and his first question was, "Hey, white boy, what you in for?"

I looked at him and said, "Um, possession of marijuana."

"Oh yeah, how much did you have?"

"I had seven grams."

"Oh, shit, boy, you got yourself a damn felony charge, then don't you? Because five grams or less is a misdemeanor now, isn't it?"

"Yeah, that's what they told me."

"Damn, boy, you'll get about two years for that."

I looked at him with a look of disbelief and said, "Two years! I'm gonna get two years for three fucking joints, man?"

"Yeah," he told me, "but don't worry about it, you can probably get out in about one, if you get your early release for good behavior."

"Well, damn, that doesn't sound much better, man!"

"Shit, boy, one year ain't shit, don't worry about it."

But I did worry about it, and I worried about it a lot. A minimum of one whole year locked up in this shit hole with these evil-looking guys seemed to me to be an eternity.

Of course, I got the one phone call that they allowed me. And so I called my dad at the number I had for him in Juana's house in Texas.

"Hello," she answered.

"Hi, Juana, this is Ron, is my dad around?"

"No, honey, he isn't. He's in Spain right now."

"In Spain! What's he doing there?"

"Well, he went on ahead on a Space A flight, to try to find us a place to live. And I'm going to join him in Madrid in a couple of weeks after I go to Hawaii to visit my daughter Linda, and her son Billy for a little while. What do you need, honey?"

So I told her all about what had happened to me and the fact I was sitting in the Hillsborough County Jail, and I was facing a felony charge and it looked like I might be there at least a year and possibly more.

She sounded very worried and told me, "Well, hold on, Ronnie. We can get you out of this mess, I'm pretty sure. You say you're in the Hillsborough County Jail. Is that in Tampa?"

"Yes, it is."

"I'll tell you what, honey. When I get back from Hawaii, I'll stop by there on my way to Spain and I'll see what we can do to get you out of there, okay?"

"Oh, wow! That would be great, Juana, and I'd really appreciate it a lot. I don't know how long I can handle being in this place, it's awful."

"I can only imagine, Ron. But you just hold on and I'll be there in a couple of weeks or so and I'll do what I can to get you out of there, so don't worry, okay, honey?"

"Okay, Juana, I really do appreciate it a lot."

"All right then, I'll contact your dad and let him know what's happening, okay?"

"Okay," I said.

"You hang in there and I'll see you in a couple of weeks or so, okay, honey?"

"Okay, and thanks again, Juana."

"You're welcome, Ron, and try not to get in any trouble there, okay?"

"Don't worry about that, I'll be fine; just try to hurry, please."

"Okay, I'll see you soon. Bye for now."

"All right, bye."

This conversation gave me an enormous amount of hope and I realized that I wasn't really totally abandoned and maybe I would be able to get out of jail before a year had passed after all, or at least I really hoped so.

In the meantime, I had to survive in this place before she got there and got me out. So I kept to myself as much as possible but when you're locked up with forty other guys for twenty-four hours a day, that's pretty hard to do. Three times per day we lined up like soldiers and marched down to the chow hall to get fed, and we were still together. Even using

 the bathroom, there wasn't any privacy, since there was always someone else in there.

But I tried to make the best of my situation and not totally lose my mind while I was locked up, which is easy to do when it feels like there is no hope or end in sight. I kept telling myself that I'd be out of there soon, that it was just a matter of time.

One thing that the guys in my cell liked to do to pass the time was to play cards, and usually the game was poker. I had been playing poker since I was a young boy because my dad was a semi-professional poker player who had played most of his life starting when he was just a raw recruit in the Army Air Corps in World War II. He had played the game for fun and profit ever since those days and had become very good at it and had won many thousands of dollars over the years.

I learned the game when my brother and I were the other "players" when he'd practice playing the game around the house. He'd deal the cards and the chips out and we'd play for hours learning all the different variants of the game, and the different strategies involved, and if one of us boys won, he'd pay us in cash, not a lot, but enough to make it worth our time and effort.

So when I was asked to join the jailhouse poker game, I accepted. One young black guy a little older than me with a wild Afro by the name of Willy, was the guy that always had a game going on around his bunk, and I spent many hours playing with him and his friends. We'd play for matchsticks which we used for chips and even though we didn't have real money to pay for the chips, we used a credit system that was based on real funds.

In the jail, it was possible to buy certain items if one had money in one's "account." This account was the amount of money that you had in your pocket when you were arrested, or sometimes, money that your friends or relatives had deposited into your account. The inmates used this money to purchase items that were allowed in the jailhouse, such as cigarettes, matches, sodas, candy, and other snacks. A "trustee" walked up to the cell doors every other day with a wagon called the "canteen," with an assortment of things to buy, and he had a list of the account of each inmate and he'd subtract the amount of any new purchase from that inmate's account.

Since I had a few dollars with me when I was arrested, I had enough to buy a few items that were rather essential to me and made being locked up just a little more tolerable. I smoked like a chimney mainly because there was little else to do, and I enjoyed an occasional candy bar or soda. But I was lucky because a lot of the guys in there had nothing in their account because they had used up any money that they happened to have with them at the time of their arrest, and they had no one on the outside to add anything to their accounts.

So if someone lost playing poker, they usually paid it off with cigarettes and these winnings were one way that an inmate who didn't have any money in his account was able to acquire certain items that he'd otherwise have no way of getting. So the poker games were serious and did involve considerable financial interest. A lot of the guys refused to play due to either already having lost a lot or having no interest or skill in the game. But to me it was a way to help pass the endless hours of being locked up and also to occasionally add to my stash of cigarettes.

It always started with a "buy-in," which is how you got into the game. Willy was the banker, and you bought so many "chips" by trading something of value, usually cigarettes, for so many matchsticks, which were valued at one penny each. So if a pack of cigarettes cost forty cents from the canteen, then that could get you forty matchsticks. Of course, matches were available to purchase from the canteen along with packs of cigarettes, but you couldn't just use your own matchsticks—only the ones that Willy would hand out. And any winnings were paid in cigarettes, which was the real jailhouse currency.

I'd usually do a buy-in of one pack and rarely did I ever have to make another buy-in for that session. I usually came out ahead after playing for several hours, but not always. I did lose sometimes but overall over a period of several days; I averaged out to be almost always at least a little ahead. I had learned a lot from my dad and knew all the different games as well as certain other skills that the game of poker required in order to win, such as the different odds involved and how to "read" other players. A lot of the games got down to being between Willy and me, and he quickly realized that I was a formidable opponent, and not just some skinny, long-haired white kid with glasses.

We played the regular poker games such as five-card stud, seven-card stud, five-card draw, and a few others such as "baseball" (with threes and nines wild), and a few games of low ball, and the deal always went around clockwise, so everyone playing got a chance to call the game when it came around for him to deal.

One afternoon, when it got to be my turn to deal, I asked the four or five guys playing at the time if any of them had ever played the game of "Three Toed Pete." None of them had ever heard of it, so I showed them the game, which was a low-ball game and really easy to learn and a lot of fun to play. Every player got three cards dealt down and then got three deals, with betting between each deal. The pot could get quite large with so many bets so it could be a very lucrative game to play. The object (as in all low-ball games) was to get the lowest hand; in this case, the best hand possible would be an ace, deuce, and trey. Any pair would be high and would be a loser.

So an average good hand in this game would be ace, trey, five for an example. But what made it exciting was, if a player had an ace, deuce and an eight by his second deal, and he threw away the eight trying to get a lower card, he very well might pair up the ace or deuce and lose, or catch an even higher card than the eight, like a face card, and also lose.

I seemed to win a lot playing this game, so I'd call the game quite often when the deal came around to me. Willy never seemed to like the game very much because he'd never stay on the second deal but would almost always take a card through the third deal, trying to hit a lower card, and he'd almost always lose. So he started to call me "God damn Pete" as in "Three Toed Pete." This nickname stuck and before too long I was known as "Pete" to almost all the other inmates.

Time passed slowly while I was locked up. I really wished that the time would go by faster, but the days seemed to drag by. I was feeling a lot less intimidated by my fellow prisoners though. My poker-playing abilities seemed to give me a little respect among some of the inmates who would otherwise have found me an easy target to pick on or try to exploit. And since the majority of the population was black, I was in the minority and I realized early that usually the races tended to stick with themselves, mostly. But I ended up hanging with Willy and his buddies instead of socializing with the other white guys most the time, who frankly seemed to be mostly rednecks.

There was one white guy about my age who had a top bunk near me by the name of "Fast Eddie," at least that is what he wanted people to call him. He was a chubby guy with thick glasses and dark slicked-back hair. He was always bragging about his car and telling anybody that would listen to him all about it. He claimed to have a metallic blue 1968 Camaro Z-28 with a 396, and that it was the fastest car in the entire state of Florida, and that he had won lots of money by street racing this super-fast car.

He also claimed that he loved "speed," as in the drug as well as in a car's velocity. He said that he got busted for possessing over a thousand hits of "white crosses," which he said were his favorite form of speed. And he couldn't wait to get out of jail and get back to racing his fast car while speeding on white crosses. I tried to argue with him that speed can be a dangerous drug and maybe he should go easy on it, but he just claimed that it made him go faster both in his mind and in his car. All I could do was wish him luck.

Eighteen long days after being arrested for a felony charge of possession of marijuana, a guard came and got me and told me I had a visitor and to come with him. I followed him to a small room they used for inmates to have visits from their lawyers and when I walked in; I saw Juana sitting there with an older man with a dark suit and tie on. She greeted me with a hug and introduced the man with her as Mr. Brown, and that he was the lawyer who was going to get me out of jail. He had some papers in his briefcase and so the three of us sat down to discuss my case.

It was quite simple really. There would not be a trial at all, but instead I would appear in front of a judge and he would release me into the custody of my family. Mr. Brown assured both Juana and me that he could get the judge to release me with time served if I agreed to leave the state. We also discussed how I was to always address the judge as "your honor" and I was to show him the utmost respect at all times.

After a few more minutes of discussion, with a guard accompanying us, we walked outside the jail and across the parking lot to where the judge's chambers and various courtrooms were located. We went into a judge's office and the three of us sat down in front of the judge who was behind a large brown desk that had a big nameplate on it saying in gold leaf, "The Honorable James P. Kirkland."

After shuffling some papers around on his large desk, Judge Kirkland took a long look at me and said, "Mr. Walker, I understand that you have been charged with felony possession of an illegal substance, in this case, marijuana, as well as possession of drug paraphernalia. I further understand that if you are to be released at this time, you will be remanded to the custody of your family, in this case your father, who I understand resides in Spain. Your stepmother is present, and she has assured me that she will make sure that you are transported to that country as soon as possible upon your release, and then directly into your father's custody. Furthermore, you are not to return to the state of Florida for a period of twenty years, and if you comply with these instructions and requirements, any record of your legal problems here will be expunged. Do you understand these terms and conditions, Mr. Walker?"

"Yes, sir, your honor, I understand," I replied.

"Very well, I hereby release you from the Hillsborough County Detention Center into the custody of your father, Mr. John Walker, who lives in Madrid, Spain. And you are to return to that country to be in his custody as soon as possible. Now please sign here."

And he handed me a paper to sign, which I did.

"That is all. Good day and good luck to you."

"Thank you, your honor," is all I said.

The three of us got up and walked out of his chambers. The guard who had been accompanying us earlier was waiting outside, and he told me to follow him.

Juana said, "Don't worry, honey, he's just going to take you back to the jail to get your clothes and other things. I'll be waiting for you in the parking lot and I'll see you when you come out. It'll only be a few minutes."

"Okay," I told her as I started walking with the guard back to the jail area.

About fifteen minutes later, I walked out of the jail with the clothes on that I had been wearing when I was arrested, along with my backpack with most of my things in it. The only things that were missing were the pot and my pouch with the rolling papers and my sebsi pipe, but everything else seemed to be there. And I was a free man! What a relief! I felt that I was not only released from jail, but also from the deep and dark despair that was threatening to overcome me while I was in my jail cell.

Juana was standing by her little rental car in the parking lot and I put my pack in the back seat and I got in the passenger seat. She started the car, and we drove away.

"Juana, I can't tell you much I appreciate what you've done for me today. I want to thank you from the bottom of my heart."

"I understand, honey, I'm just glad that it went so well. It just goes to show what some money can do to get someone out of trouble, huh?"

I looked at her closely and asked "Money? How much money did you have to spend for all this?"

"Well, altogether it was $3500, half went to the lawyer and the other half to the judge, I believe. But it was well worth it to get you out of jail now wasn't it, honey?"

"Yeah, absolutely! I don't know how much longer I could have handled it in there."

She smiled and said, "Yep, the best justice money can buy, right?"

"Yeah, I guess so."

This was a very profound lesson to learn for someone as young as I was. The rest of the guys whom I had gotten to know while in jail were still in there because they had no one on the outside who was willing or had the means to buy them their freedom, and that's why they were still sitting in there. Me, I was very lucky that Juana's ex-husband had left her well off when he had died suddenly a few years before and so she had the money to pay the right people to not only get me out of jail but also to erase any trace of my legal problems.

This was to be only the first of several other legal issues that I was to encounter in my life and in absolutely every case, the only real justice involved was controlled only by money, not by anything else.

At this point I was counting my blessings, because I was a free man again, and it felt absolutely wonderful.

Juana drove to a very nice restaurant not far from the motel rooms that she had rented for us in Tampa, and we celebrated with a steak dinner and a bottle of wine. The next day, we caught a flight from Tampa to Miami and after a short layover there; we were on a direct TWA flight from Miami International Airport all the way to Barajas Airport in Madrid, Spain.

Ah! On the way home again

Chapter 18. Back in Spain Again

"The holy passion of friendship is so sweet and steady and loyal and enduring in nature that it will last through a whole lifetime, if not asked to lend money."
— Mark Twain

By the time Juana and I returned to Madrid, it was the fall of 1971, just a little over one year since I had left Spain with my family. It appeared to me that Spain had not changed much at all, but I sure had. During the fifteen months or so that I had been in the States, I had attended college in San Antonio, moved to Denver and gotten a job, went to Myrtle Beach and broke my arm, worked for a carnival traveling all over several eastern states, went to Florida and got busted for possession of marijuana, and spent eighteen long days in jail.

No, the United States had not treated me very well during the short time I had been there, and as far as I was concerned, they could keep the place. I was back in the country where I had grown up, and it was great to feel the warm embrace of the Spanish culture and friendly people once again. I felt like I had returned not only to my home but to civilization itself!

My mom and Jim had settled into a very nice *piso* in Canillejas, on the fifth floor of a six-story building, close to my mom's friend, Maruja, who lived nearby in *Las Palomas*. The *piso* was a two-bedroom place, but they had turned the second bedroom into an office with a large desk and a hide-away bed that came out of the couch. It was on this sofa bed that I slept during most of the time I spent in Madrid over the next six months.

My dad and Juana, by contrast, had bought an old *finca* or farmhouse on the outskirts of Marbella, on the *Costa del Sol* in southern Spain, not far from the city of Malaga. It was originally a very small and ancient farmhouse on a few acres of land, in the hills overlooking the Mediterranean Sea, just north a few kilometers from the main town of

Marbella. They were renovating the old house and making it more modern and livable by adding a two-story addition, and an enclosed courtyard with a small pool. The plan was to upgrade the plumbing and electricity as well. My dad had hired a couple of local *obreros* (workers) to help, and they were making steady if slow progress.

My mom and Jim were very happy to see me and were surprised when I told them about my adventures in Myrtle Beach and in Florida. They thanked Juana repeatedly for her help when they picked me up at Barajas and while she was waiting for her transfer flight to Malaga. It was the first time they had met her, but after a while, my four parents became close friends, with my dad and Juana often visiting them in Canillejas, as well as my mom and Jim visiting the place that my dad and Juana had bought in Marbella.

Not long after I returned to Madrid and settled in somewhat sleeping on the couch, my dad and Juana came up for a visit and my mom made a nice paella dinner for everyone. We all discussed my future, but failed to come up with anything that seemed to be an answer, or even a good idea, so it was more or less decided that we'd just wait and see what happened.

It was great to have both sets of my parents living in the same country as me, and I felt more secure than before when I was trying to make it on my own in a strange country where I didn't feel like I belonged, and where I had never really lived before. And I knew that in my own small way, I was helping all four of these people out as well as them helping me. Jim had broken his leg shortly before I got there, and

he had difficulty getting around, so I'd help him whenever I could. He was still drinking quite heavily, which had contributed to his bum leg issue, but he was trying to get help with his problem at the Base hospital at Torrejon.

One of the first things I did after returning to Spain was look up my old friends who were still in town, including Andy and J.P. Andy was still finishing high school at THS (they had changed the name that year from Madrid High School to Torrejon High School for some reason). And he was still pretty much the same, and still indulging in the same things that he used to do when I lived there before, including smoking a lot of hash, and listening to rock music, which I started to do again as well.

Since I was out of school, I had a lot more times on my hands than he did, and frankly, I started smoking hash more than he did. But we still got together quite often and lit up. I spent a lot of time at his house in *Chamartin* and I got to know his family very well. He had two sisters and two brothers, and for a while I felt that I was almost a part of their large family.

His older sister had gotten pregnant with a guy by the name of Nick who had been a very good friend of my brother's while they were in school, but it turned out that he was actually really a bum. In the end, he didn't want much to do with her after he found out about the pregnancy, and he ended up returning to the States soon after to escape the responsibilities of fatherhood. But she eventually had her son who became yet another member of their already large family. Their father was still absent most of the time, still in Madagascar I suppose, but his mom was still working on base as a teacher at the junior high, and they seemed to get by okay.

I managed to get away from my mom and Jim's place in Canillejas every so often by taking the train down to Marbella and stay a while at my dad and Juana's place. The construction was still going on, but they had completed the addition so there was enough room for me to stay for a while. I helped out some with the manual labor involved with the construction of the pool and the courtyard and I enjoyed the work a lot. My dad and I both working side by side with the Spanish *obreros* was a challenge sometimes, but I felt that I was contributing somewhat towards my room and board.

I did find time occasionally to go to the beach nearby and enjoy everything else that beautiful Marbella had to offer.

Once the pool was done, I could cool off without having to hike down to the beach, but of course the view was not nearly as nice as it was on the beach with the countless girls in bikinis, along with the wonderful view of the coast of Africa right across the sea.

When the place was finally completed, my dad christened the house with the name "Villa La Juana," and it became a splendid home, and a far cry from the small typical Spanish farm house that it originally had been. In fact, it became a villa of great beauty and grace and eventually worth a considerable number of pesetas. Only if he had kept it for another couple of decades instead of selling it when he and Juana split up just a few years later, it might be worth millions, considering what Marbella has become today.

They kept a small garden on the property and grew a few vegetables such as tomatoes, lettuce, and squash and that kept them busy weeding it and watering. But when they were originally clearing some land for the garden by pulling out by hand, the numerous long pale green plants that grew everywhere that they considered to be weeds, their neighbor approached them to have a word.

She was an older Spanish lady who, like the original owners of the place, was a farmer's wife. She walked up to my dad and after watching him for a couple of minutes, asked him, in Spanish of course, "Excuse me sir, don't you like asparagus?"

My dad replied, "*Caramba!* Of course, I love asparagus. Why do you ask, ma'am?"

She gave him a funny look and said, "Well, I can see that you're pulling up all those asparagus before they are ripe and it looks like you are getting ready to discard them. Why is that, may I ask?"

He laughed and replied, "Oh, my! I didn't realize that these plants were asparagus! I thought they were merely weeds. Thanks so much for letting me know."

She gave him another funny look and just said, "You're very welcome, sir." And she slowly walked away.

After that, and after letting the crop ripen, they had fresh asparagus regularly as part of their menu for a long time. Sometimes lessons are learned the hard way indeed.

Not too long after finishing the construction, my dad and Juana took the short trip to Gibraltar from Marbella to get married. But to get there, even though it was less than 80 kilometers away, they were required to go from Algeciras to Tangiers, and then from there to Gibraltar, and then the same thing again for the return trip. This was due to *"La Linea"* still being closed between Spain and Gibraltar. It ended up being a two-day trip, and it got my dad thinking about Morocco again, and the next time I visited, he asked me if I'd like to accompany them on a trip to Morocco. Of course, I said that I'd love to, and so we started making plans.

After studying the map and doing some research locally on the ferry schedules, we realized that we could take a ferry from Malaga to Melilla, which is the Spanish enclave just two hundred kilometers or so directly across the Mediterranean Sea from Malaga, and about an equal number of kilometers down the Mediterranean coast from Tangiers. It was about a five-hour sea voyage, but our plan was to land in Melilla and then drive to Tangiers and come back to Spain through Algeciras and then back to Marbella.

On my previous trip to Morocco with my dad, we had gone with my brother and my friend Andy, and we all had a very wonderful and educational experience, but this time it was to be just my dad, his new wife, and me. I remembered from our earlier trip he had told us that he would like to try having sex while high on pot, so perhaps this could be his opportunity to do so.

The ferry ride was much longer than the short trip from Algeciras to either Tangiers or Ceuta, of course, and it seemed to take forever to make the crossing. The ship had a nice restaurant aboard where we had a leisurely lunch, and once again the ship was accompanied by a school of dolphins riding the bow. The views were magnificent of both southern Europe and northern Africa as we headed south across the blue Mediterranean Sea.

Upon landing in the port of Melilla, and once we drove off the ferry and headed into the town, again we were struck by the vast differences between Africa and anywhere else that we knew, especially Juana, since she had never been there before. And since it was getting late, and we were quite tired from our long sea voyage, we decided to find a hotel for the night and head into Morocco the next morning.

It was decided that I would be the one to acquire the *kif* that we would consume during our trip since my dad thought it would be easier for a younger person like me to score than an older man like him, and he was probably right. Nevertheless, since we were still technically in Spain, this would have to wait until we hit Morocco the next day. After finding two hotel rooms near the port area, we went out and had a nice seafood dinner, and then went to bed early.

The next morning, after going through the border checkpoint on the outskirts of Melilla, we headed directly south to the town of *Taourirt*, which is famous for its magnificent *Kasbah*, and this is where we decided to make our first stop for the night in Morocco. After finding one of the few nice hotels in the town close to the *Kasbah*, with the name of *Le Palace Berbére*, we had a leisurely lunch and, while my dad and Juana took a nap, I went out to investigate getting some *kif* for us.

As I expected, this was not at all difficult to do so. As soon as I started walking around the area with the little shops and cafes, I was approached by a young boy of around twelve or so who asked me if he could help me find something. I told him what I was looking for and we went to a small shop not far away that sold carpets and other typical Moroccan items, and after chatting with the owner, he sold me about five-dollars-worth of *kif*, and he wrapped it in a small piece of newspaper for me. My next stop was a shop that sold *sebsis* and I bought two and a few *skuffs* to go with them, and then back to the hotel.

When I got back to the hotel, I indulged in a little to test the quality, and it turned out to be fine and quite suitable for the two older folks in the other room. So after dinner that night, I gave my dad one of the *sebsis* and some *kif* and told him to let me know in the morning how it went with him.

The next morning, he reported that it went fine, but he still preferred a glass or two of cognac. He did say that the sex was far different that any he had ever had before, and that it seemed to be a little more intense and vivid but that it wasn't really all that special or mind-blowing. But he did seem to have his curiosity about it satisfied. And it appeared that Juana didn't seem to like smoking *kif* very much at all. She preferred her booze, which she drank plenty of almost every day and night.

From Taourirt we headed to Fez and then on to Meknes. When we reached Rabat, we headed north to Tangiers and landed there on the fifth night of our trip. We stayed in Tangiers two nights before taking the ferry across the Straits to Algeciras.

While in Tangiers, I bought a very small amount of hash to bring back with me, even after assuring and promising my dad that I would not be so stupid as to try anything so foolish. But I did so anyway. I still had a little of the *kif* that I had bought in Taourirt and I wasn't about to throw it away, and I figured that if I was going to bring the *kif* back, then a little hash wouldn't be any worse. I also felt that crossing the border with these two older people would make it a breeze going through customs in Algeciras, and it was, fortunately.

Also in Tangiers, I had a rather unusual experience of a different kind. Since the old folks were in bed by nine every night, I went out about the town to see what I could see after dark. The last night we were in Tangiers, I went to a bar/nightclub called *La Luna Club* in the newer quarter of town not far from the port area. While drinking a beer, I was approached by a young lady at the bar perhaps five years or so older than I was, with long dark hair and a very nice friendly smile.

We struck up a conversation in Spanish, and she told me her name was Fatima and she really liked foreigners. When I told her I was an American, she seemed to get even more excited and interested. I bought her a couple of drinks and we had a long conversation about her life and where she was from, and before I knew it, one thing led to another, and we had left the bar and we were walking towards her apartment. I couldn't believe my apparent good luck until we reached the entrance to her apartment building. That is when she brought up the question of her fee.

"Your fee?" I asked her.

"Yes, my love, if we are to go upstairs to my bed, then it is required that I receive payment of two hundred dirhams."

I looked at her with bewilderment and asked, "You mean you are a working girl then?"

"Oh, yes, my love, of course I am. Did you not know this?"

Not wanting to seem ignorant or naïve, I replied, "Well, of course I knew that, but I just wasn't certain about the fee. So, two hundred dirhams, you say, huh?"

I did a quick calculation in my mind and realized that two hundred dirhams was about twenty dollars!

She smiled sweetly at me and said, "Yes, for only two hundred dirhams, I will take you to paradise, young sir, to a place you have never been before! A place of wonderful delights and pleasures!"

I scratched my head for a moment and told her, "I'm sorry, Fatima, I don't have that much money with me. I spent a lot on the drinks tonight."

"Well, young sir, I can't possibly give you a discount. That is not my way, I am sorry."

"Yes, well, I am sorry as well, Fatima," I said with a frown.

She nodded and said, "Yes, I am sorry as well, young sir. But thank you for your kindness and for walking back with me to my home. Perhaps we can meet tomorrow night at *La Luna* and you can bring more dirhams with you then."

"Yes, perhaps," I said.

"Well, goodnight then, young sir. Perhaps I shall see you another time."

"Very, well, Fatima," I said with a shrug, "Goodnight to you as well."

I started walking away after I watched her climb the stairs to her apartment, and I wondered what kind of paradise of delights and pleasures I had just missed out on. I walked down to the water near the port area, sat on a large rock, looked over the lights of the city of Tangiers, and thought a long time about my life and my future, and I tried to figure out the complex intricacies of human relationships, but to no avail. I realized that I still had a lot to learn about the ways of the world. But I knew that I had a lot of time to do so since I also realized that I was still young and I still had most of my life in front of me to explore this most interesting but complicated of topics.

We all made it back to

Marbella without incident and soon after I took the train back to Madrid and went back to sleeping on the fold-out bed in Jim's office. Lucky I was a late sleeper and I could stay up late at night because some nights, there would be a group of friends over, and sometimes the parties would go on until the wee hours of the morning.

My mom's friend Maruja was usually the center of these get-togethers, with her singing and playing songs on the guitar and entertaining the group of assembled people. Being a fledgling guitar player myself, I carefully studied her technique and her presentation. Of  course, her style differed greatly from what I was into, since she mostly played Spanish folk songs and popular songs she knew. Still, it was a great lesson for me just watching her perform with such warmth, charisma, talent, and professionalism.

Another interesting visitor to the *piso* in Canillejas was a neighbor who lived in the *piso* directly downstairs from my mom and Jim's place. His name was John Malik, and he was a teacher at the high school on base. Even though I never had him for any of my own classes, I remembered him very well from my high school days just a couple of years before. It was quite interesting for me to sit around and have a few drinks with Mr. Malik (as I remembered him) and talk about everything under the sun, including a lot of insights into my old school.

He did like to drink quite a lot as well, and he and Jim quickly became great drinking buddies. He'd come up for dinner a couple of nights per week and usually stay until he and Jim were quite lubricated. He'd stumble back to his home, but luckily he only had to ride the elevator one story down to get to his place. At times, I felt a little pity for the students  that he would be teaching the next day at the high school, knowing he would be suffering from an enormous hangover after consuming so much Scotch and gin with Jim the night before.

It was only a few months after I got back from the States that my friend J.P. returned from a grand adventure he had experienced after graduating from high school along with me the previous summer. Right after graduating, he just took off for quite a while and headed south from Madrid, and while visiting Gibraltar, he met two British guys there who owned a large sailboat and were involved in bringing hash from Tangiers into Gibraltar. He wasn't involved in the actual smuggling operation, but his job was to "house-sit" the boat while it was in the harbor in Gibraltar, while the two Brits took the goods into Spain and distributed them in Madrid, Barcelona, Malaga, and other large cities where they had connections.

He really liked to hang out on their yacht and got to learn a little about seamanship just by living aboard the boat for a while. They paid him for his care-taking services as well as the basic maintenance that he performed on the boat. Eventually the Brits decided to not push their luck anymore and got out of the smuggling business before they ended up regretting it.

J.P. ended up going to Morocco for quite a while, and after some time in Tangiers and other places in northern Morocco, he made his way to Marrakech and then all the way south to Agadir. Agadir is located on the Atlantic Ocean near the foot of the Atlas Mountains, about five hundred kilometers south of Casablanca.

Speaking several languages, he was able to get along with just about anyone just about anywhere, and for a while he worked for a Moroccan fellow he had gotten to know fairly well. J.P. helped out with the cafe that the guy owned, by serving tea and helping with the cooking. His language abilities enabled him to converse with almost any of the various tourists who came through the cafe, whether they were French, Spanish, German, American, British, or wherever else. The cafe owner payed him in food and *kif*, and he slept in the back of the cafe.

After a while, he heard from some travelers about a large drum festival that was going to be held soon in the country of Senegal, in West Africa. Since he considered himself a drummer of sorts, he decided that he would go down there and partake in this International Festival of Drums. But after the town of Goulimime, just south of Agadir, there weren't buses or trains or any other form of public transportation that headed south. The only mode of transportation was getting rides on top of open trucks that were hauling produce and other goods down to the Spanish enclave of Sidi Ifni, in far southern Morocco just across from the Canary Islands, and not far from Spanish Sahara, which is now called Western Sahara.

There were other Spanish troops stationed further down the coast in Spanish Sahara, so he kept getting rides on these trucks delivering goods. He would pay the drivers a few dirhams, and they would allow him and a few other intrepid travelers to ride on top of the trucks while holding onto the loads of oranges, figs, grapes, and other produce that they were hauling. As a bonus, he could help himself to all the produce he wanted.

Since there were no roads at all along this coastline, the trucks would drive right on the beach at low tide and always travel in a convoy of at least two trucks, just in case one got stuck in the sand, in which case, the other could pull them out. At night, J.P. would camp out on the beach under the stars with the drivers and build bonfires of driftwood and discuss the world and all its complicated affairs.

After several days of this, the trucks finally made it to the border between Spanish Sahara and the country of Mauritania. There was a border station and inspection stop and a small guardhouse on both sides of the border. But upon attempting to enter the Mauritanian side, they told him that he could not enter the country of Mauritania because he did not have the required amount of money on him to enter the country, which was the equivalent of around two hundred dollars.

But he was determined to get across because the next country south of Mauritania was Senegal and that is where the festival was to be held. So he camped out on the Spanish Sahara side of the border-crossing for several days, trying to determine if one of the several border guards working their various shifts could be bribed and it could allow him to get into Mauritania. Every time a shift change occurred at the guardhouse, he would approach the new guard and offer him a few bills to allow him in, but every one of them refused. So it forced him to give up on his dream of attending the drum festival in Senegal, and back north he had to go.

This time he got a ride heading north on an empty truck, and made it back to Sidi Ifni and, looking at the map, he decided that the Canary Islands would be a great place to visit, being a part of Spain and only about one hundred kilometers west of the African mainland. He found out that there was a ferry that left every other day for a reasonable fare, so he just went for it.

He arrived at Las Palmas de Gran Canaria with very little money left of the original two hundred dollars that he had left Madrid with about six months earlier, so he was uncertain about what he was going to do to survive.

But being a very resourceful person, he found a group of hippies hanging around the main port area where the rich tourists congregated and these people had found a way of making some money to survive. They sold handcrafted items that they made themselves to the throngs of foreign visitors getting on and off the various ships in the port area and to many others who were just wandering around sightseeing, trying to find something to spend their money on.

He met a Swiss hippy there who was into making items out of hand-tooled leather, as in leather belts, purses, handbags, wallets, and vests. These items were created with a lot of time and work, but they could be sold for a handsome profit. He was able to acquire some leather-working tools, bought some leather, and he was in business. Of course, he could not afford the expensive housing that was available to the rich tourists on the island, so he found a small cove on a beach quite a distance outside of town where there was a small cave, and this is where he lived for two months. He was able to acquire some snorkeling gear and a spear gun and was able to spear his own dinner almost every night, usually a nice fish or two or an occasional octopus. He worked the leather goods and went into town every other day to sell what he made and to purchase a few supplies and then headed back to his secret cove.

One day while in town selling his wares, he met an American girl from upstate New York by the name of Sarah, and they really hit it off. She had been backpacking around Europe between high school and college and someone suggested she go to the Canaries and so she did. She ended up living with J.P. on the beach and then after a month or so, they went to Madrid together and stayed for a while at his *piso* near Las Ventas. His mom had been away for a while in the States visiting her sister so it worked out quite well for them there. But Sarah had made earlier plans to meet some of her American friends in Greece, so she went ahead without him to Athens, but only after making plans to meet up with him in Athens at the beginning of the summer.

It was only the beginning of spring so in the three months or so he had to kill before hooking up again with Sarah; he decided to go to Amsterdam. He had heard about the scene going on in that city from several different people during his travels and he was determined to go there and see it for himself. So he got hold of his mom in the States and she sent him a couple of hundred dollars and off he went.

He had some amazing adventures trying to survive in Amsterdam along with the recent influx of thousands of hippies into the city that had made housing almost impossible to find and the competition for jobs made finding one almost impossible as well. After a couple of months had passed, and after he was done struggling to survive in Holland, he made it back to Madrid and that is when I got together with him again, the first time since we had been in school together, almost two years earlier.

I'm mentioning the adventures that J.P. had because when I finally met up with him again in Madrid and he began to tell me a little about them, I got quite excited and I too wanted to experience such fantastic adventures, and it motivated me to go out and explore some more of the world around me. I needed something to do and somewhere to go besides hanging around Spain with my folks. So I decided to go to Amsterdam and see what the place was all about.

J. P. and I left Madrid together at the beginning of the summer of 1972. Our plan was to go to Barcelona together, and from there, he had plans to take a boat to Athens to meet up with Sarah again, and I had plans to head up to Amsterdam. My mom dropped us off on the highway heading north out of Madrid and our plan was to hitchhike all the way to Barcelona together and then each go our own way from there. We had our backpacks, and I had convinced my mom to give me two hundred dollars for my trip, so I was ready to embark on my grand adventure.

Hitchhiking in Spain during that time was nearly impossible, especially for a couple of long-haired fellows like us. The first day, after standing for long hours in the sun, we only got one ride, but it got us as far as the town of Teruel, which is the capitol of the providence of Aragon, about three hundred kilometers from Madrid. This city is quite mountainous and has a quite low population for being a provincial capital. Its remote location and low population have led to the town being relatively isolated within Spain.

I'm certain that not only were we the only foreigners or tourists in the city that night, but most likely the only ones in quite a long time. We spent the night there in a small *pensión* and went out to eat that night at a local restaurant, and we almost felt like we were Martians that had just landed in this town, by the number of strange looks we received during our brief stay.

But knowing the language always helps in these situations, and once we started chatting with some of the locals, they realized that perhaps we were not from another planet after all and they began to not only treat us with some respect, but soon it seemed that half the town had gathered around the outdoor cafe where we were having a beer and were all there listening to what we had to say. Two long-haired hippy types traveling through their town was such a rare occurrence that they wanted to make sure that they all got a good look at us and could hear what we were talking about with the locals. After a while, their curiosity was satisfied, and they wandered off and left us alone to discuss our plans for the next day.

Because of our difficulty in trying to get rides the day before, we decided that we should spring for taking the train the rest of the way to Barcelona. But due to the relative isolation of Teruel, we found out that there were no direct trains to Barcelona. Instead, we would have to take a train to Castellón de la Plana, a town north of Valencia on the Mediterranean Sea, and from there we could catch the train all the way into Barcelona.

So the next day was a long one, but we did finally make it to Barcelona where once again we found a cheap *pensión* for the night. The next day I went down to the port and saw J. P. get on the ship that he had arranged passage on that was to take him to Athens. We said our goodbyes and good lucks and promised to keep in touch, and that we would see each other again one day soon, which we actually did before too long.

Then I got on the train headed for Amsterdam, ready for the next chapter of my life and a brand-new adventure.

Chapter 19. Amsterdam

"As I play the game of life, I try to make it better each and every day. And when I struggle in the night, the magic of the music seems to light the way."
— JOHN LENNON

After riding the train all the way from Barcelona to Paris, my original plan was to hitch hike the rest of the way to Amsterdam to conserve some of my ever-dwindling cash supply. But when I got off the train in Paris and walked around for a while, trying to get my bearings, I realized that it would be a major undertaking just for me to find a way to get out to the edge of town and on the highway heading north to Holland. I returned to the *Gare du Nord* train station in the center of the city, after wandering around for a while. There I checked the price of a ticket all the way to Amsterdam and it wasn't that unreasonable, so I decided I'd just go for it.

While waiting the few hours for the train to Holland, I walked around this "City of Lights," and I was not all that impressed, frankly. I had been to Paris as a youngster with my parents, and I had already seen the Eiffel Tower, the Notre-Dame Cathedral, and some of the other sights. Paris gave me the overall impression of being loud and crowded, and the people were rude and not at all friendly. While buying a beer and a sandwich for dinner at a little cafe near the station, I tried to converse with the waiter in French, but he acted like he could not understand what I was saying, even though I spoke fairly good French, even with the *Pied Noir* accent I had learned as a student in Alicante.

I suppose since I didn't speak French the way he did or the way he liked to hear it, he simply pretended not to hear me. I managed to get my order cross somehow, and when he brought the final bill which was about three times what I estimated that it should be, I declined to tip him, which I'm sure added to his ill humor and belligerence towards future American customers.

The train to Amsterdam left right after dark and arrived very early the next morning, so I didn't get a chance to see much of the countryside along the way besides the lights of the towns and the various train stations where we stopped. Fortunately, it was a sleeper car, so I was able to catch a few hours of sleep during the trip. It's about five hundred kilometers from Paris to Amsterdam and we stopped at the Belgian border where a custom inspector boarded the train and stamped everyone's passports, and then the same thing happened when we reached the Holland border, so my sleep was interrupted at least twice during the trip just to have my passport stamped.

I disembarked from the train at the *Amsterdam Centraal Station*; the weather was sunny and warm and inviting, and when I exited the station and looked around, I was pleasantly surprised. When I started to walk, I realized that I was in a much different place than I had ever been before. Everywhere were waterways or "canals" as the Dutch called them, and they seemed to be almost as plentiful as the streets. Bridges spanned all these canals, and there were plenty of them, usually built with a slight arch to enable boats to go underneath them.

I had done a little research, and I knew that the country of Holland (also known as the Netherlands) is quite low indeed. In fact, in the French language the country is usually called *"Les Pays-Bas,"* which translates to "the low countries." About a quarter of the nation is below sea level and thanks to the diligent work of the very capable Dutch engineers; they managed to keep the sea at bay through an elaborate system of dikes and pumps.

The more I walked around, the more impressed I became. There seemed to be a feeling in the air of openness, tolerance, and lifestyle freedom. I had also never seen so many bicycles before in my life. Since Holland is almost perfectly flat, it's a perfect place to get around on two wheels. This mode of transportation made the streets much less crowded with much less vehicular traffic than a similar-sized city elsewhere would have had. Some streets allowed pedestrians and bicycles only, and this made them even more pleasant, safe, and inviting to stroll. There was also an electric streetcar system that got people around efficiently and rapidly and further helped to reduce congestion, noise, and pollution.

The canals themselves served as a means of transportation as well. Boats and barges of all kinds travelled up and down the various canals, delivering goods and services to all parts of the city. Some of the boats were obviously the live-aboard kind which people had fixed up to become very comfortable and efficient floating homes. Holland was clearly one of the most beautifully organized countries I had ever seen.

While walking around the city, I noticed more and more people who looked a lot like me. Almost everywhere, I saw long-haired people of every description wandering about with contented looks on their faces and wide smiles. It had been five years earlier, in another city far away on the west coast of the North American continent, where a similar kind of environment of acceptance had occurred.

In San Francisco, California, in 1967, there was a time that is now referred to as "The Summer of Love," when thousands and thousands of young people descended on the city and created a counter-culture scene that, although it was brief, left a lasting impression on the local culture and, indeed, the very history of the world. Although I was not in San Francisco that summer, my understanding is that for that one brief season, things were just about perfect, because this all happened before the scene became commercialized, televised, and then overblown with the homeless, bums, drug addicts, and violence.

The summer of 1972 in Amsterdam could have been "The Summer of Love" for Europe and the rest of the world. What happened in

Amsterdam was that due to the Dutch government's relaxed drug laws (especially regarding cannabis) and their tolerance for all kinds of people, thousands of hippies from all over the world found their way to Amsterdam. This created a scene, and eventually word got out and even more people showed up. The few months I was there, I met young people from the following countries: Holland, Germany, France, Spain, Great Britain, Italy, Greece, Sweden, Norway, Denmark, Belgium, Switzerland, the United States, Canada, and many more, including one guy by the name of Samson who was from Aruba, in the Dutch West Indies.

Everyone was there for the same reason, it seemed and that was to experience this scene, and this place and time, and to feel that we were all participating in trying to change the world into a better place. The ideals of the American hippies, such as peace, love, and brotherhood were shared with their European cousins in Amsterdam. Since these hippies came from so many different countries and cultures, it created a mix that differed greatly from the Haight-Ashbury version.

Everyone I met was a new experience and presented the challenge not only to try to communicate but also to try to find common ground. With a dozen languages being spoken and so many backgrounds of all the different kinds of people there, it created quite a stew of cultures, unlike anything any of us had ever seen before. And almost always we found that the things we had in common were our love of cannabis, modern music, and the hippy ideals that we were trying to implement and live by.

One of the first places I hung around regularly was one of the main  squares in the center of Amsterdam called Dam Square. This was a popular gathering place where people would sit on the steps by the statue in the middle of the square and chat, socializing and discussing everything from the evils of the Vietnam War, to where a good place in town to crash would be. It was not far from the American Express office that was just down the street. Many Americans and Canadians hung out at the American Express office a lot because it was one of the few places in the city where money could be sent to them from home, similar to the operation of a Western Union office in the States. Usually there was a line of long-haired young people waiting to get their money transfer from their parents, and it became a sort of meeting place in itself.

Another place I discovered very quickly was a park in the city's center by the name of Vondel Park, also known by many people as "Wonder Park." This is where many of the young people camped out when they could not afford anywhere else to crash. The Dutch authorities allowed this because the alternative would have been to try to lock up these thousands of people every night, so they tolerated, but did not encourage, these people camping out in one of the main parks of the city. Wonder Park became a gathering place for everything else as well. This was one of the primary places where drugs could be bought, sold, and consumed, and the smell of cannabis floating around and music playing from somewhere, along with a Frisbee or two flying around as well.

I found myself laying my sleeping bag down on the ground in the park many times that summer when I was unable or unwilling to spend the three guilders (about one dollar) for a youth hostel for the night. The Dutch government had the wisdom and the means to set up a series of these hostels all over the city for the particular purpose of trying to accommodate this influx of young tourists on stringent budgets. The rate was usually set at three guilders, and for that it was possible to get a bunk bed in a large dormitory-style room.

There were separate dorms for males and females and the cost also allowed the use of one of the showers too. The hostels also usually had a cafe on the ground floor where it was possible to get a relatively cheap breakfast or lunch. The one I stayed at most often was not far from the park and I stayed there whenever I felt I could afford it or when I really needed to get cleaned up and take a shower. Also, the fresh coffee and *muesli* for breakfast was always a treat.

There was a book that was very popular at the time called, "Europe on Five Dollars per Day," and it showed the would-be budget traveler in detail where and how to live on that amount, while traveling around and seeing the sights of Europe. It described the various youth hostels and cheap places to eat, along with other travel tips, such as using the "Euro-Rail" pass for transportation. So it was possible to live on that amount everyday by staying in youth hostels and eating at very low budget places, or by buying food from stores and making one's own meals.

My problem was that at this point at the beginning of the summer, I only had a little less one hundred and fifty dollars left to last me the rest of the summer, and if I was to use the "Europe on Five Dollars per Day" method, I would be broke after about one month. So I was forced to go on an even tighter budget than that book recommended. If I was to last the rest of the summer, I would be forced to spend only fifty dollars per month, or roughly a dollar and a half per day. And if I spent one dollar on a bed, I wasn't going to be able to eat much that day, not to mention my smoking materials (both tobacco and hash) and an occasional beer or two.

As far as my being able to get a job of some sort in Amsterdam, it was nearly impossible to do so due to the large numbers of hippies in the same boat as I was. The local Dutch people all had jobs of course, and they would continue to have them long after the hippies were gone, but there was just not any work at all for tourists. So getting work to add to my finances was not an option, so I'd be forced to try to live on what I had, because there were two things that I did not want to have to do.

One was to go back to Spain after a few weeks with my tail between my legs knowing that I just could not make it on my own. The other was to call my parents and end up standing in line at the American Express office with the rest of the people waiting for a handout from the folks.

I clearly wasn't the only person in this situation. I met lots of folks who had found other methods of surviving on very limited funds. Some resorted to selling drugs as a way of earning some money, but there was just not that much money to be made with all the competition involved. Besides, it was possible to just walk into a cafe and purchase whatever kind and amount of cannabis you wanted legally. And other drugs were available, but again there was not much money to be made; the best one could hope for, really, was to sell just enough to provide some free for oneself.

And although I saw it happening around me a little, I did not want to resort to a life of crime to survive. I was smart enough to realize that if I was caught committing a crime, I might be able to survive, but from inside a prison cell, and since I had already been there and done that in Florida, (though I didn't buy the T-shirt), I knew that a life of crime was not a life for me at all. I realized that there were many people around who were breaking into and stealing from cars, pick pocketing, and committing all kinds of crimes, but I wanted no part of it.

I was bound and determined to survive without having to take the risk of committing crimes. Of course, I had to eat, so the only wiggle room I had was with my accommodations. I could sleep in Wonder Park, but it was miserable whenever it rained. Some people had small pup-tents so they could sleep outdoors in the rain, but I didn't have this luxury. Besides, the park could be disconcerting with hundreds of people sleeping all around and always having to be on guard at all times.

There were some people who had taken over certain areas of the park and were living there on a semi-permanent basis with even some of the trappings of home. They would do their laundry in the waters of the small lake in the park, and hang it on lines between the  trees, and just generally made themselves right at home. Occasionally, the local authorities would come by and make everyone leave, and they would do so, but only to return a day or two later.

After a couple of weeks of splitting my nights between sleeping under a tree at the park and splurging for a hostel, I met two guys who seemed willing to provide a solution for my housing problem. For some reason, I kind of shied away from a lot of the Americans that I met, partly because of my experiences in the States, but also because I felt more comfortable with Europeans.

I met these two Spanish guys one day while hanging out in the park, and we got to talking. They were Spanish hippies from Barcelona and were also on a tight budget. They told me that they stayed at abandoned houses around town. There were many of them all over the city and they just walked in and made themselves at home. Once in a while, the police would come around and kick them out, but they would just find another one to move into. There was no running water or electricity, but at least these houses were dry and most importantly they were free, as well as offering a lot more privacy than the park ever could.

These two Spaniards were named Antonio and Ramón, but since they were trying to learn to speak English, they insisted on being called Tony and Ray, and once they discovered that I was an American, they wanted me around to help them learn English. They both had very long hair and rather fancy clothes with very nice leather boots, colorful scarves and leather vests. After talking to them for a while, they invited me to stay at their place.

When I got there, I realized that it wasn't strictly their place because there were at least a dozen other people there as well, but Tony and Ray did have their own room of the large two-story abandoned house. There were several old mattresses lying on the floors but not much other furniture in the entire house. I found a corner of their room to lay my sleeping bag down along with the rest of my stuff, and I made myself at home.

I soon realized how these guys were able to survive on so very little money. Early every morning before daylight, they would wake up and prowl the streets around their neighborhood and steal dairy products from the doorsteps of peoples' houses. The local dairies would deliver various products very early in the morning, and these guys would just help themselves to whatever they wanted, including milk, yogurt, and cream. They would chip in a few coins and buy a loaf of bread and that is what they would eat on all day long.

I was reluctant to participate in this type of petty crime, but I did indulge occasionally in the spoils of their efforts, but in turn I'd be required to provide something as well, usually some *muesli*, fruit or cheese that I would buy at the local store. And it was a kind of communal effort to feed us all with what we could gather, steal or purchase.

I suspected from the first time I met them that Tony and Ray were gay, and my suspicions were verified one afternoon when they started have sex together in the room the three of us shared. I politely left at that time to give them some privacy, and I went to the park to get out of their hair for a while. After that, I would do the same whenever they started to indulge in this type of activity; even if it was late at night, I'd always leave and just let them do their thing.

Before too long I realized another thing about these two guys, and what they did with the little money that they did have. They would purchase black opium and inject it into their veins. I watched them do this a couple of times and I was both amazed and repulsed at the same time. They'd cook the black shit up in a spoon with water, filter it through a cigarette filter, put it into a syringe, and inject each other with it.

As soon as the needle was pulled out, the guy who had gotten the shot would fall back and collapse onto the mattress and just pass out. Then, after several minutes, he'd get up and cook a batch for his partner and then he would do the same thing for him. Sometimes they would do this over and over again until they finally ran out of the shit. I had seen people shoot heroin but never had I seen anyone use opium in this way before.

All this eventually became a little too much for me and so after a couple of weeks, I moved out and found another abandoned house to move into. This new one was occupied mostly by Brits and Danes and all they did was sit around and smoke hash all day which was more to my liking. And once again, meals were usually made up with whatever the group had communally and could get together, mostly bread and cheap cheese and lunch meat, and the occasional stolen dairy products.

Once I found out about this way to sleep for free, I spent most of my days wandering the streets of the city or hanging out at Vondel Park, where there was always something going on. Groups of freaks would gather and just sit around, smoking hash, talking in several languages and just feeling very mellow together. Occasionally there would be a guitar or two, and the musicians would be making beautiful music together, and people would all start singing along if they knew the song. Other times somebody would have a radio or another source of music, and the sound of music would permeate the park for everyone's enjoyment.

The instrumental song by Jethro Tull titled, "Bourée," which I have mentioned before, was very popular around Amsterdam that summer, and I'd often listen to it as colorfully dressed girls with flowers in their hair and long flowing skirts would dance around, as if they were floating on the air to the magical melody coming from Ian Anderson's flute. There was a feeling in the air of oneness and community that radiated elements of times long gone and from an older, simpler and more real way of life, before modern society, greed, and money corrupted the communal nature of mankind. Love was definitely filling the air, and it could be felt by anyone who was there. It was a magical and enchanting time indeed.

While hanging around Vondel Park, I soon discovered a very popular smoking device that people were using a lot. It was called a *chillum,* and it turned out it was one of the oldest utensils used by mankind for smoking, dating back to prehistory. It consists of a long cone-shaped tube made of various materials that is tapered at one end and wider at the other end where the substance to be smoked is inserted. A small pebble is usually inserted at the wider end to keep the ash from coming

through and entering the smoker's mouth. It's a very simple apparatus, but a very functional one as well.

The most beneficial thing about smoking with a *chillum* was that it can hold an enormous amount of substance, or a very little, depending on the size of the chamber and the size of the pebble inserted into the wider end. A smaller pebble would fall lower into the chamber and allow more material to be filled into the opening and a larger pebble would allow less room and therefore less material.

And this wasn't the only thing that made this smoking device so remarkable and so popular. The way that one smoked with it prevented the passing of germs from one smoker to another. When a regular pipe or joint is passed around, everyone puts their lips on it to take a toke, and then passes it on to the next person, and then that person in turn puts their lips onto it, passing germs all the way down the line. If someone is sick with a cold or some other communicable sickness, then it can be passed around to everyone.

But smoking with a *chillum* is different, because the proper way to smoke a chillum is to put the narrow bottom end into your hands or between your fingers, make a chamber, and draw the smoke into your lungs that way. This way your lips never actually touch the device itself at all, but instead your lips touch your own hands only, and never the pipe itself.

This method was also used for smoking joints as well. A very popular way of smoking hash, if it was to be passed around to many people, was to roll a very large joint, using many rolling papers. You could roll a sixleafer or an eight-leafer or even a twelve-leafer, depending on the number of people that might be smoking it. The leaves of the rolling papers would be stuck together to form a longer and wider rolling surface and usually the roller would insert a small tube of cardboard (perhaps from a matchbook or a similar item) at the end, to form a type of filter and these kinds of joints would usually be tapered and cone-shaped like a *chillum*. These joints would be rolled with tobacco (in Holland, the most popular being *Drum*-brand rolling tobacco) and the hash would be broken up and sprinkled over the tobacco and it could be made as strong or as weak as desired. These large joints were perfect for passing around when there were larger groups of people sharing the same spliff, and they were smoked *chillum*-style for the same sanitary advantages of an actual *chillum*.

I tried to keep myself on my budget, but it was hard to do. Every so often, I felt compelled to have a shower and to get myself cleaned up. And the only way to do this was to stay in a hostel for a night and use their facilities. The hostels usually had a washing machine for their guests to use as well, so I could wash my few clothes occasionally, in my ongoing effort to keep myself from stinking quite so much. And in the mornings, it was always nice to wake up refreshed and have a nice hot cup of coffee and a bowl of *muesli* with yogurt for breakfast.

Also in most of the youth hostels, there was a common room for the guests to use and it was always interesting to hang around in these rooms and chat with some of the other folks there, sharing information, and perhaps a toke or two of hash. There was always great music playing in these common rooms and I would have liked to stay there all day except they were for ongoing guests only.

Along the many canals in Amsterdam, there were private barges that were turned into "sleeping boats" where for a small fee (usually around the same as a hostel) you could sleep on board one of these floating homes. Although I saw them on a regular basis, I never tried one out, because they always seemed to be very crowded and fully occupied, and also because they appeared to have much less room than the hostels, with everybody crammed below

decks in the cargo area of the boat and without a cafe for breakfast or lunch. And I doubted that they had laundry facilities or a decent shower system either for that matter.

Another thing that Amsterdam was very famous for was their "Red Light" district. Almost every large city in the world (and many smaller ones) had these certain areas of the city where prostitution could be found, but what made the one in Amsterdam so unusual is the fact that it was all legal. And not only legal, but the government had a well-regulated system in place to assure that the ladies were clean and disease-free and not subject to exploitation by pimps, so the criminal element of the pay-for-sex business had been removed.

In fact, in Amsterdam, instead of hanging around street corners, the prostitutes had their own shop windows to show what they were selling. There was a several-block area nor far from the center of town, along a quiet canal where the ladies of the night sat behind windows and showed you their wares. It was the ultimate in window shopping to just walk down the street and see countless ladies of all sizes, races, and ages selling themselves. The windows had curtains over them, and when a curtain was closed, then she was obviously with a client and unavailable, but when it was open, she would do whatever she could to entice potential customers to choose her over the competition.

The ladies sat around in the skimpiest and sexiest of outfits and made all kinds of gestures to lure customers their way, and it became a very good-natured competition between them, and a visual delight for the shoppers, including window-shoppers like myself.

I had seen a lot of this type of thing in Madrid but never quite so open and obvious as it was in Amsterdam, and this was what made the displays so special and unique. It was good to see that it wasn't illegal and hidden as it was in most other places, and it was refreshing to see it as just another type of business, selling a service to potential customers.

Not only was prostitution legal, but live sex shows were as well. It was possible to walk into a "private club" after paying a nominal cover charge and watch a couple having sex "live" on a stage right in front of you. I was amazed the first time I went into a place like this because I had never seen anything like it before. But the thing I couldn't understand was how the couple was able to perform all day long.

I asked the fellow who was working at the door this question as I was leaving, and he told me that they changed couples throughout the day and night, and that each couple was usually scheduled a one hour shift per day to do their thing, and then the next couple would take over when they were done, to assure a constant show was going on the entire time they were open.

I asked him where they got so many people to "perform," and he told me that there were plenty of people willing to get paid to do what they enjoyed doing anyway, so why not get paid for it? This all made sense to me and I finally understood how the business worked. I'm sure that some of their employees were some of the many hippies in town who needed to make a little money and were willing to do this type of work.

Another thing I'd indulge in now and then when I felt like I could splurge on something was a concert. There were rock-and-roll shows quite often in Amsterdam that summer, and they were enormously popular, for both locals and tourists alike. There were two clubs that usually had most of the big-name touring bands playing, along with a variety of local bands on other nights.

The first was called the *Paradiso Club*, and it had bands playing almost every night of the week. There was a nominal cover charge for the local bands, of usually around two or three guilders, but when a famous band came from out of town, the entrance fee went way up and I could not afford it. I missed seeing Pink Floyd perform there one night because I wasn't willing to pay the fifteen guilder cover charge. But I'm sure it would have been worth it considering the reputation of their live shows.

The other place in the city which featured regular rock-and-roll shows was a place called the *Melk Weg*, which translates into English as the Milky Way. Both places had large stages where the bands would perform and nice dance floors as well. Of course they served alcohol, mostly good Dutch beers such as Heineken and Amstel, and cannabis was smoked almost as much as tobacco it seemed. Every night of the week, there was something going on at either or both of these clubs, but they did require a little money to enjoy and, unfortunately, I was on my very low budget, and couldn't partake in these types of activities as much as I would have liked to.

Another place to hang out in Holland was the coffee shops that seemed to be just about everywhere. These cafes usually had a counter as you walked in and would offer just about every kind of cannabis in the world for sale. Different kinds would sell for different prices, depending on the quality, the potency, and the availability of that particular variety. For example, Moroccan double-zero hashish would sell for around three or four guilders per gram, while Lebanese gold or Afghan black would usually run a little more. Moroccan *kif* and other grass were rare to find anywhere, due to the difficulty of importing larger quantities.

Although it was technically illegal to sell or even to smoke cannabis in Holland, it was "tolerated," which meant that the authorities could still bust a person for it if the need arose for some reason, or if one began to deal in very large quantities. But this was rare and usually most people just bought a little and smoked it until they ran out, then just bought some more, knowing that the next day, there would always be more to buy at a similar price.

What a lot of people did was just go into the different cafes, sit down and order a tea or a coffee and sample what they had for sale at the counter at that particular cafe. For the price of a beer or two, one could buy a gram of something and try it out and find a variety that was likeable. This to me seemed to be a very civilized way of doing things and that's one reason that I liked Holland so well, because it was so damn civilized!

But after less than two months of living in Amsterdam, I was reaching a critical point with my finances. I either had to find a job soon, or I'd be forced to return to Spain or worse yet, call the folks and ask them for help, neither which I wanted to do.

However, while talking to some local Dutch guys one day at a cafe, I was told that it was possible to find work in the city of Rotterdam, which is about sixty kilometers south of Amsterdam. There was much less of the hippy tourism in that city and therefore much less competition for work, and jobs were much easier to find. So I headed for Rotterdam, to try my luck and see what might happen there.

Chapter 20   Rotterdam

"What we see depends mainly on what we look for."
— John Lubbock

I was able to find my way to the main highway between Amsterdam and Rotterdam fairly easily and started hitchhiking, and I got a ride within a few minutes, and less than an hour later I found myself right in the heart of Rotterdam. The city had a much different vibe and feel than Amsterdam. The most noticeable thing was the lack of hippies everywhere!

But being Holland's second largest city and one of the largest ports in the world, it was quite busy, with a lot of traffic and people everywhere. It's an ancient city dating back to the year 1270, when a dam was constructed on the *Rotte* River which people settled around for safety.

The reason it is Europe's largest and busiest port is that the city sits on the delta of the Rhine, Meuse, and Scheldt rivers and gives waterway access into the heart of Western Europe. This extensive waterway system, railroads and roads have given Rotterdam the nickname "The Gateway to Europe." The center of the city sits on the north bank of the *Nieuwe Mass* River and is built mostly behind dikes, and much of the city actually sits about six meters below sea level. The harbor area extends for many kilometers into the interior and makes it the major shipping port for the Netherlands with its proximity to the North Sea.

What all this meant to me was that with all this industry, shipping, and other related activities, it increased the possibility of my finding work of some kind which I desperately needed to do since my financial situation was growing quite severe. I made some inquiries of some locals and they told me that daily work could be had at the main train station very early in the morning. Employers would arrive with their vans at the station between five and six in the morning and hire men for day-labor jobs. The number of laborers they'd hire would depend of the particular jobs they had to get done that day, so sometimes they would hire quite a few and other days, not very many at all.

Before long I found out where the main station was and found an abandoned house not too far away. The house had been in a fire sometime in the past, but the roof and walls were still standing and this is where I made my home, along with a few other homeless and unemployed men. There were several guys, including me, who stayed there off and on because it seemed like if we got work for the day, then we might stay at a hostel instead of the abandoned house. But, unlike Amsterdam to the north, Rotterdam didn't have the multitude of youth hostels to house all the hippy tourists, so even when we had the minimum of three guilders a night to spend on a bed, at times it was still difficult to find accommodations.

Most of the men hanging around the main train station every morning hoping for work were from countries nearer the equator, like Moroccans and Egyptians, or from various other Arab countries, and there were also black guys from countries even further south in Africa. The great advantage I had was that I looked rather like a Dutchman, with my blondish hair and blue eyes, so I got chosen more often than my darker-complexioned cohorts. Many a time, when the van pulled up, and the driver said he needed eight men for work that day, I was one of the eight chosen, out of twenty or more who might have been standing there.

But every time this happened, as soon as I got in the van and we headed for the job site, the foreman would start speaking to me in Dutch, and of course I replied in English saying I didn't speak Dutch. Then when he asked me where I was from, the reaction would almost always be the same: a big smile and, "Ah, a Yankee, huh? That's okay." And then he'd talk to me in English, which almost all Dutch people spoke.

I was lucky that I got chosen as often as I did because most of the other guys were older than I was and appearing to be stronger and more capable of doing a really hard day's labor. But it was not hard to blame the Dutchmen for attempting to hire and help one of their countrymen over an obvious foreigner.

The pay was not great, but it was a lot better than nothing. The set pay was five guilders per hour, or roughly $1.60, pretty much the same as the minimum wage was in the States at the time. But they didn't take taxes or other deductions out of the pay, so we ended up with about forty guilders for an eight-hour workday, or about thirteen dollars. It seemed like a lot of money because I would have been happy earning absolutely anything at that point.

I averaged about two or three days of work every week if I went to the station every morning, except for me to live on, but I still slept in the abandoned house most nights because it was difficult to find one of the few hostels in the town that had openings. But I got a bunk often enough to take a shower and get cleaned up on a semiregular basis. It was great to be working again and taking care of myself and having a little money on me.

The actual jobs varied, but they were all difficult and physically demanding work. These were the jobs that the locals didn't want to do because of their difficulty and because of how backbreaking the work actually was to perform. They almost always involved the shipping industry in one way or another. Many were just grunt work of lifting and carrying various cargos from one place to another, but some were even worse and even downright dirty. One type of job I always dreaded getting involved with was cleaning out the giant cylinders that the pistons went into inside the engines of huge ocean-going vessels.

The engineers would temporarily remove the pistons from these giant engines and our job was to go inside these huge tubes and clean the inside walls of them by removing the grit, grime, and old burnt oil that was caked on, using old rags, solvents, and elbow grease. We had to wear full coveralls, masks, and goggles to protect us from all the crap that had accumulated inside these things.

When we started first thing in the morning, our coveralls were pure white, but by lunchtime, they were solid black from the soot, grime, and old burnt engine oil. The cylinders were about four feet in diameter, so the job required bending over or being in a squatting position for hours at a time, and we would all end up with sore backs by the end of the day.

But not all the jobs were this brutal and back-breaking. Sometimes we'd work on the decks of the ships, cleaning various pieces of machinery or work with the loading crews getting items on and off the ships. And despite all the discomforts, I was just happy to have some money in my pocket, and to be able to do a solid and honest day's work.

I got to talking to some dockworkers I met, and I asked them what it took to get a job working as an able-bodied seaman on one of these ocean-going vessels. They told me about a place in downtown Rotterdam near the old original dock area that was the Seaman's Union Building. This was the place where seamen would go to get jobs aboard all kinds of ships. They kept a list of ships that were hiring and they helped sailors to get hired. There was also a gathering place there where seamen could hang around, have a bite to eat or a beer perhaps and converse with other like-minded people in the same profession.

I found the place with no problem and approached the desk where the recruiting was done and where they kept the list of the various ships that were currently hiring, where they were headed, the cargo the ship carried, and the expected length of the voyage. I was ready to go absolutely anywhere, on any ship, and I told the man behind the desk this.

He then asked to see my "seaman's book," which of course I didn't have. This book was a resume of sorts, or a log of all the ships that the seaman had  worked on in the past and what kind of work he had done aboard the various vessels. I found myself in a similar position to where my brother had found himself in Barcelona a couple of years earlier, and he even had a letter of recommendation from the owner of the shipping line, and he still didn't get hired.

The man explained that indeed I would need to have this "seaman's book" to get hired aboard any vessel at all. When I asked him how one is to get their first job on a ship in order to start building this book, the only response I got was a shrug. So the "Catch 22" about getting hired aboard a ship was also alive and well here in one of the largest ports in the world, and I realized that it was nearly impossible to get hired even as a cabin boy on any ship going anywhere.

I asked a couple of the old sailors hanging around the place about this strange rule and how is one supposed to go about getting their first job, and one old guy told me that he **had gotten** his first job on a ship as a member of the Merchant Marine many years ago. I soon realized that perhaps a life at sea was not in my cards. Well, at least I could say that I had tried.

I did get another type of job while in Rotterdam though. Early one morning while waiting in front of the train station hoping to get hired for day labor, a very large older man with a big bushy black beard approached me. He asked me if I was Dutch and I said no but that I was an American and then we began to speak in English.

He said to me in very bad English, and with a very strong German accent, "So you're a yank, yes?"

I sighed and said, "Yes, I am."

"And you are looking for work, yes?"

I thought that was pretty obvious, but I replied, "Yes, sir, I am."

He looked at me more closely and asked, "Have you ever worked with animals before?"

I shook my head and said, "No, not really, but I am a fast learner. And I worked for a carnival one time and I was with animals all the time around the fairs where we worked."

He finally got around to introducing himself and said, "My name is Hans and I work for a German circus by the name of The Circus Maximus, and we are here in Holland touring the countryside and we are in the need of good workers to help with the animals. Are you interested, young man?"

I studied him closely and replied, "It is nice to meet you Mr. Hans, my name is Ron, and yes, I might very well be interested. What does the job entail exactly?"

"You will be taking charge of some of the animals we have in our show and seeing that they are cared for, fed and clean. We will be traveling and you would be living with us and traveling with us as a member of our Circus. Is this something you think you might like?"

I shrugged and said, "Yes, maybe, but what does the job pay, may I ask?"

"The same as you get paid as a day-laborer here, five guilders per hour, but we work very long hours so it will be considerably more than just eight hours per day, up to twelve or even more, perhaps."

I thought to myself that this might be fun and maybe even be quite an adventure. Besides, anything had to be better than breaking my back doing this day labor work on the ships, so I looked Hans right in the eye and replied, "Okay, I'll do it, sir. When do I begin?"

"Right now. I need someone to start today since we are traveling to Delft today to set up our show, so you must come with me now if you are to begin."

"Okay, but I must pick up my backpack that I have left in my place."

"Yes, no problem, we can go by there for you to pick up your things, is it near?"

"Yes sir, just a couple of blocks from here."

"Very well, let us go then."

So that is how I got a job working for a German circus in Holland. How exciting! I was going to be in *Show Business!*

I hopped in the front seat of his car and we drove over to the abandoned house where I was leaving my stuff, and as soon as I grabbed my pack, we were on our way.

It didn't take long to get to Delft, less than an hour or so, and when we got there, I saw that the circus was setting up on the outskirts of the town in a large empty field. The big top was in the middle of being set up and there were quite a few vehicles parked all around the area. Hans took me to a trailer where he said I would be sleeping, and I put my backpack on top of one of several small cots that were set up in the trailer.

He asked me to follow him so we walked the entire area while he showed me around. There were people everywhere doing various jobs including setting up the Big Top, along with various other tents and buildings, including a ticket booth, food and snack bars and other structures. Then I followed him over to where they kept the animals that they used in the circus. There were various pens and cages where they were housed, and most of the animals were inside their enclosures. I saw two tigers in separate cages, both looking quite ferocious, and a large brown bear inside his cage looking quite bored. Another smaller cage had several monkeys inside chattering away at each other.

Then off in another area nearby, I saw several open pens with other kinds of animals in them. One had several horses of different colors and sizes in it, wandering around their small enclosure, and another had about a dozen strange-looking cows, all of different exotic breeds, standing around munching on hay, each with their distinct kind of horns waving around in the air. Most I had never even known existed before and to me just barely looked like cattle, or at least the kind that I had ever seen.

We kept walking as Hans went on and on about the circus and how much it was loved by everyone wherever they traveled and set up their show, and how it performed a great service for the people by bringing both joy and knowledge to the customers that came to enjoy the circus, especially the children,  who always find it to be fascinating, exciting, and very educational.

We kept walking a little further, and we came to another large pen where there were several elephants, including one baby elephant.

He stopped and said, "So, Ron, this is where we will start you, tending to the elephants we have here. Your job will be to both feed and water them and also take care of their manure, you understand?"

"Um, yes, I guess so."

"Let us see if we can find Klaus. He is the elephant trainer and you will work under him and he will show you exactly what you have to do."

"Very well, Mr. Hans," I said.

So I followed him behind a building and he introduced me to Klaus, a large middle-aged fellow with a huge mustache and a very heavy build.

Hans looked at me one final time and told me, "Well, I leave you now in the very capable hands of Klaus here, and if you need anything else from me, I shall be in my office near the ticket booth that I showed you earlier and good luck to you, my young man. I hope you like it here at Circus Maximus."

"Thank you, Mr. Hans," I said as he walked away, leaving me alone with Klaus.

Klaus took a long look at me and said, "So, you are an American, is this correct?"

"Yes sir, I am."

"Ah, I have known many Americans during my life. There are many American military that have been occupying Germany since the end of the big war, you know this, no? Some of them I find to be decent people and others not so much. So what kind are you, young man?"

I shrugged and said, "Well, Mr. Klaus, actually I've only lived in the States just a few years of my life since my father was in the Air Force and we traveled around a lot when I was younger."

He gave me a strange look and said, "Ah, a Military Brat, as they say, hey? Yes, I have known many such young people when I lived in Stuttgart. Very well, let's get started, shall we, young brat?"

"Okay, I'm ready," I replied, trying not to return the strange look that he gave me.

"Now, the first thing to know about the elephants is that they eat very much and they also shit very much of course, and your job here will be both to feed them and clean up their shit. You understand?"

"Yes sir, Mr. Klaus."

"Very well, follow me then."

I followed him as we walk over to a shed where inside several large bales of hay were stacked up, and he reached inside and picked one up and told me to do the same. I struggled with it, but I was just barely able to lift it.

He looked at me struggling and said in a very stern voice, "Oh, I see we have a weakling here, yes? Are you not capable of lifting this?"

"No, I can get it, hold on."

And I finally lifted it up a few inches off the ground and I looked at him and asked, "Okay, where are we going with these?"

He lifted his over his head and said, "This way, yank."

I followed him over to the pen where the elephants were held, still struggling with the bale of hay. There were four elephants altogether including the baby. And they were huge. Even the baby seemed to be the size of a large horse, and the adults were each the size of small buildings. He sat his bale down and opened the gate of the pen, picked his bale up again and walked in and I followed him, still struggling with my bale, barely able to get it above my knees, but I was managing to transport it and somehow getting it to where it needed to be.

Finally he sat his bale of hay down inside the pen and I did likewise. I looked closely at the four elephants and I could tell that they were not happy creatures at all. Each one of them had a rope tied around one of their feet which was attached to a stake in the ground and

the largest of them had two ropes attached, one on his front left foot and the other on his back right one, so he could barely move in any direction.

And when I looked into his huge eyes, I could feel the sadness, the stress, and the intense anger there, and it almost broke my heart. I've always considered myself to be a sensitive person, and I started to feel the same feelings that this poor creature was feeling. I remember the few times I had gone to zoos when I was younger and what I was feeling was a similar but more intense feeling to what I had felt at the zoos.

Every time I had gone to a zoo, I had always felt so sad for the animals there in captivity. And I wondered to myself and I would ask anyone who would listen, "What crime did these animals enact to deserve to get locked up in jail like this besides just being born a different species than us humans? And how can we as the human race and as fellow inhabitants of this Earth, justify putting these fellow earthlings in cages simply for being a different species from us?"

The answer I always got was that the reason for animals being in zoos was for educational purposes, and so that people could get a chance to see these creatures that they would never see otherwise. My argument was always, well, aren't photographs and movies good enough to see them by? Other times the response I received was that they had to be kept for scientific and zoological studies and research.

My response was then: how come so many? Aren't just a few of each species good enough for this purpose? No, the plain answer was plain and simple, it was for money. People are willing to pay good money to see these animals and that is why they were captured by the thousands and put into cages in zoos all over the world.

So as I watched these elephants standing there in a vacant lot near a circus being set up on the outskirts of the town of Delft, Holland, all these emotions and feelings I had about animals that I had felt my entire life came back to me, and I felt shame, not only for myself, but for the entire human race. I saw the baby trying to hide between its mother's legs and trying to get some comfort there. But soon he was removed and put in an area away from her, and he just stood there with a lonely and neglected look on his face.

Klaus finally came over and

started telling me what my job would entail and I seriously thought about just walking away from all this, just turning around, getting my backpack and getting away from this cruel and pitiless spectacle in front of me, but I also realized that it would continue whether or not I was there, and that my being there or not would not make any difference. So I decided to stick around for the time being and see what happened.

I was quickly shown the tools of the job which were a wheelbarrow, a large shovel, and a large baling fork. The first two of these items were used to remove the huge amounts of elephant dung that was created every day, and the third item was used to break up the bales of hay and feed it to the animals. The sizes of these elephant turds were unbelievably huge as one can imagine. Even the baby's were the size of bowling balls and the large ones were the size of beach balls or even larger. Elephants eat a fantastic amount of food, and a three-ton elephant eats at least one hundred pounds of hay every day, along with fifteen to twenty pounds of produce as well. They are also fed about ten pounds of special pellets that contain essential nutrients and vitamins to keep them healthy.

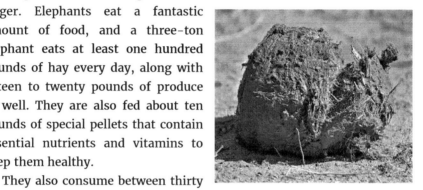

They also consume between thirty and sixty gallons of water every day. And all this has to come out eventually, and my primary job was to dispose of it. Hour after hour, I would load the wheelbarrow up, push it over to the dumpster and shovel the shit in. The countless gallons of urine would end up on the ground or onto the hay lying around and again my job was to rake it all up and dispose of it in the same way.

I think I could have handled the job for a while since I had already done much worse kinds of work doing the day-labor jobs, but the thing that got to me was the look in the eyes of the elephants that I just couldn't ignore. What finally really clinched my decision to quit the job was on my third day on the job when Klaus approached me while I was taking a short break from shoveling elephant turds and asked me to follow him. So again, I followed him, wondering what he had in store for me now.

We went over to the corral-like structure where the strange cattle were kept. I had watched the circus completely through by this time and I knew what the purpose was of having all these different kinds of cattle around. One of the "spectacles" the circus features between the lion-tamer and the elephant show was when they brought out a dozen or so of these exotic cattle. They would all be wearing very fancy bright red and gold halters, with bells and other shiny objects around their necks and they would run around in a circle with the trainer holding a whip urging them on. After a few runs around a circle, and a smattering of light applause from the audience, they were led back to their pens to await the next day's show.

So Klaus was going to show me how to put these halters onto these beasts, which had to be done each day before the show started and again once their part of the show was over. They were led one at a time into a small containing pen where it was easier to strap the halters around their necks and tightly under their bodies. Of course, they hated this treatment, and were constantly shaking their heads with their horns flying all around while Klaus somehow managed to get the halters around them. After he got the first few done and led them out so he could bring the next one in to get it dressed and ready to perform, he told me to try my hand at it. And the next one was a Texas longhorn.

As soon as I put my hand near the beast's head to try to get the halter around the horns, it started mooing and shaking its head around and the tip of the left horn barely missed my right eye by less than an inch. I looked at the beast, then at Klaus and handed him the halter and told him I wasn't about to risk my eyesight or something worse trying to get this damn cow dressed. And I just walked away, headed back to my cot, grabbed my backpack and sleeping bag, and walked over to Hans' office to talk with him.

I looked him in the eye and said quite firmly, "Mr. Hans, I don't think this job is for me. Could I have my final pay, please, because I just quit."

He asked me, "Why is that, young man? So you do not like working with the magnificent animals then?"

"Well, to be frank with you, sir, I don't like the way the animals are treated here and I feel too much pity and compassion for them. But besides that, Klaus just asked me to do something that I refused to do, because of concerns for my personal safety, so I must leave at this time. Again, may I have my final pay please?"

He gave me his funny look and said, "Well, I knew that Americans have no work ethic and are lazy as dogs. So it is good to see you go. Let me get you your money."

He walked over to his desk and took out a bank bag and counted out the few guilders they owed me for that day's work, handed them to me, and said, "Here you go, young American, now make yourself scarce. You little *scheiskopf!* Away with you now! *Arschloch!*"

I was tempted to return some choice words of my own that I knew, but since I didn't speak any German at all, I wasn't exactly sure what he had said to me. But I could tell by the tone of his voice that the words he had used were probably not compliments. So I shrugged, put my money in my wallet, and walked away, without turning around and without any regrets.

It wasn't hard to hitchhike back to Rotterdam, and I was back at my abandoned house by nightfall and at the train station early the next morning hoping to get hired for the day-labor jobs again. I was lucky and got an entire week's worth of work with the same employer and at the same job site. It was nasty work involving scraping and painting but I felt lucky to get it, and by the week's end, I had quite a few guilders in my wallet, so I decided to take a little mini-vacation and not work or even look for work for a few days.

I was lucky again and found a hostel near downtown that had an available bunk, so I paid up for four days and got some good sleep and got myself cleaned up. I went to a nearby cafe and spent about fifteen guilders on some excellent Lebanese hash, and I finally started to relax a little.

While hanging around the old part of town one evening, I met a local fellow about my age by the name of Louis and we started talking. I shared a joint with him and we became quite friendly. He was interested in all things American and asked me a lot about life in the United States. But he was a little disappointed when I told him that although technically I was an American; I had only lived a couple of years in the States during my entire life. But I told him a little about what I did know and about the visits I had made to my relatives both in Texas and in Oklahoma. His typical reaction of reaching for an imaginary six gun when I told him about Texas was not surprising to me at all.

He told me he had recently been released from the Dutch Army after spending two years in it and asked me if I had spent any time in the American military. I told him that I hadn't, and that I didn't really want to either, considering the situation that was going on in Vietnam. He said he could relate to that and then he told me he felt lucky that the Dutch were not involved in any wars and that he had spent most of his time in the Dutch Army washing dishes and patrolling empty fields.

He looked at the clothes I was wearing and asked me why I was wearing the old sports jacket I had on and asked if I didn't know that it was really out of style, and that it looked like something that his grandfather would wear. I just shrugged and told him it was all I had and it did seem to function all right and kept the chill off me at night.

At this point, he took off his dark green Dutch Army jacket, handed it to me, and said, "Here, you can have this coat. It is a little more in style, and I think it should fit you okay."

I took it from him after removing the ratty old gray sports jacket I was wearing and I tried it on, and it fit perfectly.

I asked, "Hey, are you sure you want to give this to me, man? Don't you want to keep it as a souvenir from your military service?"

"No, my friend, I do not. I would like to forget those two years of my life if I can. Besides you need it much more than I do. And look at you; you look very nice with it on, and so much more stylish."

"Okay, then I'll keep it. It feels very nice on me and I really do like it. How can I thank you? I have nothing to give you in return, man."

"Don't worry about it, my friend. When you wear it, just think about me and remember that you have a real army jacket now, so you don't have to join the American Army and go to Vietnam, okay? Ha ha!"

I laughed as well and said, "Well, thank you so much, Louis, I really do appreciate it a lot. It is very nice and I will think of you whenever I wear it." I rolled up another three-leafer, and we sat back and watched the boats in the old harbor as the sun began to set and we started relaxing even more and chatted about other topics. The jacket that my friend gave that night was one of the nicest presents I have ever received, and I kept it for a very long time. Actually, I wore it almost every day for several

years before it got a little tight on me. I even had it on a couple of years later when I had returned to the States and was hanging out in the mountains of New Mexico, and it was still very much in style.

There was a little cafe in Rotterdam near the downtown area where I spent a lot of time. It was a Turkish cafe owned by an older Turkish fellow with a big mustache by the name of Mustafa, and I came to really like the place a lot. It was dark and cozy and had several small brass tables and a lot of Turkish rugs on the floor and various colorful tapestries on the walls.

Mustafa always played the latest rock-and-roll records on his very nice stereo system and, of course, it was permitted to smoke all kinds of things while inside his cafe, which I would do regularly while drinking strong Turkish coffee or sweet Moroccan mint tea. He also sold several kinds of cannabis at his cafe and his prices were as reasonable as just about anywhere else.

Another reason I liked the place so much was that there was a very pretty girl who worked there off and on. Her name was Lydia and we would always have a very pleasant conversation whenever she served me my tea or coffee. She told me she was from a small town just outside of Brussels, Belgium, and that she was in Rotterdam because she liked Holland very much but couldn't put up with all the crowds of tourists in Amsterdam. She liked to smoke hash as well, and often she would sit down and share a little smoke with me.

She was interested in all things American like most European people were, and we talked a lot about the little that I knew about my own country. She had long dark hair and always wore brightly colored long flowing dresses and skirts and always had long interesting jingly earrings dangling from her ears. She was very pretty, but she had one tooth on the top front of her mouth that was quite crooked. I thought it looked marvelous and gave her a unique look, but I could tell that she was a little self-conscious about it, because she would sometimes cover her mouth when she smiled or laughed.

There was one album that Mustafa would play quite often on his stereo by the American band from San Francisco called Jefferson Airplane, and there was one song on it that was called "You're Only as Pretty as You Feel," and the lyrics went like this...

> "You're only as pretty as you feel, only as pretty as you feel inside,
> You're only as pretty as you feel, just as pretty as you feel inside,

When you wake up every morning, run the sleep from your eye,
Look inside the mirror, comb your hair,
Don't give vanity a second thought, no, no, no,
Beauty is only skin deep, it goes just so far because,
You're only as pretty as you feel, only as pretty as you feel inside."

Whenever this song came on the stereo at Mustafa's cafe, Lydia would stop whatever she was doing, stand up, and dance around with a big smile on her face. She floated around the room as if she was on a cloud of her own, and she would never cover her mouth but instead smile her biggest and sweetest smile.

I figured that this was her song, and she related to it so much that she couldn't help herself but to get up and dance away with the music. She looked so beautiful to me and often I would tell her so but being the shy and inexperienced young man that I was, I never pursued my feelings for her. Instead, I was always the perfect gentleman around her and we remained just friends, but I still remember her vividly to this day, and that beautiful smile of hers. She truly did melt my heart.

One sunny afternoon I was coming out of the Turkish cafe after spending a couple of hours there sipping mint tea and smoking hash, and frankly I was quite stoned. As I left the cafe, I was crossing this small open field heading back towards the main part of downtown, when a uniformed Dutch policeman approached me. He was wearing his official light green police uniform and had on the typical round short brimmed hat that policemen and military officers wear the world over. He asked me something in Dutch and when I told him I didn't understand; he spoke to me in English.

He asked in a very gruff and unfriendly voice, unlike most Dutch people I had met who were always very nice and friendly, "So, where are you coming from?"

I told him, "I just left the Turkish cafe right over there," and I pointed to the place I had just came from that was only fifty feet away or so.

He gave me a very stern look and asked, "And were you smoking hashish there in that cafe?"

I looked at him closely and I figured that if I lied, it would only make things worse for me. Besides, I'm sure he had smelled it on me, so I was truthful and replied, "Yes, sir, I was, a little."

Again he gave me a very stern look and asked, "And where is this hashish now? Do you have some with you now?"

I shrugged and reached into my pocket and pull out the tiny nugget that I had with me and showed it to him. It was about the size of my thumbnail, maybe a gram or so perhaps, wrapped in a small piece of aluminum foil.

He took it from me, unwrapped it from the foil, looked at it closely, sniffed it, and then reached his arm back and threw it as far as he could out into the open field, and told me, "You should not smoke such substances. They are illegal and are not good for your health. Go along now and do not return to that cafe. There are bad people that go there. Now go along your way."

I just looked at him and shrugged and said, "Okay."

And I walked away, rather angry that he had just thrown away a perfectly good gram of Lebanese gold that I had purchased from Mustafa earlier. But I knew better than to push my luck and not to ever anger any officer of the law in any way, so I just walked away from him.

After about a half hour, I returned to the field, making sure he was not around the area, and tried in vain to find the gram of hash but I had no luck. It blended in with the dirt in the field and I gave up trying to find it after a few minutes. This was the first and only time that I had been hassled by the cops during my entire stay in Holland. I'm not sure what his deal was, but I guess I was lucky.

Maybe he thought I was a big-time dealer, and he wanted to make a big bust, or maybe he was just having a bad day or maybe he was just bored. I guess I'll never know for sure. Or maybe he saw me wearing the Dutch Army jacket and thought I was a Dutchman and wanted to give me some health advice to one of his countrymen. I would never know.

Shortly after this confrontation with the cop, I called my mom in Madrid collect, just to let her know how I was doing, and she told me she and Jim were headed to Frankfurt the following week in order to re-register their car. They had bought an Opel in Germany when they first came to Europe and since it had German plates on it, it required them to register it every year in Germany. So they had planned a trip to Frankfurt for a few days in order to take care of the car's registration.

She asked me if I was ready to return to Madrid yet and told me that if I was, I could meet them there and get a ride with them back to Spain. I thought about it and told her that maybe I would since it didn't seem like I was doing all that wonderfully in Holland because I was sleeping in abandoned houses and could barely get enough work to survive. She told me the days that they would be there, and the hotel they'd be staying at near the *Hauptbahnhof* (the main train station) in downtown Frankfurt and I told her I would meet them there.

I knew that I had enough guilders for the train since it wasn't really all that far, only about four hundred and fifty kilometers. I wrote down the name of the hotel and the dates they were to be there and said that I'd see her and Jim the following week. She seemed happy to hear that I was planning to return to Spain, and that I was going to give up my plan of trying to make it on my own in Holland since she knew well by then the problems I had been having.

So I went to the train station in Rotterdam and bought a one-way ticket to Frankfurt for the next day, and I got on the train and I headed off for my next adventure, this time to Frankfurt, Germany, of all places.

Chapter 21. Frankfurt

"I have seen the sea when it is stormy and wild;
when it is quiet and serene;
when it is dark and moody.
And in all these moods, I see myself."
— *Martin D. Buxbaum*

I got off the train from Rotterdam at the *Haupbahnhof* (the main train station) in the center of *Frankfurt am Main*, which is the official name of the city, to distinguish it from *Frankfurt am der Oder*, a town located on the Oder River near the Polish border. Its history dates back to the Roman Empire, as many places in Europe do, and today it's the bustling center of the Frankfurt Rhine-Main Metropolitan Region. This area is named after its core city of Frankfurt and the two rivers, the Rhine and the Main. It's the fifth-largest city in Germany and a center of commerce, culture, transportation, and banking. It was built on both sides of the Main River, but the northern side is where the center and the downtown area is located, while the south bank has more parks and has much less congestion and crowds.

    I had gotten there a couple of days before my mom and Jim were scheduled to arrive, so I had to find a cheap place to stay until they got there. I walked around the downtown area for a couple of hours trying to get my bearings in this huge city. It was very congested with a lot of traffic, trams, and people everywhere. I got hungry, so I stopped at a little bar just off the main drag and I ordered a beer and a frankfurter which turned out to be a long and very skinny sausage served on an equally long bun, and it was served with a side of *pommes frites*, which were French fried potatoes.

The reason they were called this was because in French, potatoes are called *pommes de terre*, or literally "apples of the earth," so when they are deep fried they become *pommes frites* or fried apples, and they are served in Germany with a glob of thick creamy mayonnaise. And even though it's a French phrase, this is what Germans call fried potatoes.

After being fortified with some local cuisine, I continued to walk towards the south and towards the Main River. As I reached the river, I stopped at a grassy area by one of the bridges and I saw two long-haired fellows sitting around, so I approached them and started up a conversation. They could tell I was a traveler with my backpack with my sleeping bag attached to it, so our conversation led to my travels and the adventures I just had.

They were Germans but spoke excellent English so the conversation flowed very smoothly. I told them I had just arrived from Holland after spending the summer in both Amsterdam and Rotterdam. They seemed impressed and asked me questions about the scene there, especially about Amsterdam. They had heard about it and were happy to get news of that city from someone who recently been there.

I told them a little about what I had experienced: about Vondel Park, and the different nightclubs in the city, and some of the bands that had played there. After a while of conversing, I asked them about cheap places to stay in the Frankfurt area and if there were any youth hostels as there were in Amsterdam. They told me that the youth hostels were few and far between, but there were other kinds of cheap accommodations if I was willing to rough it. I told them that indeed I was, so they told me about a campground that was located on an island in the Main River just over the bridge from where we were. They pointed downriver, and I saw a rather long narrow island near the other bank connected to the mainland by a small bridge. They told me it was possible to camp there for a very reasonable sum of money. So I thanked them, said goodbye, and walked across the bridge heading for this island.

It was only about a five-minute walk to the small

bridge that connected the island to the mainland on the other bank of the river. There was a building near the entrance to the campground, and from there I could see a large grassy area with a lot of trees along the riverbank and with quite a few tents set up all around, and also various kinds of cars parked here and there, including an assortment of vans, buses, and some strange-looking vehicles as well.

Inside the building, behind the counter was a man about thirty years old with very long blond hair tied back in a ponytail. He looked at up me, smiled, and said, *"Guten Tag, Wie geht's?"* (Which translates to, "good day, what's up?")

I looked at him rather blankly and said in English, "I'm sorry, I don't speak German. Do you speak English perhaps?"

He looked at me more closely and gave a little laugh and said, "Ah yes, I do, a little. Where are you from?"

"Well, I'm an American, and someone told me that this campground might be a cheap place to stay. Is this true?"

He laughed again and said, "Yes, you are correct. This is one of the most inexpensive places to stay in the entire area. If you don't mind camping that is."

I smiled and told him, "No, I don't mind camping at all. I've recently done a lot of it, as a matter of fact."

He looked at my backpack with just my sleeping bag attached to it and said, "Well, it looks like you don't have a tent with you, is this the case?"

I hadn't thought of that, so I shrugged and told him, "Um, no, I don't have a tent."

He gave me a sad look and said, "Well, you need a tent of some sort in order to camp here. We can't have people just sleeping out in the open, now, can we?"

So I smiled and replied, "Well, I've just arrived from Amsterdam and many people were sleeping out in the open in the park there."

"Well, this is not Amsterdam, and this is a campground, not a park, so here you need a tent. I'm sorry."

I gave him the most disappointed look I could muster and said, "Yes, I'm sorry as well, but is there someplace nearby where I can buy a tent, perhaps?"

He looked at me and smiled again and said, "Well, young man, you are in luck, because I happen to have a small tent here that was left by two Dutch tourists who decided to not to take it with them when they left. Also, there is some other camping gear they left that you might be able to use. I can sell it to you perhaps if you're interested and have enough money."

I smiled back and said to him, "Well, that depends on how much you're asking for, I suppose. Can I take a look at it?"

"Absolutely; just follow me, please," he said, and I then followed him around to the back of the building to a small storeroom.

He unlocked the door, and we walked inside. The little room was crammed with all kinds of gear and supplies of all sorts. He reached up on a shelf and pulled down a small bundle of dark green canvas wrapped in rope and with poles sticking out of it and handed it to me and said, "Here is the tent; it is a small pup tent that was left here recently by the Dutch couple I told you about."

I looked at it and thought to myself that it certainly didn't look like very much all rolled up like that, but if it would allow me to stay in this campground, it just might work.

I asked him, "Okay, how much do you want for this, sir?"

He laughed and said, "Oh, please, don't call me sir. After all, I am not many years older than you are. Call me Olaf; that is my name. And what is yours, may I ask?"

I smiled. "It's nice to meet you, Olaf. My name is Ron," I said as I shook his hand with my free hand.

"And where are you from Ron, may I ask?"

"Well, as I said, I'm an American and I've been traveling around Europe for a while now."

"And you don't have a tent? That is surprising because camping is the only way to travel, I think."

"Maybe you're right, Olaf, maybe so."

"I can sell you this tent for twenty marks. Does that sound good to you, Ron?"

I calculated quickly in my head and I knew that German marks had about the same exchange rate as Dutch guilders, so twenty marks would be a little less than seven dollars.

I looked him in the eye and said, "Well, that seems a little steep to me, Olaf, considering the shape this thing is in."

I opened the tent just enough to inspect it and I noticed the manufacture's label on the inside of it and it read in both Dutch and English: "**Official Dutch Army Pup Tent, date of manufacture, 1953."**

"It says here that it was made in 1953. That makes it almost twenty years old now," I told him.

Olaf looked at the label as well and then said "Okay, Ron, if you like I will throw in for free these other items the Dutch couple left behind. Here is a one-burner propane stove and a perfectly good air mattress that looks like it will still hold air, and a small tarp big enough to put under the tent. How does that sound?"

I thought about it for a moment and said, "Okay, we got a deal. Oh, and by the way, what is the rate for the camping space?"

"The daily rate is three marks, but there is a special rate for long-term stays," he said.

"So the rate is cheaper if you stay longer?" I asked.

"Yes, if you pay for six nights, the seventh night is free, so that makes the weekly rate eighteen marks, and also there is an even cheaper rate by the month."

"And what would that be?" I asked.

"The monthly rate is seventy marks," he said with a smile. "We have guests who have been here for many months now."

"I see. Okay, Olaf, I'll go ahead and buy this gear from you plus pay a week's rent in advance, okay?"

"Very well, Ron. Let's go back to the office where I can write you a receipt and you can choose which space you would like. We also have very nice and clean bathrooms and showers here for the use of our guests, with plenty of hot water."

As we walked back over to the office, I calculated in my head how much money I'd have after paying him the rent for a week plus the money for the camping gear. Altogether, I'd have to pay him thirty-eight marks, and I had a little over one hundred marks with me that I had changed from guilders earlier that day, so I would have about sixty marks left over. But my mom and Jim were to be here in a couple of days, and if I decided to go back to Madrid with them, I still got a great deal on the camping gear which I could always use, and there would be plenty of room in their car to take it back to Spain if I wanted to go.

But I think I must have decided about that point that I wasn't going back with them to Spain after all. I didn't want to accept defeat, which to me meant that I couldn't make it on my own in the world. After seeing Frankfurt a little by then, I realized that it was a large city, and they probably had a similar day-labor situation as they had in Rotterdam, and I wanted to prove to myself and to my parents that I could survive on my own. Besides, this campground looked wonderful, with beautiful green

grass growing everywhere and the tall trees lining the beautiful riverbank and a wonderful view of the Frankfurt skyline.

When we got back to Olaf's office, he asked to see my passport, and I signed in and paid him for the gear and for one week's rent and then he asked me what space I would like to set up my tent. When I told him that I wasn't sure, he told me to just walk around the grounds and find one that I liked and then come back and let him know.

So I took a walk around the campground and realized that it really was a very nice facility. There were probably around forty spaces altogether scattered around the entire park. Most had electric outlets near each space, where it was possible to hook up a full RV, or an electric light, or another electric appliance of some sort if the camper so desired. There were also very nice picnic tables evenly spaced between every other campsite or so. I also noticed that it was about evenly split between tent campers and people who were obviously living inside their vehicles. And the park looked to be about half-full at the time.

I found one space that was a little away from the other occupied spaces and noted the number that was written on a small white stone next to it and returned to the office to talk to Olaf, and to get my gear, including the stuff I had just purchased from him.

I gave him the number of the space I had chosen, got all my gear together and carried it back to the space to set it all up. By the time I was done, I had a very cozy little tent with a nice tarp between the ground and me, and the air mattress that I had blown up using lung power was holding air. On top of the mattress, I laid out my sleeping bag and there was also room to put my pack along with the rest of my things. It was my own little space, and I actually owned it.

I liked my little home, and I noticed that the color was almost the exact shade of olive green as that the jacket I was wearing, which was not surprising since they were both Dutch Army issue. I set up the little Coleman one-burner stove and realized that I didn't have a propane cylinder for it. So I walked back to the office and told Olaf my situation. He told me that he sold the small propane cylinders for three marks each, so I bought one from him so I could use the stove.

Again I thanked him, and told him he was very kind for helping me out the way he had, and I walked away with the small metal object in my hand. I hooked up the cylinder to the stove and turned it on, hearing a slight hissing noise coming from it. I lit a match and put it to the stove and I saw blue flames emerging from the device. All right! Now I was cooking with gas! No more steady diet of cold sandwiches and cold drinks. I could now heat up anything I wanted and I could even make my own coffee. Ah! What luxuries I had attained!

By this time, I had to use the restroom, so I walked back to the building where the restrooms were located near the office. Olaf was right; they were large, clean, and they even had mirrors over the sinks. I tested the hot water in one of the sinks and it came out quite hot indeed. I looked inside one of the several shower stalls and noticed that it was spotlessly clean and even had a little bench to sit on while taking your clothes off before showering. There was even a rubber mat to stand on to prevent slipping while showering. I was quite impressed by the luxury that this campground offered. It certainly beat lying on the floor of abandoned houses like I was used to, and I really liked the fact that I had a little space of my own with my own little tent.

I took a little walk and after heading down-river for a few blocks; I discovered a small store that sold all kinds of goods. So I made a few purchases of some things to eat such as canned soups and then I realized that I needed a pot to cook them in. Fortunately, they sold such items as well, so I bought a small pot with a lid, a can opener, a coffee cup and a small jar of instant coffee and some sugar. I also bought some apples, two cans of tuna and a loaf of bread. I even celebrated and bought two bottles of good Heineken beer. I returned to my campsite and had a small celebration by myself, thanking the powers that be that I had found such a nice situation.

After I had finished a can of chicken noodle soup for dinner, I washed up the pot in the bathroom sink and I was sitting back on a picnic table near my tent as the sun was going down drinking my second Heineken when a nice-looking young lady approached me. She looked around thirty, maybe a little older, and she had an exotic look about her. She looked almost Japanese, though not completely, and she was very beautiful.

She walked right up to me and said in perfect English, "Hello there, you're new here, aren't you?"

I looked at her and smiled and said, "Well, yes I am, I just checked in today as a matter of fact."

She smiled as well and said, "My name is Mioshi, welcome to the campground. How do you like it so far?"

"Hello, Mioshi, it's very nice to meet you. My name is Ron," I replied, still grinning. "Yeah, I just checked in today and I like it a lot; it seems like a very nice place so far."

"Well, it kind of grows on you after a while. So where are you from, Ron?"

"Well, I'm an American but I've never really lived in the States very much since my dad was in the Air Force and we traveled around the world a lot while I was growing up. How about you? Um, Mioshi? Did I get that right?"

"Yes, you got it right. And I'm also an American, Ron. I grew up in San Francisco. My mom is Japanese and my dad is a Mexican-American. That's why I got the funny Japanese name."

"Well, I really like it, it's a beautiful name, Mioshi," I replied.

"I'm glad you like it; many people have a hard time pronouncing it but you don't seem to, do you?"

"Well, I speak three languages, so I pick up on sounds pretty well I guess," I said to her.

"Oh, really? What languages do you speak, may I ask?"

"Well, English obviously, Spanish, and pretty good French as well."

"It's too bad you don't speak German, that would certainly come in handy around here, wouldn't it, huh?" she said, smiling.

I smiled back at her and said, "Yeah, I guess it would. I'm trying to learn it little by little, but I just arrived today, so I haven't had a chance to learn that much yet besides how to ask for a beer, ha!"

She laughed a little and said "Yeah, that's about the first thing you gotta learn, isn't it?"

We sat there talking for about two hours or so about all kinds of things and we got to know each other quite well before she finally said she had to go to bed since she had to go to work early the next morning. So we said our goodnights, and she headed over to her own tent which was set up just a few spaces down from mine.

It turned out that she worked as a waitress at the service club at Rhein-Main Air Force Base, just outside of Frankfurt. It is one of the largest and most important American Military bases out of the many located in Germany. She also told me that it was possible to get work like she had done, with the AAFES, the Army Air Force Exchange Service.

This was a huge organization that maintained and serviced all the American Army and Air Force bases in Europe. They did just about everything for the American servicemen and their dependents including running the commissaries, the PXs, and all of the other services for the American military personnel. It turned out there were many thousands in the Frankfurt area alone. There were both Army and Air Force bases and other American Military facilities all around the area including in Bad Nauheim, Gelnhausen, Darmstadt, and Offenbach, along with many other bases and smaller posts all over Germany.

So falling asleep that first night in the campground, I was feeling pretty good about myself. I had not only found a great place to stay for very little money, but it was run by a very nice young fellow who seemed to want to help me out in any way he could. On top of that, I had made a new friend who seemed to be not only very beautiful, but also very nice and friendly as well. Maybe I would like it here in Frankfurt.

I had two days to kill before I was to meet my folks at their hotel, so I spent them wandering all around the city. I discovered that the *Strasenbahn* (the streetcar) system was not only very efficient and connected the entire city together, but it was also very reasonably priced. For less than half a mark, one could get anywhere in the entire area and very quickly. But it was very nice walking as well, since it was the beginning of September and it was still summer in Germany. The days were long and sunny and the temperatures were still quite pleasant. So I enjoyed walking around the city and getting to know it a little better. I soon discovered that most Germans speak at least a little English, probably due to the high numbers of Americans (mostly military) who have been in their country since the last World War.

By talking to Olaf for a few minutes one morning, I quickly learned how to count and how to understand numbers in German, since I knew this would be very important every time I purchased anything at all. I needed to know what the price was for something, and most importantly, I needed to know that I received the correct amount of change in return. I also learned a few expressions from Olaf that I knew would be necessary, such as *"Ja, nein"* (yes, no), *"Danke"* (thank you) and *"Bitte,"* (please).

Also, the most important phrase I learned was "Sprechen Sie Englisch?" (Do you speak English?) I used this phrase more than any other during my entire stay in Germany.

The day my mom and Jim were to arrive at the hotel downtown, I got there early and talked to the hotel clerk, explaining to him that my parents were to arrive some time that day but I was not sure exactly when. He looked it up and found their name on the reservation list and told me I could wait in the lobby if I liked. I thanked him but told him that I would just walk around the downtown area until they arrived.

I found the *Haupbahnhof* again easily enough since it was just a few blocks from the hotel so I was gradually getting my bearings around the city. I checked back with the clerk every hour or so until around six in the afternoon, when he told me that they had just checked in and he gave me the room number. I took the elevator upstairs to the fourth floor and found their room. I knocked on the door a little timidly, not knowing exactly what to expect. Jim opened the door with a gin and tonic in his hand and a big smile. He welcomed me in and gave me a big hug and a handshake. Then my mom came out of the bathroom with a big smile and a big hug as well. They were very happy to see me and I was happy to see them as well.

We sat down and talked for quite a while and I told them a little about the adventures that I had in Holland and how hard it was to get work there, but that I had somehow made enough to keep me alive and out of trouble. I also told them about the great luck I had in finding a place to stay in Frankfurt at the campground and about the tent I had bought and the rest of the gear that came with it. I also told them that I had changed my mind about returning to Madrid with them. I tried to explain that I was still trying to make it on my own and I needed to prove to them and to myself that I could do it. I mentioned the friend I had met at the campground who seemed to be positive that I could get work, as she had, with the AAFES here in Germany.

My mom looked at me closely and told me that I was twenty years old now and it was up to me what I wanted to do with my life. If I really thought I could get a job and make my way in Germany, then who was she to stand in my way. She also told me that if it turned out that I couldn't get a job or if I changed my mind about living in Germany, and needed help in getting a train ticket back to Madrid, she would be more than happy to send me the necessary funds for the ticket south.

I thanked her again for all the help that she and Jim had given me and told them that it was great to know that if I got in a jam, I could count on them to help me out. But again I told them that I really needed to prove this to myself: that I could make it on my own, and make my way in the world and in my life, and that maybe Germany was the place to do it.

We went out for dinner at a nearby restaurant shortly after that and when we finished eating; I told them that I'd see them the next day because they weren't leaving to return to Spain until the day after. Jim insisted that instead of going all the way back to the campground for the night, they would just pay for another room for me at the hotel and I could stay there. Then the next day, after they took care of the car registration, we could drive together out to the campground and they could see the place and know exactly what I was talking about. So I agreed, and I ended up spending a very nice night in the hotel in an excellent room, on a real bed, and I got the best night's sleep I had in many months.

The next morning, we went together to get the car registered and then we drove out to the campground and they were able to get a good look around. They saw my tent and my gear and realized that I was doing okay. They even met Olaf briefly and chatted with him a little. And before they went back to the hotel that evening, we went out for dinner again and when they dropped me off at the campground; we said our goodbyes then because they would be driving back to Spain early the next morning.

As I was giving my mom a big hug goodbye, I told her to not worry about me too much, and that I would be fine. And that I would write or call often and let them know how I was doing. She started to tear up a little bit and told me to take care of myself and to keep out of trouble because there were a lot of strange people in the world and some of them were not all that friendly sometimes. I told her I understood that, but I had to learn for myself the ways of the world and that was exactly what I was trying to do here.

She asked me if I needed any money, but I told her I had plenty. Still, she handed me two twenty-dollar bills and told me to keep them for an emergency. I took the bills and thanked her and Jim, and gave them final hugs and then they got in their Opal and drove away, leaving me standing there waving at them with small tears forming in my eyes. I never felt so alone in my entire life, but also knowing deep inside that this is what I needed to do: to become a man and to know what it was like to be on my own and to take care of myself.

The next day, I did a little more grocery shopping at the little store down from the campground and later that afternoon, when Mioshi got home from work, I had a long talk with her about where exactly I was to go to see about getting a job with AAFES. She told me that I would have to go out to the Rhein-Main Air Base and go to the civilian personnel office. She also told me I would have to get a visitor's permit at the front gate in order to get on base. But I told her that I still had my military dependents ID card from Torrejon so that ought to allow me entrance onto the base. She told me to try that, but if it didn't work, I could get on base by showing them my American passport and telling the guard at the gate that I was just going to the AAFES employment office to look for work.

So the next day, after taking some time figuring out which *Strasenbahn* would take me to the front gate, and riding it for a while, I arrived at the base. I ended up showing both my passport and my American Military dependents ID card to the guards at the entrance and they were fairly friendly towards me, being only a few years older than I was, but happened to be in the Air Force. After I explained why I was there, they not only issued me a temporary pass to get on base, but they also gave me a small map of the base and told me where I was to go to find the employment office for AAFES.

I found the employment office easily enough, and after about an hour of filling out applications and showing my IDs again, I walked out with a job. This was so easy to do most likely because they really needed help in different locations and with various jobs. The job I landed was with the AAFES Fresh Food Warehouse, which was located in the small town of Offenbach, about ten kilometers from downtown Frankfurt. The Fresh

Food Warehouse was where they stored and distributed fresh and frozen food for the commissaries and other facilities for all the surrounding American bases. My job title was "warehouse worker," and I was to report the following Monday at eight in the morning to the warehouse itself in Offenbach to begin work.

Monday morning I met with a man by the name of Mike Preston, who was the foreman of the warehouse. He was an ex-Master Sergeant in the U.S. Air Force who had been stationed in Germany, and had liked it so much that when he got out of the service, he stayed on, married a German girl, and got a job with AAFES. He was a very nice guy with longish hair and a trim goatee, around thirty years old and he was happy to have the extra worker assigned to his warehouse facility because there really was a lot of work to be done.

It was a huge warehouse with many thousands of square feet of storage space and since it was a *fresh* food warehouse, the entire area had to be kept at around the same temperature as inside a regular refrigerator. This warehouse was where they received, stored, and distributed all the fresh food for the various American facilities all over Germany. These items included eggs, dairy products of all kinds, cheeses, meats, fruits and vegetables and any other kind of perishable food that could not be stored "dry," meaning at regular room temperature. There was another warehouse somewhere else that handled the dry goods.

Also at the Fresh Food Warehouse they handled all the frozen food items, and there was a huge walk-in freezer where all the frozen foods were received, stored, and distributed. And this is where Mike needed the most help. He had only one employee to handle the frozen items, and I was to become his helper. He introduced me to Singh, who was the fellow in charge of the frozen foods. Singh was a Pakistani fellow in his mid-thirties and he welcomed me as his helper with open arms since he had been handling all the frozen food items himself up to this point and really needed the help.

The first thing he did was to get me my own heavy duty, arctic-weather-style coveralls, since I'd be spending most of my time inside the deep freeze walk-in. He also supplied me with a pair of heavy-duty gloves to keep my hands from freezing, and a watchman's cap. The job was quite simple, really. Every day we received a stack of order requests from the various outposts, and our job was to enter the freezer and put the requested items onto pallets and transport them to the trucks waiting at the docks to be loaded. These trucks also received fresh food items as well, so rarely did we fill a tractor trailer full of frozen items, but usually our load was just a part of the total order from the warehouse.

We also had to handle the incoming loads, but fortunately there was a crew of forklift drivers who unloaded the trucks and distributed the items around the warehouse, and all we had to do was direct them where to put their loads in order to keep everything organized and easy for us to reach, count, and load. We usually used hand-trucks and rarely did we require a forklift because we only had a few pallets at a time, but when we needed one, one of the forklift drivers would handle it for us.

We would take one of the orders we received, enter the deep freeze, load the requested items onto pallets, and put them in the trucks. There were a surprising number of frozen food items that we handled including various ice cream products, TV dinners, frozen vegetables, frozen meats of all descriptions and kinds, seafood, deserts, pizzas and every other sort of frozen food imaginable. The pallets would have to be wrapped in large sheets of plastic to keep everything on the pallet, and then a copy of the order form would be attached to the pallet.

I caught on to the job pretty quickly, and within a few days I was handling pallets on my own while Singh was doing a stack of orders himself. Between the two of us, we were able to handle the orders much more quickly, and they were being filled in a matter of days from the day of the original request, instead of up to a week as it had taken before I started.

Since I was working for the U.S. Government, I was paid in U.S. dollars and my pay was $1.60 per hour which was the minimum wage in the States at the time. I worked Monday to Friday, eight hours per day, and forty hours per week. Overtime was rarely allowed, but I still got a decent paycheck every Friday afternoon. I liked the job well enough, but as one can imagine, I was often very cold. It was still September, so my living situation in my little tent wasn't too bad yet, but they told me that Germany can have some cold and rainy winters and I was not looking forward to that. But in the meantime, life was good, I enjoyed was I was doing, and I always had enough money in my pocket for a change.

Before too long, I got to know some of the guys I worked with pretty well and I became friends with two of them. I rode the *Strasenbahn* every morning and evening with three of my co-workers and we would talk about all kinds of things on the twenty-minute trip to and from work every day. Two guys were American tourists who had come to Europe to travel around and had run out of money and taken jobs with the AAFES in order to extend their stay in Europe. They were both a couple of years older than I was and they were from somewhere in Maryland. They roomed together and worked together as well so they were great friends, obviously.

They both were big heavy-set guys with big beards and longish hair. The leader of the pair was named Dan and his sidekick was called "Lightening." When I asked about his unusual name, Dan told me that he got the nickname because he was so quick and fast. But I soon realized that they called him "Lightening" the same way that a really huge guy is often called "Tiny." That is to say that he was *not* what he was named for, but instead just the opposite: rather slow, sluggish, and dull.

But they were both really nice guys, and I found out they liked to smoke hash as well, so we got together occasionally at the little apartment they rented and drank a couple of beers and shared a toke or two. But we never indulged in dope while at work, since the three of us believed the same thing: that getting stoned at work was like stealing from your employer in a way, and besides it didn't make the job easier, but instead much harder to perform. So we waited until we were off work to indulge in this type of activity.

It turned out that many of the people with whom I worked were ex-military, either Army or Air Force, and had been stationed in Germany, and for one reason or another had decided to stay instead of returning to the U.S. Another guy that worked with us and rode the *Strasenbahn* every day was named Alfred. He was a very unusual fellow and hard to be friendly with. He had been in the Air Force and had gotten out and stayed in Germany like many of the guys, but he was not the typical ex-military type. He was a little skinny guy in his late thirties or so, with a shaved head and a long, straggly and ugly beard all the way down to his chest. And he stuttered severely. His stutter was so bad that he could barely make himself understood in any situation. He rarely, if ever, spoke, and the only time I heard him try to say anything was when he was asked a question by someone. And that was when his stutter got so bad that usually people would just give up instead of waiting for him to get it out.

Dan and Lighting would make fun of him all the time, both on the job and on our commute to and from work, but I didn't partake in it. I felt pity for Alfred, maybe because when I was a young boy, I stuttered for a while before I finally outgrew it, and I could relate to what he was going through. I also felt sorry for him because his stutter prevented him from having any kind of normal life. He didn't speak much German, so I wondered what kind of world he occupied, a world in which he couldn't communicate really with anyone.

His life must have been a lonely and isolated one indeed. I tried to befriend him the best I could, but he wanted no part of me and he refused all my attempts at kindness or compassion. So after a while, I ended up ignoring him mostly, much like Dan and Lighting did. But I still felt very sorry for him and wished I could do something to help him, but I never could figure out exactly what I could do.

One benefit of the job was that I got an ID card that allowed me to go on base and shop, or hang out at the service club, see a movie or anything else that a serviceman was able to do. I did some shopping at the commissary and at the PX, but the base was not exactly in my neighborhood, so I wouldn't go out there with any regularity, but only occasionally to buy groceries or some other items I needed. I still bought a lot of my groceries at the little store just down from the campground since it was so close and I didn't have to carry them very far.

I got to know some other folks at the campground besides Mioshi. There was an Italian guy from Naples by the name of Frederico whom I got to know pretty well. I would speak to him in Spanish and he would talk to me in Italian and we could communicate reasonably well that way. He lived in his VW bug, of all things. He had removed the front passenger seat and by doing so; he could lie down in it and that is where he slept. Often, we would share dinner together and he was an excellent cook, so I always enjoyed our dinners together. He worked at a factory somewhere, but after a month or so, he left to return to Italy.

I also got to know a nice young couple who were also fellow campers. They were living in the back of his rather large Mercedes van. They had fixed it up with a nice bed in the back and they seemed to be very comfortable in it. His name was Steve, and he worked for AAFES as a truck driver, and occasionally I would see him as he made deliveries to the warehouse where I worked.

His girlfriend's name was Susie, and she was very pretty with long hair and a nice smile. She worked at the PX on base in the clothing department and they both were saving as much money as possible because they had a big trip planned. As soon as they had saved a certain amount of money, they were planning on driving their van all the way to Kathmandu, Nepal. They told me this one night after sharing a couple of joints; and their plan was to drive all the way there.

They got the map out and showed me the route they had planned, which was to take them all across Europe to Istanbul, then across Turkey to Iran, then through Afghanistan, Pakistan, India and then to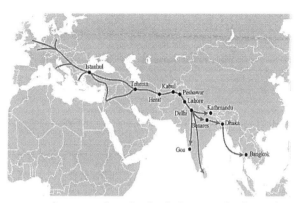
Nepal. They had met some people recently who had done a similar trip, and they had told them what a great adventure it and that Nepal was an absolutely fascinating and wonderful country. Steve told me that there exists this route, or a road, that goes almost around the entire world, blazed by the many people that have done it before. They called it the Hippie Trail, but it was also known as "the overland."

This trail was a form of alternative tourism and one of its key features was to travel as cheaply as possible. In every major stop along this trail, there were hostels, restaurants, and campgrounds that catered almost exclusively to Westerners, who networked with each other as they traveled from east to west or vice versa. Ideas and experiences were shared and discussed along the way in the series of hostels and other gathering places and this same route had been taken before by thousands of travelers before them. The Beatniks had done it in the 1950s and early 60s and now the hippies had started the tradition. Some take the trail all the way to Thailand where the trail unofficially ends.

Sometimes people would hitch hike this route, but usually they would go by private car or van, or sometimes a bus would be acquired and a large group would travel together and share expenses. People would travel lightly and by believing that the trip itself is the point of travel, not the destination, they made it a great adventure. The destination of Kathmandu was where they would usually end up and congregate, and there was even a road in that city called Freak Street named after the thousands of hippies that had made the journey and had finally reached their ambitious destination. Of course, the idea was to sample all the different kinds of cannabis available along the way and to really experience a true adventure and something completely out of the ordinary and far different from anything the average tourist would ever experience.

I wished them the best of luck and within a few weeks, they had finally saved up enough money and were heading out. Before they left one morning for their big trip, again I wished them all the luck in the world and told them that not only were they incredibly brave and daring for undertaking such a trip, but quite adventurous as well. I also told them that I wished I could go along, and who knew, maybe if I got it together, I just might meet them along the trail someday. Then we said our goodbyes and they slowly drove out of the campground and I waved at them and they waved back and I felt a great degree of envy. Now that would be a true adventure!

I had a rather true adventure myself one day not too long after they had left. Mioshi came over to my tent one sunny Sunday morning, the only day we both had off from work together, and she asked me if I'd like to go swimming with her. Since it was still September, it was still rather warm and so I agreed to go with her. She had been to the swimming place a few times before and so she knew how to get there. It was located by an old rock quarry that had filled up with water from a nearby stream and now it was used for swimming and sunbathing by the local people living in the area.

We had to take a bus to get there because the *Strasenbahn* didn't go that far out of town. So we boarded the bus and within about twenty minutes, we arrived at the place which was out in the country and surrounded by grasslands and woods. It was a beautiful day and quite warm and there wasn't a cloud in the sky. We had to walk a little distance from where the bus dropped us off, but before too long we were at the edge of a small lake surrounded by the rocks and the huge boulders of the original quarry.

I looked around and realized that there was something she had not told me about the place: that it was clothing optional. Almost everybody who was there sunbathing and swimming was nude. Mioshi proceeded to take off all her clothes and lay her towel down on the sandy area near the water and then lied back to enjoy the warm sunshine.

She looked at me, smiled her big smile and said, "Well, Ron, aren't you going to join me?"

At this point I realized that she hadn't brought a swimming suit along and neither had I, so I just shrugged and said to her, "Sure, in a little while, okay?"

The first thought that entered my mind was that I'd just strip down to my underwear and just sunbathe that way, but then I remembered that I wasn't wearing any underwear. Sometimes when I didn't have any clean clothes to wear, I'd just chose not to wear any underwear at all rather than wearing my dirty and stinky drawers. And unfortunately, on this day, I was wearing a rather tight-fitting pair of jeans and no underwear.

The thing is, if I had stripped down to nothing, I'm sure she would have noticed the huge erection which I could not seem to contain at this point, caused not only by my raging hormones and her being naked only a few feet from me, but also by the many other naked females all around the place. I knew that it would embarrass her and I would be as well, so I tried to do what I could to avoid either one of us becoming too uncomfortable.

I looked at her as I took off my shirt and shoes and said, "You know, I think I'll keep my pants on, if that's okay?"

"Sure, Ron, whatever you want to do is fine with me," she said with a big smile. "The beauty about this place is that you can do whatever you want to do. But I just like to feel free and being nude allows me to feel that way. You don't mind, do you?"

I looked at her wonderful naked body lying there, shrugged and said, "Um, no, I don't mind at all."

She just smiled and turned over on her back to get some sun on the front of her body.

I noticed that she did as most European girls did, or rather she didn't do what most American girls do, and that was to shave various parts of her body, such as her legs, armpits and crotch area. And looking around I could see that most of the other dozen or so nude females hadn't seen razors for a while either. Which was fine with me; I rather liked the natural look anyway, especially while doing what naturalists do.

But I couldn't seem to control my raging erection, and it was becoming very noticeable even through my jeans. I thought if I just lay down on my front side, and thought of other things, maybe it might diminish somewhat and no one would notice. I tried this for a while but it just didn't seem to work for me at all.

After some time had passed, I realized that I couldn't just lie there on my front side the entire day, and that eventually I'd have to get up and move around, and then people would most likely notice the huge bulge in my tight trousers.

I looked around and noticed that not a lot of the people there were actually swimming in the water and, knowing how well Germans could handle the cold,

I concluded that it must have been quite cold indeed. And that's when I got my idea: I'd go in the water and hopefully the cold water would help to shrink my throbbing manhood somewhat.

I looked at Mioshi lying there and told her, "Um, I'm getting a little warm here. I think I'll take a little dip, okay?"

She smiled at me again and said, "Sure, Ron, but I bet that it's pretty damn cold, don't you think?"

"I'll let you know," I said with a smile as I approached the water's edge and put my foot in, making sure I was facing away from her.

I realized that the only way to do this was to just take the plunge, that any other way would be pure torture. So I held my breath and jumped in all at once. Ow! Man, was it ever cold! I was used to swimming in the warm Mediterranean Sea, not this freezing cold water. Of course, I had the natural instinct to get out as soon as possible to avoid any prolonged exposure to this extreme cold and pain, but I stuck it out for as long as possible and after a few minutes, I started to feel the swelling in my groin area doing exactly what I wanted it to, and to an alarming degree. In fact, I wondered if I would be able to even find the thing if I had to go pee anytime soon.

But it seemed to do the trick and when I finally got out of the water, I felt that I could walk around a little without embarrassing myself too badly. But before too long, the swelling started up again and when that happened, I'd just jump back in the water for a few minutes until it was under control again. I ended up performing this maneuver several times over the entire afternoon, and I was pretty sure that no one was the wiser for my motives, especially Mioshi.

We never went back to the quarry after that one time, due to summer ending shortly after that, and it began to get cold and rainy once autumn arrived. Towards the end of October, I felt like I could never get warm. I worked all day in a deep freeze and then when I got off and went home; I was quite miserable and cold inside my little tent. And when it rained, which was often, the tent would leak a little and I was then not only very cold, but wet as well.

I finally called my Mom and let her know of the situation and she felt very sorry for me, and she insisted that I get a room somewhere. I told her that I wasn't making enough money to afford an apartment, but she told me that there must be rooms for rent somewhere in the city where at least I could be out of the cold and rain. She insisted that I find somewhere to stay besides the tent, because she was concerned about my health, and if I was to get sick, I would become even more miserable inside my little cold wet tent. She told me she would send me some money in order to get me a dry and warm place, and I reluctantly agreed. The next day, I went downtown to the American Express office, and I had a money order waiting for me for sixty dollars.

I immediately bought a local newspaper and started looking for a room. Even though I didn't speak very much German, and could read it even less, I could somehow decipher the gist of what was written under the "for rent" ads and circled a couple of addresses. The first one I found was just a block from the *Strasenbahn* line and it was a four-story building on a quiet street in a residential neighborhood, close to the downtown area.

I knocked on the door of the downstairs apartment and an elderly lady answered. She spoke very little English and with my limited German; we had a little trouble conversing, but eventually by me pointing to the newspaper ad in my hand, she got the idea I was looking for a room. She gestured for me to follow her and she led me up the three flights of stairs until we reached the top floor, then we kept climbing more stairs until we reached the attic of the building. This is where the room for rent was located. She showed me the room which was only about twenty feet by fifteen feet square, and I was rather disappointed, but I took a good look at it, anyway. The attic was divided into four separate guest rooms and each of them had a slanted ceiling because it was the attic, and almost all houses in Germany had highly slanted roofs due to the quite heavy accumulation of snow in the winter.

So in half of the room, it was impossible to stand up all the way, due to the slant of the ceiling, and there was one window that opened to the sky and it was so low in the slanted part of the room, that it was possible to stand up in it, put your head out of it and look around with the top half of your body sticking out. There was no furniture at all; just a bare wooden floor. There was one bathroom in the entire attic which I would be required to share with the three other guests in their separate rooms. There was no heat in the rooms, but the bathroom had hot water, a toilet, and a small shower stall.

The only good news about the place was (according to the ad in my hand) was that it rented for only one hundred and fifty marks (about fifty dollars) per month, a price I could just barely afford. I made a quick decision and considering what I was facing back in my cold and wet tent; I told the lady that I would take it. We went back downstairs to her apartment, and I showed her my passport and paid her a month's rent and signed an agreement of some sort, and she gave me the keys, one for the main door downstairs and the other for my private room in the attic. And for the first time in my entire life, I had my own actual place to live. It wasn't much, but it was all mine.

It didn't take long to get my few belongings over to my new place and get moved in. I ended up going out to the base shortly after moving in and I bought a folding lawn chair and a small folding cot, and a small electric heater that I set up in my room. I had my camp stove to cook with and I set up a small pantry in a corner with a few canned food items, and I kept my fresh food such as meats and cheese in a bag attached by a nail to the roof right outside my window.

My building was on the other side of the river from the campground and was much closer to the downtown and the *Hauptbahnhof* area, so the area where I was now living was much more crowded and congested than where I was before. The good thing was that I only had to take one *Strasenbahn* to get to work and back which saved me a little time on my daily commute.

As the winter set in on the city, it seemed to transform, from a mostly warm and sunny place to a place that was dark, gray, and rainy. I was used to the mild winters in Spain, but I soon discovered that Northern Europe was much different. I rarely saw the sun, and the atmosphere became bleak and dreary. The industrial aspect of the city became more obvious and the constant overcast and cloudy conditions added to my somewhat cheerless outlook.

But one good thing about my new location was that I could easily walk to the places in town where much of the nightlife was located. I started to frequent some of the local nightclubs around the downtown area and there was one where I became almost a regular. The name of the place was the "King's Club," and I liked it because not only did they have great local bands playing there regularly, but it also was one of the few places in town where it was okay to smoke cannabis inside the place. Like in Holland, there were many people who liked to smoke hash and enjoyed doing so in public places and sharing what they had with others. The King's Club was one of the few places in town I found where this was tolerated.

So on many a weekend night, I found myself at the King's Club listening to a great band perform and sitting around sharing a *chillum* or a joint with the many locals and foreigners who frequented the place.

This free and open atmosphere reminded me a lot of Amsterdam, and that is why it became my favorite hangout.

Another place that I discovered was a park known to the locals as "Shit Park." It was a small park not far from the main center street and the reason they called it this was because it was known all around as the place to buy "shit," which was slang for drugs. Almost any time of the day or night, and seven days a week, there were people hanging around the little park who sold drugs of all kinds. This is where I usually went to purchase the small amounts of hash that I smoked. Of course, I saw people selling every other kind of drug as well including such hard drugs as methamphetamine and heroin. Every now and then, a pair of German cops with their green uniforms would patrol the park, but I never saw anyone ever actually get busted, neither dealers nor buyers.

One night at the King's Club, I had an interesting experience. It was a typical Friday evening for me and I had spent a few hours in the club at a table near the stage, listening to a good local German band covering the latest songs by Neil Young, the Rolling Stones, Pink Floyd, and Led Zeppelin among others, and passing the chillum around with the rest of the people in the club. The place was crowded, but at two in the morning the club closed, so as usual, right after closing time, a crowd of people gathered right outside in front of the entrance of the place. Some people were probably hoping to get invited to an after-hours party, or just weren't quite ready to go home yet.

Being a people-watcher, I'd usually hang around the place after closing time just to see what happened and because I usually wasn't ready to go home just yet either. On this particular Friday night, I was just standing around helping to hold the wall up, when I saw an attractive woman standing by herself off to one side. I knew that she hadn't been in the bar earlier because I'm sure I would have noticed her, as she had a most unusual appearance.

She was tall, almost six feet, and had very short dark hair, almost a crew cut, and was wearing a large white cowboy hat, western-style boots, and tight fitting black jeans and jacket. She was obviously German because I had heard her speaking fluent German to a few of the other stragglers around. I watched her for about ten minutes until the crowd began to thin out considerably. Then she walked right up to me and started speaking German to me. I just smiled and used the most useful phrase that I knew in German which was, "*Sprechen Sie Englisch?*"

She smiled and said in a very thick German accent, "Yes, I do, a little. You are not German?"

I smiled back, shrugged, and said, "No, I'm an American."

She looked at me more closely and said, "Oh, I thought you were German. You don't look like most of the Americans that I meet."

I smiled again and asked, "So what do most of the Americans that you meet look like?"

She took off her cowboy hat and said, "Some have hair like mine," and she laughed a little. "And most of the others have hair not much longer, this is this right, no?"

I looked at her head and said, "Yes, but none of them have such a pretty head for their hair to grow out from."

She laughed again and said, "Oh, you are so kind, thank you."

I smiled again and told her, "Well, most of the other Americans you have met have probably been military, right? I'm not."

"Yes, I have met many American militarys, and I'm glad you are not."

"Um, why is that, may I ask?"

She laughed and said, "Because most are, how do you say? Assholes?"

I continued laughing and said, "Yes, you got it right, I think."

"So, what is your name, American guy who is not military?"

"Well, my name is Ron, and what is yours? Beautiful German girl who speaks pretty good English?"

She replied, "My name is Erika, very nice to meet you."

She put out her hand, and I shook it warmly.

She then asked, "So, Ron, what are you doing on this night? Where do you go now?"

I smiled again and said, "Well, Erika, I was getting ready to go back to my place and try to get warm, would you like to join me? I have a couple of cold beers there if you'd like one."

"Well, I don't know, is your place very far from here?"

"No, it's just about a ten-minute walk or so. Would you like to come over for a while?"

"Very well, for a little while would be okay, I guess."

So we walked back to my little room, talking and laughing the whole way.

She seemed to be a little drunk because I could smell alcohol on her breath, but she was not staggering or showing any other signs of being really wasted. I couldn't believe my good luck. Sometimes you just have to be in the right time at the right time, I told myself.

We reached my building; I took out my key, opened the main door on the ground floor, and I started walking up the stairs.

She frowned at me and said, "Oh, there is no, what do you call it, elevators here?"

"No, but it's only four flights of stairs." I laughed and kept climbing.

When we reached the attic of the building and the floor where my room was, we were both a little out of breath. I opened the door to my room, and she walked inside, looked around, and said, "Oh, this is not too bad; I have seen much worse place."

I invited her to sit on my lawn chair and I opened the window and reached into the outside shopping bag where I kept my cold things. I pulled out two cold bottles of Heineken, opened them, and handed her one.

She took a long swig and leaned back in the chair, said, "So, Ron, do you like to smoke the hash?"

I smiled and said, "As a matter of fact, I do. And I even have some right here."

I broke out my little pipe and my little chunk of Moroccan. I filled up a big bowl, lit it up, and passed it to her. She took a big toke and exhaled with a very satisfied sigh.

After a while we both got onto my little cot and things proceeded as they often do when two people get together for some fun and for sharing passions. In this case we did so three times in the next couple of hours, and finally she seemed satisfied and fell asleep on the cot with an old blanket over her while I crashed out on the floor next to her in my sleeping bag.

I woke up early in the morning and she was still asleep, so I quietly boiled a pot of water on my little stove and made myself a cup of coffee. After a while, she woke up, went outside to use the bathroom and when she got back, I had a coffee ready for her as well.

I asked her if she was hungry and she told me she was, and that she hadn't eaten since lunchtime the day before, so I looked in the small stash of food I had in the corner and all I saw were a few canned items. I saw that I had a can of Hormel chili with beans and I asked her if she liked chili. She just shrugged her shoulders, yawned, and said, "Yeah, I guess so, Ron."

After thinking about it, I decided that just one can of chili probably wouldn't fill both of us up, so maybe I should add something to it. I found a can of Van Camp's Spanish rice, so I combined the contents of these two cans. The only other options were a can of sardines and another one of tuna.

We chatted while the foot was warming up and when it was hot enough to eat; I dished about half of it into the one bowl I had, handed it to her with my one spoon, and I began eating the rest right out of the pot with my fork.

I noticed the mixture did have a rather original and distinct flavor, but I didn't think it to be too bad, and Erika apparently didn't either because she gobbled down everything that was in the bowl. After we were done eating, I sat back in my chair smoking a cigarette and she was lying back on the cot, when suddenly, she jumped up holding her stomach and yelled, "Oh, my stomach is hurting! What was that shit that I ate?"

I got up and went over to where the two empty cans were sitting in my little trash bag by the door, and I showed them to her and said, "This is what it was Erika, just a can of chili with a can of Spanish rice with it. And both these cans are fine and not expired or anything."

She started moaning while still holding her stomach and said, "Oh, it hurts so bad, you must have poisoned me!"

I tried to reason with her and said, "But Erika, I ate the same damn thing and I'm fine. I don't understand what could have happened."

She suddenly got up, grabbed her purse, put her shoes and jacket on and said, "Oh, shit, you have poisoned me with that shit, I can feel it. I have to get to hospital!"

She opened the door and started running down the stairs. I followed her trying to reason with her, trying to get her to relax and come back to my room.

"But Erika, it'll be all right, maybe it's just a menstrual cramp or something like that, huh?"

She glared at me with fire in her eyes and yelled, "No, you stupid man! I know what a menstrual cramp feels like and this is not that!"

I was trying to keep up with her as she was taking two stairs at a time and I said, "But you saw me eat the same thing as you did; how could you get sick and not me, it just doesn't make any sense!"

"I don't know, but I have to get to hospital now!"

We reached the ground floor, and she flung open the door and ran outside to the street with me still behind her. She started to run down the sidewalk yelling, "I have been poisoned! I have been poisoned!" Then she yelled some other things in German that I didn't understand. I was just about out of breath at this point so I slowed down to try to catch my breath but she kept running as fast as she could and was still yelling at the top of her lungs. I'm not sure who she was yelling at because I when I looked around I noticed that there were very few people out this early in the morning, but she kept on running and yelling.

I took one last look at her hauling ass down the sidewalk and that was the last time I saw her. And I thought to myself, "Well, that certainly didn't go very well, now, did it?"

And to this day, I still don't know if she really was sick or was faking it the whole time just to be able to make a quick and easy exit out of my life. If that really was her intention, then she could have done it a little more easily and with a lot less hassle. She could have gotten up at any time, said, "Okay, see you around, Ron," and just left.

I digested the contents of my stomach without any problems at all and had no pain, or stomach cramps, or any other issue. The entire ordeal is still a mystery to me, like the female of the human species was in general in those days, and still remains so to this day, in so many different ways.

I continued going to the King's Club regularly, and I even stood outside of the place after closing on many occasions, hoping to see her again, if nothing else just to find out if she was all right or not. I never saw her again, but I figured if she had really suffered from food poisoning that morning, I'm sure I probably would have heard about it one way or another, after all she did know where I lived and where I hung out.

...

The streets of Frankfurt were full of young American servicemen, both Army and Air Force, and I would see gangs of them prowling the streets downtown at all hours of the day and night looking for three things that young people the world over seemed to be looking for: sex, drugs, and rock-and-roll.

You could tell these were Americans from a long way off even though they rarely, if ever, wore their uniforms off base. But the way they looked might as well have been a uniform. They all had the same haircut, which was always the longest possible but still conforming to military regulations, which was very short in the back and the sides, and in the front, only reaching to the eyebrows, and no longer. And most of these guys, who were just barely older than I was, if at all, had the same regulation mustache, just short enough to pass inspection. And they all seemed to wear the same clothes which consisted of bell bottom Levi's jeans and T-shirts with various band logos on them.

I'd see groups of up to a dozen of these guys walking together down the main street downtown, usually drunk as hell and just looking for "action," which usually comprised one of the three above-mentioned things.

Sex could be bought easily and relatively cheaply in many areas of Frankfurt, and prostitution was semi-legal and more or less accepted and tolerated. In fact, there was a large two-story building that covered an entire square block in the downtown area that was one large red-light district. Inside on the ground floor, there were hundreds of working girls hanging around, and the upstairs area was where I assumed they went to service their customers.

There was an enormous amount of competition, so the prices were rock-bottom, I was told. There were girls from all over the world, not just from Germany and the rest of Europe, but I also saw a lot of oriental girls from Asia and others who were obviously from Africa.

I never did purchase what any of these women were selling mainly because of two reasons. First, even the rock-bottom price of thirty marks was a little out of my budget, just for a few minutes of fun. With that same amount of money, I could buy quite a lot of hash and I thought a purchase like that would provide me with more pleasure for my buck.

The second reason was, frankly, I was a little concerned about catching something that I didn't want. This was before the days of AIDS, of course, but it still was possible to walk away from an encounter with more than what you paid for. Condoms were used, but I still had my concerns. So, much like I did in Amsterdam, I just window-shopped.

But the thousands of American servicemen apparently didn't have such concerns because they were the prime customers for these working girls. They would come from all the various bases and other American military facilities around the entire area to partake in the pleasures that the city of Frankfurt offered. A little R & R in Frankfurt is what many servicemen waited for all month and was one of the main things they spent their paychecks on, I'm sure.

Another thing they spent their money on was drugs. Whenever I went to Shit Park to make a score for myself of a little hash, I would see lots of these same guys there with their regulation haircuts purchasing drugs of all kinds. I'm sure that some purchased enough so that they could take some back to their bases and re-sell them to guys who either couldn't get off base to do so themselves or didn't know how to go about doing it. And I'm sure that there were hundreds if not thousands of dollars' worth of American military paychecks spent in that one small park on a daily basis.

The third thing that these Americans were looking for in Frankfurt was rock-and-roll. There were concerts by big-name performers regularly at different venues in town. And not only were these shows attended by Germans, of course, but American servicemen would always make a point of showing up in droves as well. After all, rock-and-roll is the universal language and can be enjoyed by anyone, of any background, regardless of the language spoken. Both British and American bands would play big concerts in Frankfurt knowing there would be a full house for their performances and lots of tickets sold. Unfortunately, due to my meager earnings, I was unable to attend most of them, even though there were many bands that I would have loved to see perform live.

When Pink Floyd played Frankfurt in November, I again missed them, unfortunately. I had a chance to see them live in Amsterdam a few months earlier and missed them due to lack of funds, but this time the show was sold out when I tried to purchase my ticket.

One concert that I managed to attend was Alice Cooper when he played Frankfurt just nine days later at the same venue, the *Festhalle*. Alice had been one of my favorites ever since I listened to his song, "I'm Eighteen," over and over again on the midway of the carnival I had worked just a year and a half before. And I liked a lot of his other songs such as "Be My Lover," "School's Out," and "Under My Wheels." And he did not disappoint! He played all these songs and many more, and his stage show was visually exciting as well, with the guillotine, the live snake, and his bizarre makeup. As I walked into the venue, there were hundreds of American servicemen walking in with me, recognizable with

their identical regulation haircuts, but many were wearing makeup similar to Alice's, with the dark eye shadow and all the rest. The concert was chaotic and crazy, just as Alice and his band intended I'm sure.

One of the guitar players in his band had hair literally down to his knees, and he played the solo on "Be My Lover," right after Alice's line in the song, "And I play guitar in long-haired rock-and-roll band."

The tickets were slightly cheaper than the Pink Floyd show for some reason, but they still put on quite the spectacle, and everybody there enjoyed themselves immensely. Alice Cooper at the time was one of the strangest and exciting bands around, not only because of their great

music which young people the world over could relate to so easily, but also because of their spectacular live shows and performances, which, seemed to be more theater than just merely rock-and-roll. "Welcome to My Nightmare," indeed.

For the rest of that winter, I was still cold most of the time at work, but at least for the most part I was dry and warm in my little room. I went to work every day and then, on the weekends, I could usually be found at the King's Club enjoying myself, listening to bands, smoking hash, and drinking good German beer.

I did cross the bridge occasionally and visit my friend Mioshi, who was still living at the campground, but shortly after the New Year, I visited her for the last time. She told me that she felt she had been in Europe long enough and she was ready to go home to San Francisco. She gave me the address and the phone number of her parents' place, and told me that if I ever wanted to visit her or if I happened to come to San Francisco for any reason, to look her up and she would show me around that fabulous city.

She said that even if she wasn't living with her parents, they would always know where she was and how to get ahold of her. I also gave her the address of my mom and Jim's place in Madrid and told her the same thing. We hugged each other and said our goodbyes and promised that we'd see each other again one day, which I tried to do a couple of years later after I went to the States to live.

I can't say that I liked the weather in Germany, but I did like the openness and the freedom I felt while living there. I did try to save some money, but it seemed like all I made, I managed to spend somehow. My expenses included my rent, of course, but also other things that I couldn't avoid spending money on, such as the *Strasenbahn* fares, food, beer, and hash.

I ate out more often than I cooked at home, due to my limited cooking arrangements, and I got to know where all the cheap places to eat were located, and managed to try almost every kind of sausage made in the entire country including the *bratwurst, rostbratwurst, blutwurst, bregenwurst, knackwurst, landjager, leberwurst, leberkase, teewurst,* and of course my favorite: the *frankfurter*. They made some of these from such strange things like blood or liver, but the Germans always had a way to  make them all delicious. And served with an order of *pommes frites*, they always made a tasty and nutritious meal.

I very well might have stayed in Frankfurt for the rest of my life, or at least longer than the six months that I did stay there, if it wasn't for what happened one night in the King's Club.

One Friday night I was sitting at a table inside the King's Club, listening to a band that was covering Neil Young quite well, and accepting the *chillum* full of hash that was being passed around the club, when suddenly in walked two German policemen in their green uniforms and nightsticks. As I have already said, while it was accepted and tolerated it was by no means legal to smoke dope in the club, or even to possess it.

So suddenly a very dark and somber mood permeated the patrons of the club when the *polizei* started walking through the place. I'm not sure what they were looking for, perhaps a criminal suspect or maybe just to display their power, which Germans seemed to love to do on regular occasions. Everyone who happened to have in their hand something illegal, immediately put it out and tried to conceal it as well as possible.

As for me, I had my small hash pipe and a small amount of hash in my pocket and I suddenly became very paranoid.

So I got up and walked to the bathroom to see if I could hide my stash until the heat was gone. I walked into one of the toilet stalls in the men's room and looked around. There was a small sort of pipe thing about four inches in diameter sticking out of the wall about six inches below the ceiling of the restroom right above the stall. I looked around, making sure I was alone in the bathroom, and stood on top of the toilet and reached my hand up into the hole to see if it could be a place to put my stash, when lo-and-behold, my hand found a Marlboro pack. I opened it and looked inside and I saw that it was stuffed with twenty-eight individual packs of one gram each of pure methamphetamine: crystal meth.

Even though I was not a user of this particular drug, I realized the street value of an ounce of pure meth, so I just went ahead and put the Marlboro pack down the front of my jeans resting on my crotch, along with my pipe and my hash and casually walked out of the club, knowing that I had found a gold mine.

Obviously, someone else who had a reason to be even more paranoid than I was, had entered the same stall right before I did, had seen the pipe sticking out of the wall as well, and had gotten the same idea, which was to hide his shit until the *polizei* had left.

From spending time hanging around Shit Park, I knew that a gram of pure meth sold for around fifty dollars, and I had twenty-eight of them. I was going to be rich!

At first I wasn't totally sure what I had found, but I suspected what it was due to the fact that there was a lot of this drug around, especially around the King's Club. There was one guy by the name of Franz who would hang out in front of the club after it closed, along with me and a few dozen other people, and he would just stand there and shout

pathetically, "I need my shot, I need my shot!" I guess he was just hoping for some sympathy from someone.

And everyone around there knew that Franz was a meth head and would do absolutely anything to get it. He looked like one also, with only about half of his teeth left in his mouth, long stringy hair, extremely skinny and always with a vacant and a lost look in his eyes.

So my plan was to wait awhile until things cooled off and whoever it was who had lost the shit wasn't searching for it as hard anymore, and then I'd sell it. In the meantime, I had an ounce of this stuff. I was curious about it since I hadn't really done many hard drugs before, so I decided just to try it. I waited until the following Friday night when I'd have the entire weekend to get over it before work again on Monday morning.

I knew that a lot of users of this shit would shoot it in their vein, in order to get the rush from it and also so it would go further and not to waste any since it was quite expensive. But I wasn't about to do that; I hated needles and besides, I had plenty of the stuff. I was just planning to snort it.

Friday evening came around and I went out on the town as I usually did but this time with one of the little baggies of the stuff. I stopped at my favorite place and had a *frankfurter mit pommes frites* and eventually made my way down to the King's Club. After ordering a beer, I went to the bathroom and went into the same stall that I had found the stuff in and opened the baggie. I rolled up a ten-mark bill and put one side of it in my nose and the other into the baggie and sniffed. Wow! It went right to my brain instantly, and I felt a tingling rush all around the inside my head. And suddenly I felt incredibly energized, confident, and powerful, as if I could do anything, absolutely fucking anything!

I walked back out to the bar and looked around. Things seemed different, more alive, and everything was shimmering, electric, almost vibrating. Now I can see why people liked this shit so much. I sat back down and sipped my beer and listened to the band performing "Born to Be Wild," by Steppenwolf, and it sounded surreal, like I had never heard the song before. I got up on the dance floor and started to dance by myself, which I otherwise would never have done, but I didn't care. I just had to move, or I felt that I would explode.

I ended up dancing by myself to almost every song the band played until closing time, just taking one five-minute break to go to the bathroom again and do some more of the shit. When the club finally closed, I wasn't ready to go home and sleep. I was way too wound up and sleep was the last thing on my mind. So I walked and kept walking, and ended up walking all night long, all around the city. My teeth were clenched together and my fists as well, but I couldn't stop moving. I just had so much energy, and I was trying to walk it off and to make myself tired. Finally, the sun started to rise, and I found myself inside the

Haupbahnhof still gritting my teeth and full of energy. A few people were there waiting around for early trains and I was sure they were all looking at me and they all knew I was wired out of my mind.

Finally, I decided to just go home and see what would happen if I just lied down and tried to sleep. But once I walked back to my little room and sat down, I started to feel really shitty and really down. I tried smoking some hash but no matter how much I smoked, I could barely feel it, and couldn't seem to get stoned. So I took one more sniff of the other stuff and I felt great again.

I ended up sniffing more of the stuff every few hours the entire day and didn't sleep or eat anything at all. Saturday night came, and I went back to the King's Club and repeated what I had done the previous night and walked around the city again all night until dawn. Finally, on Sunday morning, I decided that I had to stop, no matter how shitty I felt. So I crashed all day Sunday. I felt terrible all day long, like I was sick with the flu or something, but eventually when nightfall came around, I could eat a little something and finally fell asleep very late at night, and I was able to make it to work on Monday morning.

The worst thing about doing all this stuff was that it accumulated inside my nostrils and the "crystals" of the shit would not dissolve. It felt like having tiny little rocks in my nose all the time, and no matter how much I would blow it, I couldn't seem to get it all out of me.

I don't know why, but I repeated this pattern every weekend for the next six weeks. I finally realized that if I stopped on Sunday morning, and forced myself to relax, by the afternoon, if I smoked enough hash, I could finally start to feel a little stoned and it would mellow me out somewhat, at least enough to be able to fall sleep by around midnight. But I really wouldn't start to feel normal again until around Tuesday afternoon or so.

Finally, after a month and a half of doing this shit every weekend, I realized that I had to quit it, and that if I sold all I had left, I couldn't do any more of it, so that is what I did.

I went down to Shit Park one Saturday afternoon and sat down on one of the benches there and waited. I didn't have the stuff with me because I didn't want to get ripped off, and I knew I had to be careful of that possibility, as well as being busted by the cops. So my plan was to find a buyer, offer him a great deal on it, and then meet up with him later to do the deal.

Before too long, I saw a guy walking around obviously looking for something or someone. He was an Airman; anyone could tell with his regulation haircut and mustache, his bell-bottom jeans and with his Alice Cooper T-shirt.

As he walked by me, I asked him, "Hey buddy, what you looking for?"

He gave me a good look and seemed to realize that I wasn't a cop, and so he said, "Meth. You know where I can get some?"

"Yeah, as a matter of fact, I do. How much you looking for?"

"As much as you got, man."

I looked at him closely and said, "Well, I know a guy that has about twenty-five grams that he wants to get rid of real quickly and he's willing to sell it pretty cheap. You interested in that much?"

"Oh, hell yes I am," he replied. "How much does he want for that much?"

"Well, thirty bucks a gram, so it would come to seven hundred and fifty. Can you handle that?"

"Shit man, that's a little more than half of what it usually goes for; is it good shit or what?"

"Yeah, it's good, but he just has to get rid of all of it at once. He doesn't want to sell it by the gram."

He looked at me closely again and said, "All right. But I'd have to come back tomorrow with the money, I don't have that much with me; would that be okay?"

"Yeah, that would be great, since I gotta get it from him, anyway. How about tomorrow at the same time and at this same bench? Will that work for you?"

"Yeah, man, that'll work, I'll see you then, okay?"

I nodded, and he walked away.

The next day, I was there on the bench at the same time and here he arrived wearing the same exact clothes. He sat down on the bench next to me, I looked around carefully, and I handed him one of the twenty-five grams I had and I said, "Here, why don't you go somewhere and taste it and come back if you're still interested, okay?"

He looked at me and asked, "You sure, man?"

"Yeah, go over to the bathroom over there and try it out," and I pointed to the public restroom.

"Okay, man," he said and got up and walked over to the restroom.

About five minutes later he came back with a big smile on his face and sat back down on the bench. We both looked around to make sure no one was watching, and he handed me an envelope and I handed him the shit, which was still in the same original Marlboro pack.

As I looked in the envelope and counted the money, he opened the Marlboro pack and looked inside. We both nodded at each other and he got up and before he walked away, he looked at me and said, "Thanks a lot for this, bud, this shit is going to make my work and a lot of other guys I work with jobs a lot easier. I really appreciate it."

"Hey, no problem man, I'm glad to be of service."

He walked away, and I realized that I had seven hundred fifty dollars in my pocket. That's more than I've ever had at one time in my life.

The next day, it was Monday, and I went to work as usual, but as I entered the warehouse, I went to Mr. Preston's office and told him that I was planning on quitting my job and that this would be my last week. We got paid every Friday, so I told him I'd work until then, so he had my one week's notice. He looked at me and asked why I was quitting, and I told him I was planning to return to Spain where my parents were. He nodded and said he understood and that if I ever wanted to come back and work, I'd always have a job waiting for me. I thanked him, walked out of his office and that Friday was the last day I worked for AAFES.

When I got back from work on my last day, I talked to my landlady and told her I'd be moving out that Monday and that she could keep the one week's worth of rent or so that I was owed since it wasn't quite my time to pay the monthly rent yet. She nodded that she understood; I'm not sure how since her English hadn't improved any and my German hadn't much either, but somehow she got the idea.

The next day, I went down to the *Haupbahnhof* and bought a one-way ticket from Frankfurt to Barcelona on a train that was leaving early the following Monday morning.

I was heading home to Spain once again after another adventure and another chapter of my young life. I felt quite a bit wiser than I was before I came to Germany and I had done what I wanted to do. I had proved to myself that I was able to not only live on my own, but I was also able to take care of myself. And I was returning to Madrid with a pocket full of money, instead of poor and broke with my tail between my legs. I had done it!

Chapter 22. Barcelona

"Experience is a truer guide than the words of others."
— *Leonardo Da Vinci*

On my way back to Madrid, I decided to spend a week or so in Barcelona since I had only stayed one night there with J.P. on my way north before I got on the train to Holland the previous summer. I had heard a lot about Spain's second-largest city almost my entire life. My brother John had stayed in the city for a week when he went there trying to get a job aboard a ship during his last year in Spain and had told me a little about it. On my way back to Madrid, I had the time and the money, so I stayed for about a week to get a chance to explore the city somewhat and get to know it a little.

Barcelona is a port city, unlike Madrid which is in the center of the Iberian Peninsula and is quite a distance from the sea. I was eager to investigate the port and the different ships in the harbor area since I had always been interested in ships and all things nautical.

The first thing I did when I got off the train was find a place to stay. I had just arrived from *Le Gare du Nord* in Paris where I had changed trains coming from Frankfurt. I had purposely gotten a sleeper car from Paris so I arrived in Barcelona early in the morning relatively well-rested. As in probably every major city in the world, in Barcelona there are a lot of cheap hotels around the major train stations for travelers. But I wanted to be closer to the downtown and the port area, so when I got off the train, I just started walking, and it didn't take long before I found my way to the center of the city to the famous promenade known as *Las Ramblas*.

This is the main street that leads down to the port area from the center of the city. There are two lanes for traffic going in each direction, but in between there is a very wide walkway that is the cultural center of

Barcelona. Along this walkway are countless outdoor cafes, small shops, and stands selling all kinds of items, and thousands of people strolling about. From this road, other smaller side streets lead off from it.

Once I found *Las Ramblas*, I got my bearings easily. As I was walking down each side of this thoroughfare, I looked up the side streets and this is where I saw quite a few small *pensiones* that looked rather inexpensive and therefore to my liking. I chose one at random. After talking to the proprietor, I paid for five nights and left my pack in the little room I had rented. As with all *pensiones*, it was just a small room with the bathroom down the hall, but it was quiet and safe and above all quite inexpensive at only one hundred pesetas per night or around $1.60 or so.

I had learned that the best way to find out about a place was by just walking around. The next couple of days, I spent a lot of time walking around the city and exploring it. One of the first places I wanted to see was the port area, so I spent a lot of time around there. It is a rather large harbor with all kinds of ships and vessels from all over the world. There were huge commercial cargo ships all the way down to a little dingy used to carry a yachtsman from his vessel to shore, and everything in between. There were even naval ships I assumed were from the Spanish Navy, and even one that I thought to be an American Navy vessel in port.

But there was one that really caught my eye; it was an exact replica of the Santa Maria, the ship in which Columbus sailed to the New World. Its official name was *"La Santa Maria de la Inmaculada Concepción,"* or "The Holy Mary of the Immaculate Conception." And here it was floating right next to the dock in the port of Barcelona. The Spaniards had found the original blueprints for the ship and they had painstakingly rebuilt a replica of the original ship, down to the very last detail.

Christopher Columbus is revered all over Spain as being not only a great ship captain and navigator but also as the man who "discovered" the New World. In Spanish, he is known as *Cristobál Colón*, and there are statues honoring him all over Spain from Barcelona to Cadiz.

The *Santa Maria*, as every school kid learns, was the flagship of the expedition and was only one of the three vessels that were under Colón's command, which included *La Pinta* (the Painted) and *La Niña*, (the Girl). The *Santa Maria* was the largest of the three and the one that Colón himself captained. It  had a single deck and three masts and was seventy-three feet long, comparable to an average-sized modern cruising yacht.

For a few pesetas, it allowed me, along with many other travelers to climb aboard her and look around. What surprised me the most was how primitive everything was, from the living quarters for the sailors and the captain's cabin, to the size of the rigging, the sails, and the almost complete lack of any navigational instruments. But above all, what impressed me the most was the size of her. For a ship like this to be able to cross the Atlantic was unbelievable to me, especially on a voyage where the captain and crew had no idea exactly where they were going or if they'd even reach land again after setting sail.

People can say what they will about Colón "discovering a new world," which of course had been inhabited by many people for many centuries long before he arrived, but no one can deny that it took an extreme amount of bravery and fortitude to do what he did. But, of course, this courage was mustered by the extreme poverty that was gripping Spain and all of Europe at the time, and this I'm sure contributed to his being as intrepid as he proved to be. I'm also sure that his greed and desire for riches and fame propelled him as much as anything else, as well as his crew. The fact that he died without even knowing what he had "discovered" makes the story even more interesting and intriguing.

I quite enjoyed exploring this replica of the *Santa Maria*, and it was quite an educational and eye-opening experience for me. While in Barcelona, I also had the opportunity to explore a much different type of sea-going vessel. It all started simply with a drink at a cafe.

I spent a lot of time in Barcelona sitting at outdoor cafes, partaking of two of my favorite activities: drinking, and people-watching. The city was perfect for this because along *Las Ramblas*, there were countless outdoor cafes up and down the thoroughfare. While living in Madrid for many years, I had perfected the art of making a drink last for quite a long time, but in Barcelona I discovered a new way of doing this. If I ordered a beer or coffee, the beer would get warm or the coffee would get cold after a short while, and it would require me to then order another one or get up and leave my table for a customer who was still consuming something. So what I would do was order a glass of cognac, with a glass of water as a chaser, and I could make it last for hours if I so desired.

I spent several sunny afternoons sitting at a table in an outdoor café along *Las Ramblas*, nursing a glass of good Spanish cognac, watching people walk by, and trying to imagine what their lives were like. This activity is an old European tradition which certainly predates the invention of television, and is probably just as entertaining, if not more so.

One day I was sitting at my table sipping my cognac when my attention was drawn away from the pedestrians walking by towards another table just a few feet away from mine. I heard voices conversing in English, and not the British kind, but instead the American variety. I turned to look in the direction of these voices and I saw two young guys about my age, talking and drinking bottles of *El Aguila* beer. They were obviously Americans, but I didn't get the impression that they were typical tourists. They both had rather short hair, and one guy had a full beard, while the other had a nicely trimmed goatee. And they were both wearing what looked like Navy-style, dark blue bell-bottom pants.

After a few minutes, one of the guys noticed me glancing at them occasionally and turned to me and said, "Hey, man, where you from? Are you American?"

I responded, "Yep, as a matter of fact, I am. Where you guys from?"

The guy who had spoken smiled and said, "Yeah, we're Americans too, we're both in the U.S. Navy and our ship is docked here in Barcelona and we're just enjoying a little shore time. You want to join us?"

I picked up my snifter of cognac and my glass of water and walked over to their table and said, "Okay, don't mind if I do. So you guys are in the Navy, huh?"

They both stood up, stuck out their hands and the guy who first spoke said, "Yeah, my name is Larry and this here is Bob, how you doing?"

I shook their hands and told them, "Nice to meet you guys, my name is Ron. So, what are you guys up to today?"

Larry smiled again and said, "Just enjoying a couple of cold ones before we gotta get back to our ship before dark."

"Yeah, I think I saw a Navy ship out there yesterday when I was hanging around the docks. So you guys are shipmates on that big ass ship, huh?"

Bob spoke up and said, "Yep, the LSD U.S.S. Hermitage. The best damn ship in the entire U.S. Navy!"

"LSD?" I asked with a big smile, "What the hell does that mean?"

Bob smiled back and told me, "Not what you're thinking, man. LSD stands for 'Landing Ship, Dock,' it's the type of vessel it is. Like almost everything in the military, it's ass backwards, or bass ackwards, like they always put the adjective after the noun, kind of like, 'Uniform, khaki' or 'Meals, ready to eat.' In this case it's a 'landing ship, dock.' Get it?"

"Yeah, I guess so, man. I know the military can get some things fucked up. My dad spent twenty years in the Air Force."

Bob smiled again and said, "Ah, so you're an Air Force brat, huh? But hey, don't worry, we won't hold it against you! What are you drinking? Let us buy you a drink."

"Okay, sure, I'm drinking *Fundador* brandy, but those *Aguilas* look pretty damn good."

"All right, let's get another round here," and he signaled to the waiter, by pointing to his half-empty bottle and raising three fingers in the air.

Larry looked at me and asked, "So Ron, what the hell is an American Air Force brat doing here in Barcelona? There's no Air Force base around here, is there?"

"No, but there's a big base just outside of Madrid called Torrejon, that's where I went to school."

"Oh, yeah, I've heard of that place," he said, "but you're still a long ways from home, aren't you?"

"Well, actually, I just returned from Frankfurt where I was working for AAFES for a while. And now I'm just getting ready to go back home to Madrid."

Larry nodded and said, "Well, it sounds like you get around somewhat, that's for sure."

"Yeah, and before that I spent all last summer in Holland, both in Amsterdam and in Rotterdam. Now that's a very cool place."

Bob chimed in and says, "Yeah, I heard that Amsterdam was full of freaks, is that right?"

"Yep, the whole city is full of them. There were so many heads there that they were sleeping in the fucking park, man!"

Bob smiled and said, "Wow, that has got to be pretty cool, man!"

I shrugged and said, "Not too cool if you were trying to get a job like I was; that's why I ended up going to Frankfurt and working for the damn American military."

By this time, the waiter had brought three iced cold *El Aguilas* over to our table and Larry reached into his wallet and handed him a fifty peseta note and told him to keep the change.

"*Muchas gracias, señor,*" the waiter said with a big smile.

The three of us lifted our beers and Larry said, "How about a toast, guys, to the United States Military! If it wasn't for them, we wouldn't be here!"

We all clicked our bottles together and then I said, "I got a toast for you guys; it goes like this, '*Salud, pesetas, amor y tiempo para disfrutarlas!*'"

They both looked at me with strange looks and Bob said, "Um, Ron, we're both still trying to learn Spanish, man. Would you care to translate?"

I smiled and said, "Health, pesetas, love, and time to enjoy them!"

They both smiled back and Bob said, "Now that's what I call a great toast, I'm going to have to remember that one."

So the three of us sat back, and we ended up having another couple of rounds and talking about all kinds of things, including a lot about their ship and about what life in the U.S. Navy was like, and in turn I told them a little about my adventures traveling and working in northern Europe.

Before too long, the sun was started to get low on the horizon and Bob said, "We gotta get back to the ship, our shore leave was only supposed to be until dark, so we ought to get going."

Larry agreed and said, "Yeah, that's the way it is when you're in the fucking military; there's very little freedom, but hey, it got us here, didn't it?"

I smiled and said, "Well, it was really great getting to meet you guys, man. And thanks so much for the beers, I'm going to have to return the favor sometime."

Then Larry said, "Hey, I got an idea, Ron. How would you like to see the Hermitage in person? We're allowed to bring visitors on board, you know. We could show you around if you're interested."

"Wow, that would be really cool, man," I said "I think I'd like that. When can we do it?"

"Well, let's see," Larry said, "my next day off is the day after tomorrow; will that work for you?"

"Yeah, sure, man, why not?"

"Okay, Ron, let's say I meet you right here at this cafe around noon the day after tomorrow, all right? And I'll take you aboard and show you around, okay?"

"Yeah, that sounds great. I'll be here. I'm really looking forward to it. I've never been aboard a ship like that before."

Bob looked at the both of us and said, "Well, shit, I gotta work that day, but I'll see you on board because that's where I'll be all day, anyway."

I smiled at them and said, "This has been really great, guys, I'm so glad I met you. And I'm really going to enjoy looking around your ship."

They both smiled and then Larry said, "Well, we gotta go, Ron, but I'll see you here at noon on Thursday, okay?"

"Yep, I'll be here, man."

They got up, and we shook hands all around again and we said our goodbyes and they walked back down to the port area.

I finished my beer, and I thought to myself, "Well, that was cool, and we'll see if Larry shows up or not."

And indeed he did. I was there waiting for him at the noon hour when he showed up and the first thing he said was, "Hey, Ron, good to see you. I wasn't sure you were gonna show, man."

I smiled at him and said, "Hey, man, I wouldn't miss it for the world." And off we went heading down to the dock area.

When we got to the ship, Larry and I walked up the gangplank and before actually boarding the ship, he told me, "Hold on a second, Ron, I just gotta get you checked in as a visitor; it'll just take a minute. You got your passport with you?"

"Uh, yeah, I also got my Military ID, if that will help."

"Yeah, that should work, give them to me and I'll get you checked in, okay?"

So I handed them to him and off he went, and in a couple of minutes he returned with a laminated badge with a clip which I attached to my shirt and then off we went, climbing down into the innards of the huge ship.

We went through gangways and hatches and up and down ladders and Larry was talking the entire time, telling me all about the ship. He explained that the ship was designed to load and unload cargo, vehicles, and just about anything else from the cargo hold area directing onto a dock and had the capability to do so both rapidly and efficiently. He went on and on about the number of sailors and officers aboard and many other details and information about the ship.

I was both fascinated and impressed because I had never seen anything like it before in my life and I told him so. He seemed to be proud, not only about the ship that he served on, but the U.S. Navy in general.

Finally, we got down to where the sailors' quarters were located and he showed me where he and his shipmates slept and lived and then I wasn't so impressed. I saw an area where the bunks were stacked three high and he told me that his bunk was where he slept, read, and hung around at while not working. I told him that at least when I was in jail; the bunks were only two high. But he told me that one gets used to it after a while and that the Navy believed it helped to create camaraderie between the sailors. I had to agree with him there.

Then he showed me the bathrooms that he along with the rest of the sailors used and again I was not very impressed. But I surmised that everything was so cramped because of the crowded conditions onboard a ship and I was sure it would be even worse on a submarine.

He also mentioned that the officers had much nicer "berths," as they were called in the Navy, and some even had their own private cabins. I told him that if I was in the Navy, I sure would prefer being an officer and he laughed and told me that he would have to agree with me on that.

He continued to show me around and we went to the galley which is Navy-speak for the kitchen area, and it looked very impressive with large tables and a spotlessly clean cooking area. I noticed two sailors preparing food, and they just smiled at me, shrugged and went back to what they were doing. Finally, we went up to the bridge, and I saw a couple of the officers looking at screens and doing something I couldn't figure out, but I noticed that they had the best view from anywhere on the entire ship because from up there they could look around and see a complete 360 degrees, not only of the deck of the ship but also all around the entire port area.

After about an hour, it seemed that there wasn't much more that Larry could show me, so we finally got off the ship and walked back towards *Las Ramblas,* talking all the way. We got back to our favorite cafe, and we sat down and the same waiter as the day before served us two cold beers.

Larry took a big swig and asked me, "Well, Ron, my friend, what did you think of the U.S.S. Hermitage?"

"Wow, I was really impressed. Thanks for showing me around; that was a real eye-opening experience, that's for sure. So tell me something, Larry, what made you join the Navy anyhow?"

"Well, I knew that I was going to get drafted, and so I joined the Navy instead of being forced into the Army and end up going to Vietnam, you know."

"Yeah, I know what you mean. I had a good friend who made it back from there, but it was in a fucking body-bag, man!"

"Yeah, I've known guys that the same thing happened to, or they come back really fucked up in the head, you know. How about you; how come you didn't get drafted, Ron? You're about the same age as me, right?"

"Well, I'll be twenty-one this summer, how about you?"

"Yeah, I turned twenty-one right before Christmas. But I got no regrets about the Navy, man. I joined up when I was eighteen, just a few months out of high school. And I've been able to see a lot of places and do a lot of things that otherwise I'd never be able to, you know?"

"Well, I signed up for the draft right after I turned eighteen right before I started going to college in San Antonio, Texas, where my dad's family is from."

And I told him briefly about what happened to me in the year or so that I was in the States after I finished high school at Torrejon, including my quitting college after one semester and then working in Denver for a while and then going to Myrtle Beach and working there for a while and a little about my traveling with the carnival and finally about ending up spending eighteen days in a Florida jail before returning to Spain where both sets of my parents lived.

He looked at me closely and said, "Wow, man! It seems like you've already had some adventures, both good and bad, right?"

"Yeah, and I still think this draft thing is going to come back and bite me one of these days because they don't really leave you alone or forget about you, do they?"

He shook his head and said, "Unfortunately they don't, my friend. They'll find you one way or another and if you don't comply with what they want you to do, you'll be a fucking draft-dodger. And you can go to prison for that, man."

"Damn, I've already had a taste of that of shit, and I know I can't handle it. I'll just have to wait and see what happens. But I haven't heard anything from them since the day I signed up for the selective service and I hope it stays that way."

"Well, good luck to you, Ron, however it turns out. But at least you were able to see a little of what it's like being in the Navy anyways, right?"

"Yeah, thanks to you, my friend. What's cool is that you guys can grow beards in the Navy. I remember all those Army and Air Force guys in Germany with their regulation mustaches and haircuts, and I felt sorry for them because they all looked alike, you know?"

"Yeah, the Navy lets us grow beards at least, but only so long, and they will hassle any guy that grows it too long. And they're also a little more relaxed on the hair, which is good. I couldn't stand it if we weren't at least allowed that, man."

"Well, I'll tell you one thing, if I had to join the military; it would either be the Navy or the Air Force. I couldn't stand to be in the Army or the Marines."

We sat at the cafe for the rest of the afternoon and drank several more beers each. We traded off buying rounds as is customary in Spain and in most civilized places. And by the time it got dark, Larry said that he had to get back to his ship once again, but the next night he would free because he would be working all day, so we agreed to meet up again, shortly after dark at the same cafe and we would go out and experience a little of Barcelona's night life.

So the next evening, I was at the cafe again right before dark, when Larry showed up again and we had a beer together and then he asked me, "Hey Ron, you ever heard of the *Barrio Chino* here in Barcelona?"

I looked at him and shrugged and said, "Um, no, can't say that I have. I didn't know Barcelona had a Chinatown."

"Well, according to some of the guys on the ship, it's not really a Chinatown, but more of the city's red-light district. You interested?"

"Well, I don't know man. I've seen a lot of red-light areas. Hell, at the one in Amsterdam, the girls just sit there in front of open windows and you can just walk by and take your pick."

"Well, some guys were telling me that the *Barrio Chino* here in Barcelona is one of the best in the world. And some of those old-timers have literally been around the world, and they'd know."

"Okay, sure, I'm interested. Let's do it, man."

"All right, I know it would be a lot easier to go with someone that speaks Spanish like you do. That way I'll know what the hell the girls are saying, not that I want to have a really long conversation with them, I'd rather be doing something else, right?"

And he smiled his big grin, and I smiled back.

So we finished up our beers and walked up *Las Ramblas.* It didn't take long because he seemed to know more or less where he was going and soon we were in a very seedy and poor-looking area of the city. There were a lot of old and decrepit buildings around and a lot of ancient looking bars along the very narrow streets that we were walking through. Every so often, there would be a couple of sleazy-looking women standing around, leaning up against a wall or meandering down the sidewalk with apparently no destination in mind.

We went ahead and entered one of the bars and I realized that it wasn't too much different from the *Bar Americanos* that I was familiar with in Madrid, except this was a lot more run down and not as nearly as nice as some places in Madrid that I remembered. We walked up to the bar and ordered a couple of beers and took a good look around. The place wasn't really that crowded but there were a lot of women hanging around who were obviously working-girl types. They were wearing very skimpy outfits with plenty of flesh showing and lots and lots of makeup. But unlike the *Bar Americanos* in Madrid, these girls weren't working behind the bar, but instead were just standing or sitting around the place.

There was music playing from somewhere and a couple of the girls were off to one side, swaying slowly to the music and trying to look as sexy as possible. But I noticed that they all had a profound look of boredom on their faces.

Larry was grinning ear to ear and said "Wow, man, this place is full of pussy, isn't it? We really got our pick here, don't we?"

I nodded and said, "Yeah, it sure looks that way, doesn't it? Quite a few to choose from, huh?"

Before too long, one of the girls ambled over to us at the bar and said, "*Hola muchachos, que están haciendo esta noche? Quieren comprarme un trago?*" "Hey guys, what are you doing tonight? You want to buy me a drink?"

Larry looked at me and asked, "What did she say, Ron?"

I looked back at him and replied, "She wants us to buy her a drink."

"Well, all right, let's buy her one then."

So he signaled the bartender who came over and he gestured to him for another round of beers and to include one for her as well.

But she looked at him and said, "*No, para mi, whiskey!*"

Larry shrugged and said to the bartender, "Okay then, one whiskey for the señorita."

He came back with two beers and a small shot glass of whiskey and Larry asked him, "How much, señor?"

The bartender said, "*Dos cientos cincuenta pesetas, señor.*"

I looked at him and said, "*Dos cientos cincuenta pesetas! Para dos cervezas y un whiskey. Caramba! Que caro!*" "Two hundred and fifty pesetas for two beers and a whiskey? Wow! How expensive!"

The bartender said with a sigh, "*Es un whiskey especial para las señoritas, señor.*" "It's a special whiskey for the young ladies, sir."

I looked at Larry and told him, "It's two hundred and fifty pesetas, he says it's a special whiskey for the girls, Larry."

He reached into his wallet and said, "Well, shit man, we're definitely not going to buy her another one at that price, that's for sure."

So I became the translator between the girl and Larry. She told us her

name was *Clarita* and before too long, Larry wanted to know what her price was, so I tried to delicately ask her this information. But she was very upfront about it, very much like the vendor at a market telling me the price of a kilo of tomatoes. She told me it was five hundred pesetas and they could go to her little room which was just down the street.

Larry looked at me and then at her and said, "Okay, you wait here Ron, I'll be back in a little while. And if you decide to take one of these girls for a ride and if I get back while you're gone, I'll just wait for you here, okay?"

I looked at him, smiled and said, "Okay, Larry, have fun, man."

He and Clarita walked out of the place after she chugged her shot of whiskey and Larry downed the last of his bottle of *El Aguila*.

So I was by myself now, but not for long, because almost as soon as Larry and Clarita walked out of the place, another girl came up to me with a big smile and said, *"Hola, mi amor, tu tambien quieres ir al cielo?"* "Hello, my love, so do you want to go to heaven as well?"

I looked at her and smiled and said, *"Porque no? Y tu como te llamas, señorita?"* "Why not? And what is your name, young lady?"

She smiled again and said, *"Me llamo Maribel, porque no vamos ya, mi amor."* "My name is Maribel, why don't we go already, my love."

So after assuring that the price of her tomatoes was the same as Clarita's, I finished my beer and we headed out the door. While walking the block or so to her room, I looked closely at her face and noticed that underneath the makeup, she was probably pushing forty years old or more, and at one time was quite the beautiful woman, but the life she had lived had left its toll on her. The wrinkles on her face and the bags under her eyes were a testament to the hard life she had lived. She is also at least several kilos overweight from an ideal figure.

She was not much for chit-chat; she was all business and didn't care to indulge in any small talk. We climbed the two flights of stairs of her building and she unlocked a door and we entered a small room that was obviously where she lived and where she conducted her business. There was a large cross hanging over the single bed and a small dresser against one wall and a closet in the corner. On the dresser were several small picture frames with black and white photos of family members, I assumed. There was a sink and a toilet behind a curtain in the other corner, but no shower or bath that I could see.

She asked me for the five hundred pesetas and she took it and went over to the dresser and put it in the top drawer in a little box. She took off her clothes, and I did the same, and before long we were both naked and on the bed. She slipped a condom over me and we got down to business, or rather her business. Things progressed as they normally do in a situation like this, but I noticed one big difference between having sex with a working girl and one who was not getting paid.

She seemed to be in a major hurry to get it done and as quickly as possible, and even though she acted like she was having a great time, I suspected that it was just an act to spur me on and to get me to get it over with quicker. Her moans of delight and ecstasy were not exactly an academy-award-winning performance to say the least, but in the state of lust I was in, I was not exactly a good judge of this by any means.

Within a few minutes, it was all over and so was I. She slowly took the condom off me and reached over and put it in a wastebasket near the bed. Then she got up and went over to the toilet and began to clean herself. When she had finished, she got up and grabbed a robe from a hook on the wall, put it on and looked at me still sitting on the bed and said *"Vamanos! Ya esta hecho, tienes que irte ya, muchacho."* "Let's go! It's done, you gotta go now, kiddo."

So I put my clothes back on and walked out the door, feeling a little ashamed and somewhat guilty for reasons I couldn't understand, but I managed to shake it off by the time I got down to the bottom of the stairs.

I got back to the bar and Larry was waiting there for me drinking another beer and he had a big smile on his face.

"So you went for it, did you man?" he asked me.

I smiled sheepishly and said, "Yep, I guess I got an offer I couldn't refuse!"

"So how was it?"

"Well, not too bad, I guess, how about you?"

"Not worth writing home about, but not too bad either. She certainly had a way with her mouth though, that's for sure!"

I frowned and asked him, "With her mouth? Damn, I didn't get any of that, man!"

"Well, I had to tip her another hundred pesetas, but it was well worth it."

"Shit, I didn't think of that, man."

He smiled, took a big swig of his beer and asked me, "Hey, Ron, you know how to make a hormone?"

"Um, no. How do you make a hormone?"

"Well, there's two ways, you can either give her a great tip, or refuse to pay her! Ha!"

I laughed and ordered another beer from the bartender who was doing his best to ignore us, for some reason. We each had one more beer, and we headed out and walked back to *Las Ramblas* and found our favorite cafe and sat down for one more cold one.

He looked at me seriously and said, "You know we ship out of here the day after tomorrow, right?"

"Shit, I didn't know that, Larry. Where you all heading next?"

"To Italy, to Naples I think they said. You ever been there?"

"Um, no, can't say that I have. You looking forward to it?"

He smiled and said, "Well, another port and another girl, or another girl with some port in her, ha!"

I laughed and told him, "Well shit, Larry, I'm going to miss you, buddy."

"Well, I'll tell you what, amigo, I can meet you one last time tomorrow evening if you'd like and I'll bring a present for you to remember me by, okay?"

"Sure, Larry, that sounds great man. But you don't have to do that, you know."

"No, I want to, man. It's just something for you to have as a souvenir, okay?"

"All right, man, if you want to, I guess."

So the next night, I met up with Larry one last time at our favorite cafe and he had a bag with him in his hand. He gave it to me and I opened it up and looked inside and I took out a brand-new pair of official U.S. Navy bell-bottom dungarees, with the button-up front, dark blue in color, and just my size, thirty by thirty.

I smiled and said, "Wow, Larry, what a very nice present, how did you manage to get these for me? Don't they assign certain uniform items to you?"

He shrugged and said, "Well, I work in the ship's laundry sometimes and those are real easy to come by, so don't worry about it."

"Okay, well thanks very much, Larry. I really appreciate it, amigo."

"Well, you're welcome. Wear them in style and think of me and our good times together, okay?"

"Yep, I'll do that."

Before he left, he gave me his F.P.O. address, which is the Navy's version of the A.P.O. and I gave him my mom's address in Madrid and we told each other that we'd keep in touch.

We ended up exchanging a couple of letters over the next several months and then we lost touch and I never heard from him again, and all I have left are the memories.

I ended up staying in Barcelona a few more days after Larry's ship sailed and I indulged in buying tomatoes a couple of more times from other vendors, but it never seemed to get all that much better. I even took Larry's tip of a tip, but it still felt contrived and artificial in so many ways. But when you've had a lot of drinks along with the raging hormones I had going on at that age, it was fun, exciting, and an adventure to be had. I also learned a lot about women in general and the female side of things and I considered it all to be a part of my education and part of becoming a man.

I checked my money supply and realized that I had spent over half of the stash I had from Frankfurt, and I didn't want to get back to Madrid dead broke, so I decided to call it quits and head home before I had nothing left. And I was feeling perhaps a little wiser in the ways of the world and with a really nice pair of new genuine U.S. Navy bell-bottoms as well.

Chapter 23. Madrid Once Again

*"Everybody's youth is a dream,
a form of chemical madness."*
— F. Scott Fitzgerald

Returning to Spain always felt like a homecoming to me. It is the only real home I ever knew and the only place where I felt like I somewhat belonged. And this makes sense, because at this point of my life, I had spent just over half of it in this beautiful and wonderful country.

Getting back to Canillejas where my mom and Jim were living and looking around and seeing the flat mesa near Torrejon on the horizon made me feel something deep and profound, a real sense of belonging and knowing that these were the only roots I ever had really dug in my entire life.

But almost immediately, I was faced with a couple of problems. It turned out that somehow, the Selective Service had gotten my mom's address and they had sent a letter to me, in care of her, at her local address in Canillejas, Spain, while I was living in Germany.

Basically, what this letter said was that I was to report for my Selective Service induction on a certain date that had already passed at this point. I had signed up for the Selective Service a few days after my eighteenth birthday in the summer of 1970 when I was in San Antonio, Texas, preparing to enroll in college there. And as far as they were concerned, I was trying to avoid my selective service commitment by being out of the country in Europe.

With my mom's help, I composed a letter to the draft board in San Antonio telling them the actual truth of my situation. These facts were as follows: that I was born in Europe and had spent most of my life here, and I considered it to be my home. And although I did return briefly to the States right before my eighteenth birthday to attempt going to college at S.A.C. in San Antonio, that had not worked out for me. So even though that is where I turned eighteen and where I had signed up for the Selective Service, I had now returned to my home here in Spain where I lived. And that I was sorry, but I just didn't have the funds to pay for a round-trip ticket to San Antonio merely to go through their induction process. I asked if there was any way I could do this process in Europe, perhaps at one of the bases in Germany, if it was not possible to do it here at Torrejon Air Base.

I sent off the letter and hoped for the best. At least I can say that I was in communication with them and that I was not really a draft dodger because if I was, I wouldn't be sending them letters, I figured.

In the meantime, the question still arose of what I was going to do with my life. I was back sleeping on the couch in Jim's office in their small *piso* in Canillejas and although I did feel welcome; I knew it was only temporary at best and that I needed to do something else with my life.

Of course, I looked up my old friends. Andy was in his last year of high school and again I hung around with him and his family a lot. And I met someone through him who had a big impact on my life for several years to come. Andy asked me to meet him one Friday evening at a little bar right below the *piso* where a mutual friend of ours lived by the name of Carmelita. She was an American girl about the same age as Andy who had had gotten kicked out of MHS the year before, and was living with her mom and her sister at their place near *Estadio Bernabeu* (the soccer stadium), which was right on Avenida Generalissimo, not too far from Plaza Castilla.

The little bar was right below their apartment building and he had asked me to join him there that evening because he wanted me to meet someone. I had already known Carmelita for a while when I lived in Madrid before when I was going to school, so she was an old friend, and I knew that it couldn't have been her that he had wanted me to meet.

I got there a little early, and I was sitting at a table in the bar chatting with Carmelita, who was a very nice girl and was a real pot head. And even though she was a good friend, and we enjoyed each other's company a lot, she was not really my type. She had a very rebellious type of personality and had got kicked out of school for having gotten caught smoking in the restroom too many times, along with other violations of the school's rules. She always wore black and a lot of dark makeup and had a unique and distinct personality.

After a little while, Andy walked into the place with a girl whom I had never met before. They sat down and he introduced her as his new girlfriend, Lizzy. Her real name was Elizabeth, but everyone just called her Lizzy, he told me. We chatted a little, and it turns out she was in her last year at MHS just like Andy, and she lived out at Royal Oaks with her family. She told us that she spoke perfect Spanish because her mother was Spanish and her father was a Mexican-American from southern California who was in the Air Force and stationed at Torrejon.

I think from the moment she spoke that I was smitten with her. She seemed to have a personality that for some reason I was attracted to. Not only did she have this certain way of talking and carrying herself, but she was beautiful as well. And she seemed not to be the typical girly girl, who was mostly concerned about her clothes and her makeup being just right, but instead she was more like a guy, with an old army jacket and tattered blue jeans on and she looked rather disheveled to put it mildly. She had no makeup on and her hair was long and frizzy and reached down to the middle of her back, and to me she looked like a real true hippy chick and she was absolutely beautiful in my eyes.

Andy and Lizzy were sitting very close together, and he had his arm around her and I could tell that they were quite into each other. We all had a few drinks and then we went upstairs to Carmelita's place and smoked a few tokes of some Moroccan hash and we all relaxed. She went over to her record player and put on a few albums and told us that her older brother Jack was a musician and was in a pretty good local band and not only were they playing around town quite a lot but they were also trying to cut a record.

After a couple of hours had passed, our little party had broken up and the three of us left Carmelita's house and went home. But I still couldn't seem to get Lizzy out of my mind. I felt guilty about it because she was the girlfriend of one of my best friends, and I really felt bad about the feelings I had. But because of the respect and the deep friendship I had for Andy, I kept my feelings to myself.

A few weeks later, I was with Andy over at his house and I asked him about Lizzy, and he told me that they had broken up. When I asked him why, he just mumbled something about them not being very compatible with each other. When I pursued this line of questioning a bit further, he finally admitted that she just wasn't really into the sex thing very much like he was, so they just decided to split up.

When I heard this news, I felt very conflicting emotions going on. First, it was great news that she was not with him anymore and therefore available, but on the other hand, if she wasn't into the "sex thing" very much, then how would I be able to handle something like that, because I definitely was into it, or at least I wanted to be.

But I didn't see her for quite a while after that because I got some rather alarming news right around that time. I received a letter from the Selective Service Board in San Antonio, Texas and they had obviously received the letter I had sent to them a short while earlier. Their letter said that even though it appeared that I was a resident of Europe, I had signed up for the draft at their office there in San Antonio, and as far as they were concerned, my permanent place of residence was Texas and therefore I was in violation of military selective service laws and I was still ordered to report for my induction process into the United States Military as soon as possible or I'd be considered to be a draft-dodger and face appropriate charges and consequences. The letter also said that regardless of my circumstances concerning my inability to pay for an airline ticket to Texas that was no excuse and also they did not allow the induction process to be done at any American Military facility overseas.

I discussed this letter with my mom and Jim and we decided that it might be better if I returned to the States to see what I could do to straighten this whole thing out. They agreed to pay for a one-way ticket to Dallas and from there my brother John would pick me up at the airport and I could stay with him until I got this mess fixed.

My brother had his own adventures since I had seen him last in Denver in 1971. After I had left that city and went to Myrtle Beach, the girl he had been seeing in San Antonio had came up to Denver and shortly after that, they drove the "blue beast" out to San Diego to try to make their lives there. He was able to get a job washing dishes at a Mexican restaurant and for a while he was able to save a little money.

She was able to collect food stamps and after a couple of months; they loaded up the car with lots of beans, rice and canned goods that she was able to get with her stamps and they headed south into Mexico for a grand adventure. They were gone for about three months, camping out along the way and they made it all the way down to Mazatlán, before running out of food and money and heading back north.

They entered the States again at the port of entry of Nogales, Arizona, and were almost totally broke, both sick from Montezuma's revenge, and barely made it to Phoenix where they looked up my Mom's good friend, Josie, who was living there. She helped them out a little, and they then drove back to Texas and settled at a little town about twenty miles outside of Fort Worth called Cleburne. He got a job, and they found a great place to live. It was an old farmhouse on 35 acres of mostly wooded land between Cleburne and another little town called Keene, Texas. The rent was only sixty-five dollars per month, so they were thrilled with the place. They started a garden and raised rabbits in the large barn on the property and Janie took care of things around the property while he worked.

When I arrived at the Dallas/Fort Worth airport from Madrid, John was there to pick me up. It was great seeing him again after such a long time and we had a lot of catching up to do. He told me all about his adventures traveling in Mexico and I told him a little about my travels and adventures since I had seen him last. He was working at the time as a bricklayer's helper and he told me he was sure the bricklayer could use some more help, so the next day I went with him to the job site, which was a large house being built in a nearby town and the guy hired me on the spot.

The job paid $2.50 per hour, but it was backbreaking work. Our job was to provide Barney, the bricklayer, with the supplies he needed to get the walls of the house built. We had scaffolding set up, and he stood on it to lay the bricks while we supplied him with both the bricks and the mortar to build the walls with. The mortar which we called "mud" had to be mixed in the portable cement mixer he pulled behind his truck and set up at the job site. After mixing a batch, we would load it into a wheelbarrow and take it over to where he was on the scaffolding, and shovel it up to him. And we had to lift a load of bricks over our heads as well to put them on the scaffolding for him to be able to lay them. It was very hard work, but we were both young, fairly strong and had a lot of energy and determination to get the job done.

We got paid weekly, and we usually got some overtime which helped a lot. Barney just wrote us each a check every Friday for the hours we had put in for the week and he didn't take any deductions out, but instead told us that our taxes were up to us to pay at the end of the year. And in the evenings, we would kick back in the living room of the old farmhouse, smoke a little Mexican weed, drink a couple of Lone Star beers and watch the old black-and-white TV they had. On the weekends, we would drive the "blue beast" into the city of Fort Worth and find something interesting to do. Sometimes we would go to a movie or go to see a band play or just hang around with some friends that John had made in town. They had parties regularly which were always a lot of fun.

I was saving as much of my money as possible by not having to pay rent and only contributing for groceries, beer, and weed. I was still reluctant to go to the Selective Service board in Dallas because I wasn't sure what to expect, and frankly because I really didn't want to be drafted, which I'm sure is what they had in mind for me.

One afternoon something happened that once again proved to change my life forever in a very big way. It was a typical day at work for John and me, but when we got home, we were dealt with a big surprise. As we walked into the door, Janie told us that she had two visitors at the house that morning while we were at work. Two men wearing black suits, white shirts, and black ties had knocked at the door of the house and had asked her about me.

They said they were from the FBI and were looking for me for draft evasion and they asked her if she knew of my whereabouts. Being the quick-thinking young lady that she was, she realized that I was in some deep trouble, so she just told them that all she knew was that I was living in Spain where my parents were. And that every once in a while, John would get a postcard or a letter from me postmarked from Madrid. This seemed to satisfy them because all they had to say to her after that was for my brother to contact them if he heard anything from me, and they left their business card with the address and phone number for the FBI office in Dallas.

When she told me this, I absolutely freaked out, as one can imagine. And suddenly I realized that I really was on the FBI's infamous "black list" and I was a *wanted* man. I couldn't go to the induction center now because I'd be charged with draft evasion and possibly thrown in jail. I had to come up with some kind of plan, so I decided I would just go back to Spain yet again.

By this time, I had worked almost a solid month as a bricklayer's helper and had I saved up quite a lot of money and it was just about enough for a one-way ticket from Dallas back to Madrid. So within three days of this unexpected visit from these men in black, I was on an airplane flying back to Spain. I was silently panicking before boarding the plane and when I showed my passport to board the international flight; I was sure I'd be hauled away in handcuffs. But I got on the plane without a problem but I didn't relax until I went through customs and got my passport stamped and was walking out of the terminal at Barajas.

I felt that I had avoided a major catastrophe, and I was so relieved to be back on Spanish soil. The very next day, again with the help of my mom, I composed another letter to the draft board saying in effect that here I was, still living in Spain and that I still couldn't afford the round trip flight to the States and back just to go through their induction process and asked them what they thought I should do. Again I settled back in the life I had a month or so earlier, but I was very determined to do something with myself besides worry about the draft.

I had a friend whom I had met through Juan, who was Maruja's son, who was my Mom's best friend in Spain and had been for many years. This friend of Juan's name was Raymundo and he and his family lived in Canillejas as well, not too far from Maruja and Juan's place in *Las Palomas.* Raymundo was a Puerto Rican guy whose family had lived in Madrid for many years and both his father and mother were medical doctors and worked at hospitals in the area.

He was a couple of years older than I was and he always considered himself to be a kind of Playboy type of guy. He liked fast cars and even faster women. He drove an Alfa Romeo sports car with a convertible top and five on the floor. It was not only a fast and sporty car but he was very proud of it as well, and I'm sure it helped him  with his self-image of being a Playboy and I'm also sure it helped out a lot with him getting girlfriends, which he seemed to have plenty of around most of the time.

Ray was taking some classes at the University of Maryland (Overseas Division) and they held these classes on base at the high school during the evenings when regular classes were over. Most of the students were airmen stationed at Torrejon who were trying to get an advanced education while in the Air Force. The classes offered were fully accredited, and they accepted just about anyone, active military or not.

I decided to take a few classes there to not only further my education but also to show that I was doing something constructive and creative to both sets of my parents. After all, a 21-year-old man can't just do nothing. He has to be doing something with his life besides smoking pot and listening to rock-and-roll records all the time.

I signed up for classes that were to start in a couple of weeks. I took classes I thought I'd be interested in and they even accepted my transcript from the classes that I had taken at S.A.C. so I was able to take courses that were based on the ones I already had taken and passed in San Antonio, including a writing class, a humanities class and a social studies class.

Since my friend Ray lived just a couple of blocks from me in Canillejas, I often caught rides with him out to the base where he went for his classes as well. It was great to get a ride with him because he liked to drive fast and he had the vehicle to do so. And I think he liked to show off a little about how fast his car could go, so we'd make it out to the base more quickly than I'd ever gotten there before.

I looked up Andy again, and we hung out a lot together but I never told him about the feelings I had for his ex-girlfriend, Lizzy. I saw her a few times around base but we never actually went on a date or anything like that. So, like a lot of things in my life, I decided that I would just wait and see what happened.

Jim wasn't doing any better with his battle with the bottle. Not only was his heavy drinking affecting his health but also his relationship with my mom and their marriage. Finally, she told him that he had to get professional help and quit drinking or she would leave him. At the hospital on base, there was a program for alcoholics that involved a hospital stay in order to dry out and to avoid the "D.T.s" as much as possible. So he agreed to give it a go and was admitted into the hospital for several weeks to try to get him off the booze.

My mom went out to the base every day to spend time with him and quite often I would accompany her. On many occasions, she would let me drive their Opal around the base while she was at the hospital visiting Jim. I liked to do this because I got a chance to improve my limited driving skills as well as enjoying the freedom and convenience of having a car to drive around in. But she always told me to not ever leave the base and to make sure I was there to pick her up when she was ready to go home in the evening.

One afternoon, after she went into the hospital for her daily visit with Jim, I took the car and was driving around the base as I usually did. I stopped at the service club and looked around but didn't see anyone I knew, so I went over to the bowling alley with the same result. So I was just aimlessly driving around when I drove by the front gate and I saw someone I thought I recognized sitting on the hitch-hiking bench. Just past the main entrance to the base, benches were set up with signs over them saying were the rider wanted to go. One said, "Torrejon

Apartments," another said, "Downtown," and yet another said, "Royal Oaks."

Sitting on the bench that said "Royal Oaks" was none other than the girl who I thought I was secretly in love with: Lizzy. So I made a quick decision in my mind right then. I looked at my watch and saw that it was only about 4:30 in the afternoon or so and I didn't have to meet my Mom until 7 p.m. so I had two-and-a-half hours till I had to pick her up. I knew that it was about a one-hour drive to Royal Oaks on the back road, so I'd have enough time to take Lizzy home and still make it back to the base to meet my Mom. So I just went for it.

I slowly drove through the main gate and came to a stop right in front of her on the bench. I leaned over, opened the passenger's side window and asked her, "Hey Lizzy, want a ride?"

She looked at me and said, "Sure, Ron, why not?"

She opened the door and got in and off we went. We started talking about various topics as we were driving along and soon the conversation turned to her school and the fact that she was really looking forward to graduating soon because she was tired of living at home with her parents, especially her father who was very strict and didn't understand her at all.

We talked a little about our mutual friend Andy and his family, yet I was reluctant to ask her about what happened between them and why they broke up. Being the shy and inexperienced young man that I was, I was also reluctant to actually ask her out on a date, so I just kept the chat very casual and relaxed, and I was trying my best to show her that I was not only a guy who had a car to drive her home in, but also that I was at least slightly charming and a nice and decent guy. I was honest and told her that the nice Opel GT I was driving was my mom's car and I was just borrowing it from her.

The back road from the base to Royal Oaks was a very rough road, two lanes the entire way, and there were some patches that not only had some bad potholes but also some very sharp and dangerous curves that required slowing down considerably to make safely. And what happened on that road that evening was a combination of an inexperienced driver and a driver who was trying to impress a girl whom he liked and was probably going faster than he should have been.

They called the road the "back" road because it totally avoids going "downtown" Madrid. Instead, it's an older road that goes through the countryside that lies between the base and Royal Oaks. About half way there, we came upon a sharp curve to the right and I was traveling way too fast to keep the little car on the road. So I ran off the road and ended up it a ditch. Luckily neither one of us was hurt at all, and so we just got out of the car to access the situation.

The front of the car had hit an embankment of soft dirt and the front axle was buried up to the front fender and was not going anywhere. I got back into the car and tried to back it out, but it was stuck and would not move. I was feeling shame, anger, embarrassment, and disappointment in almost equal parts, among the many other emotions going on in my head, but I tried to keep it positive and not freak out too badly.

I told Lizzy that I was very sorry about what happened, but it looked like I would not be able to give her a ride all the way home after all. About this time, another driver had stopped and had gotten out of his car to see what was going on, and it turned out that he was an American serviceman returning home from the base. I told him what had happened and asked him if he would give Lizzy a ride the rest of the way to Royal Oaks while I would see about getting a ride back to the base. He was a very nice older man who said his name was Sergeant Jackson, and he insisted on doing both. So after we got into his car, he drove the rest of the way to Lizzy's house and dropped her off, then he gave me a ride all the way back to the base hospital where I had to confront my mom and Jim and tell them what happened.

After I thanked Sargent Jackson again and even offered some money for the ride which he refused, he left me at the base hospital parking lot. Before I went up to Jim's room, I checked my watch and noticed that I wasn't really that late because barely two hours had passed since I had left the base. I walked into the room and Jim was sitting up and having dinner, so I asked him how he was doing and all he replied was that he really wanted a drink badly, but besides that he was okay. I smiled and told him I had something to take his mind off all that.

So I told them the entire story about what had happened and the fact that their car was sitting on the side of the road about halfway to Royal Oaks. My mom got furious and asked me why I would do something like that and disobey her instructions about me staying on base while driving their car. I explained about Lizzy and the fact that I really thought I was in love with her and I just wanted a chance to spend some time with her and giving her a ride was one way I could do that. She calmed down after a while and asked me what we were going to do about the car. I suggested we use the telephone at the hospital and call a *Grua*, (a tow-truck) and tell them approximately where the car was located and then call a taxi to take us out there and meet the driver and then ask him where a good place would be to take it to get fixed.

She and Jim decided that this would probably be the best course of action so we said goodbye to him and after she told him that she'd see him the next day, we went downstairs to use the phone. We contacted the *Grua* and told them where the car was located and then we called a taxi and it took us out to where the car was. We got there just before the tow-truck had arrived and soon the car was put onto the truck and we asked the driver where a good place to get the repairs done was. He told us of a body repair place he knew, so we got the address and told him to tell the shop that we'd meet them there the next day, and then we got back in our taxi, who was waiting patiently for us, and went home to Canillejas.

I felt terrible about the entire ordeal, but thankfully the next day when we went to the body shop, the damage was not as bad as it looked and after leaving the car there for a couple of days, and paying them several thousand pesetas, the car was as good as new. Needless to say, I didn't drive the Opel much after this experience.

But I wanted a car of my own, and after a little persuasion on my part, my mom and Jim decided to buy me a cheap older car for myself. Our first thought of a car for me was a SEAT 600, which were the smallest SEAT made and the most inexpensive.

They were very small two door cars with a 600 cc displacement engine and there thousands of them all over Spain, being one of the most common cars in the country. In fact, my mom had a yellow one when we lived in Alicante and it proved to be quite reliable and took us from Madrid to Alicante many times with her, my brother, me, our dog and our entire luggage all loaded into the little car. And since they were so common, parts and repairs could be found easily and were inexpensive.

But when I mentioned to my friend Andy about my possibly buying a car, he suggested that I talk to his sister's boyfriend, Antonio, whose father was the head salesmen at one of the local Citroen dealers in Madrid. So I was over at Andy's house one day when Antonio was there with Marie, Andy's sister, and I asked him if his dad could get me a good deal on a Citroen, perhaps. Of course, he said yes, and that he would talk to him and make sure I would get a great deal on one. He asked me if I wanted the *Dos Caballos* model which is the smallest and most common Citroen that is made. I told him that was probably what I was looking for since it was the most inexpensive model available too.

So the next day, I went down to Antonio's father's dealership in the *Chamartin* area of Madrid with my mom and Jim. Jim was out of the hospital by this point, but still battling the bottle, and trying desperately to stay sober. Antonio met us there, and he introduced us to his father, Señor Ramirez, and we looked at several *Dos Caballos* that he had on the lot. We ended up buying a dark blue 1964 Citroen *Dos Caballos* for 35,000 pesetas, or a little less than six hundred dollars.

The Citroen 2 CV, or the *Deux Cheveaux*, (two horses) as it is widely known in France, is an air-cooled, front-engine drive, economical car first manufactured in Paris in 1948, and has been the workhorse of many drivers in Europe ever since. It had a total of two cylinders and my model had a 450 cc engine, even smaller than the SEAT 600. It had a three-speed transmission that was controlled by a lever sticking out of the dashboard and it did not have a clutch, one just let off the gas to change gears.

It had four doors but the front ones were nicknamed "suicide doors" because they opened the opposite from a regular car door, so when both front and back doors were open, they hit against each other. It was extremely slow due to the small engine size but had amazing gas mileage, having a motor smaller than most average-sized American motorcycles. The top speed was about eighty kilometers per hour, but this speed was only reached by going downhill and with a heavy tailwind. The front windows didn't roll up or down but instead they just folded up and down, with two choices, either halfway up

or all the way down. The roof of the vehicle was made of canvas that allowed the driver to roll it back for an open top on nice days. And since the engine had only two cylinders and with such a small piston displacement, going uphill could take some time, to put it mildly, and was only achieved by constantly shifting between first and second gears. They came in two colors, either basic gray or dark blue, and mine was the dark blue which I preferred. But it was basic transportation, and it was all mine, in fact it was the very first car I ever owned. And I had a lot of fun in it during the time I owned it and drove it.

Instead of catching a ride with Ray all the time to get to my classes on base, I drove my own car out there and back. Coincidentally, one of the classes I took was a Creative Writing class, and it was held in the same exact classroom where I had spent two semesters taking and re-taking the U.S. History class with Mr. Mortimer while I was in high school three years earlier. This was the class that almost prevented me from being able to graduate if I hadn't managed to pass it the second time I took it. And since we weren't assigned seats as we were in high school, I chose the exact same seat that I sat in while I was in high school. And even though the classroom hadn't changed that much in three years, I certainly had.

There was a guy who sat directly behind me in that class that I became pretty good friends with before too long. As was the case with most of the people who were taking classes at the University of Maryland on base, he was an airman in the Air Force stationed at Torrejon and was just taking college classes to get a jump on his education once he got out of the military.

His name was Allen Harrison, but he insisted that everyone just call him "Tiny" which he claimed to be his nickname. When someone asked him where he got that particular nickname, since he was not unusually big, or small for that matter, he just said that he came from a family with nine children, and he was the youngest, and hence the smallest, so they all just called him Tiny and it stuck.

Tiny and I just seemed to hit it off, and we became good friends before the semester was even half-over. He was an African American guy from Brooklyn, New York, and at first glance, it would appear that the two of us didn't have much in common, but we both shared a love for good rock-and-roll music and smoking hash. He had his own apartment in Madrid near the *Cuatro Caminos* neighborhood which he shared with his roommate, who was another airman from the base, and I'd go over there fairly often to sit around and smoke some bowls and listen to records. Sometimes I was able to help him and his roommate score if I was able to find a good source around town, which I could sometimes do. He liked to listen to Jimi Hendrix records and so did I, so we spent a lot of time hanging around together at his little *piso*, getting stoned on good Moroccan hash and really getting into Jimi's music.

And I considered myself still hopelessly in love with Lizzy. But I couldn't see her very often because I didn't go to high school anymore, but she still did, and the only time I'd get to see her was purely by chance. Many times, I'd drive my car out to Royal Oaks, hoping to just run into her and one night I lucked out and I did.

The big red Spanish sun had just set over the small hills to the west of Royal Oaks and I was driving around the area killing time and hoping I'd see her. I first went down to the movie theater area and into the snack bar that was next to it, but I had no luck. There were lots of other people hanging around these places, but not her. I also drove by the *fruteria* to see if she was around there and even out to the horse stables to look for her.

Finally, I was just about to give up and head back to Canillejas, and I was going around a place near the center of the housing area called the "circle," which was exactly what it sounds like, when I saw her sitting on one of the sidewalk benches that were located every block or so along the streets of Royal Oaks.

I stopped the car, flipped open my window, smiled at her, and said, "Hi there, Lizzy, what are you up to tonight?"

She gave me a bored look and replied, "Oh, not too much, what are you doing?"

"Oh, I'm just driving around trying to find something to do. Wanna go for a ride?"

"Yeah, okay, sure," she said, and got in my car.

We drove around and I asked her again, "So, what do you want to do, any ideas?"

"No, not really," she said, "Do you?"

"Well, if you like we can go into town and visit a good friend of mine. He has his own apartment over near *Cuatro Caminos*. How does that sound?"

Again she gave me her bored look and said, "Okay, sure, if you want to."

"Yeah, Ron, sure, that sounds okay. I can really use a toke right about now. My old man has been giving me a lot of shit lately and it's been driving me crazy, man."

"Oh yeah? What kind of shit, may I ask?"

"Just the same old crap. He treats me like I'm ten years old, man. He wants me home before nine every night and doesn't seem to like anything about me, including my hair and my clothes, fucking everything, man!"

"Wow, that's gotta be rough, having an old man like that, huh?"

"You'd better believe it. That's why I can't wait until I graduate and can get the hell away from him and all his shit!"

"Well, it's only a few months until June and that's when you graduate, right?"

"Yep, and I'm counting the days, man!"

The entire drive into town we kept chatting about her problems at home and how she really needed to get away from all of it and get on her own as soon as possible.

The *Cuatro Caminos* area of Madrid is a working-class neighborhood not too far from *Plaza Castilla,* and there were a lot of inexpensive places to live in the area. The more expensive *Generalissimo* area, where many Americans lived, is in the other direction from *Plaza Castilla.*

Soon, I was parking the car in front of Tiny's apartment building and we got out and climbed the three flights of stairs to his *piso*. I knocked on the door and he answered almost immediately, and when he saw me, he gave me a big smile and said, "Hey, Ron, my man! It's good to see you, come on in."

I smiled back and said, "Hi, Tiny, how you doing? I brought someone over that I wanted you to meet. Tiny, this is Lizzy. And Lizzy, this is Tiny, my buddy I was telling you about."

He got a very weird look on his face and gave her an odd look too, and before we even walked in the door, he said to her in total sincerity, "Hello there, Lizzy, one day we will get married and you will have my son."

She looked at me and then at him and shrugged and said, "Okay, man, if you say so."

And she laughed a little and walked through the door.

I gave Tiny a strange look as I walked into the door behind her and said, "Well, that's rather sudden, don't you think, man?"

He still had a strange look on his face and whispered to me, "I'm serious, man. I think I just had a *déjà vu* moment or something, very weird. It's never happened to me before. Very strange, sorry."

I just smiled and shrugged and said, "Well, stranger things have happened, I guess, huh? What the hell you been smoking anyways, man?"

He smiled his big smile at me and said, "I got some double zero here that will knock your socks off, bro!"

"Cool, let's fire it up then, man!" I said with a big smile.

And so we did. And a couple of hours later when we were ready to leave, Lizzy, and I could barely navigate the three flights of stairs to get down to my car so I could drive her home. We made it, but barely. I drove very slowly and cautiously the entire way back to the Oaks, but my little car wouldn't go that fast anyway, so I couldn't have driven very fast even if I'd wanted to.

I dropped her off at her house and she thanked me for taking her into town and introducing her to Tiny, and then she told me that she was probably going to get in trouble with her old man for staying out so late. Then she asked me if I have some chewing gum to help take the smell of the hash off her breath, and I luckily found a pack in my pocket and gave her a piece. She then told me goodnight, opened the door and walked up to her place. I watched her as she opened the door and then I drove away, thinking about what a strange evening I had just experienced.

There was someone else whom I went out to Royal Oaks to see on a semi-regular basis as well. His name was Tom Green, and he also was in his last year of high school at MHS. For some reason, Tom always had hash for sale. He seemed to never run out, and he was the most reliable connection I had. I'm not sure where or how he scored but he almost always had some. And he didn't seem to mind if people just went over to his house in Royal Oaks, knocked on the door, went into his room, sampled the product, bought some, and walked out.

And usually his parents were at home most of the time and I'm sure that they must have known what he was doing, but apparently they didn't care all that much. His room would always reek of hash but they never said anything about it. Whenever we went over there to score, they were always happy to see some of Tom's friend and greeted us warmly. Tom was a very nice guy whom I really liked a lot, very friendly and rather strange looking as well. He had big thick glasses and long bushy hair that stuck out almost like an Afro and always had a tie-dye T-shirt on. And, unlike most of my other friends, instead of just buying a few grams at a time, he would buy a kilo or more at once and then sell it to his friends and acquaintances for a little profit and was also able to smoke all he wanted for free.

Before too long, Tom became famous among the American community both on base and in the Oaks and even became notorious among certain Spaniards in Madrid as well. There were many Spaniards who were beginning to smoke dope, and they began to realize that there was a reliable source of hash out at Royal Oaks at his place. Sometimes they would show up in taxis from Madrid and have the taxi wait at the curb while they went into Tom's room to score. He was known as "Tomás Verde," and always seemed to have the best "Verde" around. But this is what led to his downfall and to him eventually getting busted.

Before too long, the wrong Spaniard somehow got wind of what was happening in Tom's bedroom out in the Oaks, and one day the *Guardia Civil* showed up and took him away. This was devastating news for all concerned, not only for his friends like me and others but also to the entire scene in Madrid. But much like my good friend Bill who got busted for stealing motorcycles a few years earlier, all that happened to Tom was that they deported him back to the States to live with relatives before the rest of his family was rotated stateside later that year. Of course, he wasn't able to graduate with the rest of his classmates and had to finish school at an unfamiliar school in the States, but indeed it could have been much worse.

It was shortly before all this happened with Tom that my friend J.P. came back to Madrid from one of his great adventures, and this time he brought his girlfriend Sarah with him. His mom was still in the States living with her sister, so he and Sarah had the entire *piso* near *Las Ventas* for themselves. Since he didn't have a car, a lot of times, the four of us would get together and drive around town with J.P. and Sarah in the back seat, with Lizzy riding shotgun and me driving. Sarah really liked Madrid, and we made sure to take her around and show her the sights including the *Rastro* on Sunday mornings and the *Retiro* Park on sunny afternoons where one could go rowing on the small lake there.

J.P. and Sarah were obviously deeply in love and they seemed to really enjoy each other's company. They held hands all the time and sat very close together with their arms around each other a lot. But Lizzy's and my relationship hadn't progressed at all. In fact, the  more time I spent with her, the less she seemed to like me. Perhaps it was because of my extreme shyness and inexperience with the opposite sex that I just never could make that first essential move, to let her know that I did indeed like her in that way. So we remained just "friends" and never did we progress beyond that. I always told myself that soon, that any day now, I'd just blurt out and tell her the way I felt, but that day never arrived and I never did, much to my regret.

J.P. (being a French citizen) at this point was in the process of completing the paperwork to immigrate to Canada. He had met a Canadian fellow named Don while traveling in Morocco who had agreed to "sponsor" his immigration. Don lived in Edmonton, Alberta along with his parents and they also were helping with his immigration process. Of course, he couldn't enter France at all because he was at the age where they would have drafted him into the French Military, and that was the last thing that he wanted. So he did all the paperwork from the Canadian embassy in Madrid. Eventually the immigration papers were accepted, and he moved to Canada and he ended up making his life there for many years. This was about the same time I ended up moving to the States for good, about a year or so later.

About this time, my mom and Jim were still going through a lot of problems with him trying to quit drinking and it was decided that this effort might be a little easier if I wasn't underfoot all the time. So they decided that I would move out, and we so began to try to find a place where I could live that wasn't with them at their place in Canillejas.

My Mom's friend Maruja knew of an older Spanish couple who lived in the *Goya* area of Madrid in a large *piso* and they had been known to accept borders. This couple was in their late seventies and their names were Luz and Rogelio and both were very nice people. So after being introduced to them by Maruja and looking at the room they had for rent,

it was decided that for the sum of five hundred pesetas per week (about eight dollars), I could stay at the room at their place.

It was a very typical Spanish home with old classic Spanish furnishings and an atmosphere of the real "old" Madrid. They had been living in the *piso* for many decades and the room I had was the one that their son had lived in before he had grown up and moved out. I called the old couple Doña Luz and Don Rogelio and I treated them with the utmost respect and consideration. I rarely took my meals there, except for a coffee and a pastry for breakfast sometimes and usually ate most of my meals out, or at my folks' place in Canillejas occasionally. Of course I smoked nothing in the room, not even cigarettes, and mostly I just used the place to sleep. And I had my car which I could park downstairs within walking distance of their building and I had my own key to their place which was on the sixth floor of their apartment building.

This situation didn't last long though. After less than a month, Doña Luz asked me very politely if there was another place I could move to. It seemed that she did not like the hours I kept. I had a tendency to get home very late at night at times, and then sleep very late in the day, and she did not think this was a schedule that a young man should have. I couldn't understand why since I had my own key and came and went when I wanted to. I don't think I ever disturbed her or Don Rogelio because they slept soundly and I didn't think I woke them when I got home late, but apparently I had done so at times. This was fine, actually, because I really didn't like staying there very much, anyway. So I ended up going back to Canillejas to stay with my mom and Jim.

I tried to stay busy mostly, taking my classes during the evenings on base and hanging around different places around Madrid. There were several nightclubs I really liked going to because they seemed to be the places where things were happening around town. There was one called "Piccadilly's" that was near the road heading out to the base that I frequented quite often. This place usually had good bands playing on the weekends and was one of the happening spots in Madrid at the time. Another place that was frequented by a lot of Americans and other foreigners was called the "Stones Club" and it was another favorite of mine as well.

But the club I liked the most was downtown on the "*Gran Via*" (the Great Way) which was the main drag in downtown Madrid. The name of the place was "J. J.'s" or "*Jota Jota*" in Spanish. It was a huge place right on the main strip and it was underground, in the basement of a large office building downtown, and required walking down a flight of stairs. They always had live music and some nights there were excellent touring bands from other countries in Europe playing and then on other nights, a local Spanish band would be performing on their large stage. They had a very nice dance floor, and it was always crowded with a lot of people dancing and having a great time and was considered the place to be for the best nightlife in Madrid.

One Saturday night, a few years earlier, while I was still in high school, I went with some friends down to "J. J.'s" and as I was paying the small cover charge to the doorman at the top of the stairs, I asked him how things were going. He looked at me and told me that I should have been there the night before. When I asked him why, he told me that Jimi Hendrix had been there the previous night with his entourage and everybody had a great time. He didn't perform or anything but instead he was just partying and getting a taste of some of the famous Spanish night life, and perhaps getting inspired to write his classic song, "Spanish Castle Magic." I was devastated to find out I had missed seeing this music legend and one of my favorite musicians of all time by just one night. It wasn't too long after this that they found Jimi dead and I would never have the opportunity to see him again.

But by 1973, a lot of things had changed. My friend J.P. had almost completed the waiting period, and his paperwork for immigrating to Canada was done, and he was preparing to make the big move. Sarah had finally finished her tour of Europe, which ended up lasting much longer than she had originally planned, and had returned to her family in upstate New York. J.P.'s plan was to settle in Thunder Bay, Ontario where he had a job lined up already and was making plans to leave for North America soon, and maybe see her again in New York after he made the move.

I spent a lot of time with him at his place before he left and we promised to keep in touch. I gave him my brother's address in Texas and my mom's address in Spain and told him that she would always know my whereabouts and how to get ahold of me. He told me he felt that the only place he thought he could have a decent future in was in North America, either in the States or in Canada and that's why he was going there. I told him that I would most likely end up in the States eventually and that we'd see each other again someday.

It wasn't too long after this that I got another letter from the draft board in San Antonio, and this one was even more severe and intimidating than the previous ones. It said that even though the draft had technically ended the previous January; it still required me to report for my induction process on June 3, 1973, and be subject to being drafted or pay the penalty which included jail time, a fine, and the loss of my civil rights as an American citizen. They ordered me to report on that date at the Selective Service main office in Dallas, Texas or I would face severe consequences.

After discussing this situation with my folks, I decided that if I ever wanted to live in the United States, and try to make my life there, then I had better take care of this draft problem, once and for all. Since I was technically a dual national, having been born in Portugal to American parents, I had both American and Portuguese citizenship. And at the age of twenty-one, I had the choice of what country I wanted to owe my allegiance to and become a citizen of.

After thinking about this issue for a while, I decided (with the advice of my folks) that I'd most likely have a better life for myself if I chose to be an American, which is basically what I was, one way or another. Besides, Portugal was in the middle of bloody civil wars with their two colonies in Africa, Angola and Mozambique, and if I chose to become Portuguese, I very well may have been drafted into their military to fight in one of those wars. And since Vietnam was winding down at this point, I felt that my chances of avoiding war altogether were probably better in the U.S.

So I sold my car, got my meager belongings together and prepared to go to Dallas and take care of this never-ending nightmare which was the American military draft.

Once again, I got on a flight from Barajas to the Dallas/Ft. Worth airport and left my beloved Spain and didn't return for almost forty years.

Chapter 24. The States for Good

"Life is a hard battle anyway. If we laugh and sing a little as we fight the good fight of freedom, it makes it all go easier. I will not allow my life's light to be determined by the darkness around me."
— *Sojourner Truth*

When I got off the plane once again at the airport in Dallas, Texas, my brother John was once again waiting there to meet me. After we loaded my stuff into the old "blue beast," we headed to his house in Cleburne. I had just arrived from Spain in June 1973, about thirteen and one-half years since I had first arrived in Madrid as a seven-year-old, and where I had spent most of my young life.

I was to report to the selective service induction center two days later, or I'd be considered a draft dodger and be put onto the F.B.I.'s infamous "black list," if I wasn't already.

This did not seem to be a very good list to be on for any reason, so I made a point of making it there to Dallas for my induction date. This was the fourth notice I had received from the draft board by this point, each one giving me another date to comply, and another ultimatum, but this was the one that seemed to be the most serious and the very last chance I would have before I was subject to arrest for draft evasion.

My brother was able to get off work on the day I had to report for my induction, so he gave me a ride to downtown Dallas for this process. John had never had a problem with the draft because he had turned that magic age of eighteen while we were still in Spain and he signed up at the American embassy in Madrid and automatically got a 4-F classification, due to his obvious overseas resident status. They had never contacted him or showed any interest in him "serving" his country. They just plain left him alone.

For me, it was a different story and looking back, it probably would have been a lot easier all around, if my family had stayed in Spain just one more month during that summer of 1970, instead of coming back to the States when we did in July of that year. If we had stayed until just after my birthday in August, I could have signed up at the embassy in Madrid like my brother had, and I could have avoided this entire hassle with the draft.

The process was pretty much as I expected. They were ready to draft me into the military at this point. Even though the draft had officially ended six months earlier, I was still subject to being drafted from the previous orders and dates that I had received and had not complied with.

I was with about a dozen or so other young men, but I think I was the only one there subject to being drafted. The rest were enlisting into the Armed Forces, but we all had to go through the induction process to see if we were physically and mentally qualified to serve in the American military.

First there was a battery of written test and exams, testing our various abilities to read, write, and do simple math problems. They were not difficult at all and having a sixth-grade-level of education and proficiency in these subjects probably was sufficient to pass. I passed them all with flying colors, and then next came the physical exam. We lined up in our underwear, and the doctors went from one of us to the next, asking questions about our medical history and then giving each of us a complete physical exam.

I seemed to be passing this part of the induction process as well since I was in excellent physical shape and hadn't had any major health issues in my life. After one doctor had listened to my heart and lungs with his stethoscope and gave me the okay as far as my physical health went, another doctor began to ask me some other medical questions. He asked me if I had ever had any diseases in the past and if I had a history of mental illness in my family. I was as honest as I could be with him and replied no to all his questions.

He then looked at me closely and asked me in a very stern and authoritative voice, "Son, have you ever used any illegal drugs before?"

Ah hah! I wasn't going to start lying to him at this point, so I replied, "Um, yes sir, I have."

He looked at me closely again and then asked me, "And what kinds of drugs have you used, son?"

I shrugged and said, "Well, quite a few actually, sir."

He had his clipboard in his hand and began running down a list, "Marijuana?"

"Yes, sir."

"Hashish?"

"Um, yes, sir."

"Amphetamines?"

"Yeah, white crosses and other pills, if that's what you mean."

"Barbiturates?"

"Yep, I've taken those as well, sir."

"LSD?"

"Yeah, I've tried that too."

"Peyote?"

"Yes, sir, but just once."

"Psilocybin? Also known as magic mushrooms?"

I smiled and said, "Um, no sir, not yet."

He continued looking at me with a very stern expression and then asked, "Heroin?"

I shook my head and said, "No, absolutely not."

"Opium?"

Again I shook my head and said, "Um, no, not really."

"Methamphetamine, also known as crystal meth?"

I scratched my head and nodded and said, "Yep, I've done that some. In fact, I actually did it a little too much of it at one time."

He put his clipboard down and again gave me a very stern look and told me, "Son, due to your history of illegal drug use, in order for us to determine if you are eligible to serve in the United States Military, you are required to be examined by a qualified psychiatrist. Do you understand?"

I nodded and said, "Yes, sir, I do."

He gave me another very serious look and said, "I'm going to set up an appointment with an accredited psychiatrist here in Dallas for you to see, and based on his recommendation, it will be determined if you qualify to serve in the military or not. Do you understand?"

"Yes, I understand."

"Very well, follow me then."

I followed him over to his desk and he sat down behind it as I stood there in my underwear and he wrote something on a paper and handed it to me and said, "Okay, son, you can get dressed now. And here is the name and address of the psychiatrist you are to see tomorrow at three in the afternoon. It's located right here in downtown Dallas, and you are required to have this exam; do you understand?"

"Yes, sir, I'll be there."

And I got dressed and walked out of the place.

The next day, I was at the psychiatrist's right on time. I took the elevator up to the sixth floor of the large office building in downtown Dallas and I told the receptionist behind her desk my name and that I had an appointment with Dr. Feldman. She looked down at her paperwork and confirmed my appointment and told me to sit and wait since it would be a few minutes.

I sat down on the couch provided for this purpose and looked around. It was a typical doctor's office with a few magazines to read and I picked one up titled "Psychiatry Today" and began to thumb through it. Within a few minutes, she told me that the doctor was ready to see me. So I stood up and entered the door to his office.

A man around thirty-five years old got up from behind his desk and put out his hand and said, "Good afternoon, I'm Dr. Feldman."

I shook his hand and said, "Hello, Dr. Feldman, I'm Ron Walker, it's very nice to meet you."

He motioned to a chair in front of his desk and said, "Please, have a seat, Ron."

I smiled and said, "Okay, thank you."

I sat down in the very comfortable leather chair in front of his desk and gave him a good look. He seemed like a fairly nice man with rather long curly hair and a neatly trimmed goatee, and he was wearing wire-rimmed glasses and a dark blue suit and a bright yellow tie.

He began by shuffling some paperwork on his desk and then looked up at me and said, "So, you are here to have a psychiatric examination to determine if you are fit for military service. Is this correct, Ron?"

I nodded and said, "Yes, that is my understanding, Dr. Feldman."

"Well, then let's get started, okay?"

"Sure, whenever you're ready," I said.

He asked me all kinds of questions about my background, such as where I grew up, my family, what my father did for a living, and a lot of other personal questions.

I answered as honestly and completely as I could and he seemed to be happy with my answers as he was making notes and it went along smoothly with very little interruption for around fifteen minutes or so. He then asked me about my drug usage in the past and again I was as honest with him as I could be and told him everything I could think of concerning myself and that topic, including the time I spent in a jail in Tampa, Florida for possession of marijuana.

He went back to my dad's military career briefly and asked me what I thought of my father's attitude about the military was after being in for twenty years. I told him what my dad had told me on numerous occasions about him being very frustrated and angry that he had to salute a fellow soldier who was only half his age and with only half his experience, and he was required to call him "sir" just because he was an officer and had gone to college and he hadn't.

I also told him about how he would write brilliant letters concerning certain military subjects for the colonel he was working for and the colonel would get all the credit for the letter if it was well received and had accomplished what it was written for, but if the letter did not provide the results he wanted, then my father would get blamed for it. And how frustrated he was for having reached the highest rank he could reach very early in his career and having to stay there without promotion for the remainder of it, again because he only had a high school education.

Dr. Feldman was taking notes this entire time and nodding his head as I spoke. He then again asked me about my upbringing, so I went over the facts again in more detail about my being born in Portugal, and living most of my life in Spain and how I had turned 18 shortly after arriving back in the States, and signing up for the draft at that time. And how my brother who was two-and-a-half years older than I was, had completely avoided any draft problems at all because he had signed up for the Selective Service in Madrid and had automatically received a 4-F classification as an overseas resident. Of course, I did not mention the fact that the F.B.I. had appeared at his house looking for me while I was briefly in the States the previous year, while trying to get this issue resolved.

After another twenty minutes or so of me telling Dr. Feldman my entire life story, he quit taking notes and told me the following in a very serious voice:

"Well, Ron, this is the way it is. I'm getting my forty dollar fee from the U.S. Government for performing this evaluation of you regardless of the outcome. Frankly, it makes no difference to me what I put down on this evaluation, so I will leave it up to you."

I looked at him and nodded.

He continued, "I realize that you've had an unusual life and a background much different from that of the average American and I think the decision should be up to you if you want to be in the military or not. But I must tell you of the consequences of your decision, whichever one you make. I can put down on the evaluation that I recommend that you be drafted and that I see no reason for you not to be since many young men today have experimented with drugs of all kinds and they still become upstanding citizens and soldiers."

Again I nodded my understanding.

"On the other hand, I can recommend to the draft board that you not be allowed in the military due to several reasons and concerns. One, that your history of drug usage might have affected your ability to be able to be trained properly and to become a good soldier and also the fact you might continue to use drugs and that you might be a problem for your superiors. And second, that your father's extensive military career and his attitude towards the rank and file of military service might have influenced you to a point where you might not be an ideal candidate for military service and they should not waste their time and money with you trying to make you into a decent soldier."

"I understand, sir," I said to him very seriously.

He continued, "But I must warn you that if you choose this second option to avoid military service, there will be several consequences. This report will be on your permanent record and it will prevent you from ever being able to be hired for certain government jobs, and also it will make you unable to get clearances for many other jobs. And that this record will follow you your entire life and will never be expunged from your record. Do you understand?"

I scratched my head and said, "Yes, I think I understand."

Again, he looked at me very seriously and said, "Now do you want to have some time to think about this? After all it is a huge decision you'll be making here now, and it'll affect the rest of your life."

"No sir," I said to him. "I've already decided. I definitely do not want to go into the military, now or ever. And as far as this limiting my job possibilities in the future, well, I'm just going to have to live with it and get jobs that don't require this type of clearance, I guess."

"Well, I can see that you have made up your mind about this. I'll complete my report and I will submit it as we discussed."

"Okay," I said.

"And on a personal note, Ron, I understand that you, like so many other young men today, have no desire to be drafted and to enter a war that many people feel is disgraceful and unnecessary, but the war is winding down now and you will probably never see combat at all if you are to serve today. Are you sure you don't have any desire to serve your country?"

I looked him directly in his eye and I replied with as much seriousness and sincerity as I could muster, "Doctor Feldman, I have never had a desire to join the military, war or no war. I just want to be free and to be able to do what I want with my life without anybody telling me what to do, okay?"

He gave me another very serious look and said, "Well, you also must understand that the military can be an advantage to many people and that is why they enlist or allow themselves to be drafted. They offer great benefits, including the G. I. Bill to help you get a college education, and they even offer a great retirement plan after twenty years. And you know, as your father was obviously able to do, they also offer travel, adventure and opportunities you might not otherwise find in life, right?"

I shook my head and said, "That's okay, Doctor, I'll find my own adventures and make my own opportunities in my life and I'll do so on my terms, not the United States Military's."

"Okay, it appears that you've really made up your mind, Ron. I'd like to wish you all the luck in the world."

And he reached out his hand, and we shook hands firmly.

Again, I looked him in the eye and said, "I'd like to thank you very much, Doctor. Not only for being honest with me but also for being very nice and decent about this entire process. If it wasn't for you, I might be heading into the Army right about now."

"Well, let's just hope you made the right decision today."

I smiled at him and said, "I'm sure I did, sir. And thanks again for everything."

He smiled back and said, "Well, good luck again to you, Ron, and you take care of yourself, okay? I don't want to see you getting into any trouble, you hear?"

"You don't have to worry about that, Doctor. I'll be fine."

And I walked out of his office having no regrets and knowing in my heart I had made the right decision. And I felt free as if someone had lifted a very heavy weight off from my shoulders. Suddenly I felt better about myself and my future than I had for a long time. The future was very bright indeed and was open to all the possibilities in the world. I was not going to be drafted after all. What a relief. Finally, I was a free man!

So I settled in at John and Janie's place in Cleburne. I knew it was only temporary until I could save up enough money to get my own place. John had quit his job as a bricklayer's helper, and had gotten a job at in the small nearby town not for from Cleburne called Keene, Texas. There was a company there that built cabinets of all sorts, including kitchen, bathroom and every other kind of cabinet imaginable. They had trained him to run the counter top machine, which was a large device that adhered the laminated tops to the various cabinets. And as soon as I applied there, and after telling them I was his brother, I was hired immediately.

My particular job was not as technical or as demanding as his was since I was just a member of the assembly-line team that built the wooden kitchen cabinets. I spent most of the day sanding and helping to put together the various-sized cabinets. It certainly wasn't glamorous or all that much fun either, but it was a decent paycheck, and I saved as much as I could to get enough money together to get my own apartment in Fort Worth.

John was still raising rabbits, and it all started with buying just two and it went from there, because rabbits breed just like, well, um, rabbits. When he was working at a grocery store shortly after moving to Cleburne, he worked in the produce department, and instead of throwing away boxes and boxes of old produce that didn't sell, he would bring it home and feed it all to his rapidly expanding rabbit population. They were kept in the large barn that was on the property and he used his carpentry skills to build various hutches to keep them in, and soon it reached a point where he was butchering and eating one rabbit per week in order to keep their numbers down to a point where they would fit in the limited number of hutches that he had built.

John and Janie learned to cook rabbit in every way imaginable, including fried rabbit, baked rabbit, rabbit stew, rabbit tacos and even rabbit enchiladas. Rabbits are an excellent source of protein and a great alternative to chicken with much less fat and much tastier. And after butchering the rabbits, he would save their skins and he learned how to tan them properly and after a while, they had enough to sew together a beautiful rabbit skin cover for their couch, as well as rabbit skin purses, vests and anything else that could be made out of rabbit furs.

Whenever Easter came around, they would sell a lot of the baby rabbits to people around the area for kids to have as pets and that brought in a little extra money.

It was a very peaceful and mellow sort of existence out at John and Janie's place on the rolling hills of Northern Texas just south of Fort Worth. One of the largest cities in Texas was Dallas, and it was only an hour away, yet out in the countryside where they lived there was little traffic, crime and congestion, and it was truly a wonderful place to live.

They had a garden on the property as well and used the rabbit "pellets" as fertilizer and, as expected, everything they planted grew unusually high and thick. They grew tomatoes, peppers, squash, corn, and a variety of other vegetables. They also grew pot. He planted the pot seeds in between the rows of corn, so they could not be seen from anywhere unless you got right inside the garden to look of them. The plants grew like weeds and became almost as tall as the tallest corn plants. In the fall, they not only harvested a lot of vegetables to eat but also a lot of pot to smoke. They even had enough to give some away to friends and even sold a little for a small profit.

Within a month, I was able to save up enough money to get my own place on the south side of town. It wasn't much, but it was only sixty dollars per month including the utilities which was about all I could afford. It was upstairs and was part of a large old house that had been converted into several apartments. It had its own set of rickety stairs running along the side of the house up to the entrance and it consisted of one large room and a small kitchen and bathroom. I paid the first and last month's rent and a small deposit and moved in. The only furnishings were a bed and a desk and chair in the main room and a small table with two chairs in the kitchen. I went to a thrift store and bought a few pots, pans, dishes, and a small radio. I couldn't afford a TV set, so I spent many hours listening to the FM Rock station out of Dallas on my little radio and wishing I could afford a TV.

It wasn't much of a place, but it was all mine, and the first place I had for myself in this strange country of the United States that I found myself living in and trying so hard to adapt to.

The next thing I had to do was to get a job since I couldn't very well commute all the way to the town of Keene every day and work at the cabinet place. I didn't have a car, so I needed to find a place that was near enough that I could walk to it, or was on a bus line. I looked in the local newspaper and the first place I applied to; I got hired. It was walking distance from my small apartment and coincidentally enough it was for the Federal government. I started working for the General Services Administration, or the GSA. I guess since it wasn't a high security type of job, my recent draft problems and the reasons for my 4-F classification were not issues.

It was basically a warehouse job, loading and unloading trucks for the GSA which is an independent agency of the U.S. Government to help manage and support the basic functioning of federal agencies. It was a huge warehouse on the south side of Fort Worth and it was responsible for furnishing various federal office buildings around the country with supplies to keep them running smoothly. Everything from office desks and chairs to toilet paper and staplers went in and out of the warehouse every day and my job was to help load and unload the many trucks that were there to either unload or pick up these supplies and transport them to the different federal offices nationwide.

It was hard back-breaking work and paid only a quarter more than the minimum wage which was $2.00 per hour, so I made $2.25 before taxes and deductions. I would clear about seventy-five dollars per week but it was enough for me to live on and I even bought a car shortly after starting to work there.

I even got friendly with a couple of my co-workers at the warehouse, and before too long we were hanging out together occasionally after work. They were the only long-haired fellows I worked with and since I couldn't seem to get along very well with the typical redneck type of Texan, these two guys and I got along pretty well for the most part. They were named Tommy and Jerry and I learned later that they were both gay, but at the time I couldn't tell and if I could, I probably wouldn't have cared too much, anyway. They were just two long-haired guys like me and we all got along okay, both at work and off-hours as well. I'd go over to their place after work occasionally to drink a couple of beers and smoke a joint and they both were obsessed with Elton John and would play his albums back to back and over and over again every time I was over there.

Jerry had a 1964 Studebaker Lark that he wanted a hundred dollars for since he had bought a newer car and needed to get rid of his old one. I looked at it, took a test drive in it and told him I'd take it but I would have to make payments to him. He agreed, so I paid him twenty-five dollars per week, and after a month he turned the title over to me. It was dark green and ran pretty well and I kept it for several months before the U-joint went out on it and since the car was so rare, I couldn't find a replacement anywhere for it.

Studebaker cars were no longer being made, and I called every junk yard in the entire Fort Worth/Dallas area and I simply could not find a used U-joint for this car anywhere. So it forced me to junk it since I couldn't drive it anymore. The junkyard gave me fifty dollars for it, so I didn't lose out too much. But it was a sweet car and was the very first car I owned in the United States and of course it would be worth a lot of money today due to its rarity and uniqueness.

When I told Jerry what had happened, he didn't seem too concerned and told me he had no idea about the U-joint being ready to give out, so I just shrugged my shoulders and went on as if nothing had happened. But I did spend a lot less time over at their place after this deal with the car.

After a while, I got tired of the back-breaking work I was doing at the GSA warehouse and I was back to walking to work or riding the bus after the Lark died. I found an apartment closer to the warehouse, so it was only a ten-minute walk instead of almost a half-hour walk from my old place. My new apartment was a little nicer than the little upstairs place I had before which was really just a small part of a large old house. My new place was a little stand-alone guest house, on the same property as the landlady who was an older woman in her seventies who lived in the main house in front. She was very nice to me which was most likely due to my unusually polite manners and upbringing that demanded that I respect and honor my elders.

She rented me the little guest house for twenty dollars per week and I paid her every week instead of once per month like at the other place, and it included all utilities so I didn't have to worry about bills. And for another two dollars per week, she provided a small black-and-white TV set which I got a lot of use out of. I'd watch it every night after work and by doing so, I tried to decipher a little more of this strange land and culture I found myself living in and was finding so difficult to understand and to assimilate into.

Fort Worth, Texas had always had a reputation of being one of the most redneck cities in the country, and even has the nickname of "Cowtown, U.S.A." There were probably more people with their necks that particular color than anywhere else in the world. And because of the way I was raised, I prided myself on being a very tolerant and open-minded individual, but it had to be a two-way street for me. A lot of the Texans I came into contact with refused to accept me for who and what I was, and instead made me feel like I was less than them in some way because I was different from them, and the fact that I wasn't from where they were from and was not a native Texan.

A good example is the accent that Texans have. If I walked into a convenience store and tried to purchase a six-pack of beer—which in Texas, one has to ask the clerk behind the counter to get for you, instead of just going to the cooler and getting it yourself as they do in more civilized places—I would have to ask for it in a Texan accent. If I used my regular voice, the guy behind the counter would just act like he didn't or couldn't understand me. This happened at various places and at different times, so it wasn't just one particular clerk at one particular store. If I just used my regular voice and said, "Hello, sir, could I have a six-pack of Coors please?" the guy would just look at me and say, "Huh? Say what kid?" And so I learned to walk in and say, "Hey, bud, gimme a six of Currs, would ya?" And he would get it for me without a problem. This is just one example of the way Texans seemed to think that since their state is the biggest in the country, (except for Alaska which they believe would be smaller than Texas if all the ice and snow somehow melted) that everything is bigger and therefore better than anywhere else. There is arrogance and insolence that I found to exist in Texas that I experienced there that is like nowhere else I've ever been or lived.

But my new landlady treated me with kindness and respect and I returned the same to her. She had a grandson who had a motorbike for sale, so I made arrangements to buy it from him and then just pay her for it. So for an extra twenty dollars per week, and payments for ten weeks, I had a very nice Honda 125 to ride. It was several years old but ran great and I was happy to have my own transportation again. I was comfortable riding motorbikes from my days in Spain riding different sizes and types of Spanish-made bikes, so to me the Honda was very nice and quite a bit different because it had a four-stroke engine, unlike the Spanish bikes which were mostly all two-strokes.

The little Honda was a lot of fun and soon I was zipping all over town with it. My new wheels allowed me to look for another job and I soon found a new one by looking in the local newspaper. My new apartment was not far from the Interstate 35 and there was a bottling plant just off from one of the exits of the Interstate where I ended up getting a job. It was the Dr. Pepper Bottling plant of Fort Worth and was a large plant that supplied bottled soft drinks for most of northern Texas.

This was before soft drinks came in aluminum cans, so they were all in bottles, and consumers would return the empties to the store and exchange them for full bottles. The trucks that made the deliveries loaded up the empties and brought them back to the plant to refill them and send them out again. It was a great system because the consumer only had to pay for the beverage itself instead of the packaging for it. The added bonus to this system was that this helped cut down on waste and much less material ended up in the landfills. Empty bottles were worth money and could be brought back to any store and exchanged for cash.

This was before the days of "recycling," but recycling was totally unnecessary because the only waste involved was an occasional broken bottle. This system worked fine for many decades and I think it was the companies that eventually changed their bottling process and then the consumers went along with it instead of the other way around, the way it should have been done. And a soft drink, much the same as a beer or any other beverage, always tends to taste far better from a glass bottle than from an aluminum can.

My job title was the "lot boy" and my job was basically to keep the area cleaned up from broken bottles, cases, and pallets. The company had over a dozen large trucks designed to haul the bottles to and from the stores and each one had a certain schedule to enter the grounds of the plant to load and unload the product, so as not to create traffic jams at the several loading bays the bottling plant had for their trucks.

My job was to maintain the entire "lot" which was the area where the trucks came and went all day long. There were constantly small accidents where a pallet of bottles would overturn and break all over the yard and I was responsible to clean these messes up. They were mostly empty bottles because the full ones went directly from the plant onto the trucks waiting in the loading bays. So I'd walk around with a broom and a barrel and sweep up and discard the broken glass that regularly found itself on the lot, and I had to do it quickly because the truck drivers didn't want to drive over the broken glass for obvious reasons. Also, a great number of wooden pallets would become broken and not serviceable anymore and I would dispose of these as well whenever necessary. And lifting and stacking a lot of empty wooden pallets regularly built my upper arm strength up like it had never been before.

I liked my job quite a lot, and I was happy that I was not working on the "line" which was the assembly line where the bottles were washed out, refilled with beverage and then eventually loaded onto trucks to be transported to the stores. This kind of job appeared to me to be not only boring and repetitious but also quite noisy standing all day next to the loud machinery of the bottling operation.

My job allowed me to walk around a lot more, and sometimes when things were slow and there weren't broken bottles, cases, or pallets to clean up, I'd actually have nothing to do but wait until I had something to do, instead of constantly trying to keep up with a conveyor belt that neither rested nor was sympathetic to a man's limitations and abilities.

As an added bonus, the soft drinks were free to all employees, and there were coolers all over the plant where I could just help myself to a soft drink at any time. Dr. Pepper wasn't the only beverage that the plant bottled; there were other brands as well, such as fruity sodas, root beer and other flavors. But Dr. Pepper was my favorite, and every shift I'd drink several of the small 7 oz. "pony" bottles that were kept in the coolers for the employees to refresh themselves.

I kept this job and my little living place for quite a long time, at least long enough to pay off my Honda and to save up a little money for my next grand adventure, which began shortly after I saw my father once again.

Chapter 25. Tales of the White Mustang

"Not til we are lost do we begin to find ourselves."
— *Henry David Thoreau*

Driving down a lonely stretch of dirt road in the middle of the desert, just a few miles north of Interstate 10, not too far from Deming, New Mexico, the guy sitting in the back seat put a knife to my throat and said, "Stop the car right here, you son of a bitch." As I pulled the car over, I was almost overcome with feelings of fear, terror and apprehension. Frankly, I was scared shitless.

It had all started when I had acquired the 1966 Ford Mustang just a couple of months earlier. My father had given me the car for my 22nd birthday and almost as soon as I had the keys in my hands, I was making plans for a trip cross-country. My father had acquired the car in a trade from a car dealer in Dallas. On his last trip back from Europe, a friend of his in Madrid, who was a car dealer, had told him that the new VW van "Camp-mobiles" were all the rage in the States and they were hard to come by because each one had to be delivered from Germany which was the only place where they were being manufactured. His advice to my dad was to go to Germany, buy one brand new and take it back with him to the States for a great profit. So after having the car delivered in New York and driving it cross-country, camping out in it all along the way, he took it to a car dealer in Dallas, who offered him three cars for it in trade. A one-year-old Opel sports car, a nearly new small LUV pick up made by Chevrolet and the 1966 white Mustang.

My dad had decided that he and his wife Juana would leave their place in Marbella, Spain and have a go of living in the States, mostly to see if they could save their marriage which was having some serious issues, mostly due to Juana's serious drinking problem. The Opel was for her to drive and the small pickup would be his vehicle and the Mustang that the dealer in Dallas had thrown in to sweeten the deal was for me, knowing I really needed wheels.

The Mustang at that time was almost eight years old but had few miles on it for its age. It had a small dent in the rear fender where the previous owner had backed into a telephone pole or something, but it ran fine and made a great birthday gift for his adventurous son. It was solid white with a bright red interior and was in great shape overall and I was more than delighted to be the owner of such a really nice and sporty car.

When I saw the car in the driveway for the first time of my brother's place in Cleburne, I couldn't remember the last time I had been so excited. I had met a very nice Japanese-American lady by the name of Mioshi while I was living and working in Frankfurt, Germany a couple of years earlier and we had kept in touch. She was living in San Francisco, California and had invited me to visit her whenever I had the chance.

Well, now was my chance, now that I had wheels. So within a couple of weeks, I quit the job I had with Dr. Pepper Bottling Company, sold my motorbike, put everything I owned into the trunk of the Mustang and took off for sunny California. My plan was to stop in San Diego to visit my old friend J.P. who was living there and then eventually work my way up the coast to San Francisco. I had never been to California before so it was all going to be new to me.

I had decided to make a couple of stops in New Mexico on my way to the West Coast. My Dad and Juana had found a place in New Mexico and had settled in Tularosa, a small town just north of Alamogordo and not far from Holloman Air Force Base and White Sands National Monument. It was an old house on several acres of land and much like the place they had in Marbella, again they had plans to fix it up by adding a two story addition and other renovations and improvements. So my plan was to visit them in Tularosa on my way to California and look up an old friend of mine from Madrid who I understood was attending the University of New Mexico in Albuquerque. So by looking at the map, I realized that I'd be stopping in Albuquerque first.

My buddy Dave was going to college there so that would be my first stop. He was the fellow that had the great party at his house in Madrid where a group of us had taken acid for the first time when we were all still in high school. I had seen him in Madrid before I left and he told me he had plans to attend the University of New Mexico for four years, one reason was because it was close to the high mountains and he was really into skiing a lot.

So I made it to Albuquerque with no problems and had camped out along the way to avoid the high costs of hotel or motel rooms. I still had the original Dutch Army pup tent I had acquired while I was in Germany and it served me very well while traveling. I'd find a place off the road where no one was around and set up my tent, an air mattress and my sleeping bag, and I had free accommodations. Along with my small camp stove and some cans of food, I could eat and sleep quite well for very little. And this was of upmost importance because I left Texas with not a lot of money with me.

After arriving at Albuquerque, since I had plans to stick around for a few days, I had to find a place to pitch my tent that was close enough to the city, yet far enough away to give me the privacy I required. When I looked around for the city, I saw this huge mountain range just to the northeast of the downtown area called the Sandia Mountains. So that is where I headed for to find a peaceful place to pitch my tent for the night. Sandia Peak is the highest point in the range and sits at over 10,000 feet and so it is a very tall mountain indeed. But I found that after driving just a few miles up the road towards the top, there were plenty of places to pull over and camp and most areas had picnic tables and fire rings. And most importantly it was free.

The second day I headed down to the University area and found the campus easily enough and I went to the registration office and found a very nice lady to help me out. I explained my situation that I was looking for an old friend I knew in Spain that was supposed to be attending the University of New Mexico and after giving her his name, she gave me some bad news. It turned out he had quit school the previous semester and left no forwarding address and therefore was nowhere to be found. I thanked the lady for her help and after hanging around the campus a little longer; I left and headed back up to the mountain.

This was on a Tuesday and as I was heading back up to my camping place, I was listening to the local Rock radio station and I heard a commercial that intrigued me. It said the following Saturday night, there was to be a concert in town with Rod Stewart and his band as the headliner. I wasn't really a big fan of Rod's, but when I heard who was to be his opening band, my ears perked up. It was none other than Rory Gallagher. My friend J.P. who I had an enormous amount of respect for, had told me on more than one occasion that if I ever had a chance to see Rory perform, to don't dare miss it. J.P. claimed Rory was one of the greatest guitar players alive since he had seen him a couple of times when he was in England a few years earlier.

So I immediately decided that I'd stay in town until that coming Saturday just to see if J.P. was right or not. Besides, I was in no major hurry to get to California and I wanted a little more time to hang around the campus of the University of New Mexico because it seemed to be a very interesting place with many people hanging around that looked a lot like me and who I thought I could relate to. I had a nice place to stay for free, and I really wanted to see Rory perform, so I spent the next five days hanging around the college campus and exploring the city of Albuquerque and my nights in my little pup tent up on the mountain.

So the night of the concert, I got to the arena early enough to get my ticket, and I waited in line until they opened the doors. Since it was an open seating style concert, I was able to get down to the seats at the very front of the stage to get a good view. When Rory came out and did his set, it blew me away. He was not only a great guitarist, but an amazing performer and singer. The crowd reacted rather cool towards him because most had probably never even heard of Rory and were only there for the headliner and were eager to see the pop idol Rod Stewart. But Rod the Mod put on an amazing show as well and got the entire crowd of thousands of people on their feet and singing along with his big hit, "Maggie May." It was a strange show with an Irish rock guitarist opening for a Scottish Pop singer and both performing for a bunch of American kids in Albuquerque, New Mexico. Only in America!

The next morning I got an early start and headed towards Tularosa which was only about a four hour drive. When I got there, both my dad and Juana warmly welcomed me and before too long they showed me around the place and what they were doing to it. It was an old adobe house sitting on four acres of pecan trees just to the north of the small town of Tularosa. They had plans to add an addition to the existing house with a large bedroom upstairs and a new covered patio in the back. They had hired a local guy named Alberto who was in his seventies but knew everything about the art of building with adobe bricks, which is the principle building material used in New Mexico, since the bricks keep it cool in the summer, yet warm in the wintertime.

Alberto would show up early every morning and my dad and I would help him make the adobe bricks that were needed to build the addition. Luckily my dad had bought the small pickup truck because we spent many hours riding in it, hauling tools and supplies from the building supply store in Alamogordo to the house in Tularosa.

Adobe bricks are made on the premises instead of having to transport these heavy bricks long distances. Alberto knew how to make the bricks, so the first part of the construction process was getting the bricks made and in a sufficient quantity to do the job. An adobe brick is made of earth mixed with water and straw which is used to bind the bricks together. To allow the bricks to dry evenly, wooden frames are used to set the mixture and then are removed after the initial setting and after allowed to dry for a few hours, are turned on edge to finish the drying process.

Alberto was the expert and my dad and I were only his helpers and did whatever he said to get the bricks made. He estimated we would require around a thousand bricks for the job so we spent the next couple of weeks just getting the materials prepared for the actual building process.

It was great working right alongside my dad just like we had at his place in Marbella and the best part was that he paid me for my efforts. Not only did I get free room and board while I was there those three weeks or so, but I also got paid in cash which I put toward my traveling money.

After being there a couple of weeks and working almost every day on the construction, we got an unexpected visit from my dad's brother, my Uncle Herbert. He had came down from California where he lived with his wife and young son and to visit with my dad and his new wife for a while. Herb had spent considerable time not only in Mexico City while attending college on the G. I. Bill, but had also spent time in El Paso, Texas as well as across the river in

Ciudad Juarez, and he spoke fluent Spanish.

El Paso was only about a hundred miles from Tularosa, so we decided that while Herb was there visiting, the four of us would take a trip there for a weekend. Herb was quite the gambler and liked to bet on the racehorses which one could do easily there in Juarez. We took the little Opel down to Juarez and had a great time listening to a Mariachi band while having a fantastic meal at a nice restaurant and then stayed the night at the Hotel Juarez downtown. We all had a wonderful experience, and I got the opportunity to get to know my Uncle Herbert as an adult, because before that, I had only met him as a child.

The next day we all returned to Tularosa after experiencing a little taste of Mexico and Herb had a few dollars more in his wallet from betting on the horses. My Uncle Herbert seemed to me to have a kind and gentle soul and was obviously a quite intelligent man as well. We had several long and deep conversations about every topic imaginable, and he had very profound beliefs and was not shy about expressing them. He opened my eyes on such subjects as religion, politics, identity and culture, and I still feel his influence on my life and belief system to this day, and it was a great experience to get to know him a little better.

Within a few days, Herb headed back to California, and then I got ready to move on as well because by this time I was eager to get to San Diego. So after my dad and Juana wished me the best of luck, early one morning I took off for California, the Golden State, to make my life there with all of that wonderful sunshine, near the ocean and hopefully with more like-minded people than I had found in Texas.

Once arriving at La Jolla just north of San Diego, after a long drive through the rest of New Mexico, Arizona and Southern California, I looked up my old friend from Spain, J.P. He was working at a fancy French restaurant in La Jolla which was owned by his aunt, and it seemed to me that he was really living the great sunny California life. He had come down from Thunder Bay, Ontario after immigrating to Canada a few months earlier and was helping his aunt with her restaurant. He had a beautiful, blond-haired, blue eyed Californian girlfriend by the name of Amber, who coincidentally owned the same model year and color of my Mustang. The only difference was that hers had a blue interior and mine was red. He was living in a small house only a few blocks from the beach that he was with a French roommate by the name of Richard, who was a singer and guitar player and who also was the entertainer at his aunt's French restaurant in La Jolla.

The weekend after I arrived in California, J.P. and Amber invited me along for a trip to Baja California. The plan was to drive down to San Felipe on the Sea of Cortez for a couple of nights of fun and adventure. It was about a five-hour drive from San Diego and we decided to take Amber's Mustang because she had the Mexican Insurance for it from previous trips south of the border. So we threw sleeping bags, a cooler of beer, and some food in the trunk and off we went.

Arriving at San Felipe after driving the fairly decent paved road through the Mexican desert south of Mexicali that first evening, it surprised us to find very little there. San Felipe was hardly even a village. The only businesses in town was a restaurant and a gas station, there were no hotels, trailer parks, or any other facilities. The restaurant had a pen in the back of their property where they kept live sea turtles, which the local fishermen would catch occasionally and sell to the restaurant owner. And he would butcher one whenever he had enough customers to eat the flesh of the creature and apparently that weekend there were enough tourists around to merit butchering a fat one. So after dining on fresh turtle steak with all the trimmings, and drinking all the Mexican beer we could handle, we three young people spread our sleeping bags out on the beach a few feet above the high tide line and slept the sleep of the full, the drunk and the contented.

The next morning we were up shortly after dawn since the searing sun prevented us from sleeping in, and while having a coffee and some *huevos rancheros* at the restaurant, we talked to some American guys who were doing the same. These four guys had came down from San Diego in two separate four-wheel-drive pickups and were planning on driving that day down to the next village south called Puertecitos. Puertecitos was about fifty miles down the coast and the dirt road to get there started right outside of San Felipe.

The guys said they would take the lead and the rear if J.P., Amber and me wanted to drive our Mustang in between the trucks in a three vehicle caravan down to Puertecitos. So after loading the cooler up with cold Mexican beer and limes from the restaurant, we headed south, with the first pickup leading the way, then the Mustang, then the second pickup picking up the rear. The road (if one could call it that) was the worse that any of us had ever seen. Deep ruts, huge rocks, washboard, and sand traps were the norm and more than once one of the pickups had to winch the Mustang out of the sand to keep us all moving along.

So after over four hours of driving this hell's highway, as they called it, dodging wild burros and skinny desperate looking cattle with half their weight in *cholla* cactus stuck to their hides crossing the road right in front of us, we finally made it the fifty miles to Puertocitos. If we thought San Felipe was small, at least it had a gas station and a restaurant, but the only thing we found in Puertocitos was a bar, and a few sad looking travel trailers several decades old.

So after spending the evening in the bar, drinking and eating our fill (this time some tasty fish *tostadas* that the bartender was able to whip up), we again passed out on the sand right above the high tide line, after having a late night of dancing to the jukebox that the owner of the bar had somehow got into his little bar. We had a great time with the four guys from the trucks and with the few locals around, both gringos and Mexicans, that showed up on a Saturday night to the only bar in Puertecitos.

The next morning, after rising with the sun and a quick coffee, we headed back north to San Felipe again sandwiched between the two four-wheel drives trucks. After a quick lunch of some turtle soup at the only restaurant in town, we said our farewells and thanks to the nice guys in the pickups, then we headed back to the U.S.

On the drive back J.P. and I discussed what we had seen in Baja California and we made an agreement that someday we would drive the entire peninsula all the way to Cabo San Lucas. Baja seemed to have everything that the both of us liked so much, a lot of sun, a beautiful sea with wonderful beaches, cheap prices and everyone spoke Spanish which reminded us a lot of Spain, but Spain as it was like years before the tourists had discovered it and made it what it is today.

Shortly after arriving back in San Diego, I realized that I would have to make some more money if I was to continue on up to San Francisco to meet up with Mioshi, so I decided to get a job somewhere for a while. Unfortunately J.P.'s aunt didn't need any help because she barely had enough work for him, much less anyone else. So I went downtown to the Job Service office to see what they might have for me. It turned out that there were many people that wanted to come to sunny San Diego and make their life in this wonderful place with the nice climate and wonderful beaches. In fact, the clerk I talked to at the Job Service told me that probably the best thing for me to do would be to go back to school, because I could probably get some financial help if I was going to college full time. But I told him I wasn't interested in school at this time, that I just needed a job at this point in my life.

So he looked at all his employment referrals and told me that there just weren't *any* jobs available in San Diego for a person with my limited qualifications and experience. It devastated me and I told him to keep looking and that there must be some job somewhere that I could do.

Again he went through his listings and then he said to me, "Well, there is one job for a dishwasher, but it's in Escondido."

I looked at him and asked, "Um, where's Escondido?"

"Well, it's about thirty miles northeast of San Diego," he told me.

"Okay, I'll take it," I said immediately.

"Well, you have to get hired first, you know. But yes, I can give you a referral and send you there if you like. It's at a restaurant at the Hidden Valley Country Club up there."

"Okay, sounds great," I said.

"All right, so here's the referral slip. If you don't get hired, come on back in a few days and you never know, something else might come up, okay?"

"Yes sir, and thank you very much," I said and shook his hand and headed out the door with the slip in my hand that had the address and the contact name of the person to talk to about the job.

I easily found my way up to the town of Escondido, which is out in the hills northeast about a half hour drive from the outskirts of San Diego and I found the "Hidden Valley Country Club" which was just a few miles out of town. I parked in the parking lot of the restaurant and went in and asked for Chef Pierre who ran the kitchen of the place. After about a short five-minute interview, he told me I had the job, and I could start the next day if I'd liked. He told me that the pay was minimum wage but the kitchen staff got a percentage of the tips from the wait staff, so it would be slightly more than the minimum. The shift was Monday through Friday; from nine to six with a half hour lunch break and paydays were on Fridays. And depending on the volume of business, some overtime would be possible which paid time and a half.

I thanked Chef Pierre and told him I'd be there in the morning and left. I went back out to the parking lot of the restaurant and sat in my car for a moment to think. It was great that I had found a job, but now I had a problem of where I would stay. While I was driving up to the restaurant, I had noticed a lot of open land in the hills overlooking the town, so I took a drive out into those hills to see if I could find a place to pitch my tent. After driving on a dirt road for a couple miles I saw a turnoff that went even further back into the hills, so I took it. Before too long I found a small grove of trees with nobody around that I could see. The main dirt road was quite a ways from where I was and I had seen little traffic on it, so I thought I'd be safe camping under this small grove of trees. So I set up my camp, and that's where I stayed for the next four weeks.

I could clean myself up in the restaurant's bathroom every day, and on my days off I would go into the little town of Escondido to do my laundry and buy supplies, mostly canned food items to cook for dinner. But I got a free meal every day at work, so I didn't have to eat every meal out of a can. In fact, the food was excellent as one would expect from a first-class restaurant at a fancy country club restaurant. People left all kinds of great food on their plates, and often I would slip a half-eaten steak or prime rib and a baked potato into my pocket and take it home and have it for dinner instead of a can of soup.

I never told Pierre or anyone I worked with where I lived or where I was staying and they never asked, so it was never an issue. In fact, on most days, I wouldn't even bother breaking down my tent, but instead I'd just leave it set up all day while I was gone and nobody ever bothered it, so I felt very comfortable and safe at my campsite.

One weekend I drove back to La Jolla and saw J.P. again. He told me that his aunt really didn't have enough work to keep him on, so he had decided to leave San Diego within a couple of days and travel up to Vancouver, British Columbia and check that place out. Besides, he hadn't really entered the country of the United States totally legally, so it would probably be best if he returned to Canada for a while before that fact caught up with him. So again we said our heartfelt goodbyes and promised to keep in touch and I didn't see him again until almost six years later.

Around this time I discovered I had a problem with the manifold on the muffler of my Mustang. It had came off from the side of the engine block and was making an enormous powerful growling noise every time I started the engine, and I was afraid of getting pulled over for excessive noise or something, and the last thing I needed was trouble from the police. J.P. looked at it and advised me that to get it fixed would require a welding job and the cheapest place for that type of work was across the international line in Tijuana. There were mechanics there that would do it for a few dollars compared to perhaps a hundred or more on this side of the border. Being of limited financial means, I decided to head south to get the work done, then afterwards head north to San Francisco to see if I could find Mioshi which I was confident I could do, after all I still had her telephone number and address in my wallet.

So after working at the restaurant for four weeks, I told Chef Pierre that I was quitting and got my last paycheck. I packed up all my stuff and headed south to get my car fixed before heading to San Francisco. I crossed the border at the San Isidro crossing and drove into the city of Tijuana. It didn't take long to find a mechanic's shop that did welding and after negotiating with a mechanic for the repairs; I headed for the nearest bar to wait the few hours they told me it would take for the welding job to get done.

While standing at the bar drinking a cold beer, I struck up a conversation with two American guys about my age. They both had long hair and beards and the look of people that in my past, I had learned I could trust, just a couple more "freaks" like myself. They asked me what I was doing in Tijuana and I told them about the car repairs to my Mustang that was being performed at the nearby mechanic's shop. They asked me where I was headed after that, and I told them I was headed north to San Francisco to see an old friend.

These two guys, who said their names were Joe and Steve, said they were in Tijuana enjoying a little break after delivering a 35 foot private sail boat from Miami to San Diego through the Panama Canal. This was their business they told me, and business was good since this was the third delivery they had done this year. There were many rich yacht owners that needed to have their boats delivered from one port to another and will pay really good money to have someone do just that.

Then they told me they could use another hand on board for their next delivery and asked if I had any boating experience. I replied that as a young lad; I had spent one year on the coast of Spain and had spent time aboard boats but had never actually worked as such. I was then told that they could teach me everything I would need to know if I wanted to accompany them on their next delivery job, which was delivering a 38 foot Crist Craft power boat from New Orleans to San Francisco through the Panama Canal. It would take about three weeks and it would pay one thousand dollars each!

But they would have to get to New Orleans for the pickup, and unfortunately they had no wheels since they had just finished up a previous delivery to San Diego a few days before. They were thinking of taking the Greyhound back to New Orleans, but if I was willing to drive them, I could have the job. I told them I would have to think about it and I got up from the bar stool to relieve myself. While standing at the urinal letting go of some used beer, I told myself that if I arrived in San Francisco with one thousand dollars, not only would Mioshi be impressed, but I could relax and not have to worry about working for quite a while with that kind of money. So I walked back to the bar with a smile on my face thinking this was indeed my lucky day.

So the three of us got into the Mustang which was purring like a kitten after the recent repairs and we headed north. While waiting in line at the international border, I asked the guys what I would do with my car once we had arrived in New Orleans and we had gotten aboard the boat for the voyage.

Joe said, "Don't worry, bud, we got a storage yard down by the docks in New Orleans to leave it at, and you can pick it up the next time you're in town."

Okay, well then, that seemed like a simple solution, I thought to myself. So the first stop was the Greyhound Bus terminal in downtown San Diego to pick up their duffel bags that the guys had left in a storage locker there. After putting their bags in the trunk on top of all my gear which included my guitar, my clothes, my pup tent and everything else that I owned in the world, we got on Interstate 8 heading east, all the way to New Orleans, Louisiana. We figured we would drive straight on through, with the three of us taking turns driving while one of us crashed out in the back seat, and it would take around 30 hours for the entire trip.

When driving out of San Diego, the I-8 rises from the coastal lowlands up to a higher elevation to cross the mountain range near El Centro, and it goes through a small town in the mountains called Alpine. This is where we stopped to fill up the gas tank and to get snacks for the trip. By this time, I had started to feel somewhat uneasy about the situation I found myself in. I had a sneaky suspicion that something was just not quite right about this whole story. It was just a feeling I had but one I could no longer ignore. Besides, if I was to leave my beloved Mustang in New Orleans while we took this voyage across the hemisphere, how would I get from San Francisco back to New Orleans to recover it? I guess I could always take the Greyhound across the country, or I suppose I could sell the car before getting on the boat for the trip, and then buy another one someday, but who could I sell it to? I knew car dealers never give you what a car is worth. And besides, I loved my car, this car.

After paying the attendant for the gas, I headed back out to the pump where the car was parked and noticed that Joe and Steve were both not around, obviously in the bathroom, or in the convenience store buying cigarettes and snacks. The thought occurred to me as I was filling the tank that at this point it would be so easy to just drive to the end of the parking lot, where the entrance to the freeway began, and just stop the car there, open the trunk, grab the guys' duffel bags and throw them on the pavement and drive away. The hell with them, I thought.

Or I could just tell them that I had changed my mind, but they didn't seem to be the kind of guys that would be too happy about a change of plans like that. I realized that even though these two young men had the long hair and the look of a fellow "freak" it didn't feel quite right, that something was off. I was just about ready to put the car in gear and drive to the entrance of the freeway and execute my plan, when Joe opened the passenger door and said, "Hey, Bud, ready to go?"

So we kept heading east, and we drove through the Imperial Valley of California, through Yuma, on to Gila Bend, and then just outside of Casa Grande, we got on Interstate 10, and into Tucson along the same route I had driven only a few short weeks before. After getting a few hours sleep in the back seat while Joe drove for a while, I woke up to find ourselves just past the border into New Mexico, just a few miles before Lordsburg. At that point, I started driving again, and I took over the wheel from Joe.

Then about five or six miles before Deming, New Mexico, Joe, who was sitting in the back seat at the time said, "Hey, how about we stop at a buddy's house we know, who lives just a few miles off the interstate up here? Maybe he'll put us up for the night and I'm sure he'll have some great weed, man."

So I agreed, and we took the next exit off the highway, heading north off into the New Mexican desert. After driving on the paved road a few miles, Joe told me to take the next right on a dirt road heading east. After a few more miles of dust and bumps, Joe who is sitting in the back seat put a knife to my neck and said "Stop the car right here, you son of a bitch."

I was shocked but not totally surprised at this turn of events. I had suspected something was fishy and not quite right about this situation even before Alpine, but this wasn't what I had expected or even suspected was to happen.

I slammed on the breaks and said with the calmest voice I could muster, "What the hell do you guys want?"

Joe said, "Get out of the car right now, motherfucker," still holding the knife to my jugular.

So we all got out, and I stood there looking at Joe with the same bewildered look on my face, and before I can utter a word, Steve came up behind me and hit me over the head with an empty Coke bottle that had been rolling around on the floorboards of the back seat. I fell to the ground, with blood gushing from the wound to my head, still trying to understand what was happening.

On my knees, I cried out, "What the hell, guys, I thought we were partners! What the hell's going on?"

Steve grabbed the keys from the ignition and opened the trunk of the car, rummaged around for a few seconds, and grabbed the pup tent I had there. He then used the ropes of the tent to hogtie me, with my hands behind my back and with my hands tied to my feet, and with my face right down in the dusty dirt road.

Joe grabbed my wallet from my pants pocket, and then they both got back in the car and Joe started it up, did a quick U-Turn, and shouted "Adios, asshole!" out the window as they drove off, with everything I owned in the world, including my prized acoustic guitar, all my personal papers and photos, my passport, all of my clothing, and every other possession I had, including my wallet which had over 200 dollars in it, along with the address and phone number of Mioshi in San Francisco.

Unable to get to my feet, I spat a mixture of dirt and blood out from my mouth, cursing and asking myself how I could be so stupid, so damn stupid. After a few minutes of this, I calmed myself down a little and managed to kick my sneaker off of my right foot, and slipped my foot out from the rope that had my feet tied together, and I was able to stand up. I was barely able to slip my shoe back on my foot to be able to walk. Then with my hands still tied behind my back, and blood caking my long hair and still running down my face, I began to walk back in the direction where we had driven from and where the two criminals had headed.

After about a half an hour or so of hiking down the dirt road with blood all over my face and hair and my hands still tied behind me, I finally came to the paved road we had turned off from before. I stood there on the side of the road for a few minutes until a car approached.

But I couldn't hitchhike because my arms were still tied behind my back. The driver of the car just stared at me as he drove by, at this strange person with blood all over his hair and with a wild look of desperation on his face and just kept going, afraid of this strange apparition he had just seen on the side of the road. Another car came by within a couple of minutes with a similar reaction from the driver.

After about five minutes of this and about the same number of cars driving by, all with the same reactions, I finally just stood there in the middle of the road, forcing the next driver to stop. The driver of the pickup truck was an older cowboy/rancher type wearing a big white cowboy hat. When he saw this person standing in the middle of the road, he knew something must be terribly wrong and stopped to find out what was going on, besides he would have had to drive onto the shoulder of the road to get around me.

I was so grateful and almost in shock by this time and started sobbing when the driver stopped and got out of his truck. I quickly told the driver what had happened and the first thing he did was untie the rope binding my hands. Then he opened the passenger side of the truck and told me to hop in, that he'd take me to the Sheriff's office in town.

Within about twenty minutes, I was telling my story to Sheriff Watson who didn't seem to think what had happened out there in the desert was much of a big deal at all. He told me that the guys were probably down in Mexico by now with my car and it probably wasn't even worth it to put out an APB for the vehicle or the suspects.

"Those boys are gone by now, long gone," he snorted while spitting tobacco juice into a Dixie cup, "Long gone for sure, son, but I guess we ought to take you over to the clinic and see if they can do something about that nasty cut on your head there."

So after getting checked out by the local doctor and relieved to find out that the cut did not need stitches and would probably heal nicely, I rode with the Deputy who and given me a ride to the clinic back to the Sheriff's office.

Luckily for me, my dad and his wife were living in Tularosa at the time. And Sheriff Watson was kind enough to allow me to use his telephone as long as I called collect to talk to my father to tell him what happened. My dad told me he would be there the next day since it was almost dark by this time and it was about a four-hour drive from Tularosa to Deming.

So that night I had no other place to stay besides the jail. The Sheriff also loaned me a couple of dollars so I could walk up to the McDonald's and buy myself a hamburger and a drink for dinner before bedding down on the cot in one of the jail cells. I realized that the Sheriff didn't or couldn't recognize the extreme irony involved here, that I (the victim) was sitting in a jail cell, while the criminals drove around not only with the stolen car and all my belongings and money but also with their freedom. Well, at least the Deputy left the jail cell door open for me so not to make me feel too much like a damn criminal. Thanks so much for small favors, I thought as I fell asleep that night on the black-and-white striped mattress of the jail cell cot, wondering what the hell this country was really like where it was impossible to trust anyone, even fellow freaks.

After a sleepless night being grateful that the jail didn't haven't any other occupants besides myself that night, otherwise I'm sure I would have gotten even less sleep, my dad arrived around noon the next day and the first thing we did was head for a Salvation Army store in town to get me some new clothes since the ones I had on were dirty and had traces of my blood on them.

After buying two pairs of jeans and a couple of shirts at the thrift store, we went to another store, and I got some socks and underwear and then we headed back to Tularosa. After telling him the entire story about what had happened from the time I had left his place only a couple of months before, including my making the big mistake of trusting the two criminals that had ripped me off, I'm sure he realized, as well as I, that I had a lot to learn about life in these United States of America, and that I was a very innocent and naïve young man indeed.

I stuck around Tularosa for several weeks helping out again with the construction project mostly to save up a little money again, but also to help my Dad out because it appeared to me that not a lot of progress had been made since I had left. My plan was to return to Fort Worth and stay with my brother until I got a job and a place to live once again and having a little money would allow me to be that much closer to be able to get my own place and not have to rely so much on his hospitality and kindness. So once I was able to save a couple of hundred dollars from working every day, I said my goodbyes to my dad and Juana and took the Greyhound to Fort Worth.

It wouldn't take too long to find a job again and this time I made sure that I had a job before finding a place to live because since I didn't have a car, I wanted to live close to where I worked, so I could walk to work and not have to ride the bus which always took so much time and effort.

I looked in the newspaper and saw that a plant on the south side of town called Dairy Pack was hiring, so I went there and applied and got the job very easily. It was a lousy job is why I got it so easily, I'm sure. The plant manufactured cartons for milk and other dairy products which were printed out on a huge printing press machine and then the waxed carton paper was cut into shapes to be folded up by a machine at the dairy and then the milk or other products were placed in them and sold to the public.

They all had to be printed with the logo of the dairy and other information that a milk carton has on it, including the name and quantity of the product, and other pertinent information. So the company would have a run for a certain dairy and print thousands of sheets of special milk carton paper with that dairy's logo and information on it, and another machine would cut the sheets into separate individual pieces that would stack up on the conveyor belt and my job was to remove the stacks of flat and folded milk cartons and put them onto pallets that were then shipped to the dairy. It was back-breaking work and as boring as anything could possibly be, but it was a job. And for some reason I could never quite figure out, mostly young black guys worked there except for the forklift operators and the foremen who were all older white men. The pay was minimum wage, but it was full time with regular hours and weekends free.

I found a small apartment nearby, about six blocks away from the plant, and once again it was a large house that had been divided up into several small apartments, but at least this time my place was downstairs. The rent was reasonable and soon I was looking for a car. One of the guys at work told me about a friend of his that was selling an old car for cheap, so I went over to where the car was parked and talked to the guy that had it.

It was a 1960 Lincoln Continental 4 door hardtop, and it had seen better days, but it was only 100 dollars and it ran. I figured it would be okay to drive to work and back and go to the store for groceries and beer, so I went ahead and bought it from him. The tires were bald; the paint was fading badly, and it burned oil pretty bad but like I say, at least it ran and was cheap. And it used a lot of gas to move this tank down the road, but it was transportation and that's what I needed at this point.

So I settled into life again in Fort Worth, working five days a week and on the weekends going out to John's place occasionally to get away from the city and relax. I spent a lot of time thinking about the girl Lizzy, who I thought I was in love with in Spain. I knew she had graduated from MHS the summer before but I had no way of getting a hold of her or even where she was, but one day I had an idea.

My mom at this point was still living in Canillejas, just outside of Madrid and so I wrote her a letter and asked her to do me a favor. I asked if she would go out to the base for me and ask at the high school there if they had a record of Lizzy's whereabouts or her family's. It was a slim shot, but I thought it might be worth the effort.

My mom did what I requested and went out to MHS and talked to the lady at the office of the high school who was in charge of records and explained the situation to her, about her son being in the States but thinking he was still in love with this girl he knew from MHS. I guess the lady thought it was romantic because she broke the rules for my Mom and gave her an address in Riverside, California, where Lizzy's dad had gone to after leaving Torrejon the year before. My mom sent me the address, and I was relieved, excited and apprehensive all at the same time.

I took a long time to compose a letter to her, but I did and sent it off. But I deliberately kept the letter very open and didn't really get into my feelings for her, but more of just a friendly letter asking how she was doing. A couple of weeks later, I got a letter back from Lizzy's sister saying that Lizzy was living in New York, but she gave me her address there to write to her. Again I wrote another letter and sent it off to her address in Brooklyn, New York.

A couple of weeks later, I again got a letter, this one from Lizzy herself. She said she remembered me well, and that it was good to hear from me. She also told me she was married to Tiny Harrison, and they had a son. It was exactly like Tiny had told her the second I had introduced them together at his *piso* in Madrid. Her son's name was Allen, Jr. and they lived in a small apartment close to his family's house in Brooklyn. They had gotten married shortly after she had graduated from high school and a short time later, he got transferred back to the states, got out of the Air Force and they had settled in Brooklyn, his hometown.

She also told me some other things in that letter that made me feel some strange and conflicting emotions. She told me she was *not* happily married and that he would mistreat her regularly and spent most his time with his buddies or at his parents' house. She said he drank a lot and didn't seem to care that much about her or their baby. Then she told me some other rather strange news. She told me that she was pregnant again, but she didn't want to have another baby because she planned on leaving him soon and getting a divorce. She wanted to get an abortion, but she didn't have the money to get one. She said an abortion cost about 300 dollars and she asked me if I could lend the money to her so she could have it.

It blew my mind! This was the last thing I had expected when I had written her. That Tiny had predicted their marriage and their son the exact moment they had met was strange enough, but now she wanted me to lend her money to keep her from having another baby with him. I thought about it for several days before writing her back. In my next letter, I confessed my love for her and told her I had feelings for her from the moment I met her at a cafe near the *Estadio Bernabeu* a couple of years earlier. I told her I would see about getting the money to send her so she could get the abortion since I didn't want her to have another baby from a man she planned on divorcing soon.

In the back of my mind, I thought if she got the abortion and the divorce, then maybe, just maybe I might have a chance with her sometime in the future. I also asked her how far long she was along with her pregnancy and therefore how long I had to get the money together to send her for the abortion.

She mailed me a letter back soon after that and told me she had just found out about her pregnancy and so she had a few months yet before it was too late to get it done, and again how much she would appreciate it if I could help her out because it would really change her life for the good. So in my next letter I told her I'd send the money to her within a couple of months at the latest and for her to hang on until then, and that I would make sure I got it to her in time.

I scrimped and saved and within two months; I was able to save up the 300 dollars, and I sent it to her. In the meantime, we exchanged several more letters, and it was always the same message from her, about how he was treating her so badly and she couldn't wait until she could get away from him. She also told me that the one reason she had married him was that she really needed to get away from her family, especially her father, and that is why she accepted his proposal right before she had finished high school.

After I sent her the letter with the money, the next letter I got from her was rather disturbing to say the least. She thanked me for the money and promised to pay me back some day, but she also told me some other things that made me doubt her sincerity and honesty. She told me she was really enjoying the new ten-speed bicycle she had bought for herself because it allowed her to get around town a lot easier than walking or riding the bus. But she told me she had gotten the abortion done and was now making plans for getting the divorce done and over. She also said she had never told Tiny about the pregnancy or the abortion because she was sure that it would upset him and totally forbid her from having it because that is the way he was and the way he believed.

After this, her letters seemed to slow down considerably and became much less frequent, even though I continued to write to her regularly. When I'd write and ask her about how the divorce was going, it would take a long time to get an answer back and when I did, she was evasive and avoided the subject. I still thought I was in love and it was hard for me to see exactly what was going on and how I was possibly being duped and manipulated, but I continued to write to her, and then after a while her letters slowed down until I didn't get any response at all.

I went on with my life and within about six months of my experience outside of Deming, New Mexico, I received a letter from the California Department of Transportation, saying they had recovered my 1966 Mustang and was in a storage lot in Baker, California. They had traced the VIN (Vehicle Identification Number) and were able to find my address in Texas and were informing me that if I wanted to pick up my car, I'd be required to go to Baker and pay the storage costs owed on it, which at this point was about 100 dollars but was still accruing at a rate of five dollars per day. The letter also said all I had to do was show the letter to the manager of the storage yard and he would release the car after paying him the storage costs owed. Also, if I chose not to recover my vehicle, to please let them know, so they could dispose of it according to their rules and regulations.

This was great news to me. I could get my sweet Mustang back. All I had to do was go out to California, pay the cost of storage, pick it up and drive it back to Texas. I got out the map and found out that Baker was on the main highway between Los Angeles and Las Vegas, actually about halfway between these two cities.

After talking to my brother and some other people, I decided that the easiest and cheapest way for me to get to California was to use a service that many people were using at the time for almost free transportation. A lot of vehicles had to be transported from one area of the country to another, usually when people moved and couldn't take their car with them, so these services connected the owner of these cars with potential drivers that were headed that way and they could deliver the vehicle to the city where it needed to be. The owner of the car paid a reasonable fee to the company to have it transported, and the driver got the free use of the car to get them to the city they were headed to, one way of course.

There was one of these companies in Dallas, so I called them and they told me they had a car that needed to be transported to L.A. as soon as possible. All I had to do was to deliver it to their office in Los Angeles, and I would get free use of the car for the time I took to get there. All I had to do was pay the gas and lodging along the way.

So after telling my boss I had to take a week off from work, which he allowed me to do since I was a good worker and it was hard to find people to do the work I was doing, I packed a small bag and got my brother to drop me off at the company's office in downtown Dallas and I was off. The car was an almost brand new Buick Skylark and after signing the papers I headed out to California once again.

From Dallas I took I-20 all the way to Van Horn, Texas where I spent the night at a cheap motel and then picked up I-10 and finally on the third day I delivered the car to the company's office in downtown L.A. It wasn't hard to find the Greyhound station from there, and soon I was riding a bus out to Baker. I got there shortly before dark and found the storage yard easily. When I saw my Mustang it shocked me. Whoever had the car had changed the look of the car completely. They jacked the back end up like a drag racer and there were huge racing slicks on the back wheels. The back end set considerably higher than the front end and so the car slanted down towards the front. It looked like something one sees on a drag race track.

I had a long talk with the owner of the storage yard and he told me that his understanding was that the Highway Patrol had pulled the car over and two young boys were driving it, and neither one was over 15 years old. They had refused to tell the cops how they had been found to be driving the car on the highway between L.A. and Vegas or how and where they had acquired it. And since they were juveniles, according to the storage yard owner, they couldn't be arrested and were just released and turned over to their parents. As far as how the car got all souped up and everything, he had no clue.

I was just thrilled to get my car back even though what someone had done to it wasn't at all to my liking. I wasn't into drag racing and I had no reason to own a drag racer, but at least I had my car back and apparently it was still running okay. So after signing the papers and paying the storage yard owner the fees I owed him, I started back to Texas. The car ran fine despite its rather strange appearance and within a couple of days; I was back at my job and my little apartment in Fort Worth.

The first thing I did was sell my old clunker to a junk yard since I had no use for it anymore. I got 50 dollars for it because I could drive it to the yard instead of them having to bring their tow truck to haul it away. And while driving my Mustang around, not only did I get a lot of strange looks from people, but I even occasionally got offers to race, which I would always decline, since I was not a drag racer even though my car would say otherwise.

Within a month or two of getting back from California with my new old car, or my old new car, depending how I wanted to look at it, the automatic transmission began to go out. At first, it just shifted badly between second and third gears, and then it wouldn't shift at all, and wouldn't even go into first gear at all anymore. The only gear it would go into was reverse.

I made some inquiries at the same junk yard which I sold my other car to and I was told that a used automatic transmission for a '66 Mustang would run around 250 dollars, plus the old one for exchange, but that wouldn't include the cost of someone removing the old one and installing the new one. I didn't have the knowledge or ability to do something like this myself, so I'd have to find someone who could. I asked around at work, and one guy told me he knew a guy that did that kind of work, and gave me his number which I called. He told me he could do the job, but it would run at least 100 dollars and a couple of days of work. I told him I'd let him know as soon as I had enough money saved up to not only buy the used transmission but also enough to pay for his labor to remove the old one and install the new one.

I still had to get to work every day and since I didn't like walking the five or six blocks every morning and evening, I continued to drive my

Mustang, but in reverse! It was only a few blocks after all, and it was all back streets in a residential neighborhood so I felt fairly safe in doing so. And if a cop happened to stop me and ask why I was driving the car backwards, my plan was just to tell him that the transmission had just then went out, and I was trying to get it home so I could repair it. Luckily I didn't need this story because I never got stopped for driving my car in reverse, although I did get a lot of strange looks from people, with my neck craned around looking through the back window, driving this souped-up Mustang down the streets backwards.

But before I could save up enough money to get the transmission replaced, something else occurred that ended up with me finally losing my sweet Mustang. Since there was no place to park anywhere besides the street in front of the building where I lived, I left it parked on the street in front of the entrance to my small apartment, just a short way across the sidewalk and the small yard from my front door.

One evening after work, I was taking a bath in the ancient claw-foot bathtub in the bathroom of my little apartment, when I heard a loud smashing noise come from just outside my front door. I had a feeling that something bad had happened because the noise was so loud and seemed so close to my front door. So I put a towel around my waist and went to open the door. I saw a sight that almost brought me to tears. My beloved Mustang which had just been sitting there minding its own business in front of my house had been smashed into. I saw another car sitting there as well with its front end slightly dented but the left rear quarter panel of my car was all smashed in.

I hurriedly put clothes on and walked out to see what happened. There's a tall lanky Texan standing there looking at the damage and I approached him and asked, "What the hell happened here?"

He looked at me with a sheepish look and told me, "Well, it looks I ran into your car, buddy. Sorry about that."

I looked at him with a look of disbelief and asked, "How the hell did you do that?"

He shrugged and said, "Well, I guess I was just going a little too fast down the street here and your car was just in my way, buddy. Sorry."

"Sorry don't cut it man. Look what you did to my car!"

I looked closer at the left rear quarter panel and I saw that it was all caved in, even to a point where the over-sized tire is up against the metal of the rear fender.

I looked at the guy again and said, "Well, let's call the cops and report this accident right now, man! Look what you did to my car!"

He looked at me with a scared look and said, "Now hold on, buddy. We can handle this without the cops, can't we now?"

"No, I don't think so, man. I'm going to the phone booth down at the corner there and call the cops, this has got to be reported right now."

Again he gave me a scared look and said, "Wait a second buddy, we can handle this without the cops. Listen, I live just down the street here less than a block. Let's go over there and talk about this."

Then in a lower voice he whispered, "Buddy, I don't have any insurance, you see. I'll end up going to jail, and I got a family to support. Let's just go down to my place there and have a beer and we'll talk about this, okay? I'll make it right with you, I promise. I could have just taken off, you know?"

I looked at him and asked, "Well, where exactly do you live, man?"

"Right there, less than a block away," and he pointed down the street.

"I don't know, man. You're supposed to call the cops when there's an accident, you know."

Again he gave me this desperate look and pleaded with me, "Buddy, if the cops show up, I'm going to jail and I got a family with two little kids. You don't want to see me in jail, do you? I'll make it right with you, I promise, but no cops. Okay?"

"Well shit, all right, I guess so," I said to him.

"Okay, good, get in my car and we'll go down there and talk this out. Hop in buddy."

So I got in his car which I noticed was an older brown colored Buick, and has barely a mark on it from the accident besides a small dent in the front fender, and he turned it around and we drove down the street less than a block and he stopped at a small white house with an old sagging porch in front. We got out and walked in the front door. I saw a lady with greasy blond hair, a dirty yellow halter top on and even yellower teeth sitting at the kitchen table smoking a cigarette and drinking a Schlitz out of the can and she looked up at us as we walked in.

She looked at me and then at him and said, "So Larry, who the hell did you drag home this time?"

He looked at her and said, "Listen Marge, just forget about what was going between us on before, okay? I got some serious shit here to deal with here, so just shut the fuck up and let me handle this, all right?"

Marge took a big swig from her can of Schlitz, puffed on her Salem, sneered at him and said, "Whatever you say, asshole. You think you're the fucking boss around here anyways, so do what you gotta do. But what is this little twerp here doing in my house?"

Larry gave her a look and said, "Just shut the fuck up, would you, Marge. I just ran into this guy's car that was parked up the street and I'm trying to make a deal with him so he doesn't call the fucking cops, okay? So just be quiet while I handle this, please."

I looked around the place and wondered the hell what I had gotten myself into here. I looked at Larry and said, "Listen man, I really think we ought to let the police handle this, okay?"

"No, no buddy, it'll be all right. Here, let's have a beer, okay? Marge, get a couple of beers for us would you, honey?"

So she got up and went to the fridge and grabbed two cans of Schlitz and handed us each one, trying her best to give me a warm yellow smile.

So Larry popped open his can as we walked into the living room and said, "Here let's have a seat, buddy. What's your name anyway, can I ask?"

I followed him into the living room, opened my beer, took a long swig and said, "My name's Ron Walker, nice to meet you, your name's Larry, right?"

"Yeah, Larry Clemmons, and that's my wife Marge. We were having a little disagreement before and that's why she seems a little pissed off right now. But don't worry about her."

Marge yelled from the kitchen, "Yeah and that's why he stormed out of here like he did and hauled ass down the street in that damn car!"

He smiled a little at me and said, "Well yeah, that might have had something to do with me losing control and ramming into your car, but I'm sure you know how it is Ron, when the old lady pisses you off like that, right?"

I took another long swig of beer and said nothing.

Again he gave me his little again smile and said, "Listen Ron, I lost my job and I just don't have the money to give you for the repairs of that quarter panel, in fact I got practically no money, that's why I don't have insurance on my car. We gotta make a deal here, okay?"

I gave him my most serious look and asked, "Well, okay Larry, what kind of deal did you have in mind?"

"Well, how about if we just swap cars? That way you'll have my car, which is a good running Buick, and I'll end up with your Mustang with the busted quarter panel. How's that sound to you?"

I scratched my head and said, "Let me think about that for a minute, okay?"

"Sure Ron, take all the time you need, buddy."

Several things were going through my head at this point. If I swap cars with him, at least I'll have a good running car, at least his Buick seemed to run okay when he gave me a ride over to his house. And I won't have to drive around in reverse all the time like I have to do with my Mustang. But should I tell him about the bad transmission in the Mustang or not? I'll have to because he'll find out soon enough and he knows where I live and he'll be knocking at my door if I'm not up front with him. Besides, I am a man of integrity and honor even though I find myself at times among people who apparently lack these traits, but that doesn't mean I have to succumb to what is around me and act like they do. Okay, I'll be up front with him and see what he says about it.

So I looked him in the eye, took another swig of my beer and said, "Listen Larry, there's something you don't know about my Mustang. The transmission is acting real funny lately and I can only get it into reverse. You still want to do the deal? If not, we're still going to have to get the cops involved in this, you know."

He shrugged and said, "Hey, that's no problem, buddy. I can get the tranny swapped out easy enough. I've done that kind of work before and it'll be a piece of cake. I can handle it."

"Okay, if you're sure about that, let's do the swap then."

"All right! Great! Let's get the titles and just sign them over to each other and it'll be a done deal, okay? Mine is the car, you got yours too?"

"Yeah, it's in the glove compartment, I'll go get it now."

"Hey, I'll give you a ride back up to your place to get yours and I got mine in the Buick so we'll do this deal right now, okay? Let's go."

So within about fifteen minutes, I had signed the title of my beloved Mustang over to Larry and he had signed the title of his Buick over to me. I drove it around the block a few times before parking it back in front of my apartment, and it seemed to run okay but it felt like a tank compared to my little Mustang, but at least it went forward.

Within a couple of weeks, while driving by Larry's place one day, I saw the repairs he had done to the Mustang. First, he had put a used rear quarter panel on the car but it was a light blue color instead of the original white which made the car look even stranger than it already did. Then a week or so later I drove by his place and saw the front end jacked up and him under it apparently changing the transmission out. And a couple of days later, the car was no longer parked in front of his house, so I assumed that he got it going okay and was driving it around.

I felt terrible having to give up my beloved little Mustang like that, but it had to be done and at least I had a car that ran okay now, even though it felt like a battleship going down the road. And it was truly ugly in the worse way possible.

About a month after all this happened, I was driving the Buick home from work one day, and it just stopped in the middle of the road. When I tried to start it, it refused to turn over. It turned out that the  engine had blown a rod and had completely frozen up. I left it on the side of the road where it died, called the junk yard the next day and sold it for 50 dollars, and I was actually glad to get rid of it because I really hated it and how it drove and felt. I was a real piece of shit car and I regretted trading my beautiful white Mustang for it.

About this time, I was also sick and tired of living in Texas. I just couldn't seem to get used to living in the place. I felt like a freak because I didn't think, act or talk anything at all like the people all around me, and I couldn't seem to get used to this place I was living in no matter how hard I tried. So I decided to leave. I had still been corresponding with my friend Bill in South Carolina, so one day, I collected my last paycheck, packed a little bag and got on the Greyhound and headed back to Myrtle Beach to see if that place would treat me any better than the last time I was there, which was almost four years earlier.

Chapter 26. Myrtle Beach - ROUND 2

> *"To know oneself is, above all,*
> *to know what one lacks.*
> *It is to measure oneself against Truth,*
> *and not the other way around."*
> — Flannery O'Connor

The bus ride across the southern part of the United States from Texas to South Carolina was an interesting experience since I had never really seen this area of the country before. From Dallas, the bus went to Little Rock, Arkansas, then down through Jackson, Mississippi, Birmingham, Alabama, and then on to Atlanta, Georgia, before reaching Columbia, South Carolina, where I changed buses to make it the rest of the way to Myrtle Beach. The trip took about a day and a half in total and the only sleep I got was a few hours when I could nod out a little on the seat of the bus.

One thing I couldn't help but notice as I gazed out the window of the Greyhound was the extreme poverty I saw, especially in the states of Mississippi and Alabama, but in the other states I traveled through as well. I was amazed that this was actually part of the United States because by all appearances, it could have been a third-world country. I saw endless miles of run-down shacks, overgrown yards, rusted hulks of old cars, old buildings, and houses that looked about ready to collapse on themselves, and people just hanging out on their front porches, apparently with not a lot to do. And for some reason almost all of them were black.

I realized that what I was seeing from the comfort of my seat on the air-conditioned bus was the extreme poverty of the Deep South. I was shocked, disgusted, and ashamed that such conditions existed in this country. I was always told that America was the land of the free and the home of the brave where anyone could be what they wanted to be, and their only limitations were their imaginations and abilities. Well, I guess these people didn't get that opportunity, obviously. It was the worse poverty I had seen in my entire life and I had been to a lot of very poor countries in my travels, but nothing compared to what I was seeing in these rural areas of the south. I was glad when I finally reached Myrtle Beach and I felt I was somewhat back to real civilization again.

This was the middle of the summer of 1975 and I found myself back in South Carolina once again. I had spent the entire summer of 1971 in the town and I felt I knew it quite well from my previous stay. It didn't seem to have changed that much, actually. There were a few more high-rises being built on the beachfront and a lot more traffic and people than I remembered, but it was essentially the same as I remembered it from four years earlier.

I called Bill from the bus station and he came and picked me up and once again we went back to his family's place on the Inter-coastal waterway. He was really glad to see me and it took a while for us to catch up on all the things we had both done since we had seen each other last. It turned out he had joined the Air Force in 1972 not too long after I had left town before and had only been discharged a few months before I had arrived back this time. They had stationed him in Thailand, among other places, and part of his job was helping to get the U.S. Military out of Vietnam. He told me he had no regrets about the time he had spent in the Air Force because he was able to see some of the world that he probably never would have otherwise, and he enjoyed the benefits of being a veteran now. His older brother had joined the Army and his younger brother had joined the Navy, so it was an obvious choice for him to join the Air Force.

He had gotten a job at the convenience store on base at Myrtle Beach Air Force Base as a clerk and he seemed to like his job a lot since it wasn't far from his house and he usually worked a regular day shift with weekends off. He had recently purchased a red VW Beetle, and he loved to drive it all around the area including up and down the strip in front of the beach where people would cruise and look for fun. But being a local as compared to the thousands of tourists in town during the summer gave him a much different perspective from that of the average person cruising the "strip."

It was also great to see his family once again. His sisters had both grown up a lot and were both older teenagers by this point. His parents were happy to see me again as well and once again they treated me like one of the family. I felt very thankful and lucky that I knew such nice people who not only allowed me to stay in their home but seemed to care about me and my life. I knew my staying with them was only temporary and I needed to find my own place as soon as possible. And I also needed to find a job.

When I mentioned this to Bill's dad, he told me about a job I might be able to get. He had retired from the Air Force shortly after returning from Spain a few years earlier and had gotten a job with the City of Myrtle Beach with the Parks and Recreation Department. In fact, he was the supervisor of the "beautification" crew of the department. He had a crew of several guys and they would go around the city and maintain, clean, and "beautify" the city parks, the grounds of all public buildings, the public library, and even the local cemetery. Mr. Johnson told me to go down to the city office and apply since he knew they were hiring another full-time groundskeeper, which is basically what the job was and what it involved.

So the next day, I got a ride with Bill to the city office and I filled out an application and left the phone number at Bill's house. The next day I got a call, and I was offered the job which I accepted. I was to start the following Monday and I would work on Mr. Johnson's crew. The pay was only slightly more than minimum wage but it was full-time Monday through Friday with weekends off. I was happy with my good luck and excited to start my new job. And since I knew my boss very well, I knew I'd get along with him with no problems.

Now the next thing I had to do was find a place to live, which is not an easy thing to do in Myrtle Beach in the summer for someone on a minimum budget. There is around ten times the number of people in the city during the summer months compared to the winter months, so finding a place would be a real challenge. Luckily, I knew some locals, so a friend of Bill's knew a guy from Tennessee by the name of Carl who was in town for the summer and had rented a small upstairs apartment just a few blocks from the beach and he needed another roommate since the previous one had recently moved out. He had another roommate, so they needed a third to all pitch in on the rent which was three hundred dollars per month, so my part would be one hundred dollars per month, but Carl told me up front that it was only until Labor Day because that was when he was planning to head back to Tennessee and I would have to move out. That was fine with me because I knew after the summer was over, the rents went down considerably all over town and I was hoping to get my own place by then.

Since most of the month of July was almost over, I just gave him twenty-five dollars for the rest of the month and promised him a full one hundred for the month of August. It was only a one-bedroom apartment on the second floor of an old building, and Carl and the other roommate, Rick, were sleeping in the bedroom which had two beds in it, so I was relegated to the couch, which was fine with me and was certainly a lot better than nothing.

The apartment was not too far from the City of Myrtle Beach building where Mr. Johnson picked up the truck and the crew for the day's work every morning, so that is where I walked to begin work each day. There were three other guys on the crew besides myself and Mr. Johnson. One guy named Kenny was a local boy who had been working for the city for quite a while by then. Another guy by the name of Jimmy was from southern Ohio and was only there for the summer and was planning on returning home at the end of the tourist season. And the third guy was a Mexican American guy named Ruben who had recently gotten out of the Air Force after being stationed at Myrtle Beach Air Force Base for a couple of years. He was the only one of us who was married, and he told us that his wife was a Filipina who he had met while stationed in the Philippines before being assigned to Myrtle Beach.

The job was fairly basic and didn't really require a lot of skills. Mr. Johnson had a crew-cab pickup truck and the five of us would get in it every morning and he would take us to where we would work that day and leave us to do the job. All the tools of the trade such as rakes, shovels, lawnmowers, and waste cans were in the bed of the truck and we would work leisurely until we got the job done. It wasn't that hard a job and soon I got the hang of it pretty well. One day, we'd be working at the main public park and the next day out at the cemetery and then the next day at the City Courthouse building, mowing, raking, weeding, and beautifying the city properties.

As I expected, Myrtle Beach was still an exciting place to be in the summer, where the population swelled to 200,000 people compared to about 20,000 during the winter months. In a way, it almost reminded me of a place like Benidorm on the coast of Spain, where most of the population is from someplace else. With Benidorm, the tourists were from all over northern Europe and were there year-round. But in Myrtle Beach the tourists were mostly from the southern United States and were only there for the summer. I mostly kept away from the Grand Strand Amusement Park where I had worked for a while the previous time I had been in town because I knew what that scene was like from my experiences before and I wanted no part of it this time around.

But there were still many other things to do in town besides the Midway, the carnival, the rides, and that whole scene. There seemed to be even more t-shirt stands and souvenir stores and restaurants and bars and every other kind of business targeting the tourist industry than I had  remembered from before. Anything to get the tourist to spend their money was what the whole town seemed to be all about.

I spent a lot of time after work and on the weekends hanging around with my two roommates, Carl and Rick. They liked to drink beer and smoke pot, so I indulged in these pastimes with them regularly. Neither one of them worked, so they were usually way ahead of me by the time I got home from work. Rick was a really good-looking fellow and always seemed to have a lot of luck with the ladies. He was tall, charming, with really long dark hair and an elaborately trimmed beard. He always wore a lot of cologne and whatever he was doing seemed to work because he had all the girls around him he could handle and then some. Carl, on the other hand, was rather short and dumpy and he just tagged along with Rick but he got lucky sometimes as well.

People on vacation always wanted to have fun, and fun with the opposite sex was a big part of it. The hundreds of young girls walking the beach in their bikinis were willing and able to be with almost any guy if he was charming, sexy, and attractive enough. And if they were up to it (and many were), if nothing else just to be able to say they got "lucky  and laid" on their vacation. I met one such young lady one Saturday evening.

It was purely by chance and had nothing to do with my good-looking roommate and his considerable abilities with the opposite sex. That evening I was just hanging around "the Pavilion," which was one of largest and oldest arcades in town, and I was just watching the many tourists spend their money on such things as skeet-ball, pinball machines, and other devices made to take quarters out of people's hands, all in the name of having fun.

I happened to start chatting with a young lady about my age while watching her continue to put quarters into a skeet-ball machine and not having much luck in hitting the center hole with the ball which was worth fifty points and was what people aimed for, attempting to win tickets which were then turned in for prizes. She was by herself and that's why I ended up lucking out with her.

She told me her name was Sally Jean, and she was from Knoxville, Tennessee, and was in town with her parents and younger sister for a week. They were staying at a nearby motel and she had finally managed to get away from her family for a little while. She was a rather short and slightly chubby blond but was very pretty and had a nice smile and an infectious laugh. After talking for a while standing by the skeet-ball machine, I asked her if she'd like to smoke a doobie. She said she would really like that, so I told her I had an apartment not far away, if she'd like to go there with me to toke up. She agreed, so we walked the couple blocks to my little apartment, and I was hoping like hell that my two roommates were not there so we could have some privacy.

I was in luck because both Rick and Carl weren't home, most likely out and about on a Saturday evening doing what they did to amuse themselves, so we had the entire little place to ourselves. I got a Hendrix tape going on the eight-track deck; I grabbed a couple a cold Pabst Blue Ribbons from the fridge and after offering her one, she drank hers down even faster than I did. Then I rolled a little joint from my stash of Jamaican that I kept in the house and before too long, we were getting quite amorous on the couch, so I suggested that we go into the bedroom.

Things proceeded as they often do in a situation like this and before I knew it, we were both naked and rolling around on Rick's bed. She was very adventurous sexually, and she started off pleasuring me with her mouth and to reciprocate I did the same to her for quite a long time before she seemed to have enough. And before too long we proceeded to do the "deed" as some people called it.

Shortly after the deed was indeed done, she told me she had to get back to her motel because her folks would probably be getting worried about her. We both got dressed, and I walked her downstairs and offered to walk her back to her place, but she declined my offer, saying she didn't want to risk being seen by her folks walking with a guy because she was afraid they might get the wrong idea. I asked her what she was doing the next day. She told me that since it was her family's last day of vacation, she would have to spend it with them since they were going back home on Monday morning. So I said goodnight, and that it had been nice getting to know her, and I watched as she walked away, never to see her again.

The next morning, while brushing my teeth, I notice that something was wrong with my tongue. Looking in the mirror, I saw over a dozen small white dots protruding from all over the surface of my tongue. They looked terrible, and I didn't know what they were, but I was afraid that they might have been something I had caught from Sally Jean the night before. I took tweezers, and I tried to extract one, but it would not come loose from my poor tongue. The white things look like bugs of some kind and before long, I was freaking out considerably.

I had made plans that afternoon to meet my friend Bill at the bar where we hung out often and when I saw him; I showed him my tongue and asked him if he'd ever seen anything like it before. I also told him about my experience with Sally Jean the night before and that I was scared that I had gotten some kind of venereal disease of the tongue.

He looked carefully at my poor tongue and told me he had never seen anything like it before either and that I should go to the Free Clinic to see if the doctor could tell me what was wrong with me. He told me where the clinic was located and I went down there and to my surprise, it was open on a Sunday afternoon. After waiting around for an hour or so, I finally got in to see the doctor.

He asked me what was going on with me and I told him a little about my sexual experience the previous evening and I then told him about my tongue. He asked me to show it to him so I stuck it out at him as far as I could and he looked at it for a long time. Then he got a magnifying glass out and looked at it even closer.

He then gave me an enormous smile and said, "Son, did you have cunnilingus with that girl last night?"

I looked at him closely and I remembered that I had heard that word before and so I asked him, "You mean, did I have oral sex with her?"

"Yes, son, that's what I'm asking you."

I shrugged and said, "Well, as a matter of fact I did, and she did the same to me as well, doctor."

Again he smiled at me and said, "Well, that's what those white bumps on your tongue are: your taste buds. You see, whenever your tongue comes in contact with something very unusual or very spicy like really spicy food for an example, or a girl's vagina that might be rather pungent, your taste buds can get irritated and inflamed and that's what you have here, son."

I gave out a big sigh of relief and asked, "So it's just my taste buds that are inflamed then? And it's not some sort of bugs that have infested my tongue? Wow, what a relief! Thanks so much, Doctor."

He gave me another long look and told me, "Next time son, just try to be careful where and who you put your tongue into. Some girls are just not that clean and if you are going to indulge in that type of behavior, try to get the girl to take a bath or shower before, okay?"

"Well, thanks again, Doctor. What a relief that it's nothing serious then."

"Yes, just try to keep your tongue clean for a few days and it should go away before too long. And like I say, just try to be careful in the future, okay?"

"Okay, Doctor and thanks again for all your help. I really appreciate it."

I left the clinic with a new lesson in life learned, and a bit wiser in the ways of the world, and women. Also, I was very relieved that it wasn't anything more serious than some over-stimulated taste buds.

Before I knew it, Labor Day had arrived and the following week, Myrtle Beach felt like a ghost town. There were empty streets where once there were crowds of people, traffic, and busy businesses. Most of the tourist-oriented businesses closed up. The Grand Strand Amusement Park, The Pavilion, all the t-shirt and souvenir shops, the arcades, most of the bars and restaurants were all closed until Memorial Day when the season would start up once again.

In the meantime, the town was dead and mostly empty for the most part. A few places stayed open because the locals had to spend their money somewhere, but most businesses in town closed for the season. Even most of the hotels and motels closed for the winter, but a few stayed open. And by Labor Day, I had to move out of the little apartment I was sharing but before that happened; I easily found another place to live. The on-site managers owned and operated many of the motels, so they would stay at their motels for the winter and rent out their rooms at an incredible discount.

They figured that something was better than nothing and empty rooms did no one any good.

So I found a three-story motel right on the beach that was empty except for the owner and his wife who lived on the ground floor. I rented a room on the top floor of the Sea Palms Inn for only twenty dollars per week. It was an efficiency room, so it had a kitchen with a stove, fridge, a sink, a TV set and a great balcony overlooking the Atlantic. It was a nice little place, and the price was definitely right and within my limited budget.

Once Labor Day had come and gone and the town emptied, I found that I rather preferred it that way. The beach was almost empty and so were the streets for a change. Things were peaceful with just the locals around and the town almost became like a regular town instead of a major tourist destination. Although unlike most normal towns, Myrtle Beach in the winter seemed to be almost completely deserted, with so many places boarded up and empty.

I continued to hang out with my friend Bill on the weekends. There was a little bar we liked and where we would get together a lot called the Paradise Bar & Grill. It was right on the beach and had a great atmosphere, with a decent jukebox, several pinball machines, and live bands occasionally. We'd drink pitchers of beer and then step out onto their patio overlooking the ocean and light up a joint or two and talk about the old times we had enjoyed together in Spain, when we were swiping motorcycles and riding them all over the countryside around Madrid. We both remembered how much we loved those good times we had and how we both knew we could never return to that place and time, but it would only remain a memory in our minds for the rest of our lives.

One time while finishing a pitcher of beer together, he asked me if I had any plans for the following weekend. I told him that as usual; I didn't. So, he asked me if I'd like to make a little extra money.

I thought to myself, "Uh-oh! I hope he doesn't plan on returning to his old ways here in the States!"

But it wasn't anything like I was thinking because he just asked me if I wanted to help out picking tobacco on his Uncle Harlan's farm the following weekend. His uncle grew tobacco on ten acres of land he had out near the town of Conway, which was a several miles inland from Myrtle Beach. His uncle needed help during this time of year because this is when the tobacco plants were maturing and they could use all the help they could get. He told me it paid twenty-five dollars per day, but that it was hard work. I told him I would definitely be up for it because I could always use the extra money; besides it might be fun to see how they grow this plant which I had been smoking the leaves of ever since I was about fourteen years old.

So the next Saturday, early in the morning, he picked me up, and we drove out to the farm near Conway. His uncle had hired several other people for the job, mostly other family members, but there were a few other workers there too, about a dozen of us ready to get to work. What we would be doing this day would be walking among the tall tobacco plants and removing the flowers that the plants were producing.

The purpose of doing this was that the farmer wanted the plants to concentrate on growing their leaves as large as possible, because this is the part of the plant that was worth money, and if the plant flowered, then it would quickly die and not continue to grow its large and profitable leaves.

So we spent all day walking among these tall tobacco plants and cutting the flowers off the tops of them and discarding them. Sometimes they would be tough and we'd have to use snippers to remove them, but usually they would come off with just a little snap of the wrist. The work wasn't that hard, but it was very hot and very humid in the tobacco grove and before too long we were all sweating profusely.

By the end of the day, we had managed to remove the flowers from the entire crop of tobacco, and Uncle Harlan came around and handed each of us twenty-five dollars in cash and asked if we wanted to return in two weeks to actually pick the leaves, which was the next part of the process. We all agreed to be there and finish up the work, and he told us it might take two or three days to get all the leaves picked so we'd be working both Saturday and Sunday and even into the next week depending on how many helpers he had.

Two weeks later, we showed up again early in the morning ready to get the job done. We spent all day again walking through the tobacco plants, but this time we were removing the leaves from the plants, but only the leaves closest to the bottom and nearest the ground since these were the leaves that had turned brown and were ripe and ready to be picked. If the leaves were still green even along the bottom of the plant, we'd just leave them alone until a later date.

After the large brown leaves were picked, we would then have to string them up and hang them with their stem side up onto long wooden poles and these poles of raw tobacco would then go into the smoke barn he had on the property. Dozens of these poles of strung-up leaves would be hung at one time among the rafters of the barn, and then they would start a special fire in stoves that produced a lot of smoke inside the barn and the leaves would cure using the smoke that was produced this way.

I learned that this was how "Virginia" style of tobacco was produced. In Europe, this kind of tobacco was called blond tobacco and was always more expensive than the black tobacco that is smoked mostly in Europe, Africa, and other places. Black tobacco was just left in the sun to dry and to cure and produced a much harsher and darker kind of smoke. But blond tobacco was mild in comparison and this is what is used in almost all American cigarettes. It was rather strange working all day with these tobacco leaves puffing on a Marlboro sticking out of my mouth, but I looked around me and realized that almost everybody else was doing the same thing. After all, someone had to consume the product we were all helping to produce.

Bill's Uncle Harlan would sell the bundles of tobacco leaves once they were cured for a considerable amount of money to the Winston-Salem cigarette factory from North Carolina, who would come down in their trucks at the end of the season to buy all the tobacco he could produce.

Also at the end of the summer, there were some changes at my regular job. The job remained the same, but some people changed and this made quite a difference to me. Jimmy from Ohio had quit and gone back home at the end of the summer season and so we were short one guy on our crew. Kenny told his good buddy Bobby about the job and so he got hired onto our beautification crew of the Park and Recreation Department.

Kenny and Bobby had been good friends ever since they were kids in grade school but neither one of them had been able to graduate from high school. They were both from the Myrtle Beach area and I suspect neither one of them had ever left the county, much less the state. To put it mildly, they were a pair of ignorant, uneducated rednecks, southern style. Before Bobby joined our crew, Kenny was the only one of the four of us who was that kind of person, but once the two of them got together; it became a totally different situation. The two of them together became a redneck force to reckon with and that force was directed right at me.

There are certain kinds of people who relish in the suffering of others, especially if they have anything to do with creating that suffering. These two guys did not like me because they knew without a shadow of a doubt that I was a lot smarter, better educated, better looking, and a better human being than either one of them was or ever would be, and they resented this fact. And it became their *raison d'être* to punish me for this obvious reality.

To say they picked on me would be an understatement because what they did on a daily basis was way beyond just picking on me. They spent far more energy using their meager thought processes in conniving ways to make me feel bad, and therefore themselves better, than they spent at the menial work we were supposed to be doing. I consider myself a very tolerant person in most regards and I have dealt with all kinds of people in my life, and in my many adventures and travels, but I never had to deal with the kind of people these two guys were.

They would hide this brutal harassment and bullying from our mutual boss, Mr. Johnson. On a typical day, Mr. Johnson would pick us all up at the city building and then give us four guys a ride to wherever we would be working that day and drop us off with the equipment we needed to get the job done, and return later in the day to pick us up, leaving me alone with these two monsters all day long.

They knew I couldn't and wouldn't complain to our boss what was going on while he wasn't around because there wasn't any actual physical harm being done to me by these two guys, but only the mental and emotional kind. Besides, it would have been my word against theirs and there were two of them but only one of me.

So I never brought all this to the attention of our boss because I knew it wouldn't do any good and that if I did, and they were reprimanded by him to leave me alone, I know the bullying would only get worse (if that was possible) in retribution for my speaking up about it. So I kept silent about this and never mentioned it to Mr. Johnson.

It all began shortly after Bobby joined our crew and that's when he and Kenny became a team united against me. Bobby and Kenny were complete opposites as far as looks go. Kenny was short and chubby with dark hair and a very thick beard and his five o'clock shadow appeared right around lunchtime. And Bobby was tall, with crooked teeth and blond hair so dirty you could see the dirt in it from the raking and shoveling we had done days before. And he had a permanent scowl on his face, as if he constantly smelled something rotten and putrid, perhaps just his own B.O. And they both stunk like they took a shower once a week, whether they needed it or not, as they would often say. Neither one of them had a girlfriend or had ever even been with a girl for that matter probably.

If the harassment had been good-natured and friendly, it would have been a different situation and I probably could have handled it a lot better if I knew that it was all in good fun, but these two guys were dead serious about it and they hated me, for no other reason than because I was so different from them.

I tried to get Ruben, (the Mexican American ex-Air Force guy on our crew), to get on my side against these two assholes, but he would always remain neutral, neither backing me up nor joining them in the harassing. I attempted to befriend him frequently, even trying to speak Spanish with him on a couple of occasions and trying to get him to realize that I wasn't that much different than he was, and that both of us were way different from these guys, and that if we united together, we'd be able to put up with these guys a lot more easily. But his reaction was that since it wasn't happening to him, then he would just stay out of it and remain neutral. And he pretended like he didn't understand the Spanish I spoke to him for some reason which I could never quite understand.

I got together with him after work once before the summer was over and before Bobby started with our crew and all the hassles began. He invited me over to his place one evening after work to have a beer and I got a chance to meet his wife. To say he was henpecked and pussy-whipped would be an understatement. Her name was Lily, and she was a very mean, selfish, and small-minded Filipina whom he had met and married while he had been stationed at Clark Air Base near Manila a couple of years earlier. It was obvious to me that Ruben was being used for his American citizenship because she was in the process of bringing her entire family to the States from the Philippines. She already had her mother and sister living with them and she was trying to get more of her family to come over.

The entire hour or two I spent at their apartment having a beer, she nagged him and yelled at him the whole time. I felt sorry for Ruben but I also realized that people make their own beds and they also have to lie in them, and in this case, this was the bed that he had made for himself, and so he was forced to lie in it, both figuratively and literally.

When he was giving me a ride back to my place after the visit, he began to complain about her, and so I asked him why he just didn't divorce her if she made him so unhappy. And his reply was that divorcing her was exactly what she wanted him to do, so he wasn't about to give her the satisfaction of doing what she wanted. He told me that he would have to split everything with her, pay her alimony every month forever, and still have her in his life. He also told me they were trying to have a baby, and he thought that a baby might mellow her out somewhat once she was a mother. I thought to myself that bringing a little baby into a relationship like the one I had seen could not be good for anyone, including the innocent child, but I kept my mouth shut and my opinion to myself.

And unfortunately this is pretty much what Ruben did in the relationship between Kenny, Bobby, and me. I knew that if he would just express an opinion about what they were doing and just say one time in my defense, "Hey, guys, don't you think that's about enough?" I'm sure it would have helped me out in my predicament. But he never did, and he just totally kept out of it. So Kenny and Bobby continued with their verbal assault on me by constantly calling me names, belittling me, and doing their best to put me down in an on-going effort to bolster their own self esteem.

On several occasions, it almost reached a point where it went beyond mere verbal harassment, and almost came to blows. One time, Kenny was telling me he thought I looked like a fag with my long hair and why didn't I cut it because I looked like a real ugly girl. I replied that he just looked like a real ugly man with his short hair and he took great offense with that. He got right into my face and threatened to punch me if I didn't take it back. Of course, Bobby was right there with his fists clenched, so I was forced to back off since it would be two against one and I was bound to lose. Besides, I had always considered myself more of a lover than a fighter and I probably would have lost a fight even if it was only me against one of these bozos.

So, I learned to tolerate their abuse and insults but the injustice and the unfairness of it all got to me every single day. I told my friend Bill about what was going on at my job and he offered to back me up if I wanted to get into a real fight with these two guys, but I always declined his offer, thinking that if we did somehow manage to kick their asses, that it would only make things even worse for me at work. He also suggested that he could talk to his dad about my situation but again I knew if he did, again it would only make things worse for me.

But besides my job, I liked my life in Myrtle Beach. The town was quiet for the most part, compared to what it was like in the summer, and I really enjoyed the empty beaches and the great weather most of the time, although there were some Atlantic storms that would come in and dump rain for days at a time. I thought about trying to get a different job, but there just weren't any to be had during the winter. I looked in the newspaper and saw nothing I could possibly do, so I stuck it out and kept going to work and to another dose of bullying and harassment every day.

I put up with this for about six months before I finally had enough. I had talked to my mom on the phone at the end of February and she told me that she and Jim had returned to the States from Spain and had finally decided to settle in Tucson, Arizona, of all places. And she invited me to come to that city and see what it was like because they both really liked it a lot there, with its warm climate and nice people.

Home, to most young people, is where your mom is, and in this case, my mom was now in Tucson, so I decided to go there and maybe make my life there. Also, I was eager to finally get away from these two guys who were tormenting me daily and making my life a pure hell. I told her I wanted to come to Tucson to see what it was like, so she sent me a one way airplane ticket from Charleston to Tucson and within a few weeks I was ready to leave Myrtle Beach for good.

I gave my job a two-week notice and Mr. Johnson told me he understood that I wanted to go and live where my parents were, and he wished me good luck and told me that I would have an excellent reference from the city of Myrtle Beach. I thanked him and also told him how much I appreciated what he and his entire family had done for me and how they had made me feel so welcome and had helped me out so much, not only this last time I had been in Myrtle Beach, but the previous time four years earlier as well.

An amazing thing happened on my last day of work. It was a Friday afternoon, and I was leaving the next day for Arizona, so the guys I worked with knew they would never see me again. Kenny and Bobby approached me as I was getting ready to walk away for the last time and the following conversation ensued:

Kenny looked at me rather sheepishly and said, "Well, Ron, it's been nice knowing you and nice working with you."

Then Bobby said, "Yeah, I guess this is it, huh? You're leaving town tomorrow so we'll probably never see you all again, right?"

I shrugged and said, "Yeah, that's right, guys, you'll never have to put up with me ever again. I'm sure you'll both be happy to get rid of me, right?"

Kenny scratched his unshaven face and looked at me closely and said, "Well, that's what we wanted to talk to you about. We both want to say that we're real sorry about the way that we treated you while you were working here with us."

Then Bobby chimed in right after scratching his ass and then picking his nose, "Yeah, we want to apologize for hassling you so much and we hope that you didn't take it too personal and that you knew we were just fooling around, you know."

And he stuck out his hand for me to shake it.

I looked at them both with a look that showed no mercy, just like the ones they gave me for months and I said, "Nope, I don't accept your fucking apologies, assholes. You knew exactly what you were doing to me for months and now when I'm leaving, you want to apologize to make yourselves feel better. No, I don't think so, man. You guys can go fuck yourselves, for all I'm concerned."

They both looked really surprised, and Kenny said, "Well, shit, buddy, we're only trying to say we're sorry, is all."

"Well, sorry just doesn't cut it, man. I'll never forget what you guys did to me for the rest of my life, and I want you two to remember what you did as well. And if I accept your apology now, you'll just think that it was all okay, but it wasn't, and both you guys know it and I know it. So fuck you both!"

And I turned around and walked away from them without looking back. And the next day I left Myrtle Beach for the last time, without looking back and with no regrets whatsoever.

Bill gave me a ride to Charleston the next morning to catch my flight to Tucson and once again we said our goodbyes. He let me out of the car in front of the airport and said, "Well, Ron, old buddy, it looks like this is it once again, huh?"

"Yep, it looks that way, man. I'm going to miss you, you know. And if you ever make it out to Arizona, that's where I'll probably be, okay?"

"Okay, maybe I'll make it out that way someday, you never know. But I just want you to know that I'm really sorry about the way those two assholes treated you at your job, man."

"That's okay Bill, it wasn't your fault. And besides I'm over it now and I have to see it all as just another life lesson, right? But I just want to thank you again for all you and your family have done for me. I really appreciate it, man."

"Well, that's what friends are for, my brother. You take care of yourself now, you hear?"

"Yeah, you too Bill. Keep out of trouble and let's keep in touch, okay?"

"Yep, you got it, amigo."

And I gave him a big hug, and I walked into the airport to catch my plane and I haven't seen him since.

.

Chapter 27. Finally To Tucson

"You belong among the wildflowers.
You belong in a boat out at sea.
You belong with your love on your arm,
you belong somewhere you feel free."
— Tom Petty

I landed at Tucson International Airport, on the first of April 1976, and when I got off the plane, I felt the difference immediately. The air felt warm, dry, and with little humidity, just the opposite of what I had just left in South Carolina. Yes, the desert of southern Arizona was much different than the swamps of Carolina, with a different smell in the air and a distinctly different feeling all around me.

My mom and Jim met me, and after a great reunion, we headed from the airport out to their new house they had recently bought out on the far east side of town, near 22nd Street and Kolb Road. It was a large ranch-style house, and they had just finished the process of having a swimming pool put in the backyard. Since their place was so far out on the east side of town, there was almost nothing at all but desert from their backyard all the way out to the Rincon Mountains on the east side of the Tucson Valley. To the north, I could see the Santa Catalina Mountains dominate the skyline with Mount Lemmon, with the top of the range at over 9,000 feet above sea level. To the south were the Santa Rita Mountains almost to Mexico and to the west were the smaller Tucson Mountain range.

Tucson indeed was a desert valley surrounded by mountain ranges (sky islands) all around it.

I loved Tucson almost immediately, because for the first time since I had been living in this strange country of these United States, I felt a sense of belonging, maybe because my mom was there and once again I felt the warm embrace of her love and that very nice feeling of being "home" once again. But Arizona also had a feel about it very much different from anywhere else I had been in the entire country. Few Arizonans are natives, which are people who were actually born and raised in a state, unlike most other places I had been, where the locals had been there for generations and therefore so set in their ways. In Tucson, there were people from all over the country who had migrated to Arizona for the climate, for new opportunities, and for a new life.

Many people from the Midwest had left their homes in such places as Michigan, Wisconsin, Illinois, Indiana, Minnesota, and other states, and also many from "back east" (the East Coast), because they were tired of shoveling snow six months out of the year and wanted to live in a place where it was almost always warm and sunny.

And what they often brought with them was new ideas and new possibilities. By leaving their homes on the other side of the country to live somewhere different and new, they had opened themselves up to a new lifestyle and a different attitude towards life in general. Things seemed modern and fresh in Tucson, like almost anything was possible and indeed, it was.

When I asked my mom and Jim why they had chosen Tucson to settle down in after returning from Spain the previous year, I was told a strange story. After they had spent four years living in Canillejas near Madrid shortly after getting married in Colorado in 1971, they had finally decided to return to the States to make their lives. They stopped in New York City for a short visit with my mom's oldest friends, Felipe and Florence, and shortly after that, they bought a car and spent awhile traveling across the United States visiting relatives and trying to find a place they both liked and where they could settle down.

They went to Ohio where Jim had some family and then to Oklahoma where most of my mom's family lived and then they wandered around the western states looking for just the right place. Somewhere outside of Las Cruces, New Mexico, they stopped at a local diner for some lunch and they struck up a conversation with another couple at the table next to theirs. They

told the couple they were looking for a place in the Southwest where they could settle down and make their lives and the couple recommended Tucson to them.

The couple told them that the city had a wonderful climate, friendly people, cheap prices and an Air Force Base nearby called Davis Monthan Air Force Base. They both liked what they heard since it sounded exactly like what they were looking for. Also the idea of having an Air Force Base nearby was a bonus because Jim was a retired Air Force colonel and it would be great to shop and use the other facilities on base regularly. So they told the couple they would check it out, which they did, and the rest is history as they say.

Tucson is where they both ended up living the rest of their lives, and where I consequently ended up living most of my life as well. To think if that couple in the restaurant that day had advised them to settle in Albuquerque or Phoenix or El Paso or even Las Cruces for that matter, my life would be completely different and I most likely would have ended up living somewhere else for the next forty years or so. It is strange how sometimes the smallest things in life can have the biggest consequences.

About a week after my arrival, Tucson had a freak snowstorm on Easter Sunday. My mom had planted rose bushes all around her yard and it was strange to see snow on the ground and on the blossoming pedals of her roses as well as snow all over the many kinds of cactus around the area. And it also covered the surrounding mountain ranges with an even thicker layer of this strange unseasonable snowfall. Within a day or two, it all melted, but it left a fresh, clean, and cool feeling to the air.

Within a couple of days, I had explored the immediate neighborhood by walking around it for hours at a time, trying to get my bearings and a feel for the place. Just a few doors down from their place was a house with a two-car garage attached to it. The first time I walked by, I heard loud music coming from the garage and so I stopped to listen. What I thought at first was just a record being played quite loudly, turned out to be a band rehearsing. It was an Eagles cover band that I was hearing because all they seemed to play were songs by the Eagles over and over again.

They would play one song several times, sometimes stopping in the middle of it for a few moments, and then start it up once again. After they felt they had that song down well enough, they went onto the next Eagles song. The Eagles album, "Their Greatest Hits" had recently been released, and this garage band was intent on getting every one of those songs down perfectly. Since I had always liked the Eagles, I would stand out in front of this garage for quite a long time listening to their excellent live versions of these songs. I never got a chance to meet any of the guys in the band, but if I had, I would have told them I was their biggest fan.

My first priorities were getting three things together: a job, a car, and a place to live. And all three seemed to come quite easily and with a minimum of effort. A few days after Easter, I heard a jangling musical noise coming from down the street. When I went out to see what was causing this racket, I saw an ice cream truck slowly driving around the neighborhood. It had "Miss Sharon's Ice Cream" on the side of it and I waved my hand and the driver stopped. I bought an ice cream for myself and one each for my folks, and then I chatted with the driver who was about my age with longish hair and a big smile. I asked him what it took to get a job like his where he just drove around all day selling ice cream, and he told me that Miss Sharon's was hiring for the summer and he gave me the address of where to apply. So, the next day I went down to their office, which was close to downtown Tucson, filled out an application and within a couple of days, I got hired as an ice cream truck driver.

The job was actually rather nice, and I liked it a lot. I had a route on the east side of town and I started around ten in the morning after picking up the truck and filling it with the various cold treats we sold, put dry ice in the large cooler that  was in the back of the truck and drove around leisurely until around six in the evening when I drove the truck back and turned it in, along with my earnings for the day. They paid me fifteen percent of my sales and on a good day I could make twenty dollars or even more. But on poor days when the monsoon rains kicked up and there were few customers out and about, my sales would plummet and I would be lucky to sell a hundred dollars' worth of ice cream products and would only earn fifteen dollars or even less.

I kept the job for the entire summer until the beginning of October when they shut down for the season. I got to know the area of Tucson where my route was quite well during that time by driving around it all day long. And I even got to know some local businesses such as the convenience market I'd stop at every day for a soda and a sandwich. They called it a U-Tote-M store and again after talking to the employee on duty, this is how I got my next job as an overnight clerk.

I ran the cash register and stocked the shelves at this twenty-four-hour store, and it was an okay job except for the fact that I had several strange experiences dealing with some weird customers coming in late at night, including being robbed by gunpoint on one occasion. I also had to deal with the drunks who would come in after hours expecting to be able to buy more beer or booze and when I told them that I couldn't sell it to them, they would sometimes throw a tantrum and even threaten me. Many times I was forced to call the cops usually when some asshole drunk just walked in after hours and grabbed a twelve pack and dashed out of the place.

Shortly after getting my first few paychecks from Miss Sharon's, I had enough to look for a vehicle. I had in mind a VW van and by looking in the want-ads of the local newspaper; I found one for sale within my price range. The owner had driven it all the way down from Alaska and it had Alaskan plates on it still, and he only wanted two hundred and fifty dollars for it.

The reason it was so cheap was because it had some damage to the front of it. He had hit something obviously and the front of the van and the front bumper were dented up slightly, but it still ran fine and was in otherwise pretty good shape. Since the engine is in the rear in Volkswagens, there was no damage to the engine or transmission. I liked it a lot, and I fixed up the interior very nicely with curtains, and the fold-out bed was great for camping or just sleeping in whenever I wanted to or needed to.

Not too long after getting the van, I found a place to live that was also within my price range. It was on the north side of town off Grant Road, and it was originally a large storage shed on the grounds of a large house. The owner had fixed it up by adding a bathroom, a kitchen with appliances and had furnished it completely with a table and chairs and a large bed. Again the price was right at only ninety-two dollars per month, which was just barely within my budget.

While working for Miss Sharon's that summer, I spent considerable time at a local nightclub called "Choo-Choos" which was later called "The Night Train." This place was one of the major bars and nightclubs along the infamous "Fourth Avenue" region near downtown. This avenue was about halfway between the University of Arizona and downtown Tucson and was the area where a lot of the college students and other assorted people would hang out. There was even a "shit" park on the avenue, much like the one I knew so well in Frankfurt, where one could buy just about any illegal substance one wanted.

Before I got my own apartment, I was hanging around this place on the avenue one night and to my amazement and delight; I got lucky. I met this young lady at the bar and after drinking several rounds with her; I gave her a ride back to her place. And one thing led to another and before I knew it, I woke up in the morning and I was on her couch with her lying next to me. After a brief repeat of what we had done the night before, I told her I had to get home. So, I said goodbye, gave her a kiss, and I got in my van to drive home.

She lived in an area of the town which I was unfamiliar with and I wasn't sure exactly how to get out to the east side where I was still staying with my folks. After driving around a while, I finally found Speedway Boulevard, which is the main drag running through Tucson going east to west. I kept going down Speedway and after about twenty minutes, I still saw nothing familiar, but I kept going thinking I would, eventually.

I slowly realized that I was heading west on Speedway instead of east as I intended because I was getting to the outskirts of town near the Tucson Mountains. I saw open patches of desert with tall Saguaros and dirt roads leading up into the hills. I was just about to turn around and head back the opposite direction when I saw a sign ahead that showed a tight curve to the right and *20 mph* underneath it. I slowed down but apparently not quite enough because I couldn't quite make the turn at the speed I was traveling and I ran off the road right into the desert. The VW van is rather top heavy, so I not only ran off the road, but I flipped the van upside down.

So there I was, quite hung-over from the night before, sitting on the ceiling of my van looking out the window at the desert inches from my head. I managed to crawl out the window, and I saw that my van was sitting on its top with all four wheels still spinning in the air. I was okay and unhurt thankfully, but my van would never be the same. It had already had some major dents on the front of it and now the top of it was dented up even worse than the front.

Before too long, I somehow got a tow truck to come out and flip the van back on its wheels again, and then I added several quarts of oil to the engine (most had dripped out while it was upside down), and I drove it home. But now my poor van had a major dent in the front from before my accident, small dents on the driver's side which it had rolled onto briefly, and some major dents and damage on the roof of the vehicle, including the roof rack. So at this point, three of the five sides of the van were dented up. It looked like it had been through a war zone and back.

I kept driving it like it was and got some rather strange looks from other drivers, but by the end of the summer, the van started giving me problems with the trans-axle, which VW's have instead of transmissions, and I ended up selling it to a junkyard for fifty dollars because the cost of a new trans-axle was more than the van was worth.

I still liked the idea of the VW van because they were great for driving in the hot desert because Volkswagen engines are air-cooled instead of having a radiator with water and coolant as most vehicles do. Besides, I liked having a vehicle that served multiple purposes, in this case as basic transportation, being able to haul large items easy, and also as a portable crash pad for camping or just sleeping in whenever necessary or desirable, as when I might get lucky again and have nowhere to go.

Once again, a major coincidence occurred in my life. My folks knew a couple who they knew from Spain who were living in Tucson and they had a 1967 VW Campmobile for sale. This couple had brought this vehicle with them from Europe where they had bought it new and they had kept it for almost ten years but were now selling it. The amazing thing about it was that it was the same exact VW Campmobile I had camped out with in Benidorm on the coast of Spain when I was a teenager.

When I found out that this was the same exact van I had known so well in Spain and that it was for sale, I knew I had to own it. It was selling for seven hundred dollars and I asked my folks if they'd lend me the money for it and they did, so I bought it, and I was absolutely delighted to have it. Naturally, it was older than when I had gotten to know it so well in 1968, but it was still in great shape and everything worked as it was supposed to, including the fold-out bed, the pop-up roof, and the little sink, stove, and fridge. With this incredible little vehicle, I knew I could go anywhere I wanted to, and my accommodations were completely covered without having to set up a tent and having to sleep on the cold hard ground, as I had done so many times in the past in my travels. I really loved it.

And after all this time, I still thought I was in love with Lizzy, the girl I first met in Madrid about five years earlier at this point. I had contacted her again and found out that she was living in Riverside, California, not too far from her parents' place. She had finally gotten the divorce from her husband and was now on her own with just herself and her young son to take care of. We exchanged a couple of letters and I told her I was living in Tucson, which is only about a day's drive from Riverside. I talked her into letting me come out there one weekend to visit her, so we made arrangements for the last weekend of October. I got her address and phone number and told her I'd be out there on that Saturday afternoon.

After so long I was finally ready to let her know how I felt about her. I was either going to make her my woman, or I was going to get her out of my mind, once and for all. I was convinced that I was going to resolve this thing, one way or another. I loaded a few things in my van, including a sleeping bag, in case I needed it, but I hoped that I wouldn't, and I headed out early that Saturday, full of determination and purpose, yet with certain unavoidable and understandable fears, doubts, and anxieties.

I had been to California before but never to Riverside which was a part of that huge Metropolis which makes up Southern California. I drove out of Tucson on the I-10 through Phoenix and the Valley of the Sun, and then through western Arizona, and crossed the mighty Colorado River at Blythe and finally into the Golden State itself.

By the time I got to Palm Springs, I was feeling more and more nervous by the moment. All kinds of thoughts were going through my head, including all kinds of doubts, insecurities and fears. What if she just didn't like me or worse yet, what if I didn't really like her? Maybe this entire love thing I had for her was just something I had created in my head, and in my own mind, and it wasn't grounded in any kind of reality or even based on actual facts. Maybe I was just in love with the idea of being in love. Well, there was only one way to find out, and I was about to do it.

I found her place with no problem and discovered that it was an apartment building which was part of a low-income housing complex near a city park, not very far from downtown Riverside. I found her apartment on the second floor of one of the buildings and knocked on the door, with my heart in my throat.

She opened the door, looked at me briefly and said, "Oh, hello, Ron, come on in."

I said hello and walked into her place and looked around. It was a small one-bedroom apartment furnished tastefully and in spotless condition. I thought with a small child living there, there might be messes around, but the place was almost immaculate. She gestured for me to sit on the couch, and so I did and we started to chat.

She asked me how the drive was and I told her that there weren't any problems except for one spot outside of Palm Springs where there is quite an ascent of elevation and my little VW was straining to make it up that long and gradual gain of elevation. I told her a little about my van and how much I liked it and the history of it and within a few minutes a small boy of around three or four years of age came into the living room. She introduced me to him as her son, Allen, Junior, and I noticed that he looked very much like his father, who had been a good friend of mind in my Madrid days.

I started to feel some strange emotions, but I kept them to myself. What I was thinking was that if it wasn't for me, this little person in front of me would not be here. I was the person who introduced her to her future husband and if I hadn't done so, this child would not even exist, at least not with the same genes he had now. His father was in the Air Force and she was a high school girl when I introduced them one evening in Madrid and the odds were very slim that they would ever had met because high school kids just did not fraternize very much with servicemen at Torrejon Air Base in those days.

But who knows? When I introduced them at his apartment that first evening, the very first thing he said to her was, "Hello there, Lizzy, one day we will get married and you will have my son." So maybe they would have met and gotten married and had a child together even if I wasn't involved, but I really didn't think so.

I didn't mention this to her as we sat there on the couch looking at each other for the first time in over four years, but the thought went through my mind. We chatted some more while Junior sat on the floor playing with some toy trucks. I asked her what she was doing for work and she told me that since she had a kid, the State of California paid her a small welfare check and provided most of the cost of her housing, plus she collected food stamps and got a small child support check from Allen every month.

She told me she struggled a lot financially but somehow got by. Her family lived nearby, and they helped her out with babysitting sometimes and with rides when she couldn't get somewhere she needed to be by bus. She told me she was a lot happier now than when she was living with her husband in Brooklyn, New York. We chatted some more about the old times in Madrid and some people we both used to know, like Andy and his family, and our old mutual friend Carmelita.

Before too long, she asked me if I'd like to go outside for a while. So she took her little son by the hand, grabbed a kite that was sitting on a shelf near the door, and we walked downstairs to an open area near the apartment complex. She asked me if I knew how to fly a kite, and I told her no, but I could certainly give it a try. So with the help of Junior, I got the kite up in the air and handed the end of the string to him and he was happy and delighted to be flying it, as we watched the kite floating  magically with the wind. It stayed in the air for quite a long time as I was helping him to keep it afloat. She sat on a swing set nearby and watched us, smoking cigarettes and drinking a can of Tab.

Eventually it started to get dark, and we went back indoors and she prepared dinner for us. She took a package of chicken leg quarters out of the fridge and coated them with barbecue sauce and put them in the oven. Next, she opened a package of frozen French-fried potatoes and put them in the oven. Then she opened a can of green beans and put them in a pot on the stove. Before too long, the three of us were sitting at her small kitchen table having dinner.

When we finished, she washed the dishes, then she made a phone call to one of her friends and when she hung up, she asked me if I would mind babysitting while she went to a nightclub that evening. I shrugged and told her that I guess I wouldn't mind. So, the next thing I knew, she was in her bedroom, getting ready to go out while I was sitting on the couch watching her little black-and-white TV. She came out with a nice outfit on and her hair done up and with a pair of long earrings on, and told me that Junior was in bed, and all I would have to do is sit back and watch TV until she got home in a few hours.

Soon, there was a knock on the door and a young lady was at the door, ready to pick Lizzy up for a night on the town. I was introduced briefly to her and then they left, with me sitting there watching Saturday Night Live on her little television set, wondering what I had gotten myself into here.

Around one in the morning, she finally got home and I could tell that she'd been drinking because she was staggering and seemed to be a little out of it. She went into the bedroom and brought out a couple of blankets and a pillow and told me I could sleep on the couch if I didn't want to sleep in my van.

I chose the couch and before I knew it; it was morning and after a quick breakfast of bacon, eggs, toast, and coffee, she asked me if I'd like to go to the park with her and Junior. So the three of us got in my van and we drove a short distance to a city park on the banks of the Santa Ana River which flows through Riverside. After a nice morning of walking along the river, feeding the ducks and enjoying the nice sunshine, we headed back to her place.

She told me that her sister was planning on coming over soon to pick her up and they were going to their folk's house for a short visit that afternoon, so maybe I should get on my way. So, I said goodbye to her and her son, got in my van and drove away, never to see her again.

While driving back to Tucson, the entire visit seemed to be an anti-climax of sorts. After over four years of thinking about her and creating this whole thing about her in my head, to say it disappointed me would be an understatement. There was nothing there. No spark, no desire on her part and apparently very little on my part by the way I acted. It had felt exactly the same as when I was with her in Spain. We were friendly, but that was it. There was no evidence that she wanted to take it any further than just friendship and she acted like I was extremely lucky to even have that most basic kind of relationship with her.

For her to ask me to babysit while she went out with her girlfriend was plain evidence that once again, she was using me for her own purposes, even if in this case, it was just to babysit for a few hours. She could have invited me along; didn't she think that I might enjoy going out on the town in Riverside? And why the hell didn't I ask her for the damn money that I had "lent" her years before for her to get an abortion while she was still married to Allen? She made no mention of it at all. And I suspect that she never really had an abortion at all, but instead she just got me to give her some money because she knew that I thought I was in love with her and that I would probably do anything for her.

What the hell was wrong with me? Was I not good-looking enough for her, charming enough, nice enough, rich enough, or educated enough? How come I didn't merit at least an iota of respect from her? Was it just me, or was there something wrong with her, her values, her morals, and her upbringing? And what did I do wrong?

I got back to Tucson, and I went on with my life, finally got her out of my mind, and rarely, if ever, thought about her again, until a few decades later, when personal computers were invented, and after Facebook became so popular, one day I looked her up and found her on there.

Her Facebook page said that she was living in Fort Worth, Texas (of all places, another strange coincidence) and the description of herself was a "happy and healthy lesbian." A lesbian! Well, no wonder! Duh! Well, that certainly explains a lot, doesn't it? Obviously, she had been a lesbian her entire life, even when I knew her in Spain, and that explains her lack of "being into the sex thing" with my friend Andy when they were going together back then too.

So it wasn't just me, but instead all men in general. And it explained why she acted the way she did around me the entire time I knew her. And why she felt that by my being a man, I was just someone she could use and manipulate for her own purposes, for her to use for anything and everything that she could get out of me. I just wish I had known, is all. But maybe she didn't really know herself, or maybe she wasn't able to admit her actual sexual orientation even to herself back then, until the Gay pride thing became so prominent and she finally "came out" decades later.

Regardless, I think I finally could understand her and her motivations, her desires, and what made her act like she did with me. It wasn't necessarily me, but men in general; I was just the wrong gender. I just had the wrong genitals is all. After so long, it finally all made complete sense. And in a way I felt slightly better about the entire thing, knowing that in truth, it wasn't personal. Well, better late than never, I suppose.

The next forty-odd years, I made my life in the Tucson area. I finally did what most people do with their lives, I suppose. In no particular order: I had a few girlfriends, I fell in love a few times; I got married twice, got divorced once, worked a lot of different jobs, finally went back to school and got a degree, got a decent job and eventually a career, had a kid, and a grand-kid, bought a few houses and sold a few, traveled quite a lot (mostly in Mexico, but a lot of other places as well), played in a lot of bands over the years, spent some time in jail (again), made a few good friends and lost some, was able to retire from work at the early age of fifty-five, buried both my parents, and had a lot of good times and some great experiences, and gained quite a lot of wisdom. And throughout it all I led a fairly honest and decent life. But all of this and much more will have to be covered in another book someday, perhaps.

But even though I reached a time in my life when I finally felt like I was all grown up, I am still a "Brat" in my heart and in my mind. I had to face the inevitable and unavoidable fact of life, that everyone must become an adult eventually — if they happen to be lucky enough to live long enough — and to accept responsibility for themselves and for the life they make for themselves and for the life they live. And that is what I did. I became an adult, yet I will forever remain a Brat. Indeed, that is who I am and what I am, and will be forever.

Chapter 28. A Final Word

"Our entire life consists ultimately in accepting ourselves as we are."
— Jean Anouilh

The dandelion is the official flower of the Military Brat. Why? The plant puts down roots almost anywhere, and it's almost impossible to destroy. It's an unpretentious plant, yet good looking, and it's a survivor in a broad range of climates and environments. Military children bloom everywhere in the world where the wind carries them. They are hardy and upright and their roots are strong, cultivated deeply in the culture of the military, planted swiftly and surely. And they are ready to fly in the breezes that take them to new adventures, new lands, and new friends.

The term "Military Brat" has been around a long time. In the United States, there have been "Brats" for almost two hundred and fifty years, ever since the war between the American Colonists and England, which created this country in the first place. The term refers to both current and former children of active duty military personnel who have served or are serving in the Armed Forces, whether in the Army, Air Force, Navy, Marines, or Coast Guard.

Although no exact figures are available, the U.S. Department of Defense estimates that around fifteen million Americans are former or current military brats, or almost five percent of the entire U.S. population. Throughout my entire life, whenever I have met a fellow brat, whether overseas or stateside, we have almost always instantly connected easily on a deep and profound level. We share a tribe, a sub-culture, and a way of life that few other people can relate to or understand. And even though our particular circumstances as children might have varied widely, we still shared a common experience growing up.

Whenever I'm asked where I'm from, I have to hesitate before I can answer. My usual answer is, "Well, my dad was in the Air Force for twenty years, so I guess I'm from a lot of places and at the same time, from nowhere really at all." And I try to explain that I lived in several countries and several states growing up, and I basically never had a chance to put down any deep roots anywhere. So where am I from? That's a good question!

But my particular "Brat" experience was probably a little different from the normal one, if there actually is a normal one. Many American military brats never leave the U.S. at all, but instead travel from one stateside base to another every few years while growing up. Others, like many of the people I knew growing up in Spain, had one overseas assignment (Madrid) and they spent the rest of their time at bases stateside. But I spent over ten years in Spain alone, plus another couple of years traveling around Europe after high school, and before that when I was very young, I spent time in such exotic locales as Portugal and Turkey. So for this reason I consider myself to be an *Overseas* Brat.

Or maybe what I really am is another term I've discovered recently that attempts to explain a little better people like me, and that is a "Third Country Kid," or TCK. TCKs move between cultures before they actually have the opportunity to develop their personal or cultural identities. The first culture refers to the country from which their parents originated, the second culture refers to the culture in which the family lived, and where the kids spent a lot of time growing up, and the third culture refers to the amalgamation or a combination of these two cultures, hence a "third" culture.

In my case, since I spent so much time living in Spain and thus I speak fluent Spanish, when I finally came to Arizona to make a new life, I felt a deep kinship and connection with the many Mexican Americans who live in the state. In fact, over forty percent of the population of Arizona can claim a Hispanic background, and I guess, in my own unique way, so can I. Yet, my experience as a Hispanic American differs greatly from the one shared by my many Mexican American friends. The same, but different, as they say.

There are other groups of people with similar experiences and backgrounds as military brats, and these include: Foreign Service Brats, sometimes referred as "Diplobrats," and also Missionary kids, as well as the other TCKs mentioned above.

Regardless of what term one uses to describe someone like me, the fact is that people like me often feel we have no roots, and no real place to call home, since we never had much of an opportunity to create such things. I've met people who were born and raised in their hometown and have never left. These people have the ability as well as the luxury and the privilege to have known the same people from kindergarten, and those same people might live right down the street from them still.

They can take a drive over to the high school they attended and watch a football game on the same field where they used to play themselves perhaps forty years earlier. They can return to the same "lovers' lane" where they had their first serious kiss and re-live their earliest romantic moments from the same exact spot. They can see how their friends that they've known their entire lives change, and have families, and grow older just like they do. There's permanence and a completion there that people like myself have never known and will never experience in life.

Very few people realize that Brats serve their country also, and as honorably as any actual serviceman ever has. If a man is drafted or joins the military for a three- or four-year enlistment, afterwards he usually returns to his hometown and to his regular life, and his life resumes pretty much as it was. And the only changes he has had are a few years of a different kind of experience under his belt. He can go on with his life with little changed, unless he has been in a war zone and suffers from PTSD, physical injuries, or other consequences of actual combat and battle, but that's a different situation altogether.

For Brats, it's a different story. First, we never were asked for our participation. At least, when you're drafted, you know it will end in a couple of years and you can return to your life more or less as usual afterwards. But Brats aren't drafted; instead we are born into the service and have no choice about it at all. The average Brat moves six to nine times before finishing high school, and we have no "hometown" to call our own.

We have very limited contact with our extended families, except for an occasional visit, perhaps. Instead of being pampered by grandparents and being able to create relationships with cousins, uncles, aunts, and other extended family members, we spent our lives away from these people that most other people take for granted as being a part of their lives. We lived a quasi-military lifestyle for the most part, and this included the military hierarchy of officers and enlisted men, and the very real and obvious differences between these two groups when it came to housing, class, and social level. At times we were even made to feel almost like we were little "soldiers" ourselves.

We were constantly being reminded of the fact that as Americans living in a foreign country; we were representing America to everyone with whom we came in contact. We as children were expected to be mini-diplomats and be on our best behavior at all times. We made sacrifices that in some ways were as important and as necessary as the soldiers in uniform all over the world. But instead of medals, Veterans benefits, and honor and respect, we sometimes ended up suicidal, drug or alcohol addicted or in prison, trying to find our way in a country that we were technically a part of, yet had so little knowledge and experience of.

And other times, if we were lucky and strong enough, we just ended up mixed up emotionally, lonely, friendless, alienated and with no sense of belonging, and facing severe culture shock upon return to "our" country.

I think some of the experiences I have related here are good examples of the price that some Brats have paid in service to their country. When I finally came to the States to live my life in the country that issues my passport, I had a very hard time adapting to the culture and the way of life I found here. I was taken advantage of, abused, lied to, cheated, neglected, beaten, robbed, and literally left for dead because of my naiveté, my inexperience, and my ignorance of all things "American." In this land of the free, and this home of the brave, many times I felt much less free than I did overseas and not very brave at all. I spent almost my entire youth living in foreign countries, and to this day, unsurprisingly, I still don't feel like the United States is my home or where I really belong.

But in my case, neither is Spain. In 2013, I finally returned to Spain for a three-week trip and I traveled around to all the places I remembered so well, including Madrid and all the old neighborhoods I lived in there, as well as Peñiscola, Benidorm, Alicante, and Marbella, and I soon realized that even though Spain is still a beautiful country, full of culture and wonderful people and places, I didn't belong there either. I was just another tourist among millions of others, and although it was nice to visit and remember, it still wasn't where I belonged or where I felt at home.

Spain had changed enormously in the forty years or so since I had left, but it still kept the purity and the beauty of its ancient and wonderful culture and traditions. The Spaniards seemed to have been able to find the sweet spot between the modern and the traditional.

As a fine example, in Peñiscola, the locals have kept the original buildings and streets of the old part of the town from the days of the Moors, but have modernized them with up-to-date plumbing, electricity, and with twenty-first century technology. The Madrid metropolitan area has a population of over six million people now, but it still retains the charm, the grace, and the beauty of the city I remember so well. And above all, for the most part, Spaniards still keep that sense of honor and dignity that I admired so much.

Now, one might ask, would I trade my upbringing for a more traditional "American" one? And do I have any regrets about the places I lived and the way I was raised? Would I have preferred to have been raised in a place like San Antonio, Texas, or Grove, Oklahoma, my entire life? The answer is absolutely not. My being an Overseas Brat has made me who and what I am today. If my dad had not had his adventurous spirit, and if he had never re-enlisted in the Air Force shortly after World War II, and if he had not put in for special overseas assignments, and if he had just stayed in his hometown and settled into a typical American life, I most likely would have been raised in one of these two places I mention above.

I would still have the same body, and occupy the same physical entity, but I would not be the same person I am and who I have been my entire life. The life I lived overseas was an exciting, educational, and enlightening experience, and made me the person I am today. I speak three languages, have been to over thirty countries and about an equal number of states (including Alaska and Hawaii), and I have seen things and experienced things in my life that have not only made me the person I am, but have also given me insights, knowledge, and wisdom that otherwise I never would have had. And isn't that what life is really all about? Isn't it to live a decent and honorable life, and along the way to learn and grow and gain experiences, and the more varied the better?

If I had been born and raised in Oklahoma or Texas, for an example, I would most likely be that same redneck guy whom I detest so much today. I would be the ignorant, tobacco-chewing, gun-toting, cowboy-hat-adorned asshole whom I've met so many times and who has given me such a hard time after my returning to live in this country.

Thankfully, I am not that guy, and I thank my wonderful parents and especially my dad for having the courage, the gumption, and the desire to do something with himself and to live his life much different from what was expected of him, and what could have been a relatively easy path in life for him. I owe a great deal of gratitude to him, for not only doing what he wanted and needed to do with his life, but also for giving me the chance to become who it is that I am: an open-minded, tolerant, well-traveled, educated, wise, confident, knowledgeable, and experienced person. Someone whom I am proud to be, and always will be. An Overseas Brat!

Acknowledgements

I would like take the opportunity to thank everybody from the bottom of my heart for their support, encouragement, and assistance, who helped to make this book possible and include the following people:

Brian Jabas Smith, a fantastic local author and musician from Tucson, Arizona, and writer of a great collection of short stories, titled "Spent Saints" which was the book that actually inspired me to have the confidence and knowledge that I perhaps had the ability to do the same.

Kerry (Paul) May, author, whose wonderful collection of novels, titled "The World" (Parts 1 through 5), about living in Madrid, Spain as a Military Brat during the late 1960s and early 1970s inspired me to write my own accounts of my years living in that magical and unique time and place, but from my own particular point of view and experience.

My dear brother, John Walker, who not only lived though most of what I write about in my book, but is also the person that I was able to share my entire life with and who knows without a doubt that these "Confessions" of mine are true and all actually happened as I describe.

My oldest and dearest friend John Paul Vest, who I have known since we were both freshmen at MHS, and has continued to be my best friend ever since. His advice, counsel, support and friendship for over 50 years now has helped enormously to keep myself grounded as well as making me a wiser and more knowledgeable person.

My wonderful and beautiful wife Marilyn, who has contributed so much to the writing of this book. Her assistance with the editing, proofreading, and her great input and advice have proved to be invaluable and essential for my completing it. And her undying love and devotion for her husband has given me so much more than she will ever know.

Editor, graphic artist, book designer and my friend, Kate Horton, who without her assistance and expertise, I would never have finished this project or ended up with the great quality of book that you hold in your hands now.

A great big thanks to Marguerite Wainio, editor, writer, publicist and consultant, whose advice, criticism and final editing work and proofreading skills were invaluable in making this book what it is. Also for writing such an excellent forward to my book.

All four of my Uncles on my father's side of the family need to be mentioned and thanked, including Isaac, Herbert, Jack, and Dale. All of them (as well as my father) were writers and authors to some extent or another, and I think I inherited that writing gene (or at least the desire to be a writer) from that side of my family. All four profoundly affected me in a very positive way, each in their own unique style. And all five of these Walker brothers have books published and most are available on Amazon for purchase.

I also want to thank all of the people that I knew while growing up in Spain, including all the ones I mention in this book. All these people in one way or another helped me to become the person I was then as well as whom I am today. And they include not only my fellow students and friends at MHS and ASM, but the many great teachers I had as well, who taught me so much more than just what their subjects covered, but more importantly *how* to learn, and even about life itself.

And finally, and most importantly I want to thank my parents, John and Alice (Pat) Walker, for without them, I would not exist. They were both extraordinary people and without their bravery, courage and desire to do something different with their lives, my life would have been so much different than it was. By both of them deciding to stay in Spain and make their lives there after my dad retired from the Air Force is what enabled me to have and tell these unusual stories that I have told here.

They both lived incredible lives and strangely enough ended up living their last years together. Yes, they got divorced in 1970, but after two more marriages each during the next thirty years or so, they both found themselves single again and got re-married to each other in 2000. My mom had recently gotten divorced from her third husband, and my dad's third wife had recently passed away, so they got together once again to live their remaining years together. My mom died in 2011 and my dad in 2013, and I miss both of them dearly, but I know that they were very happy together and were truly made for each other. And they proved that Love truly is the most important thing in life.

A Note on the Pictures Used In this Book

It is said that a picture is worth a thousand words, and if that is true, then I've added many thousands of words to this book by using over 280 photographs. These pictures are used to illustrate certain things that mere words sometimes just cannot do justice to, or that I feel are a necessary ingredient to help tell the story.

Most of the pictures used are from the Walker Family archives and are used to show (in glorious black and white) certain aspects and details of what I write about. Also some pictures I got from various MHS Accolade yearbooks, and some of the other pictures I was able to "borrow" from the internet (many from certain Facebook groups pertaining to the subjects I discuss in my book) and I did purposely avoid showing most people's faces, to avoid any embarrassment or any possible legal ramifications.

I want to thank Gary C. Johnson for his permission to use the pictures of the Glass house and of Marcelino, the waiter of that establishment.

Many of the other pictures of Spain were taken by me during my last trip to Spain in 2013. While I was there, I returned to many of the places I knew so well while growing up and took many pictures. Some of these I used to help illustrate the places that I write about, but of course most of these locations have changed considerably in the last 40 or 50 years, but the reader is still able to see more or less what the place looked like.

Ronald Walker
Oracle, Arizona
December, 2018

ABOUT THE AUTHOR

Ronald Walker is an Overseas Brat who was born in Lisbon, Portugal while his father was stationed there with the U.S. Air Force. He also lived in Ankara, Turkey and then in Madrid, Spain for many years while growing up, before finally settling down to life in the United States at the age of 23.

He now lives in Oracle, Arizona with his wonderful wife and two cats, Luke and Leia, and still is trying to find his way living in the United States. This is his first book.

Made in the USA
Lexington, KY
17 January 2019